Crazy Big Book Third Grade

Thinking Kids®
Carson-Dellosa Publishing LLC
Greensboro, North Carolina

Thinking Kids®
Carson-Dellosa Publishing LLC
P.O. Box 35665
Greensboro, NC 27425 USA

ISBN 978-1-4838-4454-1
01-050187784

Table of Contents

Reading

My Story

Directions: Fill in the blanks. Use these sentences to write a story about yourself.

I feel happy when it's my birthday.

I feel sad when my brother hides my stuff.

I am good at hockey.

These words describe me: fun, nice, smart, crazy, slow.

I can help at home by ____________________.

My friends like me because ____________________.

I like to ____________________.

My favorite food is ____________________.

My favorite animal is ____________________.

Now . . . take your answers, and write a story about **you**!

Laughable Fellow

breakable
widen
readable
sinkable
harden
lighten
soften
washable
darken
enjoyable
written
straighten

Directions: Read the clues. Then, write the words in the puzzle.

Across

2. Opposite of **darken**.
4. To make wider.
5. Can be sunk.
7. To make hard.
8. Can be read.
11. Can be broken.

Down

1. Put in writing.
3. To make something not crooked.
4. Can be washed.
6. A lot of fun.
9. To make darker.
10. Opposite of **harden**.

Big B Words

Directions: Look at the picture clues. Then, complete the puzzle using the words from the word box.

Across

2. 

4. 

5. 

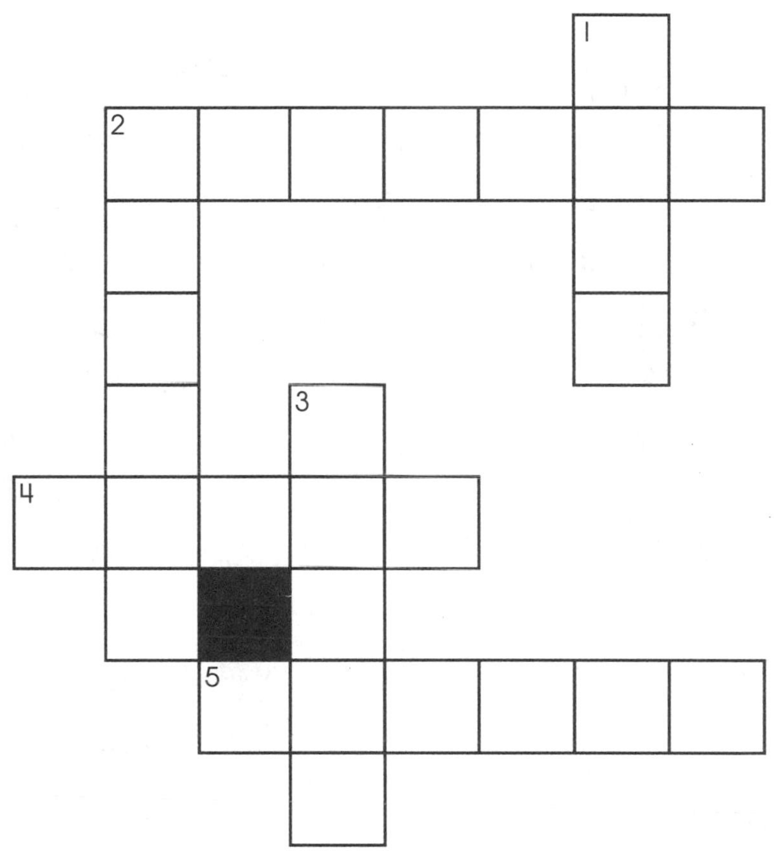

Down

1. 

2. 

3.

bend	button	boxes
bright	bubbles	bears

Phonics

Some words are more difficult to read because they have one or more silent letters. Many words you already know are like this.

Examples: wrong and **night**

Directions: Circle the silent letters in each word. The first one is done for you.

(w)rong	answer	autumn	whole
knife	hour	wrap	comb
sigh	straight	knee	known
lamb	taught	scent	daughter
whistle	wrote	knew	crumb

Directions: Draw a line between the rhyming words. The first one is done for you.

knew	try
sees	bowl
taut	stone
wrote	true
comb	song
straight	trees
sigh	home
known	great
wrong	caught
whole	boat

Phonics

Sometimes, letters make sounds you don't expect. Two consonants can work together to make the sound of one consonant. The **f** sound can be made by **ph**, as in the word **elephant**. The consonants **gh** are most often silent, as in the words **night** and **though**. But they also can make the **f** sound, as in the word **laugh**.

Directions: Circle the letters that make the **f** sound. Write the correct word from the box to complete each sentence. The first one is done for you.

ele(ph)ant	cough	laugh	telephone	phonics
dolphins	enough	tough	alphabet	rough

1. The **dolphins** were playing in the sea.
2. Did you have ______________________ time to do your homework?
3. A cold can make you ______________________ and sneeze.
4. The ______________________ ate peanuts with his trunk.
5. The road to my school is ______________________ and bumpy.
6. You had a ______________________ call this morning.
7. The ______________________ meat was hard to chew.
8. Studying ______________________ will help you read better.
9. The ______________________ has 26 letters in it.
10. We began to ______________________ when the clowns came in.

Phonics

There are several consonants that make the **k** sound: **c** when followed by **a**, **o**, or **u**, as in **cow** or **cup**; the letter **k**, as in **milk**; the letters **ch**, as in **Christmas**; and **ck**, as in **black**.

Directions: Read the following words. Circle the letters that make the **k** sound. The first one is done for you.

a(ch)e	school	market	comb
camera	deck	darkness	Christmas
necklace	doctor	stomach	crack
nickel	skin	thick	escape

Directions: Use your own words to finish the following sentences. Use words with the **k** sound.

1. If I had a nickel, I would ______________________________________.

2. My doctor is very ______________________________________.

3. We bought ripe, juicy tomatoes at the ______________________________.

4. If I had a camera now,
   I would take a picture of ______________________________.

5. When my stomach aches, ______________________________________.

Phonics

In some word families, the vowels have a long sound when you would expect them to have a short sound. For example, the **i** has a short sound in **chill**, but a long sound in **child**. The **o** has a short sound in **cost**, but a long sound in **most**.

Directions: Read the words in the word box below. Write the words that have a long vowel sound under the word **LONG**, and the words that have a short vowel sound under the word **SHORT**. (Remember, a long vowel says its name—like **a** in **ate**.)

old	odd	gosh	gold	sold	soft	toast	frost	lost	most
doll	roll	bone	done	kin	mill	mild	wild	blink	blind

LONG

bone ______________

______________ ______________

______________ ______________

______________ ______________

______________ ______________

____

SHORT

doll ______________

______________ ______________

______________ ______________

______________ ______________

______________ ______________

____

Shape Up

Directions: Write the word for each shape.

oval	rectangle
circle	square
triangle	octagon

Across

2. 

4. 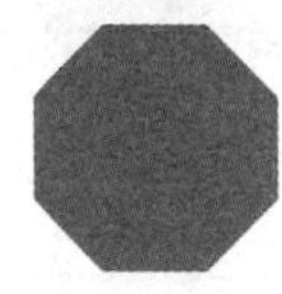

5. 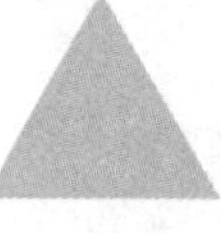

6. 

Down

1. 

3. 

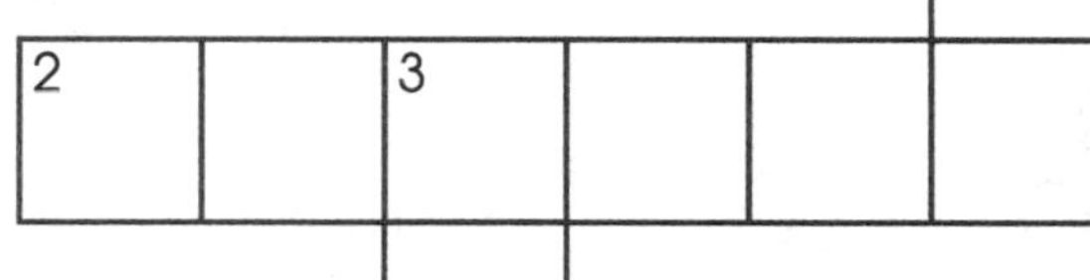

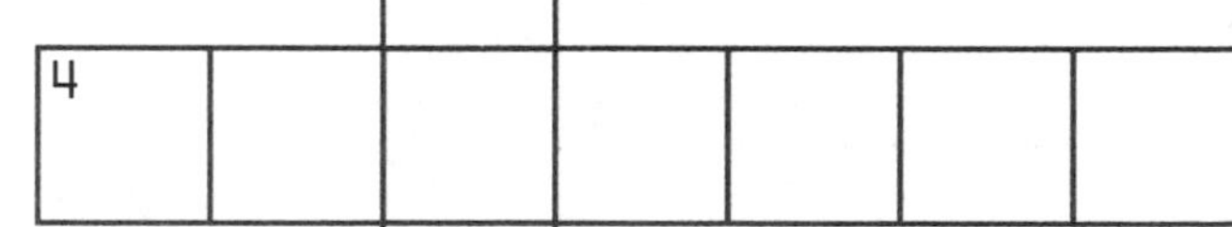

Name ______________________

Squaring Up

Directions: Use a word from the word box to finish each sentence. Then, use the words in the puzzle.

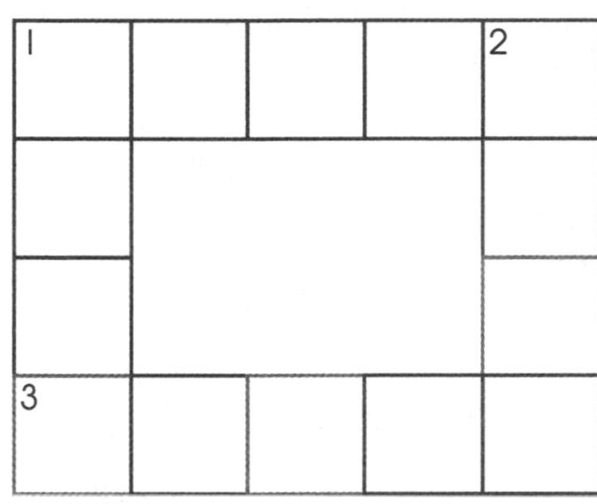

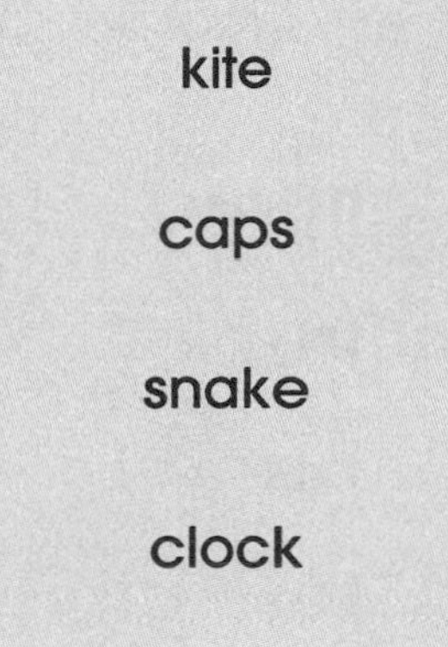

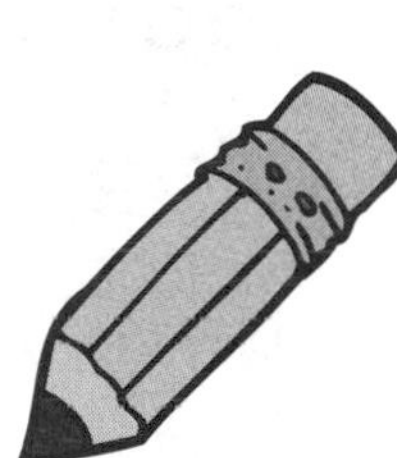

Across

1. The ______________________ said two o'clock.

3. The ______________________ slithered in the grass.

Down

1. Tommy has three baseball __________________.

2. I flew my __________________ at the beach.

Syllables

All words can be divided into **syllables**. Syllables are word parts that have one vowel sound in each part.

Directions: Draw a line between the syllables in each word, and then write the word on the correct line below. The first one is done for you.

lit|tle	bumblebee	pillow
truck	dazzle	dog
pencil	flag	angelic
rejoicing	ant	telephone

1 SYLLABLE	2 SYLLABLES	3 SYLLABLES
____________	little	____________
____________	____________	____________
____________	____________	____________
____________	____________	____________

Syllables

When the letters **le** come at the end of a word, they sometimes have the sound of **ul**, as in **raffle**.

Directions: Draw a line to match the syllables so they make words. The first one is done for you.

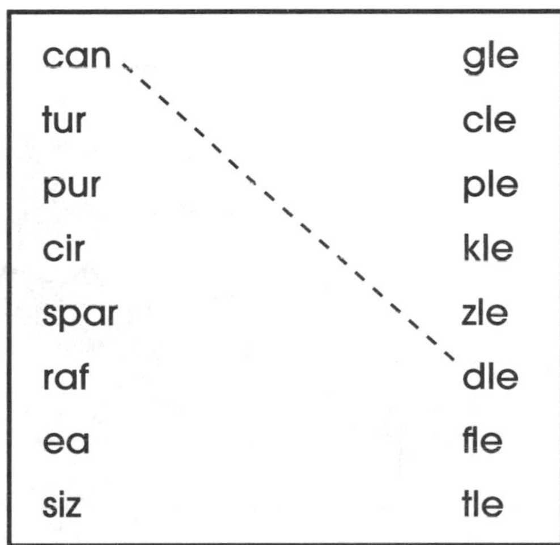

can	gle
tur	cle
pur	ple
cir	kle
spar	zle
raf	dle
ea	fle
siz	tle

Directions: Use the words you made to complete the sentences. The first one is done for you.

1. Will you buy a ticket for our school raffle?
2. The ______________________ pulled his head into his shell.
3. We could hear the bacon ______________________ in the pan.
4. The baby had one ______________________ on her birthday cake.
5. My favorite color is ______________________.
6. Look at that diamond ______________________!
7. The bald ______________________ is our national bird.
8. Draw a ______________________ around the correct answer.

A Good Scout

Directions: Read the clues at the bottom of the page. Then, write the words in the puzzle.

Across

1. A word you say when you get hurt.
3. The shape of a circle.
5. The opposite of **quiet**.
7. To find out how many, you must ______.
9. The opposite of **north**.
11. The opposite of **in**.
12. Animal like a rat.
14. A very high land form.

Down

2. Fluffy white object in the sky.
4. Ground wheat that is used in making bread.
6. Not having something.
7. A sofa.
8. A fish.
10. A home.
12. A part of your face.
13. To make a ball go down and up.

1 2 3 4 5 6 7 8 9 10 11 12 13 14

out loud south trout cloud
without flour couch ouch
bounce round mouse count
house mouth mountain

Name ______________________________

On the Farm

Directions: What would you like your farm to look like? Draw your house and barn. Color. Then, write your name on the mailbox.

Compound Words

A **compound word** is two small words put together to make one new word. Compound words are usually divided into syllables between the two words.

Directions: Read the words. Then, divide them into syllables. The first one is done for you.

1. playground play ground
2. sailboat ______________
3. doghouse ______________
4. dishpan ______________
5. pigpen ______________
6. outdoors ______________
7. beehive ______________
8. airplane ______________
9. cardboard ______________
10. nickname ______________
11. hilltop ______________
12. broomstick ______________
13. sunburn ______________
14. oatmeal ______________
15. campfire ______________
16. somewhere ______________
17. starfish ______________
18. birthday ______________
19. sidewalk ______________
20. seashore ______________

Compound Words

Directions: Read the compound words in the word box. Then, use them to answer the questions. The first one is done for you.

sailboat	blueberry	bookcase	tablecloth	beehive
dishpan	pigpen	classroom	playground	bedtime
broomstick	treetop	fireplace	newspaper	sunburn

Which compound word means . . .

1. a case for books? bookcase
2. a berry that is blue? ____________
3. a hive for bees? ____________
4. a place for fires? ____________

5. a pen for pigs? ____________
6. a room for a class? ____________
7. a pan for dishes? ____________
8. a boat to sail? ____________
9. a paper for news? ____________
10. a burn from the sun? ____________

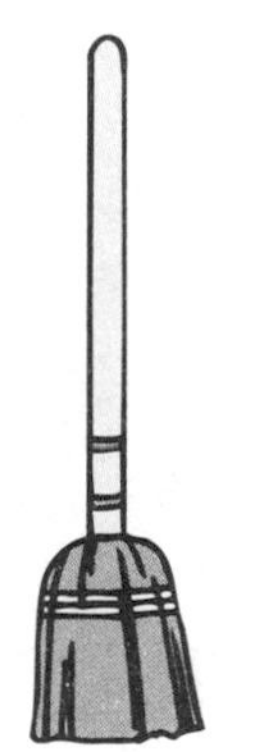

11. the top of a tree? ____________
12. a stick for a broom? ____________
13. the time to go to bed? ____________
14. a cloth for the table? ____________
15. ground to play on? ____________

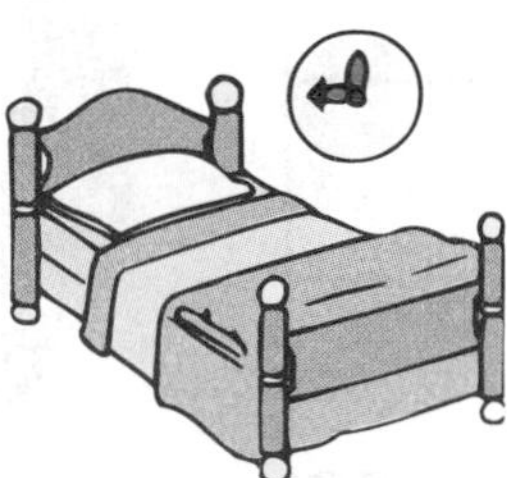

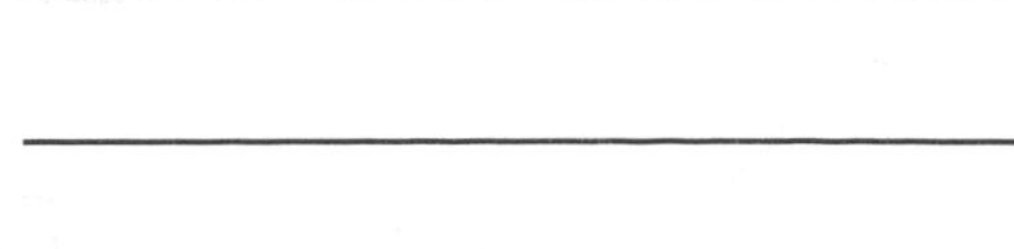

Letter Change

Directions: Starting with the top word in each square, change one letter at a time until the top word becomes the bottom word.

1.	R	I	P	E
2.				
3.				
4.				
5.	P	A	L	M

6.	M	I	C	E
7.				
8.				
9.				
10.	L	A	R	K

Crack the Code

Directions: Crack the code to reveal the words.

☺	✗	■	⚐	☆	ⓘ	○	✶	❄	❑	✎	✿	⇨	✧	✹	✓	❖	💧
c	n	k	u	a	s	j	m	l	e	r	w	o	t	p	i	g	b

___ ___ ___ ___
○ ⚐ ✶ ✹

___ ___ ___ ___
❖ ⇨ ☆ ❄

___ ___ ___ ___
💧 ☆ ❄ ❄

___ ___ ___
✎ ⚐ ✗

___ ___ ___ ___ ___ ___
⚐ ✶ ✹ ✓ ✎ ❑

Name ______________________

Transportation Vocabulary

Directions: Unscramble the words to spell the names of kinds of transportation. The first one is done for you.

behelwworar	wheel b a r r o w
anirt	t __ __ __ n
moobattor	moto __ __ __ __ t
ceicbly	b __ __ __ __ __ e
tocker	r __ __ __ __ t
etobimuloa	aut __ __ __ __ __ __ e
rilanape	a __ __ p __ __ __ e

Directions: Use a word from above to complete each sentence.

1. My mother uses a ____________________ to move dirt to her garden.
2. The ______________ blasted the spaceship off the launching pad.
3. We flew on an ______________________ to visit my aunt in Florida.
4. My grandfather drives a very old ____________________________.
5. We borrowed Fred's ________________________ to go water skiing.
6. You should always look both ways when crossing a _____________________ track.
7. I hope I get a new ___________________________ for my birthday.

Space Vocabulary

Directions: Unscramble each word. Use the numbers below the letters to tell you what order they belong in. Write the word by its definition.

i r t b o
4 2 5 3 1

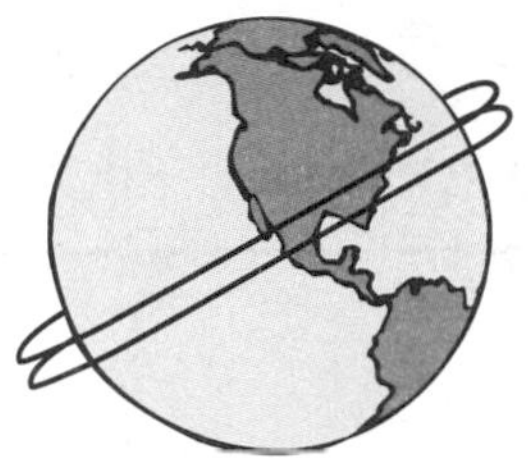

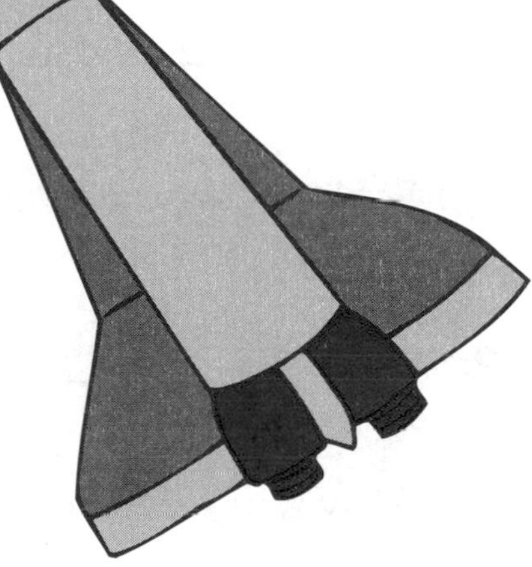

u t o n c w d n o
3 5 7 9 1 8 6 4 2

u l e f
2 4 3 1

a t s r a t n o u
7 9 2 4 1 3 6 5 8

t e h t s u l
5 7 2 4 1 3 6

A member of the team that flies a spaceship ____________________

A rocket-powered spaceship that travels between Earth and space ____________________

The material, such as gas, used for power ____________________

The seconds just before take-off ____________________

The path of a spaceship as it goes around Earth ____________________

Weather Vocabulary

Directions: Use the weather words in the box to complete the sentences.

sunny	temperature	foggy	puddles	rainy
windy	rainbow	cloudy	lightning	snowy

1. My friends and I love ________________ days, because we can have snowball fights!

2. On ________________ days, we like to stay indoors and play board games.

3. Today was hot and ________________, so we went to the beach.

4. We didn't see the sun at all yesterday. It was ________________ all day.

5. ________________ weather is perfect for flying kites.

6. It was so ________________, Mom had to use the headlights in the car so we wouldn't get lost.

7. While it was still raining, the sun began to shine and created a beautiful ________________ .

8. We like to jump in the ________________ after it rains.

9. ________________ flashed across the sky during the thunderstorm.

10. The ________________ outside was so low, we needed to wear hats, mittens, and scarves.

Name ______________________

Vocabulary Word Lists

Directions: Complete the vocabulary word lists. Be creative.

Drinks

milk
____
____
____

Lights

flashlight
____
____
____

Pets

dogs
____
____
____

School Supplies

paper
____
____
____

What other things can you think of to list?

____

Read All About It

Directions: Read the clues. Then, write the words in the puzzle.

Across

2. To send a letter.
5. Not messy.
6. What you are called.
7. A polite word.
8. Pretty.
9. Related to a donkey.
10. A kind of coat you wear around the house.
12. To sparkle.
13. Not shallow.
15. To steer a car.
16. Opposite of **dirty**.

Down

1. Used to catch a fish.
3. Jump.
4. To rob.
5. Friendly and kind.
6. Opposite of **far**.
9. Opposite of **kind**.
11. A dog's treat.
12. To slip.
13. Ten-cent coin.
14. More than one mouse.

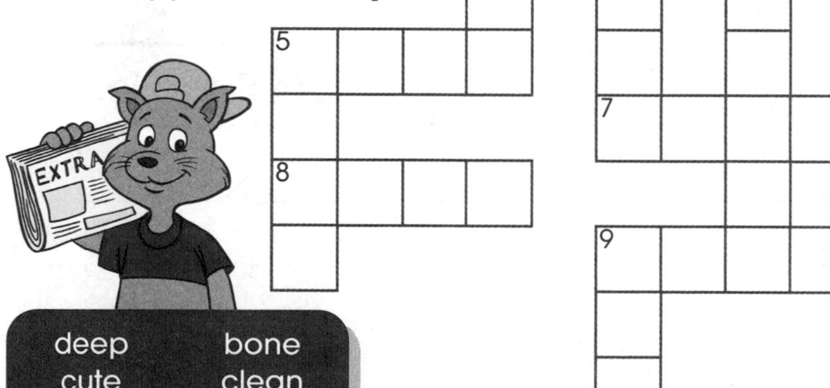

deep	bone
cute	clean
nice	steal
mail	dime
mice	name
robe	bait
near	neat
mule	mean
slide	drive
please	shine
leap	

Crack the Code

Directions: Use the secret code to unlock a silly but true fact.

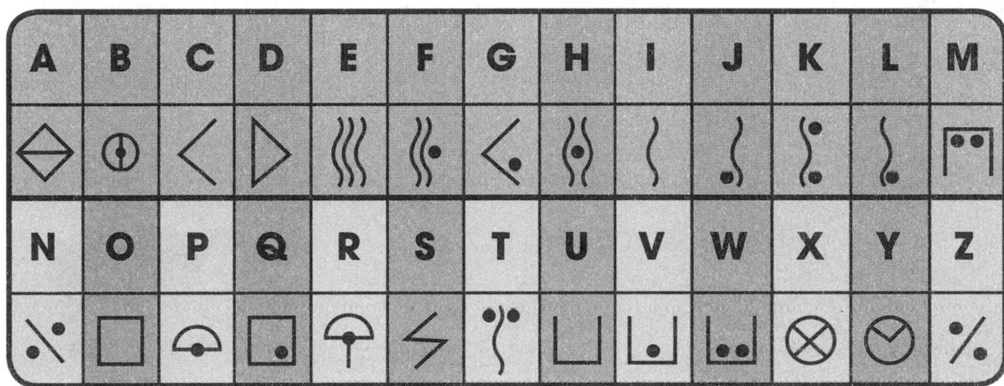

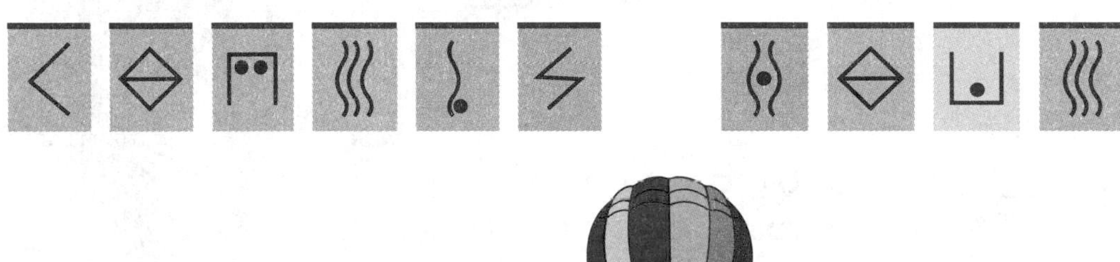

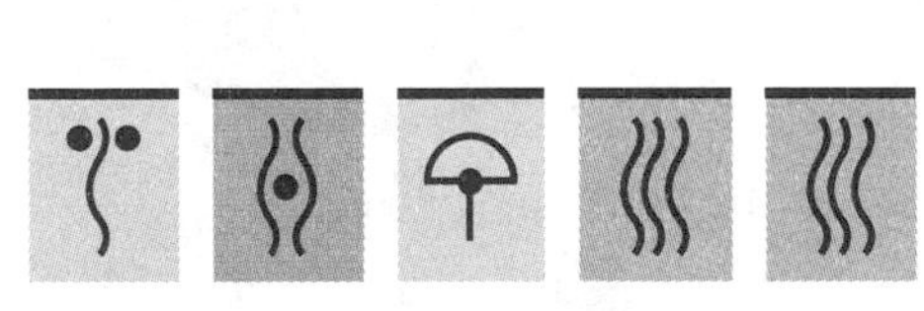

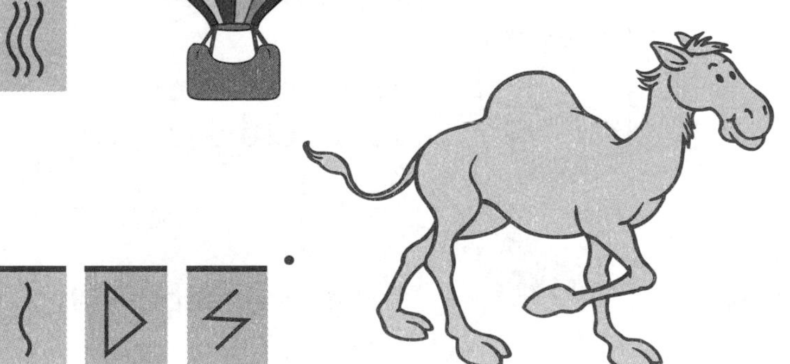

Multiple-Meaning Words

Many words have more than one meaning. These words are called **multiple-meaning words**. Think of how the word is used in a sentence or story to determine the correct meaning.

Directions: The following baseball words have multiple meanings. Write the correct word in each baseball below.

play	bat	ball	fly	run

________ This word means . . .

1. a flying mammal
2. a special stick used in baseball

________ This word means . . .

1. a small insect
2. to soar through the air

________ This word means . . .

1. a big dance
2. a round object used in sports

________ This word means . . .

1. a performance
2. to amuse oneself

Which word is left? ________ Write sentences using two different meanings of the word.

1. ____

2. ____

Multiple-Meaning Words

Directions: Complete each sentence on pages 29 and 30 using one of the words below. Each word will be used only twice.

1. The kitten watched the _______________ crawl slowly up the wall.

2. "You wouldn't _______________ me, would you?" asked Dad.

3. Do you think Aunt Donna and Uncle Mike will come to my school _______________?

4. He hit the ball so hard it broke the _______________.

5. "My favorite part of the story is when the princess goes to the _______________," sighed Veronica.

6. My brother scored the first _______________ in the game.

Multiple-Meaning Words

7. We will have to ______________ quietly while the baby is sleeping.

8. Before we go to the store, I want to get some coins out of my ______________.

9. The nature center will bring a live ______________ for our class to see.

10. We sat on the ______________ as we fished in the river.

11. The umpire decided the pitcher needed a new ______________.

12. We will ______________ in a race tomorrow.

13. "Can we please go to the ______________ after I clean my room?" asked Jordan.

14. That boomerang can really ______________!

15. Is it okay to ______________ my bike here?

16. The baby goat, or ______________, follows its mother everywhere.

Name ______________________

Large or Small?

Directions: Write the words in the puzzle.

small

large

big

little

short

tall

tiny

huge

m

n

t

g

o

a

r

b

Name ______________________

Your Body

Directions: Read the clues and use the words in the word box to complete the puzzle.

fingers
hand
nose
lips
brain
teeth
ears

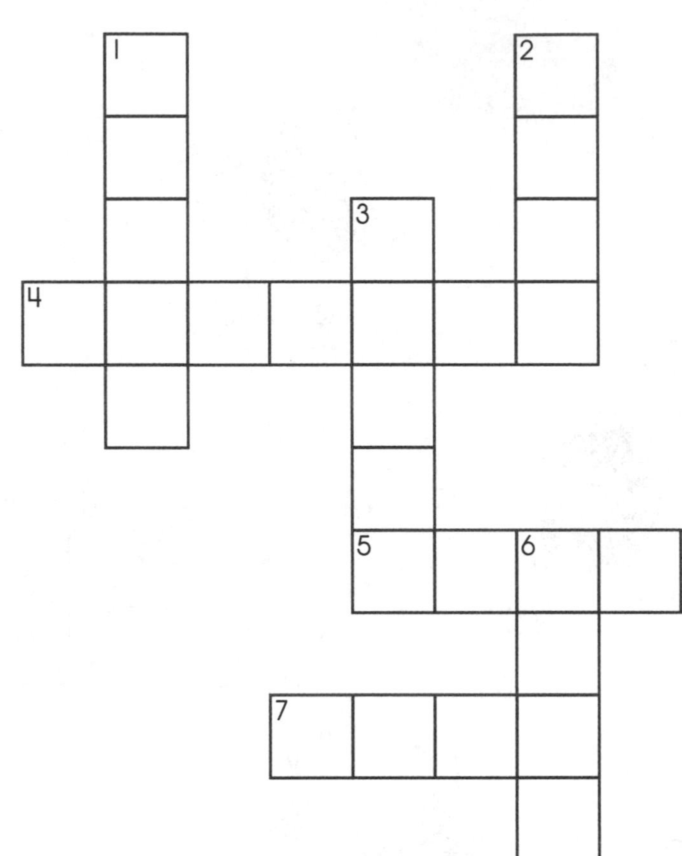

Across

4. You have five on each hand.
5. It has five fingers.
7. They help you hear.

Down

1. You think with it.
2. They smile for you.
3. They chew for you.
6. It helps you smell.

Sequencing

Directions: Fill in the blank spaces with what comes next in the series. The first one is done for you.

year	Wednesday	day	sixth	large
twenty	February	night	seventeen	mile
paragraph	winter	ocean		

1. Sunday, Monday, Tuesday, Wednesday
2. third, fourth, fifth, ____________
3. November, December, January, ____________
4. tiny, small, medium, ____________
5. fourteen, fifteen, sixteen, ____________
6. morning, afternoon, evening, ____________
7. inch, foot, yard, ____________
8. day, week, month, ____________
9. spring, summer, autumn, ____________
10. five, ten, fifteen, ____________
11. letter, word, sentence, ____________
12. second, minute, hour, ____________
13. stream, lake, river, ____________

Sequencing

When words are in a certain order, they are in sequence.

Directions: Complete each sequence using a word from the box. There are extra words in the box. The first one has been done for you.

below	three	fifteen	December	twenty	above
after	go	third	hour	March	yard

1. January, February, March
2. before, during, ____________
3. over, on, ____________
4. come, stay, ____________
5. second, minute, ____________

6. first, second, ____________
7. five, ten, ____________
8. inch, foot, ____________

Name ____________________

Sequencing: Smallest to Largest

Directions: Rearrange each group of words to form a sequence from smallest to largest.

Example:

minute, second, hour — second, minute, hour

1. least, most, more ____________________
2. full, empty, half-full ____________________
3. month, day, year ____________________
4. baseball, golf ball, soccer ball ____________________
5. penny, dollar, quarter ____________________
6. $4.12, $3.18, $3.22 ____________________
7. boy, man, infant ____________________
8. mother, daughter, grandmother ____________________

Sequencing

Directions: Read each story. Circle the phrase that tells what happened before.

1. Izzy is very happy now that she has someone to play with. She hopes that her new sister will grow up quickly!

   A few days ago . . .

   Izzy was sick.

   Izzy's mother had a baby.

   Izzy got a new puppy.

2. Sara tried to mend the tear. She used a needle and thread to sew up the hole.

   While playing, Sara had . . .

   broken her bicycle.

   lost her watch.

   torn her shirt.

3. The movers took Antonio's bike off the truck and put it in the garage. Next, they moved his bed into his new bedroom.

   Antonio's family . . .

   bought a new house.

   went on vacation.

   bought a new truck.

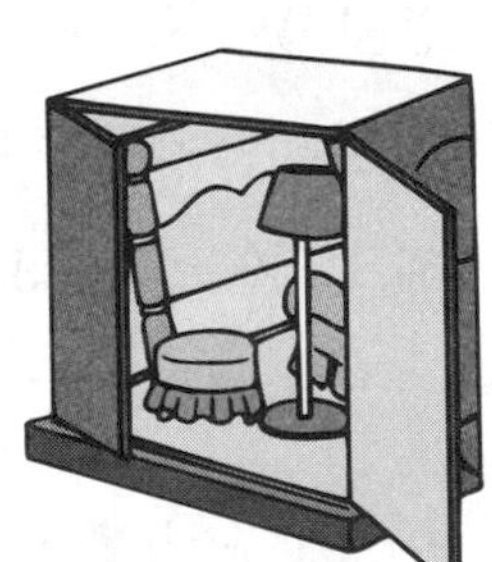

4. Katie picked out a book about dinosaurs. Luke, who likes sports, chose two books about baseball.

   Katie and Luke . . .

   went to the library.

   went to the playground.

   went to the grocery.

Sequencing

Directions: Read each story. Circle the phrase that tells what might happen next.

1. Sam and Ella picked up their books and left the house. They walked to the bus stop. They got on a big yellow bus.

   What will Sam and Ella do next?

   They will go to school.

   They will visit their grandmother.

   They will go to the store.

2. Maggie and Matt were playing in the snow. They made a snowman with a black hat and a red scarf. Then, the sun came out.

   What might happen next?

   It will snow again.

   They will play in the sandbox.

   The snowman will melt.

3. Megan put on a big floppy hat and funny clothes. She put green make-up on her face.

   What will Megan do next?

   She will go to school.

   She will go to a costume party.

   She will go to bed.

4. Mike was eating dinner. Suddenly, he smelled smoke. He turned and saw a fire on the stove.

   What will Mike do next?

   He will watch the fire.

   He will call for help.

   He will finish his dinner.

Sequencing

Directions: Number these sentences from **1** to **5** to show the correct order of the story.

Building a Treehouse

_____ They had a beautiful treehouse!

_____ They got wood and nails.

__1__ Jay and Josefina planned to build a treehouse.

_____ Now, they like to eat lunch in their treehouse.

_____ Josefina and Jay worked in the backyard for three days building the treehouse.

A School Play

_____ Everyone clapped when the curtain closed.

_____ The girl who played Snow White came onto the stage.

_____ All the other school children went to the gym to see the play.

_____ The stage curtain opened.

__1__ The third grade was going to put on a play about Snow White.

Sequencing

Directions: Number these sentences from **1** to **8** to show the correct order of the story.

_______ Jack's father called the family doctor.

_______ Jack felt much better as his parents drove him home.

_______ Jack woke up in the middle of the night with a terrible pain in his stomach.

_______ The doctor told Jack's father to take Jack to the hospital.

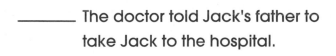

_______ Jack called his parents to come help him.

_______ At the hospital, the doctors examined Jack. They said the problem was not serious. They told Jack's parents that he could go home.

_______ Jack's mother took his temperature. He had a fever of 103 degrees.

_______ On the way to the hospital, Jack rested in the backseat. He was worried.

Name ____________________

Is It Really Magic?

Directions: Look at the picture clues. Then, complete the puzzle using the words from the word box.

Across

1.

2.

3.

5.

7.

8.

Down

1.

2.

3.

4.

6.

7.

mittens melt
map mitt
mug mop
mail moon
mask match
monster mouse

Crack the Code

Directions: Crack the code to reveal the tongue twister.

___ ___ ___
✓ ✎ ✓

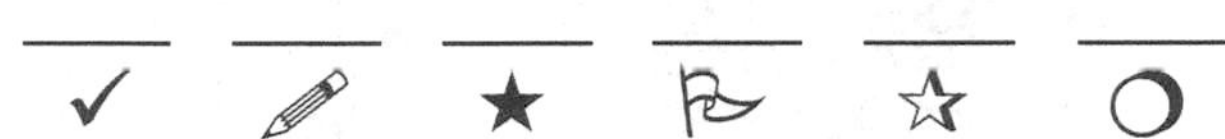

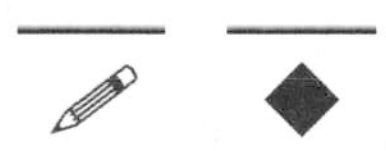

___ ___
◎ ❍

___ ___ ___ ___ ___ ___ ___
✓ ★ ✓ ✓ ❒ ❄ ■

___ ___ ___
◎ ● 💧

___ ___ ___ ___ ___ ___ ___.
✓ ◎ ★ ✓ ❒ ❄ ■

A	◎
B	✓
C	✶
D	💧
E	❄
F	◆
G	⚐
H	☆
I	✖
J	✪
K	❖
L	❒
M	⅄
N	●
O	✎
P	✋
Q	🔔
R	✦
S	■
T	❍
U	★
V	☺
W	⇨
X	⬆
Y	✿
Z	✹

Following Directions

Directions: Learning to follow directions is very important. Use the map to find your way to different houses.

1. Color the "Start" house yellow.
2. Go north 2 houses, and east two houses.
3. Go north 2 houses, and west 4 houses.
4. Color the house green.

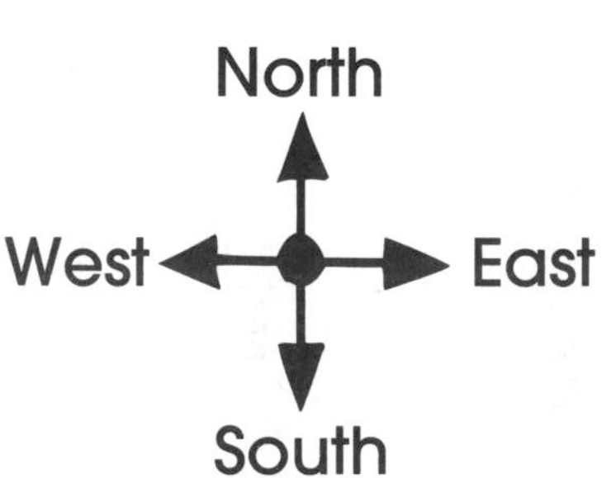

5. Start at the yellow house.
6. Go east 1 house, and north 3 houses.
7. Go west 3 houses, and south 3 houses.
8. Color the house blue.

Following Directions

Directions: Read each sentence, and do what it says to do.

1. Count the syllables in each word on the list. Write the number on the line by the word.
2. Draw a line between the two words in each compound word.
3. Draw a circle around each name of a month.
4. Draw a box around each food word.
5. Draw an **X** on each noise word.
6. Draw a line under each day of the week.

_______ April	_______ vegetable	_______ tablecloth
_______ bang	_______ June	_______ meat
_______ sidewalk	_______ Saturday	_______ crash
_______ astronaut	_______ March	_______ jingle
_______ moon	_______ cardboard	_______ rocket
_______ Friday	_______ fruit	_______ Monday

7. Write the three words from the list you did not use. Draw a picture of each of those words.

Climbing Koala

Directions: Look at the picture clues. Then, complete the puzzle using the words from the word box.

Old MacDonald Had a Code

You are looking for clues at Old MacDonald's farm. A friend sends you a note.

Directions: Use the letters and their locations on the grid to figure out the message.

B	R	E
H	M	Y
N	A	T

⌟ = B

Main Idea

The main idea of a story is what the story is mostly about.

Directions: Read the story. Then, answer the questions.

A tree is more than the enormous plant you see growing in your yard. A large part of the tree grows under the ground. This part is called the **roots**. If the tree is very big and very old, the roots may stretch down 100 feet!

The roots hold the tree in the ground. The roots do another important job for the tree. They gather minerals and water from the soil to feed the tree so it will grow. Most land plants, including trees, could not live without roots to support and feed them.

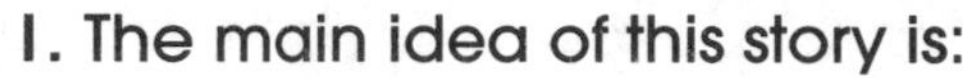

1. The main idea of this story is:

   The roots of a tree are underground.

   The roots do important jobs for the tree.

2. Where are the roots of a tree? ____________________

Circle the correct answer.

3. The roots help to hold the tree up. True False

4. Name two things the roots collect from the soil for the tree.

   a) ____________________ b) ____________________

Main Idea

Directions: Read about spiders. Then, answer the questions.

Many people think spiders are insects, but they are not. Spiders are the same size as insects, and they look like insects in some ways. But there are three ways to tell a spider from an insect. Insects have six legs, and spiders have eight legs. Insects have antennae, but spiders do not. An insect's body is divided into three parts; a spider's body is divided into only two parts.

1. The main idea of this story is:

   Spiders are like insects.

   Spiders are like insects in some ways, but they are not insects.

2. What are three ways to tell a spider from an insect?

   a) ______________________________

   b) ______________________________

   c) ______________________________

Circle the correct answer.

3. Spiders are the same size as insects. True False

 Name ______________________

Main Idea

Directions: Read about the giant panda. Then, answer the questions.

Giant pandas are among the world's favorite animals. They look like big, cuddly stuffed toys. There are not very many pandas left in the world. You may have to travel a long way to see one.

The only place on Earth where pandas live in the wild is in the bamboo forests of the mountains of China. It is hard to see pandas in the forest because they are very shy. They hide among the many bamboo trees. It also is hard to see pandas because there are so few of them. Scientists think there may be about 1,600 pandas living in the mountains of China.

1. Write a sentence that tells the main idea of this story:

____

____

2. What are two reasons that it is hard to see pandas in the wild?

   a) ____

   b) ____

3. How many pandas are believed to be living in the mountains of China?

____

Name ______________________

Main Idea

Directions: Read the story. Then, answer the questions.

Because bamboo is very important to pandas, they have special body features that help them eat it. The panda's front foot is like a hand. But, instead of four fingers and a thumb, the panda has five fingers and an extra-long wrist bone. With its special front foot, the panda can easily pick up the stalks of bamboo. It also can hold the bamboo more tightly than it could with a hand like ours.

Bamboo stalks are very tough. The panda uses its big heavy head, large jaws, and big back teeth to chew. Pandas eat the bamboo first by peeling the outside of the stalk. They do this by moving their front feet from side to side while holding the stalk in their teeth. Then, they bite off a piece of the bamboo and chew it with their strong jaws.

1. Write a sentence that tells the main idea of this story.

____

2. Instead of four fingers and a thumb, the panda has

____

3. Bamboo is very tender. True False

Puzzling Words

Directions: Fill in the blanks with **s**, **sl**, **sm**, **sn**, or **st**. Then, write the words in the puzzle.

1.  ___ ___ ed

2.  ___ ___ amp

3.  ___ ___ ow

4.  ___ ___ ide

5.  ___ eal

6.  ___ ___ ile

7.  ___ ___ ail

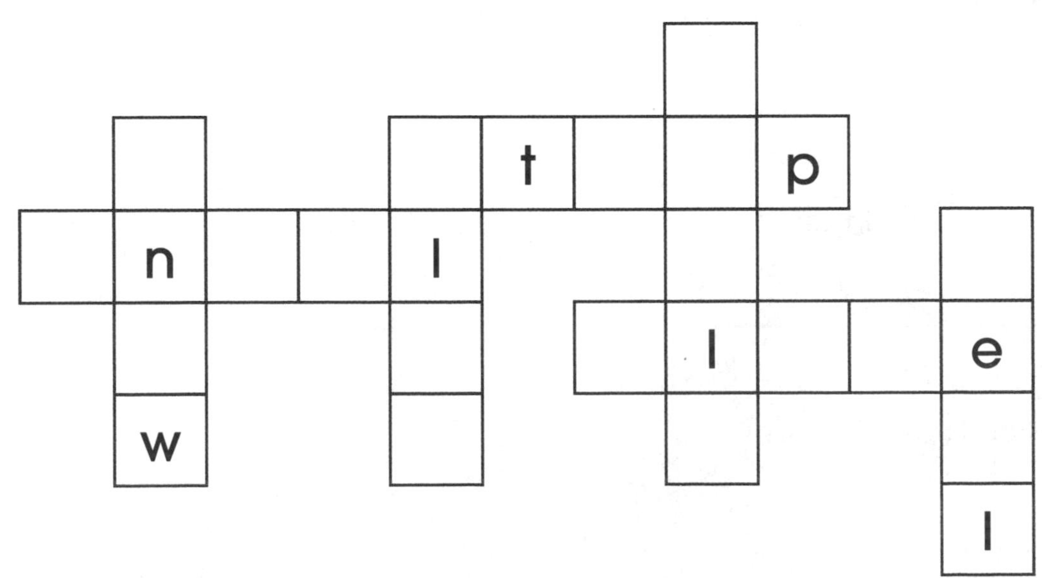

Live Via Satellite

Satellites send information about many things.

Directions: Use the code to find the different kinds of messages and information satellites send.

·	!	▭	△	(	ℸ	↓	↑	⬡	+	:	ȣ	◡	▽	#	?	□	○	><	)	[	=	ɜ	8	⊣	ᙏ
A	B	C	D	E	F	G	H	I	J	K	L	M	N	O	P	Q	R	S	T	U	V	W	X	W	X

) (ȣ (= ⬡ >< ⬡ # ▽   ) (ȣ (? ↑ # ▽ (

ℸ ȣ # # △ ><   ℸ # ○ (><)   ℸ ⬡ ○ (><

ɜ (·) ↑ (○   ? # ȣ ȣ [ ) ⬡ # ▽

? ⬡ ▭) [○ (><   # ℸ   >< ? · ▭ (

◡ # = ⬡ ▽ ↓   · ▽ ⬡ ◡ · ȣ ><

Reading for Information: Dictionaries

Dictionaries contain meanings and pronunciations of words. The words in a dictionary are listed in alphabetical order. Guide words appear at the top of each dictionary page. They help us know at a glance what words are on each page.

Directions: Place the words in alphabetical order.

apple	dog	crab	ear
book	atlas	cake	frog
egg	drip	coat	crib

Reading for Information: Newspapers

Many people learn about the day's news by reading a newspaper. Some people read a printed version. Others prefer to read a newspaper online.

A newspaper has many parts. Some of the parts of a newspaper are listed below. The parts of a paper may look different online, but the content is mostly the same.

- banner — the name of the paper
- lead story — the top news item
- caption — sentences under the picture that give information about the picture
- sports — scores and information on current sports events
- comics — drawings that tell funny stories
- editorial — an article by the editor expressing an opinion about something
- ads — paid advertisements
- weather — information about the weather
- advice column — letters from readers asking for help with a problem
- obituaries — information about people who have died

Directions: Match the newspaper sections below with their definitions.

banner	an article by the editor
lead story	sentences under pictures
caption	the name of the paper
editorial	information about people who have died
obituary	the top news item

Newspaper Writing

A good news story gives the reader important information. It answers these questions:

WHO?	WHY?	WHAT?
WHERE?	HOW?	WHEN?

Directions: Think about the story "Little Red Riding Hood." Answer the following questions about the story.

Who are the characters? ______________________________

____

What is the story about? ______________________________

____

Why does Red go to Granny's house? ______________________________

____

Where does the story take place? ______________________________

____

When did she go to Granny's house? ______________________________

____

How did the wolf try to fool Red? ______________________________

____

Fantasy and Reality

Something that is **real** could actually happen. Something that is **fantasy** is not real. It could not happen.

Examples: Real: Dogs can bark.

Fantasy: Dogs can fly.

Directions: Look at the sentences below. Write **real** or **fantasy** next to each sentence.

1. My cat can talk to me. ____________________
2. Witches ride brooms and cast spells. ____________________
3. Mom can mow the lawn. ____________________
4. I ride a magic carpet to school. ____________________
5. I have a man-eating tree. ____________________
6. My sandbox has toys in it. ____________________
7. Mom can bake carrot-nut muffins. ____________________
8. Mark's garden has tomatoes and corn in it. ____________________
9. Dmitri grows toys and balloons in his garden. ____________________
10. I make my bed every day. ____________________

Write your own **real** sentence. ____________________

____

Write your own **fantasy** sentence. ____________________

____

Parts of a Plant

Directions: Read the clues and use the words in the word box to complete the puzzle.

leaves
stem
roots
fruit
seeds
flower

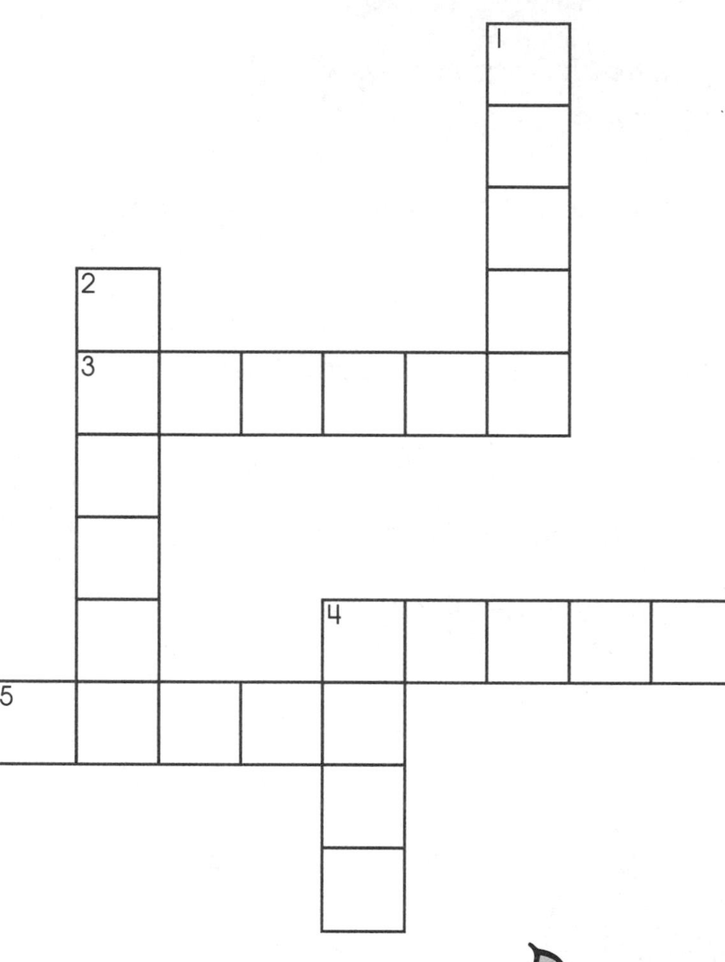

Across

3. They make food for the plant.
4. New plants grow from these.
5. This covers and protects the seeds.

Down

1. These take in water and minerals from the soil.
2. This is the part where the seeds are formed.
4. It carries the water and minerals to the leaves.

Change a Letter

Directions: Starting with the top word in each square, change one letter at a time until the top word becomes the bottom word.

1.	L	I	S	T
2.				
3.				
4.				
5.	M	A	N	E

6.	T	I	M	E
7.				
8.				
9.				
10.	F	E	L	L

Idioms

Idioms are a colorful way of saying something ordinary. The words in idioms do not mean exactly what they say.

Directions: Read the idioms listed below. Draw a picture of the literal meaning. Then, match the idiom to its correct meaning.

Idiom	Meaning
Jump on the bandwagon!	She doesn't eat very much.
She eats like a bird.	Keep the secret.
Don't cry over spilled milk!	Make sure you don't miss an opportunity.
Don't let the cat out of the bag!	Get involved!
You are the apple of my eye.	Don't worry about things that have already happened.
Don't miss the boat.	I think you are special.

Analogies

Analogies compare how things are related to each other.

Example: Finger is to **hand** as **toe** is to **foot**.

Directions: Complete the other analogies.

1. Apple is to tree as flower is to __________ .

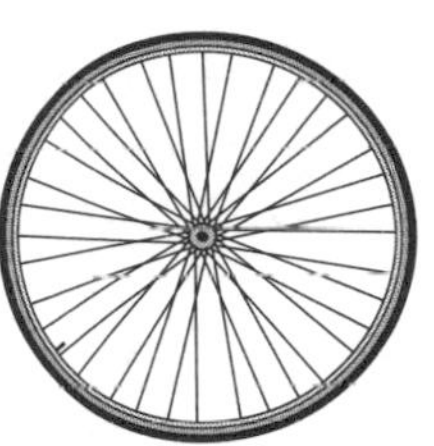

2. Tire is to car as wheel is to __________ .

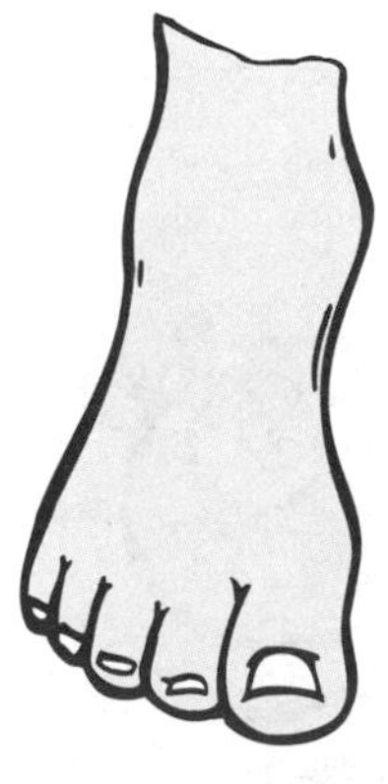

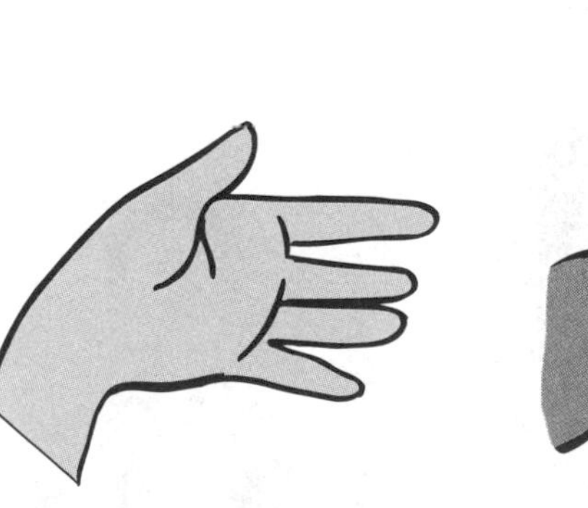
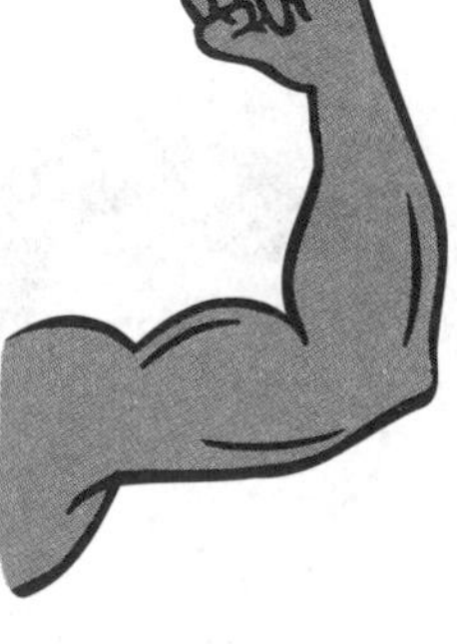

3. Foot is to leg as hand is to __________ .

Analogies

Directions: Complete each analogy using a word from the box. The first one has been done for you.

week	bottom	month	tiny	sentence	lake	out	eye

1. **Up** is to **down** as **in** is to out.
2. **Minute** is to **hour** as **day** is to ______________.
3. **Month** is to **year** as **week** is to ______________.
4. **Over** is to **under** as **top** is to ______________.
5. **Big** is to **little** as **giant** is to ______________.
6. **Sound** is to **ear** as **sight** is to ______________.
7. **Page** is to **book** as **word** is to ______________.
8. **Wood** is to **tree** as **water** is to ______________.

Toy Store

Directions: Use the word lists to fill out the grid below.

Hint: Count the squares in the grid first to see where the words will fit.

3 Letters
buy
pay

4 Letters
shop
toys
sell
sale

5 Letters
games
music
guard
clerk
hobby

8 Letters
elevator

C
L
O
T
H
E
S

A Trip to Mars

Directions: Find the Mars words from the word box. Words can be across, down, diagonal, or backward.

red	dusky	craters
windy	lifeless	volcanoes
dry	mountainous	frozen

v	o	l	c	a	n	o	e	s	c	y
r	e	d	k	m	n	a	h	e	r	a
b	v	r	w	i	h	e	a	u	a	l
i	x	y	d	n	i	w	r	f	t	i
t	t	p	l	l	k	p	r	c	e	f
y	k	s	u	d	g	o	d	g	r	e
s	g	c	s	r	z	n	v	l	s	l
h	l	r	s	e	r	e	s	c	c	e
m	o	u	n	t	a	i	n	o	u	s
a	a	m	v	u	h	r	r	h	l	s

Classifying: Seasons

Directions: Each word in the box can be grouped by seasons. Complete the pyramids for each season with words from the box.

July 4	hot	football	bike rides
kite	froze	sled ride	swimming
snowman	bunnies	ice	jack-o-lantern
windy	baseball	leaves	Thanksgiving

1. Spring

2. Summer

3. Fall

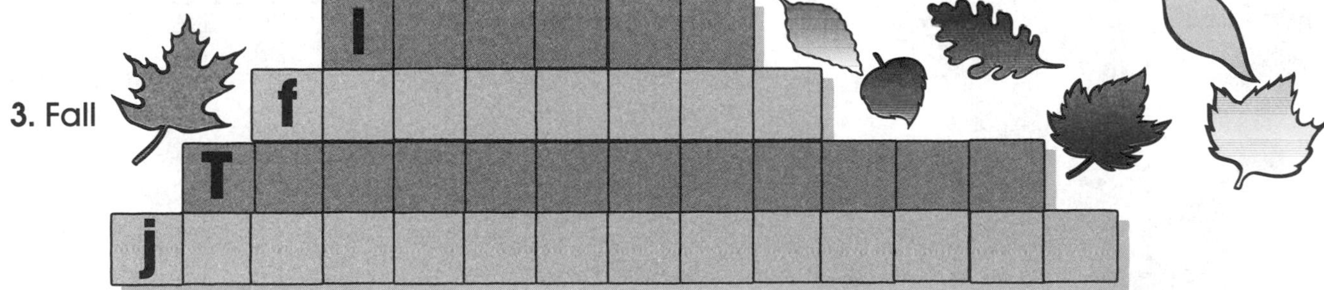

4. Winter

Classifying

Directions: Write each word from the box in the correct category.

robin	elm
buckeye	willow
sunflower	blue jay
canary	oak
rose	wren
tulip	morning glory

Trees

____
____
____
____

Birds

____
____
____
____

Flowers

____
____
____
____

Classifying

Directions: Write a word from the word box to complete each sentence. If the word you write names an article of clothing, write **1** on the line. If it names food, write **2** on the line. If it names an animal, write **3** on the line. If the word names furniture, write **4** on the line.

jacket	chair	shirt	owl	mice
bed	cheese	dress	bread	peaches

__1__ 1. Danny tucked his ______________________ into his pants.

______ 2. ______________________ are my favorite kind of fruit.

______ 3. The wise old ______________ sat in the tree and said, "Who-o-o."

______ 4. We can't sit on the ___________________ because it has a broken leg.

______ 5. Don't forget to wear your ___________________ because it is chilly today.

______ 6. Will you please buy a loaf of ___________________ at the store?

______ 7. She wore a very pretty __________________ to the dance.

______ 8. The cat chased the ______________________ in the barn.

______ 9. I was so sleepy that I went to ____________________ early.

______ 10. We put _________________ in the mouse trap to help catch the mice.

Comet Search

There are more than 800 known comets. Halley's Comet is the most famous. It appears about every 76 years. The last scheduled appearance in this century was in 1985. When will it appear next?

Directions: Circle the words from the word bank in the word search. When you are finished,write down the letters that are not circled. Start at the top of the puzzle and go from left to right.

dust	Halley	coma	snowball	melt	solar system
orbit	tail	ice	sky	shining	

S	P	M	E	L	T	L	A	N	H	E
O	T	S	S	H	A	C	O	M	A	V
L	E	N	O	R	D	B	I	T	L	S
A	L	O	I	K	U	E	C	I	L	R
R	C	W	L	E	S	S	C	O	E	M
S	E	B	T	S	T	H	A	V	Y	E
Y	O	A	R	O	R	B	I	T	B	I
S	T	L	S	S	H	A	P	E	D	L
T	I	L	K	T	A	I	L	E	A	F
E	O	O	T	I	C	E	B	A	L	L
M	S	K	Y	S	H	I	N	I	N	G

_ _

_ _ _ _ _ _ _ _ _. _ _ _ _ _ _ _ _ _ _ _ _ _ _ _ _ _ _ _

_ _.

Dino Pet!

Directions: If you could have a pet dinosaur, what would it look like? Draw your dinosaur below. Write its name on the line.

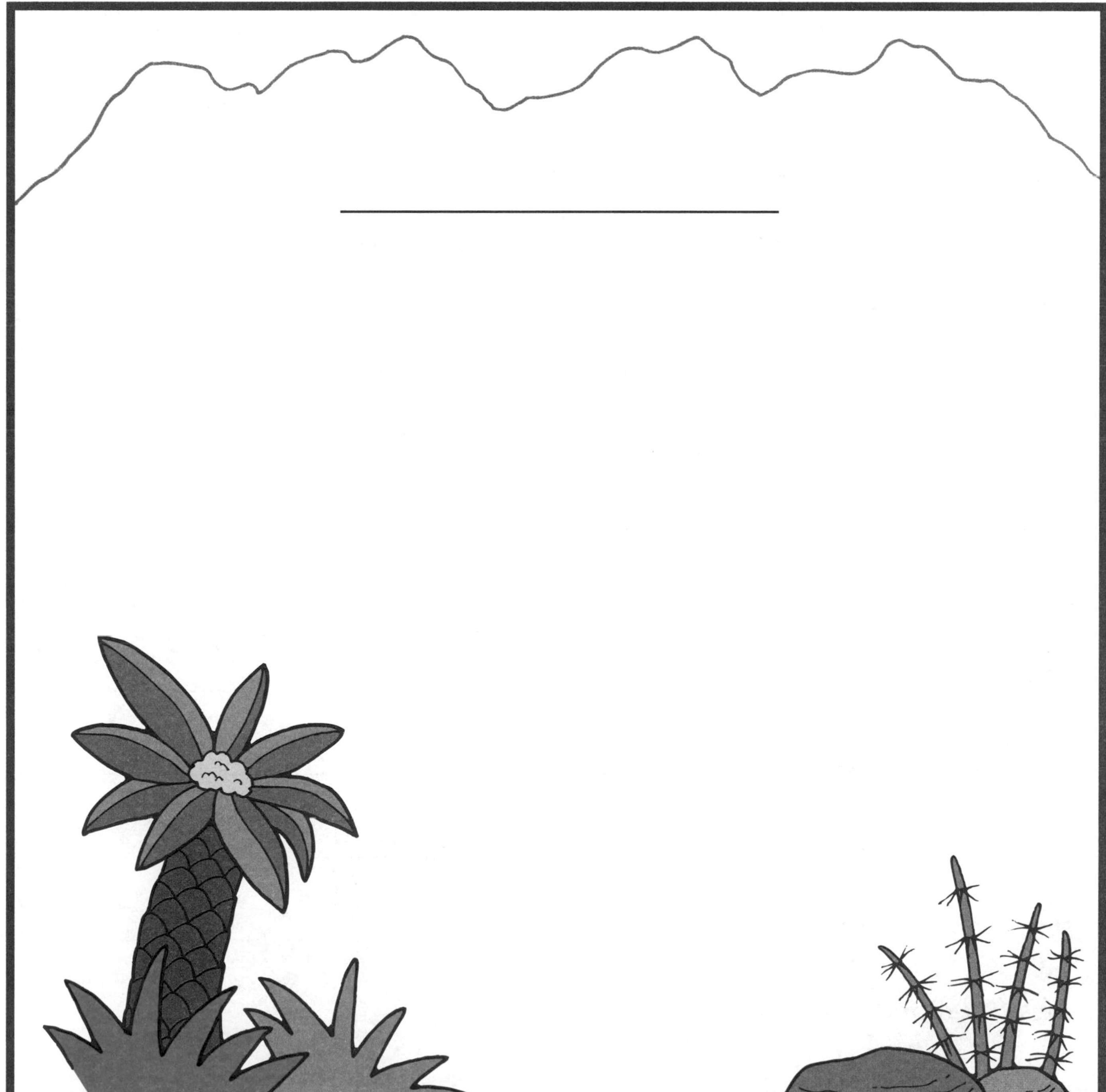

Types of Books

A **fiction** book is a book about things that are made up or not true. Fantasy books are fiction. A **nonfiction** book is about things that have really happened. Books can be classified into more types:

mystery — books that have clues that lead to solving a problem or mystery

biography — book about a real person's life

poetry — a collection of poems, which may or may not rhyme

fantasy — books about things that cannot really happen

sports — books about different sports or sport figures

travel — books about going to other places

Directions: Write **mystery**, **biography**, **poetry**, **fantasy**, **sports**, or **travel** next to each title.

The Life of Helen Keller ____________

Let's Go to Mexico! ____________

The Case of the Missing Doll ____________

How to Play Golf ____________

Turtle Soup and Other Poems ____________

Fred's Flying Saucer ____________

Fiction and Nonfiction

Fiction writing is inventing stories. The story might be about things that could really happen (realistic) or about things that couldn't possibly happen (fantasy). **Nonfiction** writing is based on facts. It usually gives information about people, places, or things. A person can often tell while reading whether a story or book is fiction or nonfiction.

Directions: Read the paragraphs below and on page 70. Determine whether each paragraph is fiction or nonfiction. Circle the letter **F** for fiction or the letter **N** for nonfiction.

"Do not be afraid, little flowers," said the oak. "Close your yellow eyes in sleep, and trust in me. You have made me glad many a time with your sweetness. Now, I will take care that the winter shall do you no harm." **F N**

The whole team watched as the ball soared over the outfield fence. The game was over! It was hard to walk off the field and face parents, friends, and each other. It had been a long season. Now, they would have to settle for second place. **F N**

Be careful when you remove the dish from the microwave. It will be very hot, so take care not to get burned by the dish or the hot steam. If time permits, leave the dish in the microwave for 2 or 3 minutes to avoid getting burned. It is a good idea to use a potholder, too. **F N**

Fiction and Nonfiction

Megan and Mariah skipped out to the playground. They enjoyed playing together at recess. Today, it was Mariah's turn to choose what they would do first. To Megan's surprise, Mariah asked, "What do you want to do, Megan? I'm going to let you pick since it's your birthday!" **F N**

It is easy to tell an insect from a spider. An insect has three body parts and six legs. A spider has eight legs and no wings. Of course, if you see the creature spinning a web, you will know what it is. An insect wouldn't want to get too close to the web or it would be stuck. It might become dinner! **F N**

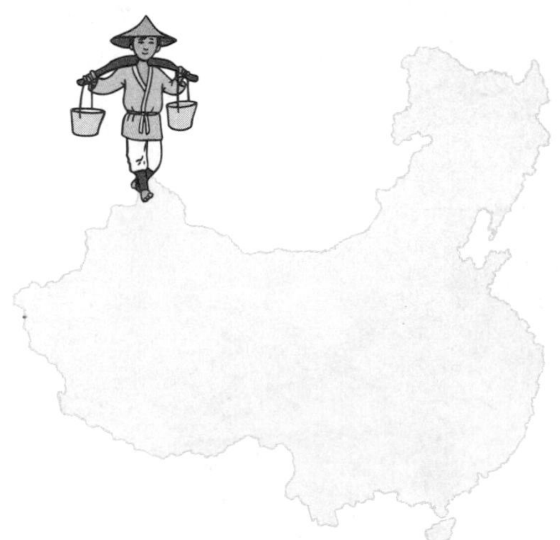

My name is Lee Chang, and I live in a country that you call China. My home is on the other side of the world from yours. When the sun is rising in my country, it is setting in yours. When it is day at your home, it is night at mine. **F N**

Henry washed the dog's foot in cold water from the brook. The dog lay very still, for he knew that the boy was trying to help him. **F N**

Mammals

Directions: Read the clues and use the words in the word box to complete the puzzle.

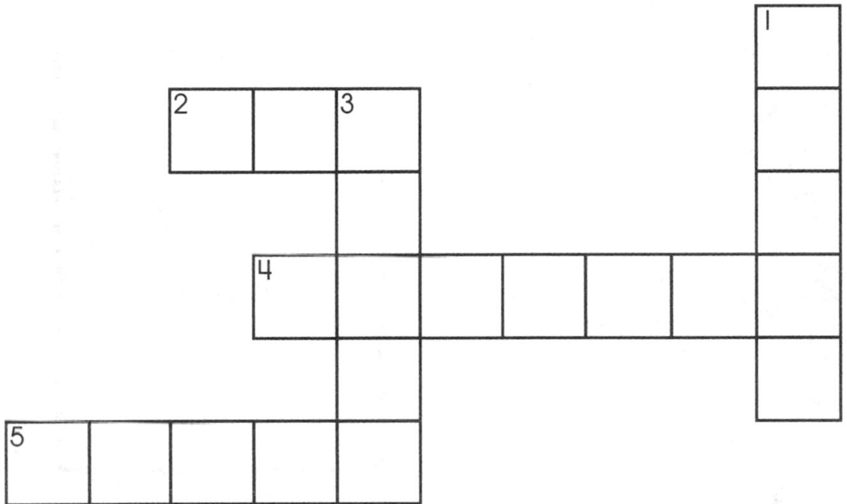

raccoon
skunk
mouse
cow
whale

Across

2. I live on a farm and give people milk.
4. I look like I wear a mask.
5. I am very small and have a long skinny tail.

Down

1. I am black with a white stripe going down the middle of my back.
3. I live in the ocean.

Q + U

Directions: Look at the picture clues. Then, complete the puzzle using the words from the word box.

Across

1. 

3. 

4. 

5. 

Down

2. 

4. 

quiet
quail
quarter
umbrella
unicorn
queen

1 2

3

4

5

English

Alphabetical Order

Alphabetical order (or ABC order) is the order of letters in the alphabet. When putting words in alphabetical order, use the first letter of each word.

Directions: Number the words in each list from **1** to **5** in alphabetical order.

___ happy	___ zebra	___ banana
___ scared	___ gorilla	___ kiwi
___ worried	___ monkey	___ apple
___ amused	___ hyena	___ peach
___ excited	___ kangaroo	___ lemon

Alphabetical Order

Directions: Alphabetical order is putting words in the order in which they appear in the alphabet. Put the eggs in alphabetical order. The first and last words are done for you.

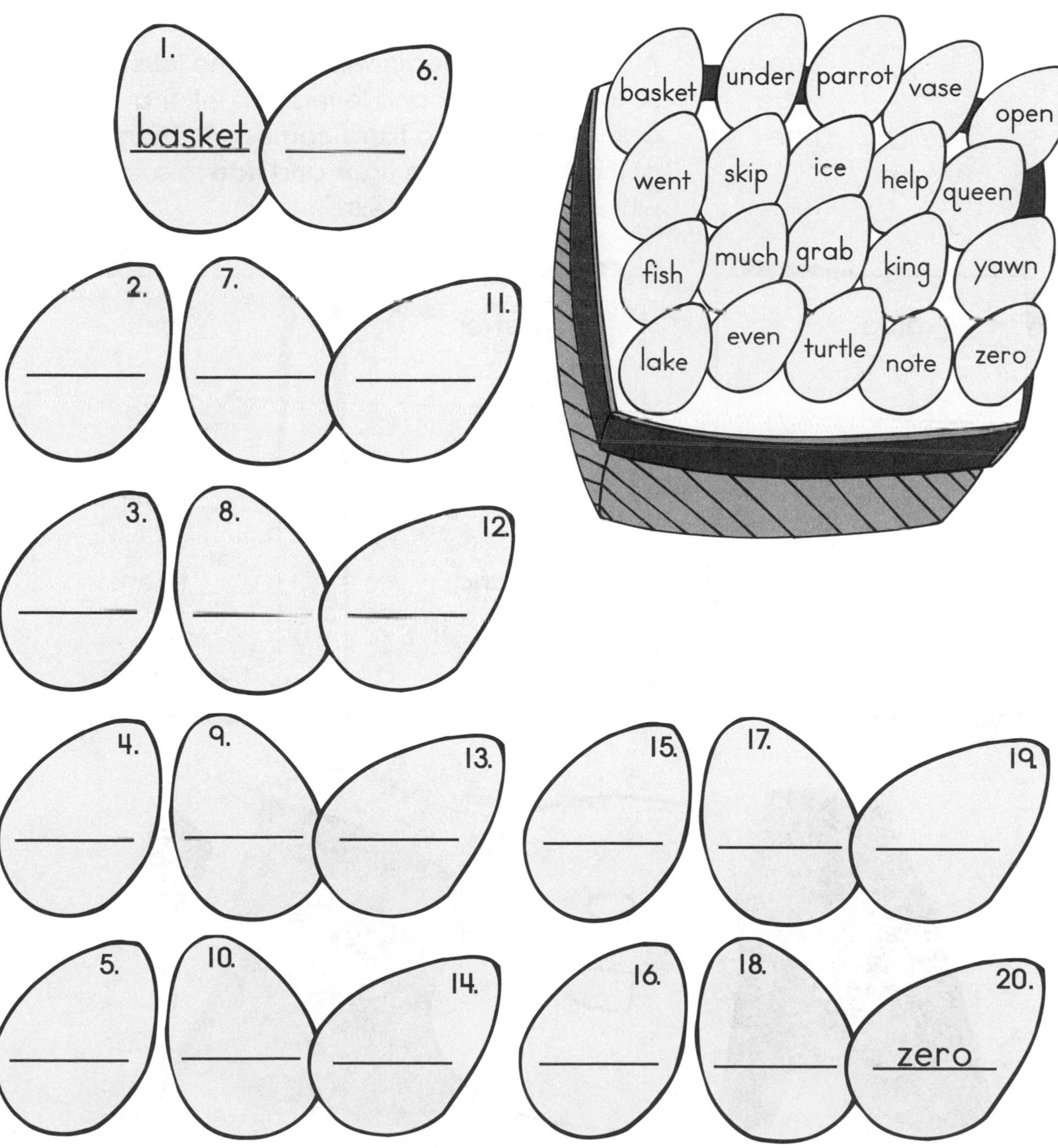

Alphabetical Order

The words in these lists begin with the same letter.

Directions: Use the second or third letters of each word to put the lists in alphabetical order.

Example:

3 tiger
1 tape
2 tide

All three words begin with the same letter **(t)**, so look at the second letters. The letter **a** comes before **i**, so **tape** comes first. Then, look at the third letters in **tiger** and **tide** to see which word comes next.

___ glad
___ goat
___ gasoline
___ gentle
___ grumble

___ answer
___ about
___ ask
___ around
___ against

___ tape
___ taste
___ table
___ talent
___ taught

Alphabetical Order

Alphabetical order is the order in which letters come in the alphabet.

Directions: Write the words in alphabetical order. If the first letter is the same, use the second letter of each word to decide which word comes first. If the second letter is also the same, look at the third letter of each word to decide.

Example: wish wasp won't 

1. w**a**sp
2. w**i**sh
3. w**o**n't

bench	flag	bowl

1. ____________________
2. ____________________
3. ____________________

egg	nod	neat

1. ____________________
2. ____________________
3. ____________________

dog	dart	drag

1. ____________________
2. ____________________
3. ____________________

skipped	stairs	stones

1. ____________________
2. ____________________
3. ____________________

Out of This World

Directions: Find the out-of-this-world space words from the word box. Words can be across, down, or diagonal.

space	alien	ship
orbit	Earth	planet
skies	stars	Mars

c	s	t	b	n	o	j	r	p	i
z	h	c	s	k	i	e	s	k	d
x	i	g	p	w	s	u	h	n	v
t	p	l	a	n	e	t	q	e	s
o	u	y	c	l	m	n	a	a	t
r	a	a	e	c	i	h	e	r	o
b	w	e	c	s	r	e	j	t	s
i	e	u	r	s	l	k	n	h	u
t	v	r	l	w	d	g	f	a	l
c	x	g	m	a	r	s	n	r	a

Climb the Tower

Directions: Look at the picture clues. Then, complete the puzzle using the words from the word box.

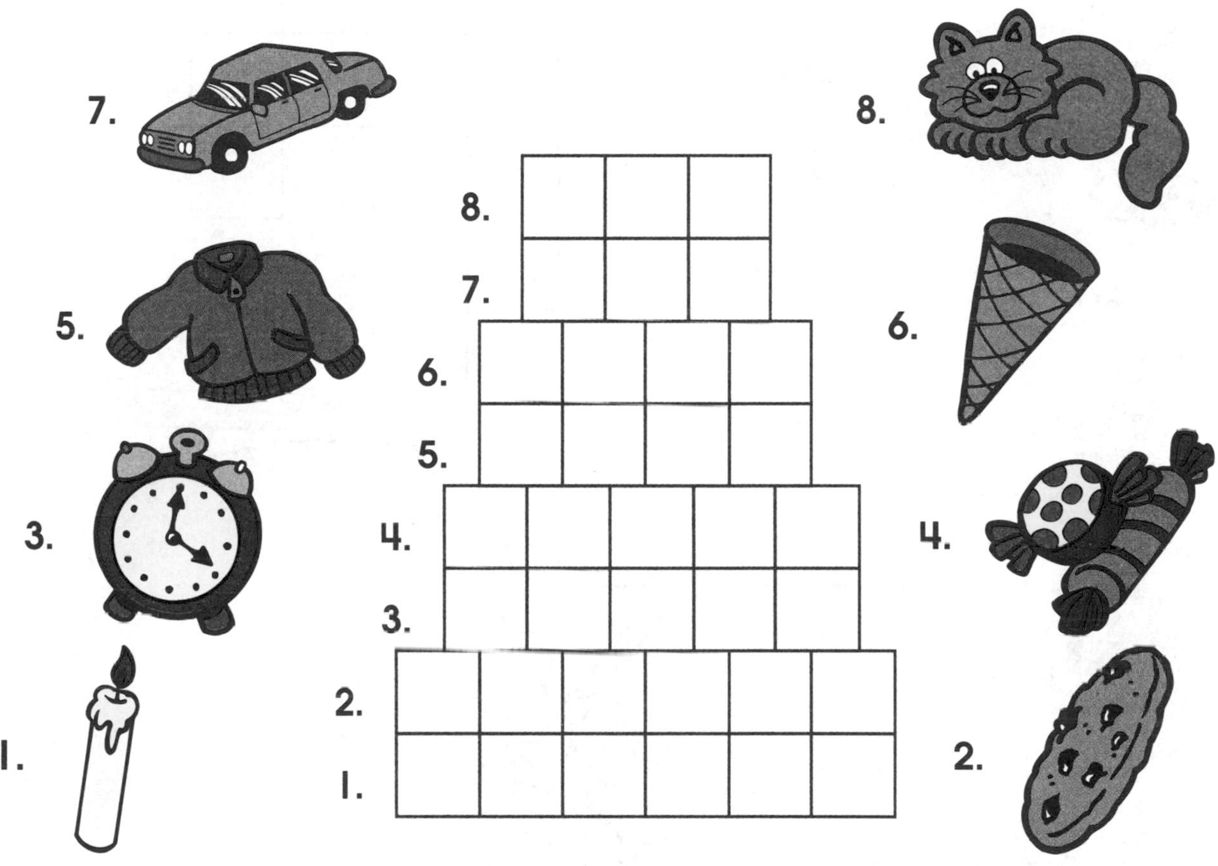

candle	cookie	cone	candy
cat	coat	car	clock

Hit the Hay!

Directions: Look at the picture clues. Then, complete the puzzle using the words from the word box.

Across

1.

3.

4.

5.

6.

7.

hop hole hill
happy helmet
hen hose
hut hay hand
hammer hat

Down

1.

2.

3.

4.

6.

7.

Antonyms

An **antonym** is a word that means the opposite of another word.

Examples:

child  adult

 hot

 cold

Directions: Match the words that have opposite meanings. Draw a line between each pair of antonyms.

thaw	same
huge	sad
crying	friend
happy	open
enemy	freeze
asleep	thin
closed	hide
fat	tiny
seek	awake
different	laughing

Antonyms

Directions: Complete each sentence with an antonym pair from page 81. Some pairs will not be used.

Example: Usually, we wear <u>different</u> clothes, but today we are dressed the <u>same</u>.

1. The ____________ cat would be ____________ if it chased more mice.
2. Mom was ______________ it rained since her garden was very dry, but I was ______________ because I had to stay inside.
3. The ______________ crowd of people tried to fit into the ______________ room.
4. The ______________ baby was soon ______________ and playing in the crib.
5. We'll ______________ the meat for now, and Dad will ______________ it when we need it.
6. The windows were wide ______________, but the door was ______________.

Now, write your own sentence using one of the antonym pairs.

____

____

____

Antonyms

Antonyms are words that are opposites.

Example:

hairy

bald

Directions: Choose a word from the box to complete each sentence below. Not every word will be used.

open	right	light	full	late	below
hard	clean	slow	quiet	old	nice

Example:

My car was **dirty**, but now it's **clean**.

1. Sometimes, my cat is naughty, and sometimes she's ________________.
2. The sign said, "Closed," but the door was ________________.
3. Is the glass half empty or half ________________ ?
4. I bought new shoes, but I like my ________________ ones better.
5. Skating is easy for me, but ________________ for my brother.
6. The sky is dark at night and ________________ during the day.
7. I like a noisy house, but my mother likes a ________________ one.
8. My friend says I'm wrong, but I say I'm ________________.
9. Jason is a fast runner, but Adam is a ________________ runner.
10. We were supposed to be early, but we were ________________.

Antonyms

Directions: Write the antonym pairs from each sentence in the boxes.

Example: Many things are bought and sold at the market.

bought	sold

1. I thought I lost my dog, but someone found him.

2. The teacher will ask a question for the students to answer.

3. Airplanes arrive and depart from the airport.

4. The water in the pool was cold compared to the warm water in the whirlpool.

5. The tortoise was slow, but the hare was fast.

Q and U Too

Directions: Look at the picture clues. Then, complete the puzzle using the words from the word box.

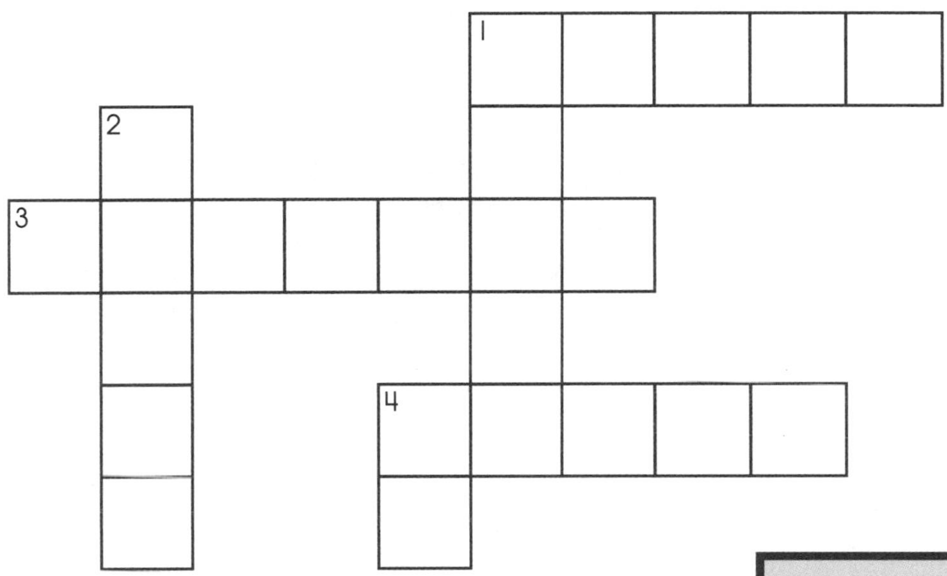

quick
under
quarter
queen
up
quack

Across

1. 

3.  

4.

Down

1.  

2. 

4. 

Build Your Dream House

Directions: If you could build your dream house, what would it look like? Draw it below. Then, write your name on the mailbox.

Starting Out

Directions: Fill in the blanks with **dr**, **fr**, **gr**, or **tr**. Then, find and circle the words in the puzzle.

1. _____ apes
2. _____ og
3. _____ ee
4. _____ um
5. _____ ain
6. _____ ink
7. _____ ame
8. _____ ess

d	h	a	g	r	a	p	e	s	k
r	f	b	f	r	a	m	e	j	d
e	r	i	n	o	t	r	e	e	r
s	o	c	d	w	m	l	p	g	u
s	g	w	d	r	i	n	k	q	m
t	r	a	i	n	s	e	w	f	r

Synonyms

Synonyms are words with nearly the same meaning.

Directions: Draw a line to match each word on the left with its synonym on the right.

infant	hello
forest	coat
bucket	grin
hi	baby
bunny	woods
cheerful	fall
jacket	repair
alike	small
smile	same
autumn	hop
little	skinny
thin	top
jump	rabbit
shirt	pail
fix	happy

Synonyms

Directions: Read each sentence. Choose a word from the box that has the same meaning as the bold word. Write the synonym on the line next to the sentence. The first one has been done for you.

skinniest	biggest	jacket	little	quickly	woods	joyful
grin	alike	trip	rabbit	fix	autumn	infant

1. The deer ran through the **forest**. ______woods______
2. White mice are very **small** pets. ____________________
3. Goldfish move **fast** in the water. ____________________
4. The twins look exactly the **same**. ____________________
5. Trees lose their leaves in the **fall**. ____________________
6. The blue whale is the **largest** animal on Earth. ____________________
7. We will go to the ocean on our next **vacation**. ____________________
8. The **bunny** hopped through the tall grass. ____________________
9. The **baby** was crying because she was hungry. ____________________
10. Put on your **coat** before you go outside. ____________________
11. Does that clown have a big **smile** on his face? ____________________
12. That is the **thinnest** man I have ever seen. ____________________
13. I will **repair** my bicycle as soon as I get home. ____________________
14. The children made **happy** sounds when they won. ____________________

Synonyms

Directions: Match the pairs of synonyms.

delight •	• discover
speak •	• tidy
lovely •	• start
find •	• talk
nearly •	• beautiful
neat •	• almost
big •	• joy
sad •	• unhappy
begin •	• large

Directions: Read each sentence. Write the synonym pairs from each sentence in the boxes.

1. That unusual clock is a rare antique.

2. I am glad you are so happy!

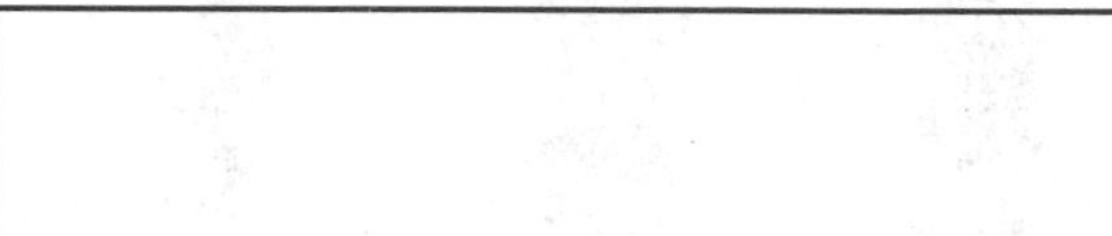

3. Ana-Maria felt unhappy when she heard the sad news.

Snow Sports

Directions: Find and circle the words in the puzzle.

lift
skate
icicle
jacket
sled
ice
ski
hockey
snowman
cold
pole
sweater
bindings
toboggan

Measurement

Directions: Read the sentences and use the words in the word box to complete the puzzle.

gallon
pound
liter
yards
inch
pint

Across

2. José ate a ____ of chocolate ice cream.
4. Mom bought a ____ of milk.

Down

1. The inchworm is one ____ long.
2. The cake recipe required a ____ of butter.
3. The length of a football field is 100 ____ .
5. Alfred bought a two-____ bottle of soda.

Sewing Search

Directions: Find and circle the words in the puzzle.

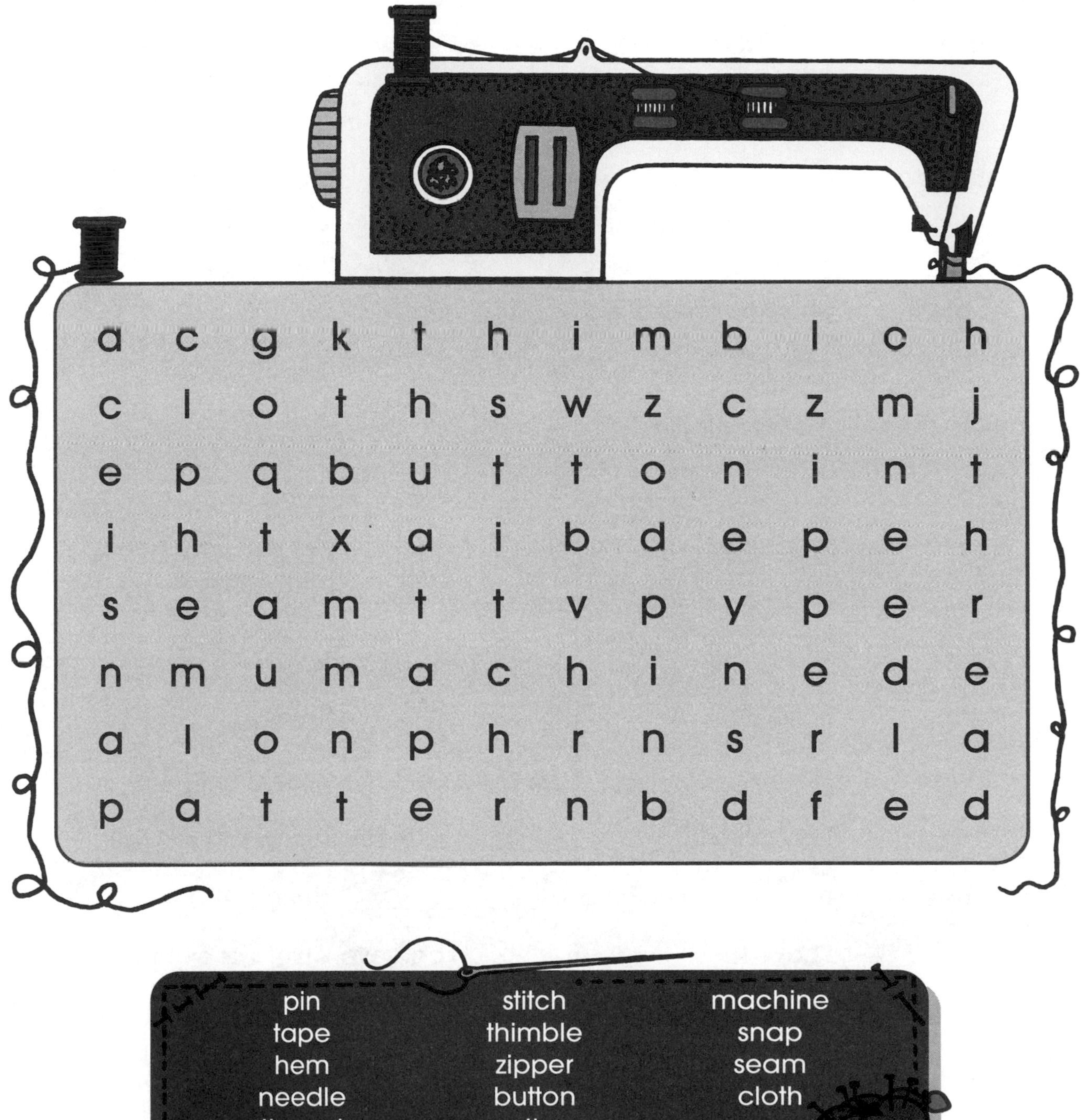

Homophones

Homophones are words that sound the same but are spelled differently and have different meanings.

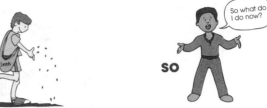

Example:

sew **sow**

so

So what do I do now?

Directions: Read the sentences, and write the correct word in the blanks.

Example:

blue	**blew**	She has **blue** eyes.
		The wind **blew** the barn down.
eye	**I**	He hurt his left ________________ playing ball.
		________________ like to learn new things.
see	**sea**	Can you ________________ the winning runner from here?
		He goes diving for pearls under the ________________ .
eight	**ate**	The baby ________________ the banana.
		Jane was ________________ years old last year.
one	**won**	Jill ________________ first prize at the science fair.
		I am the only ________________ in my family with red hair.
be	**bee**	Ivana cried when a ________________ stung her.
		I have to ________________ in bed every night at eight o'clock.
two to too		My father likes ________________ play tennis.
		I like to play, ________________ .
		It takes at least ________________ people to play.

Homophones

Directions: Circle the correct word to complete each sentence. Then, write the word on the line.

1. I am going to ______________ a letter to my grandmother.
   right, write

2. Draw a circle around the ______________ answer.
   right, write

3. Wait an ______________ before going swimming.
   our, hour

4. This is ______________ house.
   our, hour

5. He got a ______________ from his garden.
   beat, beet

6. Our football team ______________ that team.
   beat, beet

7. Go to the store and ______________ a loaf of bread.
   by, buy

8. We will drive ______________ your house.
   by, buy

9. There will be trouble if the dog ______________ the cat.
   seas, sees

10. They sailed the seven ______________.
    seas, sees

11. We have ______________ cars in the garage.
    to, too, two

12. I am going ______________ the zoo today.
    to, too, two

13. My little brother is going, ______________.
    to, too, two

Homophones

Homophones are words that sound the same but have different spellings and meanings.

Directions: Complete each sentence using a word from the box.

blew	night	blue	knight	hour	in	ant	inn
our	aunt	meet	too	two	to	meat	

1. A red ____________ crawled up the wall.
2. It will be one ____________ before we can go back home.
3. Will you ____________ us later?
4. We plan to stay at an ____________ during our trip.
5. The king had a ________________ who fought bravely.
6. The wind ____________ so hard that I almost lost my hat.
7. His jacket was ____________.
8. My____________ plans to visit us this week.
9. I will come ____________ when it gets too cold outside.
10. It was late at ____________ when we finally got there.
11. ____________ of us will go with you.
12. I will mail a note ____________ someone at the bank.
13. Do you eat red ____________?
14. We would like to join you, ____________.
15. Come over to see ____________ new cat.

Homophones

Directions: Circle the words that are not used correctly. Write the correct word above the circled word. Use the words in the box to help you. The first one has been done for you.

road	see	one	be	so	I	brakes	piece	there
wait	not	some	hour	would	no	deer	you	heard

Jake and his family were getting close to Grandpa's. It had taken them nearly an hour our to get their, but Jake knew it was worth it. In his mind, he could already sea the pond and could almost feel the cool water. It had been sew hot this summer in the apartment.

"Wood ewe like a peace of my apple, Jake?" asked his big sister Clare. "Eye can't eat any more."

"Know, thank you," Jake replied. "I still have sum of my fruit left."

Suddenly, Dad slammed on the breaks. "Did you see that dear on the rode? I always herd that if you see won, there might bee more."

"Good thinking, Dad. I'm glad you are a safe driver. We're knot very far from Grandpa's now. I can't weight!"

Homophones Sound Alike

Directions: Read the clues and use the words in the word box to complete the puzzle.

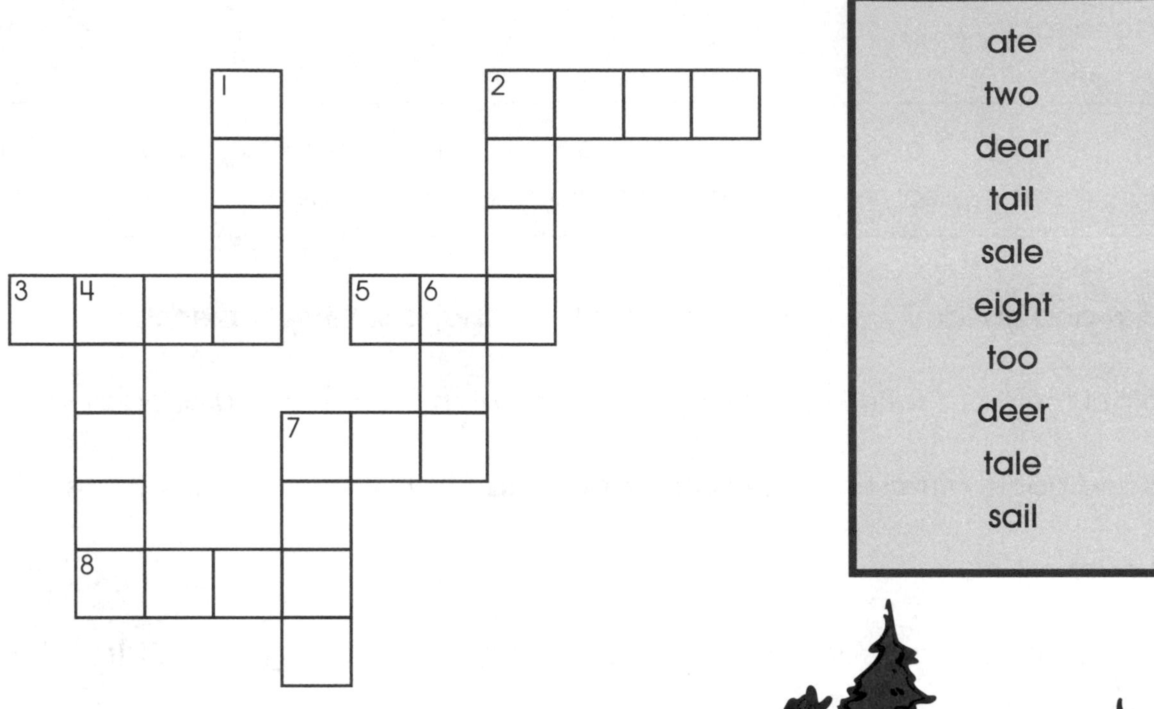

Across

2. A boat can have this.
3. This animal lives in the forest.
5. What you did at lunchtime.
7. This number is one less than three.
8. A squirrel has a long, furry one.

Down

1. This is what you say at the beginning of a letter.
2. A store can have a sign that says this.
4. This is one more than seven.
6. It is a word that means **also**.
7. This is a story.

S Blends

Directions: Read the clues and use the words in the word box to complete the puzzle.

score
swim
skate
snake
slide
stars
spoon
smile

Across

1. You glide down this on a playground.
2. Use this to eat your soup.
4. It is a boot with wheels.
6. This is fun to do in a pool.

Down

1. It is a long, thin animal without legs.
2. Keep track of points in a game.
3. These shine in the sky at night.
5. What you do when you are happy.

Nuts, Seeds, and Beans

Directions: Find and circle the words in the puzzle.

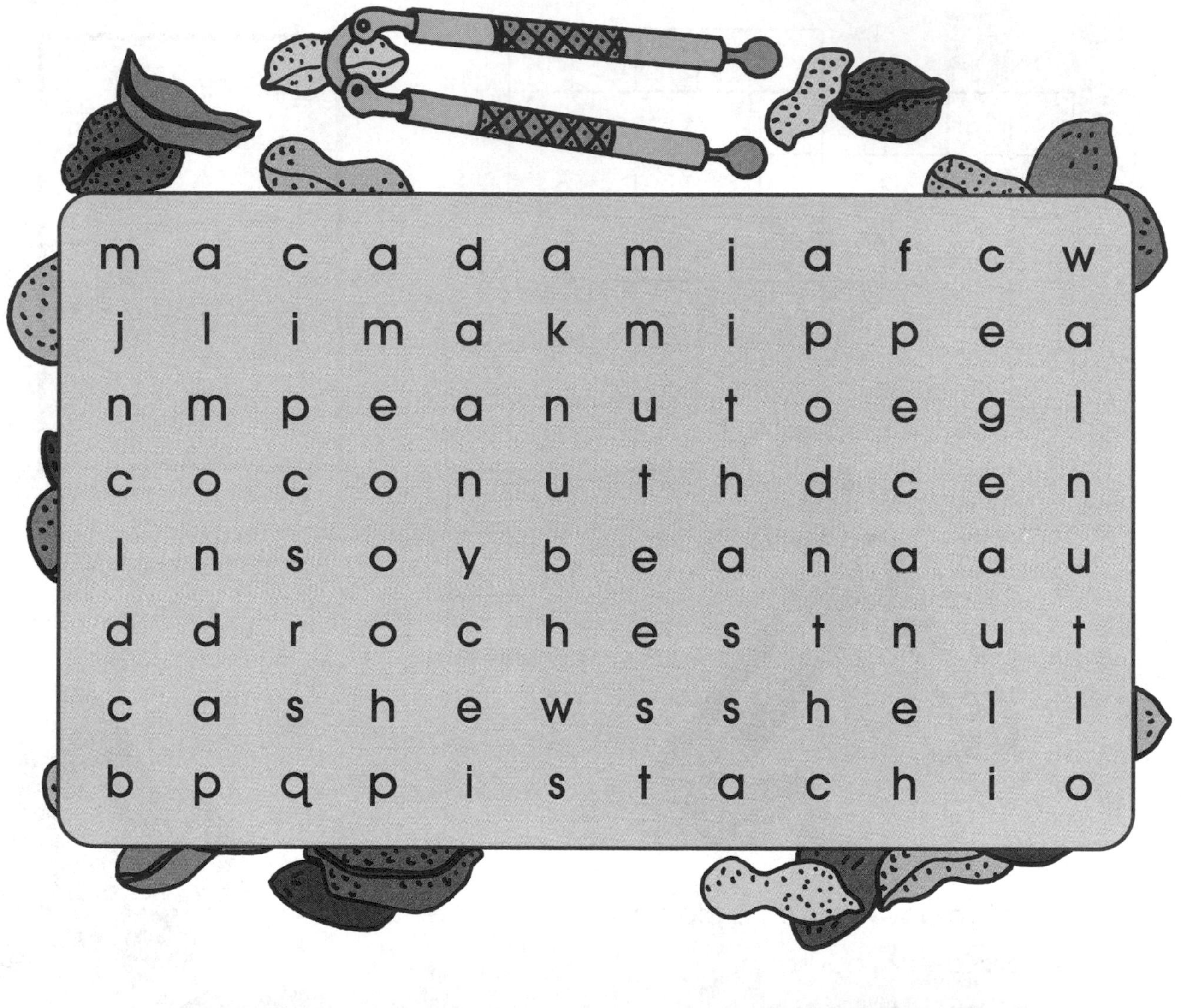

peanut
almond
soybean
lima
macadamia

pea
pecan
pod
walnut

pistachio
coconut
chestnut
cashew
shell

Nouns

Nouns are words that tell the names of people, places, or things.

Directions: Read the words below. Then, write them in the correct column.

goat	Mrs. Jackson	girl
beach	tree	song
mouth	park	Madison Rivers
finger	flower	New York
Malik Jones	Elm City	Frank Gates
Main Street	theater	skates
River Park	father	boy

Person

Place

Thing

Person	Place	Thing
______	______	______
______	______	______
______	______	______
______	______	______
______	______	______
______	______	______
______	______	______

Common Nouns

Common nouns are nouns that name any member of a group of people, places, or things, rather than specific people, places, or things.

Directions: Read the sentences below, and write the common noun found in each sentence.

Example: socks My socks do not match.

1. ______________ The bird could not fly.
2. ______________ Ben likes to eat trail mix.
3. ______________ I am going to meet my mother.
4. ______________ We will go swimming in the lake tomorrow.
5. ______________ I hope the flowers will grow quickly.
6. ______________ We colored eggs together.
7. ______________ It is easy to ride a bicycle.
8. ______________ My cousin is very tall.
9. ______________ Ted and Elena went fishing in their boat.
10. ______________ They won a prize yesterday.
11. ______________ She fell down and twisted her ankle.
12. ______________ My brother was born today.
13. ______________ She went down the slide.
14. ______________ Ray went to the doctor today.

Proper Nouns

Proper nouns are names of specific people, places, or things. Proper nouns begin with a capital letter.

Directions: Read the sentences below, and circle the proper nouns found in each sentence.

Example: Aunt Frances gave me a puppy for my birthday.

1. We lived on Jackson Street before we moved to our new house.
2. Angela's birthday party is tomorrow night.
3. We drove through Cheyenne, Wyoming, on our way home.
4. Dr. Charles always gives me a sticker after my appointment.
5. George Washington was our first president.
6. Our class took a field trip to the Johnson Flower Farm.
7. Uncle Jack lives in New York City.
8. Aliyah and Elizabeth are best friends.
9. We buy muffins at the Grayson Bakery.
10. My favorite movie is E.T.
11. We flew to Miami, Florida, in a plane.
12. We go to Riverfront Stadium to watch the baseball games.
13. Mr. Fields is a wonderful music teacher.
14. My best friend is Vik Patel.

Proper Nouns

Directions: Write about you! Write a proper noun for each category below. Capitalize the first letter of each proper noun.

1. Your first name: ____________
2. Your last name: ____________
3. Your street: ____________
4. Your city: ____________
5. Your state: ____________
6. Your school: ____________
7. Your best friend's name: ____________
8. Your teacher: ____________
9. Your favorite book character: ____________
10. Your favorite vacation place: ____________

Plural Nouns

A **plural** is more than one person, place, or thing. Add an **s** to show that a noun names more than one. If a noun ends in **x**, **ch**, **sh**, or **s**, add an **es** to the word.

Example: **pizza** 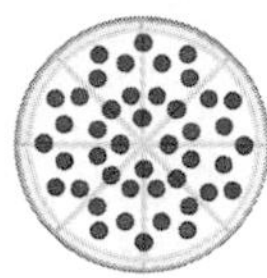 **pizzas** 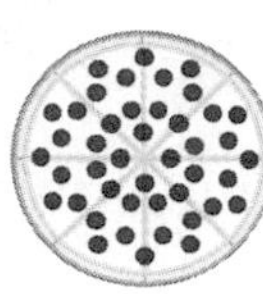 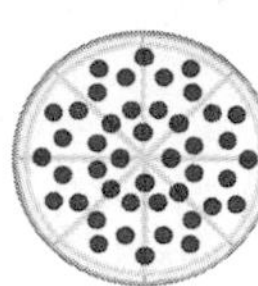 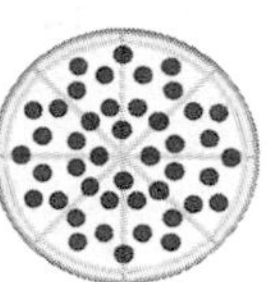

Directions: Write the plural of the words below.

Example: dog + s = dogs

cat ____________________

boot ____________________

house ____________________

Example: peach + es = peaches

lunch ____________________

bunch ____________________

punch ____________________

Example: ax + es = axes

fox ____________________

tax ____________________

box ____________________

Example: glass + es = glasses

mess ____________________

guess ____________________

class ____________________

Example: dish + es = dishes

bush ____________________

ash ____________________

brush ____________________

Example:

walrus 

walruses 

Plural Nouns

To write the plural forms of words ending in **y**, change the **y** to **ie** and add **s**.

Example: pony ponies

Directions: Write the plural of each noun on the lines below.

berry ______________________

cherry ______________________

bunny ______________________

penny ______________________

family ______________________

candy ______________________

party ______________________

Now, write a story using some of the words that end in **y**.
Remember to use capital letters and periods.

____

____

____

____

Plural Nouns

Directions: Write the plural of each noun to complete the sentences below. Remember to change the **y** to **ie** before you add **s**!

1. I am going to two birthday ______________________ this week.
(party)

2. Xander picked some ______________________ for Mom's pie.
(cherry)

3. At the store, we saw lots of ______________________.
(bunny)

4. My change at the toy store was three ______________________.
(penny)

5. All the ______________________ in Mom's book group will arrive at 7:00.
(lady)

6. Thanksgiving is a special time for ______________________ to gather together.
(family)

7. Boston and New York are very large ______________________.
(city)

Plural Nouns

Some words have special plural forms.

Example: leaf leaves

tooth	teeth
child	children
foot	feet
mouse	mice
woman	women
man	men

Directions: Some of the words in the box are special plurals. Complete each sentence with a plural from the box. Then, write the letters from the boxes in the blanks below to solve the puzzle.

1. I lost my two front ___ ___ ___ [___] ___ !

2. My sister has two pet ___ ___ ___ [___] .

3. Her favorite book is *Little* ___ ___ ___ [___] ___ .

4. The circus clown had big ___ ___ ___ [___] .

5. The teacher played a game with the

___ [___] ___ ___ ___ ___ ___ ___ .

Take good care of this pearly plural!

___ ___ ___ ___ ___

1 2 3 4 5

Plural Nouns

Directions: The **singular form** of a word shows one person, place, or thing. Write the singular form of each noun on the lines below.

cherries ______________________

lunches ______________________

countries ______________________

leaves ______________________

churches ______________________

arms ______________________

boxes ______________________

men ______________________

wheels ______________________

pictures ______________________

cities ______________________

places ______________________

ostriches ______________________

glasses ______________________

Jurassic Search

Directions: Find the hidden words in the puzzle below. The words may be written forward, backward, up, down, or diagonally. Circle the words. When you have located all the words, write the remaining letters at the bottom of the page to spell out a message.

ALLOSAURUS	APATOSAURUS	ARMORED	ARCHAEOPTERYX
BIRD HIP	COELURUS	DINOSAUR	DIPLODOCUS
FOSSIL	JURASSIC	MEAT-EATER	PALEONTOLOGIST
PLANT-EATER	PLATED	SAUROPOD	STEGOSAURUS

S	D	B	U	R	L	I	S	S	O	F	I	S	M	N
G	U	I	T	H	I	S	P	E	R	I	O	T	E	T
J	D	R	U	A	S	O	N	I	D	S	H	E	A	S
U	A	D	U	L	D	L	O	S	E	W	S	G	T	I
R	E	H	A	A	S	O	U	C	R	O	V	O	E	G
A	E	I	R	E	S	R	P	D	O	M	U	S	A	O
S	C	P	H	O	U	O	F	O	M	N	O	A	T	L
S	R	T	H	L	A	M	T	E	R	R	I	U	E	O
I	C	A	E	A	N	D	E	A	A	U	U	R	R	T
C	R	O	O	D	E	T	A	L	P	P	A	U	E	N
A	C	N	D	R	A	I	N	S	C	A	A	S	M	O
E	X	Y	R	E	T	P	O	E	A	H	C	R	A	E
T	O	T	H	D	I	P	L	O	D	O	C	U	S	L
R	E	T	A	E	T	N	A	L	P	E	D	E	S	A
E	R	A	L	L	O	S	A	U	R	U	S	T	S	P

Hidden message:

Rocks and Minerals

Directions: Find and circle the words in the puzzle.

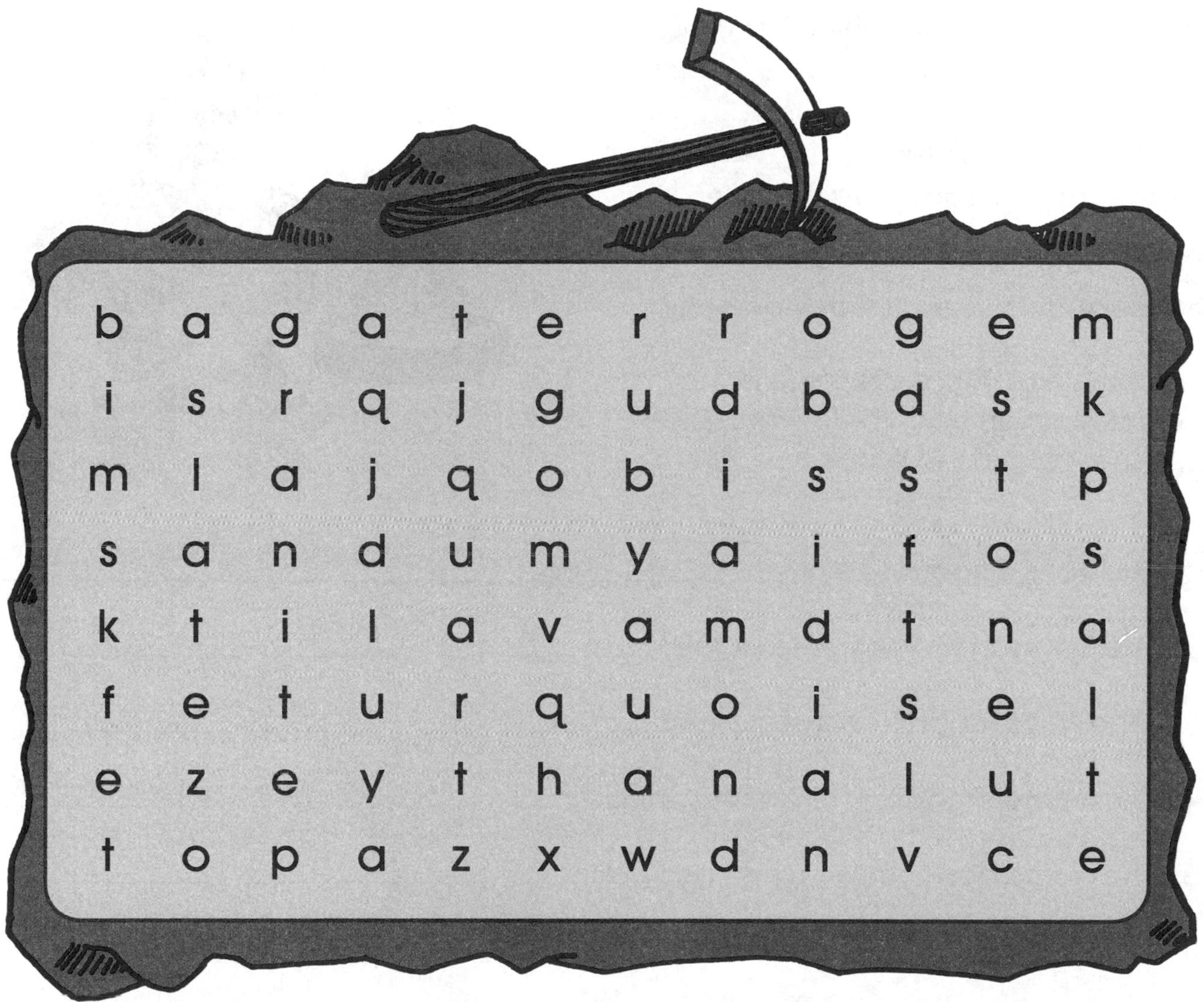

slate
agate
salt
granite
obsidian

gem
lava
sand
stone

ruby
topaz
quartz
diamond
turquoise

Possessive Nouns

Possessive nouns tell who or what is the owner of something. With singular nouns, use an apostrophe **before** the **s**. With plural nouns, use an apostrophe **after** the **s**.

Example:

singular: one elephant

The **elephant's** dance was wonderful.

plural: more than one elephant

The **elephants'** dance was wonderful.

Directions: Put the apostrophe in the correct place in each bold word. Then, write the word in the blank.

1. The **lions** cage was big. ______________________
2. The **bears** costumes were purple. ______________________
3. One **boys** laughter was very loud. ______________________
4. The **trainers** dogs were dancing about. ______________________
5. The **mans** popcorn was tasty and good. ______________________
6. **Marks** cotton candy was delicious. ______________________
7. A little **girls** balloon burst in the air. ______________________
8. The big **clowns** tricks were very funny. ______________________
9. **Lauras** sister clapped for the clowns. ______________________
10. The **womans** money was lost in the crowd. ______________________
11. **Kellys** mother picked her up early. ______________________

Possessive Nouns

Directions: Circle the correct possessive noun in each sentence, and write it in the blank.

Example: One ____girl's____ mother is a teacher.
(girl's) girls'

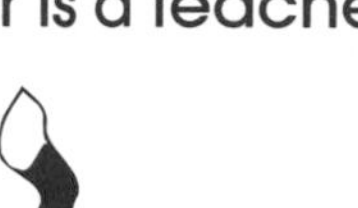

1. The ______________________ tail is long.
   cat's cats'

2. One ______________________ baseball bat is aluminum.
   boy's boys'

3. The ______________________ aprons are white.
   waitresses' waitress's

4. My ______________________ apple pie is the best!
   grandmother's grandmothers'

5. My ______________________ five uniforms are dirty.
   brother's brothers'

6. The ______________________ doll is pretty.
   child's childs'

7. These ______________________ collars are different colors.
   dog's dogs'

8. The ______________________ tail is short.
   cow's cows'

Words with *ch*, *sh*, *th*, and *wh*

Directions: Read the clues and use the words in the word box to complete the puzzle.

chick
shower
think
whale
cherry
shade
thirteen
white

Across

1. Clouds can be this color.
3. This hatches from an egg.
4. You do this with your brain.
5. It is a spray of water.
6. It is a very big sea mammal.
7. It is a red fruit.

Down

2. The number after twelve.
5. You may find this under a tree.

Pronouns

Pronouns are words that are used in place of nouns.

Examples: **he, she, it, they, him, them, her, him**

Directions: Read each sentence. Write the pronoun that takes the place of each noun.

Example:

The monkey dropped the banana. 

1. **Dad** washed the car last night. ____________
2. **Mary and David** took a walk in the park. ____________
3. **Sydney** spent the night at her grandmother's house. ____________
4. **The baseball players** lost their game. ____________
5. **Mike Van Meter** is a great soccer player. ____________
6. **The parrot** can say five different words. 
7. **Megan** wrote a story in class today. ____________
8. They gave a party for **Teresa**. ____________
9. Everyone in the class was happy for **Darius**. 
10. The children petted **the giraffe**. 
11. Miyako put **the kittens** near the warm stove. 
12. **Gina** made a chocolate cake for my birthday. 
13. **Carlos and Matt** played baseball on the same team. 
14. Give the books to **Ethan**. 

Pronouns

Singular Pronouns

I	me	my	mine
you	your	yours	
he	she	it	her
hers	his	its	him

Plural Pronouns

we	us	our	ours
you	your	yours	
they	them	their	theirs

Directions: Underline the pronouns in each sentence.

1. Mom told us to wash our hands.

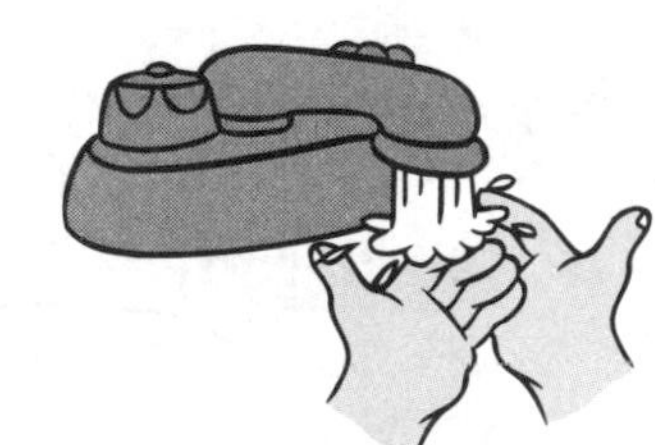

2. Did you go to the store?

3. We should buy him a present.

4. I called you about their party.

5. Our house had damage on its roof.

6. They want to give you a prize at our party.

7. My cat ate her sandwich.

8. Your coat looks like his coat.

Pronouns

Use the pronouns **I** and **we** when talking about the person or people doing the action.

Example: **I** can roller skate. **We** can roller skate.
Use **me** and **us** when talking about something that is happening to a person or people.

Example: They gave **me** the roller skates.
They gave **us** the roller skates.

Directions: Circle the correct pronoun, and write it in the blank.

Example:

___We___ are going to the picnic together. **(We,) Us**

1. __________ am finished with my science project. **I, Me**
2. Eric passed the football to __________. **me, I**
3. They ate dinner with __________ last night. **we, us**
4. __________ like spinach better than ice cream. **I, Me**
5. Mom came in the room to tell __________ good night. **me, I**
6. __________ had a pizza party in our backyard. **Us, We**
7. They told __________ the good news. **us, we**
8. Tom and __________ went to the store. **me, I**
9. She is taking __________ with her to the movies. **I, me**
10. Katie and __________ are good friends. **I, me**

Possessive Pronouns

Possessive pronouns show ownership.

Example: his hat, **her** shoes, **our** dog

Use these pronouns before a noun:
my, our, you, his, her, its, their

Example: That is **my** bike.

Use these pronouns on their own:
mine, yours, ours, his, hers, theirs, its

Example: That is **mine.**

Directions: Write each sentence again, using a pronoun instead of the words in bold letters. Be sure to use capitals and periods.

Example:

My **dog's** bowl is brown. **Its** bowl is brown.

1. That is **Beatriz's** book. ______________________

2. This is **my pencil**. ______________________

3. This hat is **your hat**. ______________________

4. Fifi is **Kevin's** cat. ______________________

5. That beautiful house is **our home**.

____

6. **The gerbil's** cage is too small.

____

Name ______________________

Don't Just Sit There

Directions: Look at the picture clues. Then, complete the puzzle using the words from the word box.

Across

3. 

7.  

4.

8.  

6. 

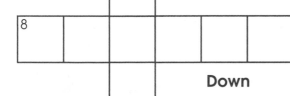

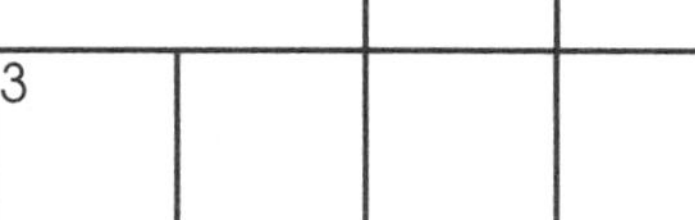

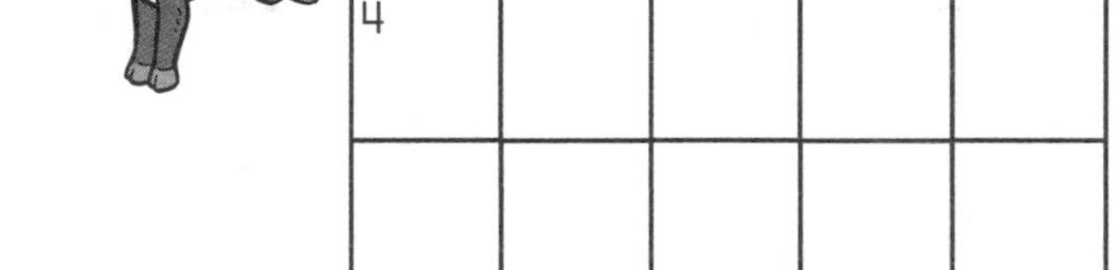

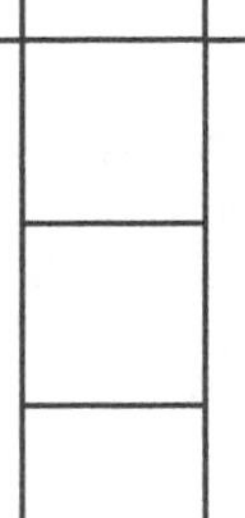

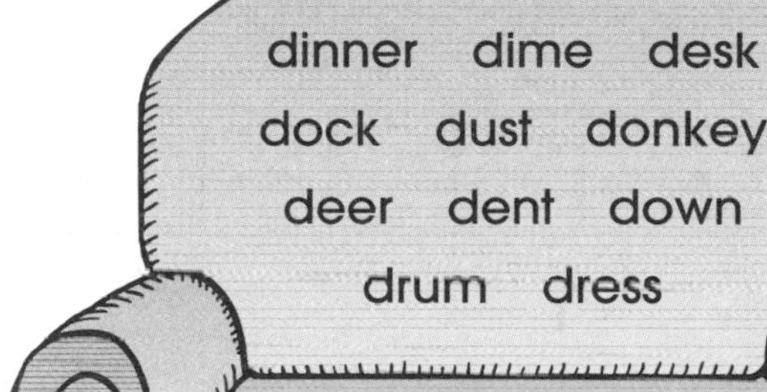

Down

1. 

2. 

3. 

4. 

5. 

7. 

 Name ____________________

Around the House

Directions: Read the clues and use the words in the word box to complete the puzzle.

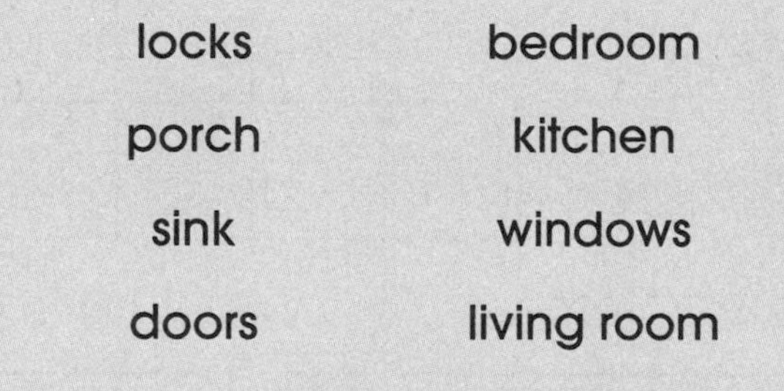

locks
bedroom
porch
kitchen
sink
windows
doors
living room

Across

3. It is a room for entertaining.
4. These keep people out.
7. It is a room for sleeping.
8. You see through these.

Down

1. It is a place to cook.
2. It is outside of the house.
5. You wash your hands here.
6. You can enter through these.

Abbreviations

An **abbreviation** is the shortened form of a word. Most abbreviations begin with a capital letter and end with a period.

Mr.	Mister	St.	Street
Mrs.	Missus	Ave.	Avenue
Dr.	Doctor	Blvd.	Boulevard
A.M.	before noon	Rd.	Road
P.M.	after noon		

Days of the week: Sun. Mon. Tues. Wed. Thurs. Fri. Sat.

Months of the year: Jan. Feb. Mar. Apr. Aug. Sept. Oct. Nov. Dec.

Directions: Write the abbreviations for each word.

Street	________	Doctor	________	Tuesday	________
Road	________	Mister	________	Avenue	________
Missus	________	October	________	Friday	________
before noon	________	March	________	August	________

Directions: Write each sentence using abbreviations.

1. On Monday at 9:00 before noon, Mister Gupta had a meeting.

____

2. In December, Doctor Carlson saw Missus Zuckerman.

____

3. One Tuesday in August, Mister Bernstein went to the park.

____

Art Words

Directions: Find and circle the words in the puzzle.

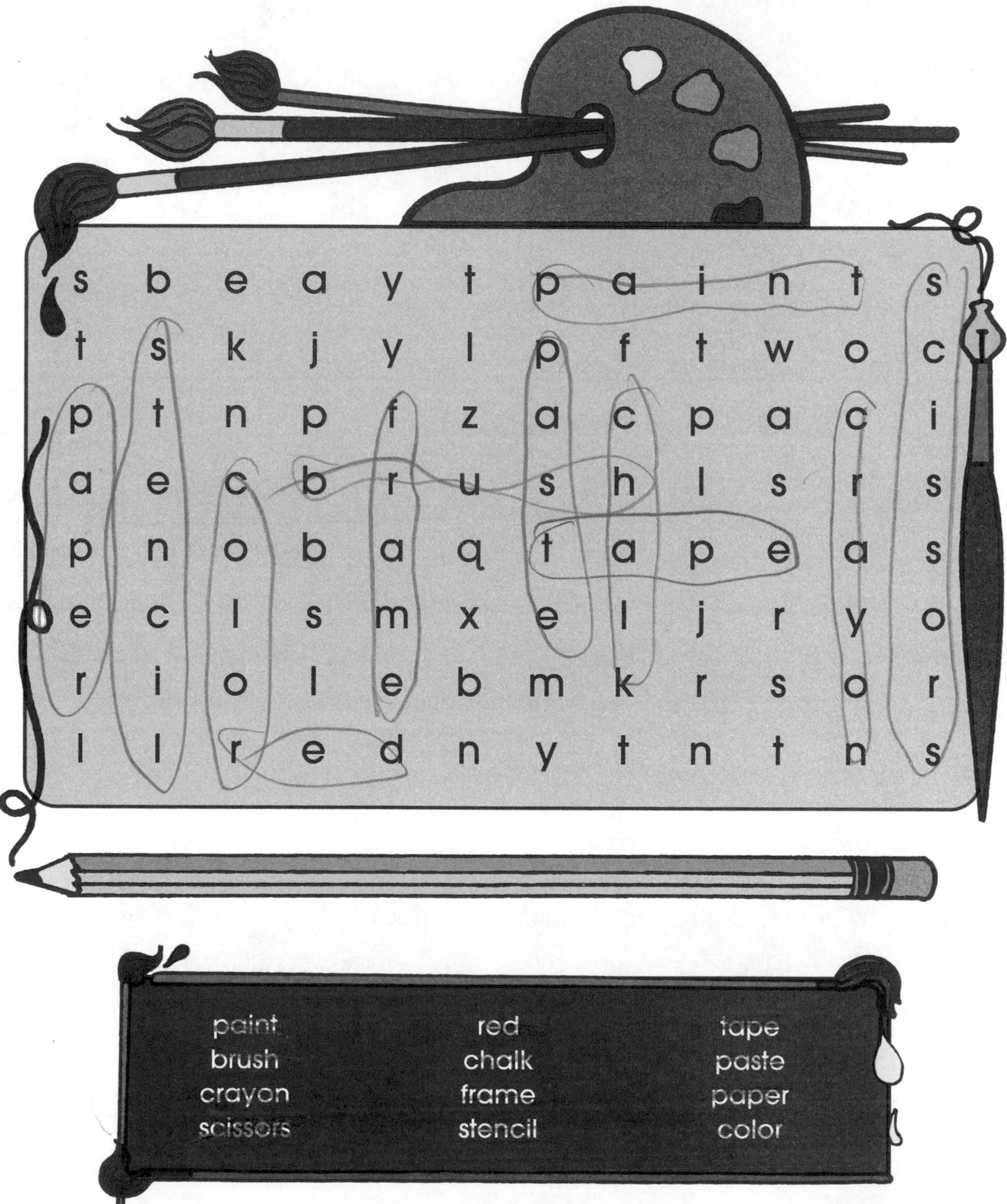

Adjectives

Adjectives are words that tell more about nouns, such as a **happy** child, a **cold** day, or a **hard** problem. Adjectives can tell how many (**one** airplane) or which one (**those** shoes).

Directions: The nouns are in bold letters. Circle the adjectives that describe the nouns.

Example: Some people have (unusual) **pets**.

1. Some people keep wild **animals**, like lions and bears.
2. These **pets** need special care.
3. These **animals** want to be free when they get older.
4. Even small **animals** can be difficult if they are wild.
5. Raccoons and squirrels are not tame **pets**.
6. Never touch a wild **animal** that may be sick.

Complete the story below by writing in your own adjectives. Use your imagination.

My Cat

My cat is a very ____________________ animal. She has ____________________

and ____________________ fur. Her favorite toy is a ____________________ ball.

She has ____________________ claws. She has a ____________________ tail.

She has a ____________________ face and ____________________ whiskers.

I think she is the ______________________________ cat in the world!

Adjectives and Nouns

Directions: Underline the nouns in each sentence below. Then, draw an arrow from each adjective to the noun it describes.

Example:

A platypus is a furry animal that lives in Australia.

1. This animal likes to swim.
2. The nose looks like a duck's bill.
3. It has a broad tail like a beaver.
4. Platypuses are great swimmers.
5. They have webbed feet, which help them swim.
6. Their flat tails also help them move through the water.
7. The platypus is an unusual mammal because it lays eggs.
8. The eggs look like reptile eggs.
9. Platypuses can lay three eggs at a time.
10. These babies do not leave their mothers for one year.
11. This animal spends most of its time hunting near streams.

Adjectives

A chart of adjectives can also be used to help describe nouns.

Directions: Look at the pictures. Complete each chart.

Example:

Noun	What Color?	What Size?	What Number?
flower	red	small	two

Noun	What Color?	What Size?	What Number?

Noun	What Color?	What Size?	What Number?

Noun	What Color?	What Size?	What Number?

Crack the Code

Directions: Use the secret code to unlock the answer to a joke.

Who is bigger, Mr. Bigger or Mr. Bigger's baby?

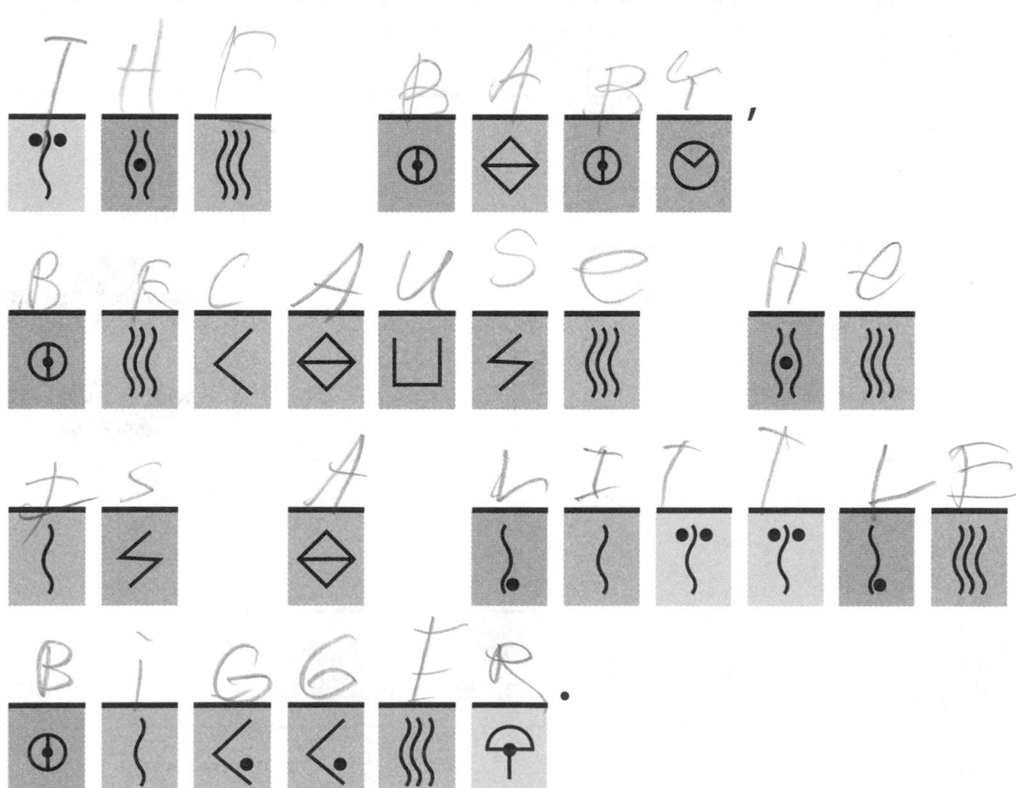

Animal Coverings

Directions: Find the type of covering for each animal to complete the puzzle.

shell
quills
fur
feathers
skin
scales

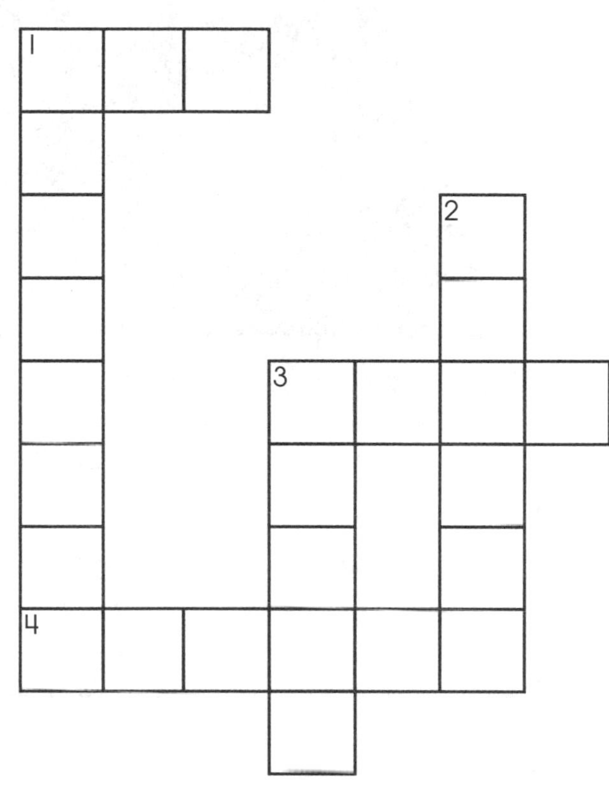

Across

1. snow hare
3. elephant
4. goldfish

Down

1. swan
2. porcupine
3. turtle

Prefixes

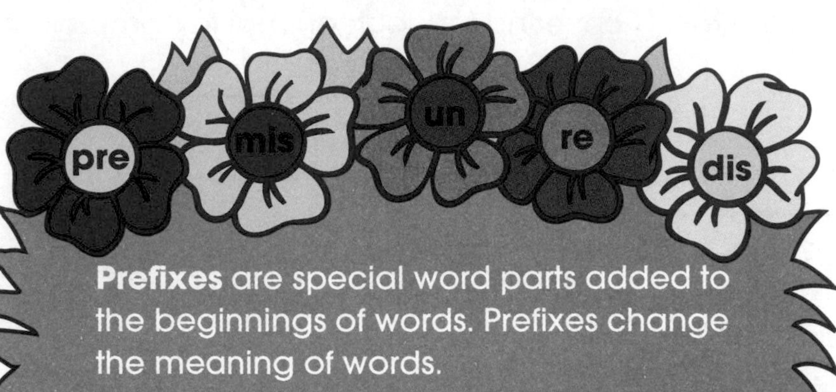

Prefixes are special word parts added to the beginnings of words. Prefixes change the meaning of words.

Prefix	Meaning	Example
un	not	**un**happy
re	again	**re**do
pre	before	**pre**view
mis	wrong	**mis**understanding
dis	opposite	**dis**obey

Directions: Circle the word that begins with a prefix. Then, write the prefix and the root word.

1. The dog was unfriendly. ____________ + ________________

2. The movie preview was interesting. ____________ + ________________

3. The referee called an unfair penalty. ____________ + ________________

4. Please do not misbehave. ____________ + ________________

5. My parents disapprove of that show. ____________ + ________________

6. I had to redo the assignment. ____________ + ________________

Suffixes

Suffixes are word parts added to the ends of words. Suffixes change the meaning of words.

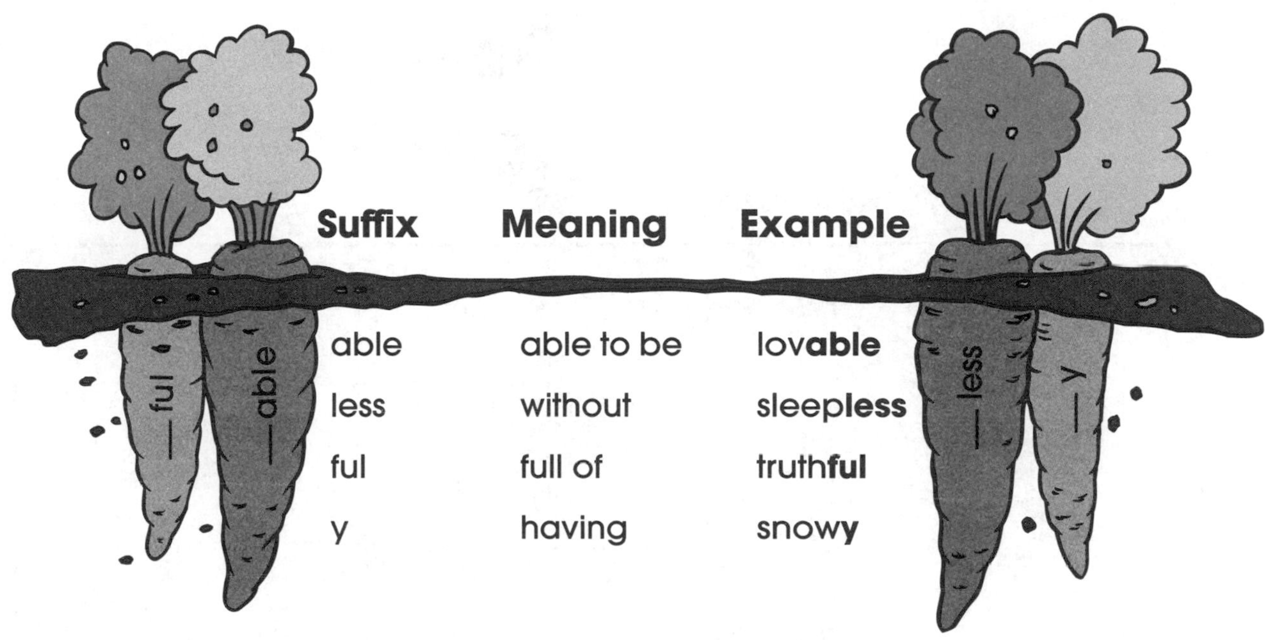

Suffix	Meaning	Example
able	able to be	lov**able**
less	without	sleep**less**
ful	full of	truth**ful**
y	having	snow**y**

Directions: Circle the suffix in each word below.

Example: fluff(y)

rainy	thoughtful	likeable
blameless	enjoyable	helpful
peaceful	careless	silky

Directions: Write a word for each meaning.

full of hope ____________________ having rain ____________________

without hope ____________________ able to break ____________________

without power ____________________ full of cheer ____________________

Bicycle Search

Directions: Find and circle the words in the puzzle.

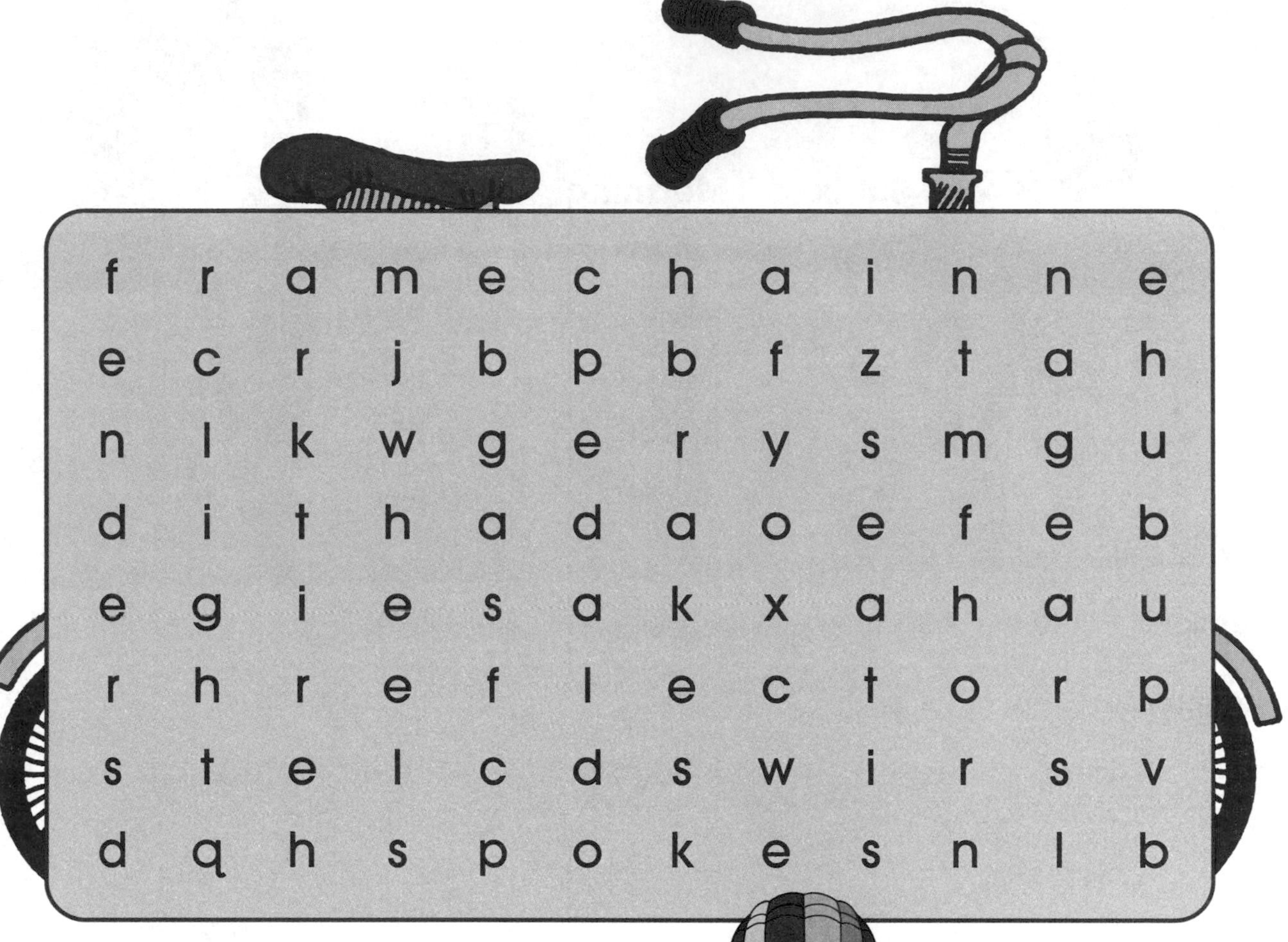

seat	pedal	tire	wheels
chain	spokes	light	horn
brakes	fenders	gears	frame
hub			reflector

Space Station

Below are hidden words that have something to do with a space station.

Directions: Circle the words as you find them.

telerobotic	battery	modular	skylab	generator
solar	heat	light	laboratory	astronauts

T	E	L	E	R	O	B	O	T	I	C	F
B	S	I	K	L	J	A	P	A	N	U	R
O	D	G	R	D	P	U	A	C	V	N	E
O	V	H	E	A	T	L	S	V	U	F	E
M	U	T	S	H	O	K	T	I	Y	T	D
T	S	K	Y	L	A	B	R	B	T	E	O
G	Q	C	R	Q	I	A	O	N	R	L	M
N	E	U	O	W	U	T	N	M	A	S	D
C	A	N	A	D	A	T	A	Q	R	T	S
A	S	A	E	P	Y	E	U	W	R	W	V
S	K	R	L	R	T	R	T	E	A	T	B
T	R	U	S	S	A	Y	S	T	Y	R	N
R	P	T	I	E	R	T	E	R	S	S	M
O	N	A	U	T	S	S	O	L	A	R	L
K	W	M	O	D	U	L	A	R	T	J	K
L	B	L	A	B	O	R	A	T	O	R	Y

Verbs

A **verb** is the action word in a sentence—the word that tells what something does or that something exists. **Examples: run, jump, skip**

Directions: Draw a box around the verb in each sentence below.

1. Spiders spin webs of silk.
2. A spider waits in the center of the web for its meals.
3. A spider sinks its sharp fangs into insects.
4. Spiders eat many insects.
5. Spiders make their nests with silk.
6. Female spiders wrap silk around their eggs to protect them.

Directions: Choose the correct verb from the box, and write it in the sentences below.

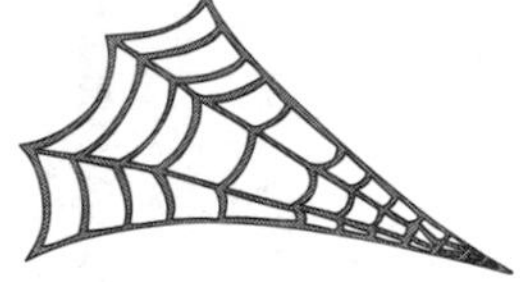

hides	swims	eats	grabs	hurt

1. A crab spider ______________________ deep inside a flower where it cannot be seen.
2. The crab spider ______________________ insects when they land on the flower.
3. The wolf spider is good because it ______________________ wasps.
4. The water spider ______________________ underwater.
5. Most spiders will not ______________________ people.

Verbs

When a verb tells what one person or thing is doing now, it usually ends in **s**. **Example:** She **sings**.

When a verb is used with **you**, **I**, or **we**, do not add an **s**.

Example: I sing.

Directions: Write the correct verb in each sentence.

Example:

I ___write___ a newspaper about our street. **writes, write**

1. My sister ____________ me sometimes. **helps, help**
2. She ____________ the pictures. **draw, draws**
3. We ____________ them together. **delivers, deliver**
4. I ____________ the news about all the people. **tell, tells**
5. Mr. Macon ____________ the most beautiful flowers. **grow, grows**
6. Mrs. Chen ____________ to her plants. **talks, talk**
7. Caleb Turner ____________ his dog loose every day. **lets, let**
8. Little Josh Cruz ____________ lost once a week. **get, gets**
9. You may ____________ I live on an interesting street. **thinks, think**
10. We ____________ it's the best street in town. **say, says**

Helping Verbs

A **helping verb** is a word used with an action verb.

Examples: might, **shall**, and **are**

Directions: Write a helping verb from the box with each action verb.

can	could	must	might
may	would	should	will
shall	did	does	do
had	have	has	am
are	were	is	
be	being	been	

Example:

Tomorrow, I ___might___ play soccer.

1. Mom ___________________ buy my new soccer shoes tonight.
2. Yesterday, my old soccer shoes ___________________ ripped by the cat.
3. I ___________________ going to ask my brother to go to the game.
4. He usually ___________________ not like soccer.
5. But, he ___________________ go with me because I am his sister.
6. He ___________________ promised to watch the entire soccer game.
7. He has ___________________ helping me with my homework.
8. I ___________________ spell a lot better because of his help.
9. Maybe I ___________________ finish the semester at the top of my class.

Camping Out

Directions: Help the camper reach the tent by finding things you would take on a camping trip.

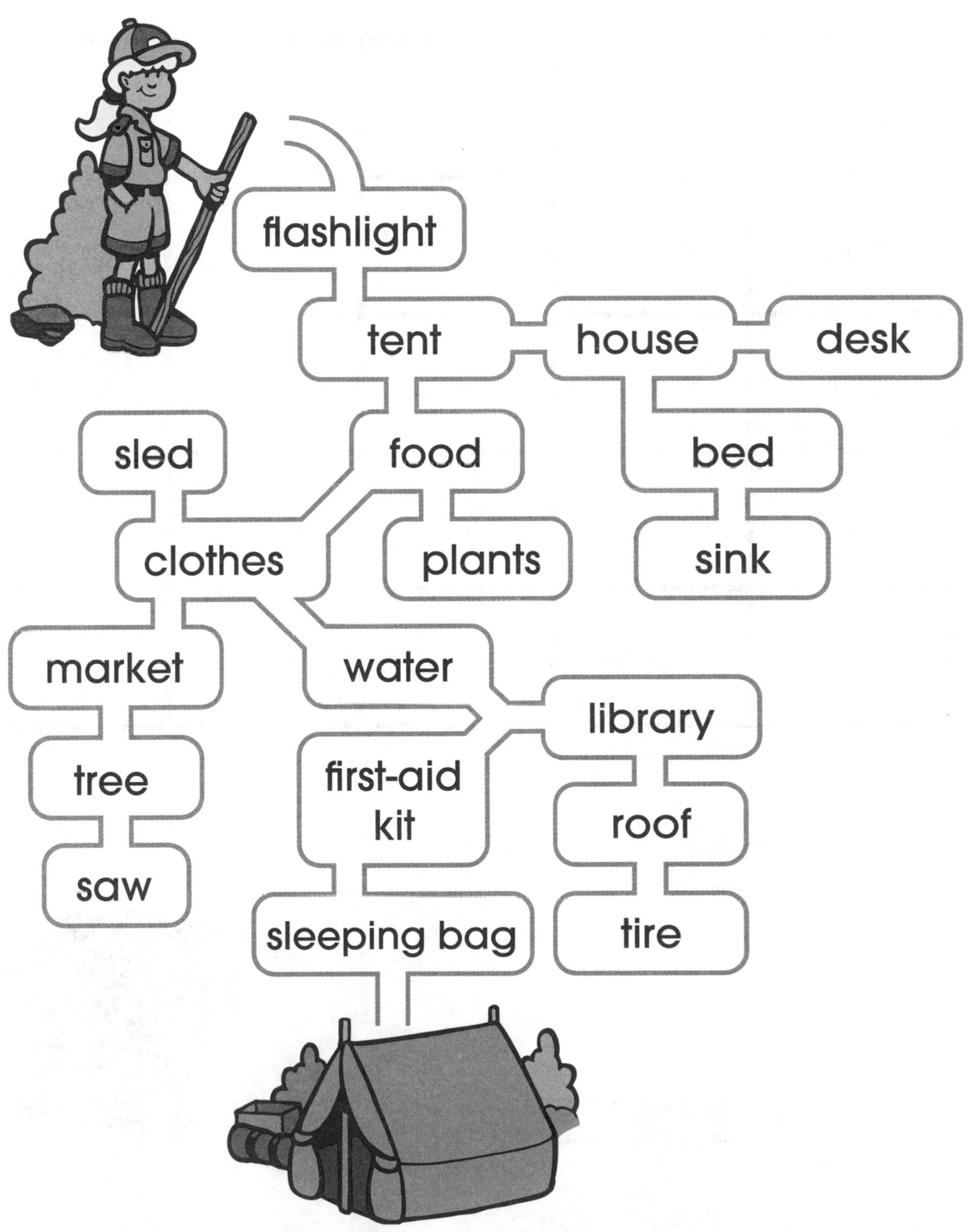

Which Letter?

Directions: Color the spaces with color words **blue**. Color the other spaces **red**.

green	home	father	happy	red
market	orange	teacher	yellow	book
child	shells	black	party	read
kitten	white	trip	purple	beside
brown	truck	sport	place	pink

What letter did you make? _____

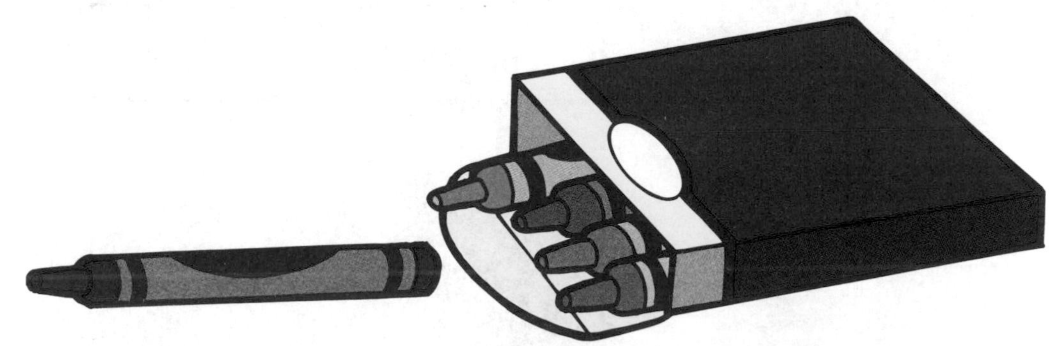

Past-Tense Verbs

The **past tense** of a verb tells about something that has already happened. Add **d** or **ed** to most verbs to show that something has already happened.

Directions: Use the verb from the first sentence to complete the second sentence.

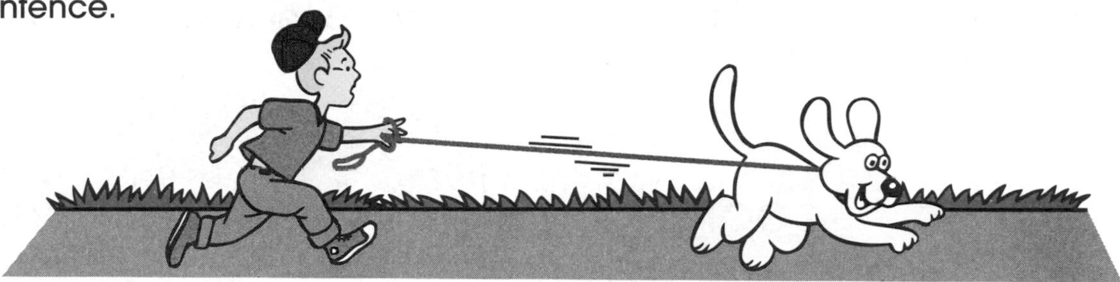

Example:

Please **walk** the dog. I already walked her.

1. The flowers look good. They ____________ better yesterday.
2. Please accept my gift. I ____________ it for my sister.
3. I wonder who will win. I ____________ about it all night.
4. He will saw the wood. He ____________ some last week.
5. Fold the paper neatly. She ____________ her paper.
6. Let's cook outside tonight. We ____________ outside last night.
7. Do not block the way. They ____________ the entire street.
8. Form the clay this way. He ____________ it into a ball.
9. Follow my car. We ____________ them down the street.
10. Glue the pages like this. She ____________ the flowers on.

Present-Tense Verbs

The **present tense** of a verb tells about something that is happening now, happens often, or is about to happen. These verbs can be written two ways: The bird sing**s**. The bird is sing**ing**.

Directions: Write each sentence again, using the verb **is** and writing the **ing** form of the verb.

Example: He cooks the cheeseburgers.

He is cooking the cheeseburgers.

1. Sharon dances to that song.

____

2. Frank washed the car.

____

3. Mr. Benson smiles at me.

____

For the sentences below, write a verb that tells something that is happening now. Be sure to use the verb **is** and the **ing** form of the verb.

Example: The big, brown dog is barking.

1. The little baby ____________________.

2. Most nine-year-olds ____________________.

3. The monster on television ____________________.

Future-Tense Verbs

The **future tense** of a verb tells about something that has not happened yet but will happen in the future. **Will** or **shall** are usually used with future tense.

Directions: Change the verb tense in each sentence to future tense.

Example: She cooks dinner.

She will cook dinner.

1. He plays baseball.

____

2. She walks to school.

____

3. Hasaan talks to the teacher.

____

4. I remember to vote.

____

5. Jack mows the lawn every week.

____

6. We go on vacation soon.

____

Irregular Verbs

Irregular verbs are verbs that do not change from the present tense to the past tense in the regular way, by adding **d** or **ed**.

Example: sing, **sang**

Directions: Read the sentence and underline the verbs. Choose the past-tense form from the box and write it next to the sentence.

blow — blew	fly — flew
come — came	give — gave
take — took	wear — wore
make — made	sing — sang
grow — grew	

Example:

Dad will make dinner tonight. made

1. I will probably grow another inch this year. ______________
2. I will blow out the candles. ______________
3. Everyone will give me presents. ______________
4. I will wear my favorite red shirt. ______________
5. My cousins will come from out of town. ______________
6. It will take them four hours. ______________
7. My Aunt Betty will fly in from Cleveland. ______________
8. She will sing me a song when she gets here. ______________

Irregular Verbs

Directions: Circle the verb that completes each sentence.

1. Scientists will try to (find, found) the cure.
2. Eric (brings, brought) his lunch to school yesterday.

3. Every day, Grace (sings, sang) all the way home.
4. Jason (breaks, broke) the vase last night.
5. The ice had (freezes, frozen) in the tray.
6. Mitzi has (swims, swum) in that pool before.

7. Now, I (choose, chose) to exercise daily.
8. The teacher has (rings, rung) the bell.

9. The boss (speaks, spoke) to us yesterday.
10. She (says, said) it twice already.

Irregular Verbs

The verb **be** is different from all other verbs. The present-tense forms of **be** are **am**, **is**, and **are**. The past-tense forms of **be** are **was** and **were**. The verb **to be** is written in the following ways:

singular: I am, you are, he is, she is, it is
plural: we are, you are, they are

Directions: Choose the correct form of **be** from the words in the box, and write it in each sentence.

are	am	is	was	were

Example:

I ____am____ feeling good at this moment.

1. My sister ____________________ a good singer.
2. You ____________________ going to the store with me.

3. Sierra ____________________ at the movies last week.
4. Oliver and Noah ____________________ best friends.

5. He ____________________ happy about the surprise.
6. The cat ____________________ hungry.
7. I ____________________ going to the ball game.

8. They ____________________ silly.
9. I ____________________ glad to help my mother.

Linking Verbs

Linking verbs connect the noun to a descriptive word. Linking verbs are often forms of the verb **be**.

Directions: The linking verb is underlined in each sentence. Circle the two words that are being connected.

Example: The cat is fat.

1. My favorite food <u>is</u> pizza.

2. The car <u>was</u> red.

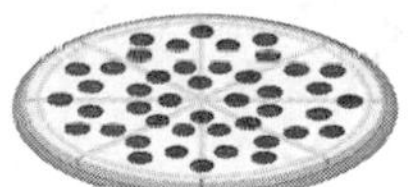

3. I <u>am</u> tired.

4. Books <u>are</u> fun.

5. The garden <u>is</u> beautiful.

6. Pears <u>taste</u> juicy.

7. The airplane <u>looks</u> large.

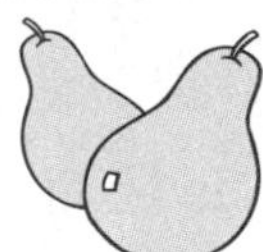

8. Rabbits <u>are</u> furry.

Let's Jog

Directions: Color the spaces with rhyming words **blue**. Color the other spaces green.

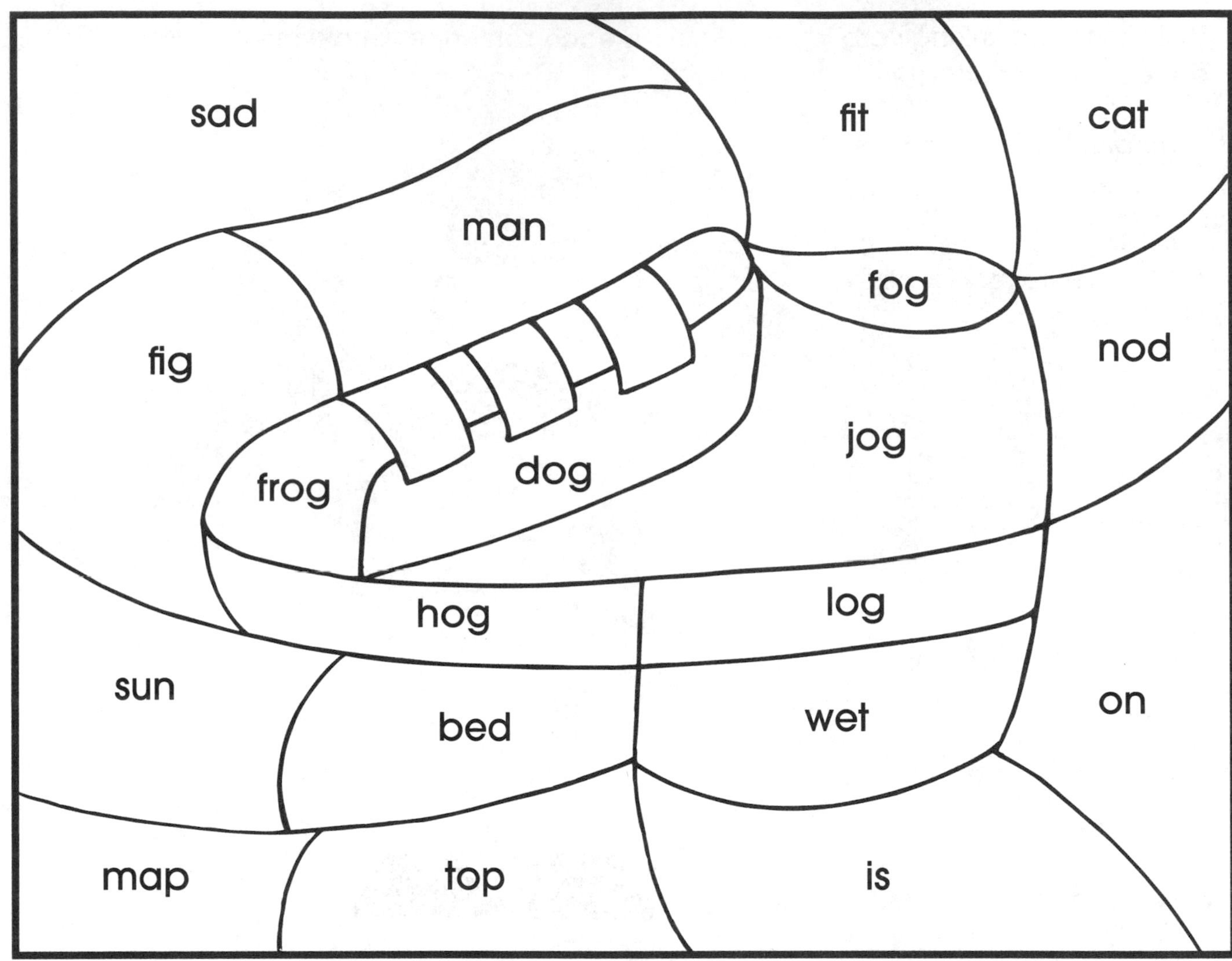

Directions: Use the rhyming words to finish the silly sentence.

Did the d ___ ___ j ___ ___ in the f ___ ___ by the h ___ ___

and the fr ___ ___ on the l ___ ___?

Ready Your Robot

Directions: Look at the picture clues. Then, complete the puzzle using the words from the word box.

Across

2. 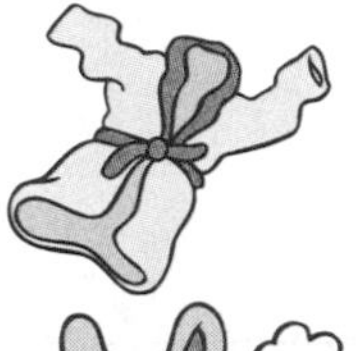

4. 

5. 

6. 

7.

Down

1. 

2. 

3. 

4. 

5.

rope
road
robe
race
rake
raft
raindrop
ribbon
rabbit
read

1 2 3 4 5 6 7

Places to Go

Directions: Look at each picture clue. Look in the word box for the place you would find that thing. Then, write the word in the puzzle.

market
bakery
bank
library
park
movies

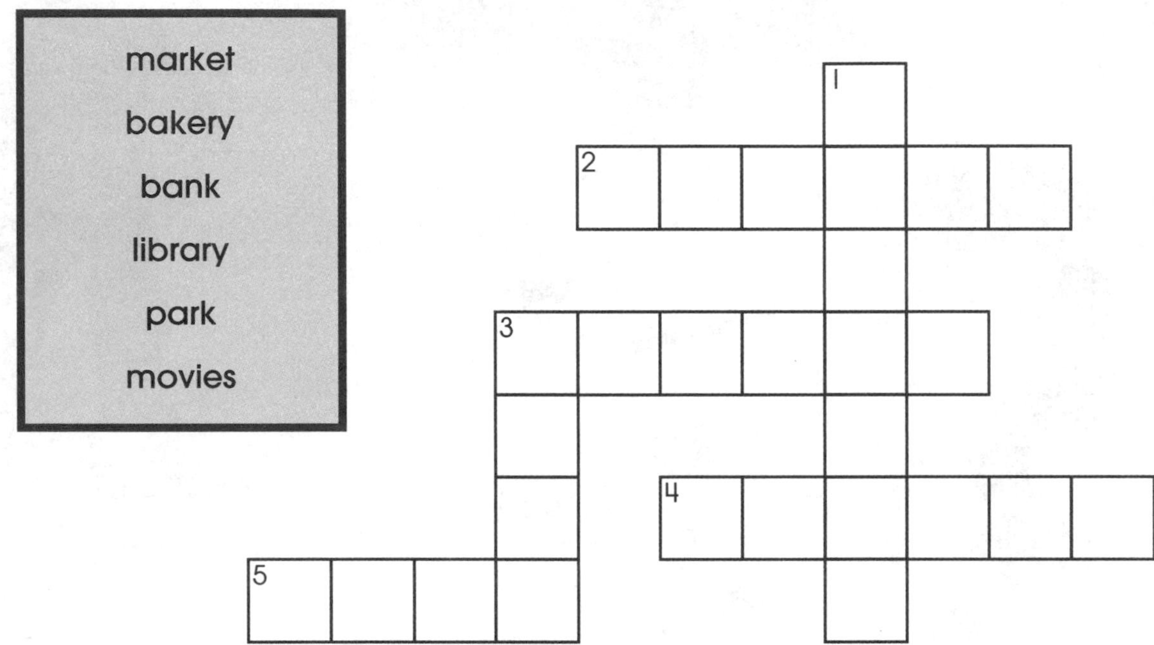

Adverbs

Adverbs are words that describe verbs. They tell where, how, or when.

Directions: Circle the adverb in each of the following sentences.

Example: The doctor worked carefully.

1. The skater moved gracefully across the ice.

2. Their call was returned quickly.

3. We easily learned the new words.

4. He did the work perfectly.

5. She lost her purse somewhere.

Directions: Complete the sentences below by writing your own adverbs in the blanks.

Example: The bees worked busily.

1. The dog barked ____________________.

2. The baby smiled ____________________.

3. She wrote her name ____________________.

4. The horse ran ____________________.

Adverbs

Directions: Read each sentence. Then, answer the questions on the lines below.

Example: Charles ate hungrily.

who? Charles

what? ate

how? hungrily

1. She dances slowly.

who? ______________________

what? ______________________

how? ______________________

2. The girl spoke carefully.

who? ______________________

what? ______________________

how? ______________________

3. My brother ran quickly.

who? ______________________

what? ______________________

how? ______________________

4. Jean walks home often.

who? ______________________

what? ______________________

when? ______________________

5. The children played there.

who? ______________________

what? ______________________

where? ______________________

Pet Shop

Directions: Read the clues and use the words in the word box to complete the puzzle.

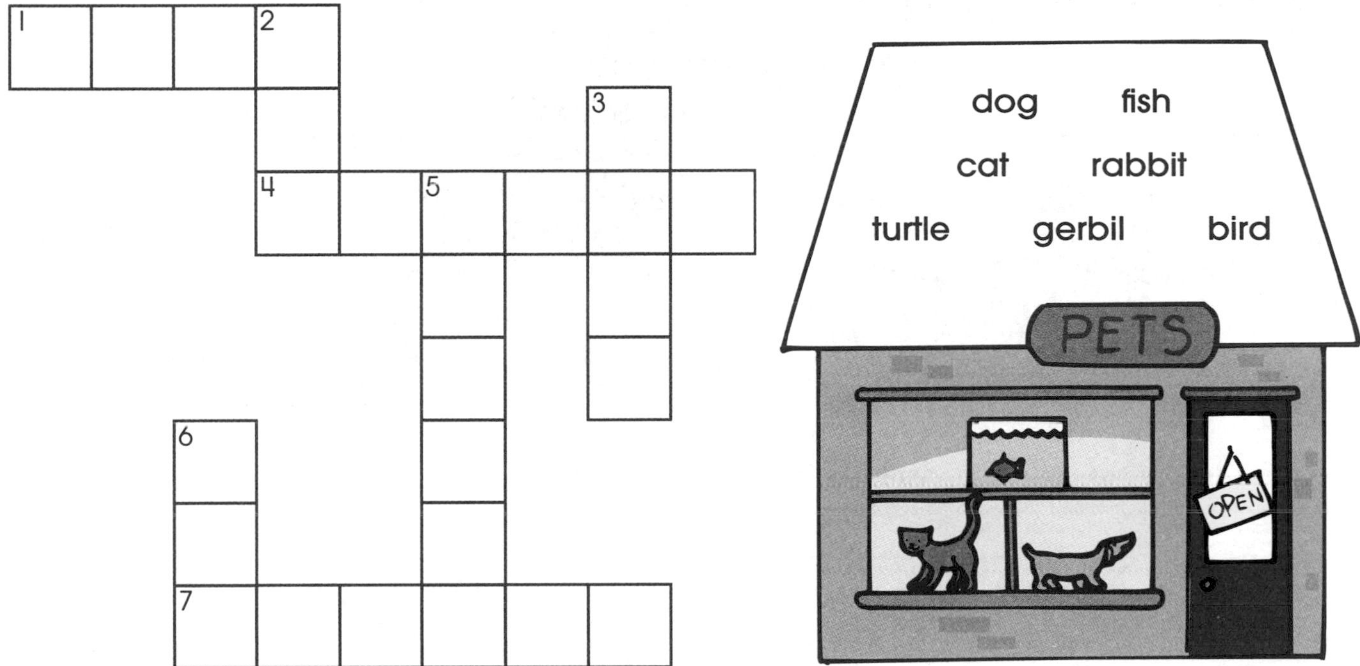

Across

1. I have feathers. I can fly and sing.
4. I am small and furry with a long skinny tail. I like running around on a wheel.
7. I have a hard shell. I walk very slowly.

Down

2. I have fur. I can bark and do tricks.
3. I am very quiet. I swim around in a bowl.
5. I have long floppy ears and a fluffy round tail. I like eating carrots.
6. I am fluffy and furry. When you pet me, I purr.

Prepositions

Prepositions show relationships between the noun or pronoun and another noun in the sentence. The preposition comes before that noun.

Example: The book is on the table.

Common Prepositions

above	behind	by	near	over
across	below	in	off	through
around	beside	inside	on	under

Directions: Circle the prepositions in each sentence.

1. The dog ran fast around the house.
2. The plates in the cupboard were clean.
3. Put the card inside the envelope.
4. The towel on the sink was wet.
5. I planted flowers in my garden.
6. My kite flew high above the trees.
7. The chair near the counter was sticky.
8. Under the ground, worms lived in their homes.
9. I put the bow around the box.
10. Beside the pond, there was a playground.

A Colorful Creation

Directions: Read the words. Color each box the same color as the thing named in the box.

banana	grass	pumpkin
carrot	strawberry	sky
water	sun	grasshopper

Articles

Articles are words used before nouns. **A**, **an**, and **the** are articles. Use **a** before words that begin with a consonant. Use **an** before words that begin with a vowel.

Example: **a peach**  **an apple** 

Directions: Write **a** or **an** in the sentences below.

Example: My bike had ____a____ flat tire.

1. They brought ______________ goat to the farm.
2. My mom wears ______________ old pair of shoes to mow the lawn.
3. We had ______________ party for my grandfather.
4. Everybody had ______________ ice-cream cone after the game.
5. We bought ______________ picnic table for our backyard.
6. We saw ______________ lion sleeping in the shade.
7. It was ______________ evening to be remembered.
8. He brought ______________ blanket to the game.
9. ______________ exit sign was above the door.
10. They went to ______________ orchard to pick apples.
11. He ate ______________ orange for lunch.

At the Beach

Directions: Read the sentences and use the words in the word box to complete the puzzle.

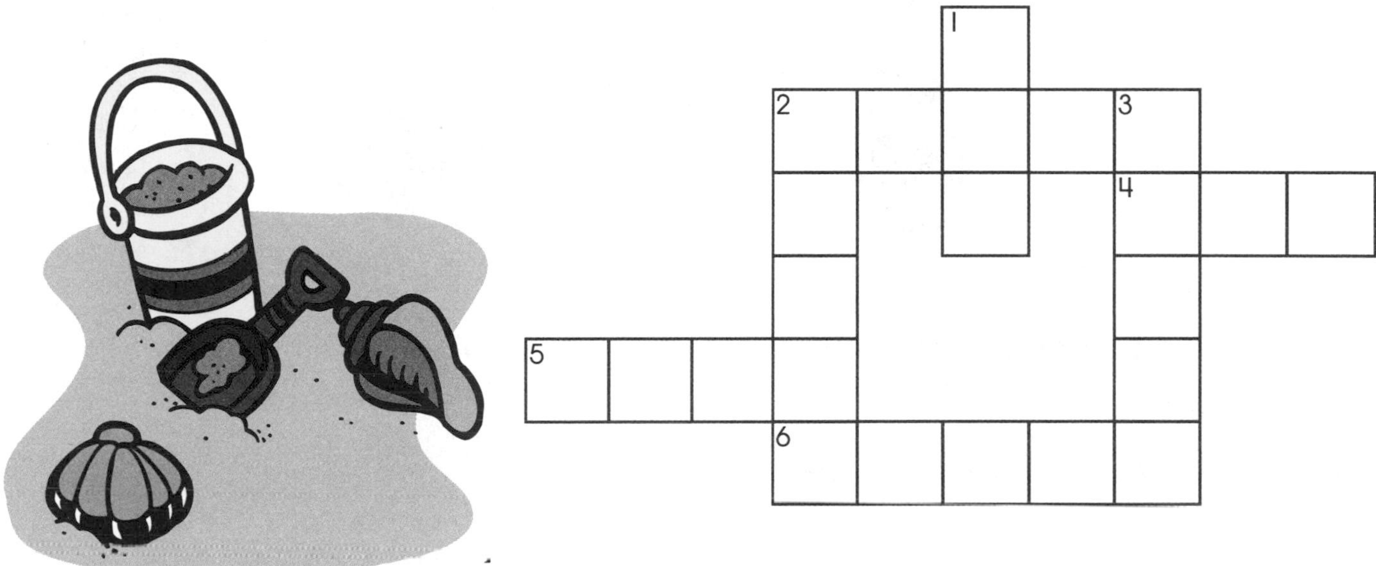

ships	shore	shell	dig	ball	large	hat

Across

2. I saw three _________ sail by.
4. I wore a _________ to protect myself from the sun.
5. I played catch with my beach _________.
6. I even saw a dolphin that was very _________.

Down

1. I used a shovel to _________ in the sand.
2. I found a _________at the beach.
3. I saw a ship float up onto the _________.

Commas

Commas are used to separate words in a series of three or more.

Example: My favorite fruits are apples, bananas, and oranges.

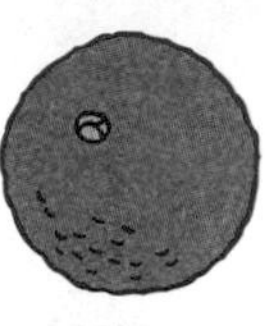

Directions: Put commas where they are needed in each sentence.

1. Please buy milk eggs bread and cheese.

2. I need a folder paper and pencils for school.

3. Some good pets are cats dogs gerbils fish and rabbits.

4. Aaron Eduardo and Matt went to the baseball game.

5. Major forms of transportation are planes trains and automobiles.

Commas

Use commas to separate the day from the year.
Example: May 13, 1950

Directions: Write the dates in the blanks. Put the commas in, and capitalize the name of each month.

Example:

Aziz and Anthony were born on february 22 2006.

February 22, 2006

1. My father's birthday is may 19 1967.

____

2. My sister was fourteen on december 13 2009.

____

3. Lauren's seventh birthday was on november 30 1998.

____

4. october 13 2012 was the last day I saw my lost cat.

____

5. On april 17 1997, we saw the Grand Canyon.

____

6. Our vacation lasted from april 2 2014 to april 26 2014.

____________________ ____________________

7. Molly's baby sister was born on august 14 2011.

____

8. My mother was born on june 22 1974.

____

Articles and Commas

Directions: Write **a** or **an** in each blank. Put commas where they are needed in the paragraphs below.

Owls

__________ owl is __________ bird of prey. This means it hunts small animals. Owls catch insects fish and birds. Mice are __________ owl's favorite dinner. Owls like protected places, such as trees burrows or barns. Owls make noises that sound like hoots screeches or even barks. __________ owl's feathers may be black brown gray or white.

A Zoo for You

__________ zoo is __________ excellent place for keeping animals. Zoos have mammals birds reptiles and amphibians. Some zoos have domestic animals, such as rabbits sheep and goats. Another name for this type of zoo is __________ petting zoo. In some zoos, elephants lions and tigers live in open country. This is because __________ enormous animal needs open space for roaming.

Fruity Fun

Directions: Look at the picture clues. Then, complete the puzzle using the words from the word box.

Across

2. 

3. 

5.

Down

1. 

2.

4.

apple
plum
orange
grapes
pear
peach

Find the Rhymes

Directions: Write the rhyming words in the puzzle boxes. Then, write the words in the silly sentence below.

1. 

2. 

3. 

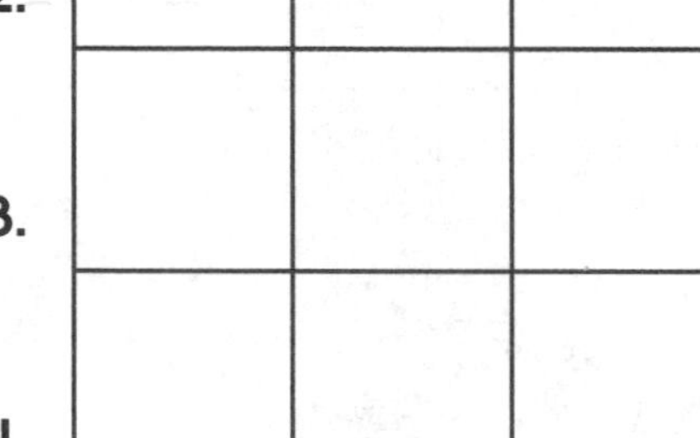

4. 

5. 

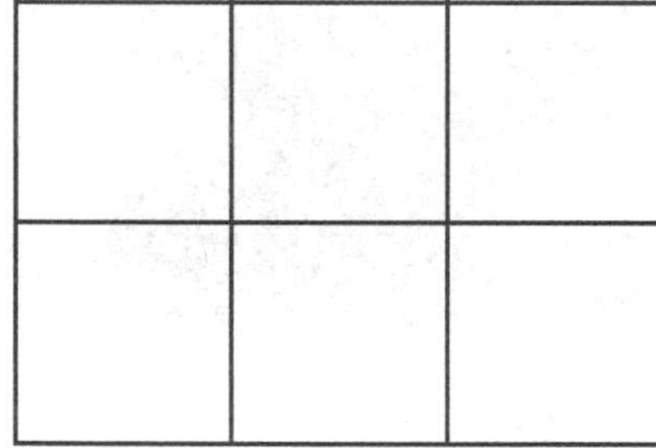

6. 

1.			
2.			
3.			
4.			
5.			
6.			

The m _____ _____ r _____ _____ to his v _____ _____, carrying a hot p _____ _____, a broken f _____ _____, and a c _____ _____ of peaches.

Capitalization

The names of **people**, **places**, and **pets**, the **days of the week**, the **months of the year**, and **holidays** begin with a capital letter.

Directions: Read the words in the box. Write the words in the correct column with capital letters at the beginning of each word.

ron polsky	tuesday	march	april
presidents' day	saturday	woofy	october
blackie	portland, oregon	corning, new york	molly yoder
valentine's day	fluffy	harold edwards	arbor day
bozeman, montana	sunday		

People	Places	Pets
______________	______________	______________
______________	______________	______________
______________	______________	______________

Days	Months	Holidays
______________	______________	______________
______________	______________	______________
______________	______________	______________

Capitalization and Commas

Capitalize the names of cities and states. Use a comma to separate the name of a city and a state.

Directions: Use capital letters and commas to write the names of the cities and states correctly.

Example:

sioux falls south dakota Sioux Falls, South Dakota

1. plymouth massachusetts ______________________

2. boston massachusetts ______________________

3. philadelphia pennsylvania ______________________

4. white plains new york ______________________

5. newport rhode island ______________________

6. yorktown virginia ______________________

7. nashville tennessee ______________________

8. portland oregon ______________________

9. mansfield ohio ______________________

Long and Short

Directions: Color the spaces with long vowel words red. Color the spaces with short vowel words blue.

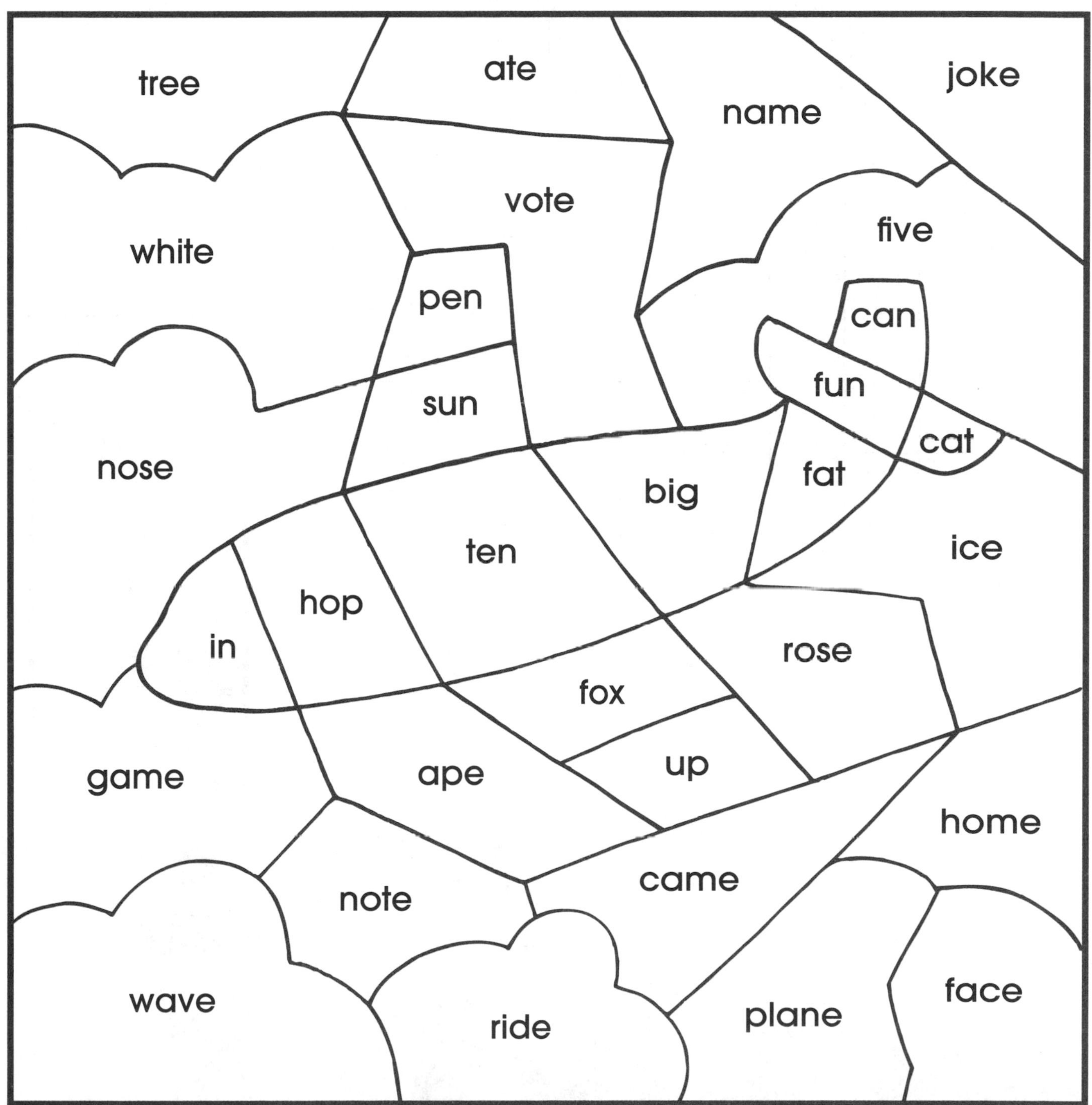

Little Ones

Directions: Look at the picture clues. Then, complete the puzzle using the words from the word box.

puppies
cub
duckling
chick
kittens
colt

Across

3. 

6. 

Down

1. 

2. 

4. 

5. 

Name ______________________________

Parts of Speech

Nouns, pronouns, verbs, adjectives, adverbs, and prepositions are all **parts of speech.**

Directions: Label the words in each sentence with the correct part of speech.

Example: The cat is fat.

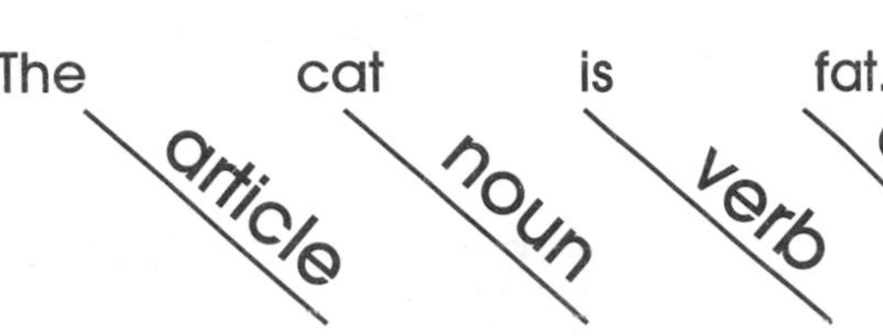

1. My cow walks in the barn.

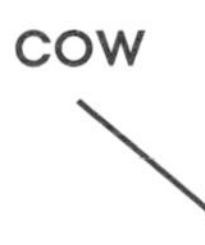

2. Red flowers grow in the garden.

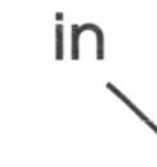

3. The large dog was excited.

Parts of Speech

Directions: Ask someone to give you nouns, verbs, adjectives, and pronouns where shown. Write them in the blanks. Read the story to your friend when you finish.

The ______________ Adventure
(adjective)

I went for a ______________ (noun). I found a really big ______________ (noun).

It was so ______________ (adjective) that I ______________ (verb) all the

way home. I put it in my ______________ (noun). To my amazement, it

began to ______________ (verb). I ______________ (past-tense verb). I took it to my

______________ (place). I showed it to all my ______________ (plural noun).

I decided to ______________ (verb) it in a box and wrap it up with

______________ (adjective) paper. I gave it to ______________ (person) for a

present. When ______________ (pronoun) opened it, ______________ (pronoun)

______________ (past-tense verb). ______________ (pronoun) shouted, "Thank you!

This is the best ______________ (noun) I've ever had!"

Parts of Speech

Directions: Write the part of speech of each underlined word.

NOUN PRONOUN VERB ADJECTIVE ADVERB PREPOSITION

There are(1) many different(2) kinds of animals. Some animals live in the wild. Some animals live in the zoo(3). And still others live in homes. The animals that live(4) in homes are called **pets**.

There are many types of pets. Some pets without fur are fish, turtles, snakes, and hermit crabs. Trained birds can fly around(5) your(6) house. Some furry(7) animals are cats, dogs, rabbits, ferrets, gerbils, or hamsters. Some animals can successfully(8) learn tricks that you(9) teach them. Whatever your favorite animal is, animals can be special(10) friends!

1. ________________
2. ________________
3. ________________
4. ________________
5. ________________
6. ________________
7. ________________
8. ________________
9. ________________
10. ________________

Feelings

Directions: Look at the picture clues and use the words in the word box to complete the puzzle.

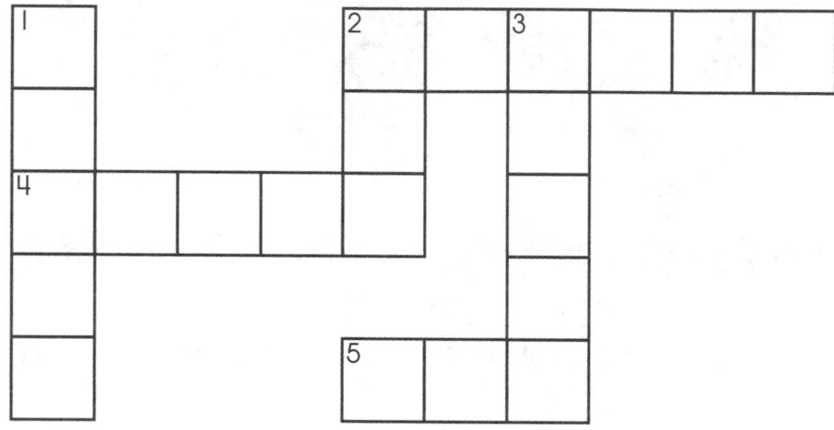

happy	sad	shy	scared	proud	angry

Across

2. 

4. 

5. 

Down

1. 

2. 

3. 

 Name ____________________

Things That Are Alike

Directions: Read the clues and find the other things from the word box that go with each group to complete the puzzle.

Across

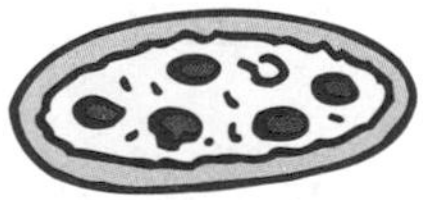

1. pizza sandwich

3. car motorcycle

5. basketball baseball

Down

1. dog cat

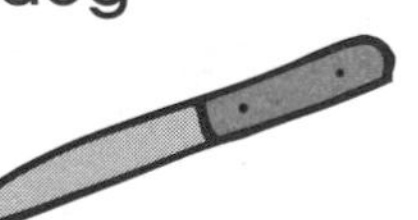

2. knife fork

4. pencil marker

And and But

The words **and** or **but** can be used to make one longer sentence from two short ones.

Directions: Use **and** or **but** to make two short sentences into a longer, more interesting one. Write the new sentence on the line below the two short sentences.

Example:

The skunk has black fur. The skunk has a white stripe.

The skunk has black fur and a white stripe.

1. The skunk has a small head. The skunk has small ears.

______

2. The skunk has short legs. Skunks can move quickly.

______

3. Skunks sleep in hollow trees. Skunks sleep underground.

______

4. Skunks are chased by animals. Skunks do not run away.

______

5. Skunks sleep during the day. Skunks hunt at night.

______

New Words

Directions: Starting with the top word in each square, change one letter at a time until the top word becomes the bottom word.

1.	C	A	P	E
2.				
3.				
4.				
5.	F	I	N	S

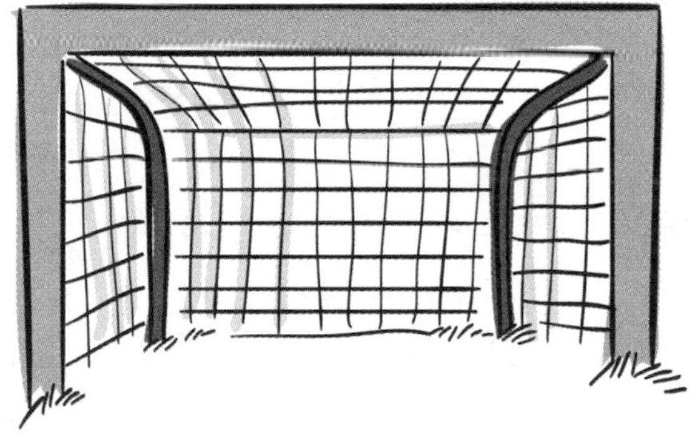

6.	G	O	A	L
7.				
8.				
9.				
10.	B	E	S	T

Subjects

A **subject** tells who or what the sentence is about.

Directions: Underline the subject in the following sentences.

Example:

The zebra is a large animal.

1. Zebras live in Africa.
2. Zebras are related to horses.
3. Horses have longer hair than zebras.
4. Zebras are good runners.
5. Their feet are protected by their hooves.
6. Some animals live in groups.
7. These groups are called **herds**.
8. Zebras live in herds with other grazing animals.
9. Grazing animals eat mostly grass.
10. They usually eat three times a day.
11. They often travel to water holes.

Simple Subjects

A **simple subject** is the main noun or pronoun in the complete subject.

Directions: Draw a line between the subject and the predicate. Circle the simple subject.

Example: The black (bear) | lives in the zoo.

1. Penguins look like they wear tuxedos.

2. The seal enjoys raw fish.

3. The monkeys like to swing on bars.

4. The beautiful peacock has colorful feathers.

5. Bats like dark places.

6. Some snakes eat small rodents.

7. The orange and brown giraffes have long necks.

8. The baby zebra is close to his mother.

Compound Subjects

Compound subjects are two or more nouns that have the same predicate.

Directions: Combine the subjects to create one sentence with a compound subject.

Example: Jill can swing.
Whitney can swing.
Luke can swing.

Jill, Whitney, and Luke can swing.

1. Roses grow in the garden. Tulips grow in the garden.

____

2. Apples are fruit. Oranges are fruit. Bananas are fruit.

____

3. Bears live in the zoo. Monkeys live in the zoo.

____

4. Jackets keep us warm. Sweaters keep us warm.

____

Compound Subjects

Directions: Underline the simple subjects in each compound subject.

Example: Dogs and cats are good pets.

1. Blueberries and strawberries are fruit.

2. Jesse, Jake, and Hannah like school.

3. Cows, pigs, and sheep live on a farm.

4. Boys and girls ride the bus.

5. My family and I took a trip to Duluth.

6. Fruits and vegetables are good for you.

7. Katarina, Lexi, and Mandi like to go swimming.

8. Petunias, impatiens, snapdragons, and geraniums are all flowers.

9. Coffee, tea, and milk are beverages.

10. Julio, Karla, and Lina worked on the project together.

Opposites

Directions: Draw lines to match the opposites. Then, write them in the puzzles.

bad	wrong
true	false
right	last
first	good
over	low
high	under

	a		
		o	

	r			
				e

		g		
w				

		r		
l				

	v			
				r

	i		
	o		

Being a Friend

Directions: Read the sentences and use the words in the word box to complete the puzzle.

respect
fairly
help
share
follow
listen

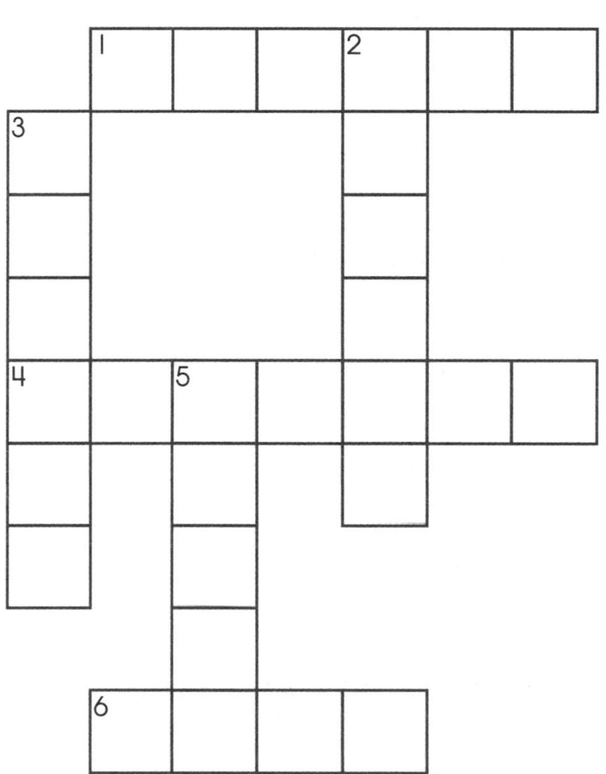

Across

1. ______ the rules.
4. ______ others' feelings.
6. ______ others.

Down

2. ______ when others are talking.
3. Treat others ______.
5. ______ with others.

Predicates

A **predicate** tells what the subject is doing, has done, or will do.

Directions: Underline the predicate in the following sentences.

Example: Woodpeckers <u>live in trees</u>.

1. They hunt for insects in the trees.

2. Woodpeckers have strong beaks.

3. They can peck through the bark.

4. The pecking sound can be heard from far away.

Directions: Circle the groups of words that can be predicates.

have long tongues

hole in bark

help them to climb trees

pick up insects

sticky substance

tree bark

Now, choose the correct predicates from above to finish these sentences.

1. Woodpeckers ______________________________.

2. They use their tongues to ______________________________.

3. Their strong feet ______________________________.

Simple Predicates

A **simple predicate** is the main verb or verbs in the complete predicate.

Directions: Draw a line between the complete subject and the complete predicate. Circle the simple predicate.

Example: The ripe apples | (fell) to the ground.

1. The farmer scattered feed for the chickens.

2. The horses galloped wildly around the corral.

3. The baby chicks were staying warm by the light.

4. The tractor was baling hay.

5. The silo was full of grain.

6. The cows were being milked.

7. The milk truck drove up to the barn.

8. The rooster woke everyone up.

Compound Predicates

Compound predicates have two or more verbs that have the same subject.

Directions: Combine the predicates to create one sentence with a compound predicate.

Example: We went to the zoo.
We watched the monkeys.
We went to the zoo and watched the monkeys.

1. Students read their books. Students do their work.

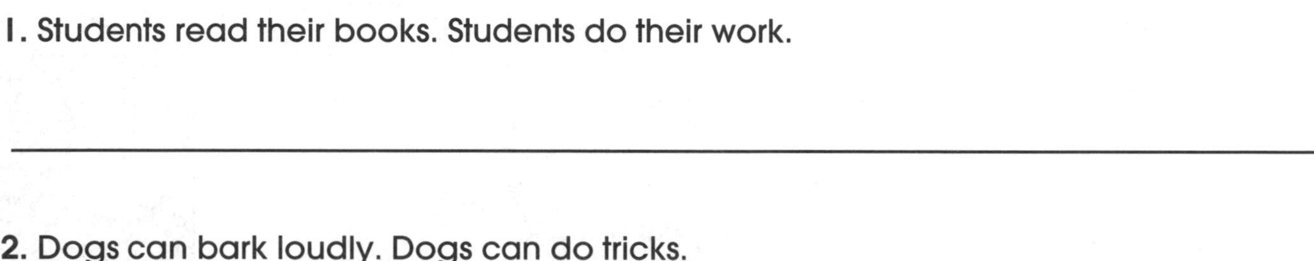

2. Dogs can bark loudly. Dogs can do tricks.

____

3. The football player caught the ball. The football player ran.

____

4. My dad sawed wood. My dad stacked wood.

____

5. My teddy bear is soft. My teddy bear likes to be hugged.

____

Compound Predicates

Directions: Underline the simple predicates (verbs) in each predicate.

Example: The fans clapped and cheered at the game.

1. The coach talks and encourages the team.

2. The cheerleaders jump and yell.

3. The basketball players dribble and shoot the ball.

4. The basketball bounces and hits the backboard.

5. The ball rolls around the rim and goes into the basket.

6. Everyone leaps up and cheers.

7. The team scores and wins!

Subjects and Predicates

Directions: Write the words for the subject to answer the **who** or **what** questions. Write the words for the predicate to answer the **does, did, is,** or **has** questions.

Example:

My friend has two pairs of sunglasses. **who?** My friend

has? has two pairs of sunglasses

1. John's dog went to school with him. **what?** ___

   did? ___

2. The Alaskan traveled by dog sled. **who?** ___

   did? ___

3. Alex slept in his treehouse last night. **who?** ___

   did? ___

4. Cherry pie is my favorite kind of pie. **what?** ___

   is? ___

5. The mail carrier brings the mail to the door. **who?** ___

   does? ___

6. We have more than enough bricks to build the wall. **who?** ___

   has? ___

7. The bird has a worm in its beak. **what?** ___

   has? ___

Subjects and Predicates

Directions: Every sentence has two main parts—the subject and the predicate. Draw one line under the subject and two lines under the predicate in each sentence below.

Example:

Porcupines are related to mice and rats.

1. They are large rodents.
2. Porcupines have long, sharp quills.
3. The quills stand up straight when it is angry.
4. Most animals stay away from porcupines.
5. Their quills hurt other animals.
6. Porcupines sleep under rocks or bushes.
7. They sleep during the day.
8. Porcupines eat plants at night.
9. North America has some porcupines.
10. They are called New World porcupines.
11. New World porcupines can climb trees.

Subjects and Predicates

Directions: Draw one line under the subjects and two lines under the predicates in the sentences below

1. My mom likes to plant flowers.

2. Our neighbors walk their dog.

3. Our car needs gas.

4. The children play house.

5. Movies and popcorn go well together.

6. Peanut butter and jelly is my favorite kind of sandwich.

7. Tyler, Flora, and Amelia ride to the park.

8. We use pencils, markers, and pens to write on paper.

9. Trees and shrubs need special care.

Name ______________________

Figure Them Out!

Directions: Unscramble each word. Use the words in the word box to help you.

teacher	ice cream	apple
mouse	jogger	tennis

1. Someone who runs is called a

   rjggeo ____ ____ ____ ____ ____ ____.

2. A game that uses a racket and a small ball is

   stinne ____ ____ ____ ____ ____ ____.

3. Something cold to eat on a hot day is

   cie ramec ____ ____ ____   ____ ____ ____ ____ ____.

4. Someone who teaches children is a

   erhteac ____ ____ ____ ____ ____ ____ ____.

5. A tasty fruit that grows on a tree is called an

   leppa ____ ____ ____ ____ ____.

6. A furry little animal that squeaks is a

   somue ____ ____ ____ ____ ____.

A Taste of Italy

Directions: Unscramble the letters to spell three different toppings on each pizza.

pepperoni
ham
mushroom

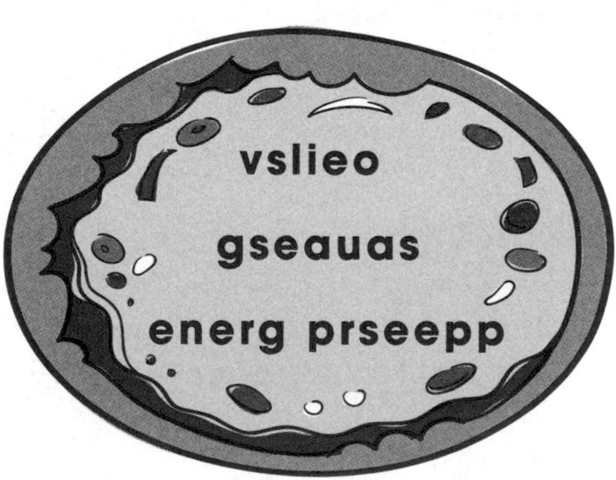

onions
ground beef
spin

____

____

____

Spring

Directions: Read the clues and use the words in the word box to complete the puzzle.

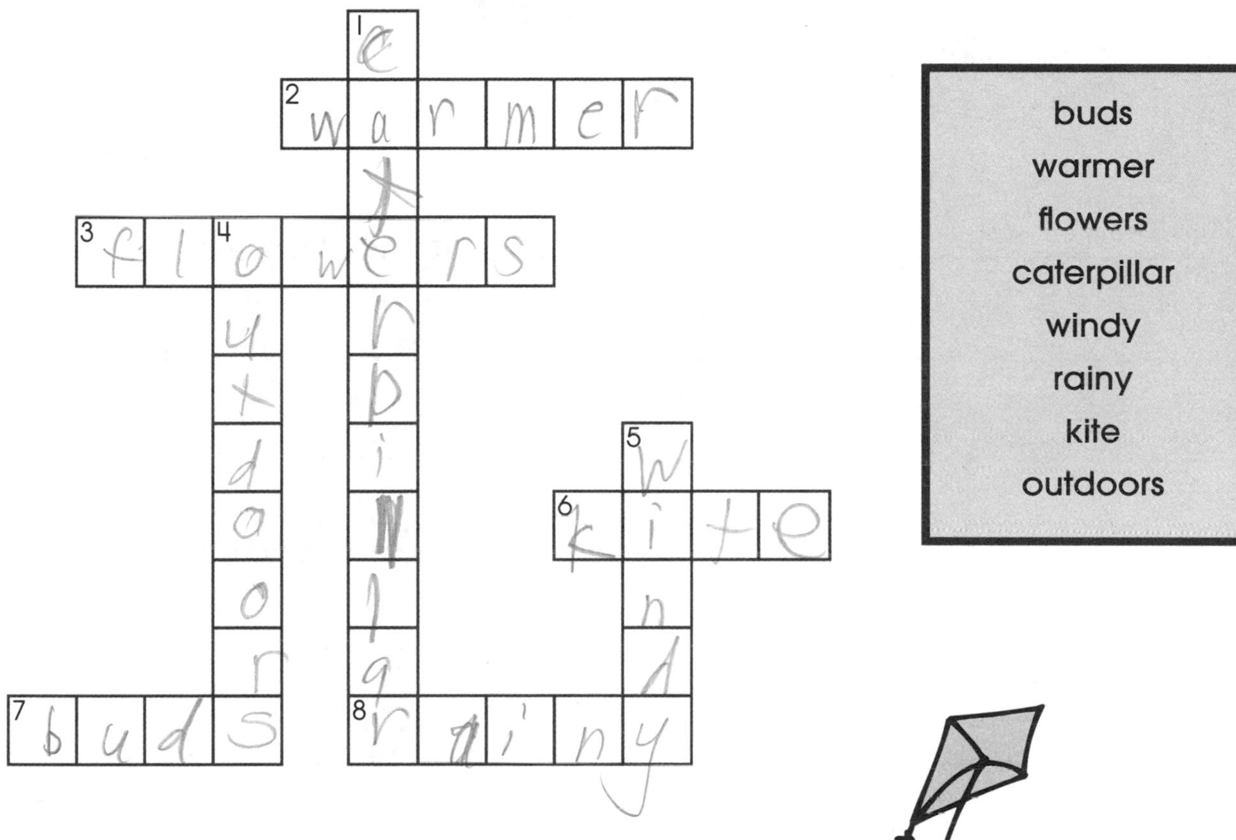

buds
warmer
flowers
caterpillar
windy
rainy
kite
outdoors

Across

2. It is the opposite of **colder**.
3. These bloom in the spring.
6. You can fly one outdoors in the spring.
7. Trees have these in the spring.
8. Take your umbrella on days like this.

Down

1. This is busy eating new leaves in spring.
4. It's fun to play here.
5. This is a good day to fly a kite.

Subjects

Directions: Use your own words to write the subjects in the sentences below.

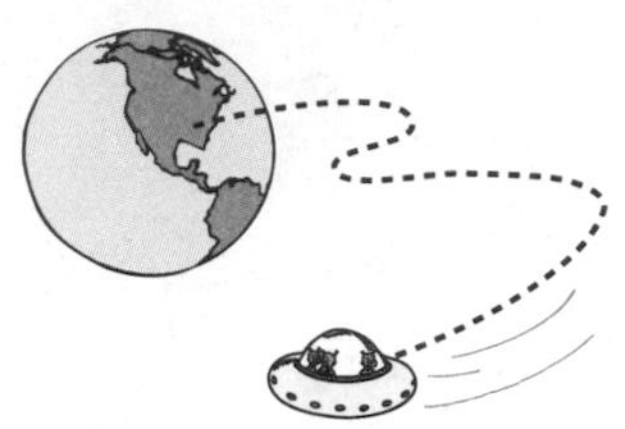

1. ____________________ landed in my backyard.
2. ____________________ rushed out of the house.
3. ____________________ had bright lights.
4. ____________________ were tall and green.
5. ____________________ talked to me.
6. ____________________ came outside with me.
7. ____________________ ran into the house.
8. ____________________ shook hands.
9. ____________________ said funny things.
10. ____________________ gave us a ride.
11. ____________________ flew away.
12. ____________________ will come back soon.

Predicates

Directions: Use your own words to write the predicates in the sentences below.

1. The swimming pool ____________________.
2. The water ____________________.
3. The sun ____________________.
4. I always ____________________.
5. My friends ____________________.
6. We always ____________________.
7. The lifeguard ____________________.
8. The rest periods ____________________.
9. The lunch ____________________.
10. My favorite food ____________________.
11. The diving board ____________________.
12. We never ____________________.

Busy Year

Directions: Use the word lists to fill out the grid below.

Hint: Count the squares in the grid first to see where the words will fit.

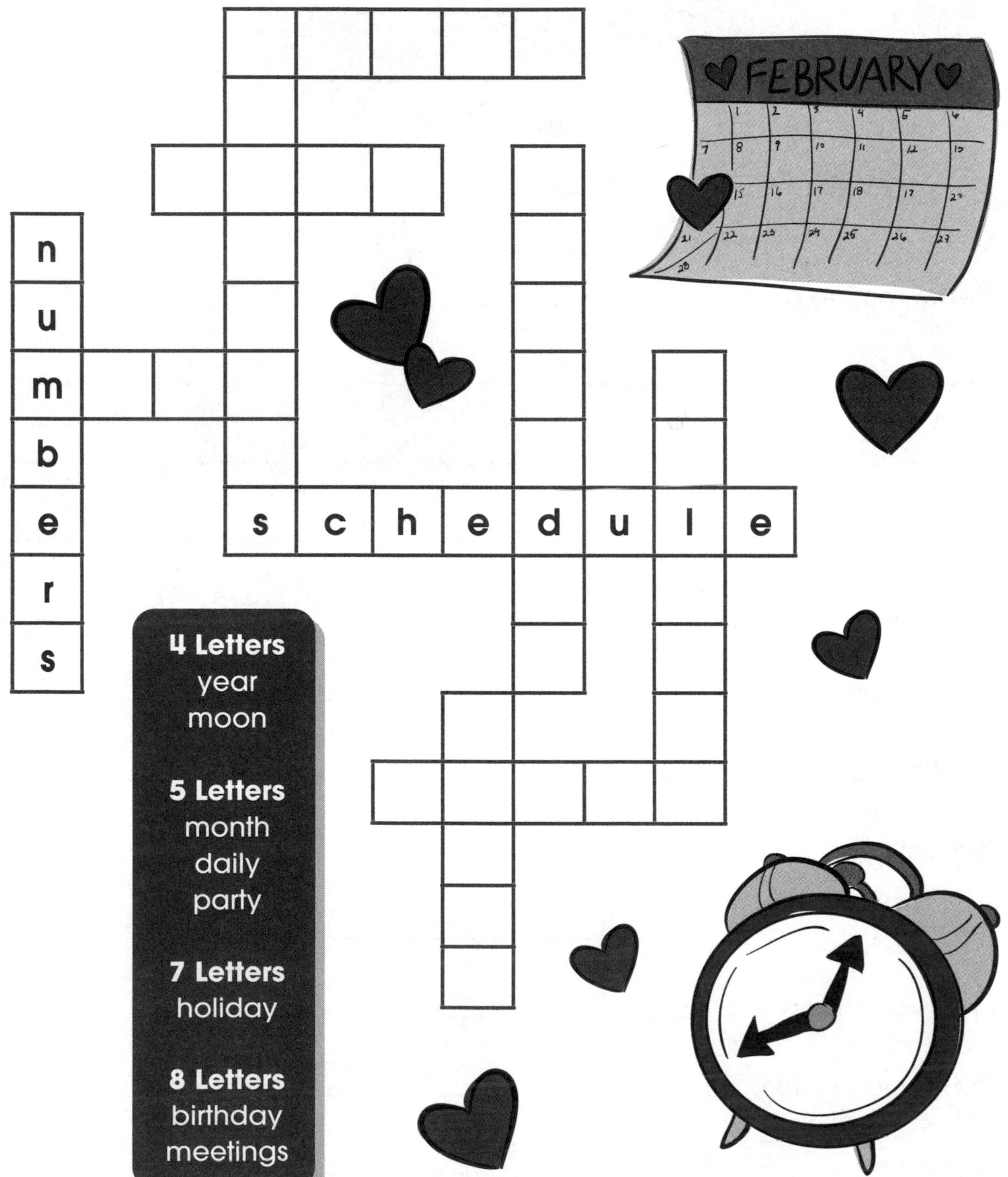

Word Order

Word order is the logical order of words in sentences.

Directions: Put the words in order so that each sentence tells a complete idea.

Example: outside put cat the

Put the cat outside.

1. mouse the ate snake the

____

2. dog John his walk took a for

____

3. birthday Maria the present wrapped

____

4. escaped parrot the cage its from

____

5. to soup quarts water three of add the

____

6. bird the bushes into the chased cat the

____

Astro Adventure

Directions: Look at the picture clues. Then, complete the puzzle using the words from the word box.

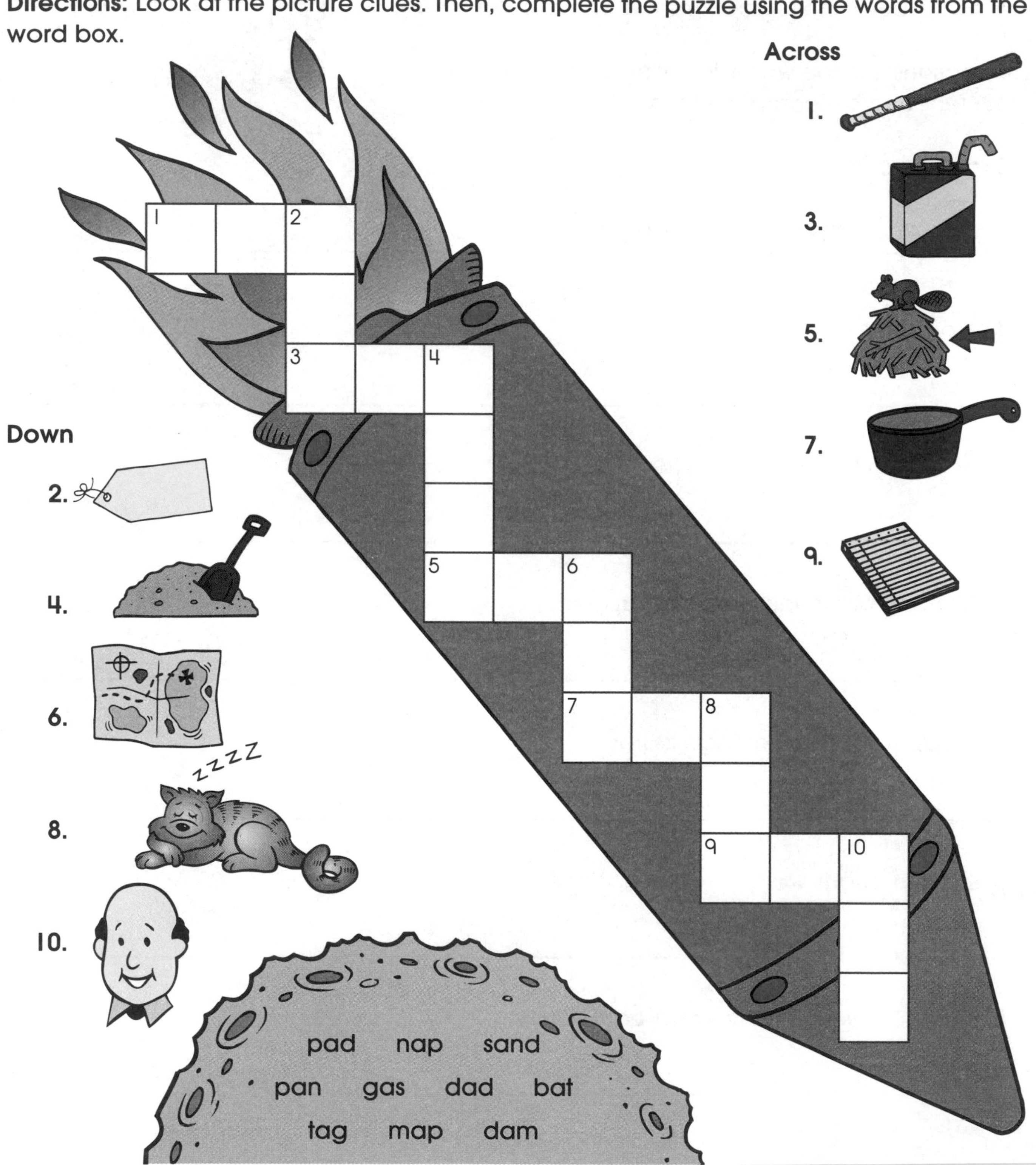

Sentence and Non-Sentences

A **sentence** tells a complete idea.

Directions: Circle the groups of words that tell a complete idea.

1. Sharks are fierce hunters.
2. Afraid of sharks.
3. The great white shark will attack people.
4. Other kinds will not.

5. Sharks have an outer row of teeth for grabbing food.
6. When the outer teeth fall out, another row of teeth moves up.
7. The ocean clean by eating dead animals.
8. Not a single bone in its body.
9. Cartilage.
10. Made of the same material as the tip of your nose.
11. Unlike other fish, sharks cannot float.
12. In motion constantly.
13. Even while sleeping.

Rhyme Time

Directions: Read the clues and use the words in the word box to complete the puzzle.

Across

1. It rhymes with cake.
2. It rhymes with day.
3. It rhymes with damp.
6. It rhymes with light.

Down

1. It rhymes with dizzy.
2. It rhymes with space.
4. It rhymes with hairy.
5. It rhymes with far.

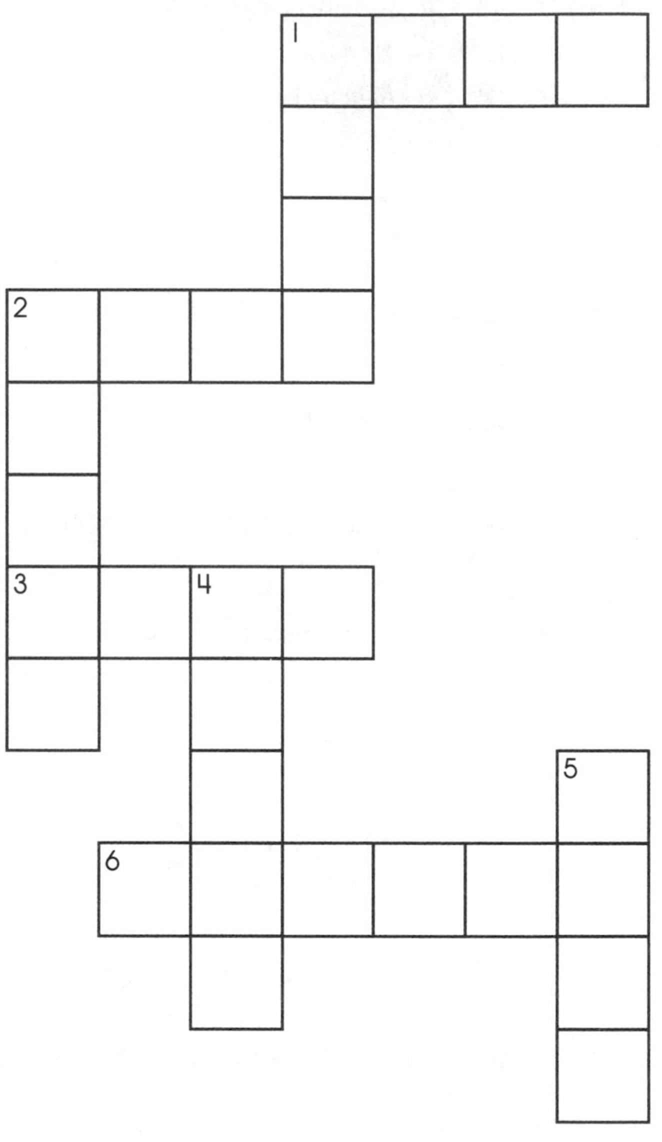

play	bake	busy	place
bright	camp	merry	star

Nap Time in the Nest

Directions: Look at the picture clues. Then, complete the puzzle using the words from the word box.

Across

2.

4.

5.

6.

Down

1. 

5.

2. 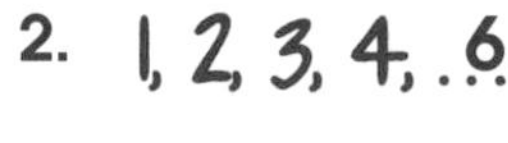

3. 

note nose numbers
needle net nail nine
nurse nest

Statements and Questions

Statements are sentences that tell about something. Statements begin with a capital letter and end with a period. **Questions** are sentences that ask about something. Questions begin with a capital letter and end with a question mark.

Directions: Rewrite the sentences using capital letters and either a period or a question mark.

Example: walruses live in the Arctic

Walruses live in the Arctic.

1. are walruses large sea mammals or fish

____

2. they spend most of their time in the water and on ice

____

3. are floating sheets of ice called **ice floes**

____

4. are walruses related to seals

____

5. their skin is thick, wrinkled, and almost hairless

____

Statements and Questions

Directions: Change the statements into questions and the questions into statements.

Example: Jane is happy. Is Jane happy?
Were you late? You were late.

1. The rainbow was brightly colored.

____

2. Was the sun coming out?

____

3. The dog is doing tricks.

____

4. Have you washed the dishes today?

____

5. Kurt was the circus ringmaster.

____

6. Were you planning on going to the library?

____

Exclamations

Exclamation points are used for sentences that express strong feelings. These sentences can have one or two words or be very long.

Example: **Wait!** or **Don't forget to call!**

Directions: Add an exclamation point at the end of sentences that express strong feelings. Add a period at the end of the statements.

1. My parents and I were watching television
2. The snow began falling around noon
3. Wow
4. The snow was really coming down
5. We turned the television off and looked out the window
6. The snow looked like a white blanket
7. How beautiful
8. We decided to put on our coats and go outside
9. Hurry
10. Get your sled
11. All the people on the street came out to see the snow
12. How wonderful
13. The children began making a snowman
14. What a great day

Color Words

Directions: Write the color of the fruit or vegetable to complete the puzzle.

red
orange
yellow
green
blue
purple

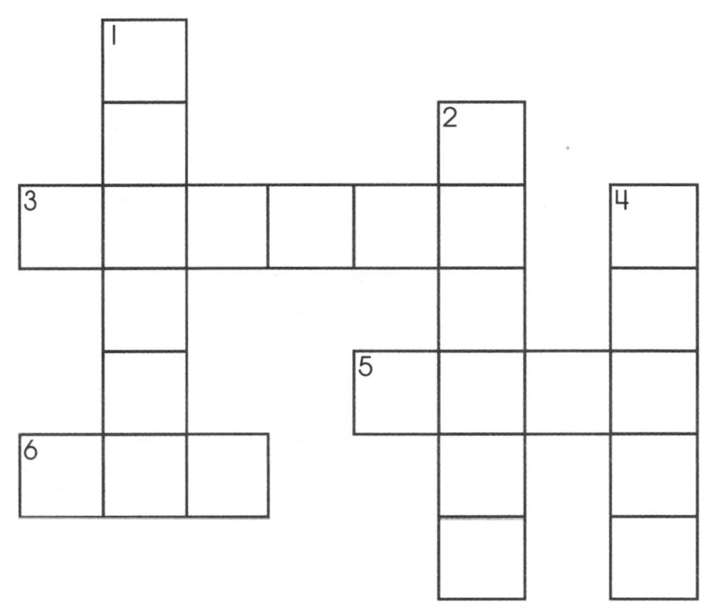

Across

3. a carrot
5. a blueberry
6. a strawberry

Down

1. a plum
2. a lemon
4. a lime

Dinosaurs

Directions: Read the sentences and use the words in the word box to complete the puzzle.

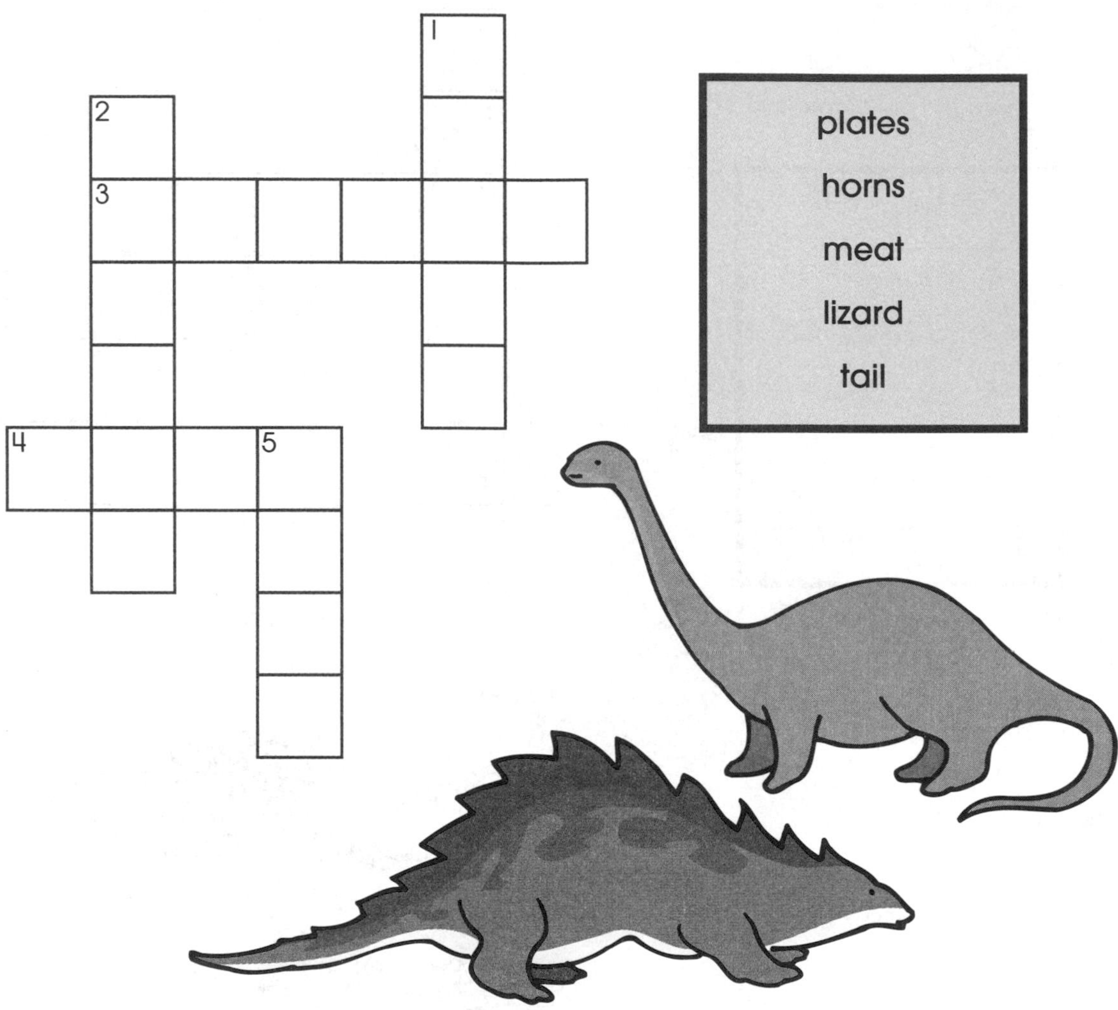

Across

3. The name **Brontosaurus** means "thunder _____."
4. A Tyrannosaurus was the largest _____-eating dinosaur.

Down

1. A Triceratops had three _____ and a massive shield.
2. A Stegosaurus had huge bony _____ along its back.
5. An Ankylosaurus had a heavy club at the end of its _____.

Contractions

Contractions are shortened forms of two words. Use apostrophes to show where letters are missing.

Example: it is = it's

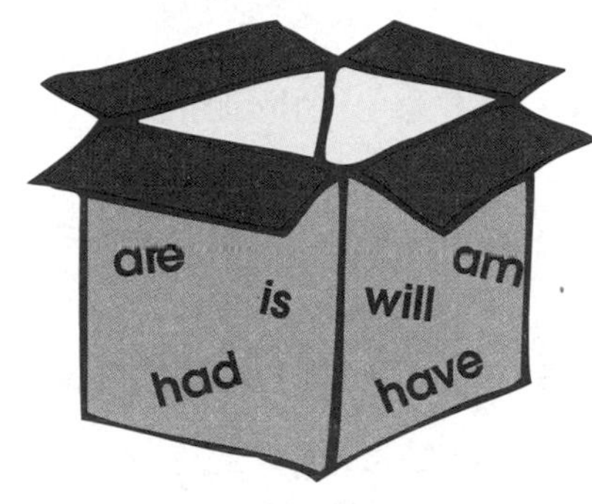

Directions: Write the words that are used in each contraction.

we're ____________ + ____________ they'll ____________ + ____________

you'll ____________ + ____________ aren't ____________ + ____________

I'm ____________ + ____________ isn't ____________ + ____________

Directions: Write the words as contractions.

you have ____________________ have not ____________________

had not ____________________ we will ____________________

they are ____________________ he is ____________________

she had ____________________ it will ____________________

I am ____________________ is not ____________________

Apostrophes

Apostrophes show where letters are missing when two words are combined to form a contraction.

Example: **would not = wouldn't**

Directions: Write the apostrophes in the contractions below.

Example: We shouldn't be going to their house so late at night.

1. We didn t think that the ice cream would melt so fast.

2. They re never around when we re ready to go.

3. Didn t you need to make a phone call?

4. Who s going to help you paint the bicycle red?

Directions: Add an apostrophe and an **s** to the words to show ownership of a person, place, or thing.

Example: Jill**'s** bike is broken.

1. That is Holly flower garden.

2. Mark new skates are black and green.

3. Mom threw away Dad old shoes.

4. Buster food dish was lost in the snowstorm.

Wild West

Directions: Use the word lists to fill out the grid below.

Hint: Count the squares in the grid first to see where the words will fit.

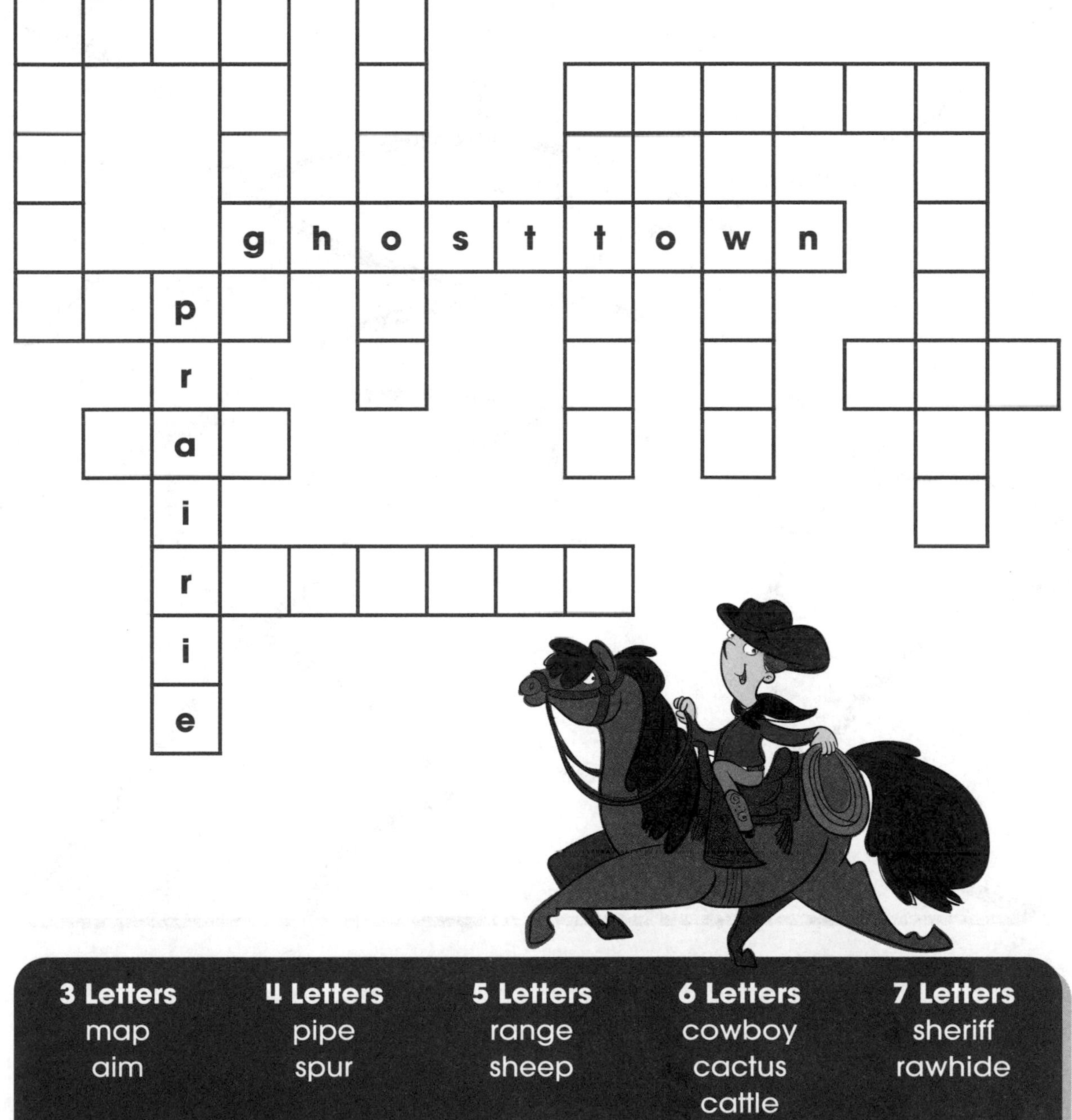

3 Letters	4 Letters	5 Letters	6 Letters	7 Letters
map	pipe	range	cowboy	sheriff
aim	spur	sheep	cactus	rawhide
			cattle	
			saloon	

Name ______________________

Splishing and Splashing

Directions: Color the spaces with rhyming words gray. Color the other spaces blue.

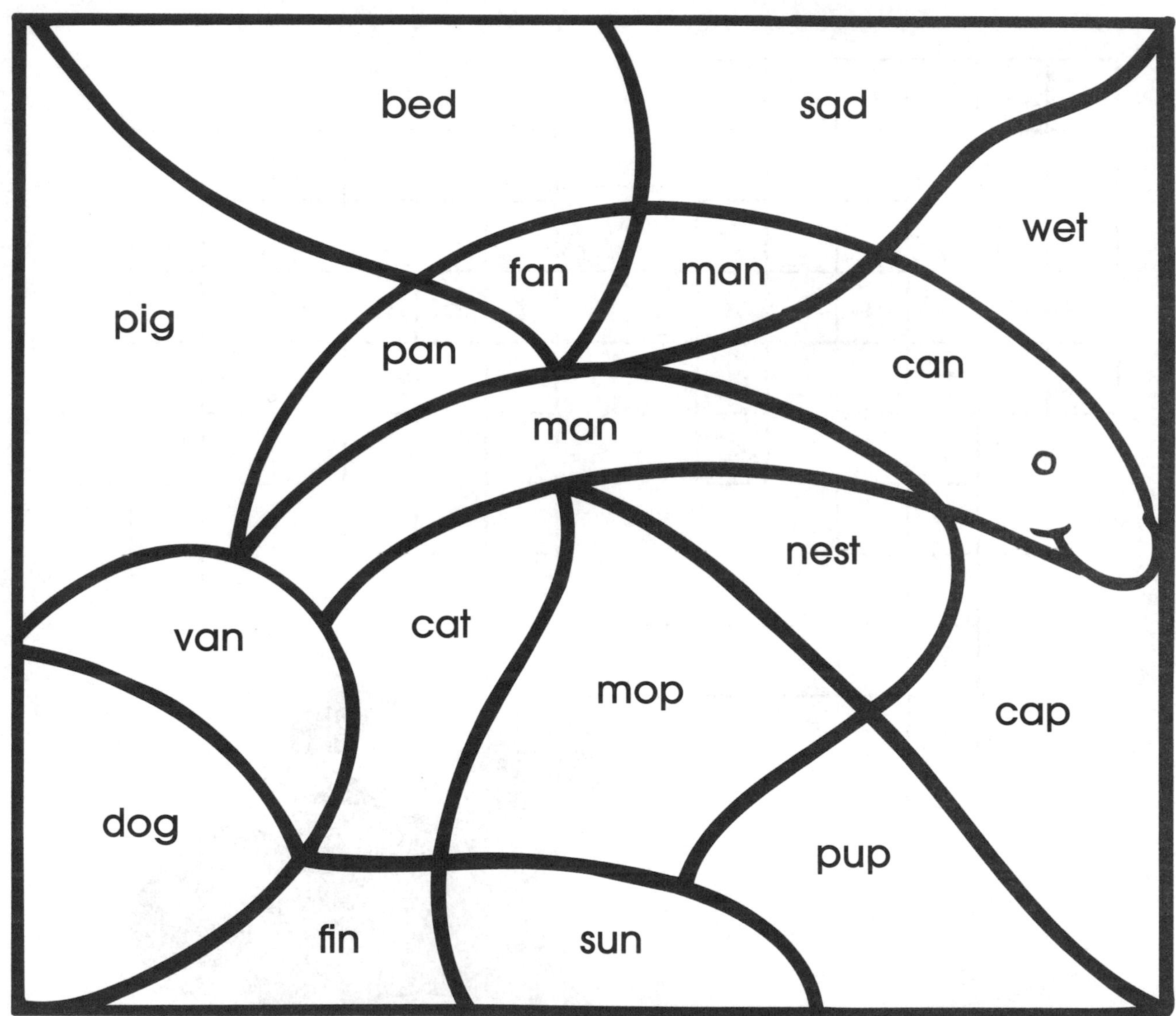

Directions: Use some of the rhyming words to finish the sentence.

C ____ ____ the m ____ ____ in the

v ____ ____ turn on the ____ an?

Name ____________________

Quotation Marks

Quotation marks are punctuation marks that tell what is said by a person. Quotation marks go before the first word and after the punctuation of a direct quote. The first word of a direct quote begins with a capital letter.

Example: Katie said, "Never go in the water without a friend."

Directions: Put quotation marks around the correct words in the sentences below.

Example: "Wait for me, please," said Laura.

1. Nico, would you like to visit a jungle? asked his uncle.
2. The police officer said, Don't worry, we'll help you.
3. James shouted, Hit a home run!
4. My friend Chloe said, I really don't like cheeseburgers.

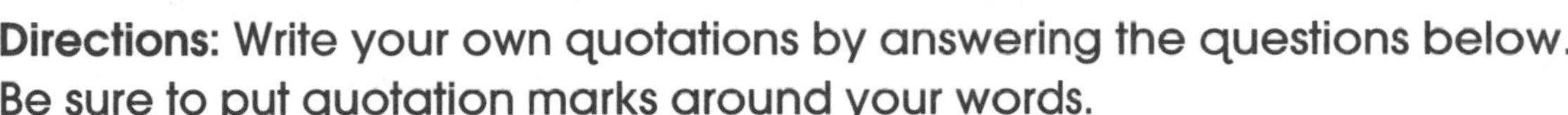

Directions: Write your own quotations by answering the questions below. Be sure to put quotation marks around your words.

1. What would you say if you saw a dinosaur?

____

____

2. What would your best friend say if your hair turned purple?

____

____

Name ______________________

Quotation Marks

Directions: Put quotation marks around the correct words in the sentences below.

1. Can we go for a bike ride? asked Katrina.

____

2. Yes, said Mom.

____

3. Let's go to the park, said Micah.

____

4. Great idea! said Mom.

____

5. How long until we get there? asked Katrina.

____

6. Soon, said Micah.

____

7. Here we are! exclaimed Mom.

____

Healthy Foods

Directions: Read the sentences and use the words in the word box to complete the puzzle.

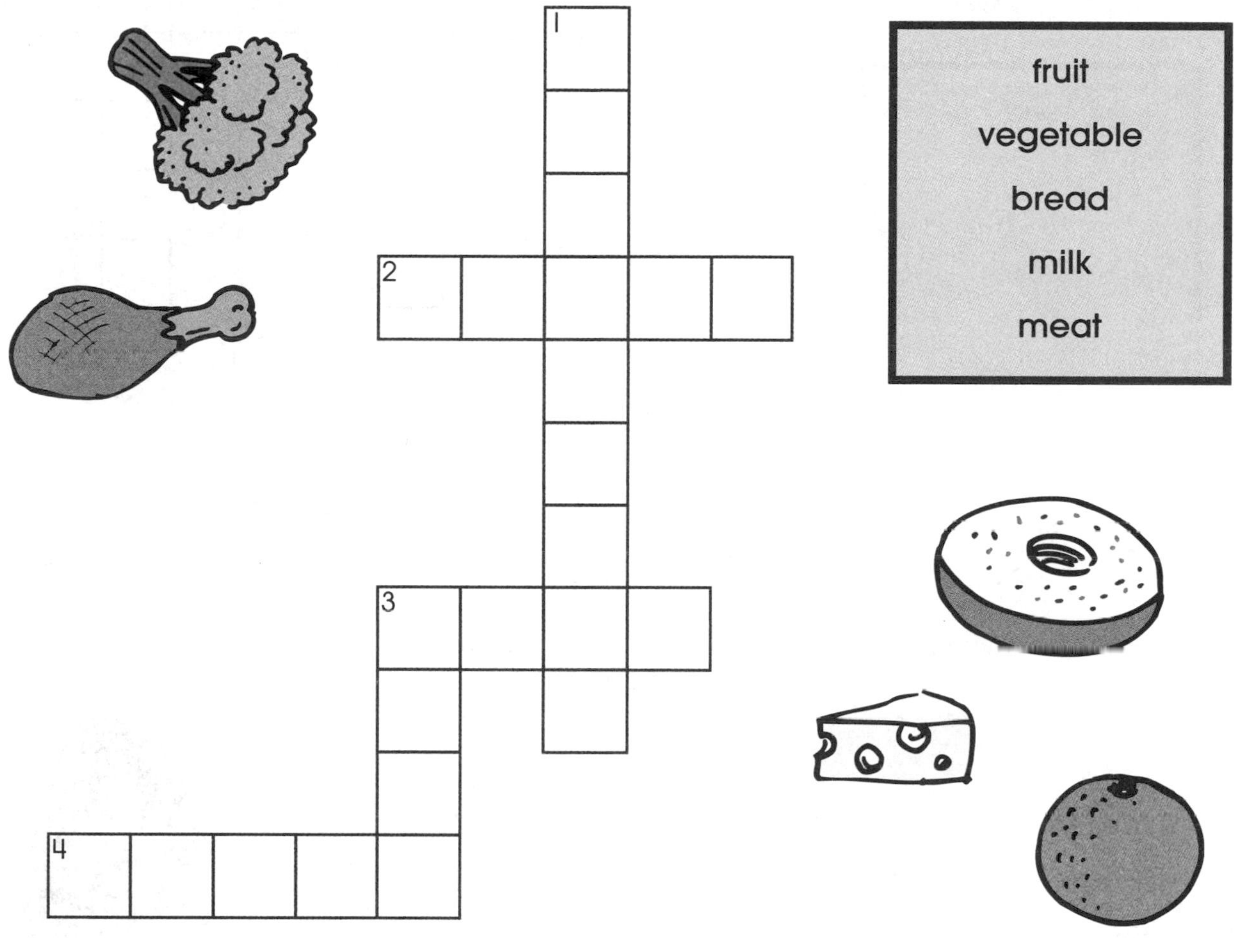

Across

2. A bagel is a food from the ____ and cereal group.
3. A slice of cheese belongs to the ____ group.
4. An orange is a food from the ____ group.

Down

1. Broccoli is a food from the ____ group.
3. Chicken and eggs belong to the ____ group.

Five Senses

Directions: Read the clues and use the words in the word box to complete the puzzle.

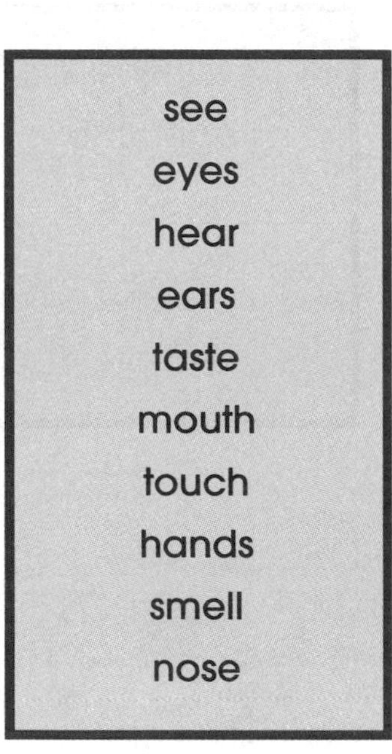

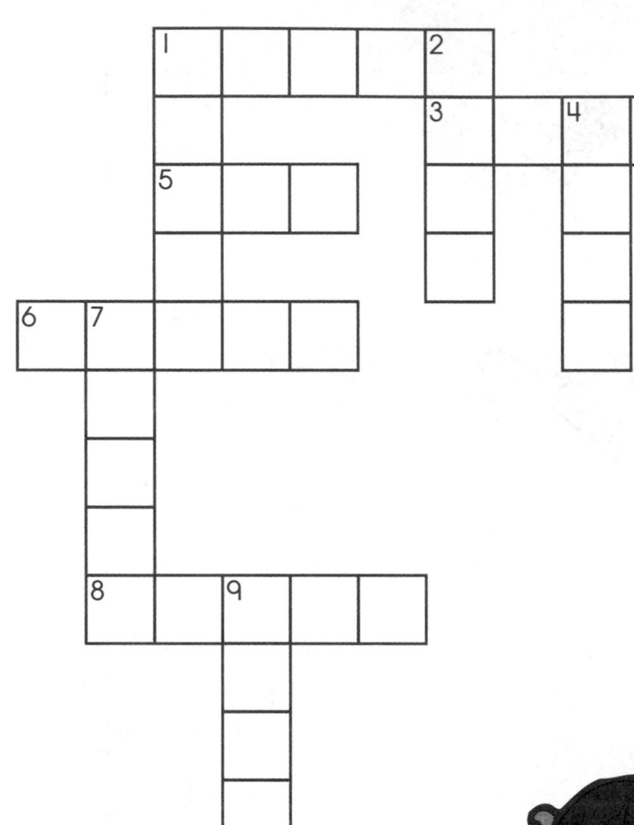

Across

1. Your hands help you do this.
3. You look at a pretty butterfly with these.
5. Your eyes help you do this.
6. You use your nose to do this.
8. You use these to touch a soft kitten.

Down

1. Your mouth helps you do this.
2. Your ears help you do this.
4. You listen to music with these.
7. You taste your favorite fruit with this.
9. You use this to smell a flower.

Alliteration

Alliteration is the repeated use of beginning sounds. Alliterative sentences are sometimes referred to as "tongue twisters."

Example:

She sells seashells by the seashore.
Peter Piper picked a peck of pickled peppers.

Directions: Use alliteration to write your own tongue twisters.

1. ____________________
____
____

2. ____________________
____
____

3. ____________________
____
____

Crazy About Contractions

Pairs of words combined into one with an apostrophe are called **contractions**.

Directions: Read the lists of words below. Combine them to make contractions and complete the puzzle.

Example: did not = didn't.

Across

2. they had
4. would not
5. you are
6. he is
7. I have
8. should have
9. could not

Down

1. will not
3. do not
4. we are
5. you have
6. have not
7. it is

Poetry

Shape poems are words that form the shape of the thing being written about.

Example:

Directions: Create your own shape poem below.

Nonliving Things

Directions: Read the sentences and use the words in the word box to complete the puzzle.

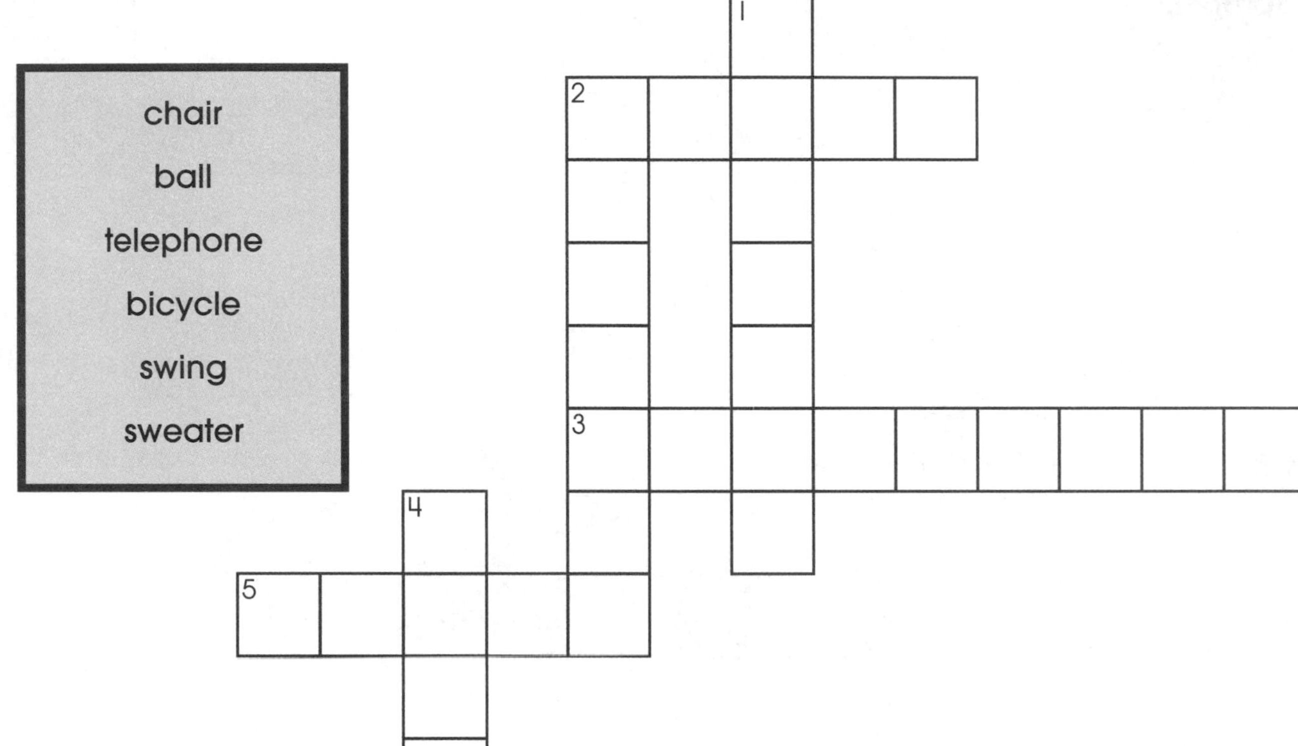

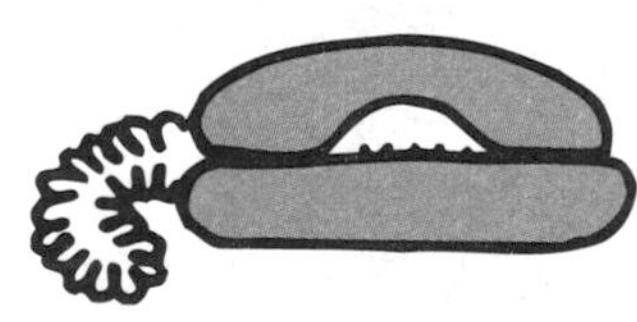

Across

2. A _____ is something you play on.
3. A _____ is something you call people on to talk to them.
5. A _____ is something that has four legs and you sit on it.

Down

1. A _____ is something you ride on that has two wheels.
2. A _____ is something you wear to keep you warm.
4. A _____ is something you can throw and catch.

Poetry: Cinquains

A **cinquain** is a type of poetry. The form is:

Noun
Adjective, adjective
Verb + ing, verb + ing, verb + ing
Four-word phrase
Synonym for noun in line 1

Example:

Books
Creative, fun
Reading, choosing, looking
I love to read!
Novels

Directions: Write your own cinquain!

____
noun

______________, ______________
adjective adjective

______________, ______________, ______________
verb + ing verb + ing verb + ing

____
four-word phrase

____
synonym for noun in first line

It's a Mystery

Directions: Fill in the puzzle with words that name the pictures below. Use the word box to help you.

1.	○							
2.		○		■				
3.	○							
4.		○						
5.					○			
6.	○							

bib
bonnet
blanket
bottles
stroller
car seat

1.

2. 

3. 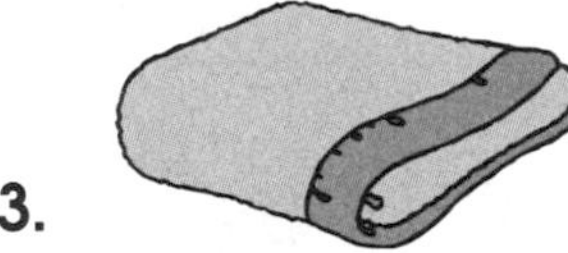

4.

5. 

6. 

Directions: The letters in the circles going down the puzzle spell a mystery word. The word names people who might use all these items. Write the mystery word.

____

Spelling

Name ____________________

Vocabulary: Beginning and Ending Sounds

Directions: Use the words in the box to answer the questions below.

ax	mix
beach	church
class	kiss
brush	crash

Which word:

begins with the same sound as **breakfast** and ends with the same sound as **fish**? ____________________

begins with the same sound as **children** and ends with the same sound as **catch**? ____________________

begins and ends with the same sound as **cuts**? ____________________

sounds like **acts**? ____________________

begins with the same sound as **coconut** and ends with the same sound as **splash**? ____________________

rhymes with **tricks**? ____________________

has **each** in it? ____________________

Compound Word Fun

Directions: Read the clues and use the words in the word box to complete the puzzle.

seashore
rainbow
footprints
sailboat
watermelon
sunburn
sandcastle

Across

1. Your feet make these in the sand.
5. You can swim here.
6. The wind helps this boat move.
7. You don't want to get this at the beach.

Down

2. Look for this in the sky after it rains.
3. You can build one of these in the sand.
4. This tastes good on a hot day.

Vocabulary: Sentences

Directions: Use a word from the box to complete each sentence. Use each word only once.

ax	mix	beach	church	class	kiss	brush	crash

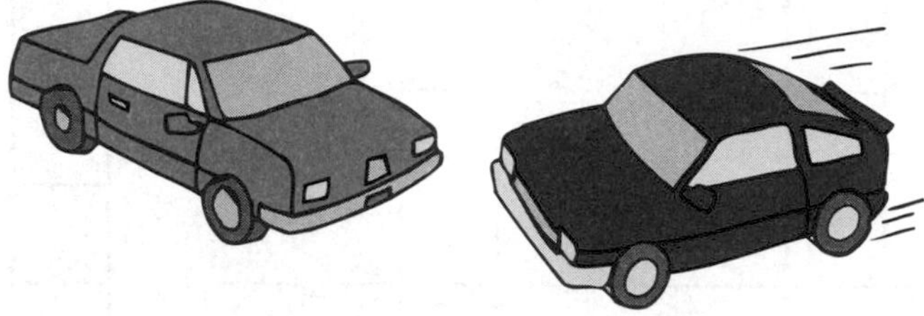

1. Those two cars are going to ____________________.

2. He chopped the wood with an ____________________.

3. Grandma gave me a ____________________ on my cheek.

4. Before you go, ____________________ your hair.

5. How many students are in your ____________________ at school?

6. The waves bring sand to the ____________________.

7. To make orange, you ____________________ yellow and red.

8. On Sunday, we always go to ____________________.

Vocabulary: Plurals

A word that names one thing is **singular**, like **house**. A word that names more than one thing is **plural**, like **houses**.

To make a word plural, add **s**.

Examples: one book — two book**s** one tree — four tree**s**

To make plural words that end in **s**, **ss**, **x**, **sh**, and **ch**, add **es**.

Examples: one fox — two fox**es** one bush — three bush**es**

Directions: Write the word that is missing from each pair below.
Add **s** or **es** to make the plural words. The first one is done for you.

Singular	Plural
table	tables
beach	____________
class	____________
____________	axes
brush	____________
____________	crashes

Name ______________________

Vocabulary: Nouns and Verbs

A **noun** names a person, place, or thing. A **verb** tells what something does or what something is. Some words can be a noun one time and a verb another time.

Directions: Complete each pair of sentences with a word from the box. The word will be a noun in the first sentence and a verb in the second sentence.

mix	kiss	brush	crash

1. Did your dog ever give you a ______________?
(noun)

I have a cold, so I can't ______________ you today.
(verb)

2. I brought my comb and my ______________.
(noun)

I will ______________ the leaves off your coat.
(verb)

3. Was anyone hurt in the ______________?
(noun)

If you aren't careful, you will ______________ into me.
(verb)

4. We bought trail ______________ at the store.
(noun)

I will ______________ the eggs together.
(verb)

Vocabulary: Beginning and Ending Sounds

Directions: Write the words from the box that begin or end with the same sound as the pictures.

stir	clap	drag	hug	plan	grab

1. Which word **begins** with the same sound as each picture?

 ______________________________

 ______________________________

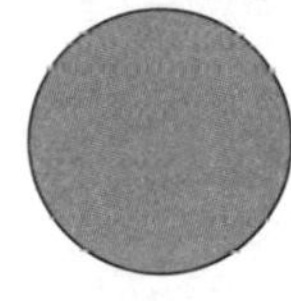 ______________________________

 ______________________________

 ______________________________

2. Which word (or words) **ends** with the same sound as each picture?

 ______________________________

 ______________________________

 ______________________________

 ______________________________

 ______________________________

 ______________________________

Firefighters

Directions: Read the sentences and use the words in the word box to complete the puzzle.

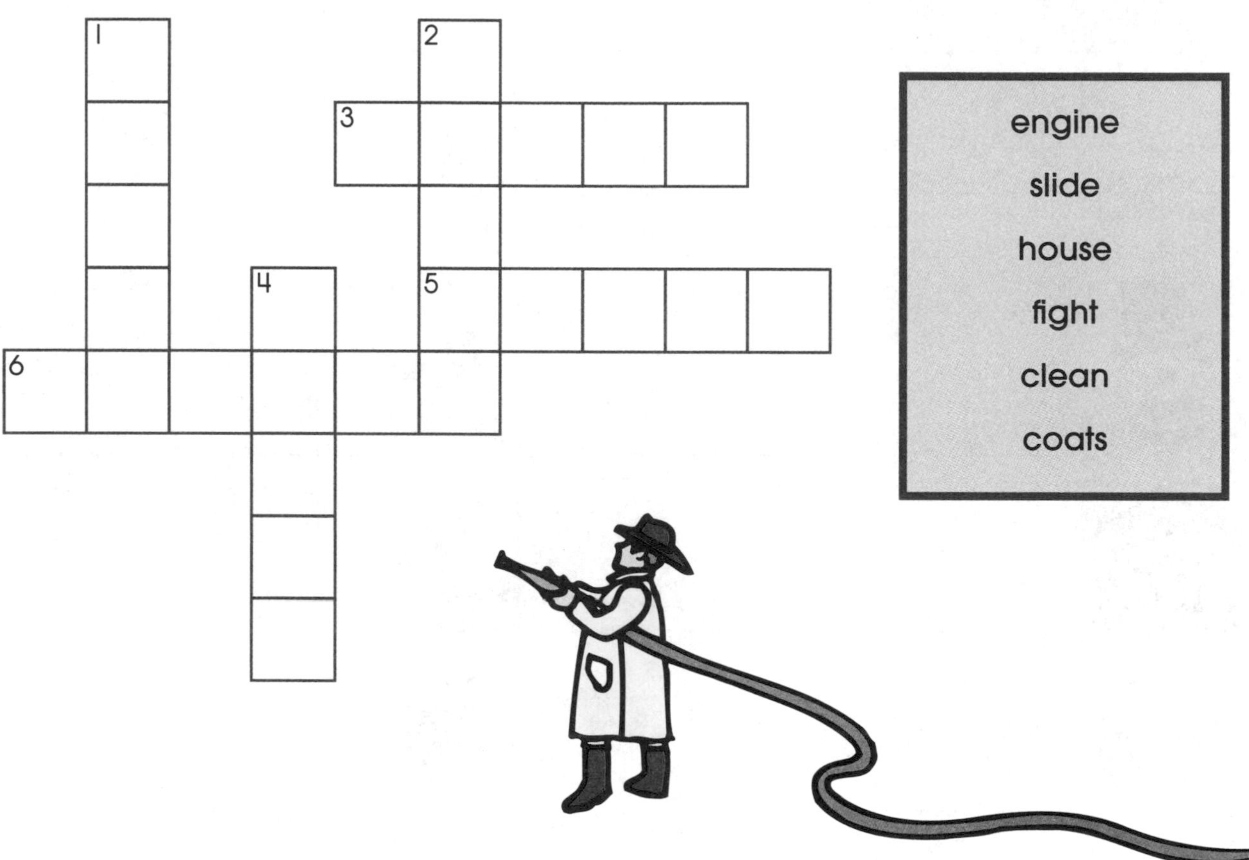

Across

3. They put on their ____ , boots, and helmets.
5. As the fire alarm goes off, the firefighters ____ down the nearest fire pole.
6. They jump onto the fire ____ .

Down

1. They check, ____ , and put away all of their equipment.
2. After the fire is put out, the firefighters go back to the fire ____ .
4. They turn on their siren and speed away to ____ the fire.

Vocabulary: Verbs

Directions: Write the verb that answers each question. Write a sentence using that verb.

stir	clap	drag	hug	plan	grab

Which verb means "to put your arms around someone"?

____

____

Which verb means "to mix something with a spoon"?

____

____

Which verb means "to pull something along the ground"?

____

____

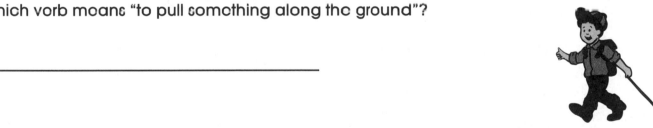

Which verb means "to take something suddenly"?

____

____

Vocabulary: Past-Tense Verbs

The past tense of a verb tells that something already happened. To tell about something that already happened, add **ed** to most verbs. If the verb already ends in **e**, just add **d**.

Examples:

We enter**ed** the contest last week.
I fold**ed** the paper wrong.
He add**ed** two boxes to the pile.

We taste**d** the fruit salad.
They decide**d** quickly.
She share**d** her sandwich.

Directions: Use the verb from the first sentence to complete the second sentence. Add **d** or **ed** to show that something already happened.

Example:

My mom looks fine today. Yesterday, she ___looked___ tired.

1. You enter through the middle door.

   We ______________________ that way last week.

2. Please add this for me. I already ______________________ it twice.

3. Will you share your banana with me?

   I ______________________ my apple with you yesterday.

4. It's your turn to fold the clothes. I ______________________ them yesterday.

5. May I taste another one? I already ______________________ one.

6. You need to decide. We ______________________ this morning.

Vocabulary: Past-Tense Verbs

When you write about something that already happened, you add **ed** to most verbs. For some verbs that have a short vowel and end in one consonant, you double the consonant before adding **ed**.

Examples:

He hugg**ed** his pillow
She stir**red** the carrots.
They clap**ped** for me.
The dog grab**bed** the stick.
We plan**ned** to go tomorrow.
They drag**ged** their bags on the ground.

Directions: Use the verb from the first sentence to complete the second sentence. Change the verb in the second part to the past tense. Double the consonant, and add **ed**.

Example:

We skip to school. Yesterday, we ____skipped____ the whole way.

1. It's not nice to grab things.

   When you ______________________ my book, I felt angry.

2. Did anyone hug you today? Dad ______________________ me this morning.

3. We plan our vacations every year. Last year, we ______________________ to go to the beach.

4. Is it my turn to stir the pot? You ______________________ it last time.

5. Let's clap for Andy, just like we ______________________ for Amy.

6. My sister used to drag her blanket everywhere.

   Once, she ______________________ it to the store.

Vocabulary: Present-Tense Verbs

When something is happening right now, it is in the **present tense**. There are two ways to write verbs in the present tense.

Examples: The dog **walks**. The dog **is walking**.

The cats **play**. The cats **are playing**.

Directions: Write each sentence again, writing the verb a different way.

Example:

He lists the numbers.

He is listing the numbers.

1. She is pounding the nail.

____

2. My brother toasts the bread.

____

3. They search for the robber.

____

4. The teacher lists the pages.

____

5. They are spilling the water.

____

6. Nikhil and Amy load the packages.

____

Name ____________________

Slumbering Slippers

Directions: Read the clues and use the words in the word box to complete the puzzle.

Across

4. Opposite of frown.
5. A small, slow-moving creature.
6. Opposite of rough.
9. Resting.
10. To slant or lean.
11. What your nose does.
13. Intelligent.
14. Ah . . . choo!

Down

1. To shut with a bang.
2. A smooth, layered rock.
3. A cracking sound.
4. Very clever, like a fox.
6. To trip.
7. A kind of shoe.
8. Reptiles.
11. Frozen white flakes.
12. Something burning gives off.

smooth	snail	sly
slam	smart	slip
slipper	snow	smile
slope	slate	smoke
snakes	smells	sneeze
snap	sleeping	

Vocabulary: Statements

A **statement** is a sentence that tells something.

Directions: Use the words in the box to complete the statements below. Write the words on the lines.

glue	decide	add
share	enter	fold

1. It took ten minutes for Kayla to ____________________ the numbers.

2. Ben wants to ____________________ his snack with me.

3. "I can't ____________________ which color to choose," said DeShawn.

4. ____________________ can be used to make things stick together.

5. "This is how you ____________________ your paper in half," said Mrs. Green.

6. The opposite of **leave** is ____________________ .

Write your own statement on the line.

____

Vocabulary: Questions

Questions are asking sentences. They begin with a capital letter and end with a question mark. Many questions begin with the words **who**, **what**, **why**, **when**, **where**, and **how**. Write six questions using the question words below. Make sure to end each question with a question mark.

1. Who ______________________

2. What ______________________

3. Why ______________________

4. When ______________________

5. Where ______________________

6. How ______________________

Vocabulary: Commands

A **command** is a sentence that tells someone to do something.

Directions: Use the words in the box to complete the commands below. Write the words on the lines.

glue	decide	add	share	enter	fold

1. ____________________ a cup of flour to the batter.

2. ____________________ how much paper you will need to write your story.

3. Please____________________ the picture of the apple onto the paper.

4. ____________________ through this door and leave through the other door.

5. Please ____________________ the letter and put it into an envelope.

6. ____________________ your toys with your sister.

Write your own command on the lines.

____

____

Vocabulary: Directions

A **direction** is a sentence written as a command.

Directions: Write the missing directions for these pictures. Begin each direction with one of the verbs below.

glue	enter	share	add	decide	fold

How To Make a Peanut Butter and Jelly Sandwich:

1. Spread peanut butter on bread.
2. ______________________
3. Cut the sandwich in half.
4. ______________________

How To Make a Valentine:

1. ______________________
2. Draw half a heart.
3. Cut along the line you drew.
4. ______________________

Name ____________________

A Neighborhood

Directions: Read the sentences and use the words in the word box to complete the puzzle.

Across

1. The children go to ____ .
4. Latasha and Ryan walked on the ____ .
5. Mom and Dad went to the____ to buy groceries.

Down

2. Tyana lives in the blue ____ on the corner.
3. The children play in the ____.
4. Cars drive up and down the ____ .

Homophones

Homophones are words that sound the same but are spelled differently and have different meanings.

Directions: Use the homophones in the box to answer the riddles below.

main	meat	peace	dear	to
mane	meet	piece	deer	too

1. Which word has the word **pie** in it? ____________________
2. Which word rhymes with **ear** and is an animal? ____________________
3. Which word rhymes with **shoe** and means **also**? ____________________
4. Which word has the word **eat** in it and is something you might eat? ____________________
5. Which word has the same letters as the word **read** but in a different order? ____________________
6. Which word rhymes with **train** and is something on a pony? ____________________
7. Which word, if it began with a capital letter, might be the name of an important street? ____________________
8. Which word sounds like a number but has only two letters? ____________________
9. Which word rhymes with **street** and is a synonym for **greet**? ____________________
10. Which word rhymes with the last syllable in **police** and can mean quiet? ____________________

Helpful Friends

Directions: Read the clues and use the words in the word box to complete the puzzle.

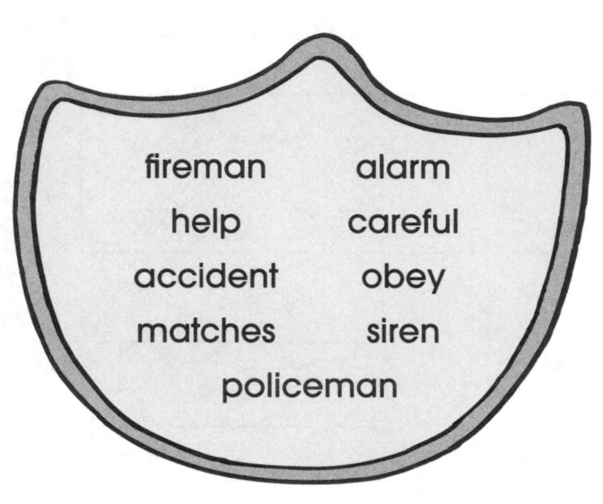

fireman
alarm
help
careful
accident
obey
matches
siren
policeman

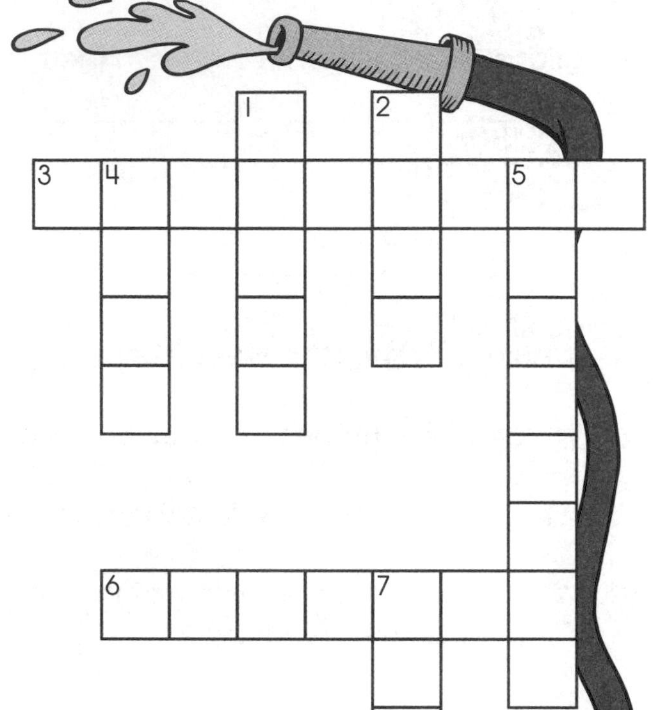

Across

3. A person who works for the police.
6. A person who puts out fires.
9. Always be ____________ with fire.

Down

1. Makes a police car's sound.
2. Policemen and firemen ____________ everyone.
4. People need to ____________ the rules.
5. Police help when there is an ____________.
7. Never play with ____________.
8. An ____________ goes off when there is a fire.

Short Vowels

Short vowel patterns usually have a single vowel followed by a consonant sound.

Short a is the sound you hear in the word **can**.

Short e is the sound you hear in the word **men**.

Short i is the sound you hear in the word **pig**.

Short o is the sound you hear in the word **pot**.

Short u is the sound you hear in the word **truck**.

fast	stop
spin	track
wish	lunch
bread	block

Directions: Use the words in the box to answer the questions below.

Which word:

begins with the same sound as **blast** and ends with the same sound as **look**? ____________________

rhymes with **stack**? ____________________

begins with the same sound as **phone** and ends with the same sound as **lost**? ____________________

has the same vowel sound as **hen**? ____________________

rhymes with **crunch**? ____________________

begins with the same sound as **spot** and ends with the same sound as **can**? ____________________

begins with the same sound as **win** and ends with the same sound as **crush**? ____________________

has the word **top** in it? ____________________

Name ______________________

Long Vowels

Long vowels say the letter name sound.

Long a is the sound you hear in **cane**.

Long e is the sound you hear in **green**.

Long i is the sound you hear in **pie**.

Long o is the sound you hear in **bowl**.

Long u is the sound you hear in **cube**.

lame	goal
pain	few
street	fright
nose	gray
bike	fuse

Directions: Use the words in the box to answer the questions below.

1. Add one letter to each of these words to make words from the box.

ray ______________ use ______________ right ______________

2. Change one letter from each word to make a word from the box.

pail ______________ goat ______________

late ______________ bite ______________

3. Write the word from the box that . . .

has the long **e** sound. ______________

rhymes with **you**. ______________

is a homophone for **knows**. ______________

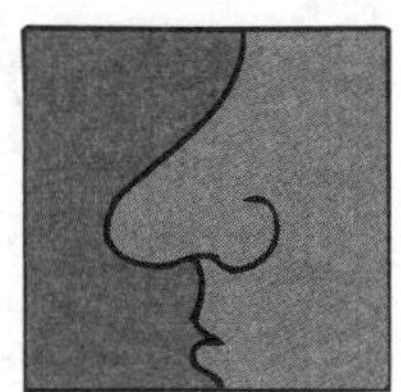

Long Vowels: Sentences

Directions: Use the words in the box to complete each sentence.

lame	goal	pain	few	bike
street	fright	nose	gray	fuse

1. Look both ways before crossing the ____________________.

2. My ____________________ had a flat tire.

3. Our walk through the haunted house gave us such a ____________________.

4. I kicked the soccer ball and scored a ____________________.

5. The ____________________ clouds mean rain is coming.

6. Cover your ____________________ when you sneeze.

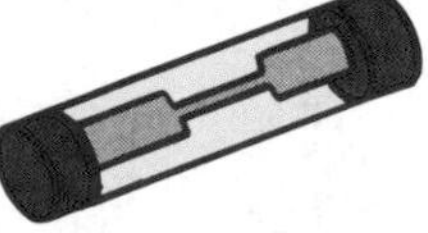

7. We blew a ____________________ at my house last night.

Around the City

Directions: Read the clues and use the words in the word box to complete the puzzle.

Across

3. You can borrow books here.
4. Teachers help children learn here.
7. You can get something to eat here.
8. This is where you can go to play or ride a bike.

Down

1. Your mother or father can get medicine here.
2. This building has things about science, antiques, or art.
5. This is where you can see a movie.
6. This is a place where people keep money.

Adjectives

Directions: Use the words in the box to answer the questions below. Use each word only once.

polite	careless	neat	shy	selfish	thoughtful

1. Someone who is quiet and needs some time to make new friends is ____________________.

2. A person who says "please" and "thank you" is ____________________.

3. Someone who always puts all the toys away is ____________________.

4. A person who won't share with others is being ____________________.

5. A person who leaves a bike out all night is being ____________________.

6. Someone who thinks of others is ____________________.

Spelling

Directions: Circle the word in each sentence that is not spelled correctly. Then, write the word correctly.

1. Zack isn't shelfish at all. ____________________

2. He sharred his lunch with me today. ____________________

3. I was careles and forgot to bring mine. ____________________

4. My father says if I planed better, that wouldn't happen all the time. ____________________

5. Zack is kind of quiet, and I used to think he was shie. ____________________

6. Now, I know he is really thotful. ____________________

7. He's also very polyte and always asks before he borrows anything. ____________________

8. He would never just reach over and grabb something he wanted. ____________________

9. I'm glad Zack desided to be my friend. ____________________

At School

Directions: Read the clues and use the words in the word box to complete the puzzle.

teacher
children
books
computer
desk
read
write
learn

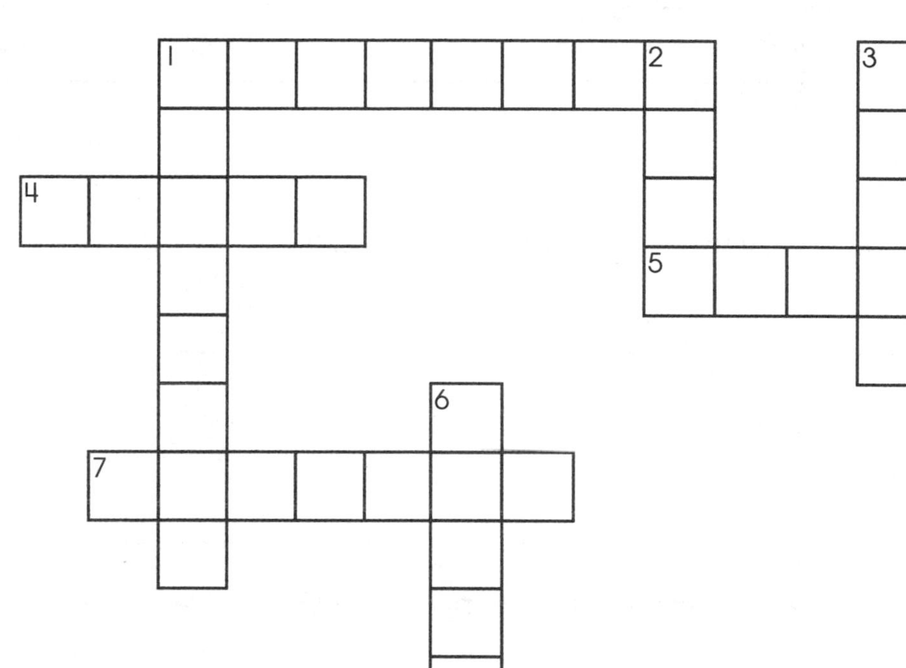

Across

1. This is a machine that helps you learn.
4. You do this with a pencil or a computer.
5. This is where you can work in school.
7. This is a person who helps you learn.

Down

1. These are young people who go to school.
2. This is what you do with a book.
3. These have words and pictures in them.
6. This means "to find out about things".

C, *K*, and *CK* Words: Spelling

Directions: Write the words from the box that answer the questions.

crowd	keeper	cost	pack	kangaroo	thick

1. Which words spell the **k** sound with a **k**?

____

2. Which words spell the **k** sound with a **c**?

____

3. Which words spell the **k** sound with **ck**?

____

4. Circle the letters that spell the **k** sound in these words:

cook black cool kite

cake pocket poke

5. Which words from the box rhyme with each of these?

tossed ____________________ deeper ____________________

proud ____________________ all in blue ____________________

S Words: Spelling

The **s** sound can be spelled with **s**, **ss**, **c**, or **ce**.

Directions: Use the words from the box to complete the sentences below. Write each word only once.

center	pencil	space
address	police	darkness

1. I drew a circle in the ____________________ of the page.

2. I'll write to you if you tell me your ____________________.

3. She pushed too hard and broke the point on her ____________________.

4. If you hear a noise at night, call the ____________________.

5. It was night, and I couldn't see him in the ____________________.

6. There's not enough ____________________ for me to sit next to you.

S Words: Spelling

Directions: Write the words from the box that answer the questions.

center	pencil	space	address	police	darkness

1. Which words spell the **s** sound with **ss**?

____

2. Which words spell the **s** sound with a **c**?

____

3. Which words spell the **s** sound with **ce**?

____

4. Write two other words you know that spell the **s** sound with an **s**.

____

5. Circle the letters that spell the **s** sound in these words.

decide kiss careless ice

cost fierce sentence

6. Put these letters in order to make words from the box.

sdsdera ____________ sdserakn ____________

clipoe ____________ clipne ____________

capse ____________ retnce ____________

C Words: Spelling

The letter **c** can make the **k** sound or the **s** sound.

Example: **c**ount, **c**ity

Directions: Write **k** or **s** to show how the **c** in each word sounds.

cave	________	copy	________	force	________
become	________	dance	________	city	________
certain	________	contest	________	cool	________

Directions: Use the words from the box to answer these questions.

center	pencil	space	address	police	darkness

1. Which word begins with the same sounds as **simple** and ends with the same sound as **fur**? ____________________
2. Which word begins with the same sound as **average** and ends with the same sound as **circus**? ____________________
3. Which word begins with the same sound as **popcorn** and ends with the same sound as **glass**? ____________________
4. Which word begins and ends with the same sound as **pool**?

   ____
5. Which word begins with the same sound as **city** and ends with the same sound as **kiss**? ____________________
6. Which word begins and ends with the same sound as **delicious**?

   ____

Name ______________________

Time to Rhyme

Directions: Use the picture clues to match the rhyming words.

1. meat 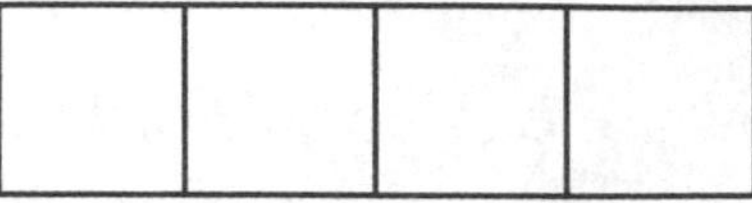

2.  seal 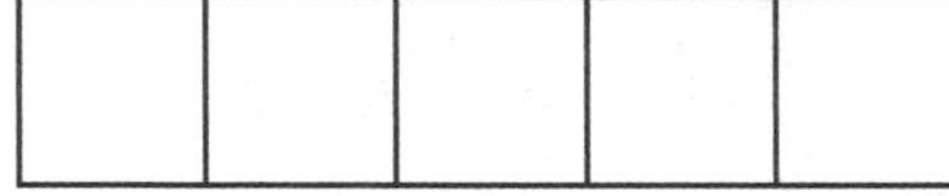

3.  king 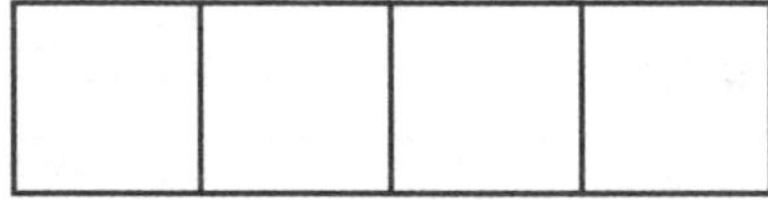

4.  mouse 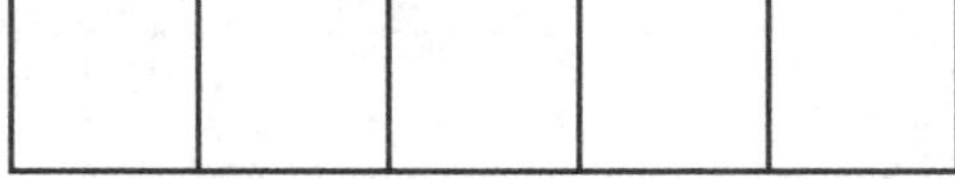

5.  clock 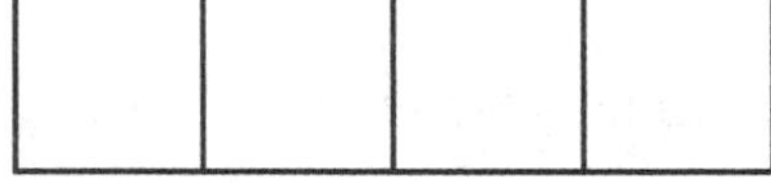

6.  hair 

7.  dog 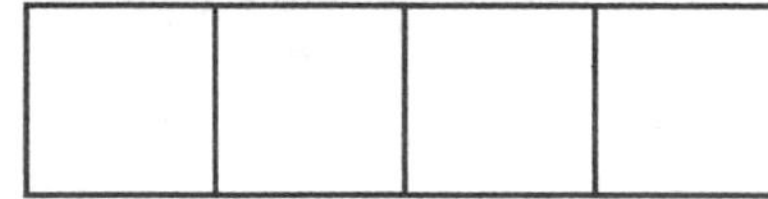

8.  boat 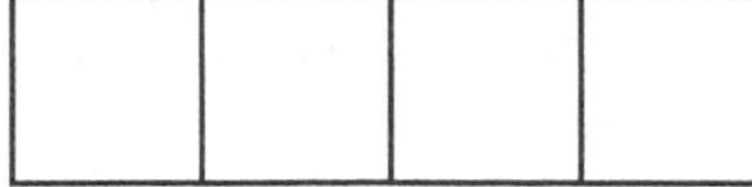

sock

 wheel

 bear

 ring

 goat

 frog

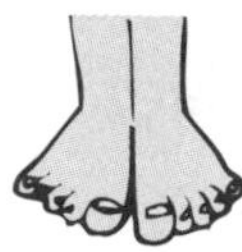 feet

 house

Name ______________________________

Suffixes

A **suffix** is a word part added to the end of a word. Suffixes add to or change the meaning of the word.

Example: sad + ly = sadly

Below are some suffixes and their meanings.

ment	state of being, quality of, act of
ly	like or in a certain way
ness	state of being
ful	full of
less	without

Directions: The words in the box have suffixes. Use the suffix meanings above to match each word with its meaning below. Write the words on the lines.

friendly	cheerful	safely	sleeveless	speechless
kindness	amazement	sickness	peaceful	excitement

1. in a safe way ___ ___(6) ___ ___ ___ ___

2. full of cheer ___ ___ ___ ___ ___(2) ___ ___ ___

3. full of peace ___ ___(4) ___ ___ ___ ___ ___ ___

4. state of being amazed ___ ___ ___ ___ ___ ___(5) ___ ___ ___

5. state of being excited ___ ___ ___ ___ ___(1) ___ ___ ___ ___ ___

6. without speech ___ ___ ___ ___ ___ ___ ___ ___ ___(3) ___

Use the numbered letters to find the missing word below.

You are now on your way to becoming a

___(5) ___(6) ___(3) ___(1) ___(4) ___(2) of suffixes!

Suffixes: Adverbs

Adverbs are words that describe verbs. Adverbs tell where, when, or how. Most adverbs end in the suffix **ly**.

Directions: Complete each sentence with the correct part of speech.

Example: Hank wrote here.

who? (noun) what? (verb) where? (adverb)

1. ____________ was lost ____________

who? (noun) what? (verb) where? (adverb)

2. ____________ ____________ quickly.

who? (noun) what? (verb) how? (adverb)

3. ____________ felt ____________

who? (noun) what? (verb) how? (adverb)

4. My brother ____________ ____________

who? (noun) what? (verb) when? (adverb)

5. ____________ woke up ____________

who? (noun) what? (verb) when? (adverb)

6. ____________ ____________ gladly.

who? (noun) what? (verb) how? (adverb)

Summer

Directions: Read the clues and use the words in the word box to complete the puzzle.

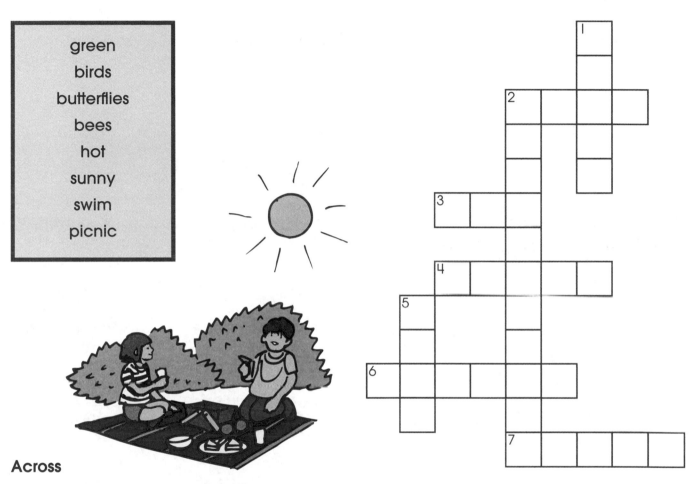

green
birds
butterflies
bees
hot
sunny
swim
picnic

1 2 3 4 5 6 7

Across

2. These buzz around flowers.
3. It is the opposite of **cold**.
4. You might hear them chirp and sing.
6. Bring your lunch outside for this.
7. This kind of day is good for playing outside.

Down

1. Leaves and grass are this color.
2. They flutter their colorful wings.
5. This feels good to do on a hot summer day.

Prefixes: Sentences

Directions: Match each sentence with the word that completes it. Then, write the word on the line.

1. The farmer was ______________ because it didn't rain. •	• input
2. The scientist tried to ______________ the secret formula. •	• redo
3. Mom and Dad asked for our ______________ about where we should go on vacation this year. •	• unhappy
4. We were ______________ to do the work without help. •	• disagree
5. My brother and I ______________ about which show to watch. •	• replay
6. The umpire called for a ______________ of the game. •	• discover
7. We had to stay ______________ when it got cold. •	• inside
8. I spilled my milk on my paper and had to ______________ my homework. •	• unable

Places, Everyone!

Directions: Use the word box and the pictures below to help you fill in the puzzle.

Across

2. frog
4. flower
6. tree
9. sun

Down

1. snake
3. bear
5. rain
6. bird
7. squirrel
8. butterfly

first	second	third	fourth	fifth
sixth	seventh	eighth	ninth	tenth

Synonyms

Synonyms are words that mean almost the same thing.

Example: sick — ill

Directions: Use words from the box to help you complete the sentences below.

glad	fast	noisy	filthy	angry

1. When I am mad, I could also say I am ____________________.

2. To be ____________________ is the same as being happy.

3. After playing outside, I thought I was dirty, but Mom said I was ____________________!

4. I tried not to be too loud, but I couldn't help being a little ____________________.

5. If you're too ____________________, or speedy, you may not do a careful job.

Think of another pair of synonyms. Write them on the lines.

____________________ ____________________

Cool Cider

Directions: Read the clues and use the words in the word box to complete the puzzle.

Across

3. A baby's bed.
5. The cost of something.
6. A castle.
8. A yellow vegetable.
9. You can mold things with this.
10. A very small house.

Down

1. Something to drink.
2. Frozen water.
4. A cold dessert that comes in a cone.
7. A very large town.
8. A desert animal with a humped back.
9. A line that goes around.

city ice ice cream
corn circle palace
cabin clay camel
price crib juice

Antonyms

Directions: Use antonyms from the box to complete the sentences below.

speedy	clean	quiet	thoughtful	happy

1. If we get too loud, the teacher will ask us to be ______________________.

2. She was sad to lose her puppy, but she was ______________________ to find it again.

3. Mark got dirty, so he had to scrub himself ______________________.

4. Janna was too ______________________ when she did her homework, so she worked slowly when she did it over.

5. Logan was too selfish to share his snack,

   but Kyra was ______________________ enough to share hers.

Think of another pair of antonyms. Write them on the lines.

______________________ ______________________

Stretch!

Directions: Read the clues and use the words in the word box to complete the puzzle.

Across

2. A shape that has equal sides.
4. A road.
5. To scatter little pieces.
7. Lightweight rope.
10. A bushy-tailed animal.
11. A stalk of grain.

Down

1. Opposite of weak.
2. The sound a mouse makes.
3. A small river.
4. Yell.
5. Opposite of crooked.
6. A season of the year.
7. To throw water.
8. Very odd.
9. To separate.
10. A homeless cat or dog.

splash	spring
squeak	square
strong	sprinkle
straight	straw
split	string
scream	squirrel
strange	stream
street	stray

Contractions

A **contraction** is a short way to write two words together. Some letters are left out, but an apostrophe takes their place.

Directions: Write the words from the box that answer the questions.

hasn't	you've	aren't	we've	weren't

1. Write the correct contractions below.

Example:

I have I've — was not wasn't

we have ________ you have ________

are not ________ were not ________

has not ________

2. Write two words from the box that are contractions using **have**.

________ ________

3. Write three words from the box that are contractions using **not**.

________ ________ ________

Contractions

Directions: In each sentence below, underline the two words that could be made into a contraction. Write the contraction on the line. Use each contraction from the box only once.

Example: The boys have not gone camping in a long time.

hasn't	you've	aren't
we've	weren't	

1. After a while, we were not sure it was the right direction. ____________

2. I think we have been this way before. ____________

3. We have been waiting, but our guide has not come yet. ____________

4. Did you say you have been here with your sister? ____________

5. You are not going to give up and go back, are you? ____________

Math

Addition

Directions: Add.

Example:

Add the ones.

```
 26
+21
---
  7
```

Add the tens.

```
 26
+21
---
 47
```

```
 18     24     38     49     52
+11    +35    +21    +50    +33
---    ---    ---    ---    ---
```

```
 75     83     67     44     28
+12    +16    +32    +25    +41
---    ---    ---    ---    ---
```

68 + 20 = ____ 54 + 25 = ____ 71 + 17 = ____

The Lions scored 42 points. The Clippers scored 21 points.
How many points were scored in all? ________

Crack the Code

Directions: Write each sum. Then, use the code to find the letter that goes with each sum. Write the letter in the circle.

	+7
3	
4	
6	
7	

	+4
4	
3	
8	
4	
8	
1	
7	
0	
2	
9	

	+6
4	
1	
6	
3	
7	

7	13	9	4	10	5	8	14	12	6	11
r	s	g	l	f	d	c	h	o	e	i

Case of the Litterbug

Who keeps littering the streets with trash? You have three suspects: Ollie Outlaw, Harry Hustler, and Connie Crook!

1. Look for numbers that become 500 when rounded to the nearest hundred. Color their boxes.

2. Look at the letter that appears to discover who the litterbug is!

545	439	464
496	527	501
483	578	470

Who is the litterbug? ____________________

Subtraction

Directions: Subtract.

Example:

Subtract the ones.	Subtract the tens.
39 -24 5	39 -24 15

48 -35	95 -22	87 -16	55 -43
37 -14	69 -57	44 -23	99 -78

66 - 44 = ____

57 - 33 = ____

The yellow car traveled 87 miles per hour. The orange car traveled 66 miles per hour. How much faster was the yellow car traveling? ____________

Number Maze

Directions: Find the shortest route in and out of this honeycomb without going through or next to any cell where a bee is.

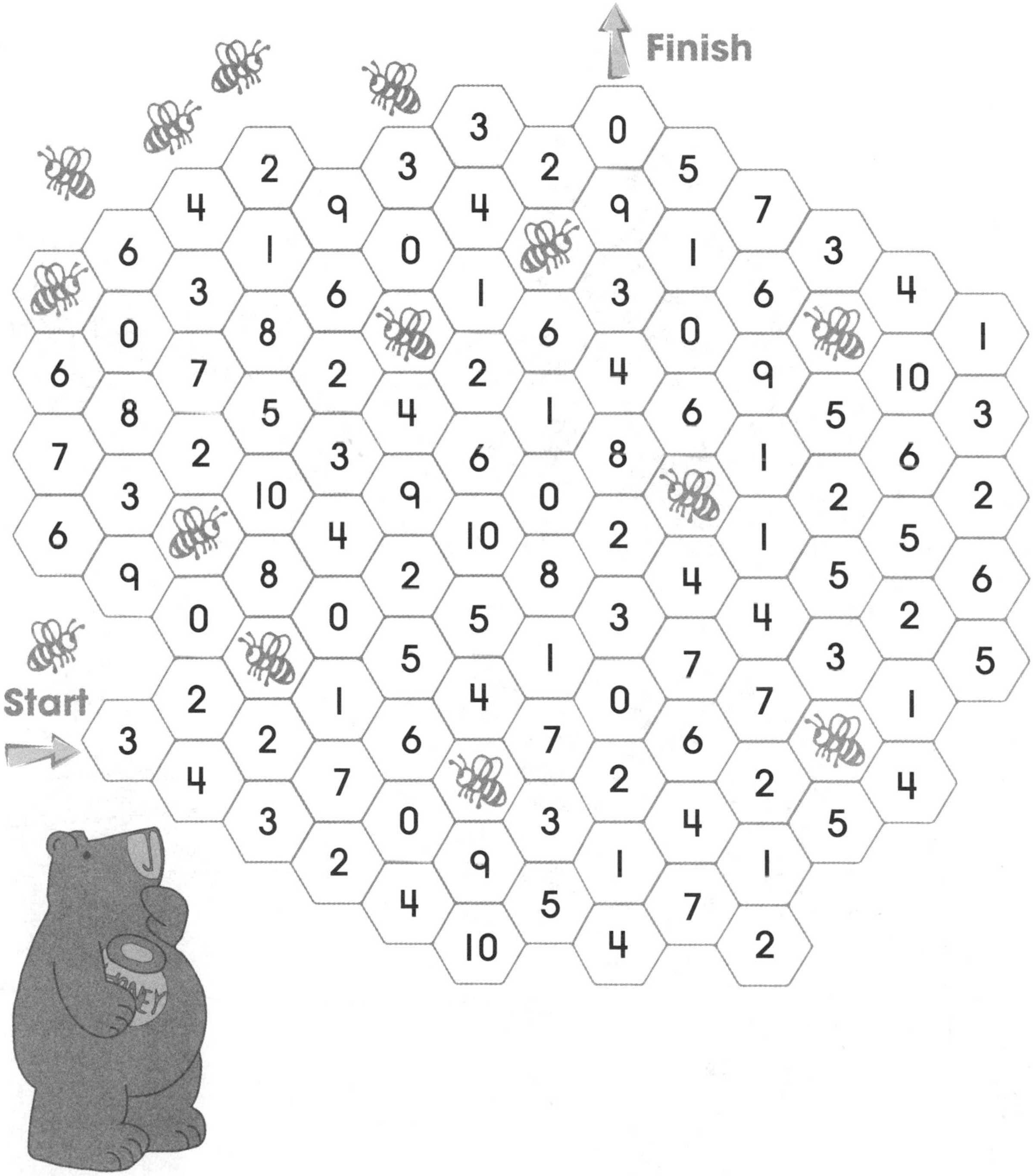

Finish

Start

Double Scoop

Directions: What is your favorite flavor? Connect the dots from **5** to **100**. Color.

Place Value

The **place value** of a digit, or numeral, is shown by where it is in the number. For example, in the number **1,234, 1** has the place value of thousands, **2** is hundreds, **3** is tens, and **4** is ones.

Hundred Thousands	Ten Thousands	Thousands	Hundreds	Tens	Ones
9	4	3	8	5	2

943,852

Directions: Match the numbers in Column A with the words in Column B.

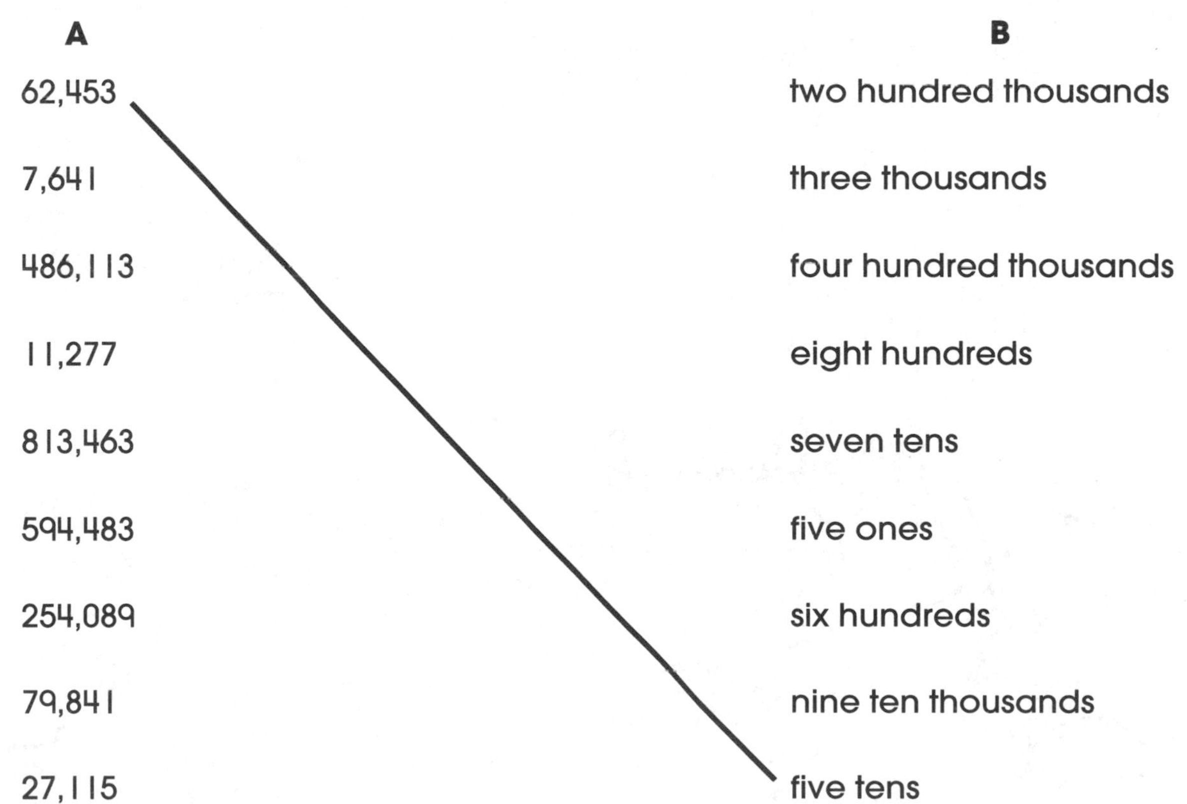

A	B
62,453	two hundred thousands
7,641	three thousands
486,113	four hundred thousands
11,277	eight hundreds
813,463	seven tens
594,483	five ones
254,089	six hundreds
79,841	nine ten thousands
27,115	five tens

Let's Ride

Directions: Monica loves to ride her horse, Spartan. Connect the dots from **100** to **2000**. Color.

Addition: Regrouping

Addition means "putting together" or adding two or more numbers fo find the sum. For example, 3 + 5 = 8. To regroup is to use ten ones to form one ten, ten tens to form one 100, and so on.

Directions: Add using regrouping.

Example:

Add the ones.	Add the tens with regrouping.
88 +21 9	88 +21 109

37 +72	56 +67	51 +88	37 +55	70 +68
93 +54	47 +82	81 +77	23 +92	36 +71

92 + 13 = ____ 73 + 83 = ____ 54 + 61 = ____

The Blues scored 63 points. The Reds scored 44 points.
How many points were scored in all? ____________

Find the Bandits

Four bandits are hiding in four different houses. You need to get their house numbers so you can check up on them.

Directions: Look at the numbers below. Use them to write four 2-digit numbers that can be rounded to 60. The numbers you make will tell you where the bandits are hiding!

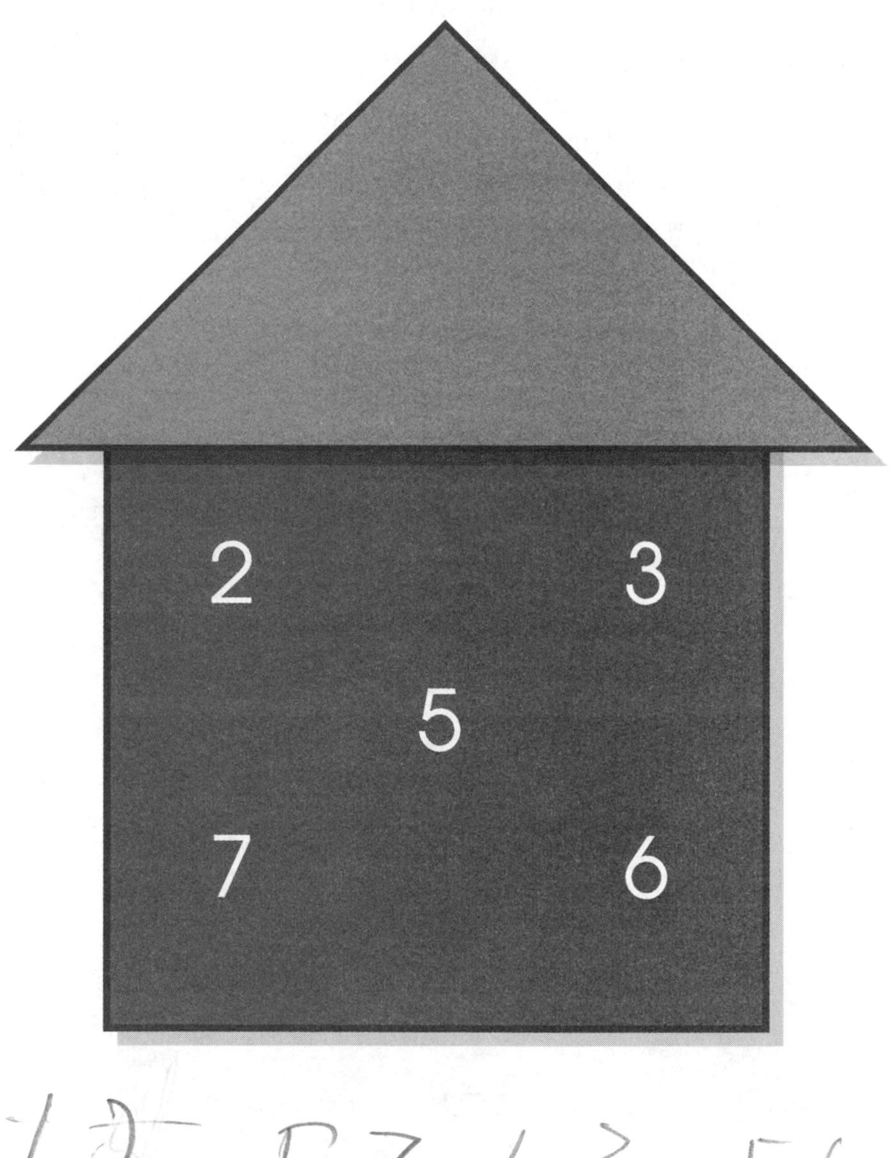

62 57 63 56

Name ____________________

Subtraction: Regrouping

Subtraction means "taking away" or subtracting one number from another to find the difference. For example, 10 - 3 = 7. To regroup is to use one ten to form ten ones, one 100 to form ten tens, and so on.

Directions: Study the example. Subtract using regrouping.

Example:

32	=	2 tens	+	12 ones
-13	=	1 ten	+	3 ones
19	=	1 ten	+	9 ones

$$\begin{array}{r} 33 \\ -28 \\ \hline \end{array} \quad \begin{array}{r} 86 \\ -59 \\ \hline \end{array} \quad \begin{array}{r} 92 \\ -37 \\ \hline \end{array} \quad \begin{array}{r} 71 \\ -48 \\ \hline \end{array}$$

$$\begin{array}{r} 63 \\ -47 \\ \hline \end{array} \quad \begin{array}{r} 45 \\ -18 \\ \hline \end{array} \quad \begin{array}{r} 31 \\ -22 \\ \hline \end{array} \quad \begin{array}{r} 55 \\ -39 \\ \hline \end{array}$$

82 - 69 = ____ 73 - 36 = ____

The Yankees won 85 games.
The Cubs won 69 games.
How many more games did the Yankees win? ____________

Barry the Beetle

Directions: Connect the dots from **10** to **200**. Then, color to finish the picture.

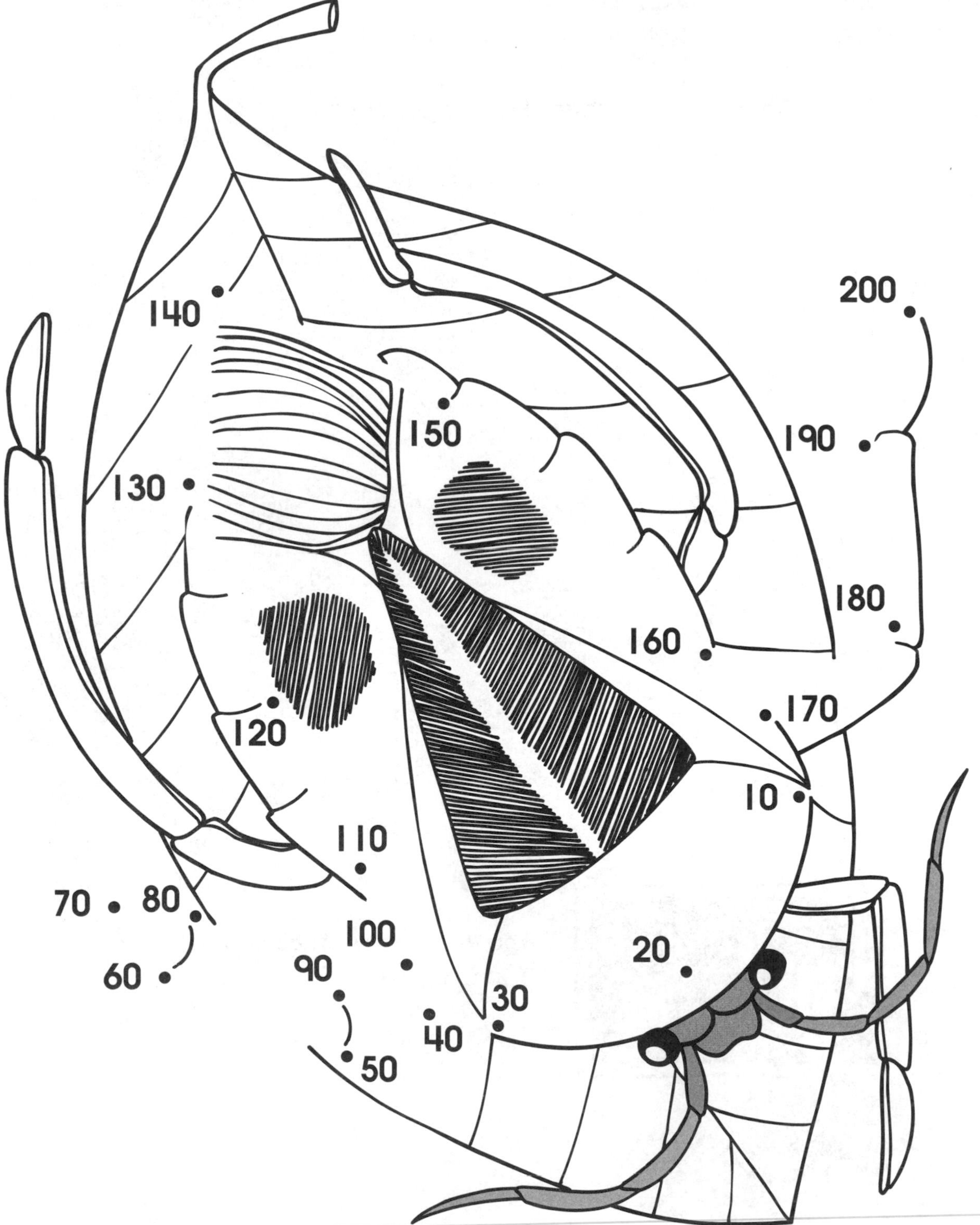

Addition and Subtraction: Regrouping

Directions: Add or subtract. Regroup when needed.

92 -47	58 +26	63 +18	77 -38
27 -17	31 +42	56 -29	67 +33
72 +19	87 -58	93 -89	54 +27

The soccer team scored 83 goals this year. The soccer team scored 68 goals last year. How many goals did they score in all? ____________

How many more goals did they score this year than last year? ____________

Addition and Subtraction: Regrouping

Directions: Add or subtract using regrouping.

28 56 +93	82 49 +51	33 75 +128	67 94 +248
683 -495	756 +139	818 -387	956 +267
1,588 - 989	4,675 -2,976	8,732 -5,664	2,938 +3,459

To drive from New York City to Los Angeles is 2,832 miles. To drive from New York City to Miami is 1,327 miles. How much farther is it to drive from New York City to Los Angeles than from New York City to Miami? ____________

Addition: Regrouping

Directions: Study the example. Add using regrouping.

Examples:

Add the ones. Regroup.		Add the tens. Regroup.		Add the hundreds.
1		1	11	1
156	6	5	156	156
+267	+7	+6	+267	+267
3	13	12	23	423

29	81	52	49	
46	78	67	37	162
+12	+33	+23	+19	+349

273	655	783	385	428
+198	+297	+148	+169	+122

Tasha went bowling. She had scores of 115, 129, and 103. What was her total score for three games? ____________

Addition: Regrouping

Directions: Add using regrouping. Then, use the code to discover the name of a United States president.

348 +752 1,100	642 +277	386 +787	184 +875	578 +874
653 +768	653 +359	946 +239	393 +257	199 +843
721 +679				

____. ____ ____ ____ ____ ____ ____ ____ ____ ____ ____

1012	1173	1059	1421	919	650	1452	1042	1100	1400	1185
N	A	S	I	W	T	H	O	G	N	G

Name ____________________

Addition: Regrouping

Directions: Study the example. Add using regrouping.

Example:

```
  5,356
 +3,976
 ------
  9,332
```

Steps:
1. Add the ones.
2. Regroup the tens. Add the tens.
3. Regroup the hundreds. Add the hundreds.
4. Add the thousands.

```
  6,849        1,846        9,221
 +3,276       +8,384       +6,769
 ------       ------       ------

  2,758        5,299        7,932
 +3,663       +8,764       +6,879
 ------       ------       ------
```

A plane flew 1,838 miles on the first day. It flew 2,347 miles on the second day. How many miles did it fly in all? ____________

Spider Math

The spider has woven its web according to number patterns. Can you discover them?

Directions: Fill in the missing numbers.

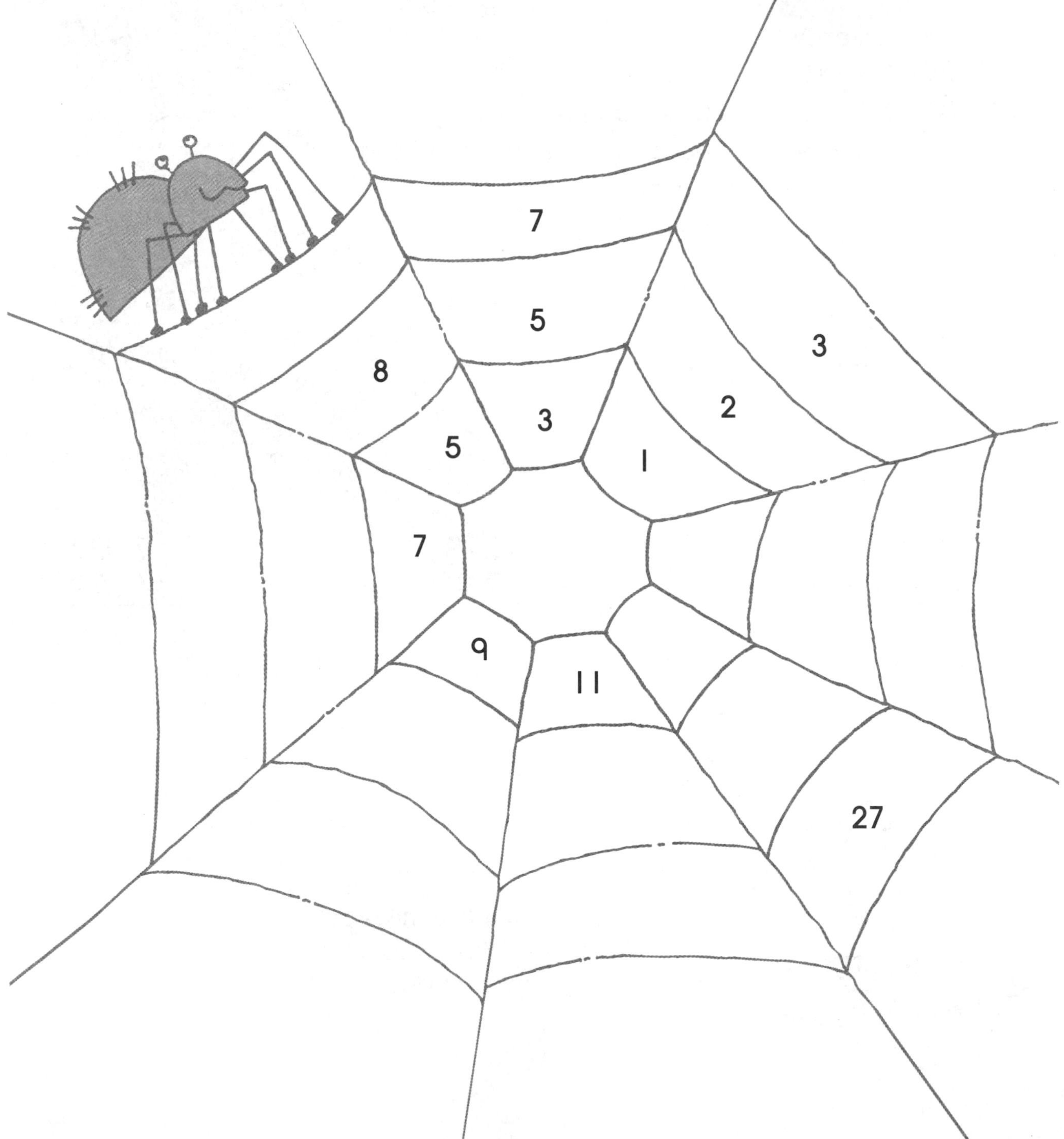

Sudoku Challenge

Directions: Complete the sudoku puzzle. Every row and column must contain the numbers **5**, **6**, **7**, and **8**. Do not repeat the same number twice in any row or column.

5			7
	8	6	
	5	7	
6			8

Addition: Mental Math

Directions: Try to do these addition problems in your head without using paper and pencil.

7 +4	6 +3	8 +1	10 + 2	2 +9	6 +6
10 +20	40 +20	80 +100	60 +30	50 +70	100 + 40
350 +150	300 +500	400 +800	450 + 10	680 +100	900 + 70
1,000 + 200	4,000 400 + 30	300 200 + 80	8,000 500 + 60	9,800 + 150	7,000 300 + 30

Name ______________________

Color Code

Directions: Solve the subtraction problems. Then, color the spaces according to the answers.

Color Code:

1 = white	**4 = green**	**7 = pink**
2 = purple	**5 = yellow**	**8 = red**
3 = black	**6 = blue**	**9 = orange**

Subtraction: Regrouping

Directions: Regrouping for subtraction is the opposite of regrouping for addition. Study the example. Subtract using regrouping. Then, use the code to color the flowers.

Example:

```
 647
-453
 194
```

Steps:
1. Subtract ones.
2. Subtract tens. Five tens cannot be subtracted from 4 tens.
3. Regroup tens by regrouping 6 hundreds (5 hundreds + 10 tens).
4. Add the 10 tens to the 4 tens.
5. Subtract 5 tens from 14 tens.
6. Subtract the hundreds.

If the answer has:
1 one, color it **red**;
8 ones, color it pink;
5 ones, color it yellow.

Subtraction: Regrouping

Directions: Study the example. Follow the steps. Subtract using regrouping.

Example:

```
 634
-455
 179
```

Steps:

1. Subtract ones. You cannot subtract 5 ones from 4 ones.
2. Regroup ones by regrouping 3 tens to 2 tens + 10 ones.
3. Subtract 5 ones from 14 ones.
4. Regroup tens by regrouping hundreds (5 hundreds + 10 tens).
5. Subtract 5 tens from 12 tens.
6. Subtract hundreds.

635 -169	553 -174	832 -563	944 -578
423 -268	941 -872	733 -498	266 -197
387 -198	594 -385	960 -759	887 -598

Eva goes to school 185 days a year. Yoko goes to school 313 days a year. How many more days of school does Yoko attend each year? ____________

Subtraction: Regrouping

Directions: Study the example. Follow the steps. Subtract using regrouping. If you have to regroup to subtract ones and there are no tens, you must regroup twice.

Example:

300
- 182
118

Steps:

1. Subtract ones. You cannot subtract 2 ones from 0 ones.
2. Regroup. No tens. Regroup hundreds (2 hundreds + 10 tens).
3. Regroup tens (9 tens + 10 ones).
4. Subtract 2 ones from 10 ones.
5. Subtract 8 tens from 9 tens.
6. Subtract 1 hundred from 2 hundreds.

602 -423	306 -128	600 -263	807 -499	703 -328
800 -557	206 -137	400 -224	508 -379	909 -769
207 -138	604 -397	308 -199	700 -531	900 -278

Subtraction: Regrouping

Directions: Subtract. Regroup when necessary. The first one is done for you.

7,354 -5,295 2,059	4,214 -3,185	8,437 -5,338	6,837 -4,318
5,735 -3,826	1,036 - 947	6,735 -6,646	3,841 -1,953

Columbus landed in America in 1492. The Pilgrims landed in America in 1620. How many years were there between these two events?

____

Mary the Millipede

Directions: Connect the dots from 100 to 900. Then, color to finish the picture.

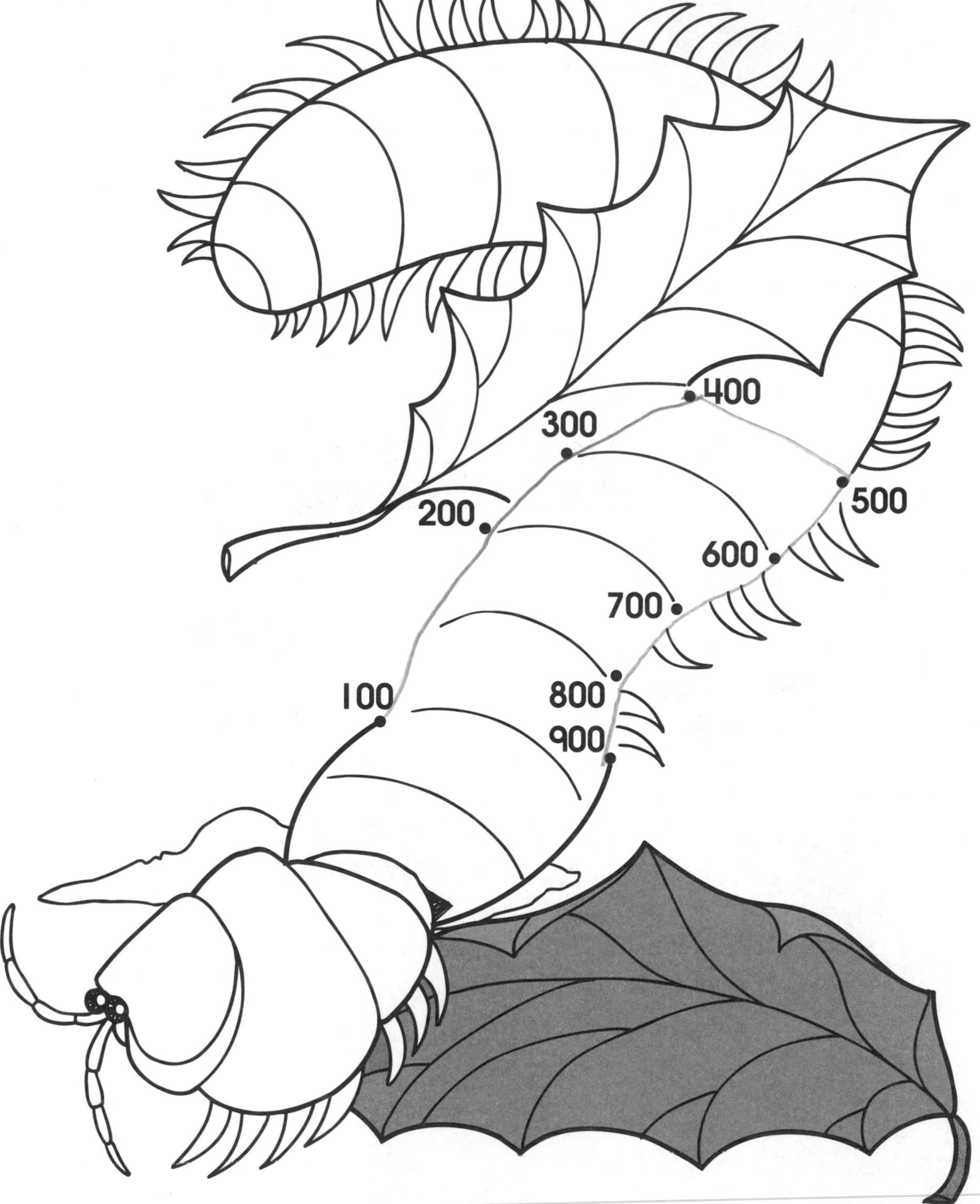

Space!

Directions: Use the word lists to fill out the grid below.

Hint: Count the squares in the grid first to see where the words will fit.

4 Letters	5 Letters	6 Letters	7 Letters	8 Letters
Mars	Venus	Uranus	Jupiter	Milky Way
star	Pluto		Neptune	
	Titan			
	comet			

A S T E R O I D

Down the Slope!

Directions: Find the differences. The number in the snowflakes will answer the question.

Denali is the tallest mountain in North America. How high is it?

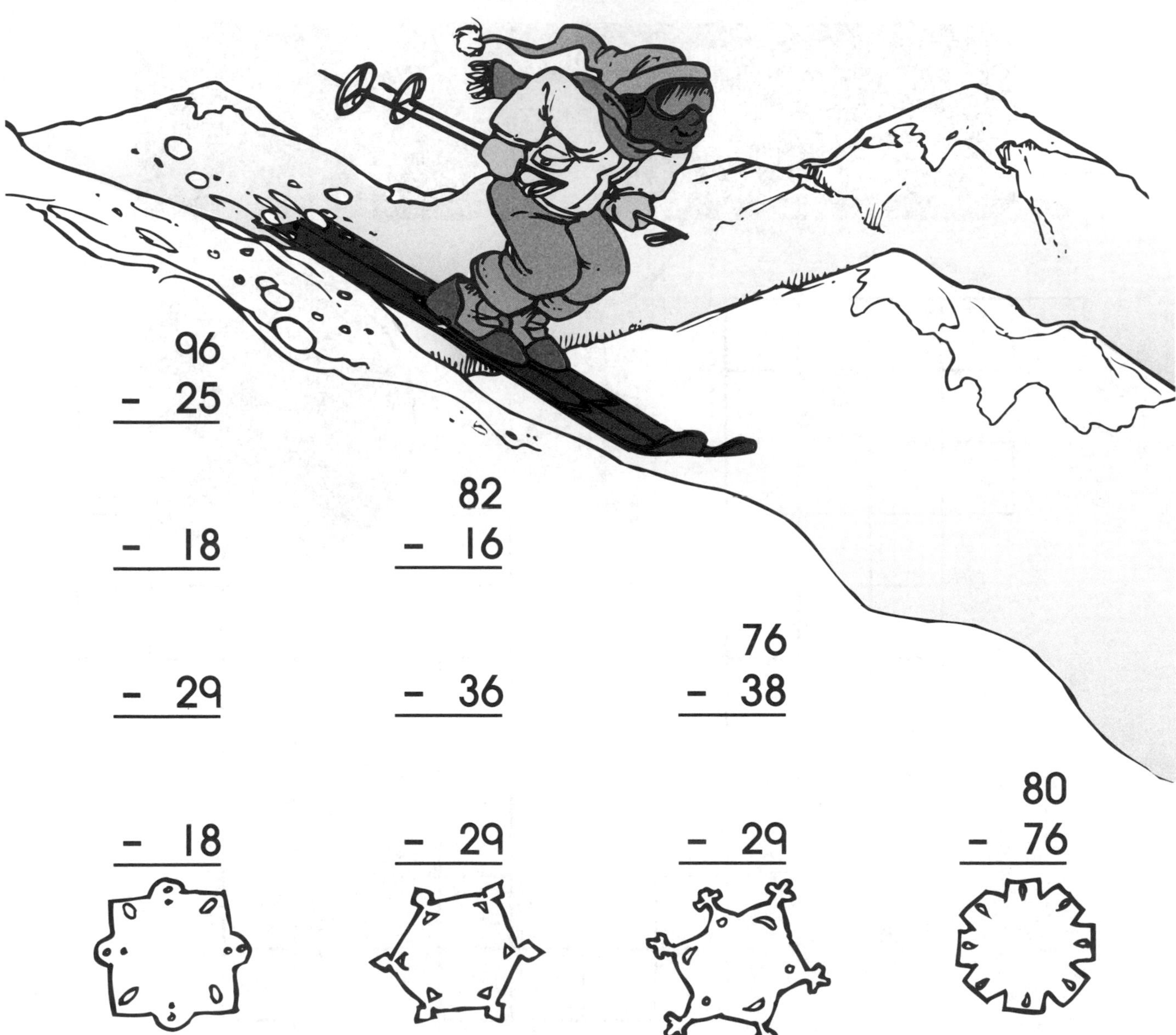

96
− 25

− 18

82
− 16

− 29

− 36

76
− 38

− 18

− 29

− 29

80
− 76

Denali is ____, ____ ____ ____ meters high!

Name ______________________

Case of the Missing Poodle

The detective sent you a note about Fifi, a missing poodle. Can you figure out her message?

1. Solve the problems. Write the answers in rows like below.
2. Write the matching letters. A clue about the poodle will appear!

Code
12 – K
18 – E
20 – P
24 – C
25 – R
32 – A
36 – H
40 – T

	8 x 3	6 x 6	2 x 9	4 x 6	3 x 4
Answers	______	______	______	______	______
Letters	______	______	______	______	______

	8 X 5	4 x 9	3 x 6
Answers	______	______	______
Letters	______	______	______

	5 x 4	4 x 8	5 x 5	6 x 2
Answers	______	______	______	______
Letters	______	______	______	______

Name ____________________

Subtraction: Mental Math

Directions: Try to do these subtraction problems in your head without using paper and pencil.

9 - 3	12 - 6	7 - 6	5 - 1	15 - 5	2 - 0
40 - 20	90 - 80	100 - 50	20 - 20	60 - 10	70 - 40
450 - 250	500 - 300	250 - 20	690 - 100	320 - 20	900 - 600
1,000 - 400	8,000 - 500	7,000 - 900	4,000 - 2,000	9,500 - 4,000	5,000 - 2,000

Looking at the Seasons

Directions: Use the fact families to subtract.

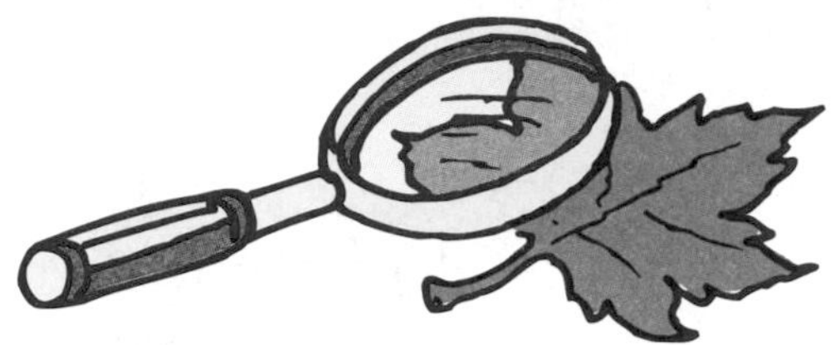

8 + 9 = 17

9 + 8 = 17

17 – 8 = ______

17 – 9 = ______

9 + 9 = 18

18 – 9 = ______

Directions: Practice.

15 – 6 = ______	13 – 6 = ______	17 – 9 = ______
11 – 5 = ______	14 – 7 = ______	15 – 8 = ______
16 – 9 = ______	17 – 8 = ______	11 – 7 = ______
16 – 7 = ______	15 – 9 = ______	16 – 8 = ______
18 – 9 = ______	15 – 7 = ______	14 – 8 = ______
17 – 8 = ______	12 – 7 = ______	14 – 9 = ______

Name ____________________

Rounding: The Nearest Ten

Directions: If the ones number is 5 or greater, round up to the nearest ten. If the ones number is 4 or less, round down to the nearest ten.

Examples: 15 round up to 20 23 round down to 20 47 round up to 50

7	_____	58	_____
12	_____	81	_____
33	_____	94	_____
27	_____	44	_____
73	_____	88	_____
25	_____	66	_____
39	_____	70	_____

Rounding: The Nearest Hundred

Directions: If the tens number is 5 or greater, round up to the nearest hundred. If the tens number is 4 or less, round down to the nearest hundred.

REMEMBER... Look at the number directly to the right of the place you are rounding to.

Example:

230 round down to 200

470 round up to 500

150 round up to 200

732 round down to 700

456 ____ 120 ____

340 ____ 923 ____

867 ____ 550 ____

686 ____ 231 ____

770 ____ 492 ____

Grid Game

1. Draw a square around the greatest number.
2. Count by 2s to 40. Underline the numbers you use.
3. Draw a triangle around the number that is 4 less than 62.
4. Draw an X over each odd number.
5. Circle all of the uppercase letters. Write the letters you circled in order, starting with the top row and moving left to right.

____

b	r	q	e	o	S	c	r	y	10	6	3
U	y	10	5	2	4	M	z	l	q	a	i
6	v	0	7	8	M	p	2	10	17	12	l
r	b	14	18	b	e	16	f	h	19	E	s
18	5	14	7	2	p	m	n	z	58	20	s
94	86	22	2	R	17	I	0	24	n	x	c
26	39	3	a	d	e	28	g	S	52	19	30
7	j	F	k	32	y	34	4	31	t	10	36
0	n	e	n	38	o	80	98	U	47	x	p
w	m	m	11	N	3	14	39	c	r	e	t
q	u	v	9	7	6	w	5	40	w	13	19

Good Shape

Directions: Use the numbers in the shapes to answer the questions.

1. Find the sum of the numbers in the circle and square.

   ____

2. Find the sum of the numbers in the circle, square, and triangle.

   ____

3. Find the sum of the numbers in all of the shapes.

   ____

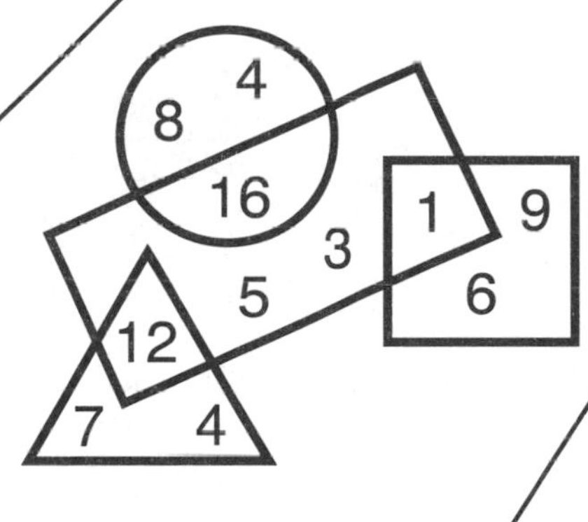

4. Find the difference between the largest number in the square and the smallest number in the triangle.

   ____

5. Divide the sum of all of the numbers by 5.

   ____

6. Find the sum of the numbers in the circle.

   ____

7. Find the difference between the largest number in the square and the smallest number in the circle.

   ____

8. Find the shape whose numbers add up to 37.

   ____

Front-End Estimation

Front-end estimation is useful when you don't need to know the exact amount, but a close answer will do.

In front-end estimation, round the front digit in each number. Then, add the numbers together to get the estimate.

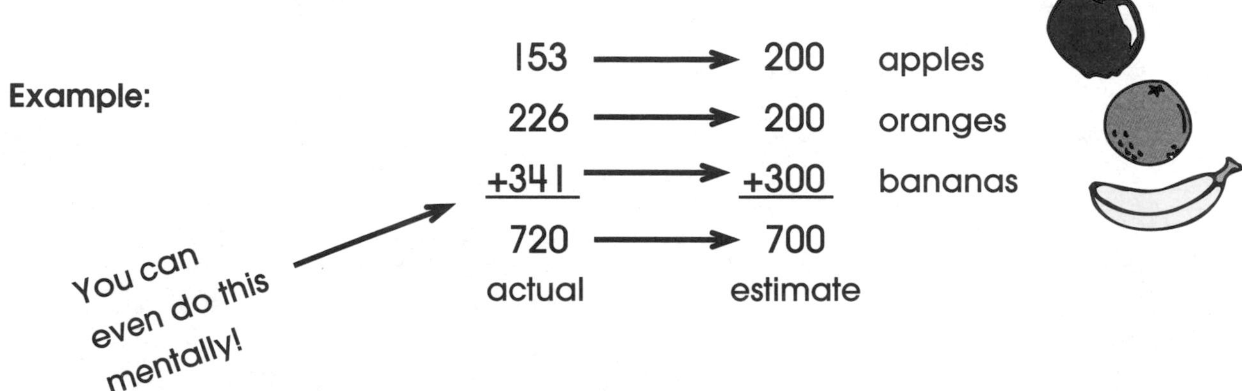

Directions: Estimate the sum of these numbers.

456 →		910 →		686 →	
121 →		280 →		307 →	
+438 →	+ ____	+320 →	+ ____	+711 →	+ ____
	☐		☐		☐

Lily Pad

Directions: Help the frog hop to the lily pad.

Multiplication

Multiplication is a short way to find the sum of adding the same number a certain amount of times. For example, write 7 x 4 = 28 instead of 7 + 7 + 7 + 7 = 28.

Directions: Study the example. Multiply.

Example:

There are 2 groups of seashells.
There are 3 seashells in each group.
How many seashells are there in all?

2 x 3 = 6

4 + 4 = ____
2 x 4 = ____

3 + 3 + 3 = ____
3 x 3 = ____

2 x3	3 x5	4 x3	6 x2	7 x3
5 x2	6 x3	4 x2	7 x2	8 x3
5 x5	9 x4	8 x5	6 x6	9 x3

Multiplication

Directions: Multiply.

3 x5	4 x6	3 x8
5 x5	4 x8	5 x4

6 x7	3 x9	2 x8	7 x6	9 x4
6 x8	5 x6	7 x7	5 x3	8 x9

A riverboat makes 3 trips a day every day.
How many trips does it make in a week? ____________

Multiplication

Factors are the numbers multiplied together in a multiplication problem. The answer is called the **product**. If you change the order of the factors, the product stays the same.

Example:

There are 4 groups of fish.
There are 3 fish in each group.
How many fish are there in all?

4 x 3 = 12
factor x factor = product

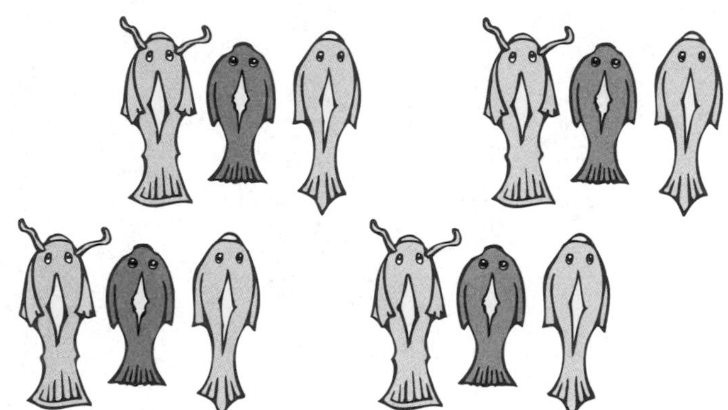

Directions: Draw 3 groups of 4 fish.

3 x 4 = 12

Compare your drawing and answer with the example. What did you notice?

Directions: Fill in the missing numbers. Multiply.

5 x 4 = _____ 3 x 6 = _____ 4 x 2 = _____

4 x 5 = _____ 6 x 3 = _____ 2 x 4 = _____

3	7	2	9	8	4
x7	x3	x9	x2	x4	x8

5	2	6	3	5	6
x2	x5	x3	x6	x6	x5

More or Less

Directions: Each letter is worth 1 to 6 points. Add the points for each letter to find out how much a word is worth. Circle the correct answer.

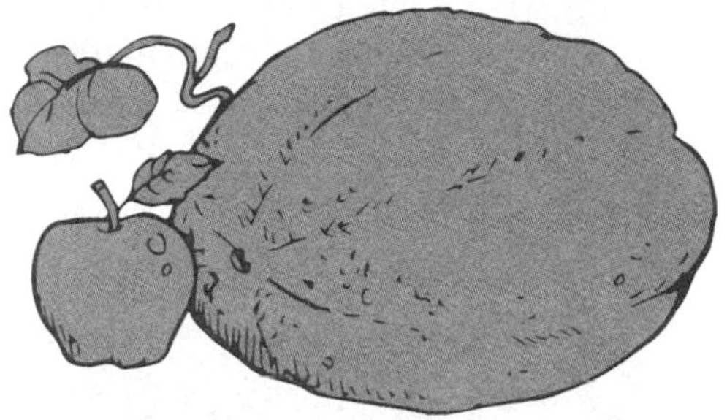

1 a	2 b	3 c	4 d	5 e	6 f	1 g	2 h	3 i	4 j	5 k	6 l	1 m
2 n	3 o	4 p	5 q	6 r	1 s	2 t	3 u	4 v	5 w	6 x	1 y	2 z

Which shape is worth more?

h e x a g o n

___ ___ ___ ___ ___ ___ ___ = ___

o c t a g o n

___ ___ ___ ___ ___ ___ ___ = ___

Which color is worth more?

p u r p l e

___ ___ ___ ___ ___ ___ = ___

s i l v e r

___ ___ ___ ___ ___ ___ = ___

Which fruit is worth more?

m e l o n

___ ___ ___ ___ ___ = ___

a p p l e

___ ___ ___ ___ ___ = ___

Dan's Footprints

Why did Dan the Dinosaur go outside with just one boot on? The answer is started for you at the bottom of the page. To finish the answer, work through these footprints. Start at the top with the letter **T**. Then, do the math problem on that footprint (7+7) and look for its answer (14) on another footprint. Then, write the letter that appears on that footprint in the next blank below.

Directions: Continue from footprint to footprint until you've covered all your tracks!

Why did Dan the Dinosaur go outside with just one boot on?
Because he heard

___ ___ ___   ___ ___ ___ ___   ___ ___ ___

___ ___ ___ ___   ___ ___ ___   ___ ___ ___ ___

___ ___ ___ ___!

Case of the Golden Egg

A thief stole a golden egg from a museum! Your job is to find out where it's hidden.

Directions:

1. Solve the problems below. Write the answers in a row.
2. Write the letter for each answer. When you're done, you'll see where the egg is hidden!

120	130	140	160	170	180
A	T	I	E	S	N

$$\begin{array}{r} 90 \\ 20 \\ +\ 30 \\ \hline \end{array} \qquad \begin{array}{r} 65 \\ 45 \\ +\ 70 \\ \hline \end{array} \qquad \begin{array}{r} 30 \\ 30 \\ +\ 60 \\ \hline \end{array}$$

$$\begin{array}{r} 50 \\ 60 \\ +\ 70 \\ \hline \end{array} \qquad \begin{array}{r} 25 \\ 40 \\ +\ 95 \\ \hline \end{array} \qquad \begin{array}{r} 10 \\ 95 \\ +\ 65 \\ \hline \end{array} \qquad \begin{array}{r} 70 \\ 35 \\ +\ 25 \\ \hline \end{array}$$

Multiplication: Zero and One

Any number multiplied by zero equals zero. One multiplied by any number equals that number. Study the example. Multiply.

Example:

How many full sails are there in all?

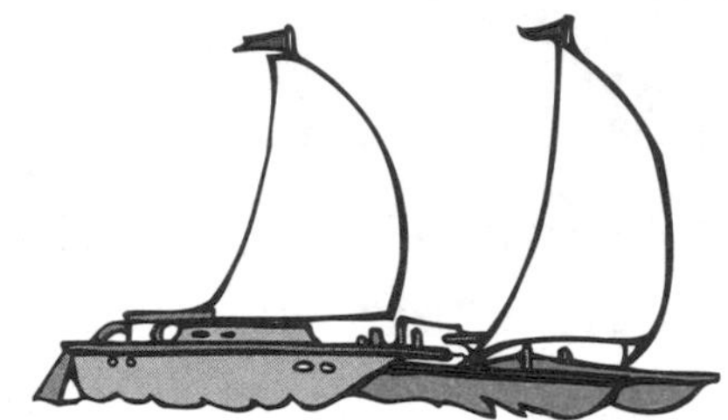

2 boats x **1** sail on each boat = **2** sails

How many full sails are there now?

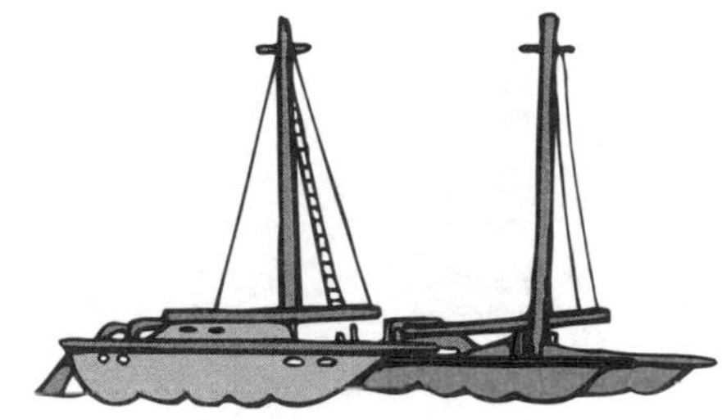

2 boats x **0** sails = **0** sails

Directions: Multiply.

1	2	3	4	0	7
x5	x1	x0	x1	x6	x0

9	8	3	4	7	6
x1	x0	x1	x0	x1	x1

Multiplication

Directions: Time yourself as you multiply. How quickly can you complete this page?

3 x2	8 x7	1 x0	1 x6	3 x4	0 x4
4 x1	4 x4	2 x5	9 x3	9 x9	5 x3
0 x8	2 x6	9 x6	8 x5	7 x3	4 x2
3 x5	2 x0	4 x6	1 x3	0 x0	3 x3

Sudoku

Directions: Complete the sudoku puzzle. Every row and column must contain the numbers 1, 2, 3, and 4. Do not repeat the same number twice in any row or column.

	1	4	
4			2
1			4
	4	2	

At the Seashore

Directions: Annie loves to build this at the beach. Connect the dots from **50** to **170**. Color.

Multiplication Table

Directions: Complete the multiplication table. Use it to practice your multiplication facts.

X	0	1	2	3	4	5	6	7	8	9	10
0	0										
1		1									
2			4								
3				9							
4					16						
5						25					
6							36				
7								49			
8									64		
9										81	
10											100

Crack the Case

Who cracked Zachary Zing's violin?

Directions: Solve the problems in order and follow the answers on the path. The last answer will lead you to the guilty bandit!

1. Start with 3 x 3.
2. Go to 2 x 7.
3. Go to 6 x 4.
4. Go to 4 x 7.
5. Go to 9 x 4.
6. Go to 8 x 6.
7. Go to 6 x 9.
8. Go to 8 x 8.
9. Go to 9 x 8.

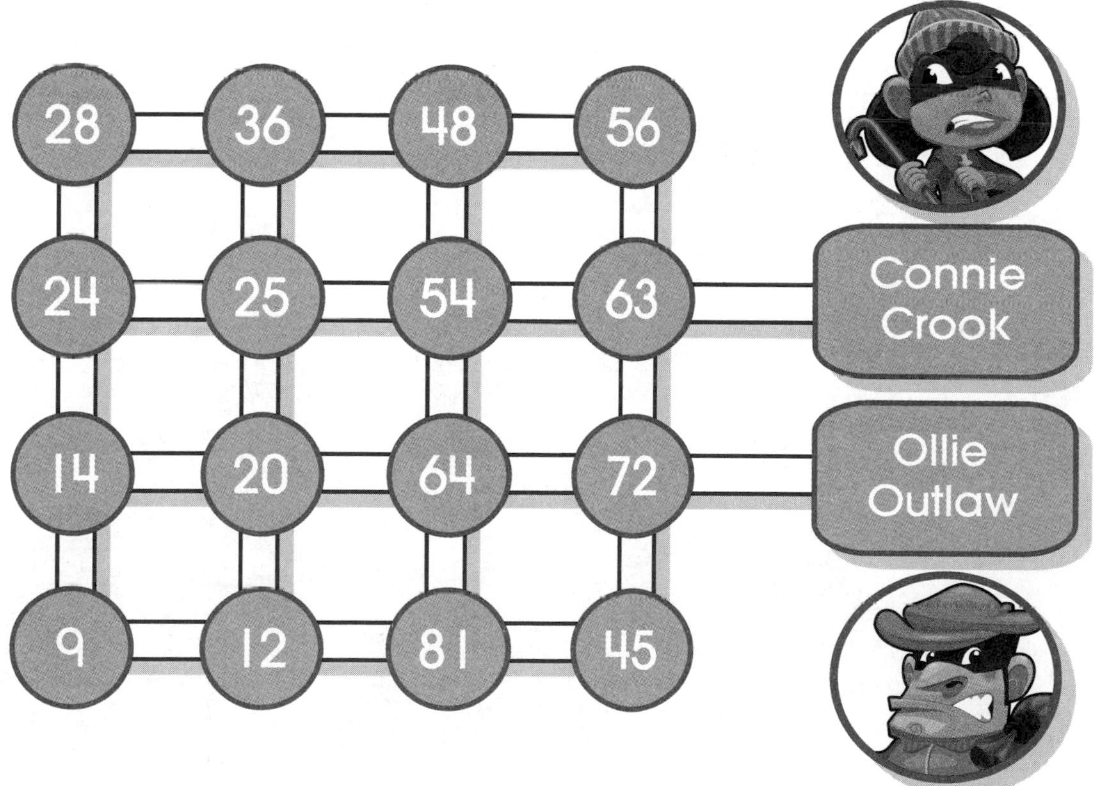

What's It Worth?

a	b	c	d	e	f	g	h	i	j	k	l	m
1	2	3	4	5	6	1	2	3	4	5	6	1
n	**o**	**p**	**q**	**r**	**s**	**t**	**u**	**v**	**w**	**x**	**y**	**z**
2	3	4	5	6	1	2	3	4	5	6	1	2

Directions: Each letter above is worth from one to six points. Add the points for each letter to find out how much a word is worth. Circle the correct answer.

1. Which animal is worth more?

s h a r k
__ __ __ __ __ = ___

w h a l e
__ __ __ __ __ = ___

2. Which gem is worth more?

d i a m o n d
__ __ __ __ __ __ __ = ___

e m e r a l d
__ __ __ __ __ __ __ = ___

3. Which flower is worth more?

t u l i p
__ __ __ __ __ = ___

d a i s y
__ __ __ __ __ = ___

Division

Division is a way to find out how many times one number is contained in another number. For example, 28 ÷ 4 = 7 means that there are 7 groups of 4 in 28.

Directions: Study the example. Divide.

Example:

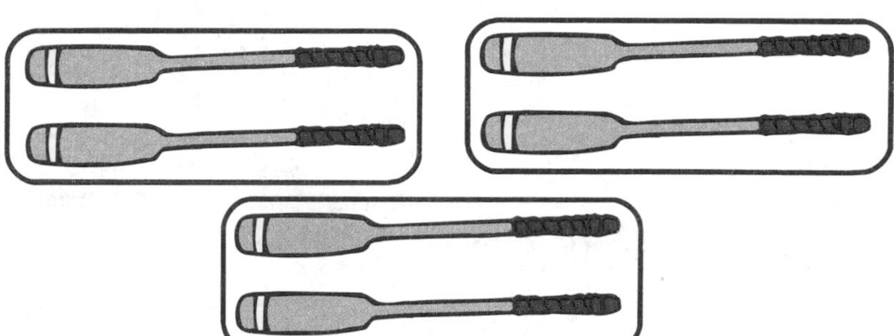

There are 6 oars.
Each canoe needs 2 oars.
How many canoes can be used?

Circle groups of 2.
There are 3 groups of 2.

6	÷	2	=	3
oars		number of oars needed per canoe		canoes

9 ÷ 3 = _____ 8 ÷ 2 = _____ 16 ÷ 4 = _____

15 ÷ 5 = _____ 18 ÷ 2 = _____ 20 ÷ 4 = _____

21 ÷ 7 = _____ 24 ÷ 6 = _____ 12 ÷ 2 = _____

Division

Directions: Divide. Draw a line from the boat to the sail with the correct answer.

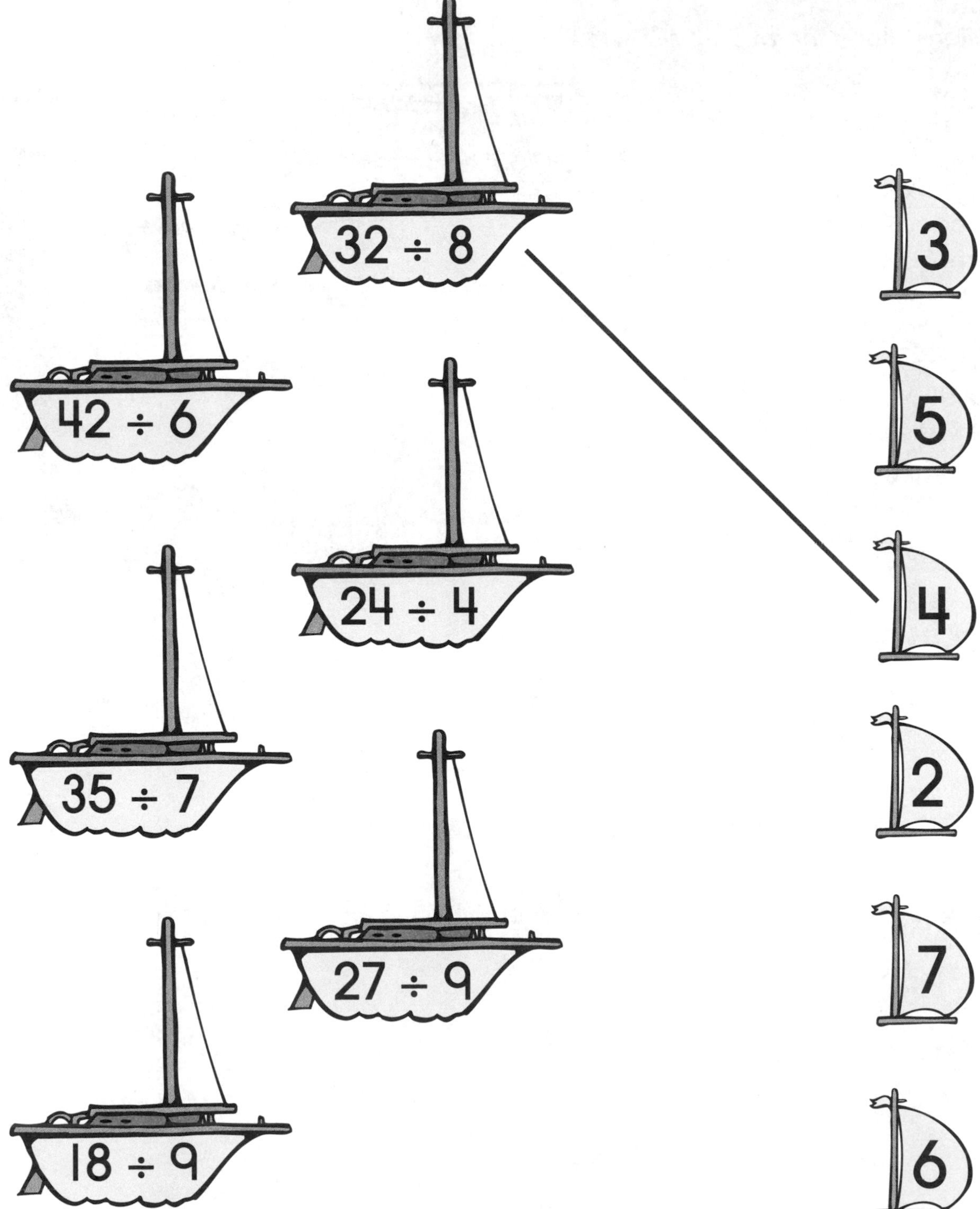

Find the Treasure

There is a compass rose in the bottom right corner of the map. The compass rose gives the eight compass directions: north (N), south (S), east (E), west (W), northeast (NE), southeast (SE), southwest (SW) and northwest (NW).

Follow the directions to find where the secret treasure is buried. Each box is equal to one step.

Directions:

1. Start at the star.
2. Go north 5 steps.
3. Go east 9 steps.
4. Go southwest 4 steps.
5. Go east 2 steps.
6. Go south 2 steps.
7. Go northeast 4 steps.
8. Dig here. You have reached the secret treasure!

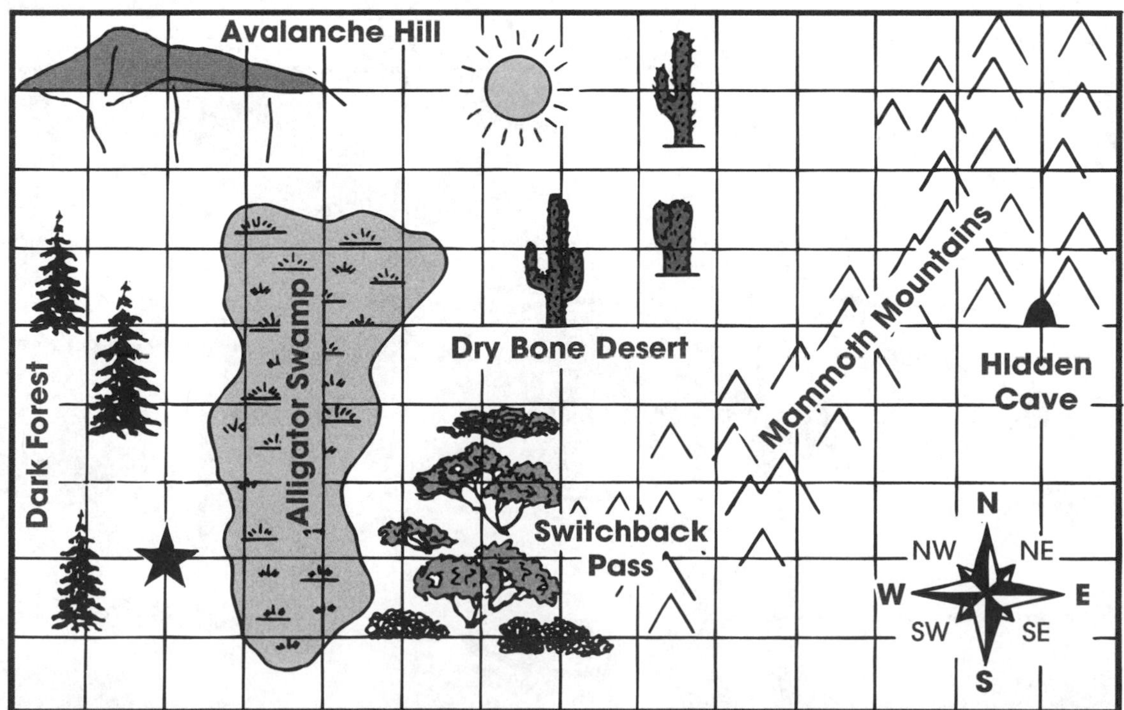

A Picnic

Directions: Add. Then, use the sums to color the picture.

96 = red 67 = brown 53 = yellow

85 = blue 78 = green

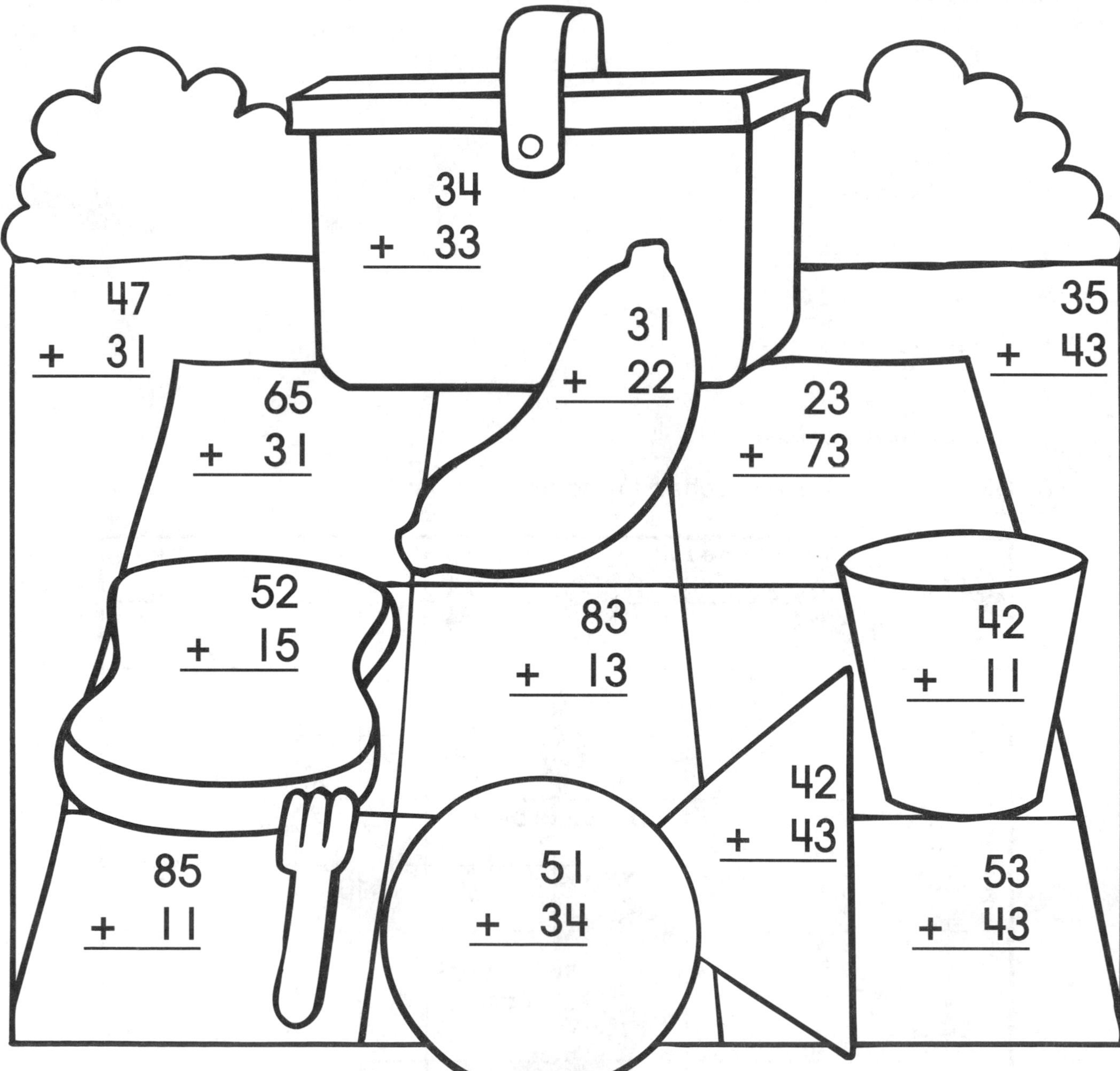

Order of Operations

When you solve a problem that involves more than one operation, this is the order to follow:

( )	Parentheses first
x	Multiplication
÷	Division
+	Addition
-	Subtraction

Example:

$$2 + (3 \times 5) - 2 = 15$$
$$2 + 15 - 2 = 15$$
$$17 - 2 = 15$$

Directions: Solve the problems using the correct order of operations.

$(5 - 3) + 4 \times 7 =$ ____

$1 + 2 \times 3 + 4 =$ ____

$6 \times 3 - 1 =$ ____

$(8 \div 2) \times 4 =$ ____

$9 \div 3 \times 3 + 0 =$ ____

$5 - 2 \times 1 + 2 =$ ____

Order of Operations

Directions: Use **+**, **–**, **x**, and **÷** to complete the problems so the number sentence is true.

Example: 4 __+__ 2 __–__ 1 = 5

(8 _____ 2) _____ 4 = 8

(1 _____ 2)_____ 3 = 1

9 _____ 3 _____ 9 = 3

(7 _____ 5) _____ 1 = 2

8 _____ 5 _____ 4 = 10

5 _____ 4 _____ 1 = 1

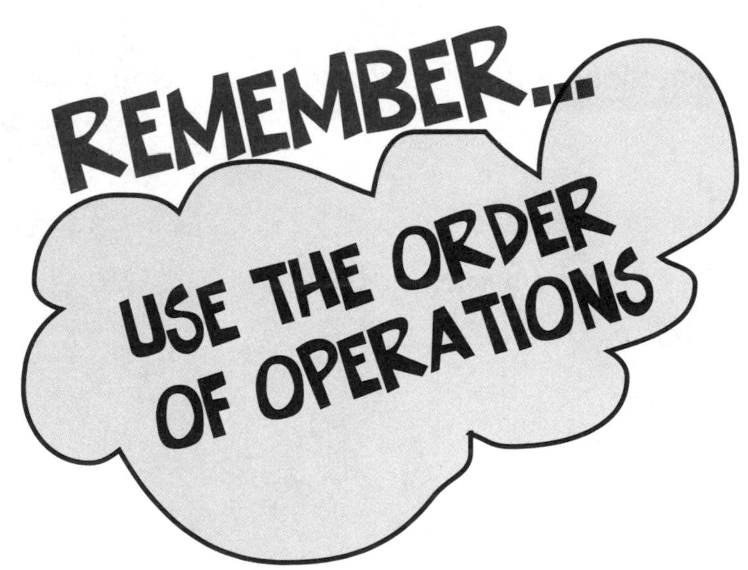
REMEMBER...
USE THE ORDER
OF OPERATIONS

Name ______________________

Number Words

Directions: Find the number words from the word box. Words can be across or down.

zero	three	six	nine	twelve
one	four	seven	ten	
two	five	eight	eleven	

t	e	a	z	w	z	x	a	b	i	g	t	e	n
o	l	z	r	b	e	r	e	v	e	d	l	a	j
t	w	e	l	v	e	a	b	o	n	e	c	d	z
i	a	r	p	q	d	p	s	u	j	x	e	i	w
c	f	o	p	l	s	c	k	i	q	u	i	i	o
m	s	t	f	v	i	o	e	t	t	f	g	h	d
t	n	u	w	u	x	g	z	w	h	g	h	r	o
n	i	n	e	k	f	d	f	o	u	r	t	j	f
a	s	g	l	q	c	w	k	o	s	n	v	m	i
n	y	c	e	b	o	n	h	h	p	o	m	p	v
b	e	x	v	s	s	e	v	e	n	w	e	n	e
t	h	r	e	e	r	t	a	l	j	k	x	q	z
m	o	a	n	e	n	i	m	u	t	w	a	y	x

Tic-Tac-Toe!

Directions: Find each sum. Color the sums on the cards as you go. Be careful! Some sums are on both cards. The first card with three numbers across, down, or diagonally is the winner!

A. $62 + 13$

B. $54 + 33$

C. $35 + 43$

D. $43 + 46$

E. $37 + 22$

F. $39 + 10$

G. $41 + 20$

H. $42 + 21$

I. $64 + 34$

60	49	87
63	75	42
73	92	59

73	78	75
49	98	89
61	59	60

Division

Division is a way to find out how many times one number is contained in another number. The ÷ sign means "divided by." Another way to divide is to use $\overline{)\quad}$.
The **dividend** is the larger number that is divided by the smaller number, or **divisor**.
The answer of a division problem is called the **quotient**.

Directions: Study the example. Divide.

Example:

20 ÷ 4 = 5

20 = dividend, 4 = divisor, 5 = quotient

$4\overline{)20}$ with quotient 5

5 = quotient, 4 = divisor, 20 = dividend

35 ÷ 7 = ____ $7\overline{)35}$ 42 ÷ 6 = ____ $6\overline{)42}$

$2\overline{)12}$ $3\overline{)18}$ $4\overline{)36}$ $5\overline{)50}$

$6\overline{)24}$ $7\overline{)21}$ $8\overline{)32}$ $9\overline{)27}$

36 ÷ 6 = ____ 28 ÷ 4 = ____ 15 ÷ 5 = ____ 12 ÷ 2 = ____

A tree farm has 36 trees. There are 4 rows of trees.
How many trees are there in each row? ____________

Division: Zero and One

Directions: Study the rules of division and the examples. Divide, and then write the number of the rule you used to solve each problem.

Examples:

Rule 1: $1\overline{)5}$ = **5** Any number divided by 1 is that number.

Rule 2: $5\overline{)5}$ = **1** Any number except 0 divided by itself is 1.

Rule 3: $7\overline{)0}$ = **0** Zero divided by any number is zero.

Rule 4: $0\overline{)7}$ You cannot divide by zero.

$1\overline{)6}$ Rule ____

$4 \div 1 =$ ______ Rule ____

$7\overline{)7}$ Rule ____

$9 \div 9 =$ ______ Rule ____

$9\overline{)0}$ Rule ____

$7 \div 1 =$ ______ Rule ____

$1\overline{)4}$ Rule ____

$6 \div 0 =$ ______ Rule ____

Division: Remainders

Division is a way to find out how many times one number is contained in another number. For example, 28 ÷ 4 = 7 means that there are 7 groups of 4 in 28. The dividend is the larger number that is divided by the smaller number, or divisor. The quotient is the answer in a division problem. The remainder is the amount left over. The **remainder** is always less than the divisor.

Directions: Study the example. Find each quotient and remainder.

Example:
There are 11 dog biscuits.
Put them in groups of 3.
There are 2 left over.

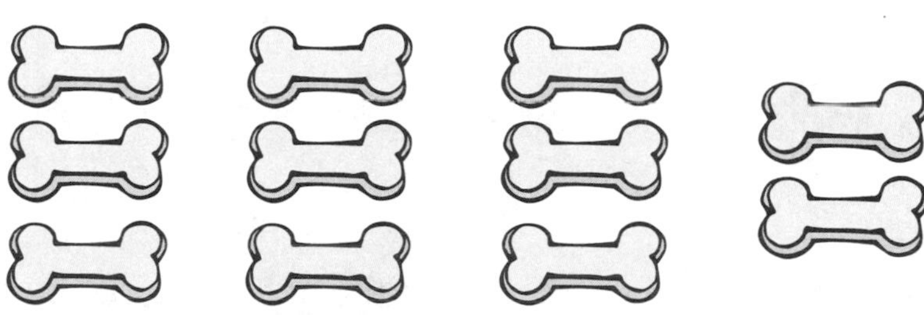

$$3\overline{)11} = 3,\quad -9,\quad 2 \text{ remainder}$$

$$3\overline{)11} = 3 \text{ r } 2$$

Remember: The remainder must be less than the **divisor**!

$3\overline{)13}$ $4\overline{)17}$ $6\overline{)32}$ $5\overline{)26}$

9 ÷ 4 = ____ 12 ÷ 5 = ____ 26 ÷ 4 = ____ 49 ÷ 9 = ____

The pet store has 7 cats. Two cats go in each cage. How many cats are left over? ____________

Divisibility Rules

A number is divisible... by 2 if the last digit is 0 or even (2, 4, 6, 8).
by 3 if the sum of all digits is divisible by 3.
by 4 if the last two digits are divisible by 4.
by 5 if the last digit is a 0 or 5.
by 10 if the last digit is 0.

Example: 250 is divisible by 2, 5, 10

Directions: Tell what numbers each of these numbers is divisible by.

3,732 ____________ 439 ____________

50 ____________ 444 ____________

7,960 ____________ 8,212 ____________

104,924 ____________ 2,345 ____________

Name ____________________

Shape Sudoku

Directions: Complete the sudoku puzzle. Every row and column must contain a ▲, ■, ♥, and ●. Do not repeat the same shape twice in any row or column.

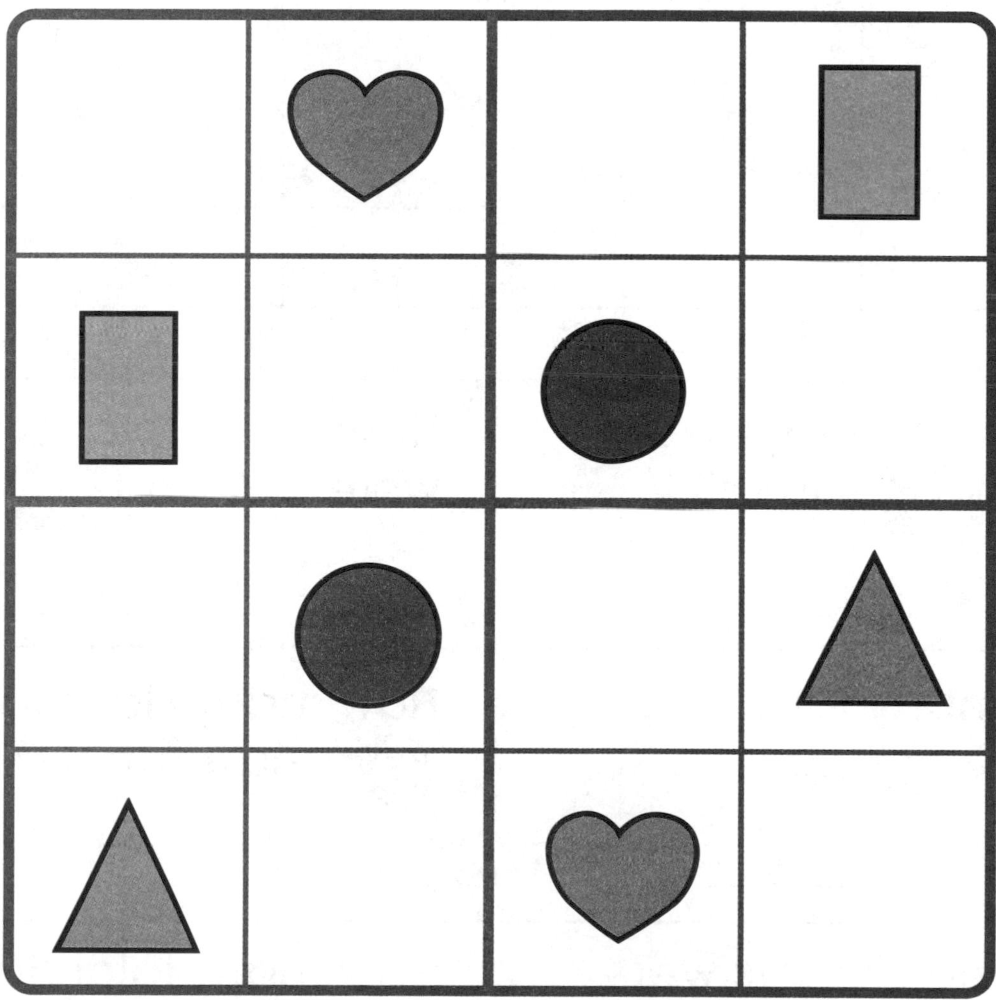

How's the Weather?

Directions: Use information from the graph to find the answers.

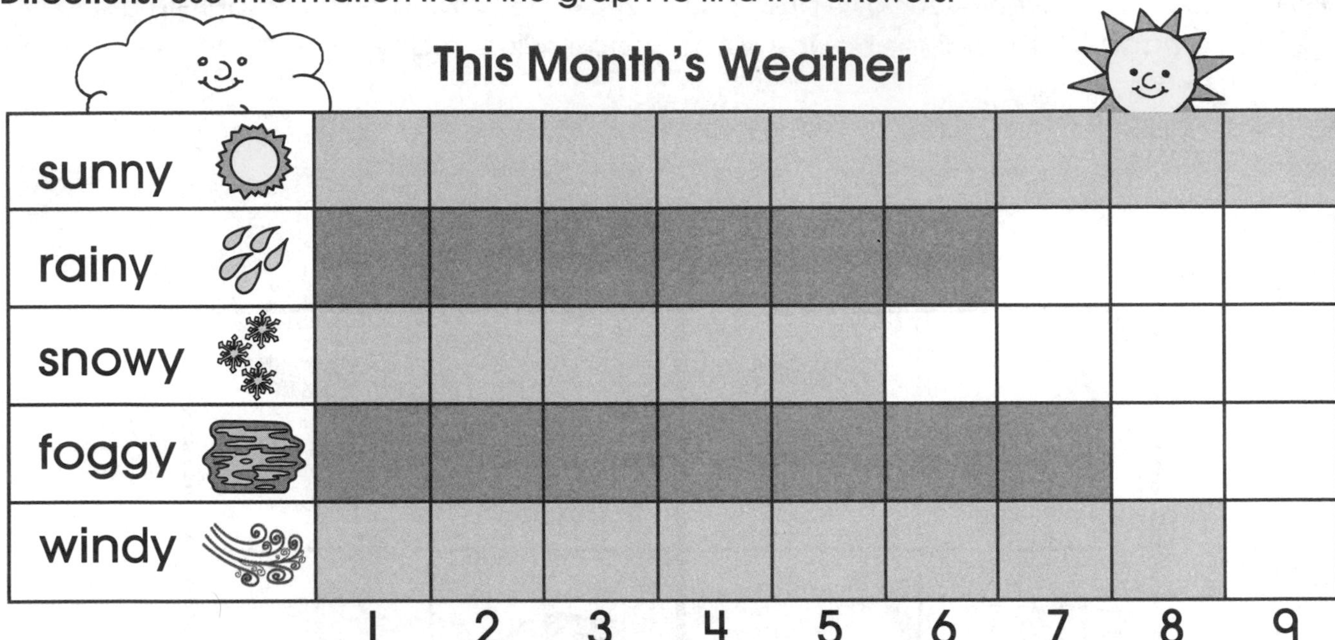

How many days were and in all? _____ + _____ = _____	How many total days were and ? _____ + _____ = _____
How many total days were and ? _____ + _____ = _____	How many days were and in all? _____ + _____ = _____
How many days were and in all? _____ + _____ = _____	How many total days were and ? _____ + _____ = _____

Family Feud

Directions: Who will win? Find each sum working from left to right. Shade the answer on a bingo board. The first family to completely cover their card is the winner!

$$\begin{array}{r} 11 \\ +\ 24 \\ \hline \end{array} \qquad \begin{array}{r} 36 \\ +\ 33 \\ \hline \end{array} \qquad \begin{array}{r} 90 \\ +\ 8 \\ \hline \end{array}$$

$$\begin{array}{r} 25 \\ +\ 51 \\ \hline \end{array} \qquad \begin{array}{r} 87 \\ +\ 12 \\ \hline \end{array} \qquad \begin{array}{r} 36 \\ +\ 3 \\ \hline \end{array}$$

$$\begin{array}{r} 29 \\ +\ 50 \\ \hline \end{array} \qquad \begin{array}{r} 28 \\ +\ 21 \\ \hline \end{array} \qquad \begin{array}{r} 80 \\ +\ 11 \\ \hline \end{array}$$

$$\begin{array}{r} 36 \\ +\ 11 \\ \hline \end{array} \qquad \begin{array}{r} 55 \\ +\ 31 \\ \hline \end{array} \qquad \begin{array}{r} 16 \\ +\ 13 \\ \hline \end{array}$$

$$\begin{array}{r} 62 \\ +\ 35 \\ \hline \end{array} \qquad \begin{array}{r} 43 \\ +\ 31 \\ \hline \end{array} \qquad \begin{array}{r} 41 \\ +\ 15 \\ \hline \end{array}$$

The Hatfields:

81	76
49	35
74	91
98	79

The McCoys:

69	56
47	97
99	29
86	39

What's Missing?

Directions: Fill in the missing numbers to make the problems work.

Factor Trees

Factors are the smaller numbers multiplied together to make a larger number. Factor trees are one way to find all the factors of a number.

Directions: Fill in each blank to complete the factor trees below.

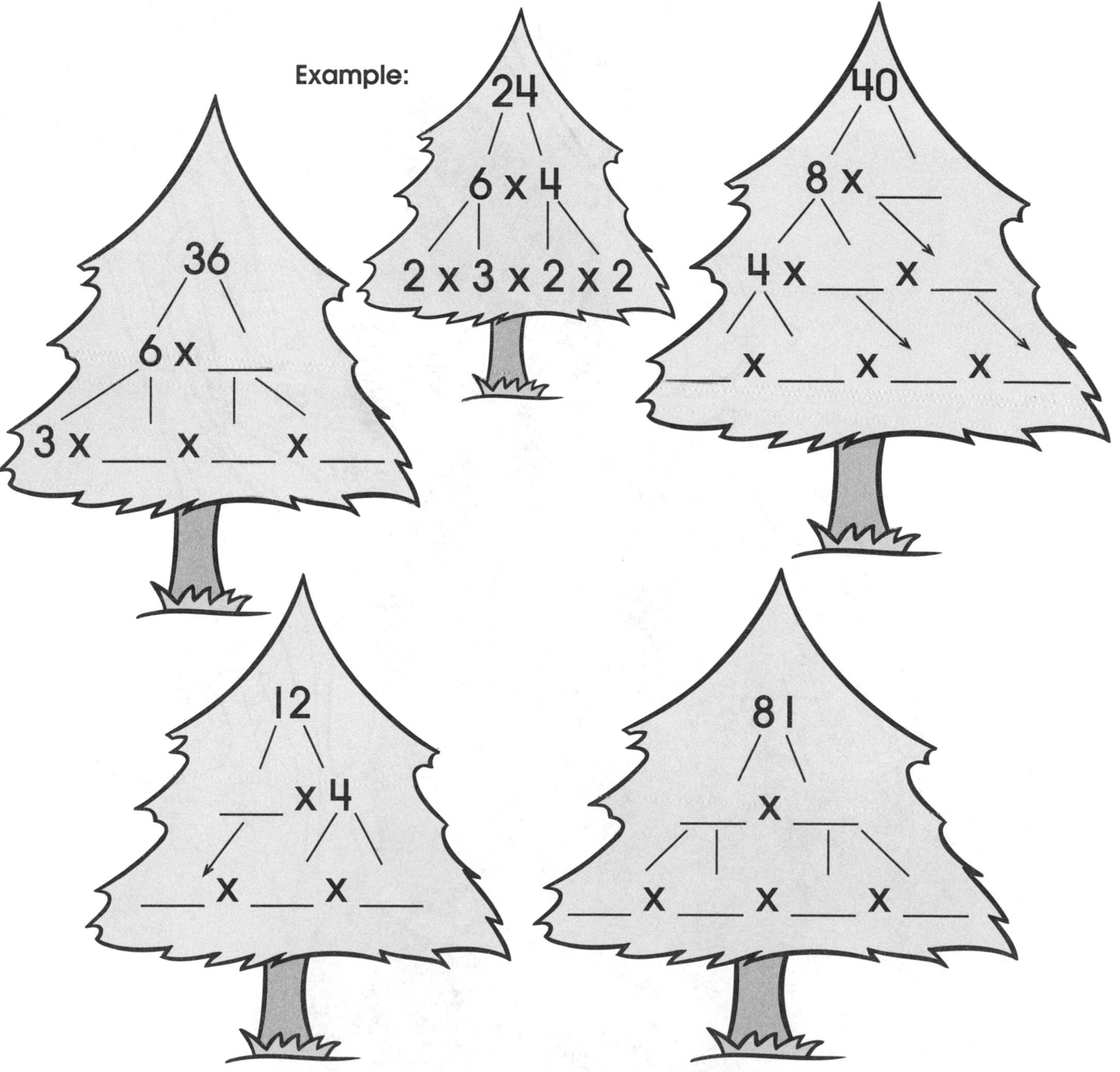

Gina the Goliath Beetle

Directions: Connect the dots from 10 to 100. Then, color to finish the picture.

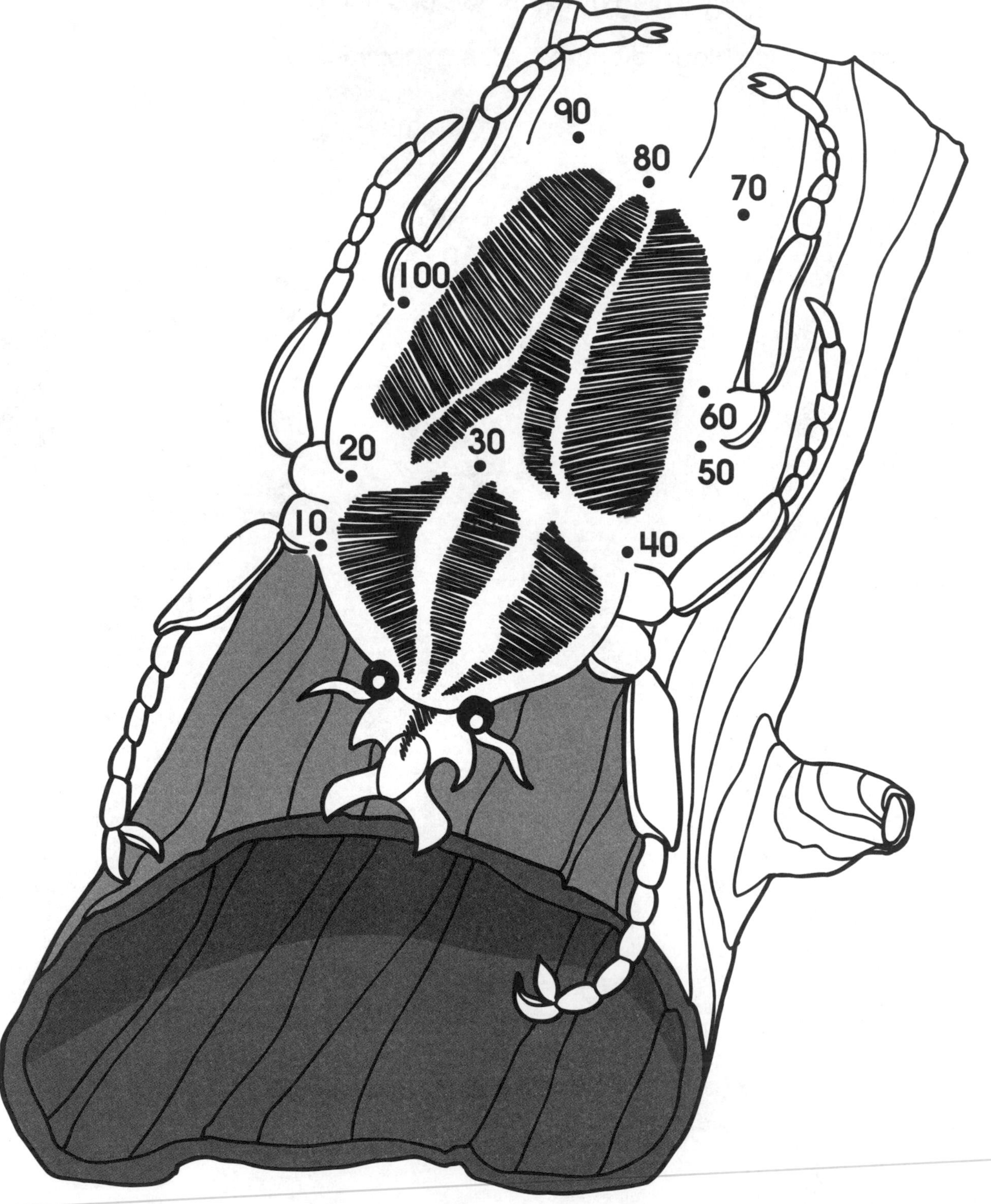

Go Bananas!

Directions: Write **<**, **>**, or **=** on each tree trunk. Color the banana with the greater number yellow. Color the banana with the lesser number green.

< less than > greater than = equal to

72 56

18 20

24 24

40 34

80 90

30 29

61 16

9 90

68 85

Percentages

A **percentage** is the amount of a number out of 100.
This is the percent sign: %.

Directions: Fill in the blanks.

Example: $70\% = \frac{70}{100}$ $\quad$ $40\% = \frac{40}{100}$

$30\% = \frac{\_\_\_}{100}$ $\quad$ $10\% = \frac{\_\_\_}{100}$

$90\% = \frac{\_\_\_}{100}$ $\quad$ $40\% = \frac{\_\_\_}{100}$

$70\% = \frac{\_\_\_}{100}$ $\quad$ $80\% = \frac{\_\_\_}{100}$

$\_\_\_\% = \frac{20}{100}$ $\quad$ $\_\_\_\% = \frac{60}{100}$

$\_\_\_\% = \frac{30}{100}$ $\quad$ $\_\_\_\% = \frac{10}{100}$

$\_\_\_\% = \frac{50}{100}$ $\quad$ $\_\_\_\% = \frac{90}{100}$

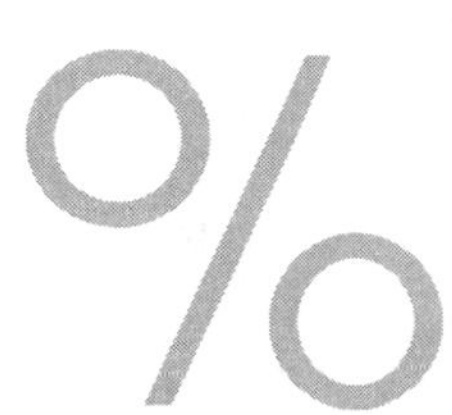

Park Here, Please

Directions: In each parking lot, the sum of each row and column should be the same. Park the cars shown to match the sum on the flag.

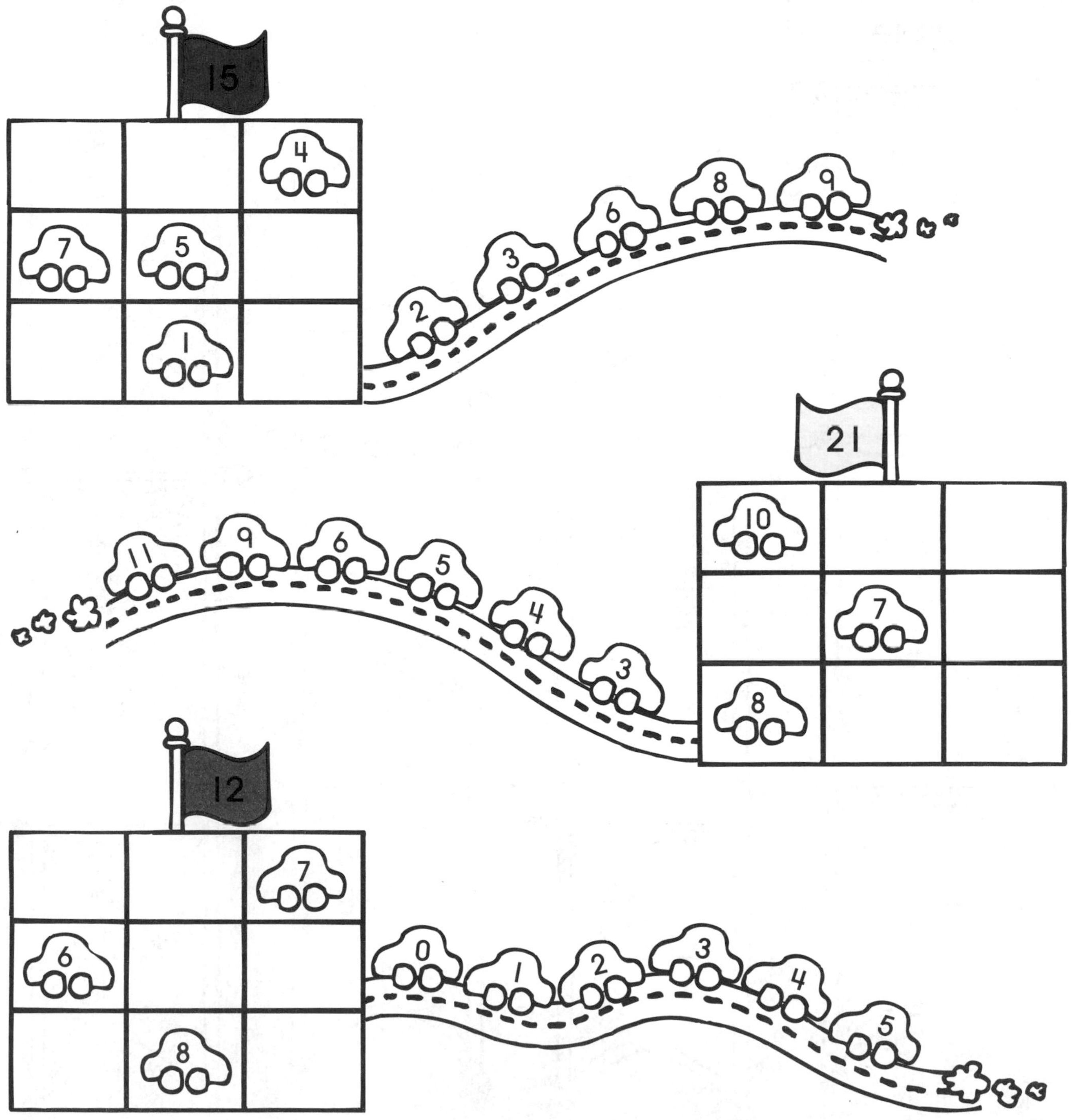

Banners High

Directions: Find the sums by regrouping. Then, color the flags by their sums.

20 to 39 purple	40 to 59 yellow	60 to 79 red	80 to 99 blue

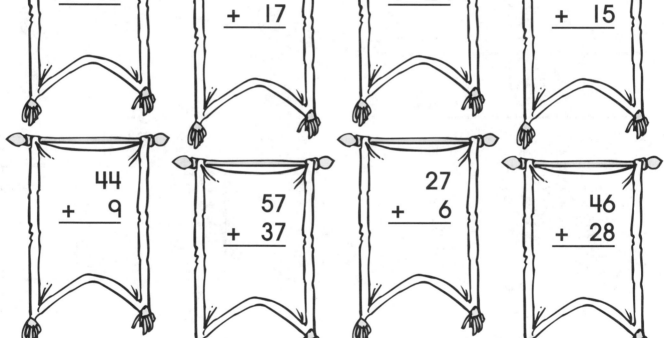

58 + 13 =

23 + 17 =

64 + 29 =

15 + 15 =

44 + 9 =

57 + 37 =

27 + 6 =

46 + 28 =

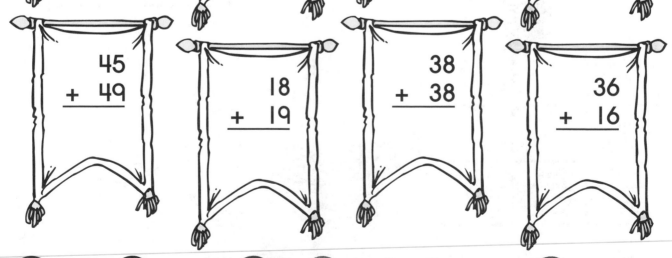

45 + 49 =

18 + 19 =

38 + 38 =

36 + 16 =

Fractions

A **fraction** is a number that names part of a whole, such as $\frac{1}{2}$ or $\frac{1}{3}$.

Directions: Write the fraction that tells what part of each figure is colored. The first one is done for you.

Example: 2 parts shaded
5 parts in the whole figure

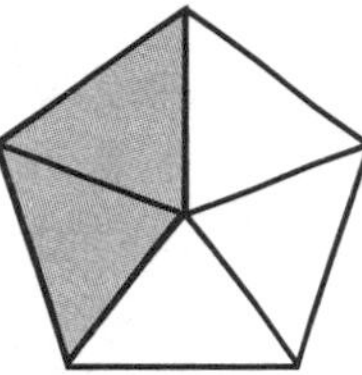

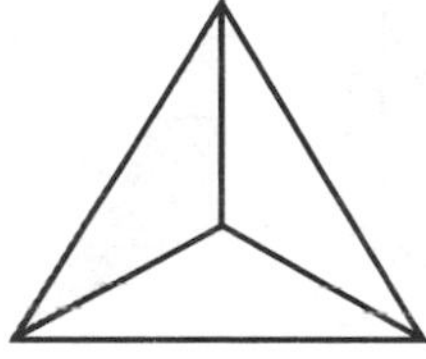

$\frac{1}{3}$ ______

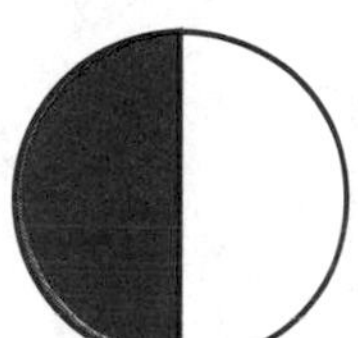

______

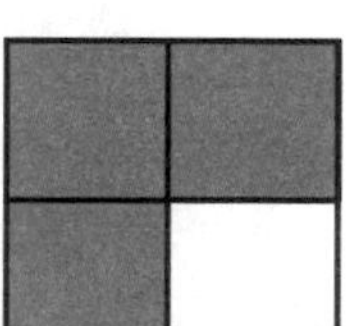

______

______

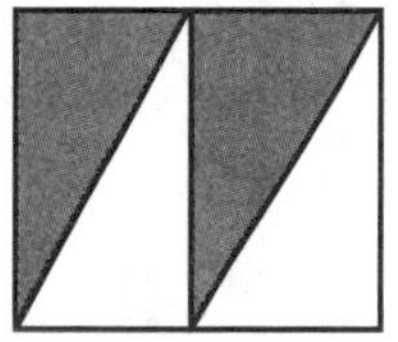

______

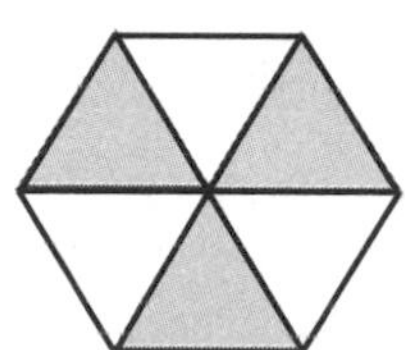

______

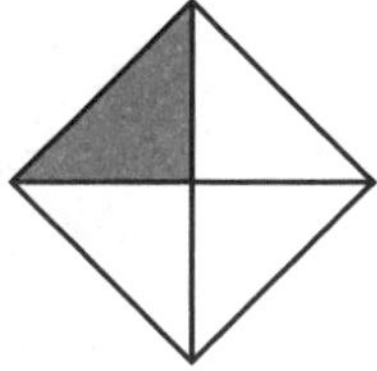

______

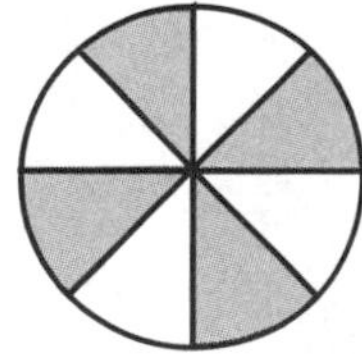

______

______

Fractions: Equivalent

Fractions that name the same part of a whole are **equivalent fractions.**

Example:

$\frac{1}{2} = \frac{2}{4}$ 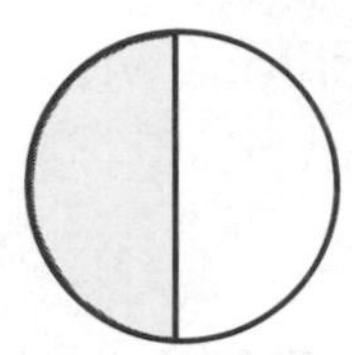 

Directions: Fill in the numbers to complete the equivalent fractions.

$\frac{1}{4} = \frac{\square}{8}$ 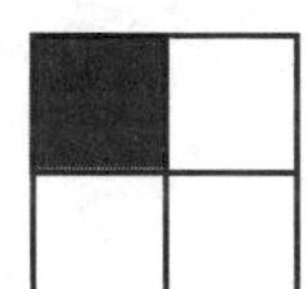 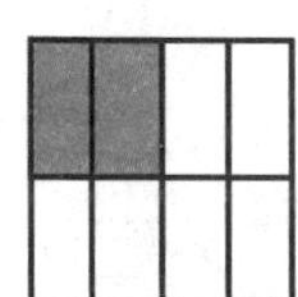

$\frac{2}{3} = \frac{\square}{6}$ 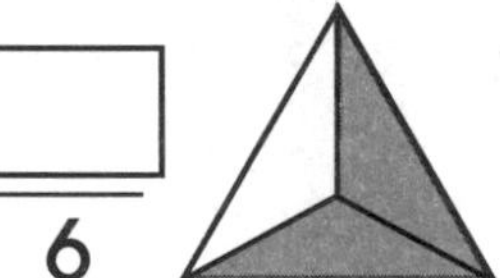 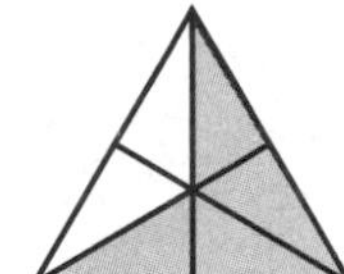

$\frac{1}{6} = \frac{\square}{12}$ 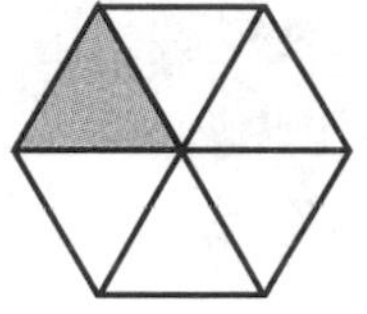 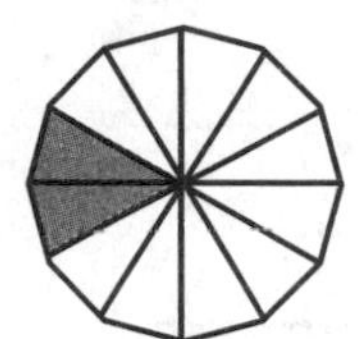

$\frac{2}{3} = \frac{\square}{6}$ 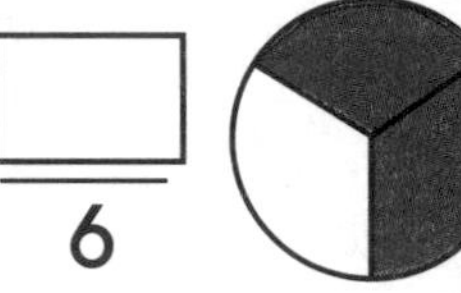

$\frac{1}{3} = \frac{\square}{12}$

$\frac{1}{5} = \frac{\square}{15}$

$\frac{1}{4} = \frac{\square}{8}$

$\frac{1}{2} = \frac{\square}{6}$

$\frac{2}{3} = \frac{\square}{9}$

$\frac{2}{6} = \frac{\square}{18}$

Fractions: Division

A fraction is a number that names part of an object. It can also name part of a group.

Directions: Study the example. Divide by the bottom number of the fraction to find the answers.

Example:

There are 6 cheerleaders.
$\frac{1}{2}$ of the cheerleaders are boys.
How many cheerleaders are boys?

6 cheerleaders ÷ 2 groups = 3 boys

$\frac{1}{2}$ of 6 = 3

$\frac{1}{2}$ of 8 = 4

$\frac{1}{2}$ of 10 = _____

$\frac{1}{3}$ of 9 = _____

$\frac{1}{5}$ of 10 = _____

$\frac{1}{4}$ of 12 = _____

$\frac{1}{8}$ of 32 = _____

$\frac{1}{3}$ of 27 = _____

$\frac{1}{5}$ of 30 = _____

$\frac{1}{2}$ of 14 = _____

$\frac{1}{9}$ of 18 = _____

$\frac{1}{6}$ of 24 = _____

$\frac{1}{3}$ of 18 = _____

$\frac{1}{10}$ of 50 = _____

Fractions: Comparing

Directions: Circle the fraction in each pair that is larger.

Example:

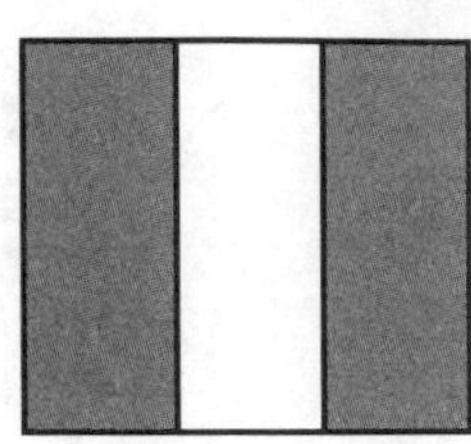

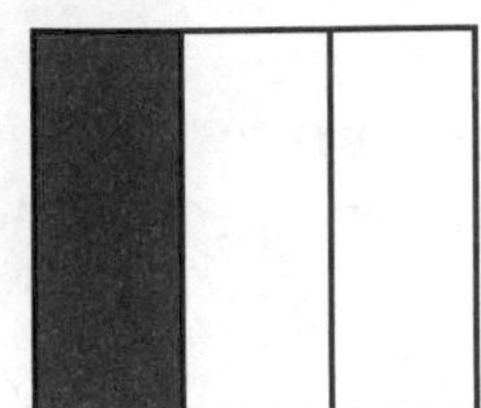

$\frac{1}{3}$

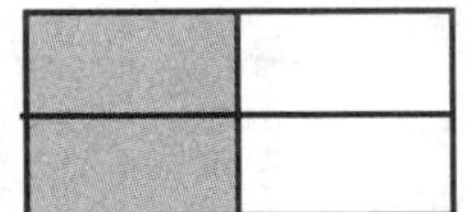

$\frac{2}{4}$

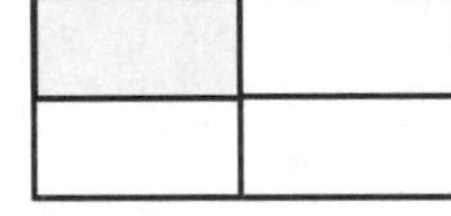

$\frac{1}{4}$

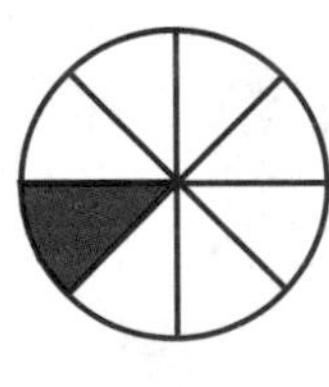

$\frac{1}{8}$

$\frac{2}{8}$

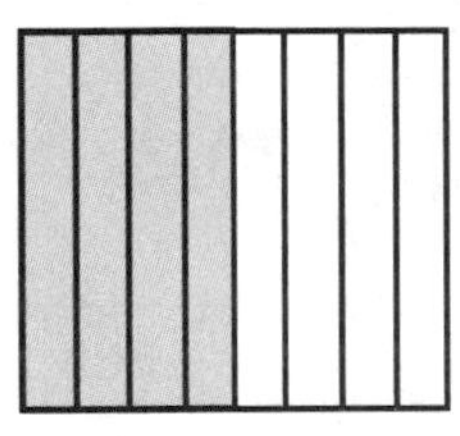

$\frac{1}{2}$

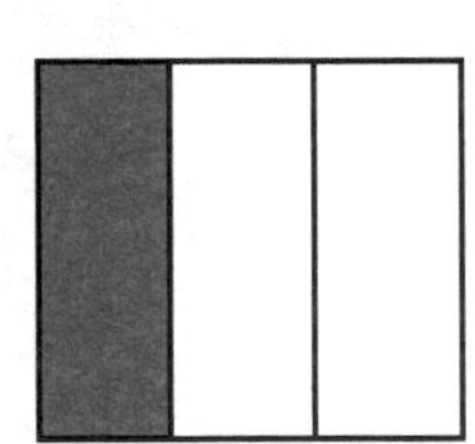

$\frac{1}{3}$

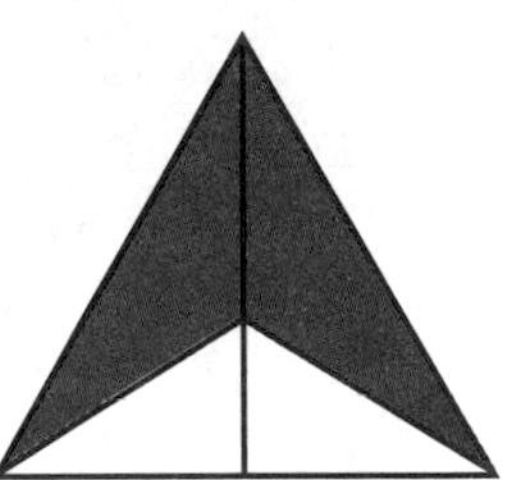

$\frac{2}{3}$

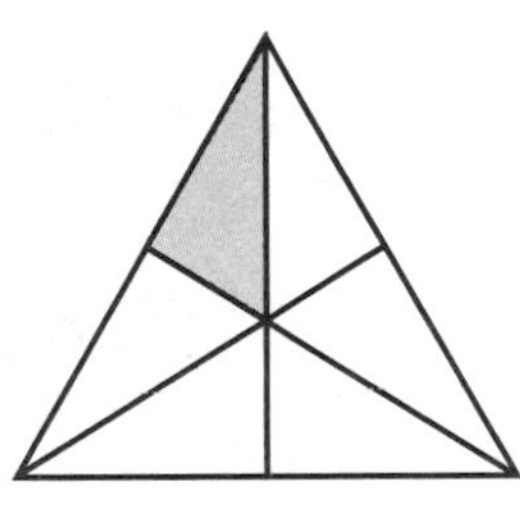

$\frac{1}{6}$

$\frac{1}{4}$ or $\frac{1}{6}$

$\frac{1}{5}$ or $\frac{1}{7}$

$\frac{1}{8}$ or $\frac{1}{4}$

Lift Off!

Directions: Subtract.

86 − 43   75 − 31

86 − 30   68 − 32   95 − 13

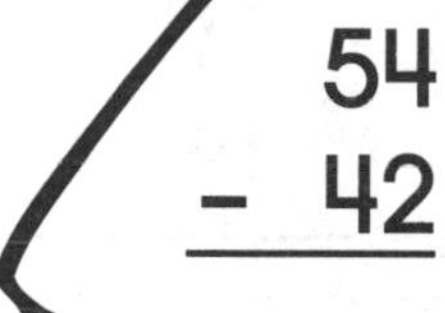

54 − 42   76 − 31   91 − 40   66 − 10   94 − 52

79 − 56   68 − 46

37 − 21

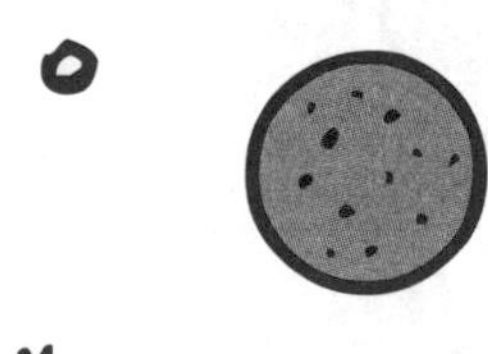

Space Travel

Directions: Marty has been traveling to the planets. Use the numbers in his space log to find the answers.

Space Log	
Planet	Days Visited
Mars	76
Earth	68
Jupiter	57
Venus	52
Saturn	49
Mercury	32
Neptune	24
Uranus	21
Pluto	13

How many more days did Marty visit Earth than Jupiter?

☐
− ☐
☐

How many more days did Marty visit Saturn than Neptune?

☐
− ☐
☐

How many more days did Marty visit Venus than Uranus?

☐
− ☐
☐

How many more days did Marty visit Venus than Mercury?

☐
− ☐
☐

How many more days did Marty visit Mars than Neptune?

☐
− ☐
☐

Batter Up!

Directions: Rename each number by regrouping. Take from the tens place and give to the ones place as shown.

36 = 3 tens and 6 ones = 2 tens and 16 ones

72 = 7 tens and 2 ones = _____ tens and _____ ones

50 = 5 tens and 0 ones = _____ tens and _____ ones

23 = 2 tens and 3 ones = _____ tens and _____ ones

85 = 8 tens and 5 ones = _____ tens and _____ ones

90 = 9 tens and 0 ones = _____ tens and _____ ones

64 = 6 tens and 4 ones = _____ tens and _____ ones

Uh-Oh!

Directions: Answer each problem by regrouping. Use the differences to answer the riddle.

Why didn't the mountain climber yell for help?

___ ___   ___ ___ ___
35 28   9 67 63

___ ___ ___ ___ ___ ___ ___
35 67 25 46 52 25 46

___ ___   ___ ___ ___
17 74   35 52 63

___ ___ ___ ___ ___ !
19 28 28 19 35

G $62 - 16$	T $48 - 29$	R $83 - 34$	W $91 - 82$	E $56 - 28$
A $74 - 7$	D $57 - 19$	H $64 - 29$	Y $92 - 18$	I $81 - 29$
B $36 - 19$	S $71 - 8$	F $54 - 49$	N $43 - 18$	C $87 - 48$

Decimals

A **decimal** is a number with one or more numbers to the right of a decimal point. A **decimal point** is a dot placed between the ones place and the tenths place of a number, such as 2.5.

Example:

$\frac{3}{10}$ can be written as .3 They are both read as "three-tenths."

Directions: Write the answer as a decimal for the shaded parts.

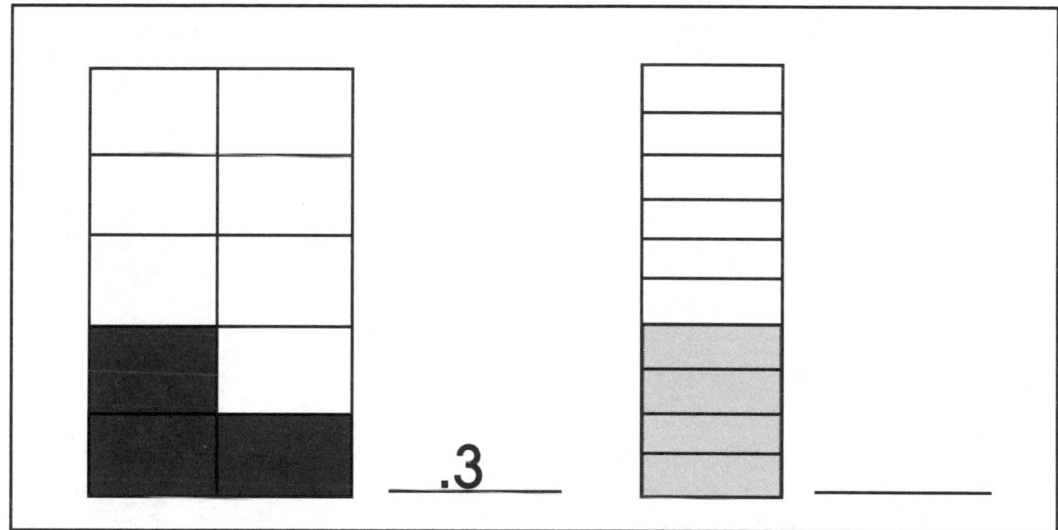

Directions: Color parts of each object to match the decimals given.

.7

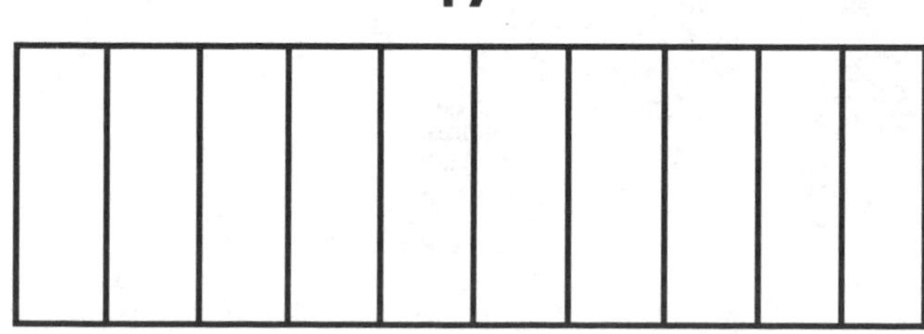

.6

.5

Decimals

A decimal is a number with one or more numbers to the right of a decimal point, such as 6.5 or 2.25. **Equivalent** means "numbers that are equal."

Directions: Draw a line between the equivalent numbers.

.8	$\frac{5}{10}$
five-tenths	$\frac{8}{10}$
.7	$\frac{6}{10}$
.4	.3
six-tenths	$\frac{2}{10}$
three-tenths	$\frac{7}{10}$
.2	$\frac{9}{10}$
nine-tenths	$\frac{4}{10}$

Decimals Greater than 1

Directions: Write the decimal for the part that is shaded.

Example: $2\frac{4}{10}$

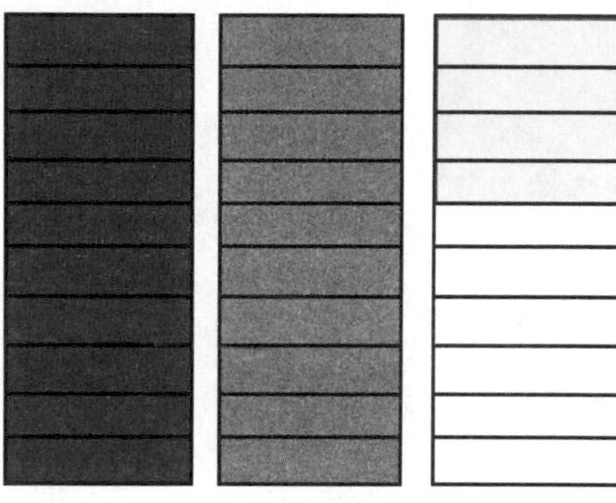

Write: 2.4 Read: two and four-tenths

$1\frac{2}{10}$ = ____

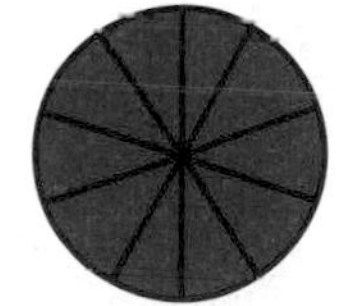

$3\frac{6}{10}$ = ____

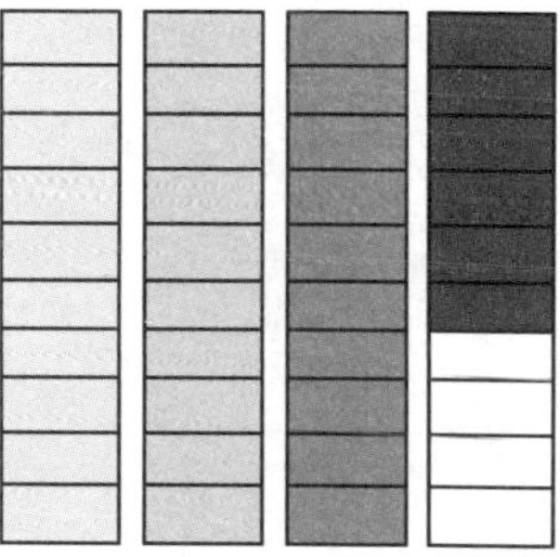

$2\frac{3}{10}$ = ____

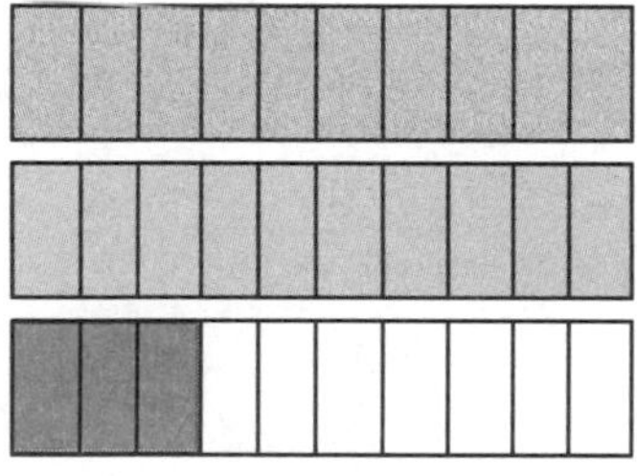

$2\frac{7}{10}$ = ____

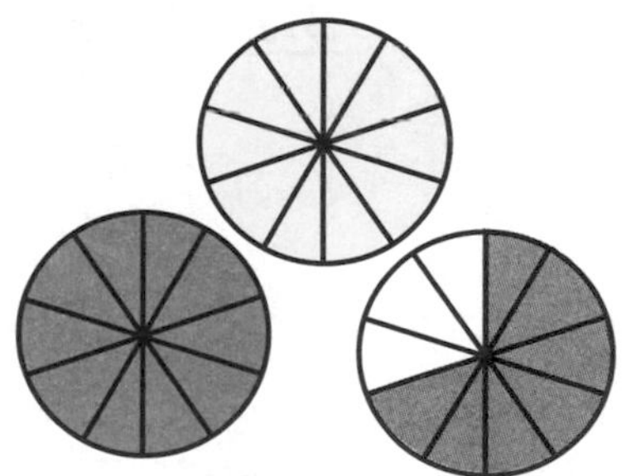

Directions: Write each number as a decimal.

four and two-tenths = ____

seven and one-tenth = ____

$3\frac{4}{10}$ = ____ $6\frac{9}{10}$ = ____ $8\frac{3}{10}$ = ____ $7\frac{5}{10}$ = ____

Decimals: Addition and Subtraction

Decimals are added and subtracted in the same way as other numbers. Simply carry down the decimal point to your answer.

Directions: Add or subtract.

Examples:

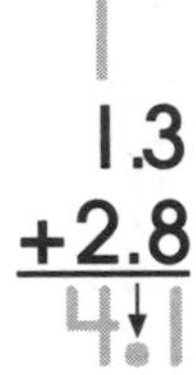

4.5
-2.2
2.3

1.3 +2.2	4.6 -3.4	5.1 +8.8	6.7 -4.3
7.9 -3.7	6.4 +8.7	11.4 - 9.5	0.5 +3.6

9.3 + 1.2 = ____ 2.5 - 0.7 = ____ 1.2 + 5.0 = ____

Antonio jogs around the school every day. The distance for one time around is 0.7 of a mile. If he jogs around the school twice, how many miles does he jog each day? ____________

Tic-Tac-Travel

Directions: Find each sum. Write **X** or **O** over the answers in the suitcase. The winner must get 3 spaces in a row or diagonally.

A. 7 + 8 = ☐ = X

B. 6 + 4 = ☐ = O

C. 3 + 3 = ☐ = X

D. 5 + 4 = ☐ = O

E. 3 + 2 = ☐ = X

F. 6 + 7 = ☐ = O

G. 8 + 6 = ☐ = X

H. 6 + 6 = ☐ = O

I. 7 + 4 = ☐ = X

10	15	13	7
2	6	14	12
5	9	8	11

Perfect Pairs

Directions: Find the pair of numbers that matches both operations in each box. Then, use the circled letters to solve the riddle below.

A sum of 8 and a product of 15

_____

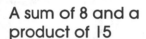

(E)

A sum of 7 and a product of 10

_____

(N)

A sum of 15 and a product of 54

_____

(S)

A difference of 27 and a quotient of 4

_____

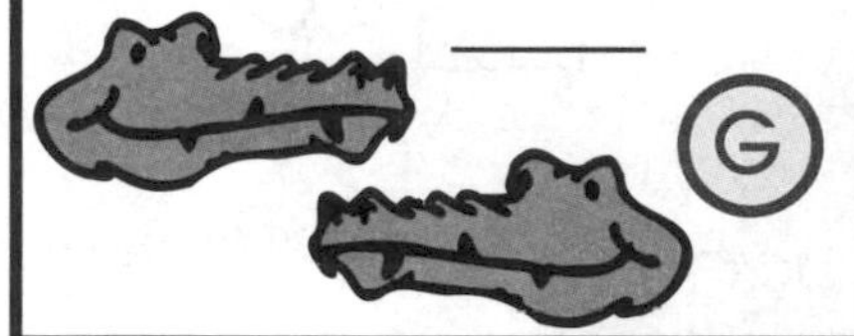

(G)

A difference of 12 and a quotient of 4

_____

(R)

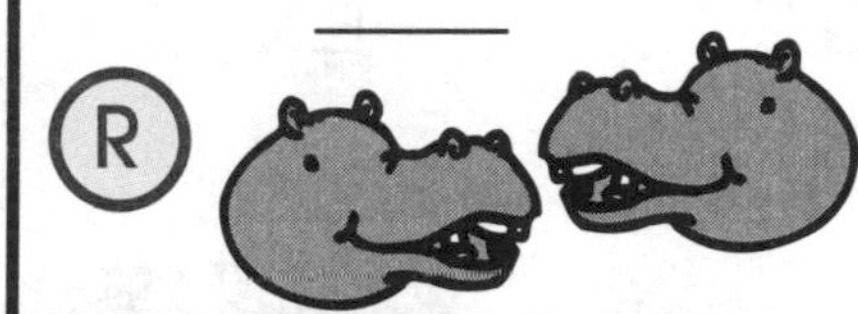

A difference of 21 and a quotient of 4

_____

(A)

A sum of 11 and a product of 28

_____

(D)

A difference of 8 and a quotient of 5

_____

(I)

Why did the inchworm get lost in the math book?

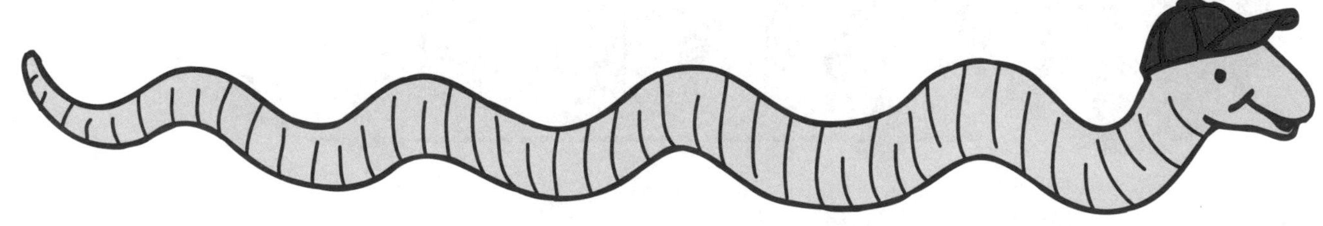

He didn't _____ _____ _____ _____ the _____ _____ _____ _____ _____!

(4, 16) (3, 5) (7, 28) (4, 7) (6, 9) (2, 10) (9, 36) (2, 5) (6, 9)

Make it Fair

Practice fair sharing by completing these problems. Circle the objects and write a division problem to go with each picture.

There are six children. Circle the number of cookies each child will get if the cookies are divided equally.

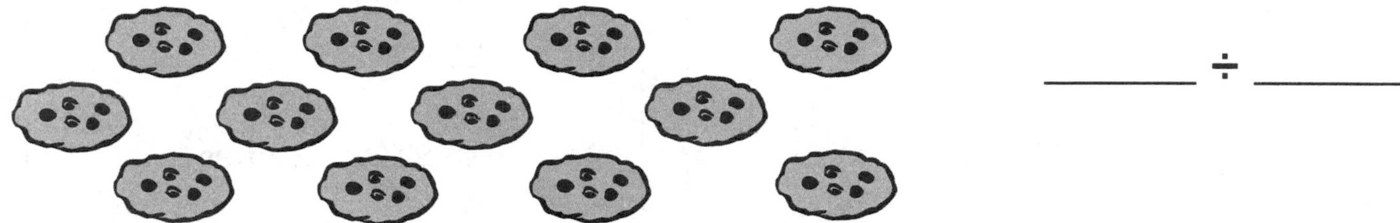

_______ ÷ _______

There are four dogs. Circle the dog bones each dog will get if the dog bones are divided equally.

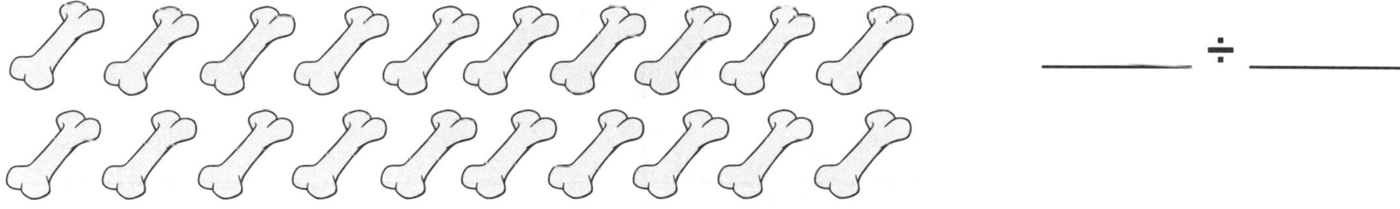

_______ ÷ _______

Divide the pepperoni so that five pizzas will have the same amount.

_______ ÷ _______

Divide the books so that there will be the same number of books on three shelves.

_______ ÷ _______

Multiplication Challenge

Directions: Solve each problem.

Kevin is 3 feet tall.

His dad is 2 times as tall as Kevin.

×

How tall is Kevin's dad?

Yesterday, Shannette drank 7 glasses of water.

Today, she drank 2 times as many.

×

How many glasses did Shannette drink today?

Emily drew 2 houses yesterday.

Today, she drew 4 times as many.

×

How many houses did she draw today?

Sarah fixed 2 lamps yesterday.

Today, she fixed 8 times as many.

×

How many lamps did she fix today?

Patterns

Directions: Write what would come next in each pattern.

0 2 0 4 0 6 ________

1 3 5 7 9 11 ________

5 10 20 40 80 ________

▽ □ ▷ ▭ ▽ □ ________

◇ □ ▽ ◇ □ ▽ ________

○ ◯ ● ⬤ ○ ◯ ________

1 A 2 B 3 C ________

A B C 1 2 3 ________

⊞ ⊞ ⊞ ⊞ ⊞ ⊞ ________

Pattern Maze

Directions: Follow the pattern: ● ■ ▲ ☆ to get through the maze.

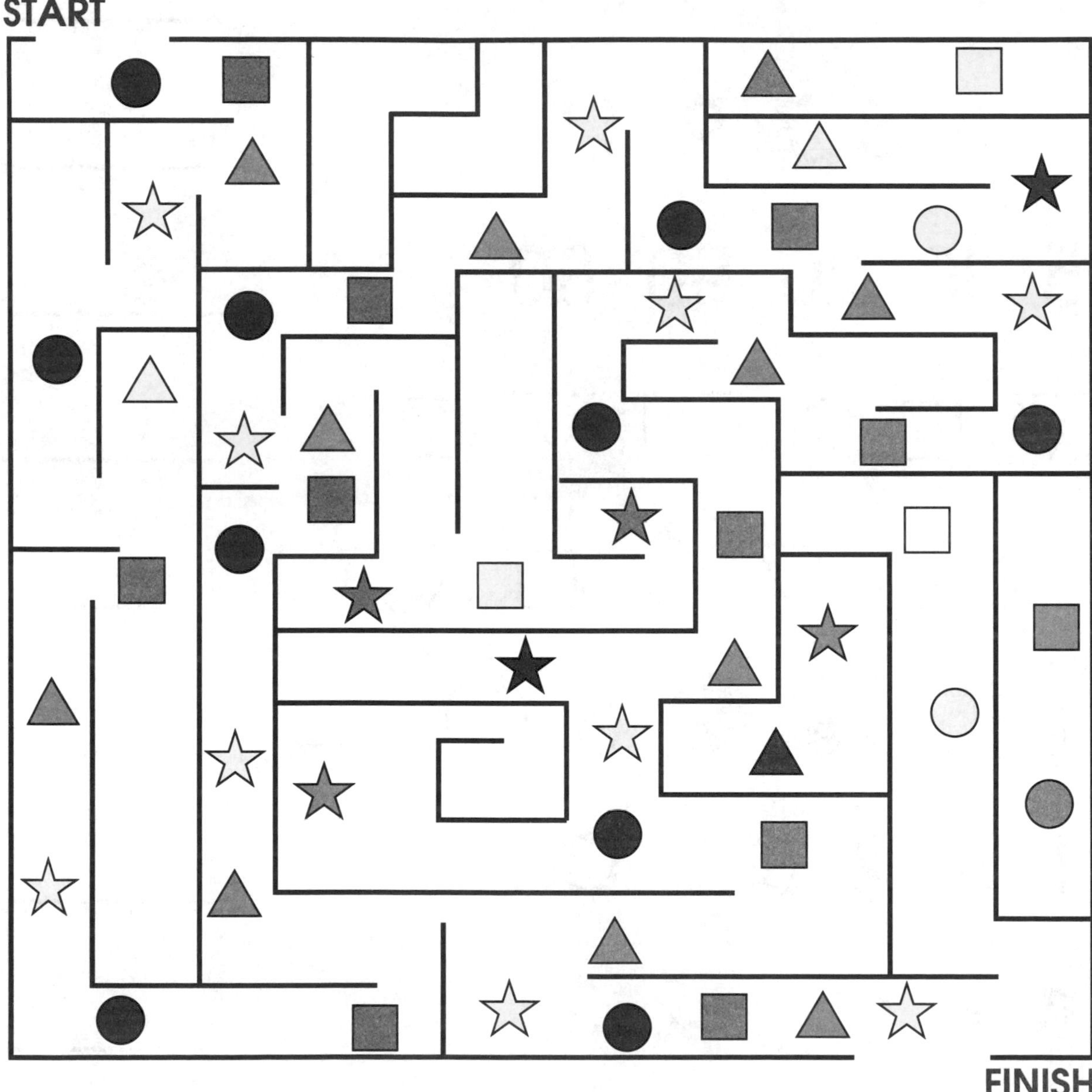

Compare Sums

Directions: Find the sums. Write **>**, **<**, or **=** in the circles to compare the sums.

231 + 445 ○ 417 + 372	244 + 323 ○ 321 + 555
136 + 247 ○ 569 + 268	678 + 316 ○ 216 + 313
635 + 218 ○ 417 + 113	141 + 132 ○ 345 + 289

Zombie Chase

Directions: Help the boy escape from the zombies.

Math Time

Directions: Use the math words in the word box to fill in the wheel. Each word starts with the last letter of the word before it.

time	sum	more	equals	less	subtract

Shape Up!

Directions: Add to find the answers. Color the shapes with even sums green and those with odd sums **purple**.

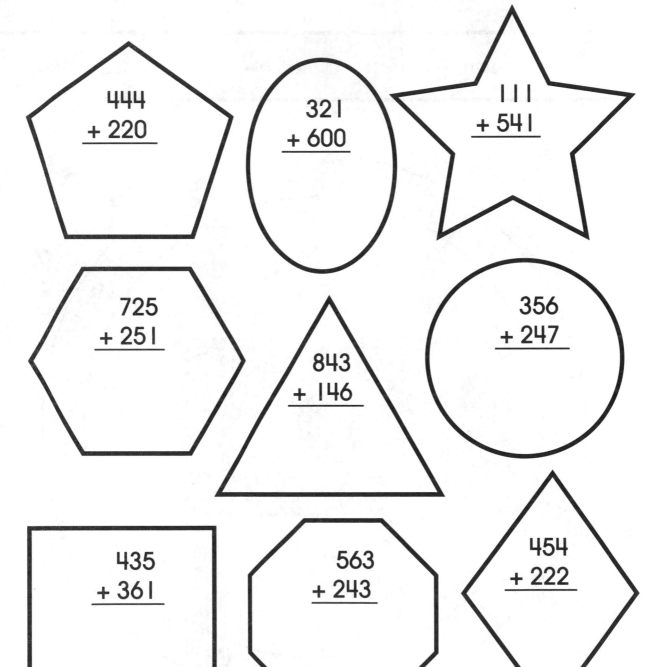

$$\begin{array}{r} 444 \\ +\ 220 \\ \hline \end{array}$$

$$\begin{array}{r} 321 \\ +\ 600 \\ \hline \end{array}$$

$$\begin{array}{r} 111 \\ +\ 541 \\ \hline \end{array}$$

$$\begin{array}{r} 725 \\ +\ 251 \\ \hline \end{array}$$

$$\begin{array}{r} 843 \\ +\ 146 \\ \hline \end{array}$$

$$\begin{array}{r} 356 \\ +\ 247 \\ \hline \end{array}$$

$$\begin{array}{r} 435 \\ +\ 361 \\ \hline \end{array}$$

$$\begin{array}{r} 563 \\ +\ 243 \\ \hline \end{array}$$

$$\begin{array}{r} 454 \\ +\ 222 \\ \hline \end{array}$$

Geometry

Geometry is the branch of mathematics that has to do with points, lines, and shapes.

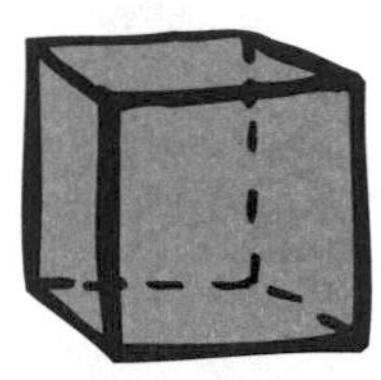

cube

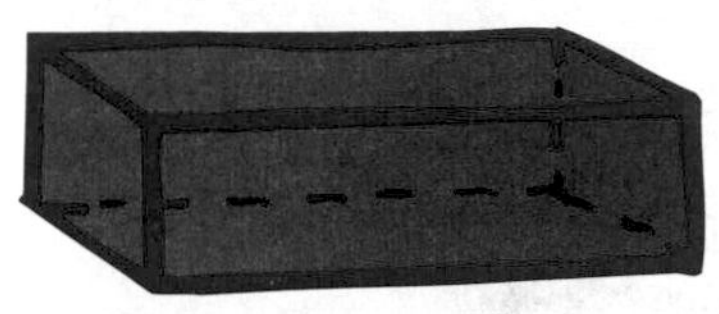

rectangular prism

cone

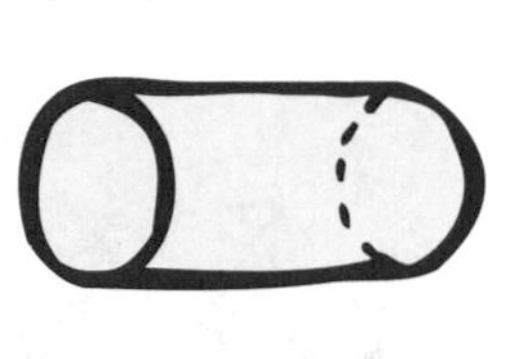

cylinder

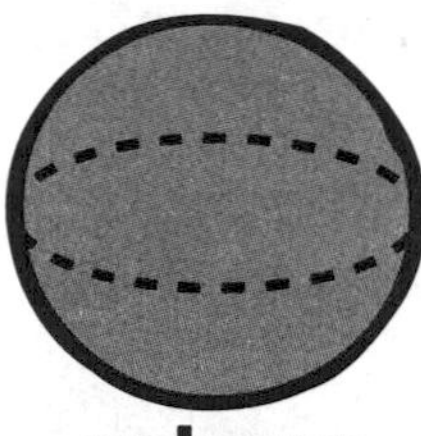

sphere

Directions: Use the code to color the picture.

Color:
cubes — blue
rectangular prisms — red
cones — green
cylinders — yellow
spheres — orange

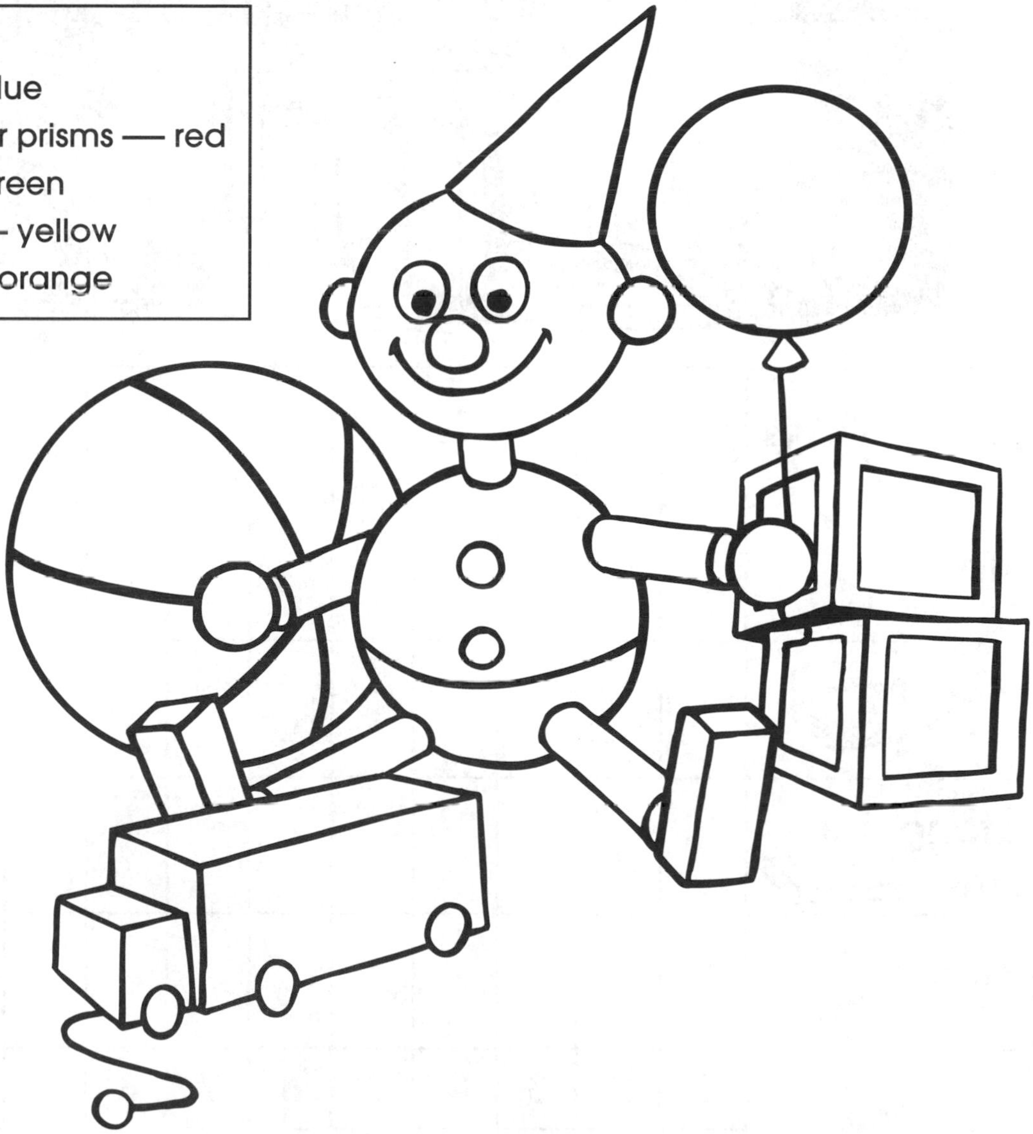

Home Sweet Home

Directions: Count the number of each kind of candy on the house. Color one part of the graph for each candy you count.

Spheres												
Cones												
Cubes												
Rectangular prisms												
Pyramids												
	1	2	3	4	5	6	7	8	9	10	11	12

Geometric Coloring

Directions: Color the geometric shapes in the box below.

Geometry: Lines, Segments, Rays, Angles

Geometry is the branch of mathematics that has to do with points, lines, and shapes.

A **line** goes on and on in both directions. It has no end points.

Line CD

A **segment** is part of a line. It has two end points.

Segment AB

A **ray** has a line segment with only one end point. It goes on and on in the other direction.

Ray EF

An **angle** has two rays with the same end point.

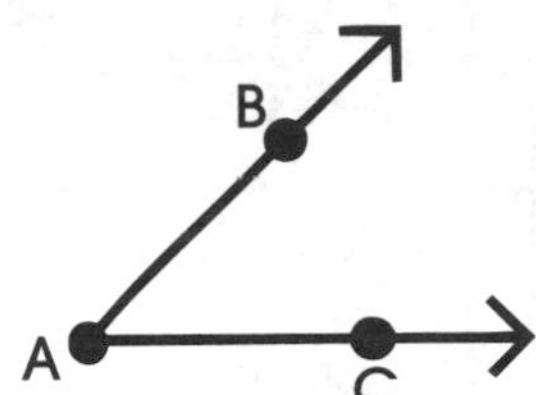

Angle BAC

Directions: Write the name for each figure.

line MN

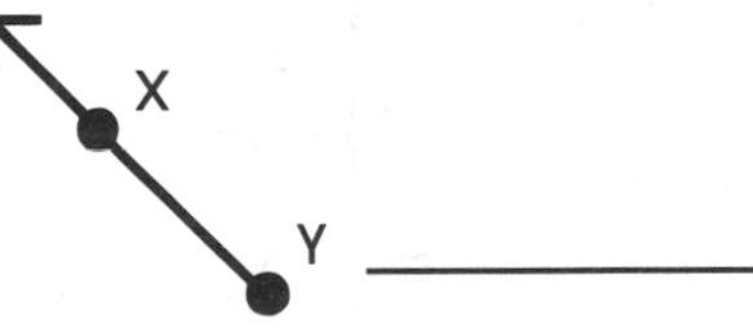

____

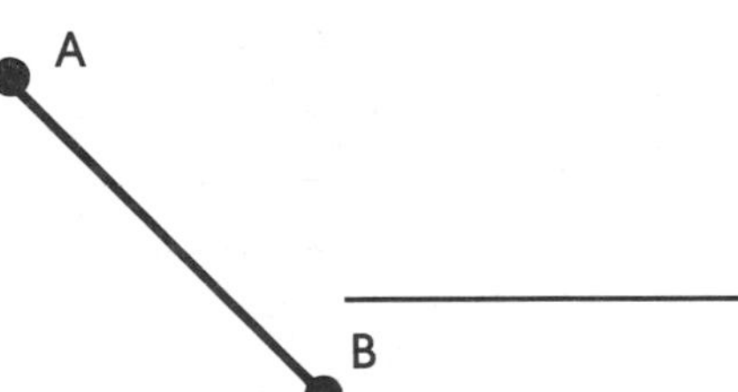

____

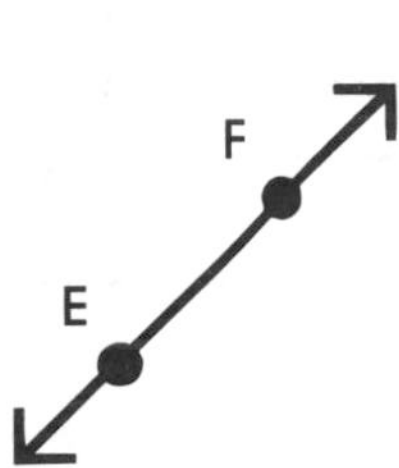

____

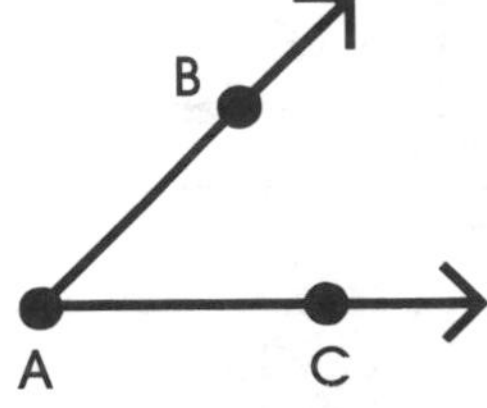

____

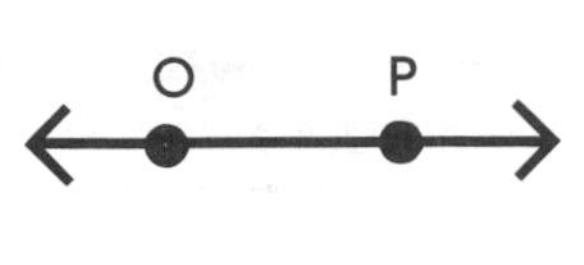

____

Geometry: Perimeter

The **perimeter** is the distance around an object. Find the perimeter by adding the lengths of all the sides.

Directions: Find the perimeter for each object (ft. = feet).

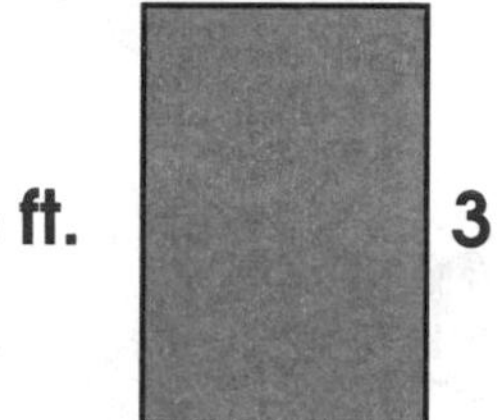

10 ft.

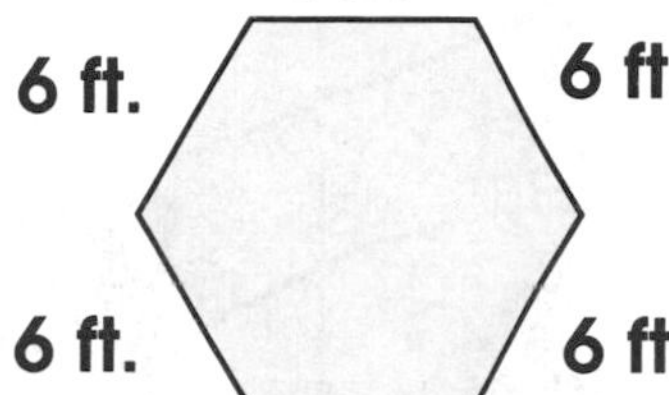

______

4 ft.
4 ft.
3 ft.

______

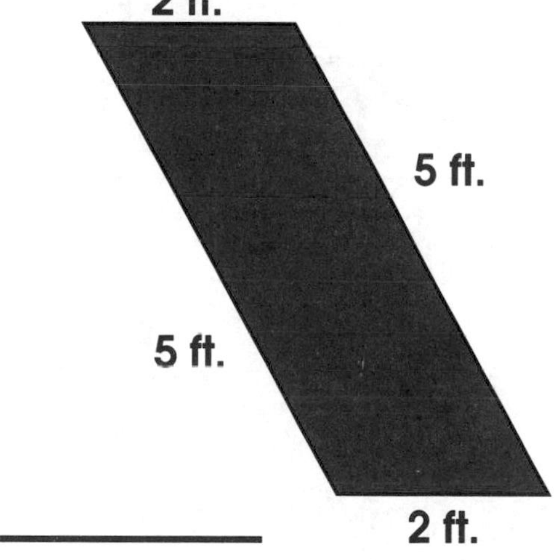

______

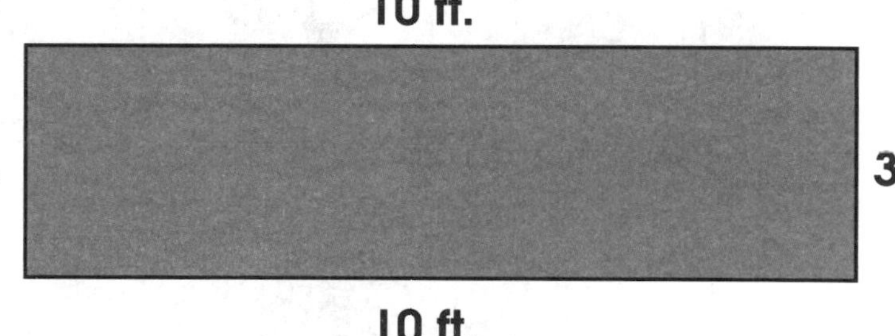

______

1 ft.
1 ft. 1 ft.
1 ft. 1 ft.
1 ft. 1 ft.
1 ft.

______

7 ft.
5 ft.
5 ft.

______

3 ft.
1 ft. 1 ft.
5 ft.

______

Flower Power

Directions: Count the flowers, and answer the questions.

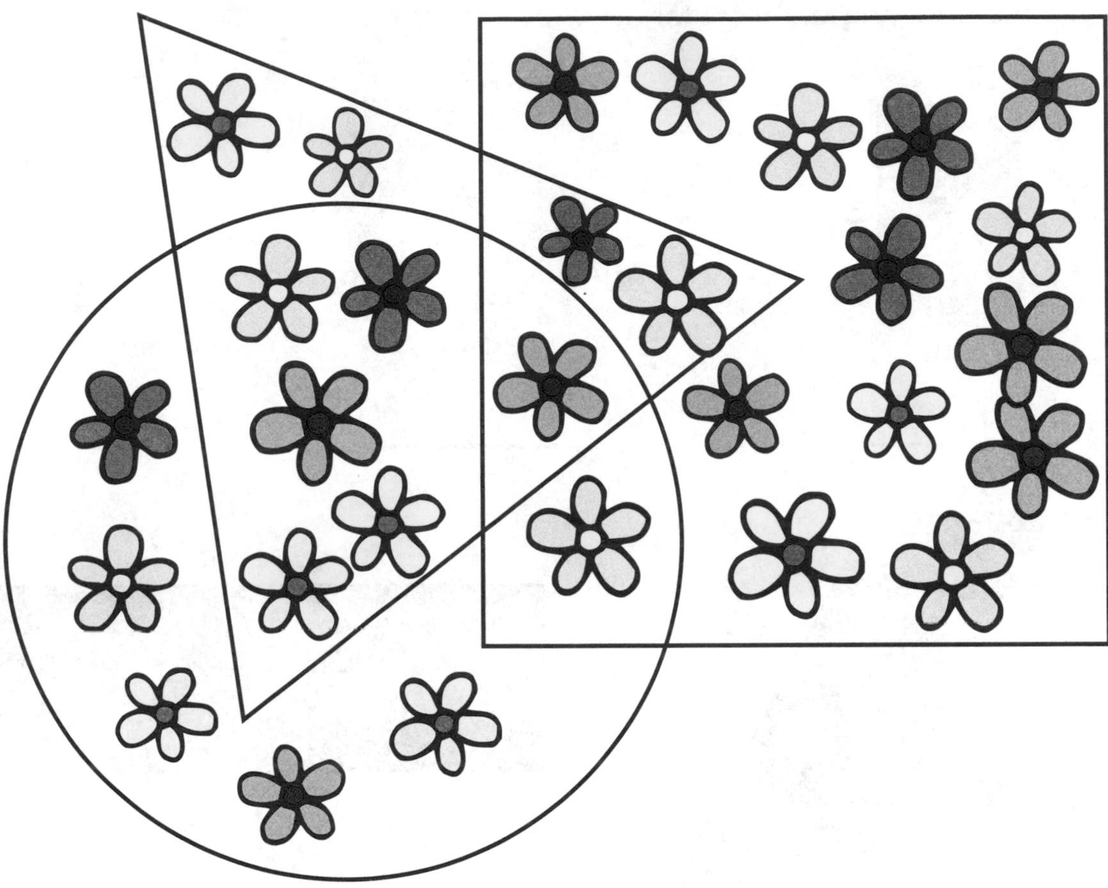

How many  s are in the circle? ________

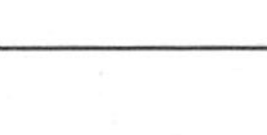

How many  s are in the triangle? ________

How many s are in the square? ________

How many  s in all? ________

Find the Mystery Number

Directions: Color the spaces with words that name shapes or colors **red**. Color the spaces with words that name numbers **purple**.

nine	circle	one	rectangle	fifteen
seven	red	nineteen	blue	eleven
two	octagon	twenty	hexagon	eighteen
eight	green	star	yellow	heart
one	thirteen	twelve	rhombus	ten
three	six	seventeen	brown	five
thirteen	fourteen	four	square	sixteen

The mystery number is ______.

Sweet Dreams

Directions: Find each sum by regrouping from the tens to the hundreds place. Then, color the pillows.

0 to 199	200 to 399	400 to 599	600 to 799	800 to 999
blue	green	purple	red	orange

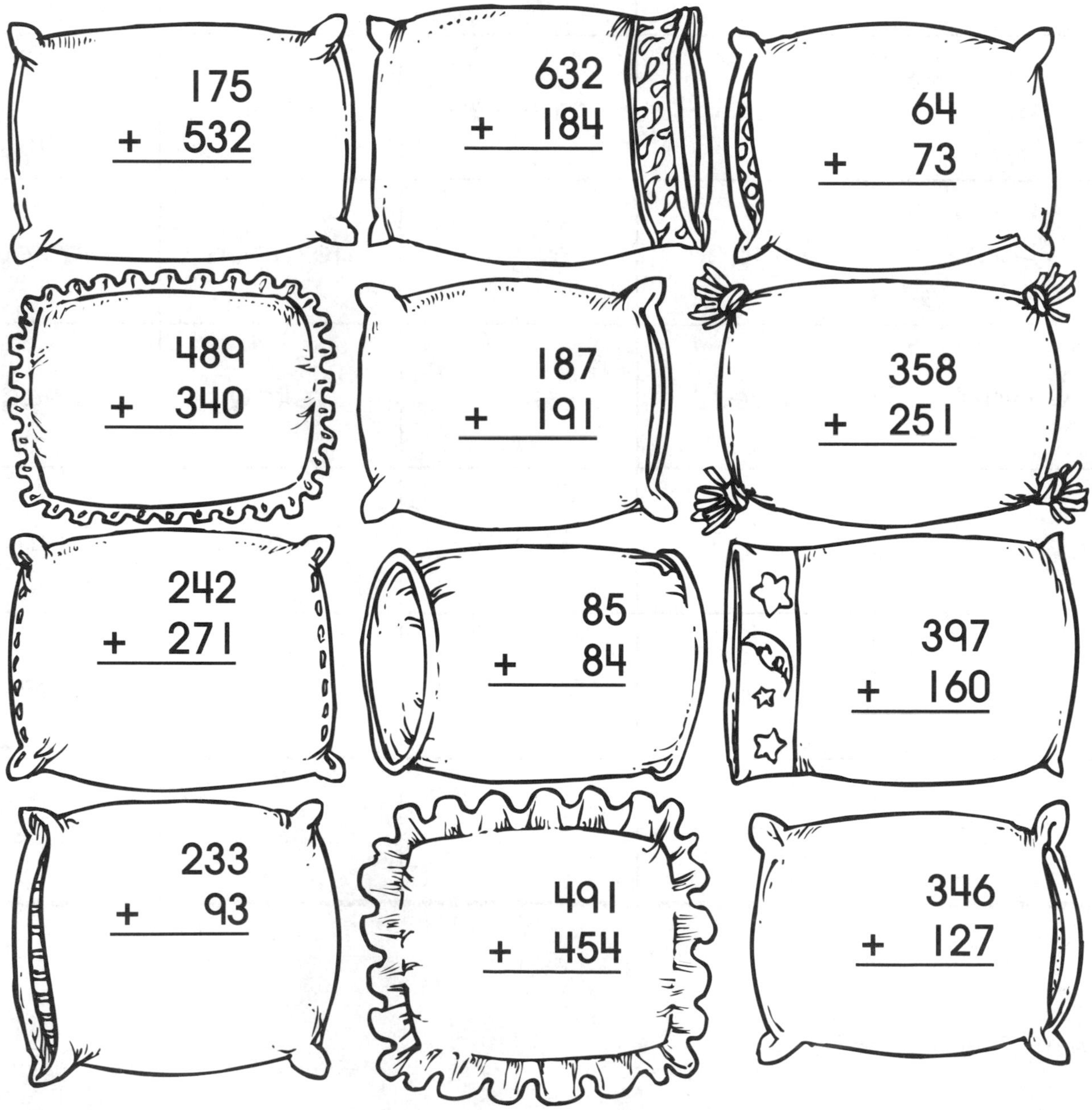

175 + 532

632 + 184

64 + 73

489 + 340

187 + 191

358 + 251

242 + 271

85 + 84

397 + 160

233 + 93

491 + 454

346 + 127

Name ______________________

Add It Up

Directions: Find the sums. Write **>**, **<**, or **=** in the circles to compare the sums.

221 + 425 ○	416 + 572	344 + 523 ○	243 + 444
671 + 304 ○	465 + 524	206 + 133 ○	347 + 212
417 + 341 ○	634 + 124	142 + 153 ○	141 + 148
281 + 612 ○	386 + 312	623 + 311 ○	502 + 432

Let's Go!

Directions: Add to find each sum. Be sure to regroup from the ones to the tens place. Then, find and circle the sums hidden in the puzzle.

345	374	175	517	632
+ 429	+ 206	+ 416	+ 406	+ 328

446	385	705	618	617
+ 129	+ 107	+ 205	+ 345	+ 177

4 0 5 1 5 8 2 5 5
9 7 9 2 3 1 9 6 9
2 9 7 6 4 6 3 4 1
2 6 1 0 3 7 7 4 7
8 3 5 7 5 9 9 3 0
5 2 8 4 0 2 4 8 9
9 6 0 1 3 4 9 1 0

Double Digits

Directions: Write how many tens and ones. Write the numbers as an addition problem. Then, write the sum.

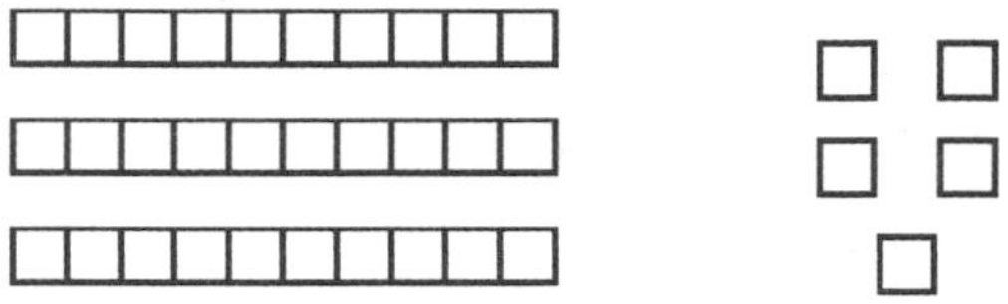

3 tens 5 ones
30 + 5
35

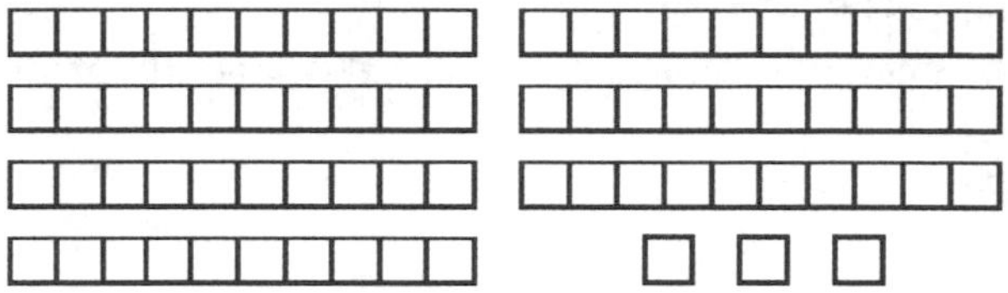

____ tens ____ ones
____ + ____
______

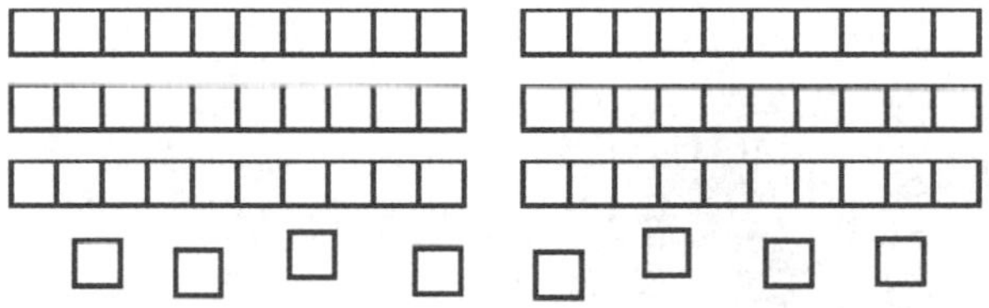

____ tens ____ ones
____ + ____
______

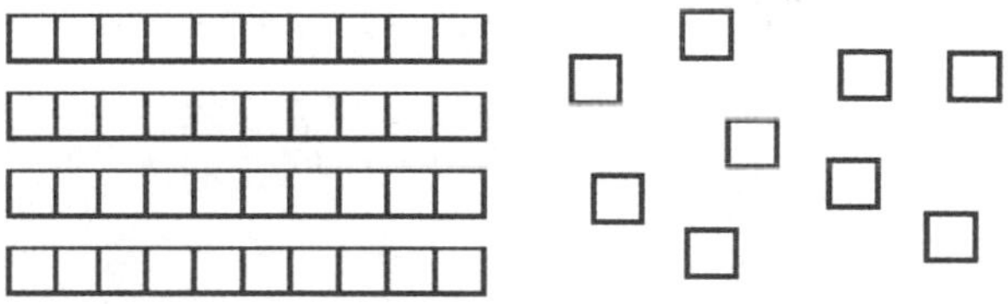

____ tens ____ ones
____ + ____
______

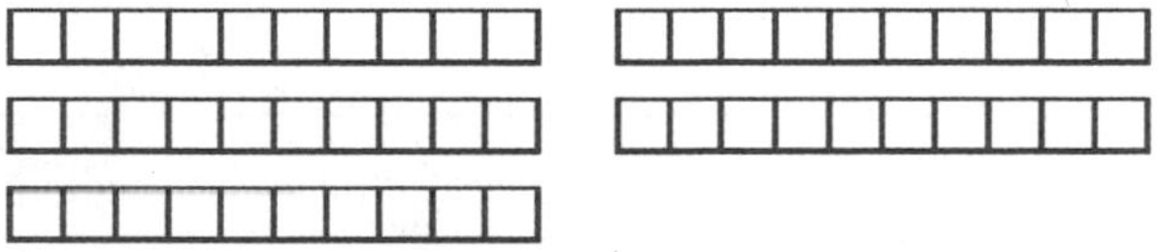

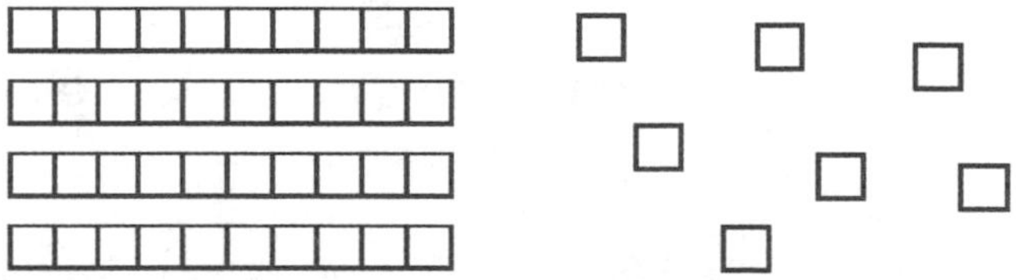

____ tens ____ ones
____ + ____
______

____ tens ____ ones
____ + ____
______

Map Skills: Scale

A **map scale** shows how far one place is from another. This map scale shows that 1 inch on this page equals 1 mile at the real location.

Directions: Use a ruler and the map scale to find out how far it is from Ann's house to other places. Round to the nearest inch.

Map Scale
1 inch = 1 mile

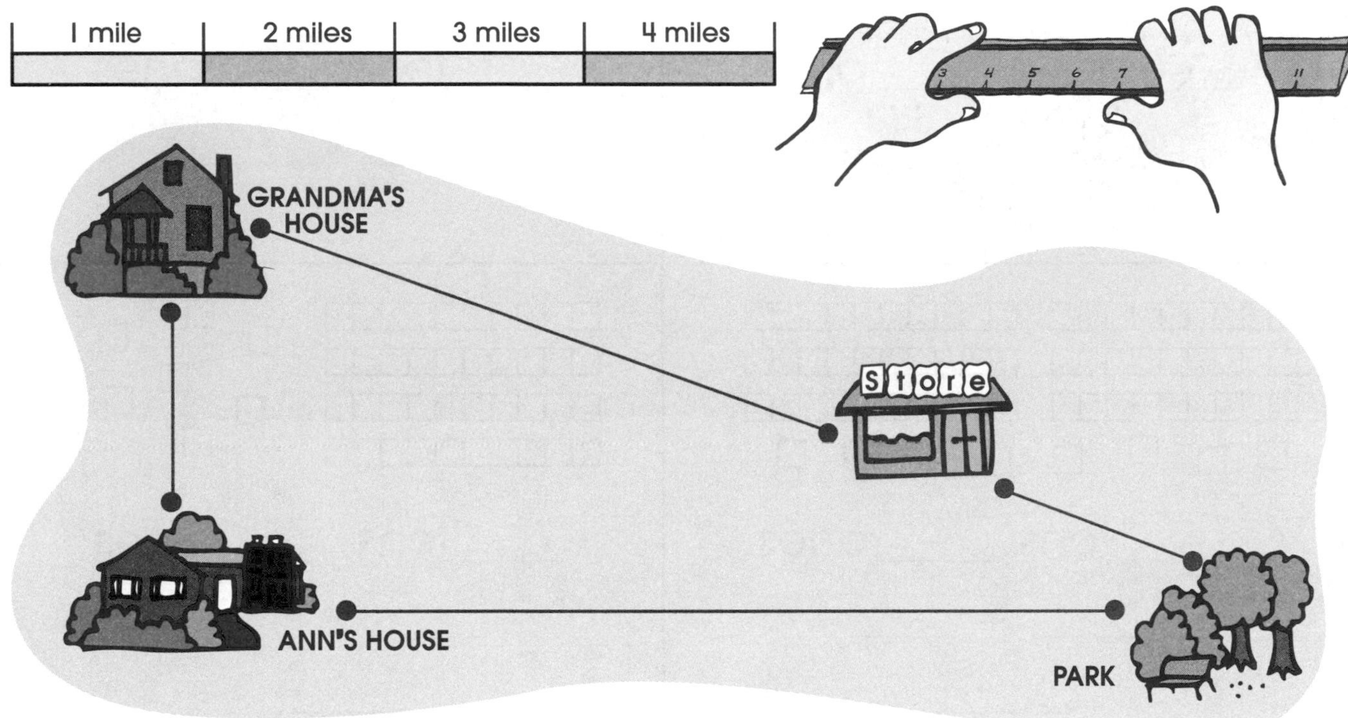

1. How far is it from Ann's house to the park? ______________________

2. How far is it from Ann's house to Grandma's house? ______________________

3. How far is it from Grandma's house to the store? ______________________

4. How far did Ann go when she went from her house to Grandma's and then to the store? ______________________

Map Skills: Scale

Directions: Use a ruler and the map scale to measure the map and answer the questions. Round to the nearest inch.

Map Scale
1 inch = 10 feet

10 feet	20 feet	30 feet	40 feet

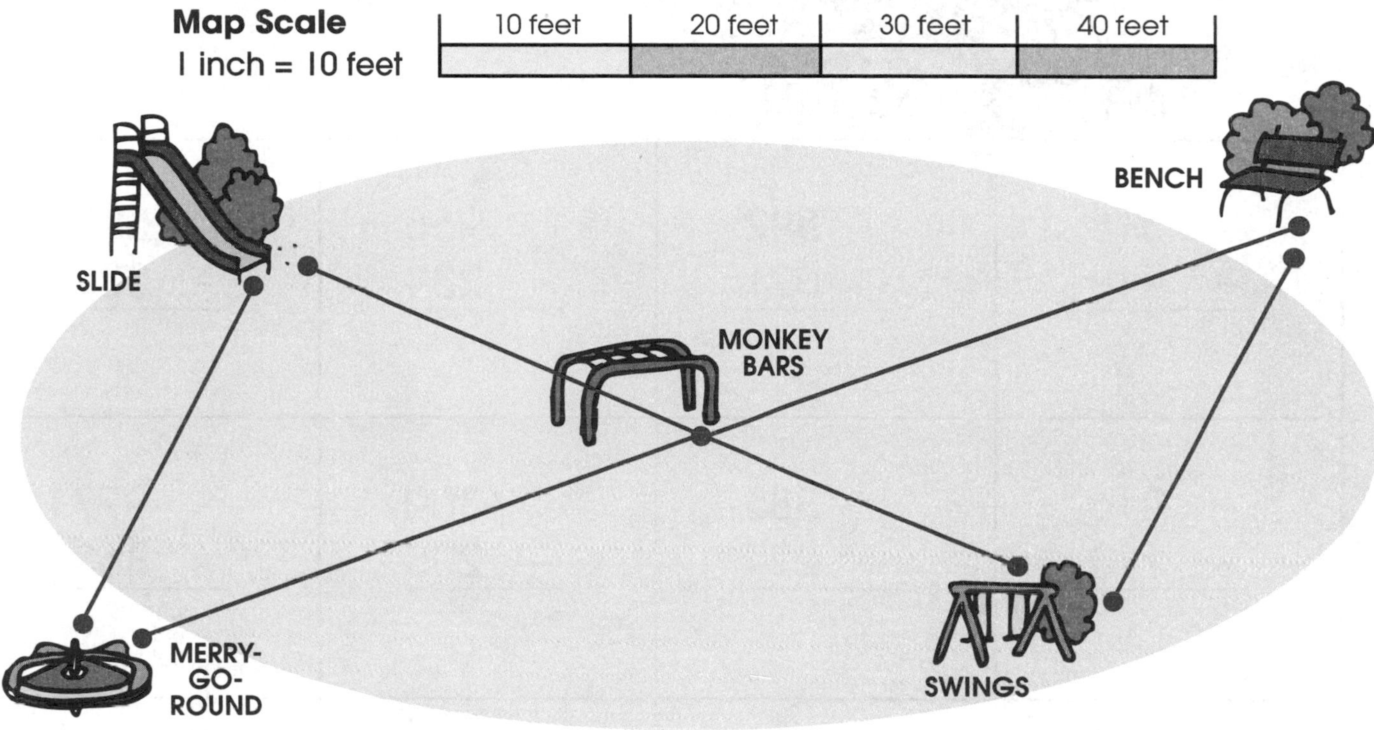

1. How far is it from the bench to the swings? ____________________

2. How far is it from the bench to the monkey bars? ____________________

3. How far is it from the monkey bars to the merry-go-round? ____________________

4. How far is it from the bench to the merry-go-round? ____________________

5. How far is it from the merry-go-round to the slide? ____________________

6. How far is it from the slide to the swings? ____________________

That Bugs Me!

Directions: Subtract. Then, color the squares with answers that are odd numbers to help the bug get to the leaf.

518 - 414	842 - 621	966 - 234	549 - 321
916 - 113	385 - 224	309 - 203	977 - 863
459 - 100	749 - 637	496 - 260	928 - 210
839 - 324	578 - 241	659 - 6	948 - 243

That's Puzzling

Directions: Find each difference. Be sure to regroup from the hundreds place to the tens place. Use the answers to complete the puzzle.

Across

1. $328 - 184$

3. $735 - 451$

4. $945 - 193$

6. $589 - 293$

8. $483 - 382$

9. $668 - 182$

10. $903 - 81$

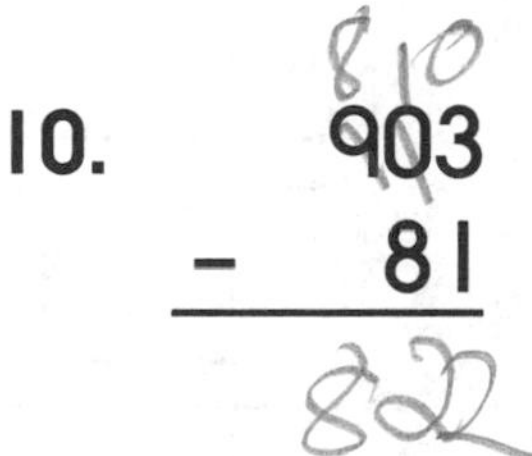

1.		2.		
		3.		
4.	5.			
	6.		7.	
		8.		
9.				
		10.		

Down

2. $612 - 190$

5. $807 - 215$

7. $959 - 269$

8. $349 - 181$

Hit the Slopes!

Directions: Use the prices to find the answers.

Suzy had $17.00. She bought a . How much does she have left?	How much more is the than the ?
How much more is the than the ?	How much more do cost than a ?
Nick had $14.00. He bought . How much does he have left?	Shane had $17.00. He bought . How much does he have left?

Find the Quotient: Drawing

You can draw a picture to find a quotient.

Example: Find the quotient. 8 ÷ 2 = ______

Step 1: Draw 8 dots. Group them into 2s.

Step 2: Count all the groups.

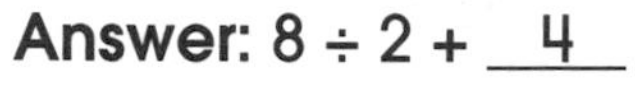

Answer: 8 ÷ 2 + __4__

Directions: Draw a picture to find the quotient.

6 ÷ 2 = ______

8 ÷ 4 = ______

10 ÷ 2 = ______

6 ÷ 3 = ______

12 ÷ 3 = ______

12 ÷ 4 = ______

Fishing Around

Directions: Write how many hundreds (h), tens (t), and ones (o). Then, write the three-digit number.

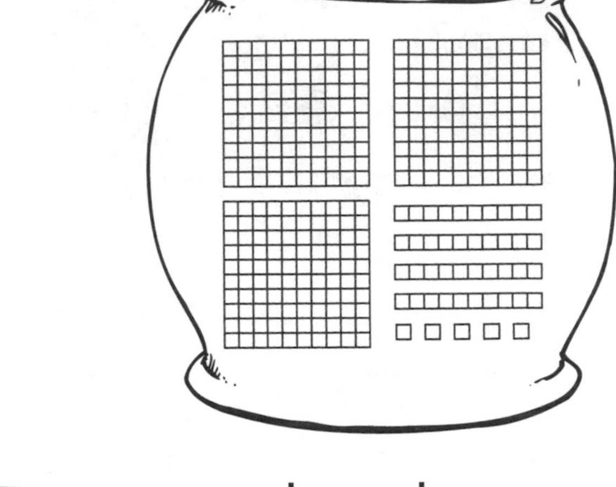

___h ___t ___o

______

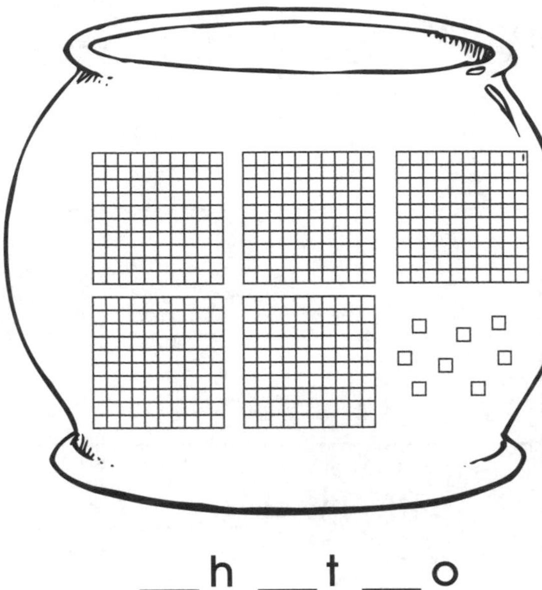

___h ___t ___o

______

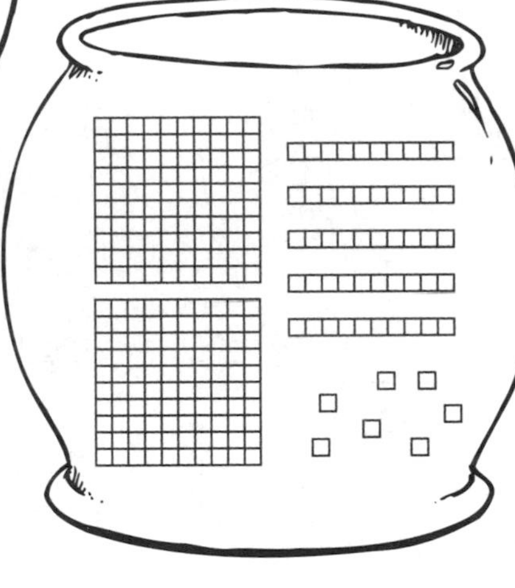

___h ___t ___o

______

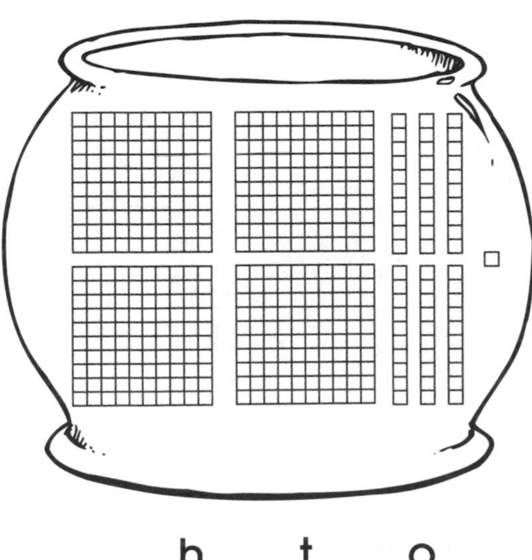

___h ___t ___o

______

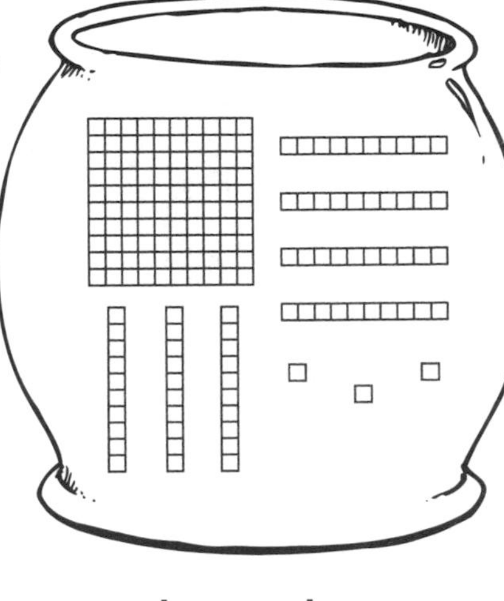

___h ___t ___o

______

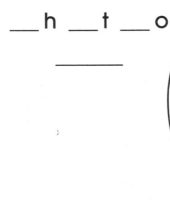

Complete the Circle

Directions: Complete this circle by dividing each of the numbers by 3.

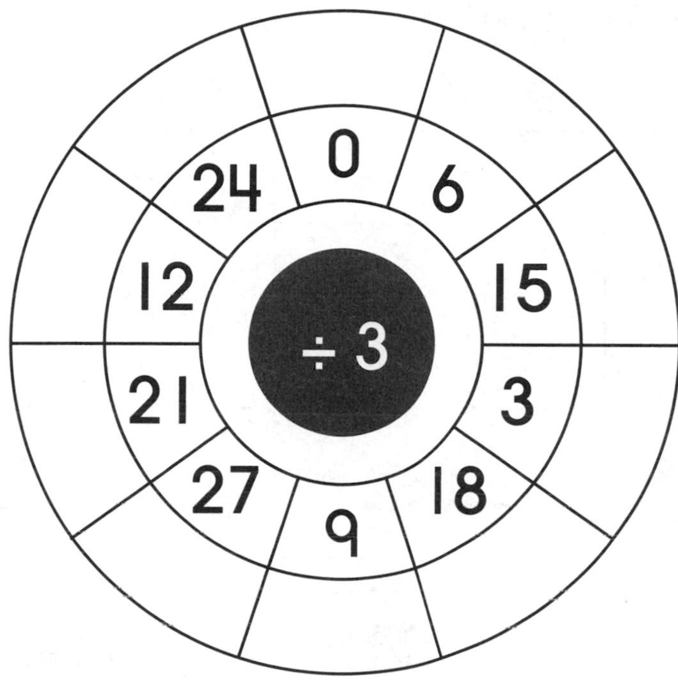

Directions: Complete these facts.

$3\overline{)3}$	$3\overline{)27}$	$3\overline{)9}$	$3\overline{)24}$
$3\overline{)12}$	$3\overline{)6}$	$3\overline{)18}$	$3\overline{)21}$

Graphs

A **graph** is a drawing that shows information about numbers.

Directions: Color the picture. Then, tell how many there are of each object by completing the graph.

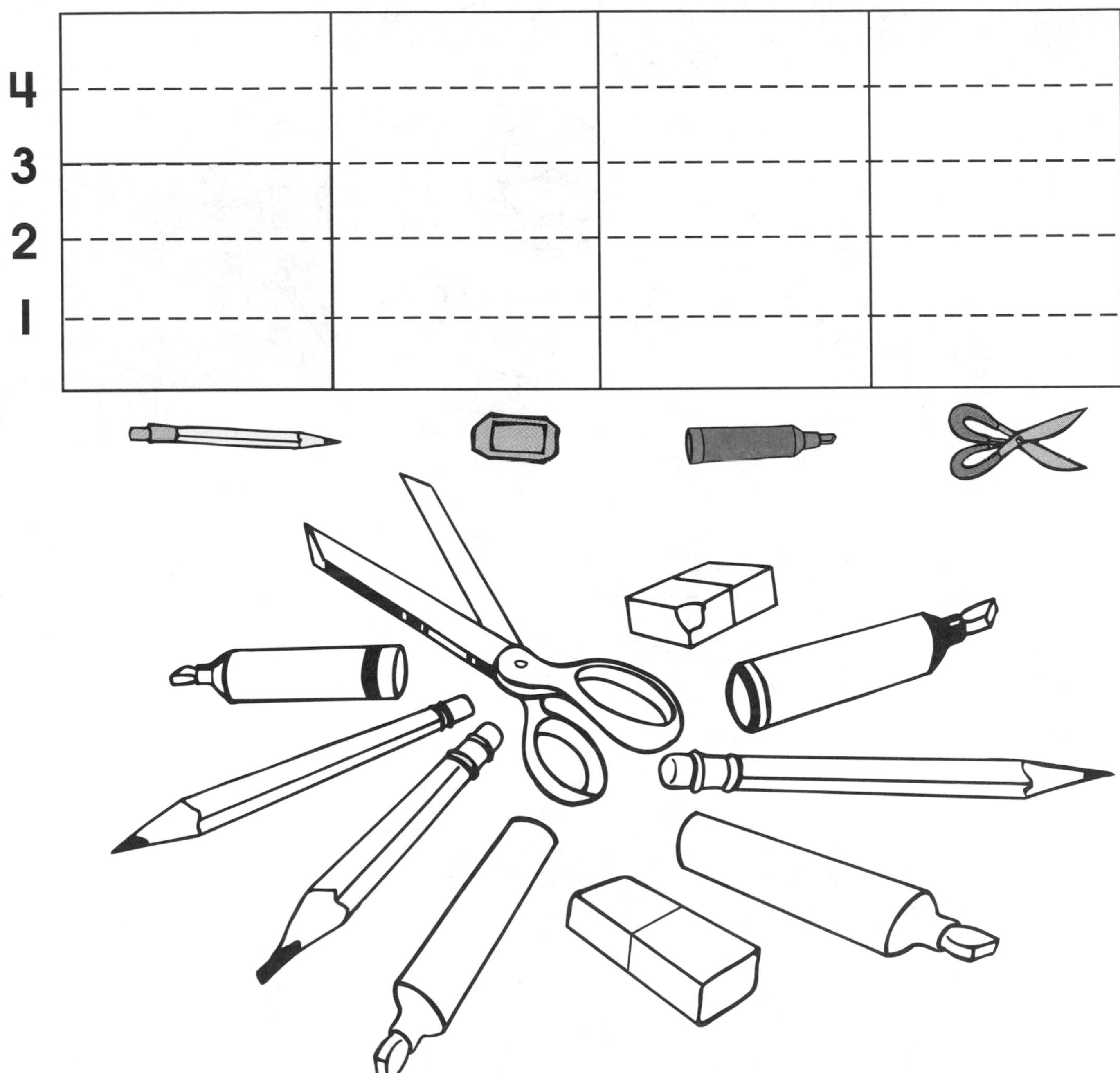

Graphs

Directions: Answer the questions about the graph.

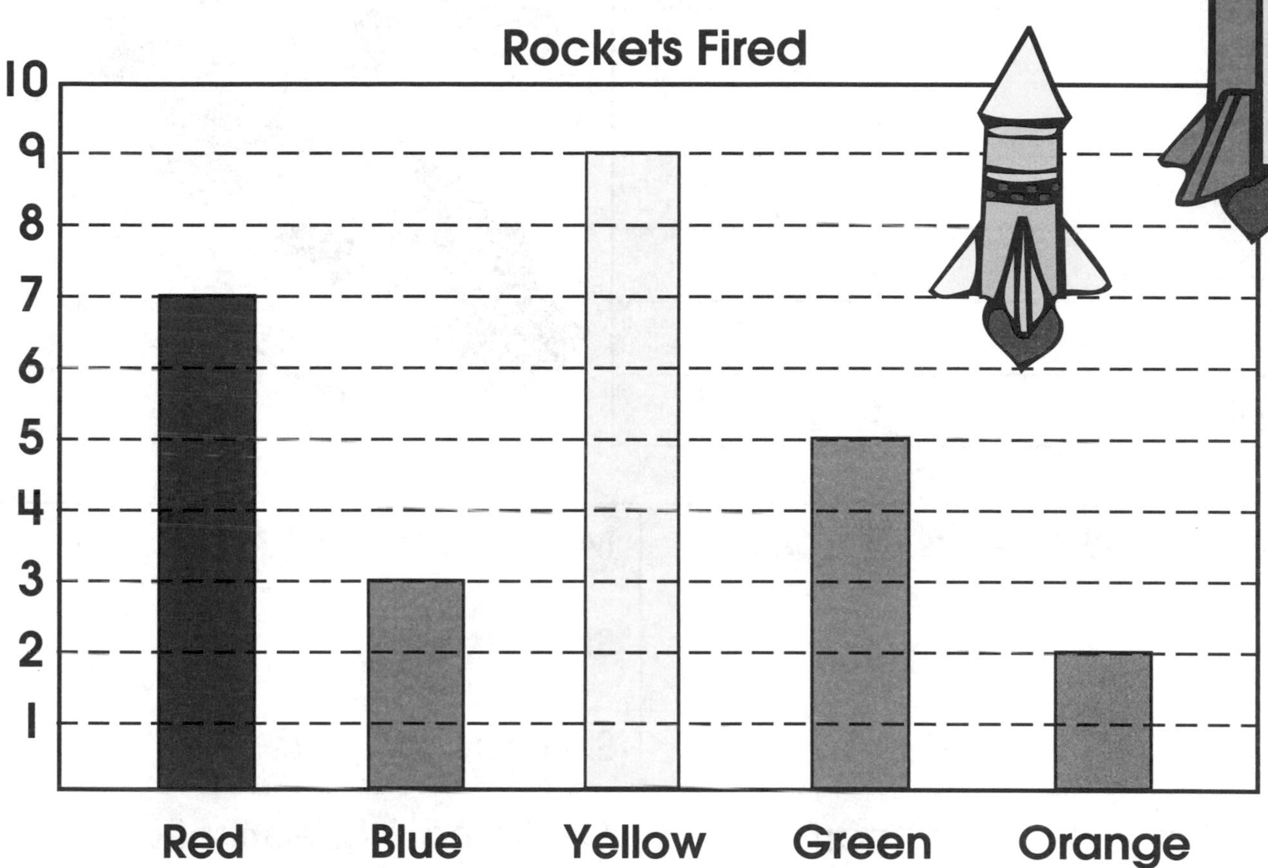

How many rockets did the Red Club fire? ____________

How many rockets did the Green Club fire? ____________

The Yellow Club fired 9 rockets. How many more rockets did it fire than the Blue Club? ____________

How many rockets were fired in all? ____________

Cows and Corn

Directions: Use information from the chart to find the answers.

Cow	Ears of Corn Eaten
Daisy	5
Clara	6
Gertie	5
Flora	7
Ida	4
Maizy	6

Clara had 11 ears of corn. She ate ______ She has ______ left.	Maizy had 12 ears of corn. She ate ______ She has ______ left.
Ida had 11 ears of corn. She ate ______ She has ______ left.	Gertie had 12 ears of corn. She ate ______ She has ______ left.
Flora had 10 ears of corn. She ate ______ She has ______ left.	Daisy had 11 ears of corn. She ate ______ She has ______ left.

Around Town

Directions: Use the fact families to subtract.

$2 + 7 = 9$

$7 + 2 = 9$

$9 - 2 =$ ____

$9 - 7 =$ ____

$3 + 6 = 9$

$6 + 3 = 9$

$9 - 3 =$ ____

$9 - 6 =$ ____

$4 + 5 = 9$

$5 + 4 = 9$

$9 - 5 =$ ____

$9 - 4 =$ ____

$2 + 8 = 10$

$8 + 2 = 10$

$10 - 2 =$ ____

$10 - 8 =$ ____

$3 + 7 = 10$

$7 + 3 = 10$

$10 - 3 =$ ____

$10 - 7 =$ ____

$4 + 6 = 10$

$6 + 4 = 10$

$10 - 4 =$ ____

$10 - 6 =$ ____

$5 + 5 = 10$

$10 - 5 =$ ____

Skipping Through the 10s

Directions: Skip count by 10s. Begin with the number on the first line. Write each number that follows.

0, ____, ____, ____, ____, ____, ____, ____, ____, ____, 100

3, ____, ____, ____, ____, 53, ____, ____, ____, ____, 103

1, ____, ____, ____, ____, ____, ____, ____, 81, ____, ____

8, ____, ____, ____, ____, ____, 68, ____, ____, ____, ____

6, ____, ____, ____, ____, ____, ____, ____, ____, ____, ____

4, ____, ____, ____, ____, ____, ____, ____, ____, ____, 104

2, ____, ____, ____, ____, ____, ____, ____, ____, 92, ____

5, ____, ____, ____, 45, ____, ____, ____, ____, ____, ____

7, ____, ____, ____, ____, ____, ____, 77, ____, ____, ____

9, ____, ____, ____, ____, ____, ____, ____, ____, ____, ____

What is ten more than . . .?

26 ______ 29 ______

44 ______ 77 ______

53 ______ 91 ______

24 ______ 49 ______

66 ______ 35 ______

54 ______ 82 ______

Backward Multiplication

Division problems are like multiplication problems—just turned around. As you solve 8 ÷ 4, think, "how many groups of 4 make 8?" or "what number 'times' 4 is eight?"

2 x 4 = 8, so 8 ÷ 4 = **2**

Directions: Use the pictures to help you solve these division problems.

9 ÷ 3 =

6 ÷ 2 =

16 ÷ 4 =

10 ÷ 5 =

20 ÷ 1 =

18 ÷ 3 =

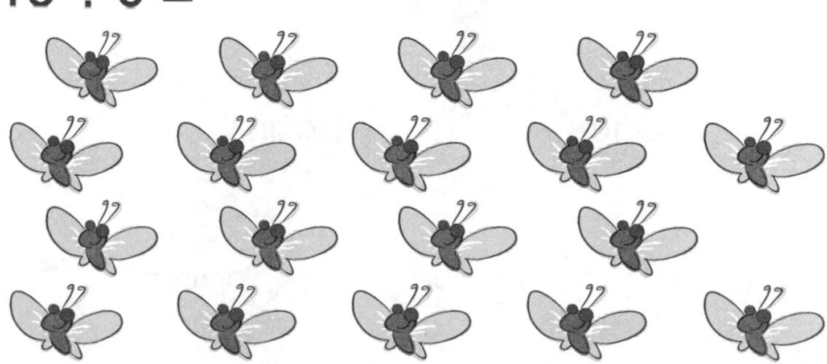

Name ______________________

Measurement: Ounce and Pound

Ounces and **pounds** are measurements of weight in the standard measurement system. The ounce is used to measure the weight of very light objects. The pound is used to measure the weight of heavier objects. 16 ounces = 1 pound

Example:

8 ounces 

15 pounds 

Directions: Decide if you would use ounces or pounds to measure the weight of each object. Circle your answer.

ounce pound

ounce pound

ounce pound

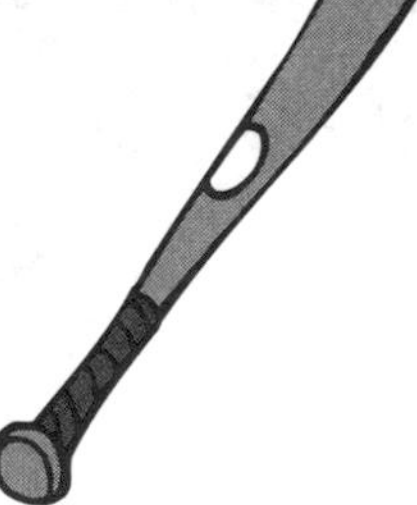

ounce pound

a chair: ounce pound

a table: ounce pound

a shoe: ounce pound

a shirt: ounce pound

Measurement: Inches

An **inch** is a unit of length in the standard measurement system.

Directions: Use a ruler to measure each object to the nearest $\frac{1}{4}$ inch. Write **in.** to stand for inch.

Example:

I in. $2\frac{1}{2}$ in.

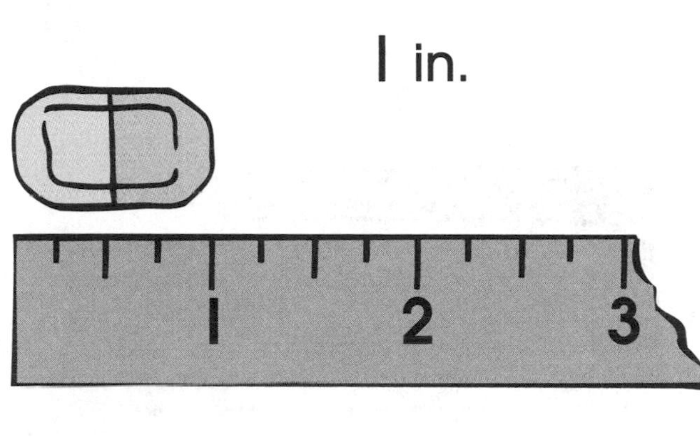

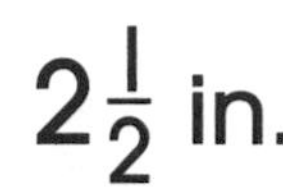

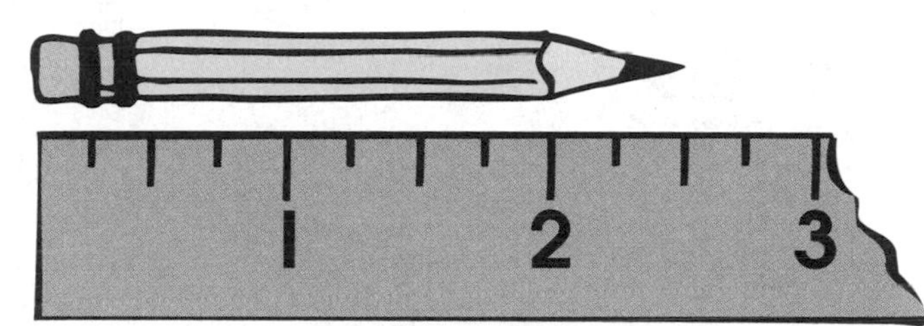

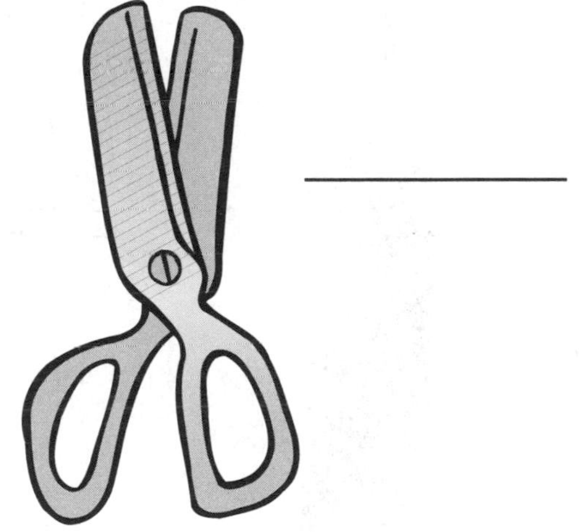

____

____

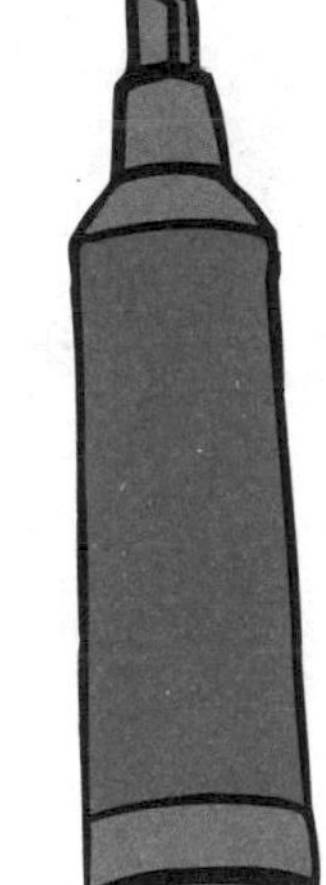

____

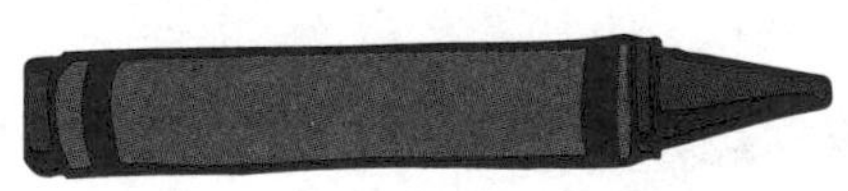

______________ ______________

Measurement: Centimeter

A **centimeter** is a unit of length in the metric system. There are 2.54 centimeters in an inch.

Directions: Use a centimeter ruler to measure each object to the nearest half of a centimeter. Write **cm** to stand for centimeter.

Example:

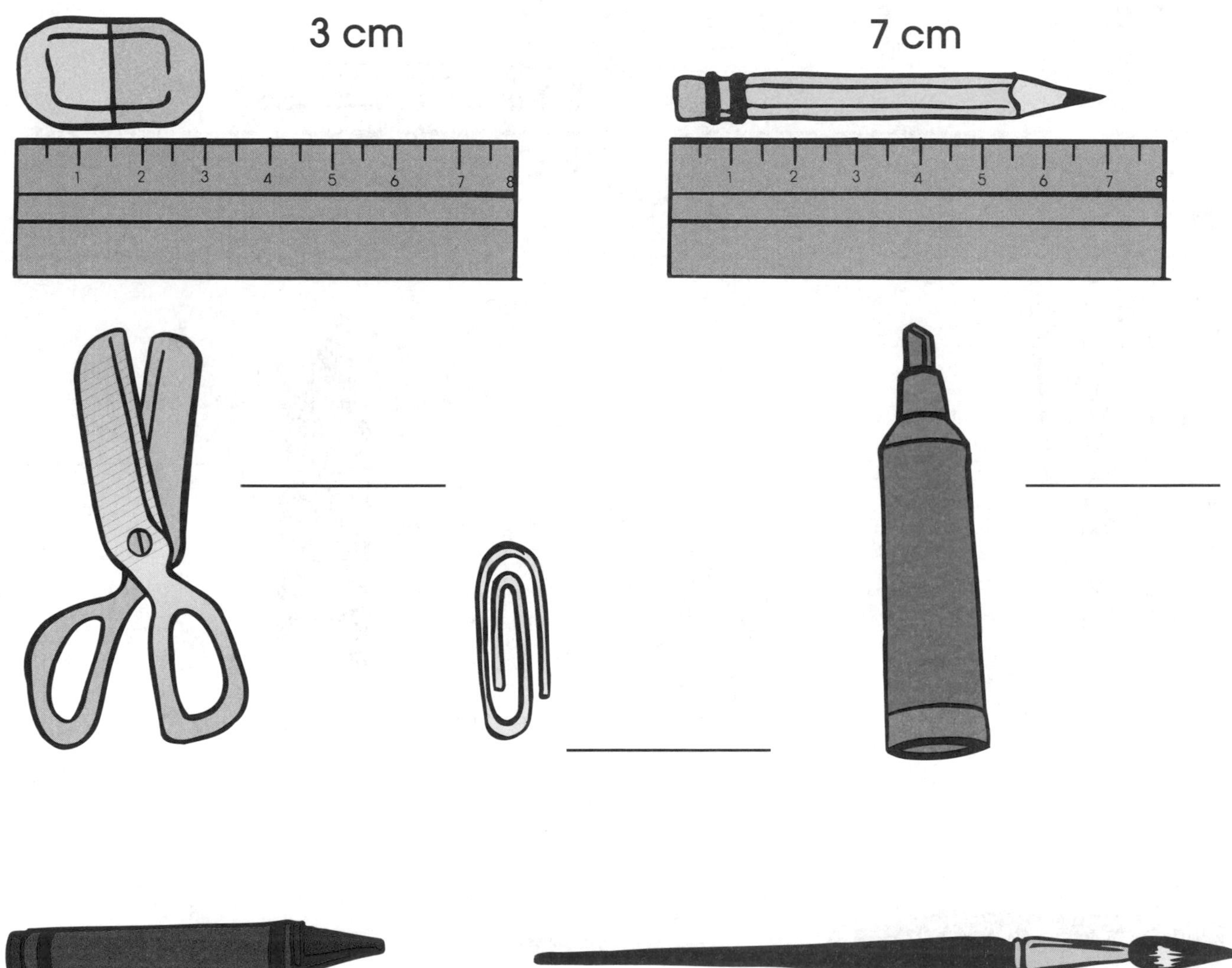

Measurement: Foot, Yard, Mile

Directions: Decide whether you would use feet, yards, or miles to measure each object.

I foot = I2 inches
I yard = 36 inches or 3 feet
I mile = I,760 yards

length of a river ______miles______

height of a tree ____________

width of a room ____________

length of a football field ____________

height of a door ____________

length of a dress ____________

length of a race ____________

height of a basketball hoop ____________

width of a window ____________

distance a plane travels ____________

Directions: Solve the problem.

Tara races Parker in the I00-yard dash. Tara finishes I0 yards in front of Parker. How many feet did Tara finish in front of Parker? ____________

Measurement: Meter and Kilometer

Meters and **kilometers** are units of length in the metric system. A meter is equal to 39.37 inches. A kilometer is equal to about $\frac{5}{8}$ of a mile.

Directions: Decide whether you would use meters or kilometers to measure each object.

I meter = 100 centimeters
I kilometer = 1,000 meters

length of a river kilometers

height of a tree ______________________

width of a room ______________________

length of a football field ______________________

height of a door ______________________

length of a dress ______________________

length of a race ______________________

height of a basketball hoop ______________________

width of a window ______________________

distance a plane travels ______________________

Directions: Solve the problem.

Cassidy races Anya in the 100-meter dash. Cassidy finishes 10 meters in front of Anya. How many centimeters did Cassidy finish in front of Anya? ______________

Miles and Miles

Directions: Use information from the map to find the answers in miles.

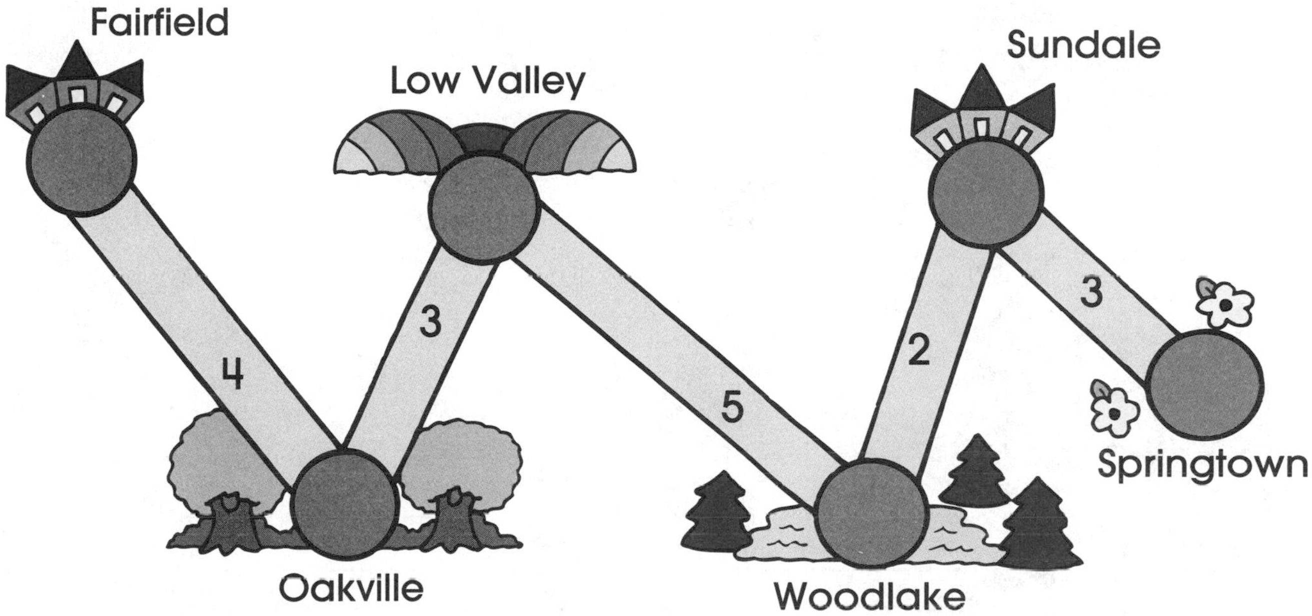

A. How far is it from Fairfield to Low Valley? ☐ + ☐ = ☐

B. How far is it from Woodlake to Springtown? ☐ + ☐ = ☐

C. How far is it from Oakville to Woodlake? ☐ + ☐ = ☐

D. How far is it from Fairfield to Woodlake? ☐ + ☐ + ☐ = ☐

E. How far is it from Low Valley to Springtown? ☐ + ☐ + ☐ = ☐

Fancy Fish

Directions: Connect the dots from 20 to 160. Then, color to finish the picture.

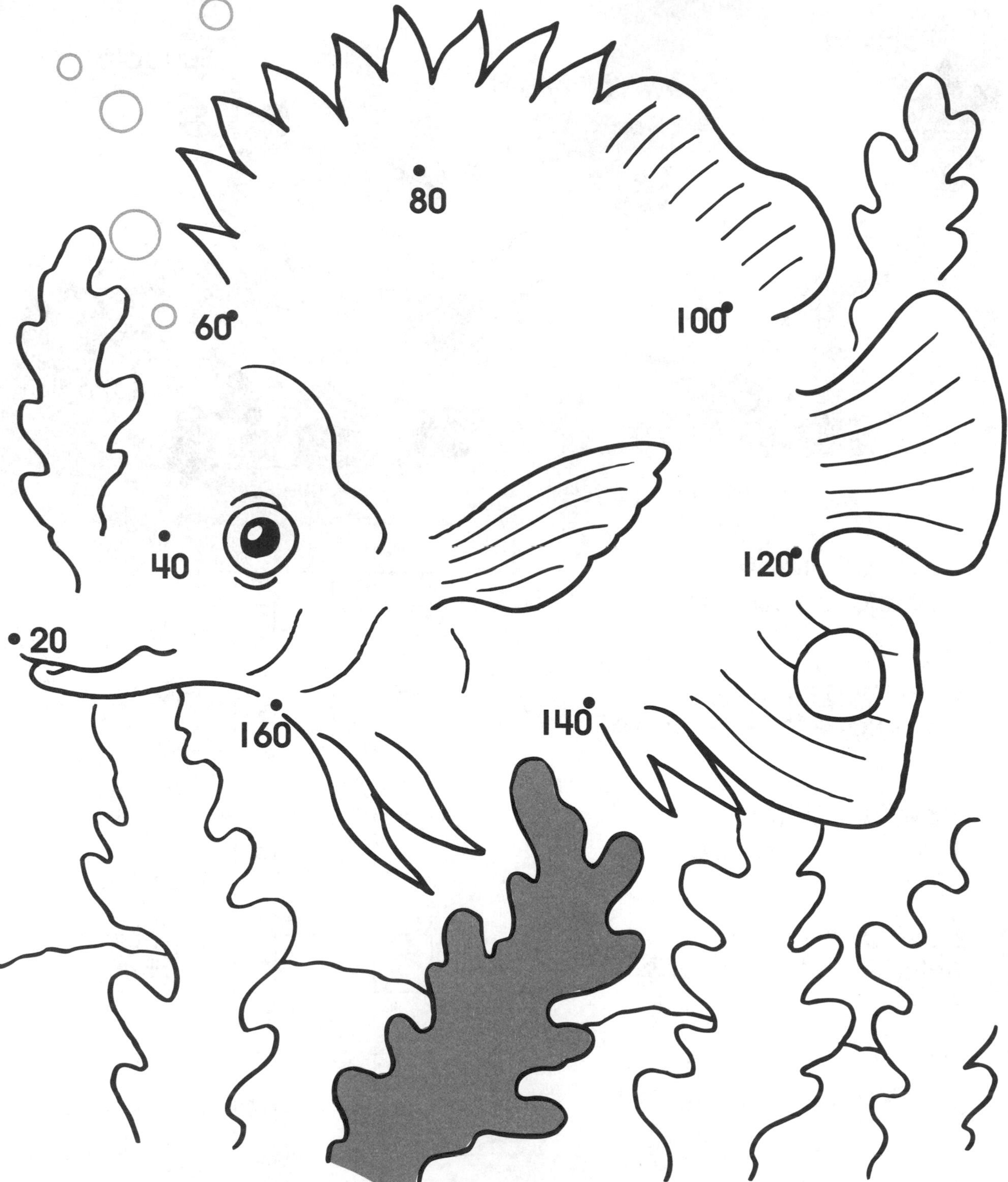

Big-Backed Bugs

Directions: Subtract. Be sure to regroup from the tens place to the ones place.

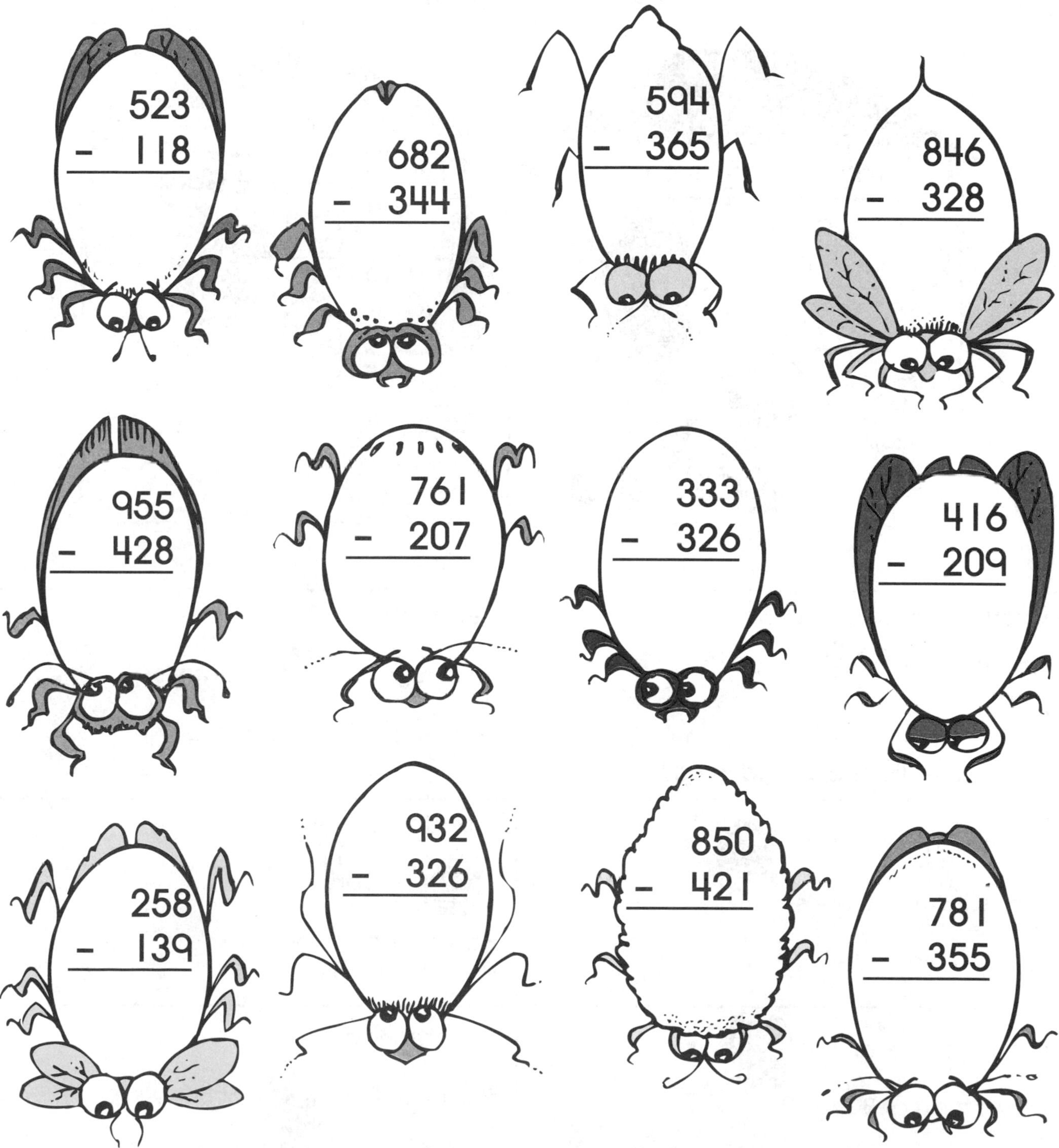

Barry's and Gary's

Directions: Read each story. Use the pictures and price tags below to find the prices. Write and solve an addition or subtraction problem.

Darcy shopped at Gary's. She bought a (glasses) and a (glue). How much did she spend in all?	Devin had $4.33. He bought a (book) at Barry's. How much did he have left?
How much more is a (book) at Barry's than at Gary's?	Brandon bought two (markers) at Gary's. How much did he spend altogether?
How much more is a (backpack) at Gary's than at Barry's?	Hannah had $7.81. She bought a (backpack) at Barry's. How much does she have left?

What a Ball Game!

Directions: Use information from the scoreboard to find the answers.

Runs scored

Inning	1	2	3	4	5	6	7	8	9
Cubs	8	14	14	5	12	6	5	13	11
Reds	13	7	8	13	6	14	12	7	5

Who scored more runs in the 4th inning? ________
How many more?

□
− □
□

Who scored more runs in the 8th inning? ________
How many more?

□
− □
□

Who scored more runs in the 3rd inning? ________
How many more?

□
− □
□

Who scored more runs in the 6th inning? ________
How many more?

□
− □
□

Who scored more runs in the 1st inning? ________
How many more?

□
− □
□

Who scored more runs in the 7th inning? ________
How many more?

□
− □
□

I Spy Something Green

Directions: To find out what I spy, color the boxes with differences of **5**, **6**, or **7**. Then, write the letters from the colored boxes in the blanks, working from left to right.

I spy a ____ ____ ____ ____ ____ ____ ____!

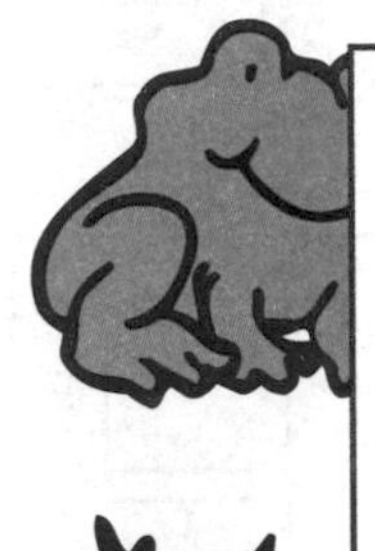

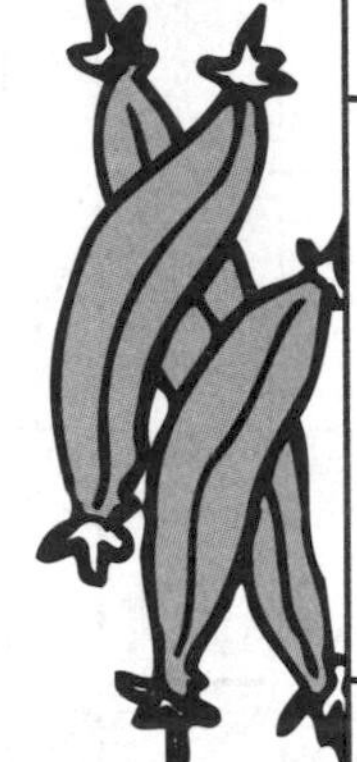

S: $12 - 9$	T: $11 - 4$	L: $12 - 8$	E: $9 - 5$
R: $12 - 7$	F: $10 - 7$	A: $10 - 3$	Q: $11 - 8$
G: $9 - 6$	C: $10 - 4$	T: $11 - 5$	O: $10 - 6$
H: $11 - 7$	M: $8 - 4$	O: $11 - 6$	R: $12 - 5$

Name ____________________

Weather Chart

Directions: Use information from the graph to find the answers.

This Month's Weather

rainy	𝍸 ||
cloudy	𝍸 ||
sunny	𝍸 |||
windy	|||
snowy	||||

How many more days were than ? ______ - ______ = ______	How many more days were than ? ______ - ______ = ______
How many more days were than ? ______ - ______ = ______	How many more days were than ? ______ - ______ = ______
How many more days were than ? ______ - ______ = ______	How many more days were than ? ______ - ______ = ______

Coordinates

Directions: Locate the points on the grid and color in each box.

What animal did you form? ______________________________

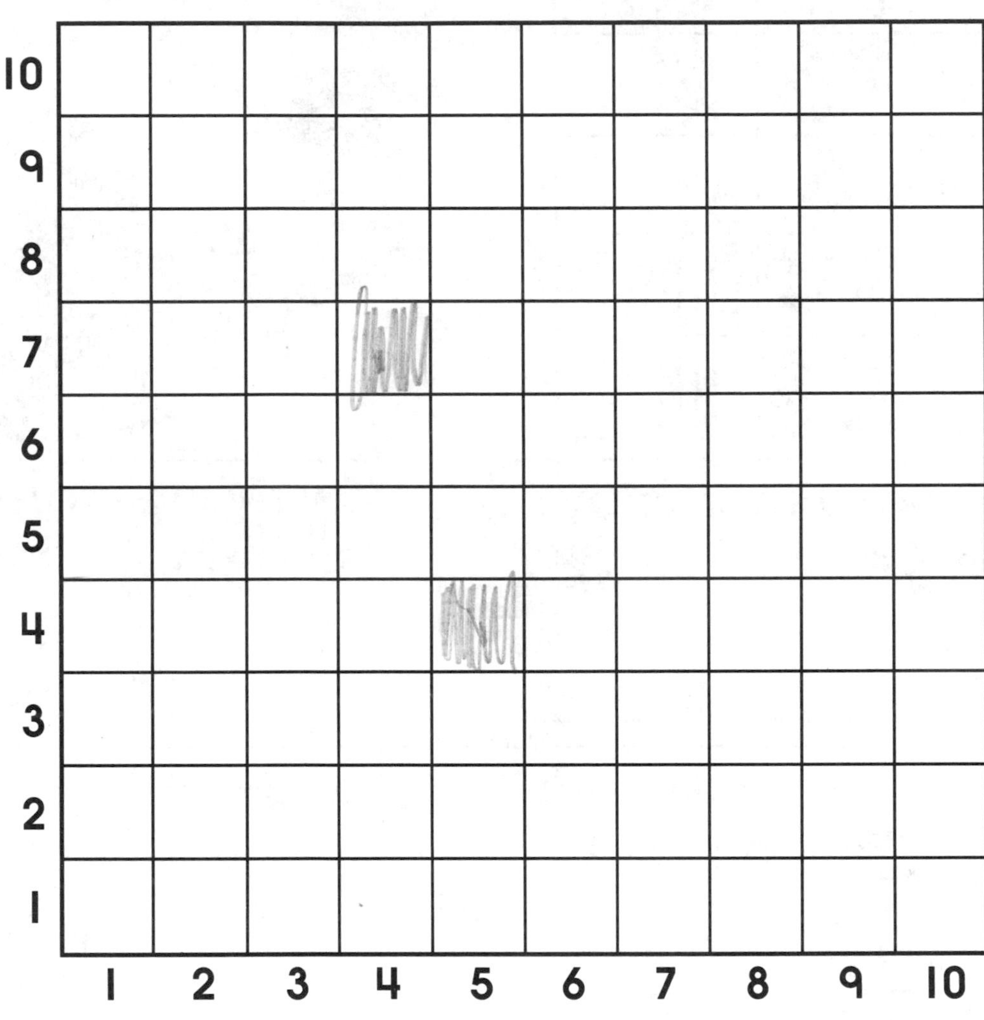

(across, up)

(4, 7)	(4, 1)	(7, 1)	(3, 5)	(2, 8)	(8, 6)	(4, 8)	(3, 7)
(5, 4)	(6, 5)	(5, 5)	(6, 6)	(7, 3)	(8, 5)	(10, 5)	(4, 3)
(7, 6)	(4, 6)	(1, 8)	(6, 4)	(7, 2)	(4, 5)	(9, 6)	(4, 9)
(3, 6)	(7, 5)	(5, 6)	(4, 2)	(4, 4)	(7, 4)	(2, 7)	(3, 8)

Time to Add

Directions: Add. Then, to answer the question, write the circled numbers in order.

How many minutes are in a day? ____ , ____ ____ ____

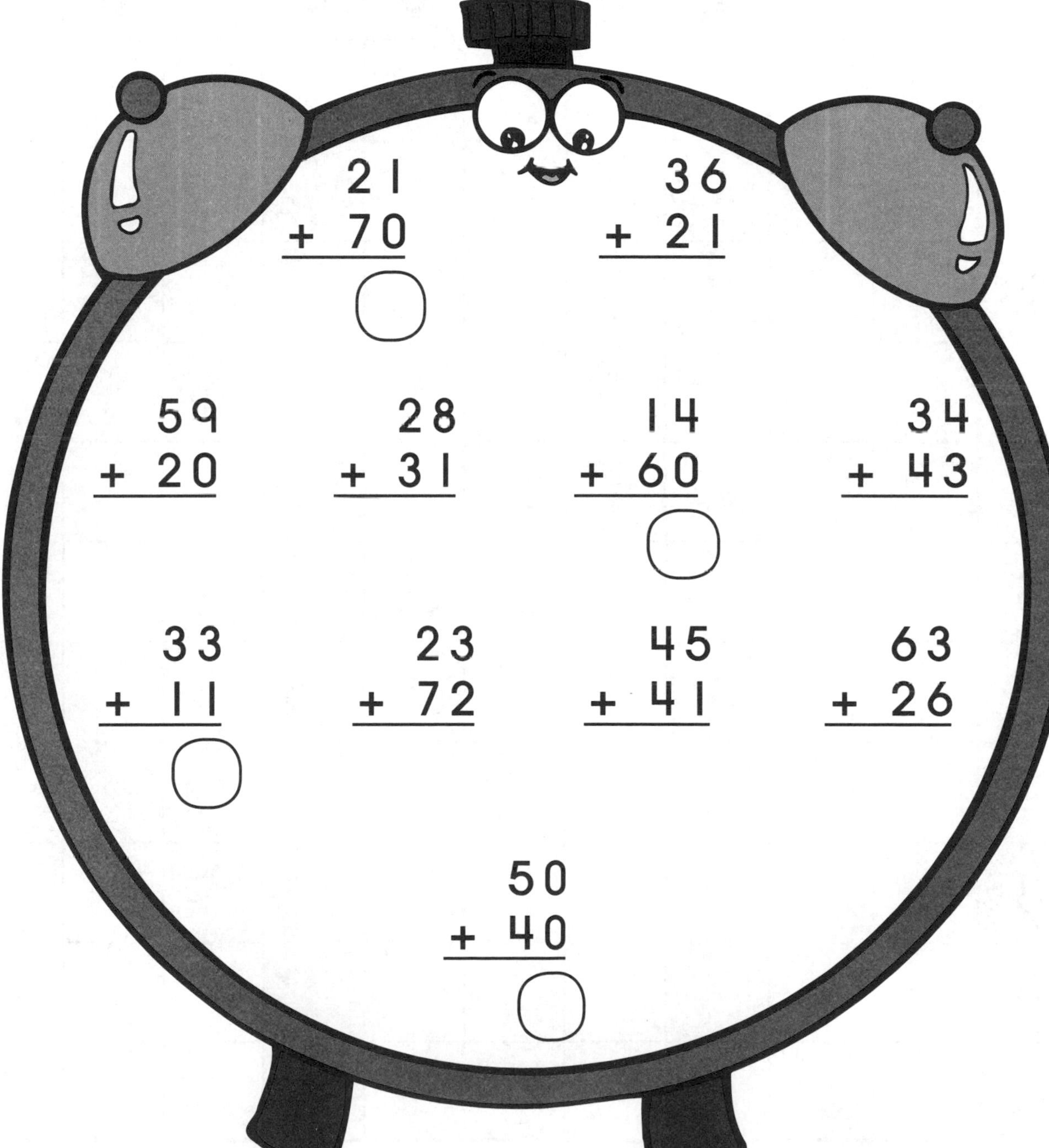

Multiplication Table

Directions: Complete the multiplication table.

×	0	1	2	3	4	5	6	7	8	9	10
0	0										
1		1									
2			4								
3				9							
4					16						
5						25					
6							36				
7								49			
8									64		
9										81	
10											100

Multiplication Challenge

Directions: Solve each problem.

Delaina saw 5 kites yesterday.

She saw 8 times more kites today.

How many kites did she see today?

$\square \times \square = \square\square$

Byron had 2 toys yesterday.

Today he has 7 times more toys.

How many toys does Byron have today?

$\square \times \square = \square\square$

Breannah has 2 children.

Her sister has 2 times as many children.

How many children does her sister have?

$\square \times \square = \square$

Yesterday, Katie had 2 bottles.

Today, she has 3 times as many bottles.

How many bottles does Katie have today?

$\square \times \square = \square$

Division Challenge

Directions: Solve each problem.

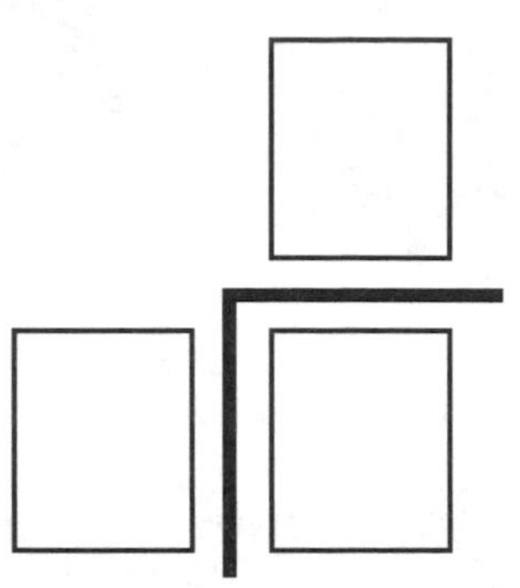

There are 12 students.

They split into 4 equal groups.

How many students are in each group?

There are 9 cars.

They park in 3 different lots.

How many cars are in each lot?

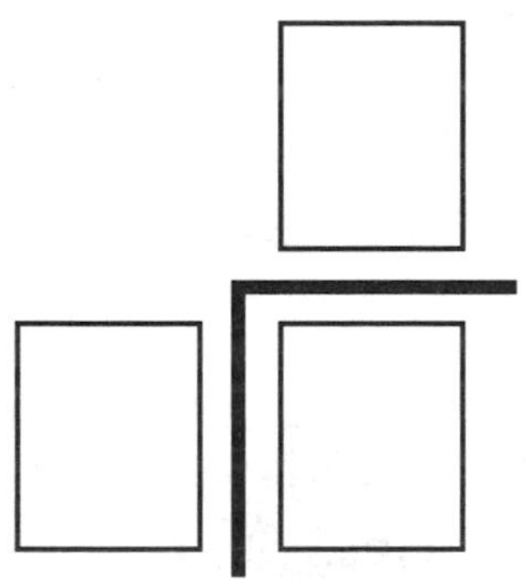

There are 10 tourists.

They split into 2 equal groups.

How many tourists are in each group?

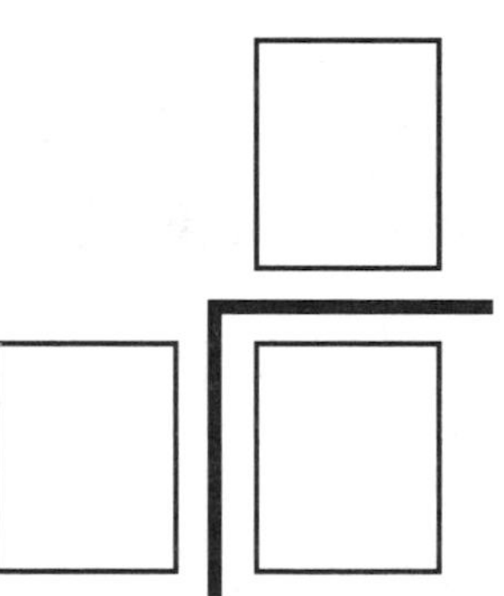

There are 6 runners.

They run in groups of 2 runners.

How many groups are there?

Roman Numerals

Another way to write numbers is to use Roman numerals.

I	1	VII	7
II	2	VIII	8
III	3	IX	9
IV	4	X	10
V	5	XI	11
VI	6	XII	12

Directions: Fill in the Roman numerals on the watch.

What time is it on the watch?

____________ o'clock

Roman Numerals

I	1	VII	7
II	2	VIII	8
III	3	IX	9
IV	4	X	10
V	5	XI	11
VI	6	XII	12

Directions: Write the number.

V	____	VII	____
X	____	IX	____
II	____	XII	____

Directions: Write the Roman numeral.

4	____	5	____
10	____	8	____
6	____	3	____

Counting to 100

Directions: Skip count to 100.

By twos:

		6	8				16			22			
30							44						56
				66						78			
							100						

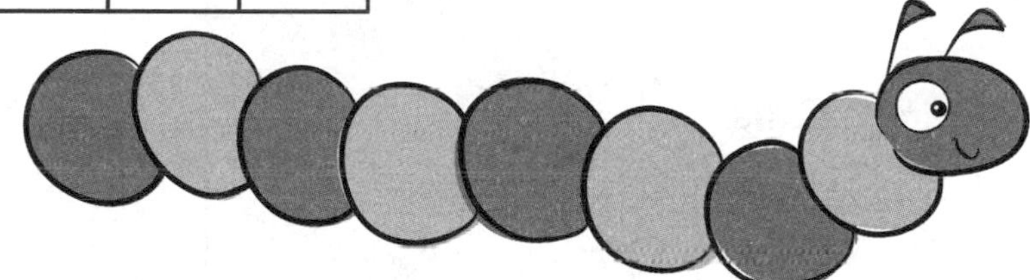

By threes:

3	6					21						39	
				57						75			
	90				102								

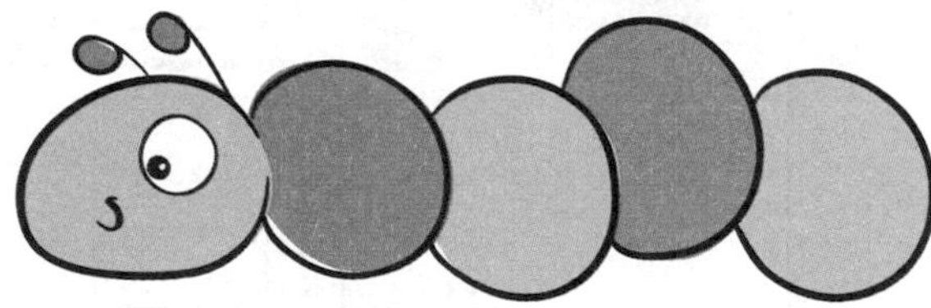

By fours:

4	8								40				
60							88			100			

On another sheet of paper, count by fives to 100.
Then, count by sixes.

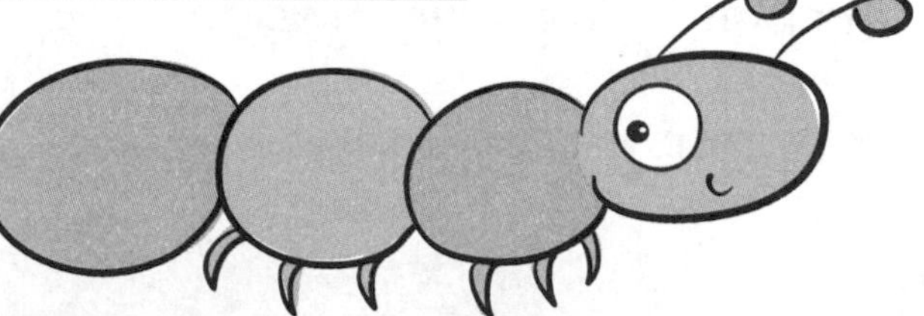

Division Challenge

Directions: Solve each problem.

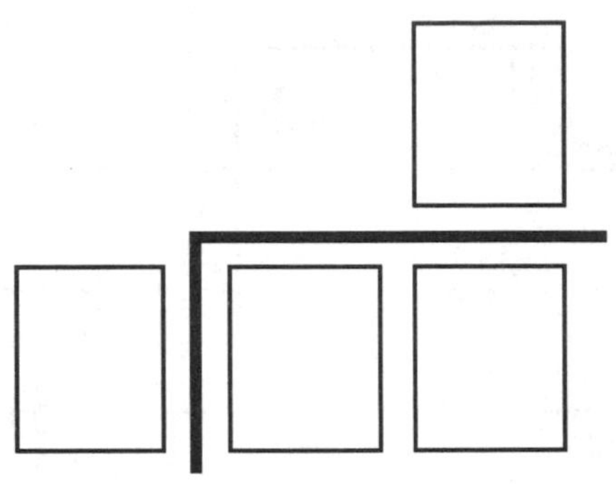

There are 64 chairs.

They are in 8 rows.

How many chairs are in each row?

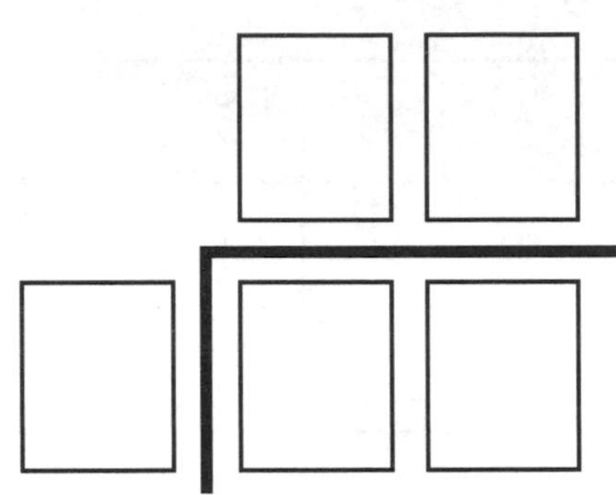

Sierra has 28 balloons.

She gives each friend 2 balloons.

How many friends are there?

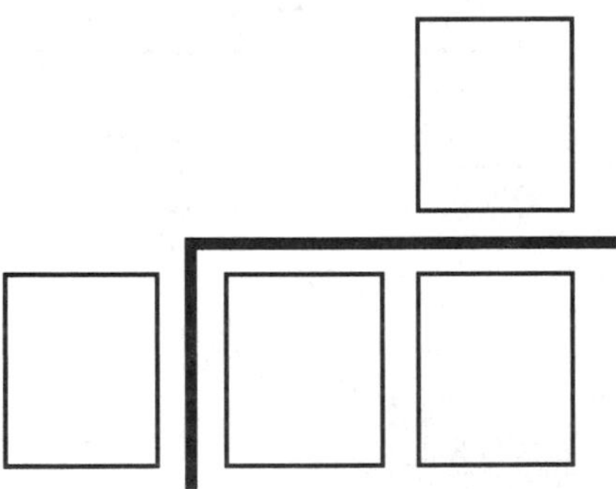

George has 18 birds.

He puts 2 birds in each cage.

How many cages does he have?

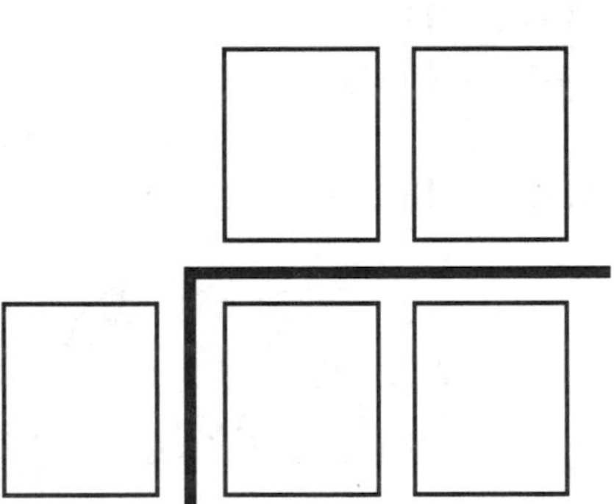

Isabel has 38 apples.

She puts 2 in each bag.

How many bags does she have?

Rhyme Time

Directions: Use the code to find the total value of each word.

a	b	c	d	e	f	g	h	i	j	k	l	m
4	2	3	4	5	7	2	9	3	8	5	6	6
n	o	p	q	r	s	t	u	v	w	x	y	z
4	4	4	6	5	4	5	1	2	8	3	9	1

cat	rat
____ + ____ + ____ = ____	____ + ____ + ____ = ____
hat	**fat**
____ + ____ + ____ = ____	____ + ____ + ____ = ____
mat	**sat**
____ + ____ + ____ = ____	____ + ____ + ____ = ____

The Great Puzzle Race

Directions: Which team will put its puzzle together first? Find each difference, working from left to right. Shade the answer on the puzzle. The first team to completely cover its puzzle is the winner!

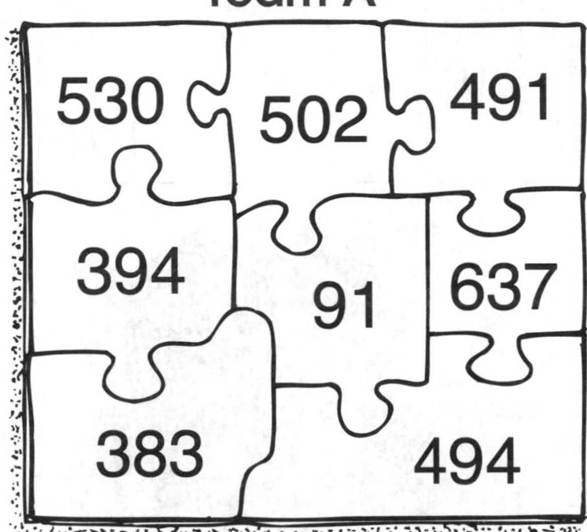

Team B

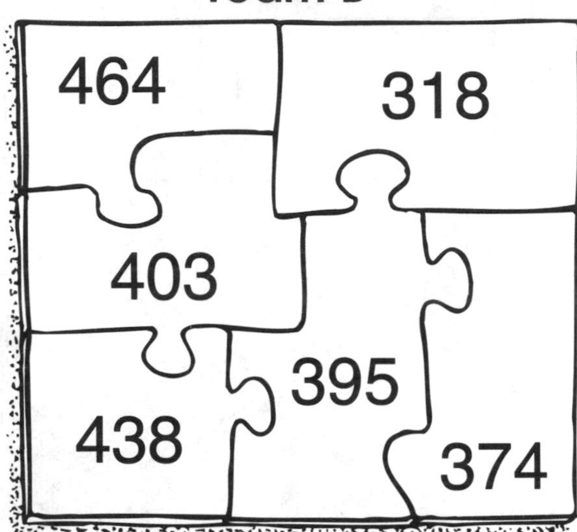

786 − 392	874 − 383	686 − 291	567 − 129
281 − 190	943 − 306	518 − 135	859 − 485
631 − 228	826 − 324	366 − 48	792 − 328

What's the Weather?

Directions: Use the fact families to subtract.

1 + 6 = 7

6 + 1 = 7

7 – 1 = ____

7 – 6 = ____

2 + 5 = 7

5 + 2 = 7

7 – 2 = ____

7 – 5 = ____

3 + 4 = 7

4 + 3 = 7

7 – 4 = ____

7 – 3 = ____

2 + 6 = 8

6 + 2 = 8

8 – 2 = ____

8 – 6 = ____

3 + 5 = 8

5 + 3 = 8

8 – 3 = ____

8 – 5 = ____

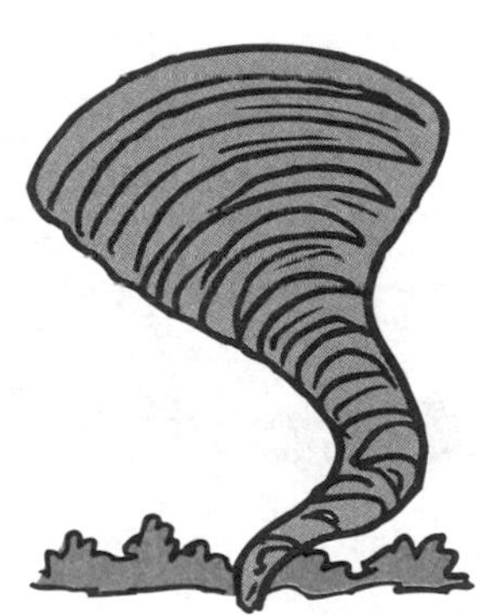

4 + 4 = 8

8 – 4 = ____

Getting Around Town

Directions: Use information from the graph to find the answers.

How People Get Around

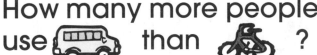

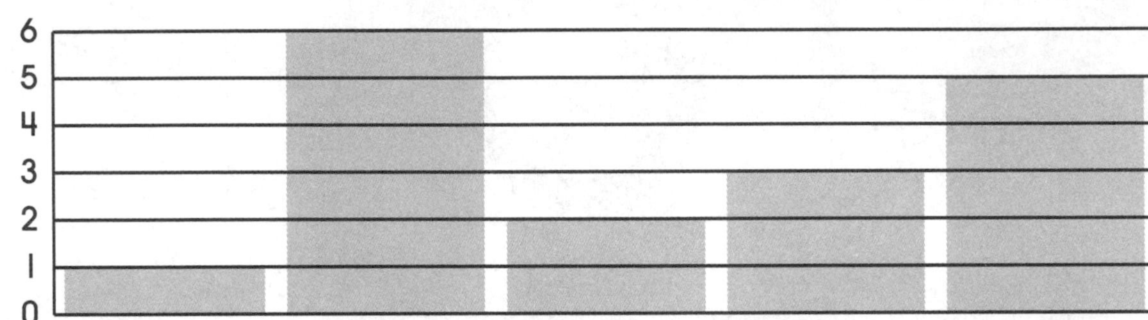

How many more people use  (car) than (train)? ______ – ______ = ______ 	How many more people use  (bus) than (plane)? ______ – ______ = ______ 
How many more people use  (car) than (plane)? ______ – ______ = ______ 	How many more people use  (bike) than (train)? ______ – ______ = ______ 
How many more people use  (bus) than (bike)? ______ – ______ = ______ 	How many more people use  (car) than (bus)? ______ – ______ = ______ 

Time: 5, 15, 30, and 60-Minute Intervals

Directions: Write the time shown on each clock.

Example:

7:15

7:00

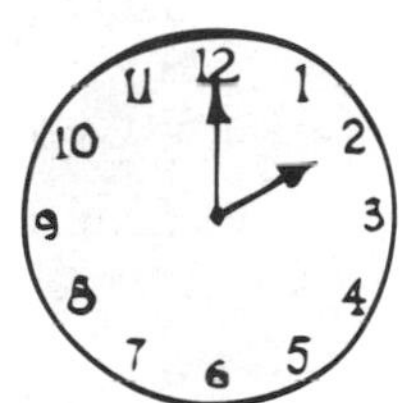

Time: A.M. and P.M.

In telling time, the hours between 12:00 midnight and 12:00 noon are A.M. hours. The hours between 12:00 noon and 12:00 midnight are P.M. hours.

Directions: Draw a line between the times that are the same.

Example:

7:30 in the morning — 7:30 A.M.
7:30 in the morning — half-past seven A.M.
7:30 in the morning — seven thirty in the morning

9:00 in the evening - - - 9:00 P.M.
9:00 in the evening - - - nine o'clock at night

six o'clock in the evening	8:00 A.M.
3:30 A.M.	six o'clock in the morning
4:15 P.M.	6:00 P.M.
eight o'clock in the morning	eleven o'clock in the evening
quarter past five in the evening	three thirty in the morning
11:00 P.M.	four fifteen in the evening
6:00 A.M.	5:15 P.M.

Time: Minutes

A **minute** is a measurement of time. There are 60 seconds in a minute and 60 minutes in an hour.

Directions: Write the time shown on each clock.

Example:

Each mark is one minute.
The big hand is at mark number 6.

Write: 5:06
Read: six minutes after five

____

____

____

____

____

____

____

____

____

____

____

____

Time: Addition

Directions: Add the hours and minutes together.
(Remember, 1 hour equals 60 minutes.)

Example:

```
   2 hours  10 minutes
+  1 hour   50 minutes
   3 hours (60 minutes)
            (1 hour)
   4 hours
```

```
   4 hours  20 minutes
+  2 hours  10 minutes
   6 hours  30 minutes
```

```
   9 hours        1 hour        6 hours
+  2 hours     +  5 hours    +  3 hours
```

```
   6 hours  15 minutes      10 hours  30 minutes       3 hours  40 minutes
+  1 hour   15 minutes   +   1 hour   10 minutes    +  8 hours  20 minutes
```

```
  11 hours  15 minutes       4 hours  15 minutes       7 hours  10 minutes
+  1 hour   30 minutes   +   5 hours  45 minutes    +  1 hour   30 minutes
```

Time: Subtraction

Directions: Subtract the hours and minutes.
(Remember, 1 hour equals 60 minutes.)
Regroup from the hours if you need to.

Example:

```
 5        70
 6 hours  10 minutes
-2 hours  30 minutes
 3 hours  40 minutes
```

12 hours - 2 hours	5 hours - 3 hours	2 hours - 1 hour
5 hours 30 minutes - 2 hours 15 minutes	9 hours 45 minutes - 3 hours 15 minutes	11 hours 50 minutes - 4 hours 35 minutes
12 hours - 6 hours 30 minutes	7 hours 15 minutes - 5 hours 30 minutes	8 hours 10 minutes - 4 hours 40 minutes

Time to Multiply

Directions: Complete the table. Try to do it in less than 3 minutes.

×	0	1	2	3	4	5	6	7	8	9
0	0									
1										
2			4							
3										
4										
5						25				
6										
7										
8										
9										

Multiplication Challenge

Directions: Solve each problem.

Andres had 39 cards yesterday.

Today, he got 2 times more cards. ×

How many cards does he have today?

Bobbi saw 29 bees yesterday.

Today, she saw 8 times more bees. ×

How many bees are there today?

Taron hit 11 home runs last year.

He hit 5 times that many this year. ×

How many home runs did he hit this year?

Last year, Ana won 32 games.

She won 2 times that many this year. ×

How many games did she win this year?

Complete the Circle

Directions: Complete this circle by dividing each of the numbers by 5. Then, divide the problems below.

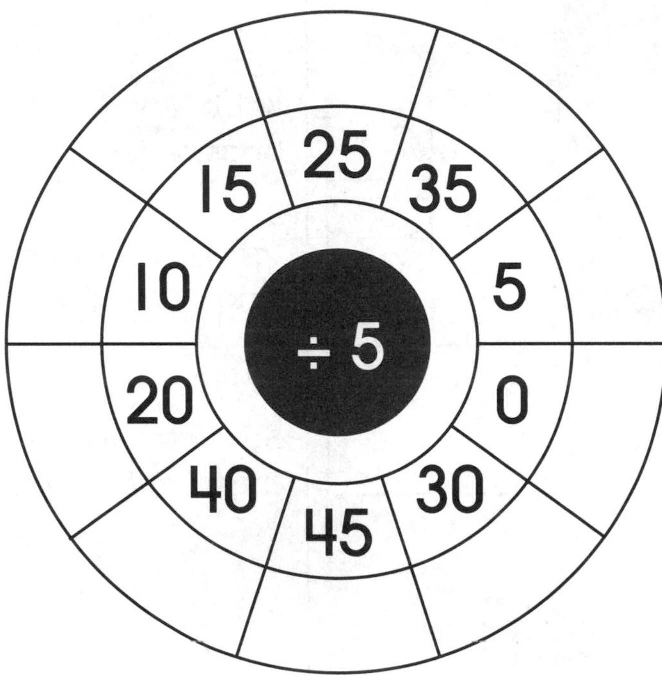

$5\overline{)15}$ $5\overline{)25}$ $5\overline{)0}$ $5\overline{)20}$ $5\overline{)40}$

$5\overline{)10}$ $5\overline{)35}$ $5\overline{)5}$ $5\overline{)30}$ $5\overline{)45}$

Division Challenge

Directions: Solve each problem.

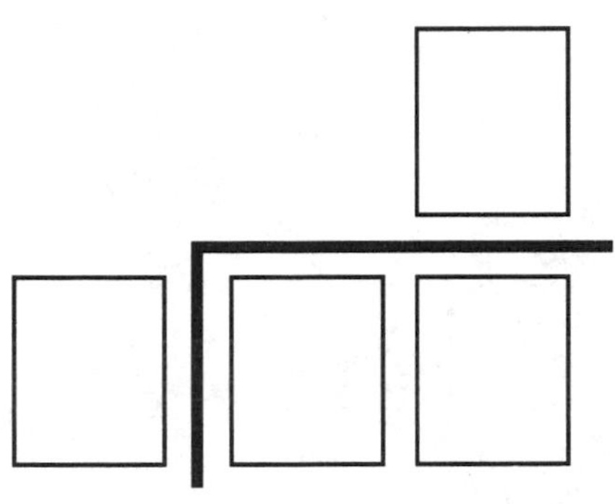

Vince read 35 pages in his book.

It took him 7 days.

How many pages did he read each day?

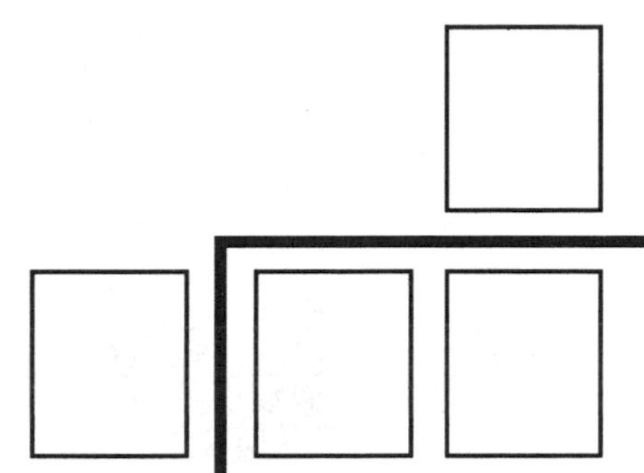

Tasha worked 18 hours.

She worked for 2 days.

How many hours did she work each day?

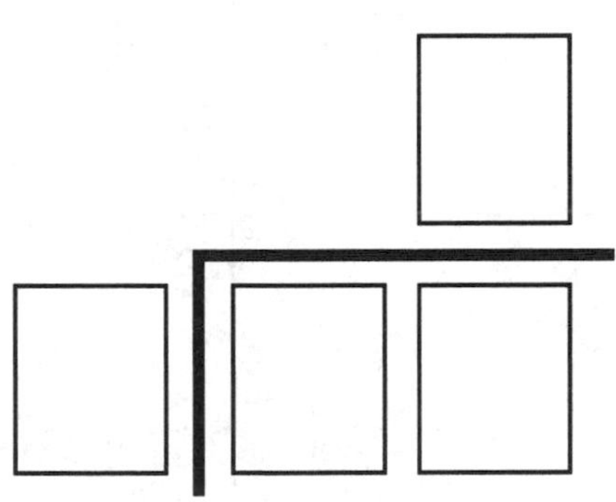

Emory bought 54 cards.

They came in 6 boxes.

How many cards are in each box?

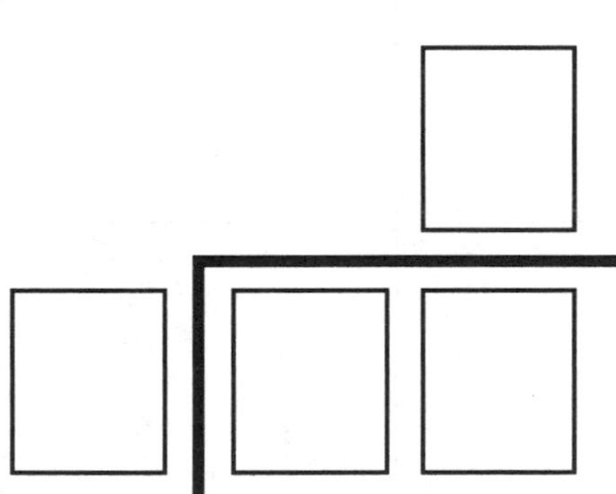

A basketball game is 32 minutes long.

The game is split in 4 parts.

How many minutes long is each part?

Counting Sheep

Directions: Add. Use the sums to answer the riddle.

Why did the sheep get a traffic ticket?

___ ___ ___
892 470 624

___ ___ ___ ___ ___ ___
681 684 936 785 712 389

___   ___ ___ ___
684   565 982 565

___ ___ ___ ___ !
577 913 624 712

M	I	U	R	E
263 + 418	304 + 481	782 + 131	517 + 107	380 + 185
K	**F**	**T**	**A**	**S**
463 + 473	806 + 86	283 + 294	435 + 249	137 + 645
N	**W**	**O**	**G**	**Y**
292 + 420	641 + 341	349 + 121	194 + 195	111 + 222

Wriggling Division

Directions: Solve the problems.

Money: Coins and Dollars

dollar = 100¢ or $1.00

penny = 1¢ or $.01

nickel = 5¢ or $.05

dime = 10¢ or $.10

quarter = 25¢ or $.25

half-dollar= 50¢ or $.50

Directions: Write the amount for each group of money shown. Use a dollar sign and decimal point. The first one is done for you.

$.07

____

____

____

____

____

Money: Five-Dollar Bill and Ten-Dollar Bill

Directions: Write the amount for each group of money shown. Use a dollar sign and decimal point. The first one is done for you.

Five-dollar bill =
5 one-dollar bills

Ten-dollar bill =
2 five-dollar bills or
10 one-dollar bills

$15.00

____

____

____

7 one-dollar bills, 2 quarters ______________

2 five-dollar bills, 3 one-dollar bills, half-dollar ______________

3 ten-dollar bills, 1 five-dollar bill, 3 quarters ______________

Money: Counting Challenge

Directions: Subtract the money using decimals to show how much change a person would receive in each of the following.

Example:

Bill had 3 dollars.	$3.00
He bought a baseball for $2.83.	-$2.83
How much change did he receive?	$ .17

Paid 2 dollars.

____

Paid 1 dollar.

83¢

____

Paid 5 dollars.

____

Paid 10 dollars.

____

Paid 4 dollars.

____

Paid 7 dollars.

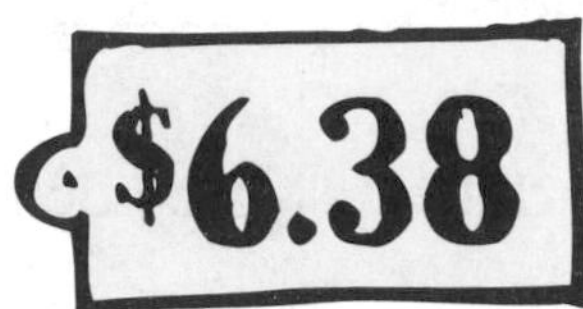

____

Money: Comparing

Directions: Compare the amount of money in the left column with the price of the object in the right column. Is the amount of money in the left column enough to purchase the object in the right column? Circle **yes** or **no**.

Example:

Alice has 2 dollars. She wants to buy a jump rope for $1.75.
Does she have enough money?

Yes No

Yes No

Yes No

I Spy Something Red

Directions: To find out what I spy, color the boxes with differences of **1**, **2**, or **3**. Then, write the letters from the colored boxes in the blanks, working from left to right.

I spy a _____ _____ _____ _____ _____ _____ _____!

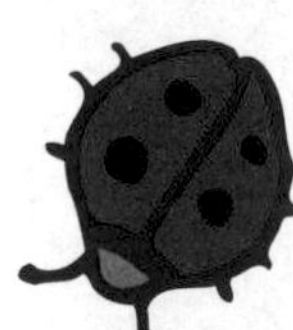

6 K - 2	4 C - 3	5 A - 3	6 T - 1
5 B - 2	4 O - 2	5 L - 1	6 R - 2
4 S - 0	6 U - 0	3 O - 2	5 W - 1
5 M - 0	4 B - 0	6 S - 3	5 E - 4

The Shoe Store

Directions: Use the prices to find the answers.

Dan buys [sneakers] and [boots]. How much does he spend in all? $☐ + $☐ = $☐	Anna buys [dress shoes] and [high heels]. How much does she spend in all? $☐ + $☐ = $☐
David buys [sneakers] and [dress shoes]. How much does he spend in all? $☐ + $☐ = $☐	Rachel buys [high heels] and [boots]. How much does she spend in all? $☐ + $☐ = $☐
Lee buys [high heels] and [sneakers]. How much does she spend in all? $☐ + $☐ = $☐	Josie buys [ballet slippers] and [dress shoes]. How much does she spend in all? $☐ + $☐ = $☐

Division Challenge

Directions: Solve each problem.

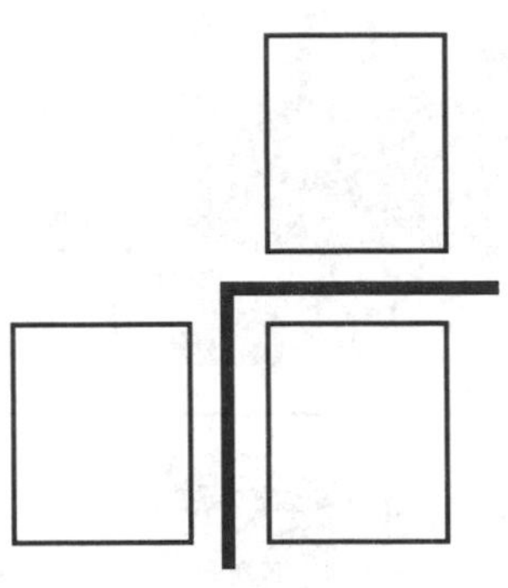

April hit 6 home runs.

She hit in 3 games.

How many home runs did she hit in each game?

Felipe has 8 pencils.

He divides them equally among 2 friends.

How many pencils does each friend have?

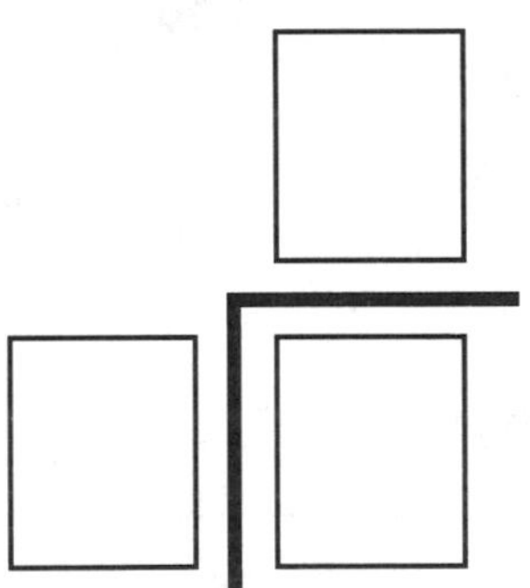

Logan has 2 presents.

He gives them to 2 friends.

How many presents did each friend get?

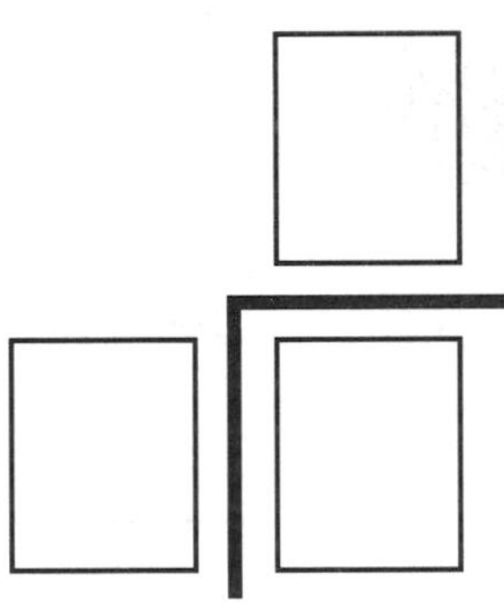

Chrissie sees 8 birds.

They fly away in 2 equal groups.

How many birds were in each group?

Division Ahoy!

Directions: Divide. Draw a line from the boat to the sail with the correct answer.

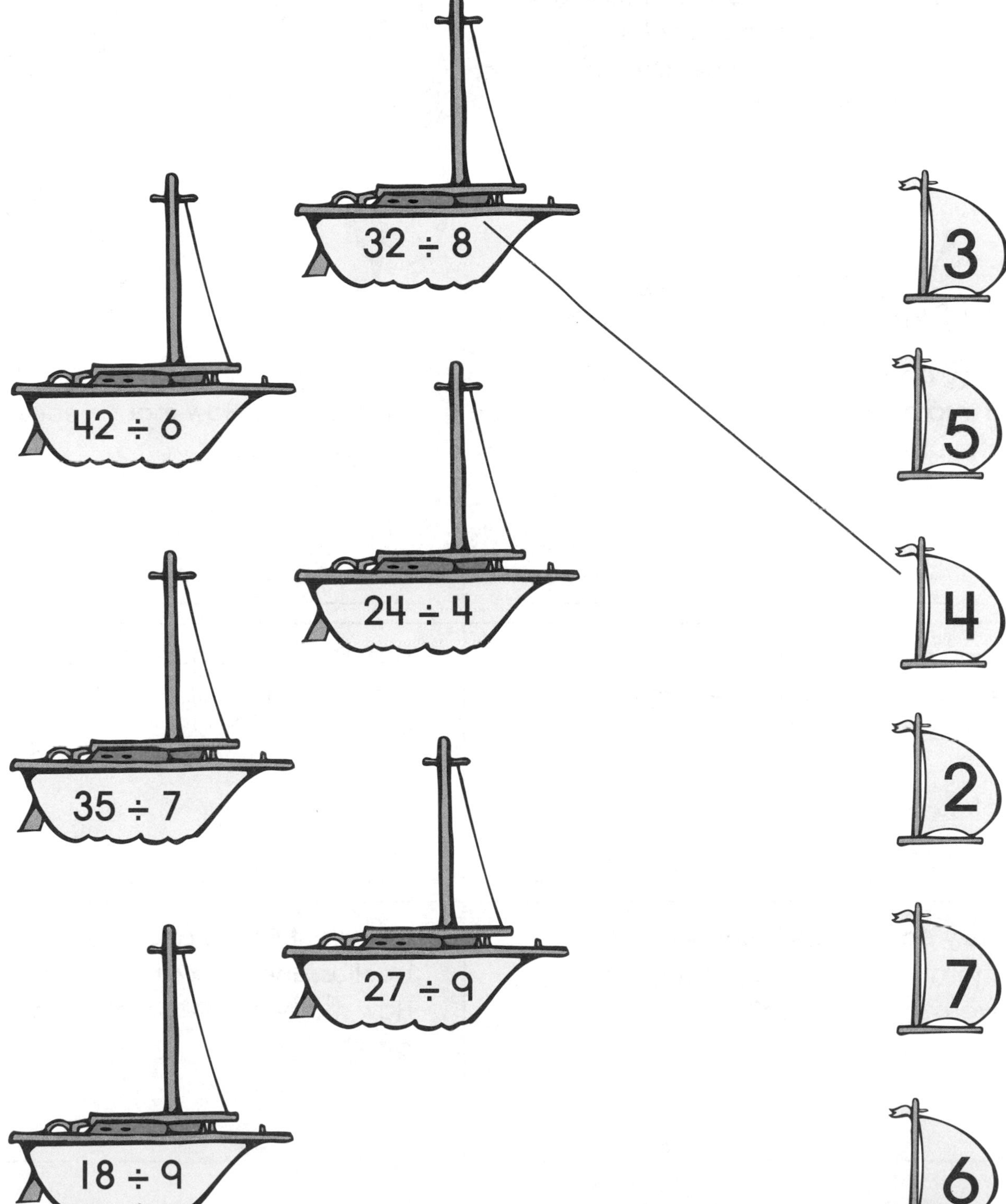

Lizzy the Lizard Bags Her Bugs

Lizzy the Lizard separates her bugs into separate bags so that her lunch is ready for the week. Help her decide how to divide the bugs.

1. Lizzy caught 45 cockroaches. She put 5 into each bag. How many bags did she use?

   _______ ÷ _______ = _______

2. Lizzy found 32 termites. She put 4 into each bag. How many bags did she need?

   _______ ÷ _______ = _______

3. Lizzy captured 49 stinkbugs. She put them in 7 bags. How many stinkbugs were in each bag?

   _______ ÷ _______ = _______

4. Lizzy bagged 27 horn beetles. She used 3 bags. How many beetles went into each bag?

   _______ ÷ _______ = _______

5. Lizzy lassoed 36 butterflies. She put 9 into each bag. How many bags did she need?

   _______ ÷ _______ = _______

6. Lizzy went fishing and caught 48 water beetles. She used 6 bags for her catch. How many beetles went into each bag?

   _______ ÷ _______ = _______

Problem Solving: Addition and Subtraction

Directions: Read and solve each problem. The first one is done for you.

The clown started the day with 200 balloons. He gave away 128 of them. Some broke. At the end of the day he had 18 balloons left. How many of the balloons broke? 54

On Monday, there were 925 tickets sold to adults and 1,412 tickets sold to children. How many more children attended the fair than adults? ____________

At one game booth, prizes were given out for scoring 500 points in three attempts. Tiana scored 178 points on her first attempt, 149 points on her second attempt, and 233 points on her third attempt. Did Tiana win a prize? ____________

The prize-winning steer weighed 2,348 pounds. The runner-up steer weighed 2,179 pounds. How much more did the prize steer weigh? ____________

There were 3,418 people at the fair on Tuesday, and 2,294 people on Wednesday. What was the total number of people there for the two days? ____________

Complete the Circle

Directions: Complete the circle by multiplying each of the numbers by 3.

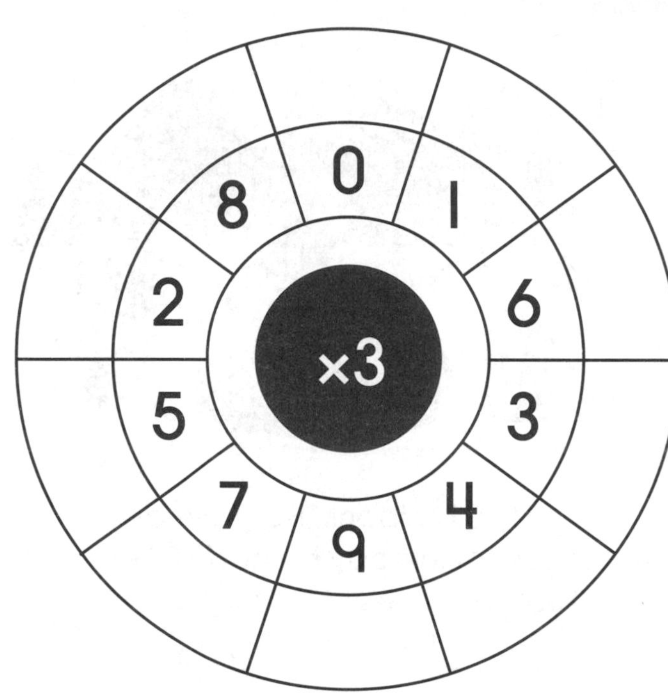

Now, complete these facts.

$$\begin{array}{r} 5 \\ \times 3 \\ \hline \end{array} \quad \begin{array}{r} 9 \\ \times 3 \\ \hline \end{array} \quad \begin{array}{r} 3 \\ \times 1 \\ \hline \end{array} \quad \begin{array}{r} 3 \\ \times 8 \\ \hline \end{array} \quad \begin{array}{r} 6 \\ \times 3 \\ \hline \end{array} \quad \begin{array}{r} 3 \\ \times 2 \\ \hline \end{array}$$

$$\begin{array}{r} 0 \\ \times 3 \\ \hline \end{array} \quad \begin{array}{r} 3 \\ \times 5 \\ \hline \end{array} \quad \begin{array}{r} 2 \\ \times 3 \\ \hline \end{array} \quad \begin{array}{r} 3 \\ \times 4 \\ \hline \end{array} \quad \begin{array}{r} 8 \\ \times 3 \\ \hline \end{array} \quad \begin{array}{r} 3 \\ \times 9 \\ \hline \end{array}$$

Double Trouble

Directions: Solve each multiplication problem. Below each answer, write the letter from the code that matches the answer. Read the coded question and write the answer in the space provided.

1	4	9	16	25	36	49	64	81	100	121	144
E	G	H	I	N	O	S	T	U	W	X	Y

10 × 10	3 × 3	6 × 6

4 × 4	7 × 7

7 × 7	4 × 4	8 × 8	8 × 8	4 × 4	5 × 5	2 × 2

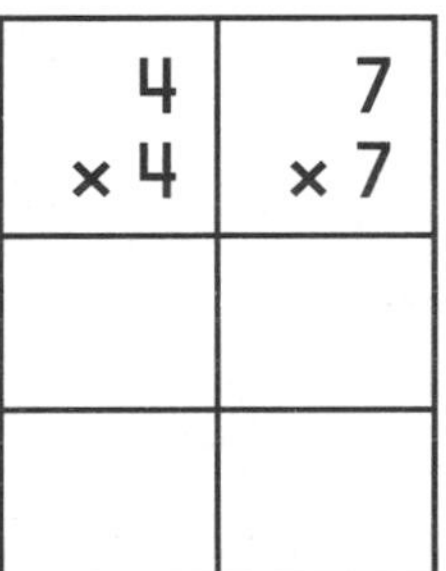

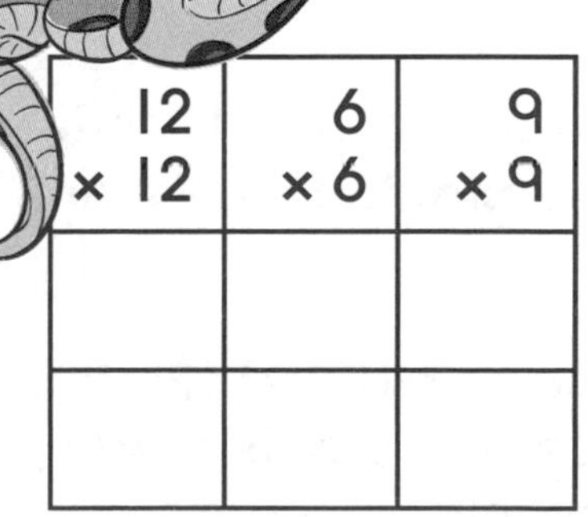

5 × 5	1 × 1	11 × 11	8 × 8

8 × 8	6 × 6

12 × 12	6 × 6	9 × 9

?

Answer: ____

Problem Solving: Multiplication and Division

Directions: Read and solve each problem.

Marco and Isaac are planting a garden. They plant 3 rows of green beans with 8 plants in each row. How many green bean plants are there in the garden? ________

There are 45 tomato plants in the garden. There are 5 rows of them. How many tomato plants are in each row? ________

The children have 12 plants each of lettuce, broccoli, and spinach. How many plants are there in all? ________

Marco planted 3 times as many cucumber plants as Isaac. He planted 15 of them. How many did Isaac plant? ________

Isaac planted 12 pepper plants. He planted twice as many green pepper plants as red pepper plants. How many green pepper plants are there? ________

How many red pepper plants? ________

Find the Product: Drawing

You can draw a picture to find a product.

Example: Find the answer. 4 × 2 = _____

Step 1: Draw 4 sets of 2 dots. ●● ●● ●● ●●

Step 2: Count all the dots.

Answer: 4 × 2 = 8

Directions: Draw a picture to find the product.

3 × 2 = _____

2 × 4 = _____

5 × 2 = _____

2 × 3 = _____

4 × 3 = _____

3 × 4 = _____

Who Will Be First?

Directions: Find the sums one at a time from left to right. After each sum, move an insect toward the center of the flower by coloring the petal with the matching number. Circle the bug that reaches the center.

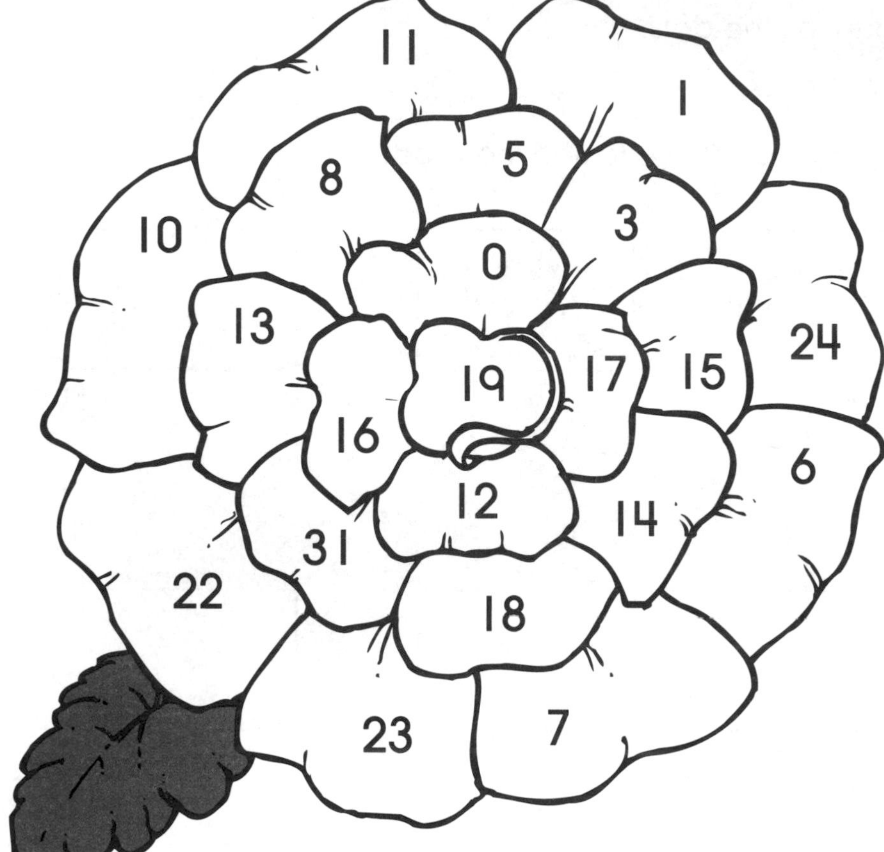

Color my path yellow.

$$\begin{array}{r} 5 \\ +\ 6 \\ \hline \end{array} \quad \begin{array}{r} 3 \\ +\ 7 \\ \hline \end{array} \quad \begin{array}{r} 4 \\ +\ 4 \\ \hline \end{array} \quad \begin{array}{r} 9 \\ +\ 4 \\ \hline \end{array} \quad \begin{array}{r} 8 \\ +\ 8 \\ \hline \end{array} \quad \begin{array}{r} 5 \\ +\ 7 \\ \hline \end{array}$$

Color my path **blue**.

$$\begin{array}{r} 3 \\ +\ 4 \\ \hline \end{array} \quad \begin{array}{r} 9 \\ +\ 9 \\ \hline \end{array} \quad \begin{array}{r} 6 \\ +\ 8 \\ \hline \end{array} \quad \begin{array}{r} 9 \\ +\ 6 \\ \hline \end{array} \quad \begin{array}{r} 9 \\ +\ 8 \\ \hline \end{array} \quad \begin{array}{r} 10 \\ +\ 9 \\ \hline \end{array}$$

Problem Solving: Fractions and Decimals

A **fraction** is a number that names part of a whole, such as $\frac{1}{2}$ or $\frac{1}{3}$.

Directions: Read and solve each problem.

There are 20 large animals on the Mendozas' farm. Two-fifths are horses, two-fifths are cows, and the rest are pigs. Are there more pigs or cows on the farm? __________

Farmer Mendoza had 40 eggs to sell. He sold half of them in the morning. In the afternoon, he sold half of what was left. How many eggs did Farmer Mendoza have at the end of the day? __________

There is a fence running around seven-tenths of the farm. How much of the farm does not have a fence around it? Write the amount as a decimal. __________

The Mendozas have 10 chickens. Two are roosters, and the rest are hens. Write a decimal for the number that are roosters and for the number that are hens. ______ roosters ______ hens

Mrs. Mendoza spends three-fourths of her day working outside and the rest working inside. Does she spend more time inside or outside? __________

Ouch!

Directions: Add. Use the sums to answer the riddle.

What happened to the human cannonball at the circus?

___ ___   ___ ___ ___   ___ ___ ___ ___ ___
18 4   15 11 14   18 17 12 4 16

___ ___ ___   ___ ___ ___ ___ ___   ___ ___
11 8 16   9 17 12 4 16   10 8

___ ___ ___   ___ ___ ___ ___   ___ ___ ___!
7 18 4   14 11 13 4   16 11 6

S $2 + 6 + 6 =$ ____	**E** $1 + 1 + 2 =$ ____	**N** $2 + 2 + 4 =$ ____
F $2 + 3 + 4 =$ ____	**O** $3 + 3 + 4 =$ ____	**Y** $2 + 2 + 2 =$ ____
H $3 + 6 + 9 =$ ____	**I** $2 + 7 + 8 =$ ____	**W** $3 + 4 + 8 =$ ____
A $2 + 4 + 5 =$ ____	**T** $1 + 2 + 4 =$ ____	**M** $3 + 3 + 7 =$ ____
R $4 + 4 + 4 =$ ____	**D** $4 + 4 + 8 =$ ____	**B** $1 + 1 + 1 =$ ____

Complete the Circle

Directions: Complete the circle by multiplying each of the numbers by 5.

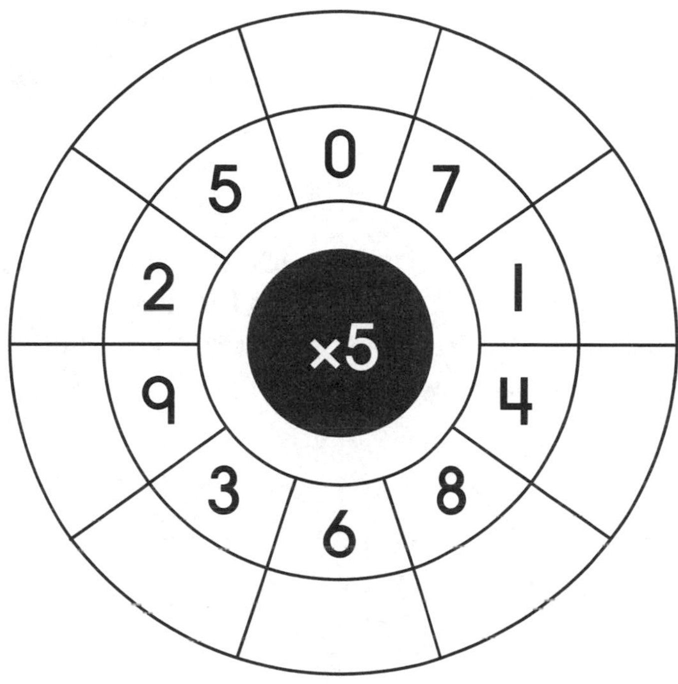

Now, complete these facts.

5 × 8	5 × 4	5 × 2	7 × 5	5 × 7	1 × 5
5 × 0	6 × 5	5 × 9	3 × 5	8 × 5	5 × 5

Problem Solving: Measurement

Directions: Read and solve each problem.

This year, hundreds of people ran in the Capital City Marathon. The race is 4.2 kilometers long. When the first person crossed the finish line, the last person was at the 3.7 kilometer point. How far ahead was the winner? ____________

Dennis crossed the finish line 10 meters ahead of Lucy. Lucy was 5 meters ahead of Sam. How far ahead of Sam was Dennis? ____________

Tony ran 320 yards from school to his home. Then, he ran 290 yards to Jay's house. Together, Tony and Jay ran 545 yards to the store. How many yards in all did Tony run? ____________

The teacher measured the heights of three children in her class. Brianna was 51 inches tall, Diego was 48 inches tall, and Owen was $52\frac{1}{2}$ inches tall. How much taller is Owen than Brianna? ____________

How much taller is he than Diego? ____________

Division Challenge

Directions: Solve each problem.

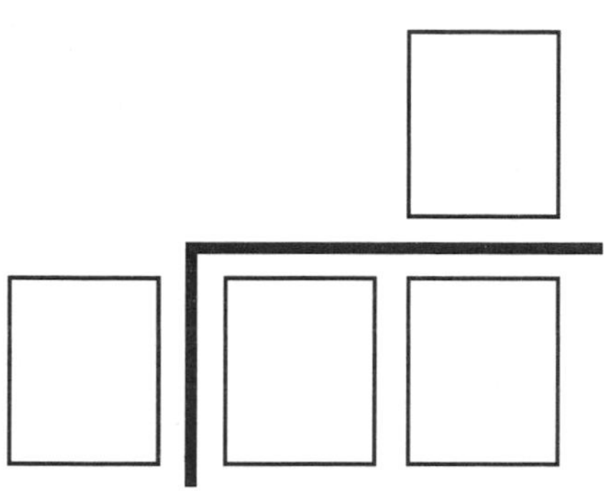

Nadia worked 49 problems.

She did 7 problems per page.

How many pages did she use?

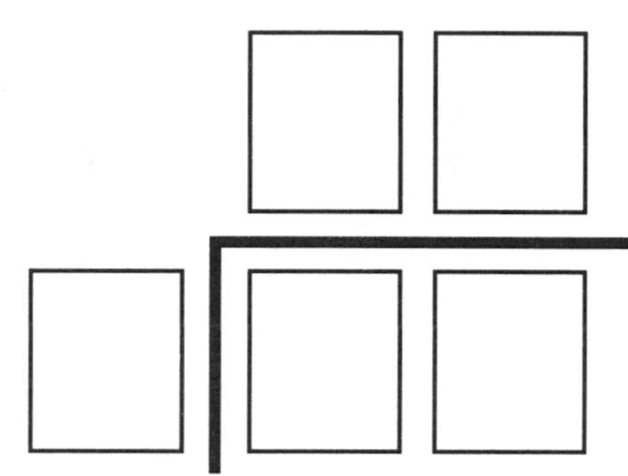

A team played 48 quarters.

There are 4 quarters a game.

How many games did they play?

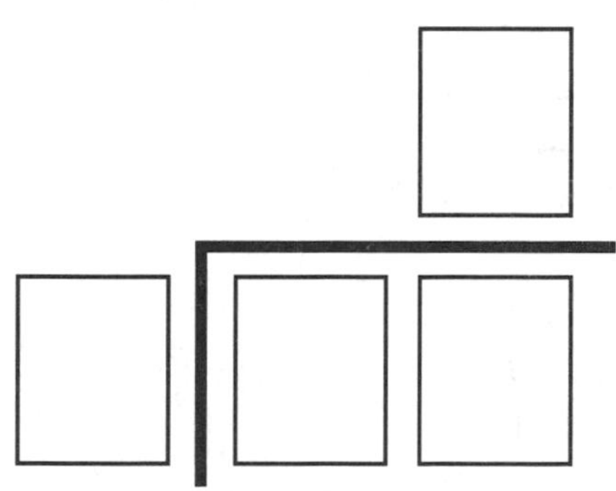

There are 20 slices of bread in a loaf.

Hunter uses 5 slices a day.

How many days will the loaf last?

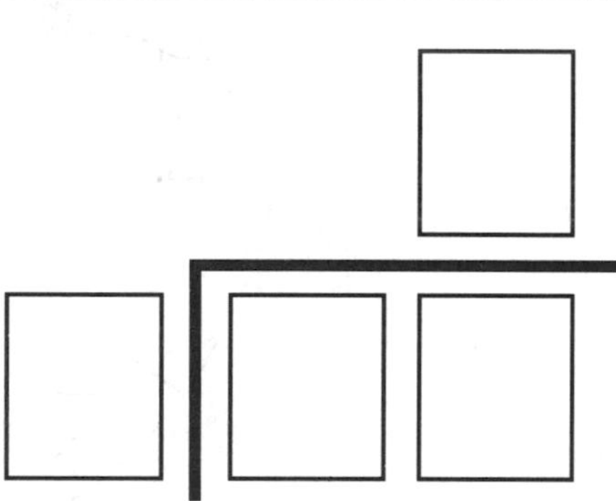

Norris has 10 books.

He puts them in 2 equal stacks.

How many books are in each stack?

Complete the Circle

Directions: Complete these facts in which 7 is a factor.

3	1	5	2	0	4	6
× 7	× 7	× 7	× 7	× 7	× 7	× 7

Directions: Complete the circle by multiplying each of the numbers by 7.

Problem Solving

Directions: Read and solve each problem.

Ralph has $8.75. He buys a teddy bear and a puzzle. How much money does he have left? ______________

Kelly wants to buy a teddy bear and a ball. She has $7.25. How much more money does she need? ______________

Lydia paid 1 five-dollar bill, 2 one-dollar bills, 2 quarters, 1 dime, and 8 pennies for a book. How much did it cost? ______________

Mei-Lin leaves for school at 7:45 A.M. It takes her 20 minutes to get there. On the clock, draw the time that she arrives at school.

Frank takes piano lessons every Saturday morning at 11:30. The lesson lasts for an hour and 15 minutes. On the clock, draw the time his piano lesson ends. Is it A.M. or P.M.? Circle the correct answer.

Division Challenge

Directions: Solve each problem.

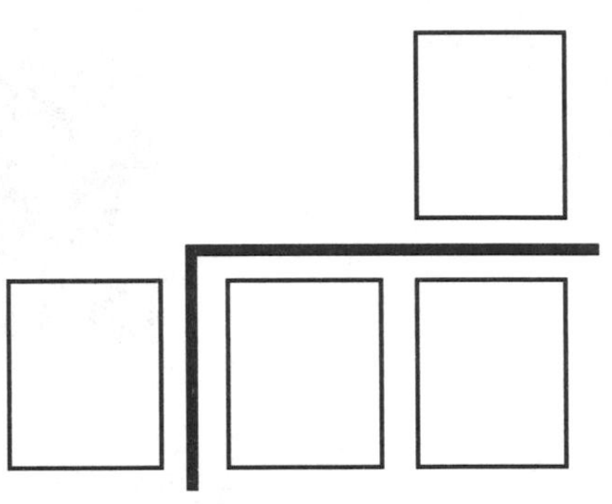

There are 15 students.

They are split into 5 equal groups.

How many students are in each group?

There are 9 students.

Javon splits them in 3 equal groups.

How many students are in each group?

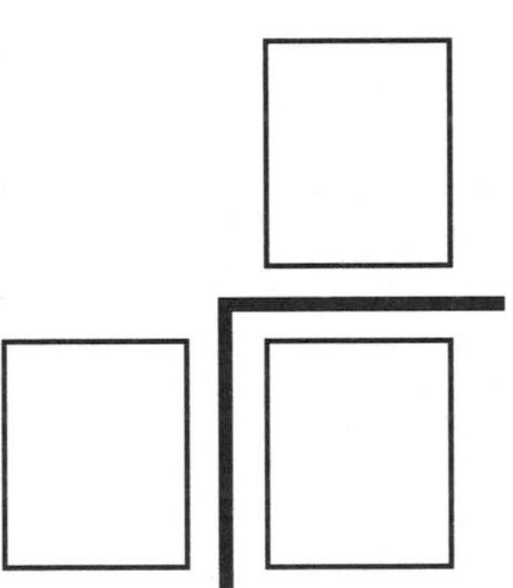

There are 6 rabbits.

Only 2 go into each rabbit hole.

How many rabbit holes are there?

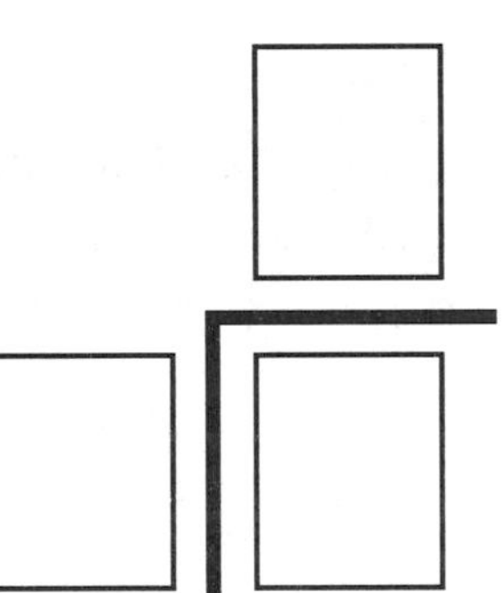

There are 9 bees.

They fly to 9 flowers.

How many bees are there on each flower?

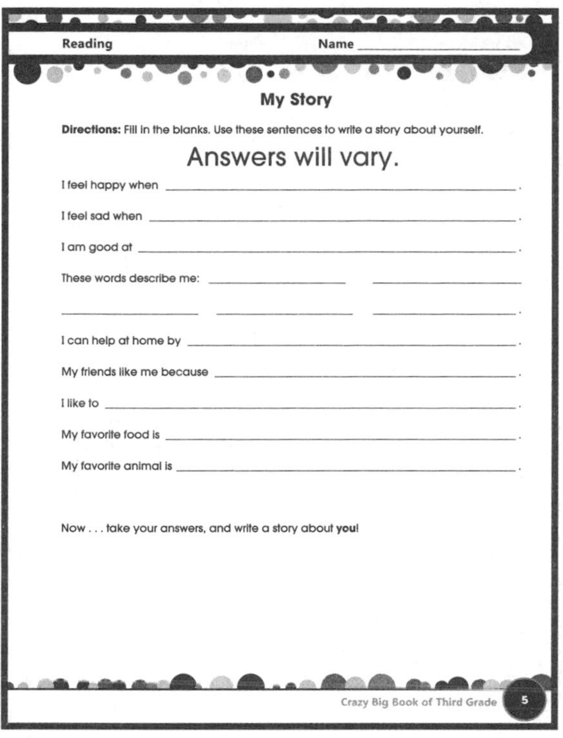

Reading Name __________

My Story

Directions: Fill in the blanks. Use these sentences to write a story about yourself.

Answers will vary.

I feel happy when __________.

I feel sad when __________.

I am good at __________.

These words describe me: ______ ______ ______ ______ ______.

I can help at home by __________.

My friends like me because __________.

I like to __________.

My favorite food is __________.

My favorite animal is __________.

Now . . . take your answers, and write a story about **you**!

Crazy Big Book of Third Grade 5

page 5

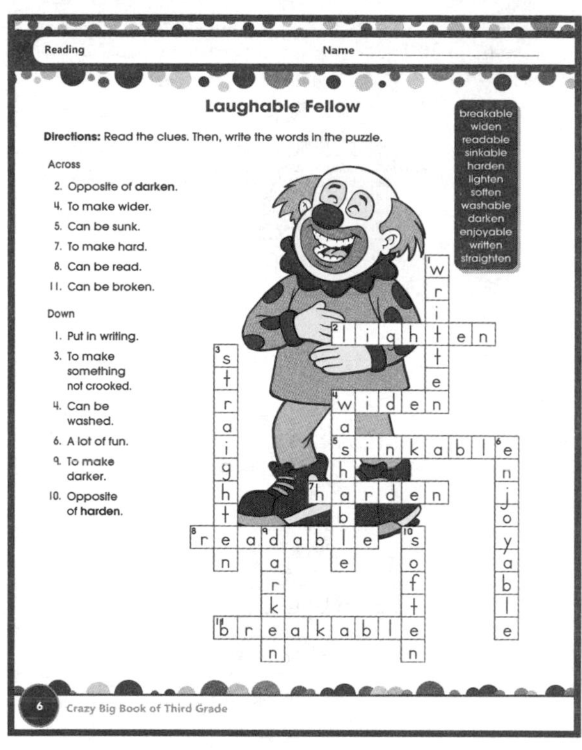

Reading Name __________

Laughable Fellow

Directions: Read the clues. Then, write the words in the puzzle.

breakable
widen
readable
sinkable
harden
lighten
soften
washable
darken
enjoyable
written
straighten

Across

2. Opposite of **darken**.
4. To make wider.
5. Can be sunk.
7. To make hard.
8. Can be read.
11. Can be broken.

Down

1. Put in writing.
3. To make something not crooked.
4. Can be washed.
6. A lot of fun.
9. To make darker.
10. Opposite of **harden**.

6 Crazy Big Book of Third Grade

page 6

Reading Name __________

Big B Words

Directions: Look at the picture clues. Then, complete the puzzle using the words from the Word Box.

Across

2.

4.

5.

Down

1.

2.

3.

1 bend
2 bubbles
2 button
3 bears
4 boxes
5 bright

bend	button	boxes
bright	bubbles	bears

Crazy Big Book of Third Grade 7

page 7

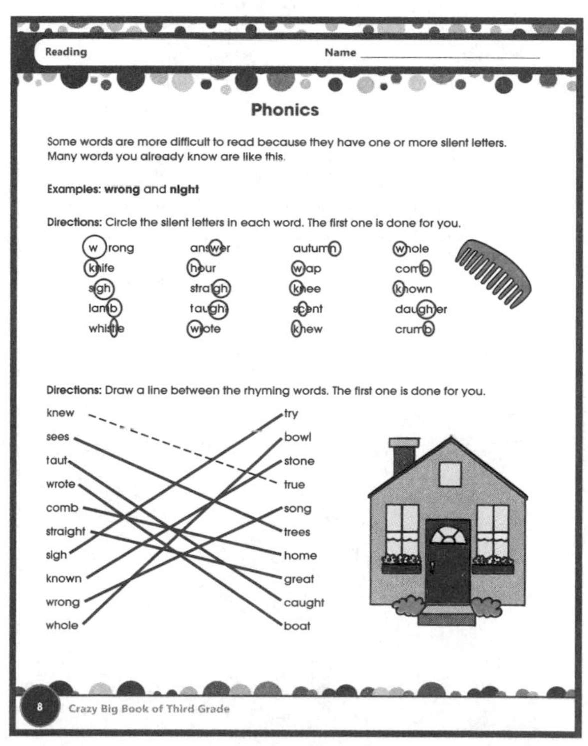

Reading Name __________

Phonics

Some words are more difficult to read because they have one or more silent letters. Many words you already know are like this.

Examples: wrong and **night**

Directions: Circle the silent letters in each word. The first one is done for you.

wrong	answer	autumn	whole
knife	hour	wrap	comb
sigh	straight	knee	known
lamb	taught	scent	daughter
whistle	wrote	knew	crumb

Directions: Draw a line between the rhyming words. The first one is done for you.

knew	try
sees	bowl
taut	stone
wrote	true
comb	song
straight	trees
sigh	home
known	great
wrong	caught
whole	boat

8 Crazy Big Book of Third Grade

page 8

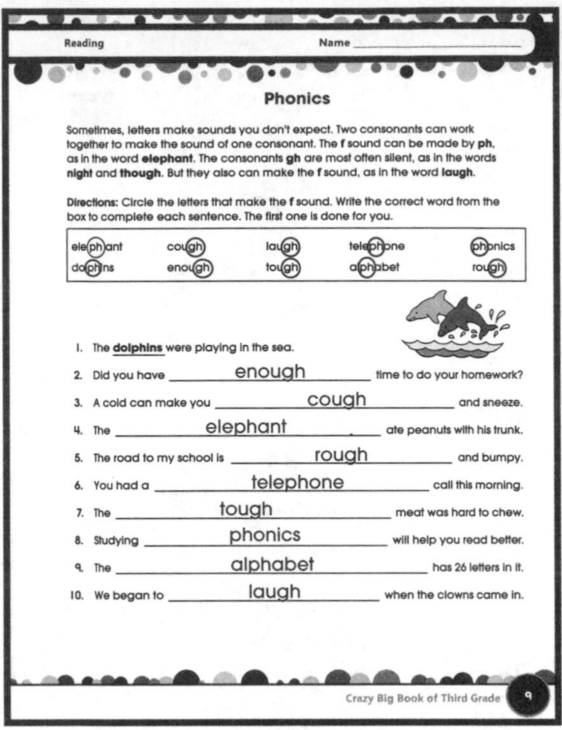

Reading Name ____

Phonics

Sometimes, letters make sounds you don't expect. Two consonants can work together to make the sound of one consonant. The **f** sound can be made by **ph**, as in the word **elephant**. The consonants **gh** are most often silent, as in the words **night** and **though**. But they also can make the **f** sound, as in the word **laugh**.

Directions: Circle the letters that make the **f** sound. Write the correct word from the box to complete each sentence. The first one is done for you.

elephant	cough	laugh	telephone	phonics
dolphins	enough	tough	alphabet	rough

1. The **dolphins** were playing in the sea.
2. Did you have enough time to do your homework?
3. A cold can make you cough and sneeze.
4. The elephant ate peanuts with his trunk.
5. The road to my school is rough and bumpy.
6. You had a telephone call this morning.
7. The tough meat was hard to chew.
8. Studying phonics will help you read better.
9. The alphabet has 26 letters in it.
10. We began to laugh when the clowns came in.

Crazy Big Book of Third Grade 9

page 9

Reading Name ____

Phonics

There are several consonants that make the **k** sound: **c** when followed by **a**, **o**, or **u**, as in **cow** or **cup**; the letter **k**, as in **milk**; the letters **ch**, as in **Christmas**; and **ck**, as in **black**.

Directions: Read the following words. Circle the letters that make the **k** sound. The first one is done for you.

ache	school	market	comb
camera	deck	darkness	Christmas
necklace	doctor	stomach	crack
nickel	kin	thick	escape

Directions: Use your own words to finish the following sentences. Use words with the **k** sound.

1. If I had a nickel, I would ____.
2. My doctor is very ____.
3. We bought ripe, juicy tom____.
4. If I had a camera no____ I would take a picture ____.
5. When my stomach aches, ____.

Answers will vary.

10 Crazy Big Book of Third Grade

page 10

Reading Name ____

Phonics

In some word families, the vowels have a long sound when you would expect them to have a short sound. For example, the **i** has a short sound in **chill**, but a long sound in **child**. The **o** has a short sound in **cost**, but a long sound in **most**.

Directions: Read the words in the word box below. Write the words that have a long vowel sound under the word **LONG**, and the words that have a short vowel sound under the word **SHORT**. (Remember, a long vowel says its name—like **a** in **ate**.)

old	odd	gosh	gold	sold	soft	toast	frost	lost	most
doll	roll	bone	done	kin	mill	mild	wild	blink	blind

LONG		SHORT	
bone	old	doll	doll
roll	bone	odd	gosh
gold	sold	done	kin
toast	most	mill	frost
mild	wild	lost	blink
blind		soft	

Crazy Big Book of Third Grade 11

page 11

Reading Name ____

Shape Up

Directions: Write the word for each shape.

oval	rectangle
circle	square
triangle	octagon

Across

2. circle
4. octagon
5. triangle
6. oval

Down

1. square
3. rectangle

12 Crazy Big Book of Third Grade

page 12

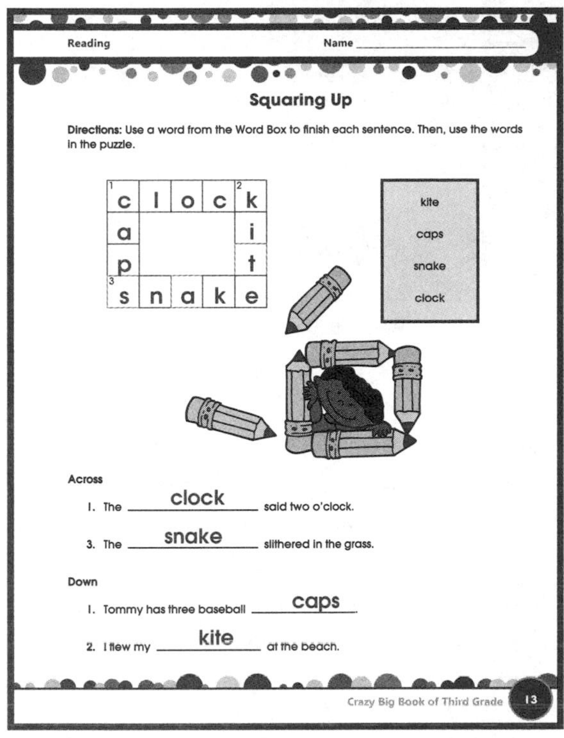

Reading Name ____________

Squaring Up

Directions: Use a word from the Word Box to finish each sentence. Then, use the words in the puzzle.

Word Box: kite, caps, snake, clock

Across

1. The clock said two o'clock.
3. The snake slithered in the grass.

Down

1. Tommy has three baseball caps.
2. I flew my kite at the beach.

Crazy Big Book of Third Grade 13

page 13

Reading Name ____________

Syllables

All words can be divided into **syllables**. Syllables are word parts that have one vowel sound in each part.

Directions: Draw a line between the syllables in each word, and then write the word on the correct line below. The first one is done for you.

lit|tle	bum|ble|bee	pil|low
truck	daz|zle	dog
pen|cil	flag	an|gel|ic
re|joic|ing	ant	tel|e|phone

1 SYLLABLE	2 SYLLABLES	3 SYLLABLES
truck	little	rejoicing
flag	pencil	bumblebee
ant	dazzle	angelic
dog	pillow	telephone

14 Crazy Big Book of Third Grade

page 14

Reading Name ____________

Syllables

When the letters **le** come at the end of a word, they sometimes have the sound of **ul**, as in **raffle**.

Directions: Draw a line to match the syllables so they make words. The first one is done for you.

can	gle
tur	cle
pur	ple
cir	kle
spar	zle
raf	dle
ea	fle
siz	tle

Directions: Use the words you made to complete the sentences. The first one is done for you.

1. Will you buy a ticket for our school raffle?
2. The turtle pulled his head into his shell.
3. We could hear the bacon sizzle in the pan.
4. The baby had one candle on her birthday cake.
5. My favorite color is purple.
6. Look at that diamond sparkle!
7. The bald eagle is our national bird.
8. Draw a circle around the correct answer.

Crazy Big Book of Third Grade 15

page 15

Reading Name ____________

A Good Scout

Directions: Read the clues at the bottom of the page. Then, write the words in the puzzle.

Across

1. A word you say when you get hurt. (ouch)
3. The shape of a circle. (round)
5. The opposite of **quiet**. (loud)
7. To find out how many, you must ____. (count)
9. The opposite of **north**. (south)
11. The opposite of **in**. (out)
12. Animal like a rat. (mouse)
14. A very high land form. (mountain)

Down

2. Fluffy white object in the sky. (cloud)
4. Ground wheat that is used in making bread. (flour)
6. Not having something. (without)
7. A sofa. (couch)
8. A fish. (trout)
10. A home. (house)
12. A part of your face. (mouth)
13. To make a ball go down and up. (bounce)

out loud south trout cloud without flour couch ouch bounce round mouse count house mouth mountain

16 Crazy Big Book of Third Grade

page 16

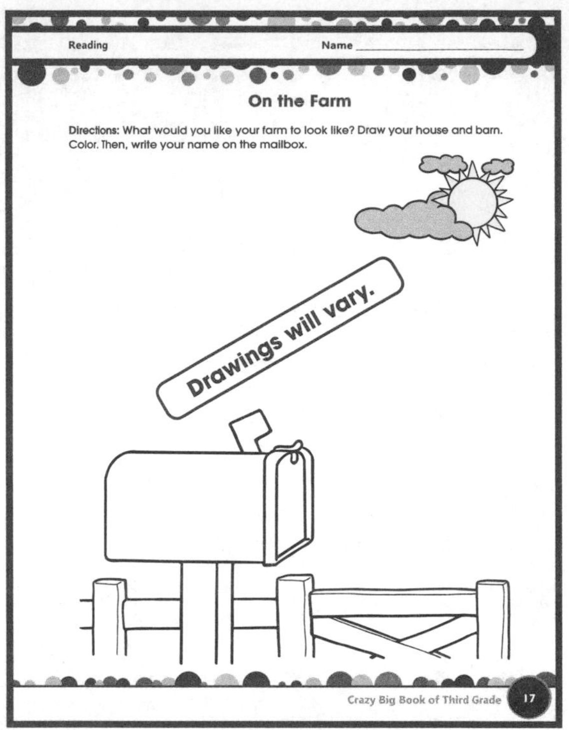
Reading Name ____________

On the Farm

Directions: What would you like your farm to look like? Draw your house and barn. Color. Then, write your name on the mailbox.

Drawings will vary.

Crazy Big Book of Third Grade 17

page 17

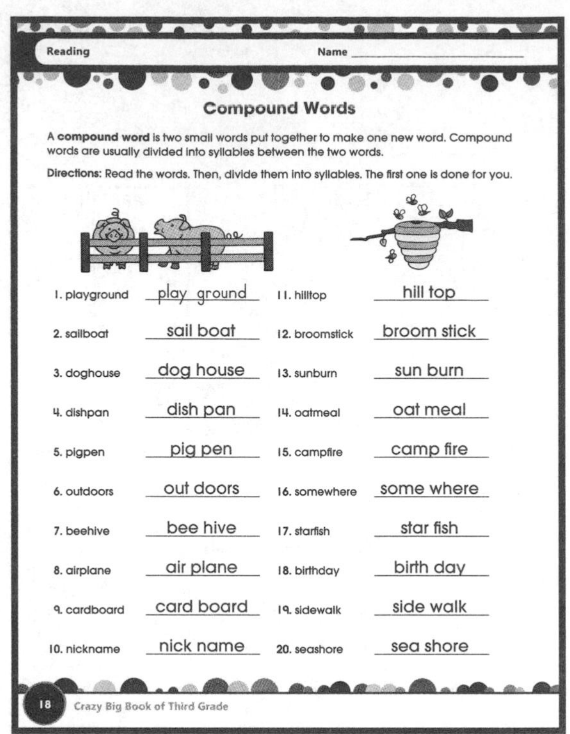
Reading Name ____________

Compound Words

A **compound word** is two small words put together to make one new word. Compound words are usually divided into syllables between the two words.

Directions: Read the words. Then, divide them into syllables. The first one is done for you.

1. playground play ground
2. sailboat sail boat
3. doghouse dog house
4. dishpan dish pan
5. pigpen pig pen
6. outdoors out doors
7. beehive bee hive
8. airplane air plane
9. cardboard card board
10. nickname nick name
11. hilltop hill top
12. broomstick broom stick
13. sunburn sun burn
14. oatmeal oat meal
15. campfire camp fire
16. somewhere some where
17. starfish star fish
18. birthday birth day
19. sidewalk side walk
20. seashore sea shore

18 Crazy Big Book of Third Grade

page 18

Reading Name ____________

Compound Words

Directions: Read the compound words in the word box. Then, use them to answer the questions. The first one is done for you.

sailboat	blueberry	bookcase	tablecloth	beehive
dishpan	pigpen	classroom	playground	bedtime
broomstick	treetop	fireplace	newspaper	sunburn

Which compound word means . . .

1. a case for books? bookcase
2. a berry that is blue? blueberry
3. a hive for bees? beehive
4. a place for fires? fireplace
5. a pen for pigs? pigpen
6. a room for a class? classroom
7. a pan for dishes? dishpan
8. a boat to sail? sailboat
9. a paper for news? newspaper
10. a burn from the sun? sunburn
11. the top of a tree? treetop
12. a stick for a broom? broomstick
13. the time to go to bed? bedtime
14. a cloth for the table? tablecloth
15. ground to play on? playground

Crazy Big Book of Third Grade 19

page 19

Reading Name ____________

Letter Change

Directions: Starting with the top word in each square, change one letter at a time until the top word becomes the bottom word.

1.	R	I	P	E
2.	P	I	P	E
3.	P	I	L	E
4.	P	A	L	E
5.	P	A	L	M

6.	M	I	C	E
7.	L	I	C	E
8.	L	A	C	E
9.	L	A	C	K
10.	L	A	R	K

20 Crazy Big Book of Third Grade

page 20

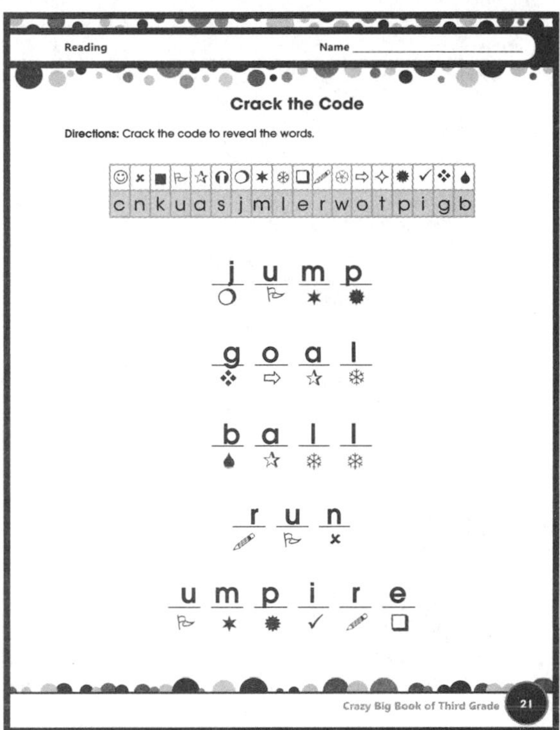
Reading Name

Crack the Code

Directions: Crack the code to reveal the words.

c n k u a s j m l e r w o t p i g b

j u m p

g o a l

b a l l

r u n

u m p i r e

Crazy Big Book of Third Grade 21

page 21

Reading Name

Transportation Vocabulary

Directions: Unscramble the words to spell the names of kinds of transportation. The first one is done for you.

behelwworar	wheel b a r r o w
anirt	t r a i n
moobattor	moto r b o a t
ceicbly	b i c y c l e
tocker	r o c k e t
etobimuloa	aut o m o b i l e
rilanape	a i r p l a n e

Directions: Use a word from above to complete each sentence.

1. My mother uses a wheelbarrow to move dirt to her garden.
2. The rocket blasted the spaceship off the launching pad.
3. We flew on an airplane to visit my aunt in Florida.
4. My grandfather drives a very old automobile.
5. We borrowed Fred's motorboat to go water skiing.
6. You should always look both ways when crossing a train track.
7. I hope I get a new bicycle for my birthday.

22 Crazy Big Book of Third Grade

page 22

Reading Name

Space Vocabulary

Directions: Unscramble each word. Use the numbers below the letters to tell you what order they belong in. Write the word by its definition.

i r t b o
4 2 5 3 1

u t o n c w d n o
3 5 7 9 1 8 6 4 2

u l e f
2 4 3 1

a t s r a t n o u
7 9 2 4 1 3 6 5 8

t e h t s u l
5 7 2 4 1 3 6

A member of the team that flies a spaceship	astronaut
A rocket-powered spaceship that travels between Earth and space	shuttle
The material, such as gas, used for power	fuel
The seconds just before take-off	countdown
The path of a spaceship as it goes around Earth	orbit

Crazy Big Book of Third Grade 23

page 23

Reading Name

Weather Vocabulary

Directions: Use the weather words in the box to complete the sentences.

sunny	temperature	foggy	puddles	rainy
windy	rainbow	cloudy	lightning	snowy

1. My friends and I love snowy days, because we can have snowball fights!
2. On rainy days, we like to stay indoors and play board games.
3. Today was hot and sunny, so we went to the beach.
4. We didn't see the sun at all yesterday. It was cloudy all day.
5. Windy weather is perfect for flying kites.
6. It was so foggy, Mom had to use the headlights in the car so we wouldn't get lost.
7. While it was still raining, the sun began to shine and created a beautiful rainbow.
8. We like to jump in the puddles after it rains.
9. Lightning flashed across the sky during the thunderstorm.
10. The temperature outside was so low, we needed to wear hats, mittens, and scarves.

24 Crazy Big Book of Third Grade

page 24

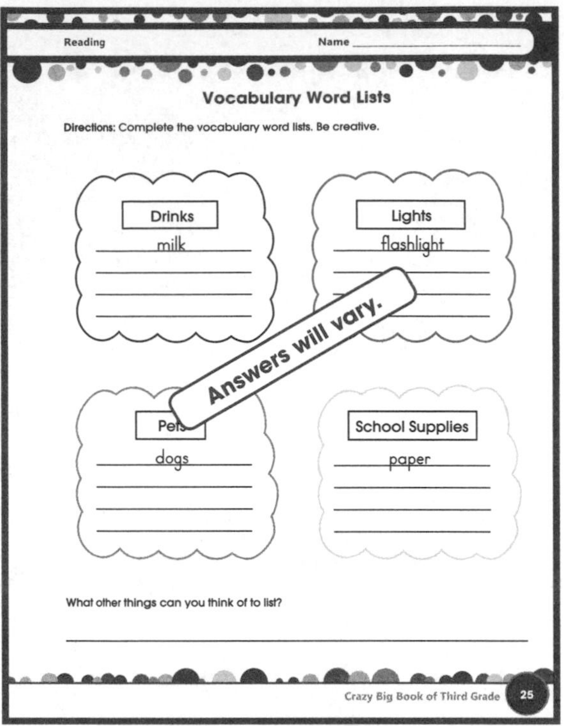
Reading Name ________

Vocabulary Word Lists

Directions: Complete the vocabulary word lists. Be creative.

Drinks
milk

Lights
flashlight

Pets
dogs

School Supplies
paper

Answers will vary.

What other things can you think of to list?

Crazy Big Book of Third Grade 25

page 25

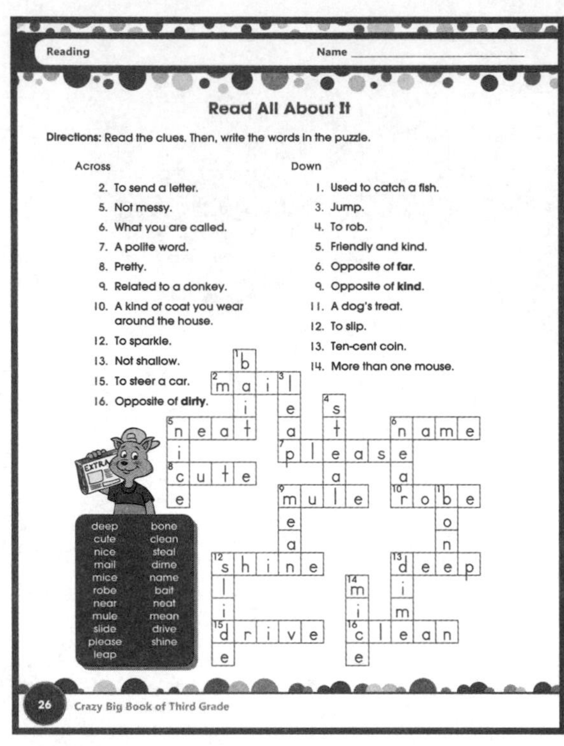
Reading Name ________

Read All About It

Directions: Read the clues. Then, write the words in the puzzle.

Across
2. To send a letter.
5. Not messy.
6. What you are called.
7. A polite word.
8. Pretty.
9. Related to a donkey.
10. A kind of coat you wear around the house.
12. To sparkle.
13. Not shallow.
15. To steer a car.
16. Opposite of **dirty**.

Down
1. Used to catch a fish.
3. Jump.
4. To rob.
5. Friendly and kind.
6. Opposite of **far**.
9. Opposite of **kind**.
11. A dog's treat.
12. To slip.
13. Ten-cent coin.
14. More than one mouse.

Across answers: 2. mail 5. neat 6. name 7. please 8. cute 9. mule 10. robe 12. shine 13. deep 15. drive 16. clean

Down answers: 1. bait 3. leap 4. steal 5. nice 6. near 9. mean 11. bone 12. slide 13. dime 14. mice

deep, cute, nice, mail, mice, robe, near, mule, slide, please, leap, bone, clean, steal, dime, name, bait, neat, mean, drive, shine

26 Crazy Big Book of Third Grade

page 26

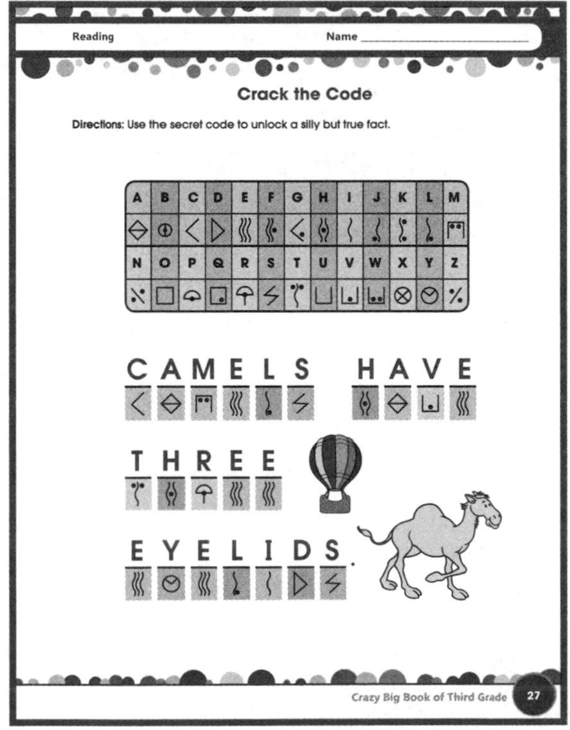
Reading Name ________

Crack the Code

Directions: Use the secret code to unlock a silly but true fact.

CAMELS HAVE THREE EYELIDS.

Crazy Big Book of Third Grade 27

page 27

Reading Name ________

Multiple-Meaning Words

Many words have more than one meaning. These words are called **multiple-meaning words.** Think of how the word is used in a sentence or story to determine the correct meaning.

Directions: The following baseball words have multiple meanings. Write the correct word in each baseball below.

play	bat	ball	fly	run

bat — This word means . . .
1. a flying mammal
2. a special stick used in baseball

fly — This word means . . .
1. a small insect
2. to soar through the air

ball — This word means . . .
1. a big dance
2. a round object used in sports

play — This word means . . .
1. a performance
2. to amuse oneself

Which word is left? run Write sentences using two different meanings of the word.

1. Sentences will vary.

2. ________

28 Crazy Big Book of Third Grade

page 28

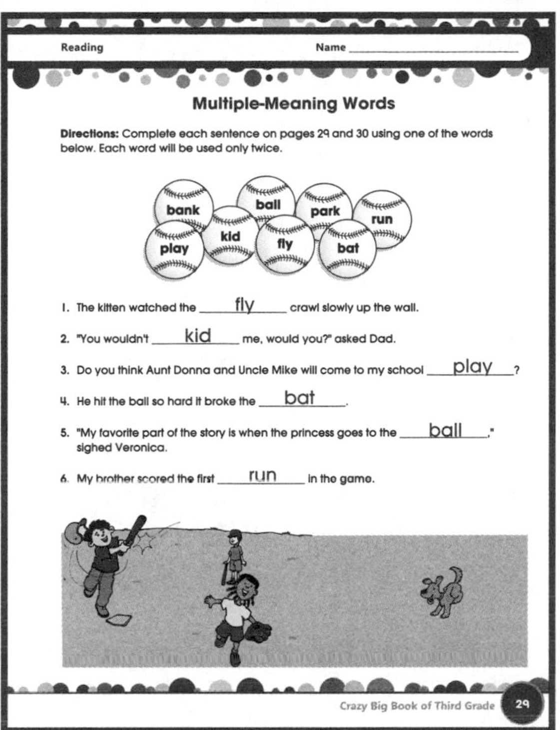

Reading Name ____________

Multiple-Meaning Words

Directions: Complete each sentence on pages 29 and 30 using one of the words below. Each word will be used only twice.

bank ball park run play kid fly bat

1. The kitten watched the fly crawl slowly up the wall.
2. "You wouldn't kid me, would you?" asked Dad.
3. Do you think Aunt Donna and Uncle Mike will come to my school play?
4. He hit the ball so hard it broke the bat.
5. "My favorite part of the story is when the princess goes to the ball," sighed Veronica.
6. My brother scored the first run in the game.

Crazy Big Book of Third Grade 29

page 29

Reading Name ____________

Multiple-Meaning Words

7. We will have to play quietly while the baby is sleeping.
8. Before we go to the store, I want to get some coins out of my bank.
9. The nature center will bring a live bat for our class to see.
10. We sat on the bank as we fished in the river.
11. The umpire decided the pitcher needed a new ball.
12. We will run in a race tomorrow.
13. "Can we please go to the park after I clean my room?" asked Jordan.
14. That boomerang can really fly!
15. Is it okay to park my bike here?
16. The baby goat, or kid, follows its mother everywhere.

30 Crazy Big Book of Third Grade

page 30

Reading Name ____________

Large or Small?

Directions: Write the words in the puzzle.

small large big little short tall tiny huge

Across: small, tiny, huge, tall, big

Down: little, short, large

Crazy Big Book of Third Grade 31

page 31

Reading Name ____________

Your Body

Directions: Read the clues and use the words in the word box to complete the puzzle.

fingers
hand
nose
lips
brain
teeth
ears

Across: 4. fingers 5. hand 7. ears

Down: 1. brain 2. lips 3. teeth 6. nose

Across

4. You have five on each hand.
5. It has five fingers.
7. They help you hear.

Down

1. You think with it.
2. They smile for you.
3. They chew for you.
6. It helps you smell.

32 Crazy Big Book of Third Grade

page 32

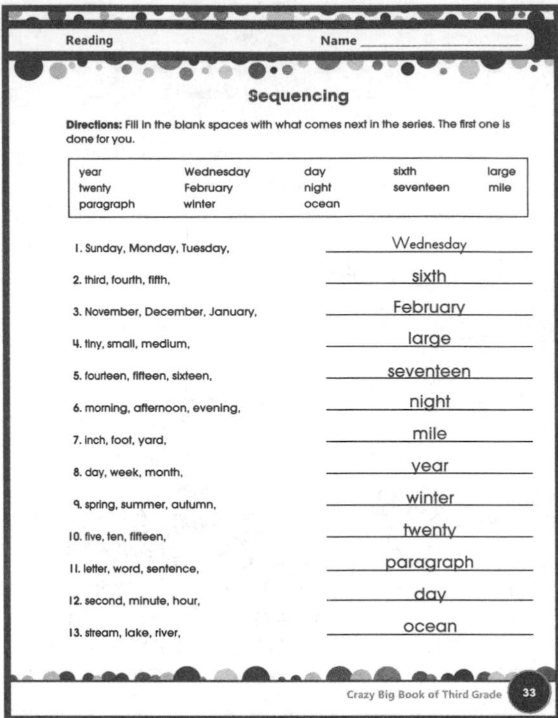

Reading Name ____________

Sequencing

Directions: Fill in the blank spaces with what comes next in the series. The first one is done for you.

year	Wednesday	day	sixth	large
twenty	February	night	seventeen	mile
paragraph	winter	ocean		

1. Sunday, Monday, Tuesday, Wednesday
2. third, fourth, fifth, sixth
3. November, December, January, February
4. tiny, small, medium, large
5. fourteen, fifteen, sixteen, seventeen
6. morning, afternoon, evening, night
7. inch, foot, yard, mile
8. day, week, month, year
9. spring, summer, autumn, winter
10. five, ten, fifteen, twenty
11. letter, word, sentence, paragraph
12. second, minute, hour, day
13. stream, lake, river, ocean

Crazy Big Book of Third Grade 33

page 33

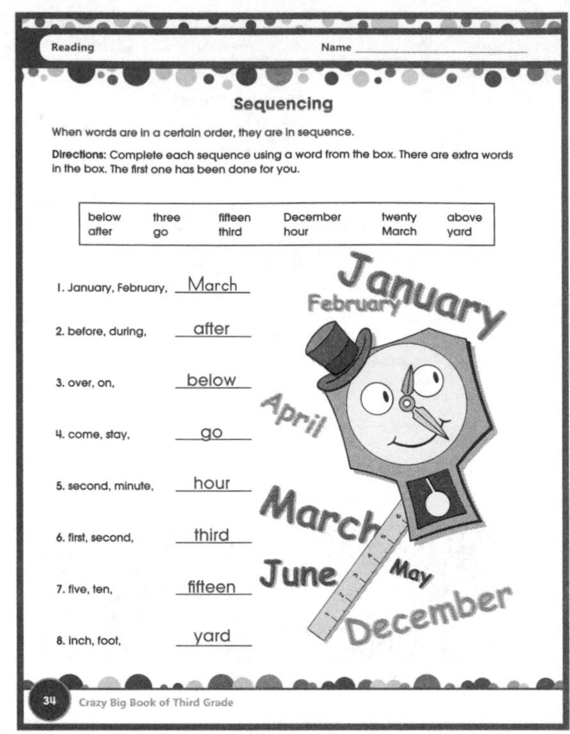

Reading Name ____________

Sequencing

When words are in a certain order, they are in sequence.

Directions: Complete each sequence using a word from the box. There are extra words in the box. The first one has been done for you.

below	three	fifteen	December	twenty	above
after	go	third	hour	March	yard

1. January, February, March
2. before, during, after
3. over, on, below
4. come, stay, go
5. second, minute, hour
6. first, second, third
7. five, ten, fifteen
8. inch, foot, yard

34 Crazy Big Book of Third Grade

page 34

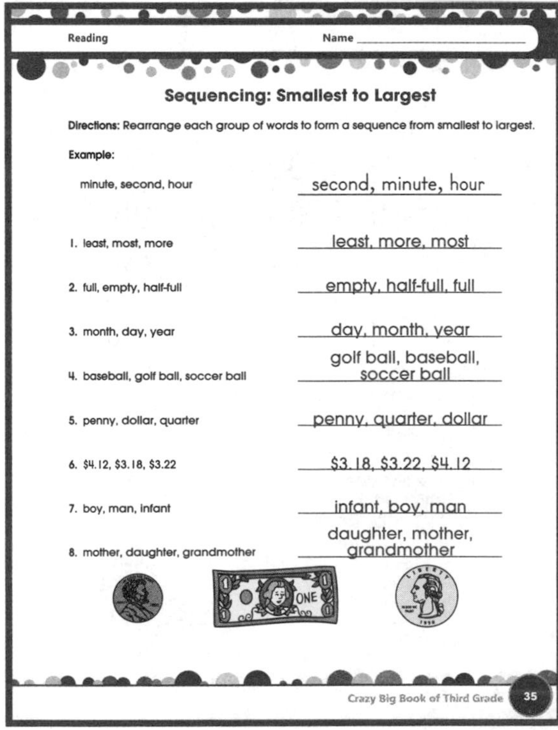

Reading Name ____________

Sequencing: Smallest to Largest

Directions: Rearrange each group of words to form a sequence from smallest to largest.

Example:

minute, second, hour — second, minute, hour

1. least, most, more — least, more, most
2. full, empty, half-full — empty, half-full, full
3. month, day, year — day, month, year
4. baseball, golf ball, soccer ball — golf ball, baseball, soccer ball
5. penny, dollar, quarter — penny, quarter, dollar
6. \$4.12, \$3.18, \$3.22 — \$3.18, \$3.22, \$4.12
7. boy, man, infant — infant, boy, man
8. mother, daughter, grandmother — daughter, mother, grandmother

Crazy Big Book of Third Grade 35

page 35

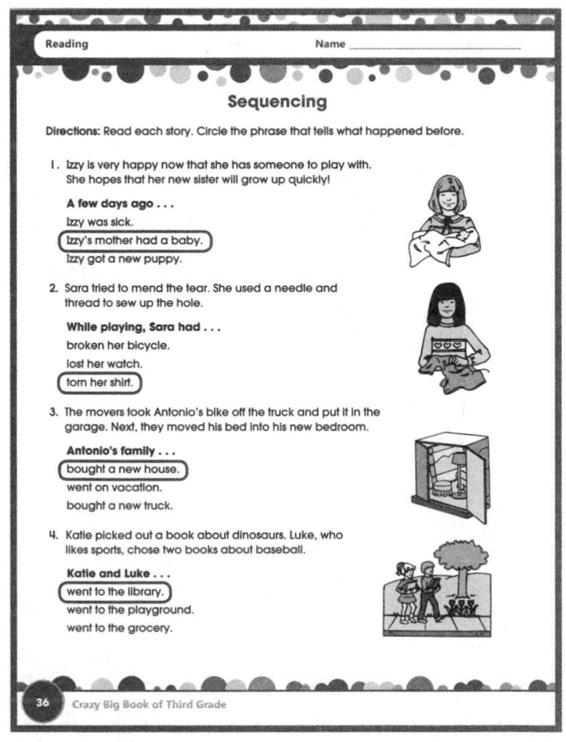

Reading Name ____________

Sequencing

Directions: Read each story. Circle the phrase that tells what happened before.

1. Izzy is very happy now that she has someone to play with. She hopes that her new sister will grow up quickly!

   A few days ago . . .
   Izzy was sick.
   (Izzy's mother had a baby.)
   Izzy got a new puppy.

2. Sara tried to mend the tear. She used a needle and thread to sew up the hole.

   While playing, Sara had . . .
   broken her bicycle.
   lost her watch.
   (torn her shirt.)

3. The movers took Antonio's bike off the truck and put it in the garage. Next, they moved his bed into his new bedroom.

   Antonio's family . . .
   (bought a new house.)
   went on vacation.
   bought a new truck.

4. Katie picked out a book about dinosaurs. Luke, who likes sports, chose two books about baseball.

   Katie and Luke . . .
   (went to the library.)
   went to the playground.
   went to the grocery.

36 Crazy Big Book of Third Grade

page 36

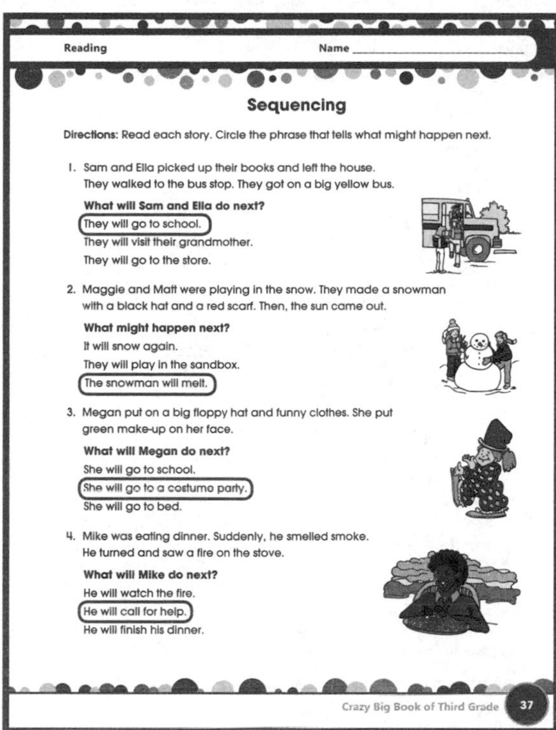
Reading Name ____________

Sequencing

Directions: Read each story. Circle the phrase that tells what might happen next.

1. Sam and Ella picked up their books and left the house. They walked to the bus stop. They got on a big yellow bus.

   What will Sam and Ella do next?
   They will go to school. (circled)
   They will visit their grandmother.
   They will go to the store.

2. Maggie and Matt were playing in the snow. They made a snowman with a black hat and a red scarf. Then, the sun came out.

   What might happen next?
   It will snow again.
   They will play in the sandbox.
   The snowman will melt. (circled)

3. Megan put on a big floppy hat and funny clothes. She put green make-up on her face.

   What will Megan do next?
   She will go to school.
   She will go to a costume party. (circled)
   She will go to bed.

4. Mike was eating dinner. Suddenly, he smelled smoke. He turned and saw a fire on the stove.

   What will Mike do next?
   He will watch the fire.
   He will call for help. (circled)
   He will finish his dinner.

Crazy Big Book of Third Grade 37

page 37

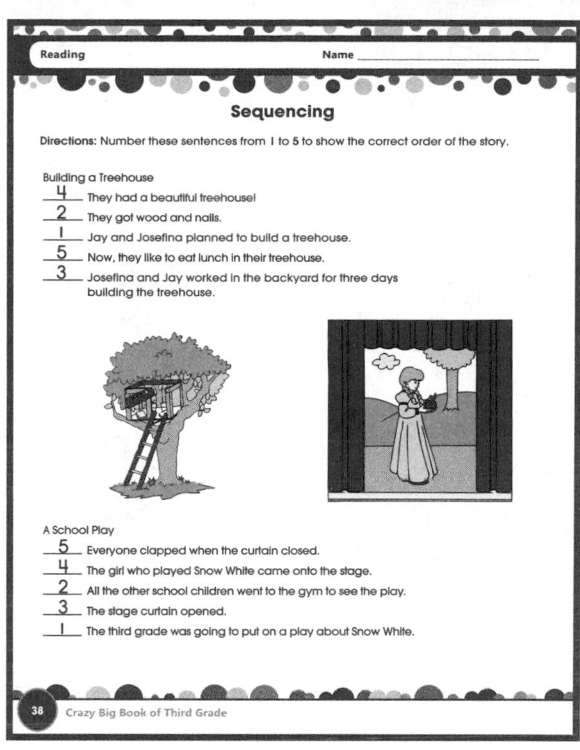
Reading Name ____________

Sequencing

Directions: Number these sentences from 1 to 5 to show the correct order of the story.

Building a Treehouse

4 They had a beautiful treehouse!
2 They got wood and nails.
1 Jay and Josefina planned to build a treehouse.
5 Now, they like to eat lunch in their treehouse.
3 Josefina and Jay worked in the backyard for three days building the treehouse.

A School Play

5 Everyone clapped when the curtain closed.
4 The girl who played Snow White came onto the stage.
2 All the other school children went to the gym to see the play.
3 The stage curtain opened.
1 The third grade was going to put on a play about Snow White.

38 Crazy Big Book of Third Grade

page 38

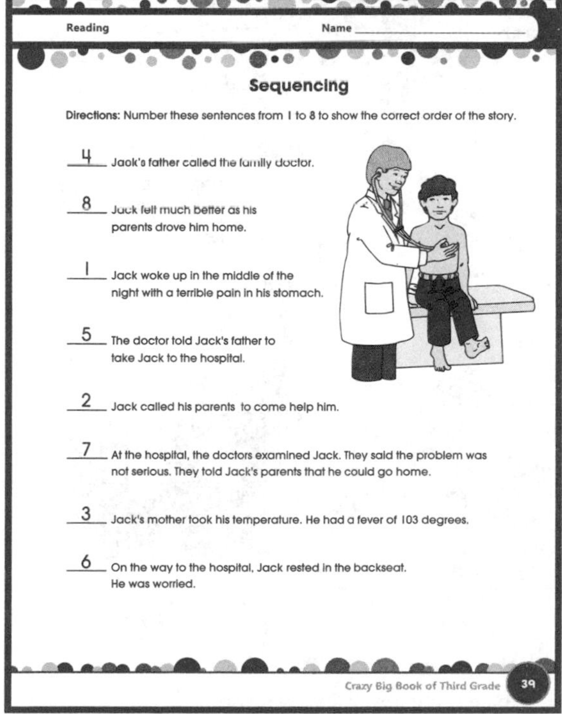
Reading Name ____________

Sequencing

Directions: Number these sentences from 1 to 8 to show the correct order of the story.

4 Jack's father called the family doctor.
8 Jack felt much better as his parents drove him home.
1 Jack woke up in the middle of the night with a terrible pain in his stomach.
5 The doctor told Jack's father to take Jack to the hospital.
2 Jack called his parents to come help him.
7 At the hospital, the doctors examined Jack. They said the problem was not serious. They told Jack's parents that he could go home.
3 Jack's mother took his temperature. He had a fever of 103 degrees.
6 On the way to the hospital, Jack rested in the backseat. He was worried.

Crazy Big Book of Third Grade 39

page 39

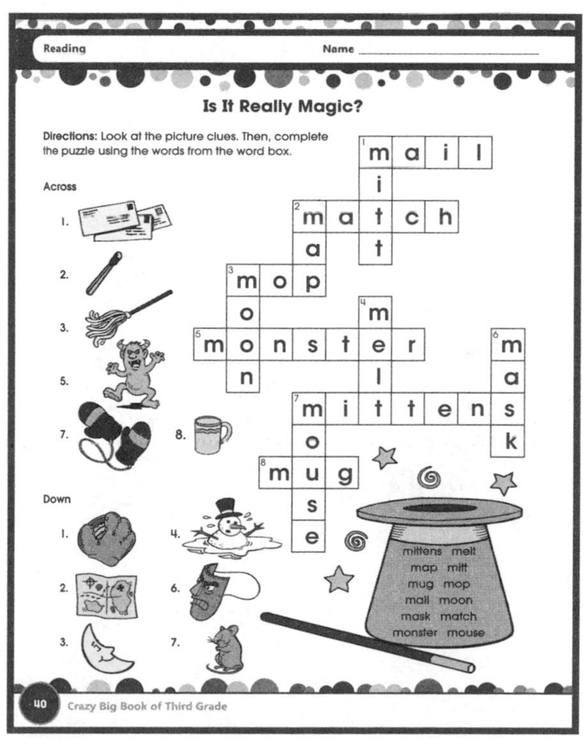
Reading Name ____________

Is It Really Magic?

Directions: Look at the picture clues. Then, complete the puzzle using the words from the word box.

Across: 1. mail 2. match 3. mop 5. monster 7. mittens 8. mug

Down: 1. mitt 2. map 3. moon 4. melt 6. mask 7. mouse

Word box: mittens melt map mitt mug mop mail moon mask match monster mouse

40 Crazy Big Book of Third Grade

page 40

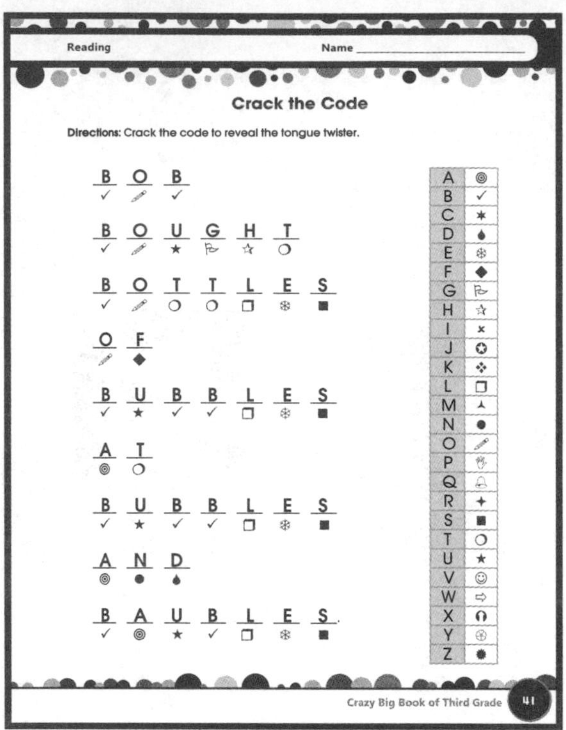
Reading Name ____________

Crack the Code

Directions: Crack the code to reveal the tongue twister.

BOB BOUGHT BOTTLES OF BUBBLES AT BUBBLES AND BAUBLES.

A B C D E F G H I J K L M N O P Q R S T U V W X Y Z

Crazy Big Book of Third Grade 41

page 41

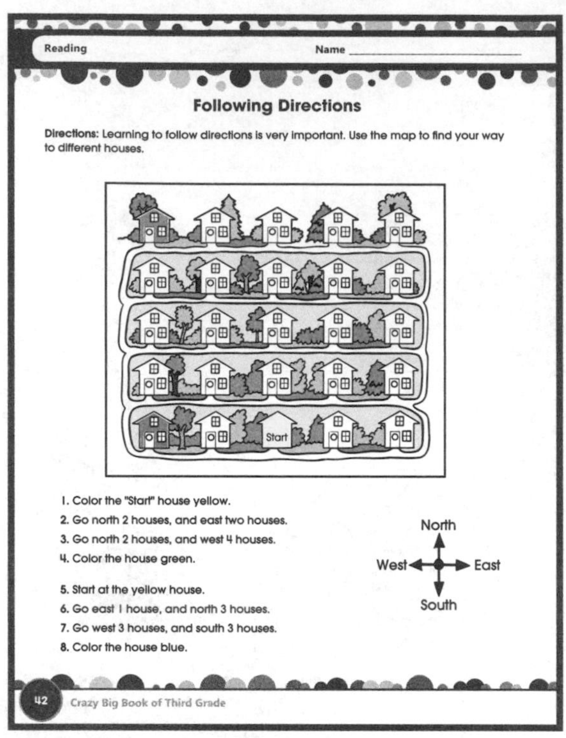
Reading Name ____________

Following Directions

Directions: Learning to follow directions is very important. Use the map to find your way to different houses.

1. Color the "Start" house yellow.
2. Go north 2 houses, and east two houses.
3. Go north 2 houses, and west 4 houses.
4. Color the house green.
5. Start at the yellow house.
6. Go east 1 house, and north 3 houses.
7. Go west 3 houses, and south 3 houses.
8. Color the house blue.

42 Crazy Big Book of Third Grade

page 42

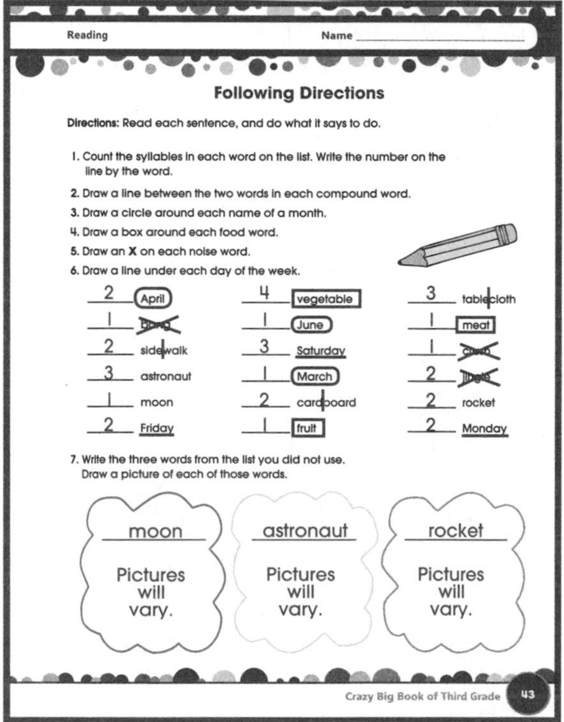
Reading Name ____________

Following Directions

Directions: Read each sentence, and do what it says to do.

1. Count the syllables in each word on the list. Write the number on the line by the word.
2. Draw a line between the two words in each compound word.
3. Draw a circle around each name of a month.
4. Draw a box around each food word.
5. Draw an **X** on each noise word.
6. Draw a line under each day of the week.

2 April	4 vegetable	3 table|cloth
1 bang	1 June	1 meat
2 side|walk	3 Saturday	1 crash
3 astronaut	1 March	2 tinkle
1 moon	2 card|board	2 rocket
2 Friday	1 fruit	2 Monday

7. Write the three words from the list you did not use. Draw a picture of each of those words.

moon — Pictures will vary.

astronaut — Pictures will vary.

rocket — Pictures will vary.

Crazy Big Book of Third Grade 43

page 43

Reading Name ____________

Climbing Koala

Directions: Look at the picture clues. Then, complete the puzzle using the words from the word box.

Across: 1. kettle 3. kangaroo 4. kite 6. kind 7. keys

Down: 1. king 2. koala bear 3. kitten 4. kick 5. kits

44 Crazy Big Book of Third Grade

page 44

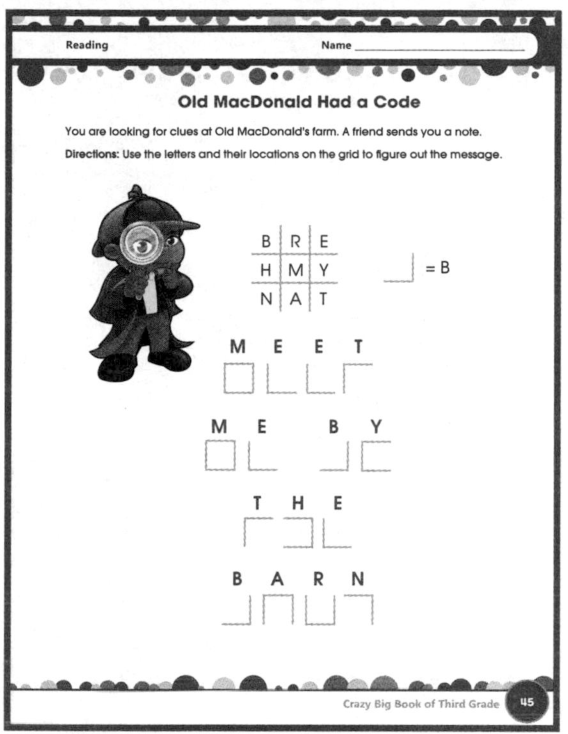

Old MacDonald Had a Code

You are looking for clues at Old MacDonald's farm. A friend sends you a note.

Directions: Use the letters and their locations on the grid to figure out the message.

B	R	E
H	M	Y
N	A	T

= B

M E E T

M E B Y

T H E

B A R N

page 45

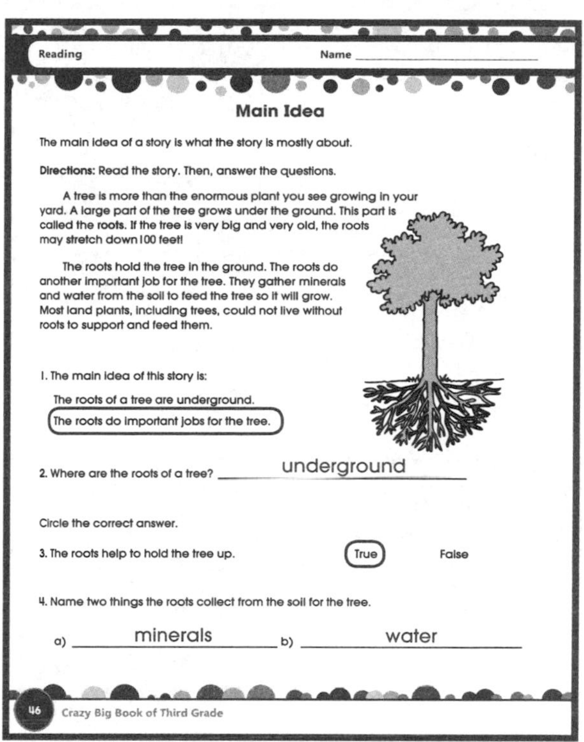

Main Idea

The main idea of a story is what the story is mostly about.

Directions: Read the story. Then, answer the questions.

A tree is more than the enormous plant you see growing in your yard. A large part of the tree grows under the ground. This part is called the roots. If the tree is very big and very old, the roots may stretch down 100 feet!

The roots hold the tree in the ground. The roots do another important job for the tree. They gather minerals and water from the soil to feed the tree so it will grow. Most land plants, including trees, could not live without roots to support and feed them.

1. The main idea of this story is:

The roots of a tree are underground.

(circled) The roots do important jobs for the tree.

2. Where are the roots of a tree? underground

Circle the correct answer.

3. The roots help to hold the tree up. (circled) True False

4. Name two things the roots collect from the soil for the tree.

a) minerals b) water

page 46

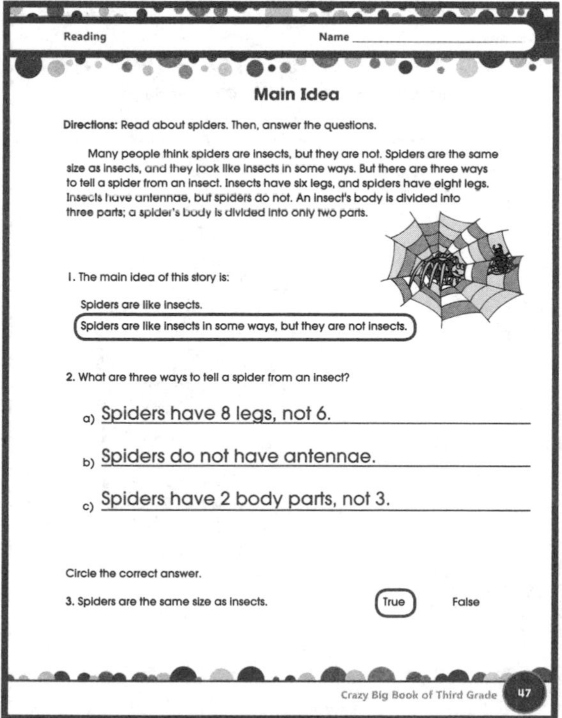

Main Idea

Directions: Read about spiders. Then, answer the questions.

Many people think spiders are insects, but they are not. Spiders are the same size as insects, and they look like insects in some ways. But there are three ways to tell a spider from an insect. Insects have six legs, and spiders have eight legs. Insects have antennae, but spiders do not. An insect's body is divided into three parts; a spider's body is divided into only two parts.

1. The main idea of this story is:

Spiders are like insects.

(circled) Spiders are like insects in some ways, but they are not insects.

2. What are three ways to tell a spider from an insect?

a) Spiders have 8 legs, not 6.

b) Spiders do not have antennae.

c) Spiders have 2 body parts, not 3.

Circle the correct answer.

3. Spiders are the same size as insects. (circled) True False

page 47

Main Idea

Directions: Read about the giant panda. Then, answer the questions.

Giant pandas are among the world's favorite animals. They look like big, cuddly stuffed toys. There are not very many pandas left in the world. You may have to travel a long way to see one.

The only place on Earth where pandas live in the wild is in the bamboo forests of the mountains of China. It is hard to see pandas in the forest because they are very shy. They hide among the many bamboo trees. It also is hard to see pandas because there are so few of them. Scientists think there may be about 1,600 pandas living in the mountains of China.

1. Write a sentence that tells the main idea of this story:

Possible answer: People love giant pandas, but it is not easy to see one.

2. What are two reasons that it is hard to see pandas in the wild?

a) They hide and are shy.

b) There are not many left in the wild.

3. How many pandas are believed to be living in the mountains of China?

1,600

page 48

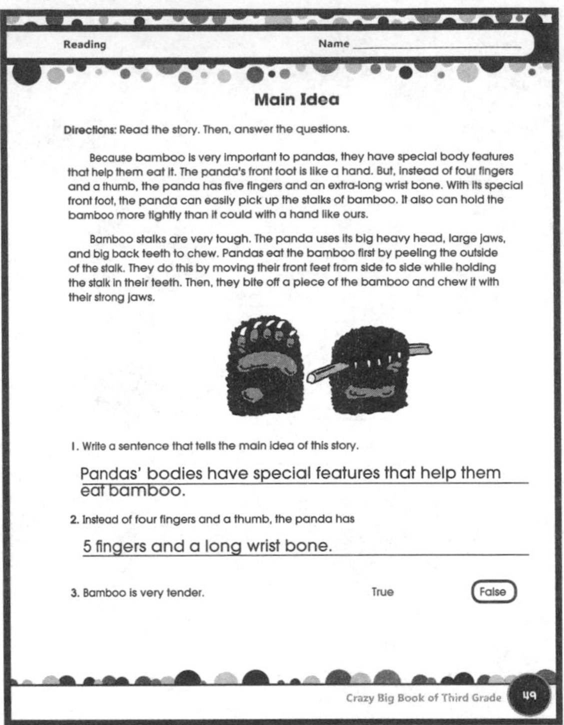

Reading Name ____________

Main Idea

Directions: Read the story. Then, answer the questions.

Because bamboo is very important to pandas, they have special body features that help them eat it. The panda's front foot is like a hand. But, instead of four fingers and a thumb, the panda has five fingers and an extra-long wrist bone. With its special front foot, the panda can easily pick up the stalks of bamboo. It also can hold the bamboo more tightly than it could with a hand like ours.

Bamboo stalks are very tough. The panda uses its big heavy head, large jaws, and big back teeth to chew. Pandas eat the bamboo first by peeling the outside of the stalk. They do this by moving their front feet from side to side while holding the stalk in their teeth. Then, they bite off a piece of the bamboo and chew it with their strong jaws.

1. Write a sentence that tells the main idea of this story.
Pandas' bodies have special features that help them eat bamboo.

2. Instead of four fingers and a thumb, the panda has
5 fingers and a long wrist bone.

3. Bamboo is very tender. True (False)

Crazy Big Book of Third Grade 49

page 49

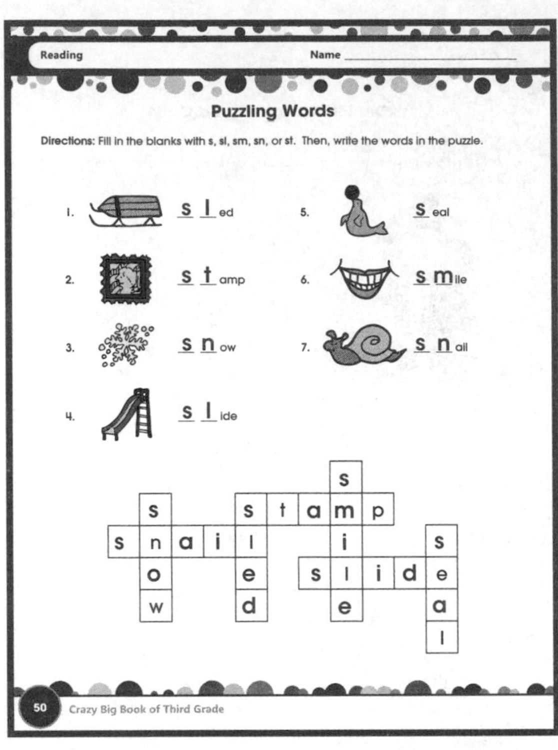

Reading Name ____________

Puzzling Words

Directions: Fill in the blanks with s, sl, sm, sn, or st. Then, write the words in the puzzle.

1. s l ed
2. s t amp
3. s n ow
4. s l ide
5. s eal
6. s m ile
7. s n ail

50 Crazy Big Book of Third Grade

page 50

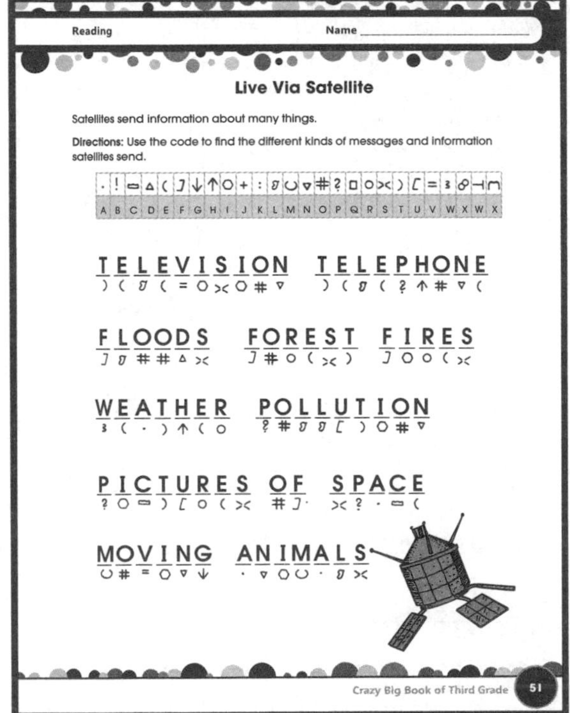

Reading Name ____________

Live Via Satellite

Satellites send information about many things.

Directions: Use the code to find the different kinds of messages and information satellites send.

TELEVISION TELEPHONE

FLOODS FOREST FIRES

WEATHER POLLUTION

PICTURES OF SPACE

MOVING ANIMALS

Crazy Big Book of Third Grade 51

page 51

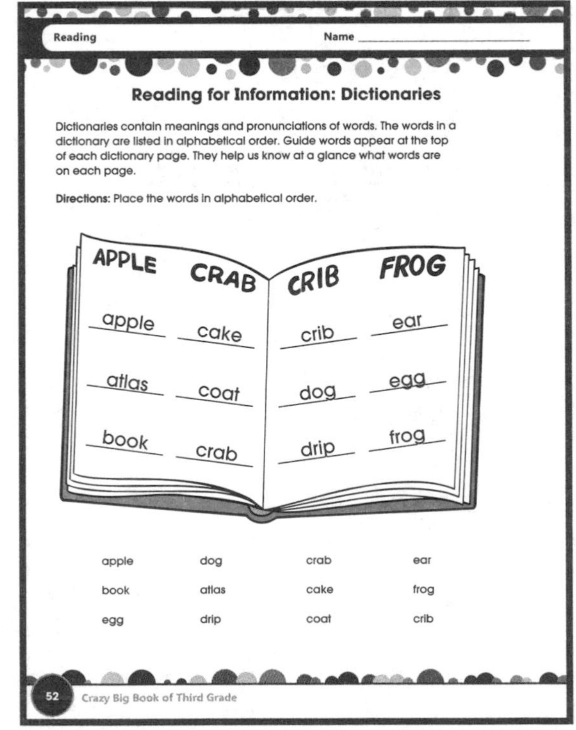

Reading Name ____________

Reading for Information: Dictionaries

Dictionaries contain meanings and pronunciations of words. The words in a dictionary are listed in alphabetical order. Guide words appear at the top of each dictionary page. They help us know at a glance what words are on each page.

Directions: Place the words in alphabetical order.

APPLE	CRAB	CRIB	FROG
apple	cake	crib	ear
atlas	coat	dog	egg
book	crab	drip	frog

apple, dog, crab, ear, book, atlas, cake, frog, egg, drip, coat, crib

52 Crazy Big Book of Third Grade

page 52

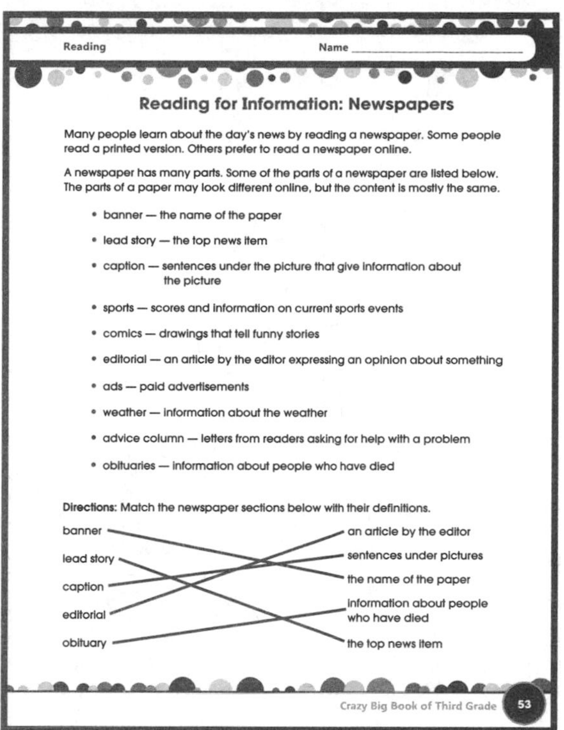

Reading Name ____________

Reading for Information: Newspapers

Many people learn about the day's news by reading a newspaper. Some people read a printed version. Others prefer to read a newspaper online.

A newspaper has many parts. Some of the parts of a newspaper are listed below. The parts of a paper may look different online, but the content is mostly the same.

- banner — the name of the paper
- lead story — the top news item
- caption — sentences under the picture that give information about the picture
- sports — scores and information on current sports events
- comics — drawings that tell funny stories
- editorial — an article by the editor expressing an opinion about something
- ads — paid advertisements
- weather — information about the weather
- advice column — letters from readers asking for help with a problem
- obituaries — information about people who have died

Directions: Match the newspaper sections below with their definitions.

- banner → the name of the paper
- lead story → the top news item
- caption → sentences under pictures
- editorial → an article by the editor
- obituary → information about people who have died

Crazy Big Book of Third Grade 53

page 53

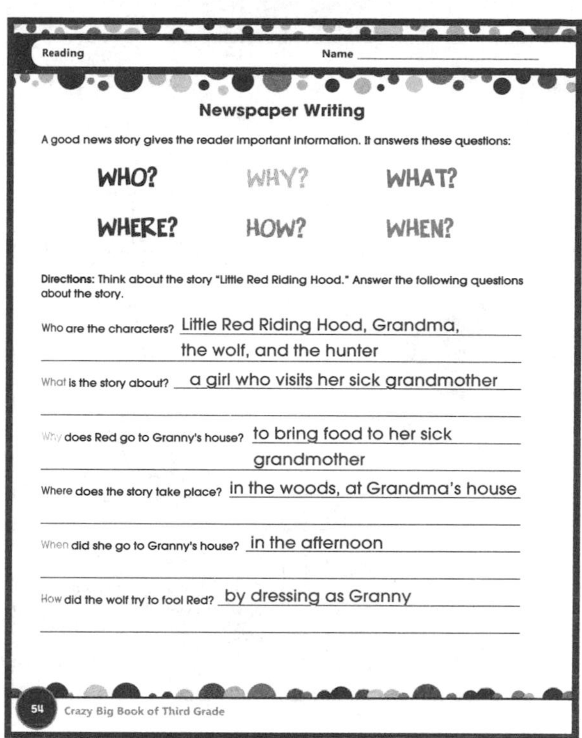

Reading Name ____________

Newspaper Writing

A good news story gives the reader important information. It answers these questions:

WHO? WHY? WHAT?
WHERE? HOW? WHEN?

Directions: Think about the story "Little Red Riding Hood." Answer the following questions about the story.

Who are the characters? Little Red Riding Hood, Grandma, the wolf, and the hunter

What is the story about? a girl who visits her sick grandmother

Why does Red go to Granny's house? to bring food to her sick grandmother

Where does the story take place? in the woods, at Grandma's house

When did she go to Granny's house? in the afternoon

How did the wolf try to fool Red? by dressing as Granny

54 Crazy Big Book of Third Grade

page 54

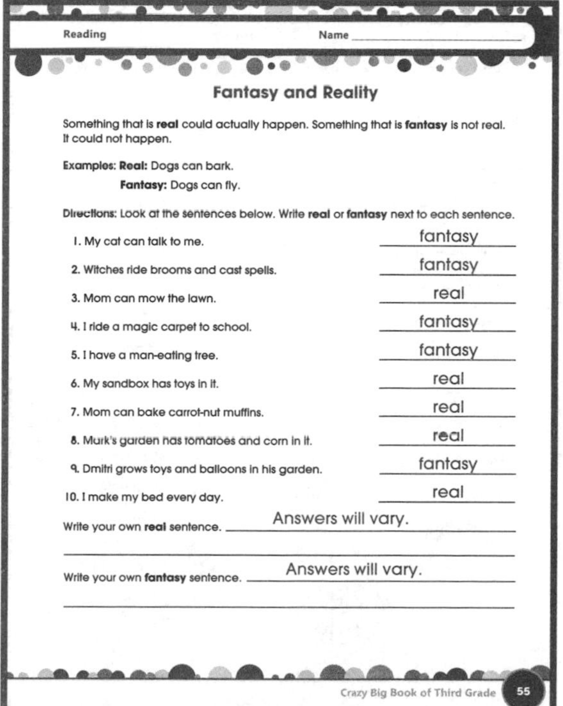

Reading Name ____________

Fantasy and Reality

Something that is **real** could actually happen. Something that is **fantasy** is not real. It could not happen.

Examples: Real: Dogs can bark.
Fantasy: Dogs can fly.

Directions: Look at the sentences below. Write **real** or **fantasy** next to each sentence.

1. My cat can talk to me. fantasy
2. Witches ride brooms and cast spells. fantasy
3. Mom can mow the lawn. real
4. I ride a magic carpet to school. fantasy
5. I have a man-eating tree. fantasy
6. My sandbox has toys in it. real
7. Mom can bake carrot-nut muffins. real
8. Mark's garden has tomatoes and corn in it. real
9. Dmitri grows toys and balloons in his garden. fantasy
10. I make my bed every day. real

Write your own **real** sentence. Answers will vary.

Write your own **fantasy** sentence. Answers will vary.

Crazy Big Book of Third Grade 55

page 55

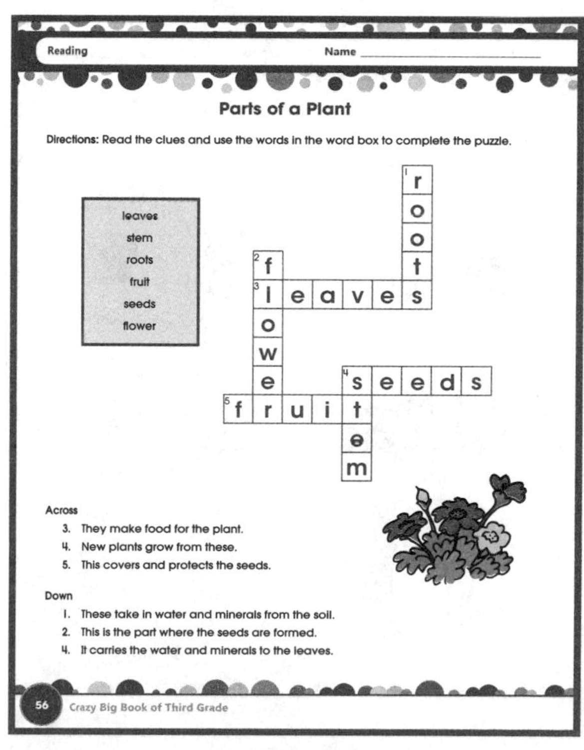

Reading Name ____________

Parts of a Plant

Directions: Read the clues and use the words in the word box to complete the puzzle.

leaves
stem
roots
fruit
seeds
flower

1 root (down)
2 flower (down)
3 leaves (across)
4 seeds (across), stem (down)
5 fruit (across)

Across
3. They make food for the plant.
4. New plants grow from these.
5. This covers and protects the seeds.

Down
1. These take in water and minerals from the soil.
2. This is the part where the seeds are formed.
4. It carries the water and minerals to the leaves.

56 Crazy Big Book of Third Grade

page 56

Reading Name ____________

Change a Letter

Directions: Starting with the top word in each square, change one letter at a time until the top word becomes the bottom word.

1.	L	I	S	T
2.	**M**	**I**	**S**	**T**
3.	**M**	**I**	**N**	**T**
4.	**M**	**I**	**N**	**E**
5.	M	A	N	E

6.	T	I	M	E
7.	**T**	**I**	**L**	**E**
8.	**F**	**I**	**L**	**E**
9.	**F**	**I**	**L**	**L**
10.	F	E	L	L

Crazy Big Book of Third Grade 57

page 57

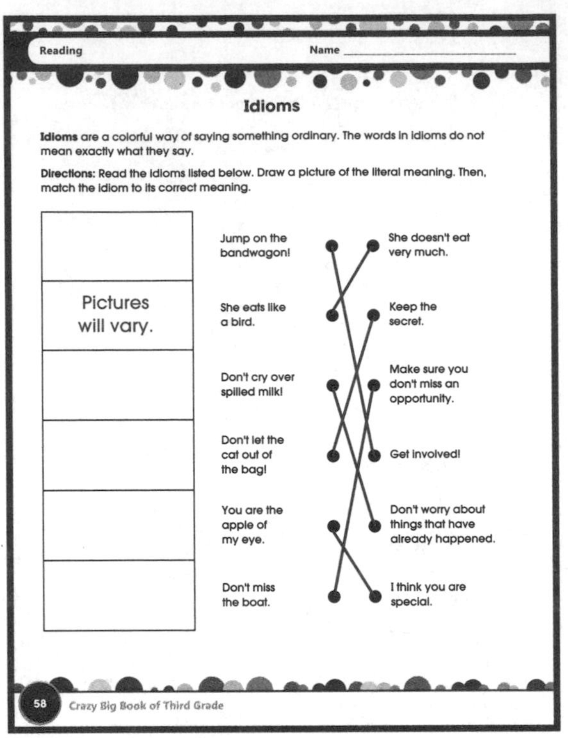
Reading Name ____________

Idioms

Idioms are a colorful way of saying something ordinary. The words in idioms do not mean exactly what they say.

Directions: Read the idioms listed below. Draw a picture of the literal meaning. Then, match the idiom to its correct meaning.

Pictures will vary.

Idiom	Meaning
Jump on the bandwagon!	She doesn't eat very much.
She eats like a bird.	Keep the secret.
Don't cry over spilled milk!	Make sure you don't miss an opportunity.
Don't let the cat out of the bag!	Get involved!
You are the apple of my eye.	Don't worry about things that have already happened.
Don't miss the boat.	I think you are special.

58 Crazy Big Book of Third Grade

page 58

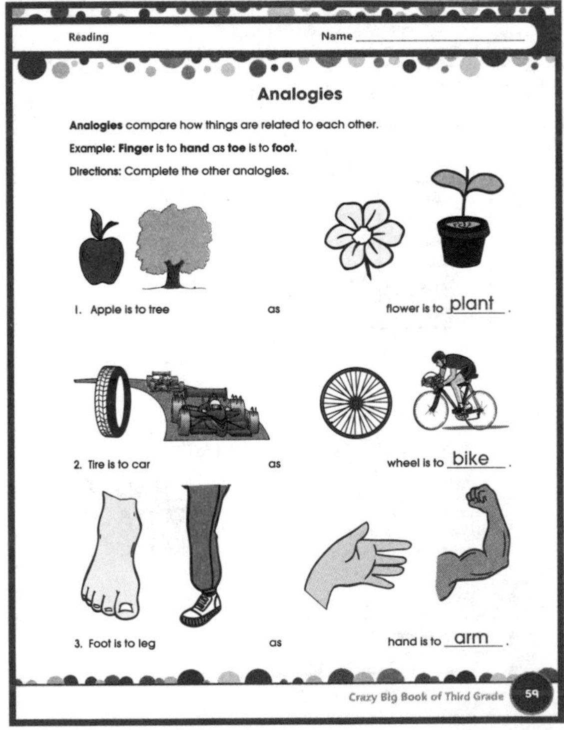
Reading Name ____________

Analogies

Analogies compare how things are related to each other.

Example: Finger is to **hand** as **toe** is to **foot.**

Directions: Complete the other analogies.

1. Apple is to tree as flower is to plant.
2. Tire is to car as wheel is to bike.
3. Foot is to leg as hand is to arm.

Crazy Big Book of Third Grade 59

page 59

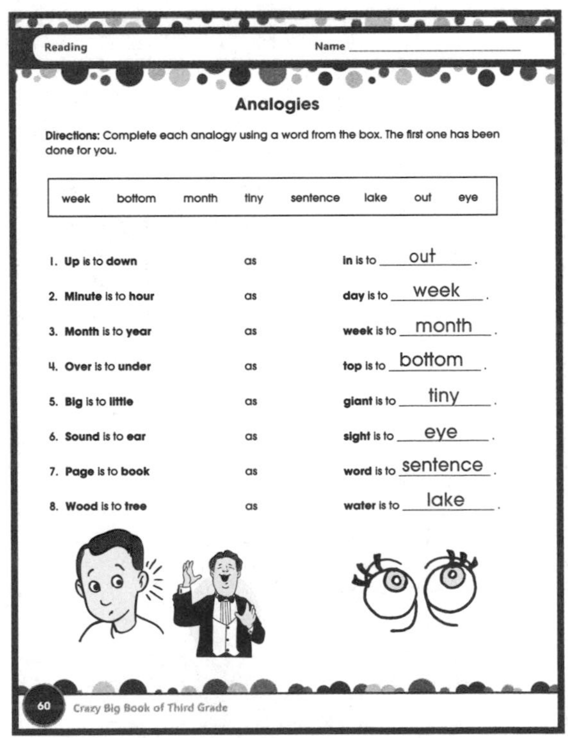
Reading Name ____________

Analogies

Directions: Complete each analogy using a word from the box. The first one has been done for you.

week bottom month tiny sentence lake out eye

1. **Up** is to **down** as **in** is to out.
2. **Minute** is to **hour** as **day** is to week.
3. **Month** is to **year** as **week** is to month.
4. **Over** is to **under** as **top** is to bottom.
5. **Big** is to **little** as **giant** is to tiny.
6. **Sound** is to **ear** as **sight** is to eye.
7. **Page** is to **book** as **word** is to sentence.
8. **Wood** is to **tree** as **water** is to lake.

60 Crazy Big Book of Third Grade

page 60

Reading Name ______

Toy Store

Directions: Use the word lists to fill out the grid below.

Hint: Count the squares in the grid first to see where the words will fit.

3 Letters
buy
pay

4 Letters
shop
toys
sell
sale

5 Letters
games
music
guard
clerk
hobby

8 Letters
elevator

Crazy Big Book of Third Grade 61

page 61

Reading Name ______

A Trip to Mars

Directions: Find the Mars words from the word box. Words can be across, down, diagonal, or backward.

red	dusky	craters
windy	lifeless	volcanoes
dry	mountainous	frozen

v o l c a n o e s c y
r e d k m n a h e r a
b v r w i h e a u a l
i x y d n i w r f t i
t t p l l k p r c e f
y k s u d g o d g r e
s g c s r z n v l s l
h l r s e r e s c c e
m o u n t a i n o u s
a a m v u h r r h l s

62 Crazy Big Book of Third Grade

page 62

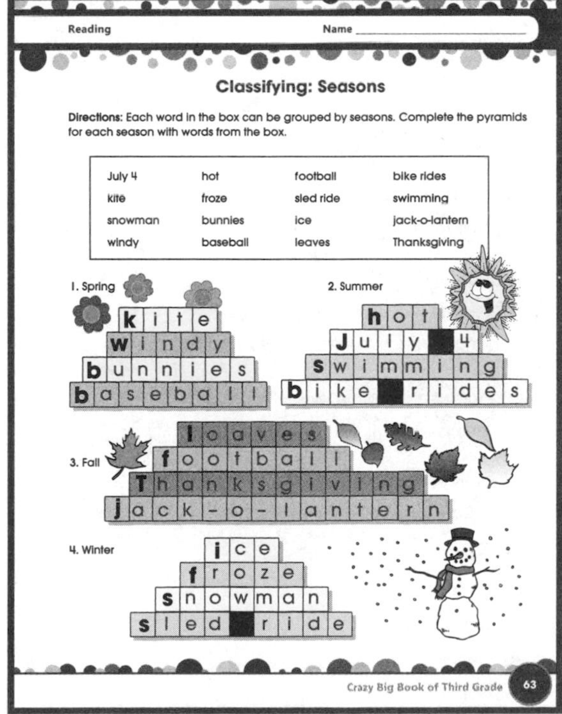
Reading Name ______

Classifying: Seasons

Directions: Each word in the box can be grouped by seasons. Complete the pyramids for each season with words from the box.

July 4	hot	football	bike rides
kite	froze	sled ride	swimming
snowman	bunnies	ice	jack-o-lantern
windy	baseball	leaves	Thanksgiving

1. Spring: kite, windy, bunnies, baseball
2. Summer: hot, July 4, swimming, bike rides
3. Fall: leaves, football, Thanksgiving, jack-o-lantern
4. Winter: ice, froze, snowman, sled ride

Crazy Big Book of Third Grade 63

page 63

Reading Name ______

Classifying

Directions: Write each word from the box in the correct category.

robin	elm
buckeye	willow
sunflower	blue jay
canary	oak
rose	wren
tulip	morning glory

Trees
buckeye
elm
willow
oak

Birds
robin
canary
blue jay
wren

Flowers
sunflower
rose
tulip
morning glory

64 Crazy Big Book of Third Grade

page 64

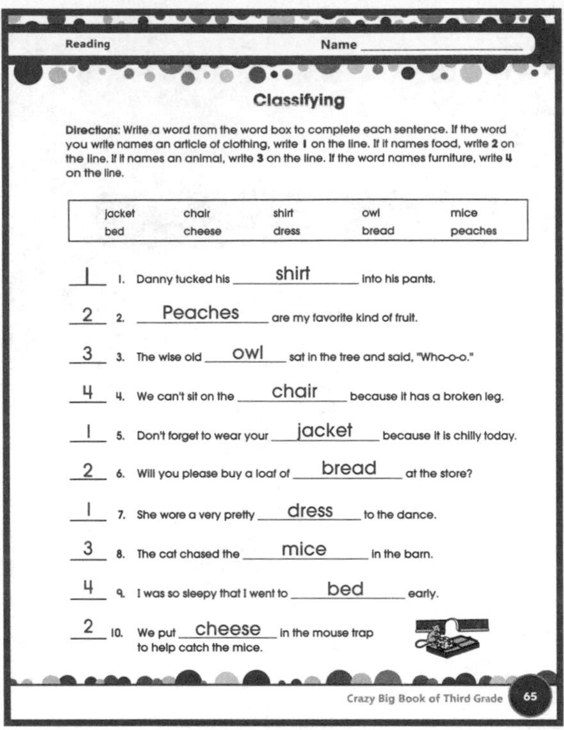

Reading Name ____________

Classifying

Directions: Write a word from the word box to complete each sentence. If the word you write names an article of clothing, write **1** on the line. If it names food, write **2** on the line. If it names an animal, write **3** on the line. If the word names furniture, write **4** on the line.

jacket	chair	shirt	owl	mice
bed	cheese	dress	bread	peaches

1 1. Danny tucked his shirt into his pants.

2 2. Peaches are my favorite kind of fruit.

3 3. The wise old owl sat in the tree and said, "Who-o-o."

4 4. We can't sit on the chair because it has a broken leg.

1 5. Don't forget to wear your jacket because it is chilly today.

2 6. Will you please buy a loaf of bread at the store?

1 7. She wore a very pretty dress to the dance.

3 8. The cat chased the mice in the barn.

4 9. I was so sleepy that I went to bed early.

2 10. We put cheese in the mouse trap to help catch the mice.

Crazy Big Book of Third Grade 65

page 65

Reading Name ____________

Comet Search

There are more than 800 known comets. Halley's Comet is the most famous. It appears about every 76 years. The last scheduled appearance in this century was in 1985. When will it appear next?

Directions: Circle the words from the word bank in the word search. When you are finished, write down the letters that are not circled. Start at the top of the puzzle and go from left to right.

dust	Halley	coma	snowball	melt	solar system
orbit	tail	ice	sky	shining	

S	P	M	E	L	T	L	A	N	H	E
O	T	S	S	H	A	C	O	M	A	V
L	E	N	O	R	D	B	I	T	L	S
A	L	O	I	K	U	E	C	I	L	R
R	C	W	L	E	S	S	C	O	E	M
S	E	B	T	S	T	H	A	V	Y	E
Y	O	A	R	O	R	B	I	T	B	I
S	T	L	S	S	H	A	P	E	D	L
T	I	L	K	T	A	I	L	E	A	F
E	O	O	T	I	C	E	B	A	L	L
M	S	K	Y	S	H	I	N	I	N	G

Planets have orbits like circles. Comets have orbits shaped like a football.

66 Crazy Big Book of Third Grade

page 66

Reading Name ____________

Dino Pet!

Directions: If you could have a pet dinosaur, what would it look like? Draw your dinosaur below. Write its name on the line.

Answers will vary.

Crazy Big Book of Third Grade 67

page 67

Reading Name ____________

Types of Books

A **fiction** book is a book about things that are made up or not true. Fantasy books are fiction. A **nonfiction** book is about things that have really happened. Books can be classified into more types:

mystery — books that have clues that lead to solving a problem or mystery

biography — book about a real person's life

poetry — a collection of poems, which may or may not rhyme

fantasy — books about things that cannot really happen

sports — books about different sports or sport figures

travel — books about going to other places

Directions: Write **mystery**, **biography**, **poetry**, **fantasy**, **sports**, or **travel** next to each title.

The Life of Helen Keller biography

Let's Go to Mexico! travel

The Case of the Missing Doll mystery

How to Play Golf sports

Turtle Soup and Other Poems poetry

Fred's Flying Saucer fantasy

68 Crazy Big Book of Third Grade

page 68

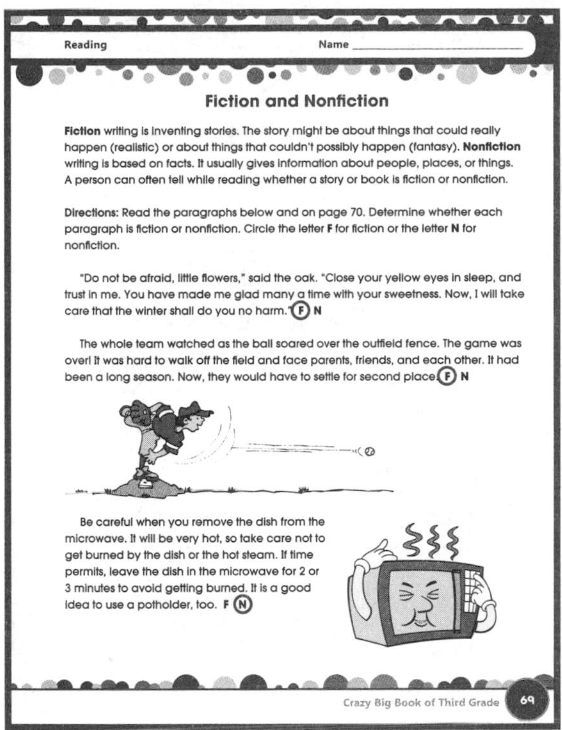

Fiction and Nonfiction

Fiction writing is inventing stories. The story might be about things that could really happen (realistic) or about things that couldn't possibly happen (fantasy). **Nonfiction** writing is based on facts. It usually gives information about people, places, or things. A person can often tell while reading whether a story or book is fiction or nonfiction.

Directions: Read the paragraphs below and on page 70. Determine whether each paragraph is fiction or nonfiction. Circle the letter **F** for fiction or the letter **N** for nonfiction.

"Do not be afraid, little flowers," said the oak. "Close your yellow eyes in sleep, and trust in me. You have made me glad many a time with your sweetness. Now, I will take care that the winter shall do you no harm." (F) N

The whole team watched as the ball soared over the outfield fence. The game was over! It was hard to walk off the field and face parents, friends, and each other. It had been a long season. Now, they would have to settle for second place. (F) N

Be careful when you remove the dish from the microwave. It will be very hot, so take care not to get burned by the dish or the hot steam. If time permits, leave the dish in the microwave for 2 or 3 minutes to avoid getting burned. It is a good idea to use a potholder, too. F (N)

page 69

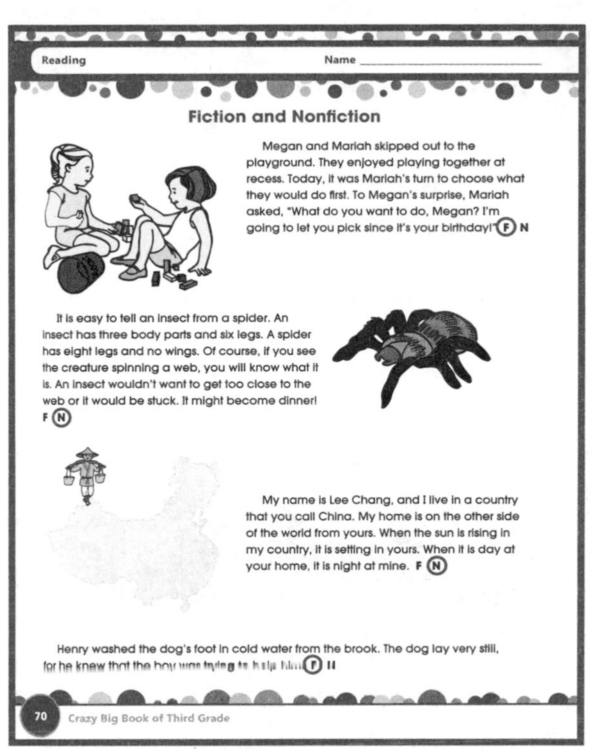

Fiction and Nonfiction

Megan and Mariah skipped out to the playground. They enjoyed playing together at recess. Today, it was Mariah's turn to choose what they would do first. To Megan's surprise, Mariah asked, "What do you want to do, Megan? I'm going to let you pick since it's your birthday!" (F) N

It is easy to tell an insect from a spider. An insect has three body parts and six legs. A spider has eight legs and no wings. Of course, if you see the creature spinning a web, you will know what it is. An insect wouldn't want to get too close to the web or it would be stuck. It might become dinner! F (N)

My name is Lee Chang, and I live in a country that you call China. My home is on the other side of the world from yours. When the sun is rising in my country, it is setting in yours. When it is day at your home, it is night at mine. F (N)

Henry washed the dog's foot in cold water from the brook. The dog lay very still, for he knew that the boy was trying to help him. (F) N

page 70

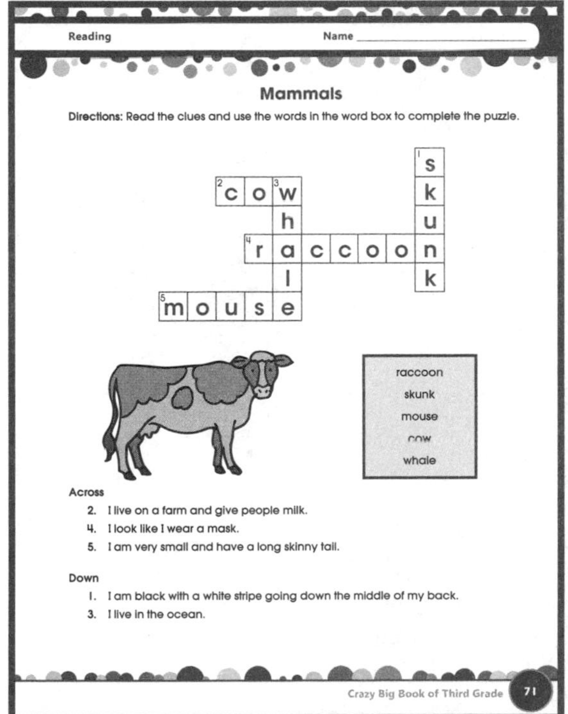

Mammals

Directions: Read the clues and use the words in the word box to complete the puzzle.

1 Down: skunk
2 Across: cow
3 Down: whale
4 Across: raccoon
5 Across: mouse

Word box: raccoon, skunk, mouse, cow, whale

Across

2. I live on a farm and give people milk.
4. I look like I wear a mask.
5. I am very small and have a long skinny tail.

Down

1. I am black with a white stripe going down the middle of my back.
3. I live in the ocean.

page 71

Q + U

Directions: Look at the picture clues. Then, complete the puzzle using the words from the word box.

Word box: quiet, quail, quarter, umbrella, unicorn, queen

Across

1. quiet
3. quarter
4. quail
5. unicorn

Down

2. umbrella
4. queen

page 72

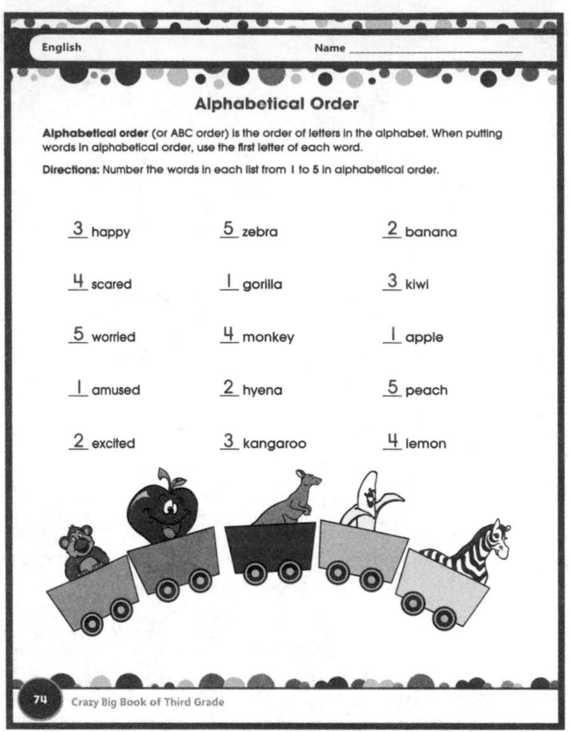

English Name ____________

Alphabetical Order

Alphabetical order (or ABC order) is the order of letters in the alphabet. When putting words in alphabetical order, use the first letter of each word.

Directions: Number the words in each list from 1 to 5 in alphabetical order.

3 happy	5 zebra	2 banana
4 scared	1 gorilla	3 kiwi
5 worried	4 monkey	1 apple
1 amused	2 hyena	5 peach
2 excited	3 kangaroo	4 lemon

74 Crazy Big Book of Third Grade

page 74

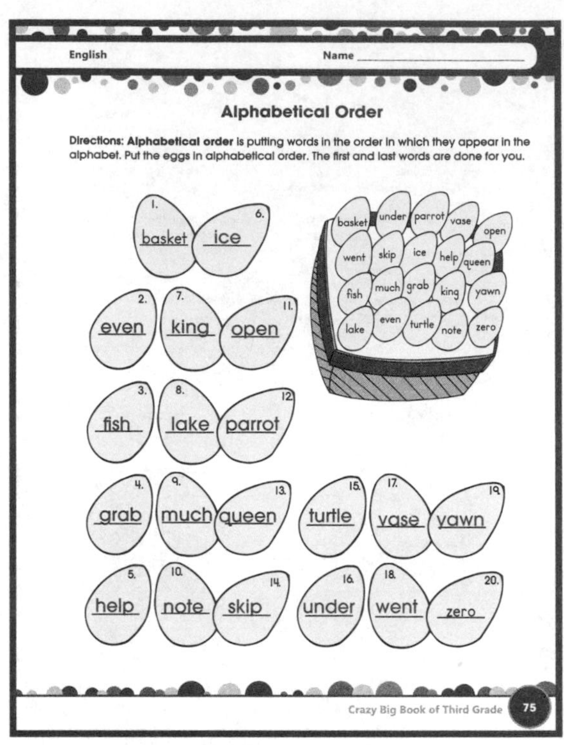

English Name ____________

Alphabetical Order

Directions: Alphabetical order is putting words in the order in which they appear in the alphabet. Put the eggs in alphabetical order. The first and last words are done for you.

1. basket
2. even
3. fish
4. grab
5. help
6. ice
7. king
8. lake
9. much
10. note
11. open
12. parrot
13. queen
14. skip
15. turtle
16. under
17. vase
18. went
19. yawn
20. zero

Crazy Big Book of Third Grade 75

page 75

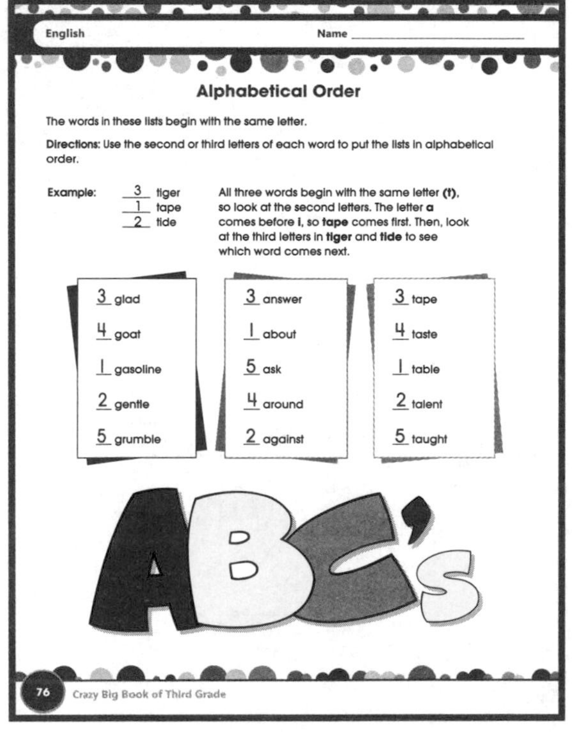

English Name ____________

Alphabetical Order

The words in these lists begin with the same letter.

Directions: Use the second or third letters of each word to put the lists in alphabetical order.

Example: 3 tiger, 1 tape, 2 tide

All three words begin with the same letter **(t)**, so look at the second letters. The letter **a** comes before **i**, so **tape** comes first. Then, look at the third letters in **tiger** and **tide** to see which word comes next.

3 glad	3 answer	3 tape
4 goat	1 about	4 taste
1 gasoline	5 ask	1 table
2 gentle	4 around	2 talent
5 grumble	2 against	5 taught

76 Crazy Big Book of Third Grade

page 76

English Name ____________

Alphabetical Order

Alphabetical order is the order in which letters come in the alphabet.

Directions: Write the words in alphabetical order. If the first letter is the same, use the second letter of each word to decide which word comes first. If the second letter is also the same, look at the third letter of each word to decide.

Example: wish wasp won't

1. wasp
2. wish
3. won't

All right! Bravo! Cool!

bench flag bowl

1. bench
2. bowl
3. flag

egg nod neat

1. egg
2. neat
3. nod

dog dart drag

1. dart
2. dog
3. drag

skipped stairs stones

1. skipped
2. stairs
3. stones

Crazy Big Book of Third Grade 77

page 77

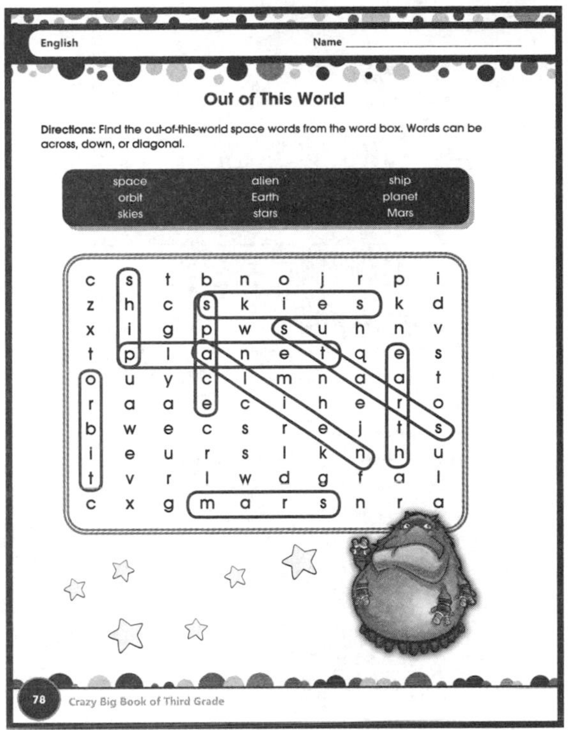

English Name ____________

Out of This World

Directions: Find the out-of-this-world space words from the word box. Words can be across, down, or diagonal.

space	alien	ship
orbit	Earth	planet
skies	stars	Mars

c	s	t	b	n	o	j	r	p	i
z	h	c	s	k	i	e	s	k	d
x	i	g	p	w	s	u	h	n	v
t	p	l	a	n	e	t	q	e	s
o	u	y	c	l	m	n	a	a	t
r	a	a	e	c	i	h	e	r	o
b	w	e	c	s	r	e	j	t	s
i	e	u	r	s	l	k	n	h	u
t	v	r	l	w	d	g	f	a	l
c	x	g	m	a	r	s	n	r	a

78 Crazy Big Book of Third Grade

page 78

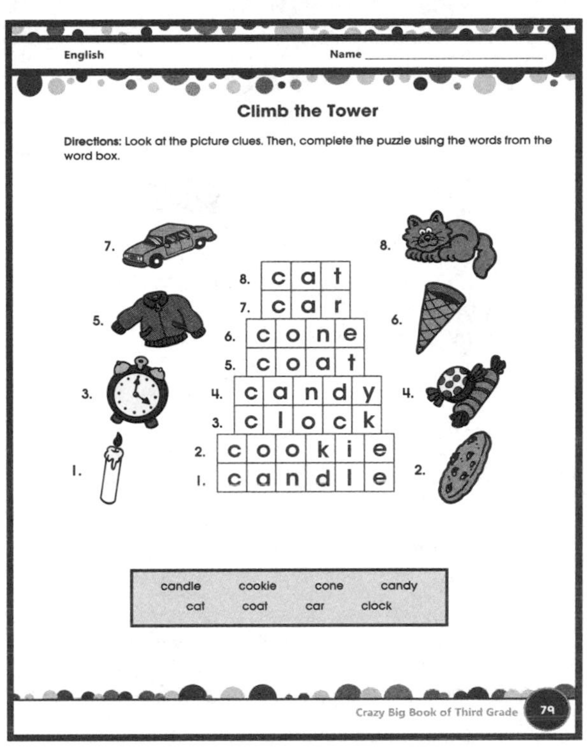

English Name ____________

Climb the Tower

Directions: Look at the picture clues. Then, complete the puzzle using the words from the word box.

8. cat
7. car
6. cone
5. coat
4. candy
3. clock
2. cookie
1. candle

candle	cookie	cone	candy
cat	coat	car	clock

Crazy Big Book of Third Grade 79

page 79

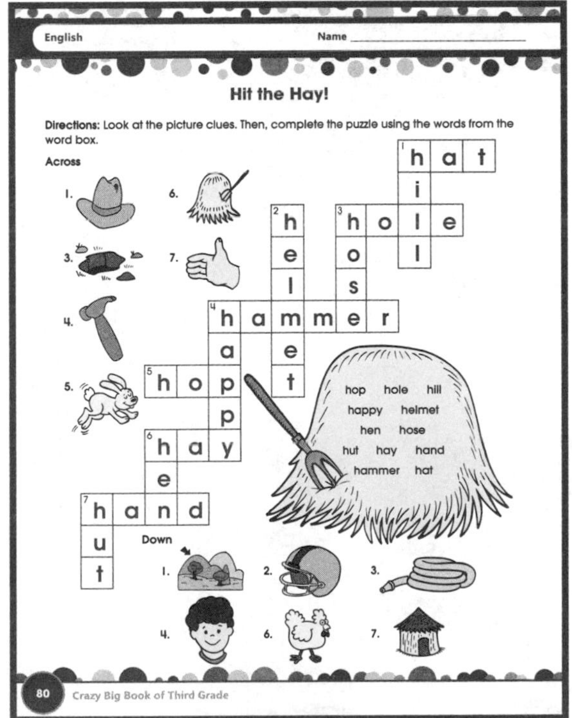

English Name ____________

Hit the Hay!

Directions: Look at the picture clues. Then, complete the puzzle using the words from the word box.

Across

1. hat
3. hole
4. hammer
5. hop
6. hay
7. hand

Down

1. hill
2. helmet
3. hose
4. happy
6. hen
7. hut

hop hole hill
happy helmet
hen hose
hut hay hand
hammer hat

80 Crazy Big Book of Third Grade

page 80

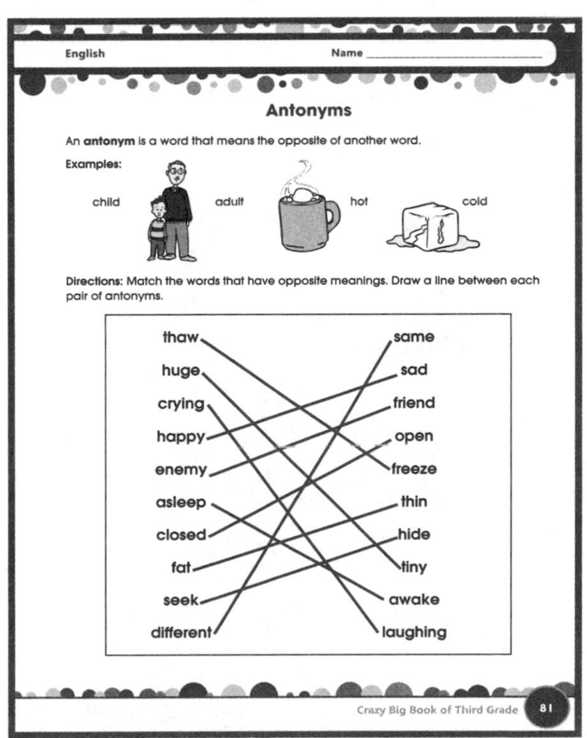

English Name ____________

Antonyms

An **antonym** is a word that means the opposite of another word.

Examples:

child adult hot cold

Directions: Match the words that have opposite meanings. Draw a line between each pair of antonyms.

thaw	same
huge	sad
crying	friend
happy	open
enemy	freeze
asleep	thin
closed	hide
fat	tiny
seek	awake
different	laughing

Crazy Big Book of Third Grade 81

page 81

English Name ______

Antonyms

Directions: Complete each sentence with an antonym pair from page 81. Some pairs will not be used.

Example: Usually, we wear <u>different</u> clothes, but today we are dressed the <u>same</u>.

1. The __fat__ cat would be __thin__ if it chased more mice.
2. Mom was __happy__ it rained since her garden was very dry, but I was __sad__ because I had to stay inside.
3. The __huge__ crowd of people tried to fit into the __tiny__ room.
4. The __crying__ baby was soon __laughing__ and playing in the crib.
5. We'll __freeze__ the meat for now, and Dad will __thaw__ it when we need it.
6. The windows were wide __open__, but the door was __closed__.

Now, write your own sentence using one of the antonym pairs.

Answers will vary.

82 Crazy Big Book of Third Grade

page 82

English Name ______

Antonyms

Antonyms are words that are opposites.

Example: hairy bald

Directions: Choose a word from the box to complete each sentence below. Not every word will be used.

open	right	light	full	late	below
hard	clean	slow	quiet	old	nice

Example:

My car was **dirty**, but now it's **clean**.

1. Sometimes, my cat is naughty, and sometimes she's __nice__.
2. The sign said, "Closed," but the door was __open__.
3. Is the glass half empty or half __full__?
4. I bought new shoes, but I like my __old__ ones better.
5. Skating is easy for me, but __hard__ for my brother.
6. The sky is dark at night and __light__ during the day.
7. I like a noisy house, but my mother likes a __quiet__ one.
8. My friend says I'm wrong, but I say I'm __right__.
9. Jason is a fast runner, but Adam is a __slow__ runner.
10. We were supposed to be early, but we were __late__.

Crazy Big Book of Third Grade 83

page 83

English Name ______

Antonyms

Directions: Write the antonym pairs from each sentence in the boxes.

Example: Many things are bought and sold at the market.

bought	sold

1. I thought I lost my dog, but someone found him.

lost	found

2. The teacher will ask a question for the students to answer.

question	answer

3. Airplanes arrive and depart from the airport.

arrive	depart

4. The water in the pool was cold compared to the warm water in the whirlpool.

cold	warm

5. The tortoise was slow, but the hare was fast.

slow	fast

84 Crazy Big Book of Third Grade

page 84

English Name ______

Q and U Too

Directions: Look at the picture clues. Then, complete the puzzle using the words from the word box.

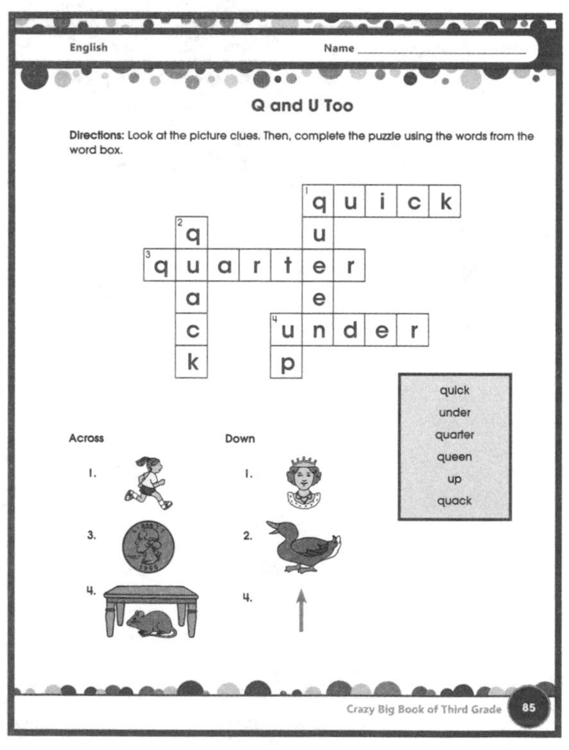

Crazy Big Book of Third Grade 85

page 85

English Name ____________

Build Your Dream House

Directions: If you could build your dream house, what would it look like? Draw it below. Then, write your name on the mailbox.

Drawings will vary.

86 Crazy Big Book of Third Grade

page 86

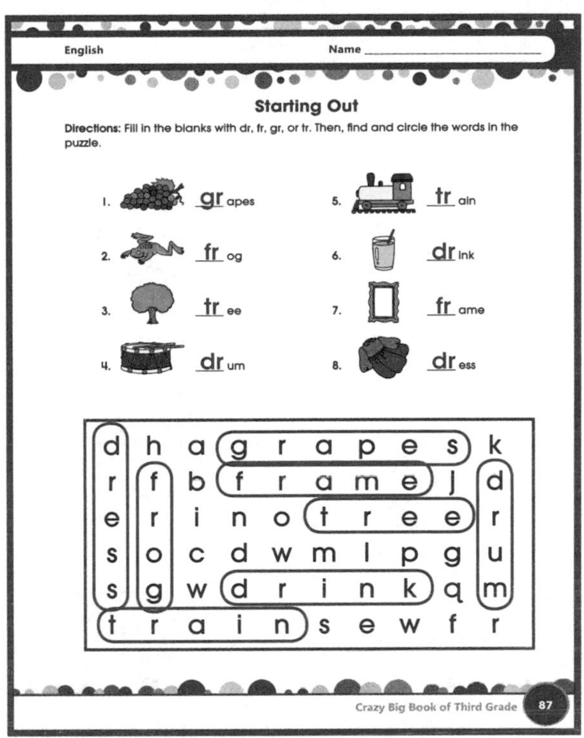

English Name ____________

Starting Out

Directions: Fill in the blanks with dr, fr, gr, or tr. Then, find and circle the words in the puzzle.

1. gr apes
2. fr og
3. tr ee
4. dr um
5. tr ain
6. dr ink
7. fr ame
8. dr ess

d	h	a	g	r	a	p	e	s	k
r	f	b	f	r	a	m	e	j	d
e	r	i	n	o	t	r	e	e	r
s	o	c	d	w	m	l	p	g	u
s	g	w	d	r	i	n	k	q	m
t	r	a	i	n	s	e	w	f	r

Crazy Big Book of Third Grade 87

page 87

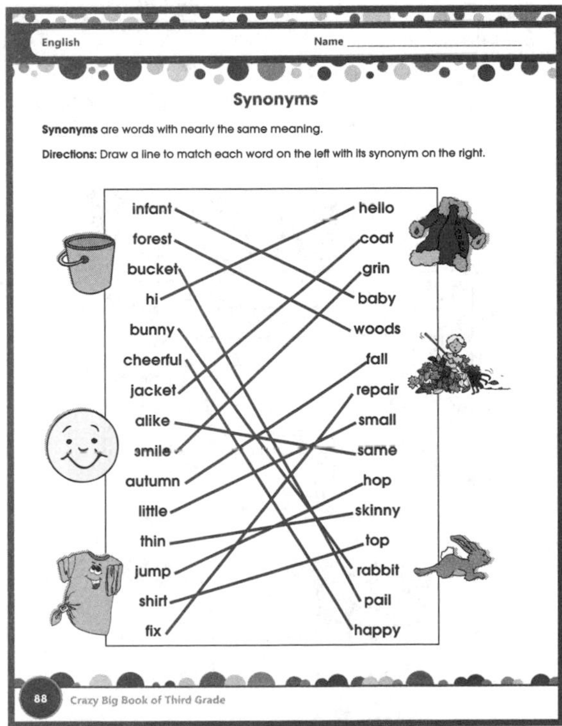

English Name ____________

Synonyms

Synonyms are words with nearly the same meaning.

Directions: Draw a line to match each word on the left with its synonym on the right.

infant	hello
forest	coat
bucket	grin
hi	baby
bunny	woods
cheerful	fall
jacket	repair
alike	small
smile	same
autumn	hop
little	skinny
thin	top
jump	rabbit
shirt	pail
fix	happy

88 Crazy Big Book of Third Grade

page 88

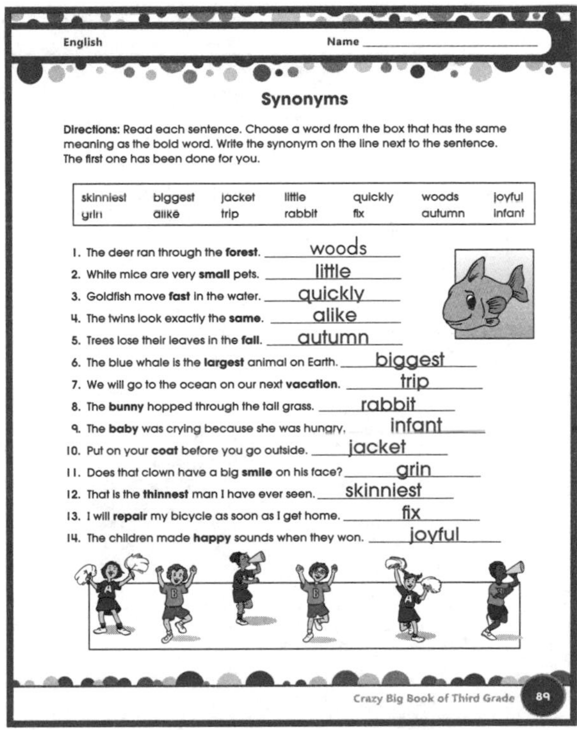

English Name ____________

Synonyms

Directions: Read each sentence. Choose a word from the box that has the same meaning as the bold word. Write the synonym on the line next to the sentence. The first one has been done for you.

skinniest	biggest	jacket	little	quickly	woods	joyful
grin	alike	trip	rabbit	fix	autumn	infant

1. The deer ran through the **forest**. woods
2. White mice are very **small** pets. little
3. Goldfish move **fast** in the water. quickly
4. The twins look exactly the **same**. alike
5. Trees lose their leaves in the **fall**. autumn
6. The blue whale is the **largest** animal on Earth. biggest
7. We will go to the ocean on our next **vacation**. trip
8. The **bunny** hopped through the tall grass. rabbit
9. The **baby** was crying because she was hungry. infant
10. Put on your **coat** before you go outside. jacket
11. Does that clown have a big **smile** on his face? grin
12. That is the **thinnest** man I have ever seen. skinniest
13. I will **repair** my bicycle as soon as I get home. fix
14. The children made **happy** sounds when they won. joyful

Crazy Big Book of Third Grade 89

page 89

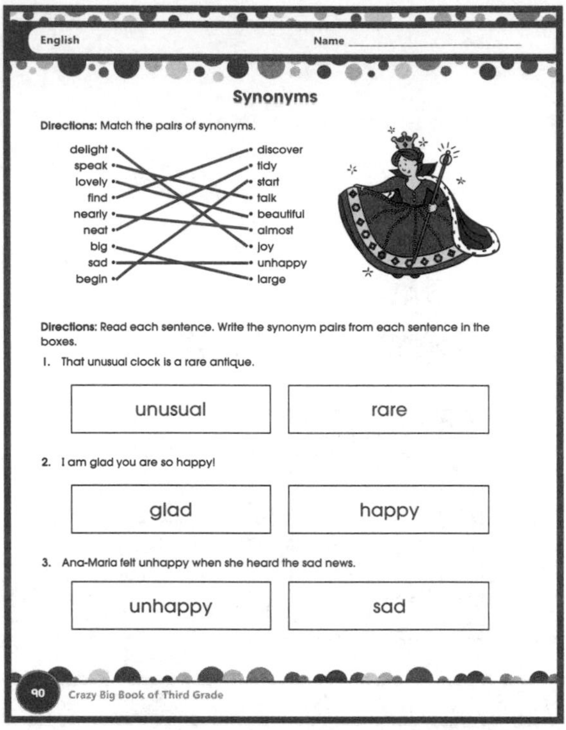

English Name ____________

Synonyms

Directions: Match the pairs of synonyms.

delight	discover
speak	tidy
lovely	start
find	talk
nearly	beautiful
neat	almost
big	joy
sad	unhappy
begin	large

Directions: Read each sentence. Write the synonym pairs from each sentence in the boxes.

1. That unusual clock is a rare antique.

unusual | rare

2. I am glad you are so happy!

glad | happy

3. Ana-Maria felt unhappy when she heard the sad news.

unhappy | sad

90 Crazy Big Book of Third Grade

page 90

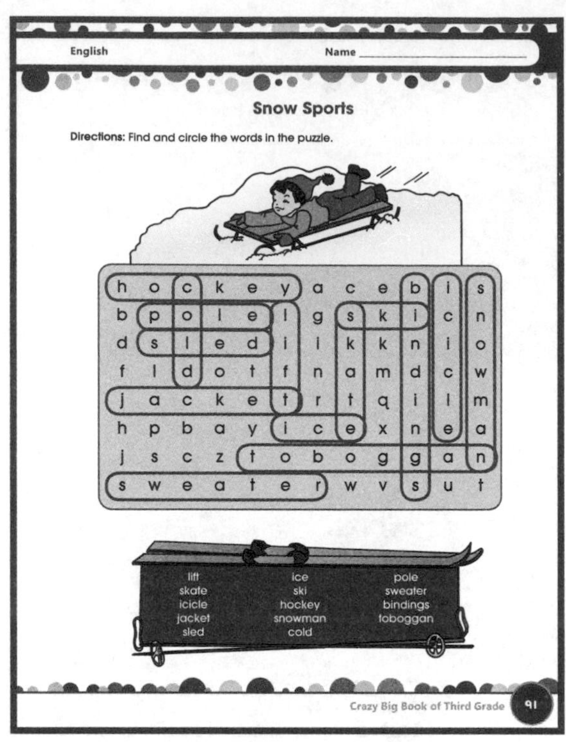

English Name ____________

Snow Sports

Directions: Find and circle the words in the puzzle.

lift, skate, icicle, jacket, sled, ice, ski, hockey, snowman, cold, pole, sweater, bindings, toboggan

Crazy Big Book of Third Grade 91

page 91

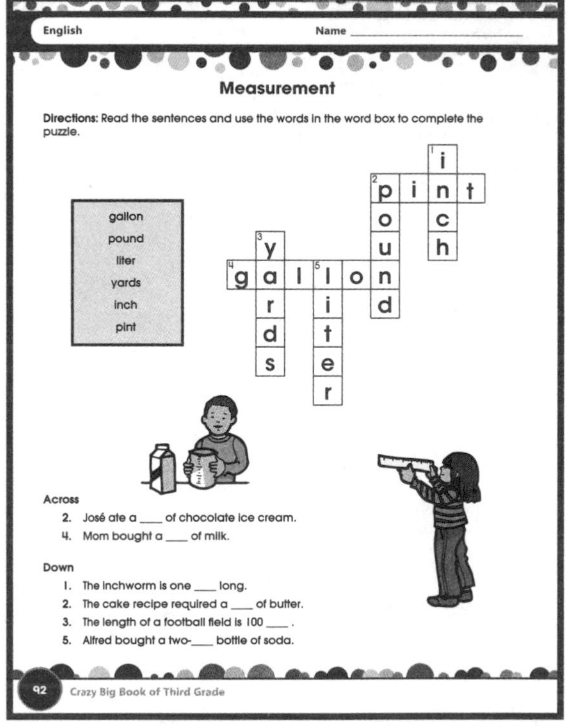

English Name ____________

Measurement

Directions: Read the sentences and use the words in the word box to complete the puzzle.

gallon, pound, liter, yards, inch, pint

Across

2. José ate a ____ of chocolate ice cream.
4. Mom bought a ____ of milk.

Down

1. The inchworm is one ____ long.
2. The cake recipe required a ____ of butter.
3. The length of a football field is 100 ____ .
5. Alfred bought a two-____ bottle of soda.

92 Crazy Big Book of Third Grade

page 92

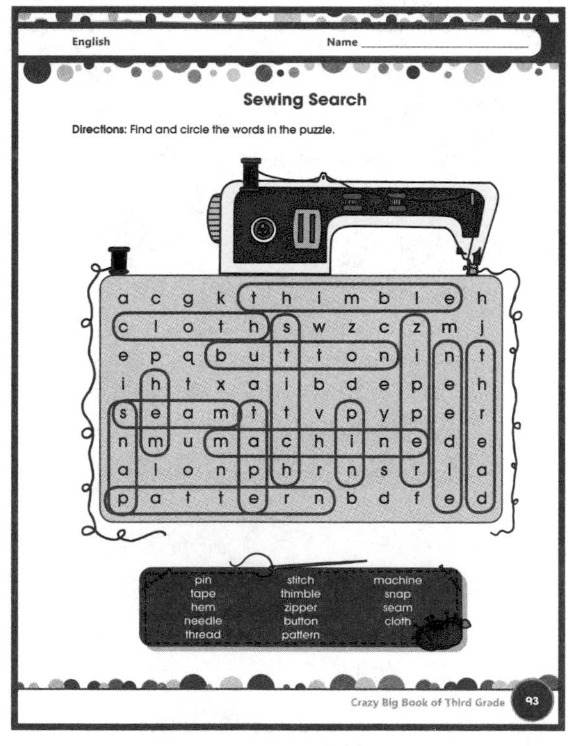

English Name ____________

Sewing Search

Directions: Find and circle the words in the puzzle.

pin, tape, hem, needle, thread, stitch, thimble, zipper, button, pattern, machine, snap, seam, cloth

Crazy Big Book of Third Grade 93

page 93

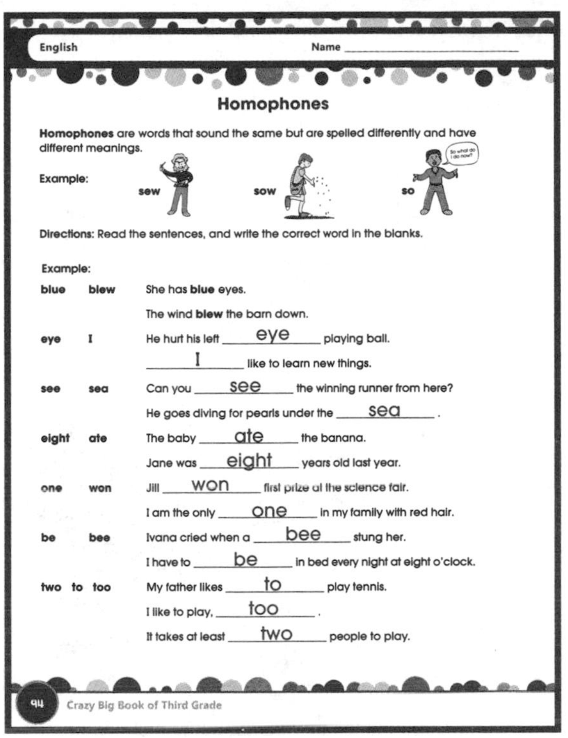
English Name ______________

Homophones

Homophones are words that sound the same but are spelled differently and have different meanings.

Example: sew sow so

Directions: Read the sentences, and write the correct word in the blanks.

Example:

blue	**blew**	She has **blue** eyes.
		The wind **blew** the barn down.
eye	**I**	He hurt his left __eye__ playing ball.
		__I__ like to learn new things.
see	**sea**	Can you __see__ the winning runner from here?
		He goes diving for pearls under the __sea__.
eight	**ate**	The baby __ate__ the banana.
		Jane was __eight__ years old last year.
one	**won**	Jill __won__ first prize at the science fair.
		I am the only __one__ in my family with red hair.
be	**bee**	Ivana cried when a __bee__ stung her.
		I have to __be__ in bed every night at eight o'clock.
two to	**too**	My father likes __to__ play tennis.
		I like to play, __too__.
		It takes at least __two__ people to play.

94 Crazy Big Book of Third Grade

page 94

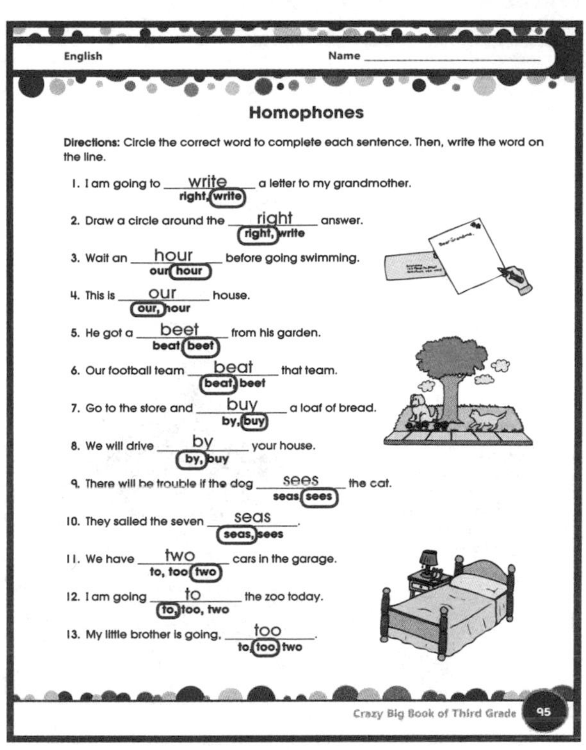
English Name ______________

Homophones

Directions: Circle the correct word to complete each sentence. Then, write the word on the line.

1. I am going to __write__ a letter to my grandmother. (right, **write**)
2. Draw a circle around the __right__ answer. (**right**, write)
3. Wait an __hour__ before going swimming. (our, **hour**)
4. This is __our__ house. (**our**, hour)
5. He got a __beet__ from his garden. (beat, **beet**)
6. Our football team __beat__ that team. (**beat**, beet)
7. Go to the store and __buy__ a loaf of bread. (by, **buy**)
8. We will drive __by__ your house. (**by**, buy)
9. There will be trouble if the dog __sees__ the cat. (seas, **sees**)
10. They sailed the seven __seas__. (**seas**, sees)
11. We have __two__ cars in the garage. (to, too, **two**)
12. I am going __to__ the zoo today. (**to**, too, two)
13. My little brother is going, __too__. (to, **too**, two)

Crazy Big Book of Third Grade 95

page 95

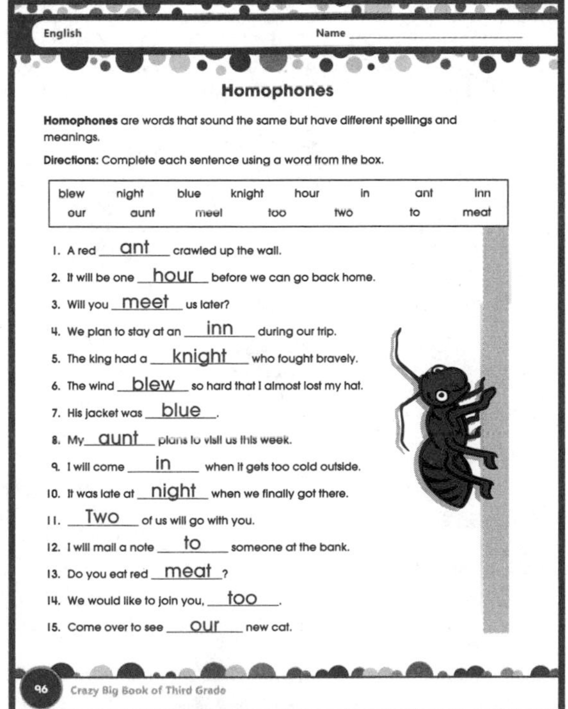
English Name ______________

Homophones

Homophones are words that sound the same but have different spellings and meanings.

Directions: Complete each sentence using a word from the box.

blew	night	blue	knight	hour	in	ant	inn
our	aunt	meet	too	two	to	meat	

1. A red __ant__ crawled up the wall.
2. It will be one __hour__ before we can go back home.
3. Will you __meet__ us later?
4. We plan to stay at an __inn__ during our trip.
5. The king had a __knight__ who fought bravely.
6. The wind __blew__ so hard that I almost lost my hat.
7. His jacket was __blue__.
8. My __aunt__ plans to visit us this week.
9. I will come __in__ when it gets too cold outside.
10. It was late at __night__ when we finally got there.
11. __Two__ of us will go with you.
12. I will mail a note __to__ someone at the bank.
13. Do you eat red __meat__?
14. We would like to join you, __too__.
15. Come over to see __our__ new cat.

96 Crazy Big Book of Third Grade

page 96

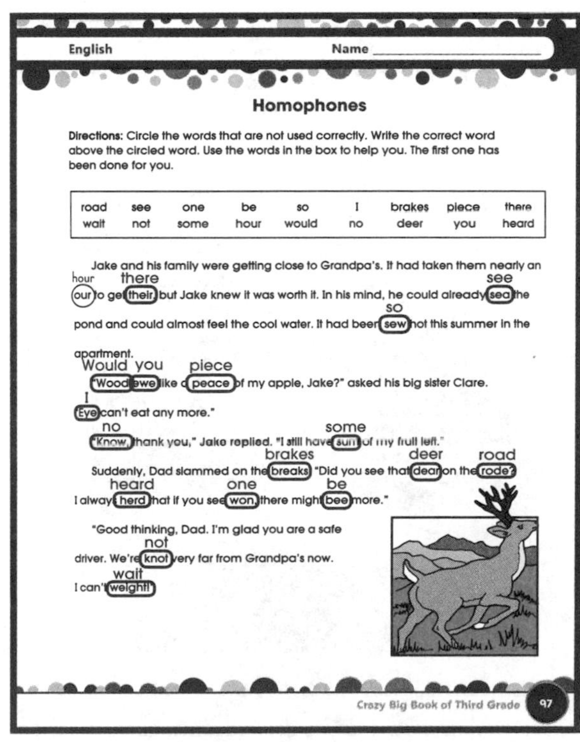
English Name ______________

Homophones

Directions: Circle the words that are not used correctly. Write the correct word above the circled word. Use the words in the box to help you. The first one has been done for you.

road	see	one	be	so	I	brakes	piece	there
wait	not	some	hour	would	no	deer	you	heard

Jake and his family were getting close to Grandpa's. It had taken them nearly an (our) [hour] to get (their) [there] but Jake knew it was worth it. In his mind, he could already (sea) [see] the pond and could almost feel the cool water. It had been (sew) [so] hot this summer in the apartment.

"(Wood) [Would] (ewe) [you] like a (peace) [piece] of my apple, Jake?" asked his big sister Clare.

"(Eye) [I] can't eat any more."

"(Know) [No], thank you," Jake replied. "I still have (sum) [some] of my fruit left."

Suddenly, Dad slammed on the (breaks) [brakes]! "Did you see that (dear) [deer] on the (rode) [road]? I always (herd) [heard] that if you see (won) [one], there might (bee) [be] more."

"Good thinking, Dad. I'm glad you are a safe driver. We're (knot) [not] very far from Grandpa's now. I can't (weight) [wait]!"

Crazy Big Book of Third Grade 97

page 97

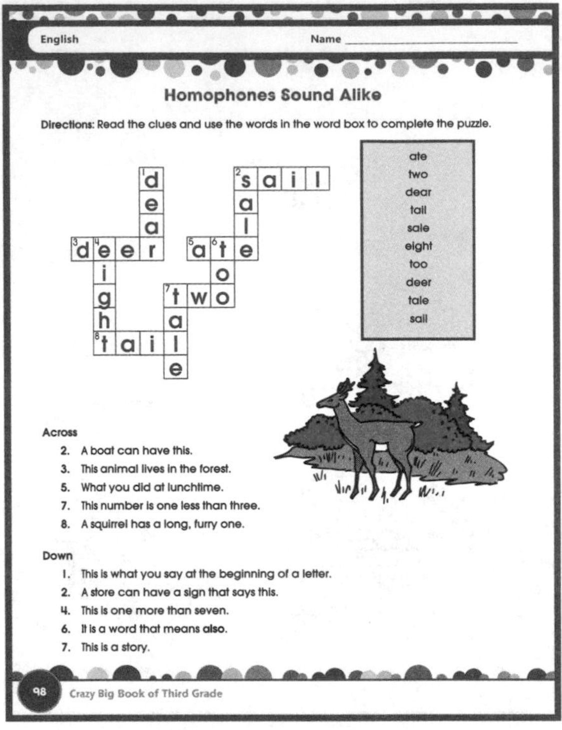

English Name ___

Homophones Sound Alike

Directions: Read the clues and use the words in the word box to complete the puzzle.

ate
two
dear
tall
sale
eight
too
deer
tale
sail

Across
2. A boat can have this.
3. This animal lives in the forest.
5. What you did at lunchtime.
7. This number is one less than three.
8. A squirrel has a long, furry one.

Down
1. This is what you say at the beginning of a letter.
2. A store can have a sign that says this.
4. This is one more than seven.
6. It is a word that means **also**.
7. This is a story.

98 Crazy Big Book of Third Grade

page 98

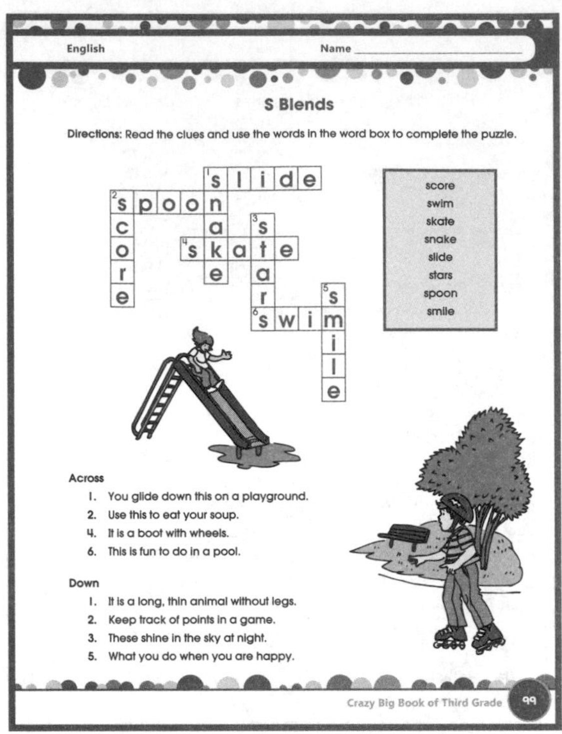

English Name ___

S Blends

Directions: Read the clues and use the words in the word box to complete the puzzle.

score
swim
skate
snake
slide
stars
spoon
smile

Across
1. You glide down this on a playground.
2. Use this to eat your soup.
4. It is a boot with wheels.
6. This is fun to do in a pool.

Down
1. It is a long, thin animal without legs.
2. Keep track of points in a game.
3. These shine in the sky at night.
5. What you do when you are happy.

Crazy Big Book of Third Grade 99

page 99

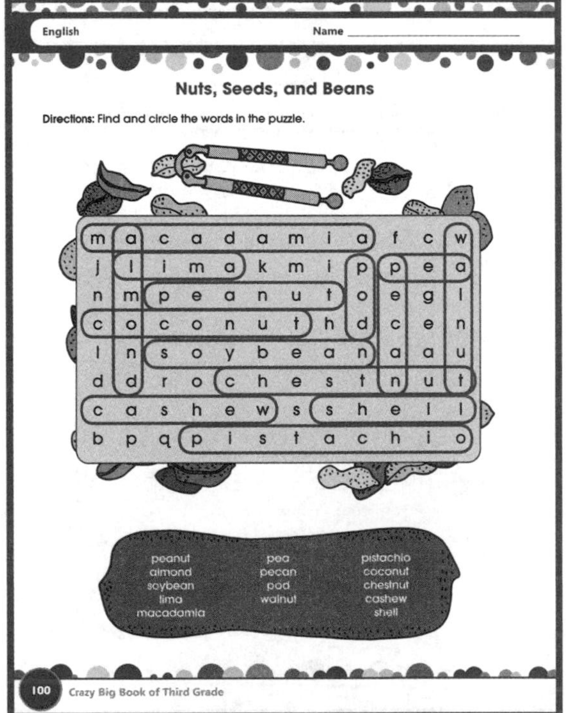

English Name ___

Nuts, Seeds, and Beans

Directions: Find and circle the words in the puzzle.

m	a	c	a	d	a	m	i	a	f	c	w
j	l	i	m	a	k	m	i	p	p	e	a
n	m	p	e	a	n	u	t	o	e	g	l
c	o	c	o	n	u	t	h	d	c	e	n
l	n	s	o	y	b	e	a	n	a	a	u
d	d	r	o	c	h	e	s	t	n	u	t
c	a	s	h	e	w	s	s	h	e	l	l
b	p	q	p	i	s	t	a	c	h	i	o

peanut
almond
soybean
lima
macadamia
pea
pecan
pod
walnut
pistachio
coconut
chestnut
cashew
shell

100 Crazy Big Book of Third Grade

page 100

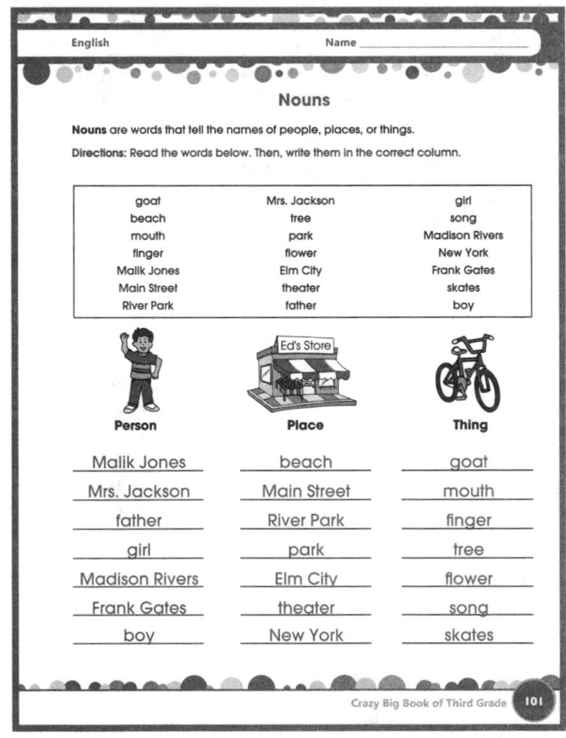

English Name ___

Nouns

Nouns are words that tell the names of people, places, or things.

Directions: Read the words below. Then, write them in the correct column.

goat
beach
mouth
finger
Malik Jones
Main Street
River Park
Mrs. Jackson
tree
park
flower
Elm City
theater
father
girl
song
Madison Rivers
New York
Frank Gates
skates
boy

Person	Place	Thing
Malik Jones	beach	goat
Mrs. Jackson	Main Street	mouth
father	River Park	finger
girl	park	tree
Madison Rivers	Elm City	flower
Frank Gates	theater	song
boy	New York	skates

Crazy Big Book of Third Grade 101

page 101

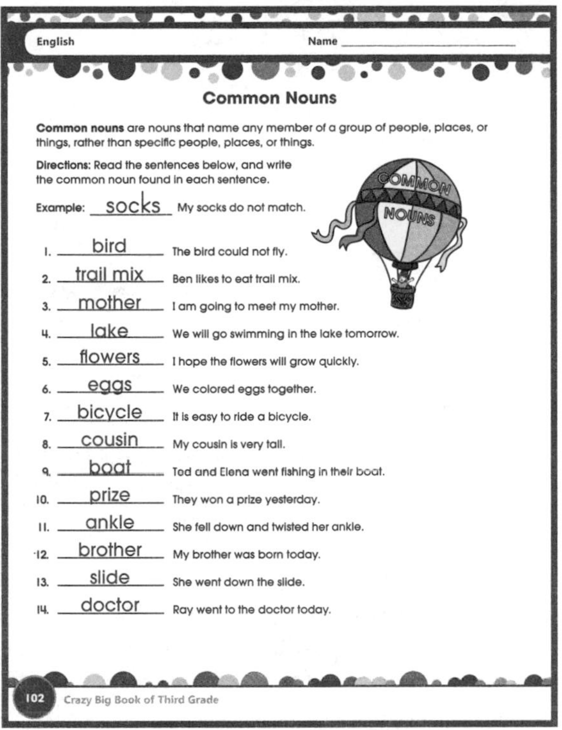

English Name

Common Nouns

Common nouns are nouns that name any member of a group of people, places, or things, rather than specific people, places, or things.

Directions: Read the sentences below, and write the common noun found in each sentence.

Example: socks My socks do not match.

1. bird The bird could not fly.
2. trail mix Ben likes to eat trail mix.
3. mother I am going to meet my mother.
4. lake We will go swimming in the lake tomorrow.
5. flowers I hope the flowers will grow quickly.
6. eggs We colored eggs together.
7. bicycle It is easy to ride a bicycle.
8. cousin My cousin is very tall.
9. boat Tod and Elena went fishing in their boat.
10. prize They won a prize yesterday.
11. ankle She fell down and twisted her ankle.
12. brother My brother was born today.
13. slide She went down the slide.
14. doctor Ray went to the doctor today.

102 Crazy Big Book of Third Grade

page 102

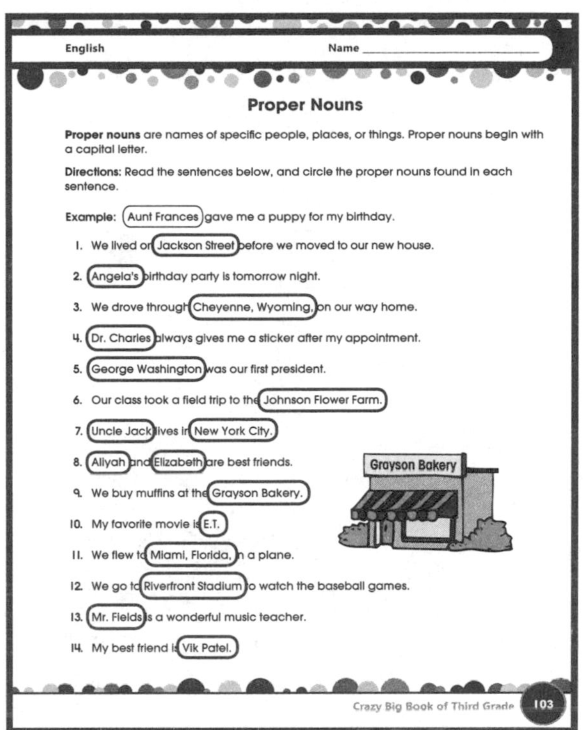

English Name

Proper Nouns

Proper nouns are names of specific people, places, or things. Proper nouns begin with a capital letter.

Directions: Read the sentences below, and circle the proper nouns found in each sentence.

Example: (Aunt Frances) gave me a puppy for my birthday.

1. We lived on (Jackson Street) before we moved to our new house.
2. (Angela's) birthday party is tomorrow night.
3. We drove through (Cheyenne, Wyoming,) on our way home.
4. (Dr. Charles) always gives me a sticker after my appointment.
5. (George Washington) was our first president.
6. Our class took a field trip to the (Johnson Flower Farm.)
7. (Uncle Jack) lives in (New York City.)
8. (Aliyah) and (Elizabeth) are best friends.
9. We buy muffins at the (Grayson Bakery.)
10. My favorite movie is (E.T.)
11. We flew to (Miami, Florida,) in a plane.
12. We go to (Riverfront Stadium) to watch the baseball games.
13. (Mr. Fields) is a wonderful music teacher.
14. My best friend is (Vik Patel.)

Crazy Big Book of Third Grade 103

page 103

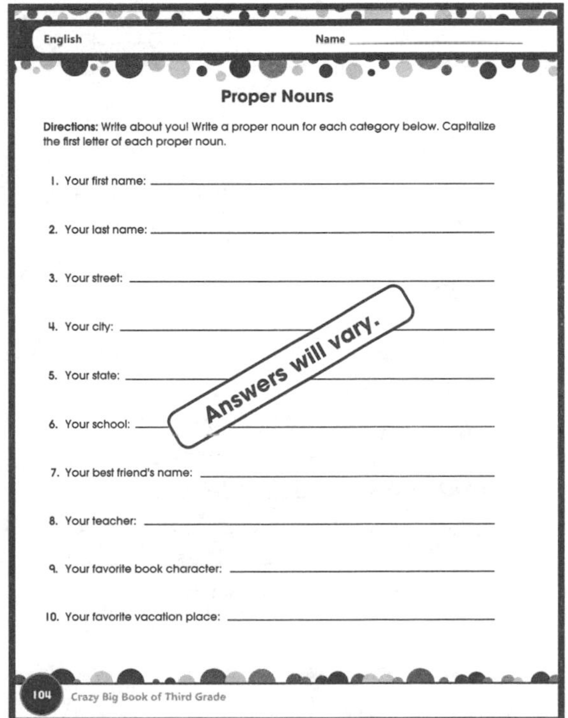

English Name

Proper Nouns

Directions: Write about you! Write a proper noun for each category below. Capitalize the first letter of each proper noun.

1. Your first name:
2. Your last name:
3. Your street:
4. Your city:
5. Your state:
6. Your school:
7. Your best friend's name:
8. Your teacher:
9. Your favorite book character:
10. Your favorite vacation place:

Answers will vary.

104 Crazy Big Book of Third Grade

page 104

English Name

Plural Nouns

A **plural** is more than one person, place, or thing. Add an **s** to show that a noun names more than one. If a noun ends in **x**, **ch**, **sh**, or **s**, add an **es** to the word.

Example: pizza pizzas

Directions: Write the plural of the words below.

Example: dog + s = dogs

cat	cats
boot	boots
house	houses

Example: peach + es = peaches

lunch	lunches
bunch	bunches
punch	punches

Example: ax + es = axes

fox	foxes
tax	taxes
box	boxes

Example: glass + es = glasses

mess	messes
guess	guesses
class	classes

Example: dish + es = dishes

bush	bushes
ash	ashes
brush	brushes

Example:

walrus

walruses

Crazy Big Book of Third Grade 105

page 105

English Name ____________

Plural Nouns

To write the plural forms of words ending in **y**, change the **y** to **ie** and add **s**.

Example: pony ponies

Directions: Write the plural of each noun on the lines below.

berry berries
cherry cherries
bunny bunnies
penny pennies
family families
candy candies
party parties

Now, write a story using some of the words that end in **y**.
Remember to use capital letters and periods.

Answers will vary.

106 Crazy Big Book of Third Grade

page 106

English Name ____________

Plural Nouns

Directions: Write the plural of each noun to complete the sentences below. Remember to change the **y** to **ie** before you add **s**!

1. I am going to two birthday parties (party) this week.
2. Xander picked some cherries (cherry) for Mom's pie.
3. At the store, we saw lots of bunnies (bunny).
4. My change at the toy store was three pennies (penny).
5. All the ladies (lady) in Mom's book group will arrive at 7:00.
6. Thanksgiving is a special time for families (family) to gather together.
7. Boston and New York are very large cities (city).

Crazy Big Book of Third Grade 107

page 107

English Name ____________

Plural Nouns

Some words have special plural forms.

Example: leaf leaves

tooth	teeth
child	children
foot	feet
mouse	mice
woman	women
man	men

Directions: Some of the words in the box are special plurals. Complete each sentence with a plural from the box. Then, write the letters from the boxes in the blanks below to solve the puzzle.

1. I lost my two front t e e t h.
2. My sister has two pet m i c e.
3. Her favorite book is *Little* W o m e n.
4. The circus clown had big f e e t.
5. The teacher played a game with the c h i l d r e n.

Take good care of this pearly plural!

t e e t h
1 2 3 4 5

108 Crazy Big Book of Third Grade

page 108

English Name ____________

Plural Nouns

Directions: The **singular form** of a word shows one person, place, or thing. Write the singular form of each noun on the lines below.

cherries cherry
lunches lunch
countries country
leaves leaf
churches church
arms arm
boxes box
men man
wheels wheel
pictures picture
cities city
places place
ostriches ostrich
glasses glass

Crazy Big Book of Third Grade 109

page 109

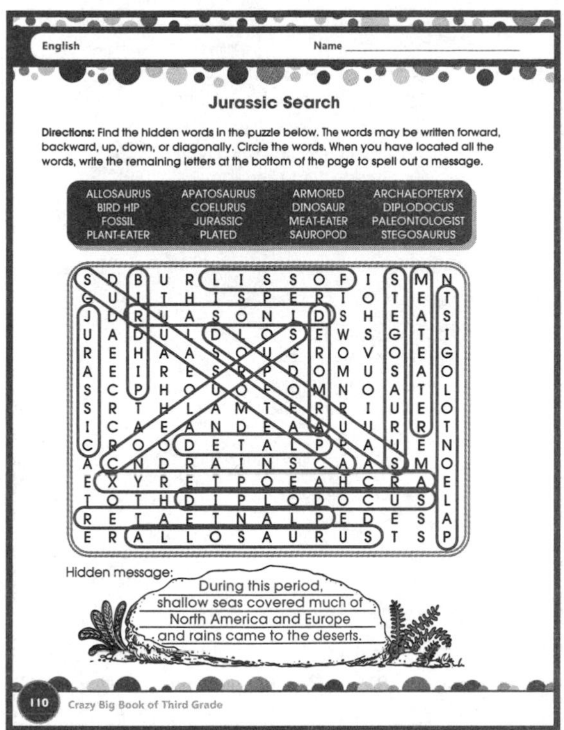

English Name ____________

Jurassic Search

Directions: Find the hidden words in the puzzle below. The words may be written forward, backward, up, down, or diagonally. Circle the words. When you have located all the words, write the remaining letters at the bottom of the page to spell out a message.

ALLOSAURUS	APATOSAURUS	ARMORED	ARCHAEOPTERYX
BIRD HIP	COELURUS	DINOSAUR	DIPLODOCUS
FOSSIL	JURASSIC	MEAT-EATER	PALEONTOLOGIST
PLANT-EATER	PLATED	SAUROPOD	STEGOSAURUS

S	D	B	U	R	L	I	S	S	O	F	I	S	M	N
G	U	I	T	H	I	S	P	E	R	I	O	T	E	T
J	D	R	U	A	S	O	N	I	D	S	H	E	A	S
U	A	D	U	L	D	L	O	S	E	W	S	G	T	I
R	E	H	A	A	S	O	U	C	R	O	V	O	E	G
A	E	I	R	E	S	R	P	D	O	M	U	S	A	O
S	C	P	H	O	U	O	F	O	M	N	O	A	T	L
S	R	T	H	L	A	M	T	E	R	R	I	U	E	O
I	C	A	E	A	N	D	E	A	A	U	U	R	R	T
C	R	O	O	D	E	T	A	L	P	P	A	U	E	N
A	C	N	D	R	A	I	N	S	C	A	A	S	M	O
E	X	Y	R	E	T	P	O	E	A	H	C	R	A	E
T	O	T	H	D	I	P	L	O	D	O	C	U	S	L
R	E	T	A	E	T	N	A	L	P	E	D	E	S	A
E	R	A	L	L	O	S	A	U	R	U	S	T	S	P

Hidden message: During this period, shallow seas covered much of North America and Europe and rains came to the deserts.

110 Crazy Big Book of Third Grade

page 110

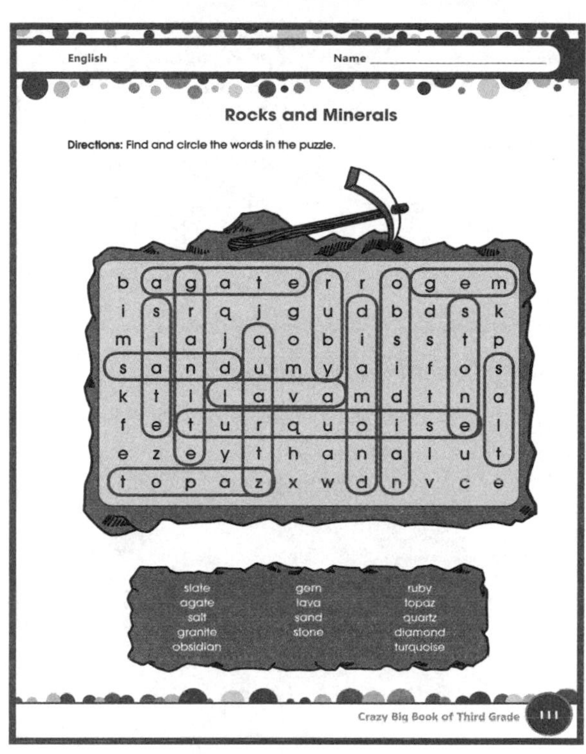

English Name ____________

Rocks and Minerals

Directions: Find and circle the words in the puzzle.

b	a	g	a	t	e	r	r	o	g	e	m
i	s	r	q	j	g	u	d	b	d	s	k
m	l	a	j	q	o	b	i	s	s	t	p
s	a	n	d	u	m	y	a	i	f	o	s
k	t	i	l	a	v	a	m	d	t	n	a
f	e	t	u	r	q	u	o	i	s	e	l
e	z	e	y	t	h	a	n	a	l	u	t
t	o	p	a	z	x	w	d	n	v	c	e

slate	gem	ruby
agate	lava	topaz
salt	sand	quartz
granite	stone	diamond
obsidian		turquoise

Crazy Big Book of Third Grade 111

page 111

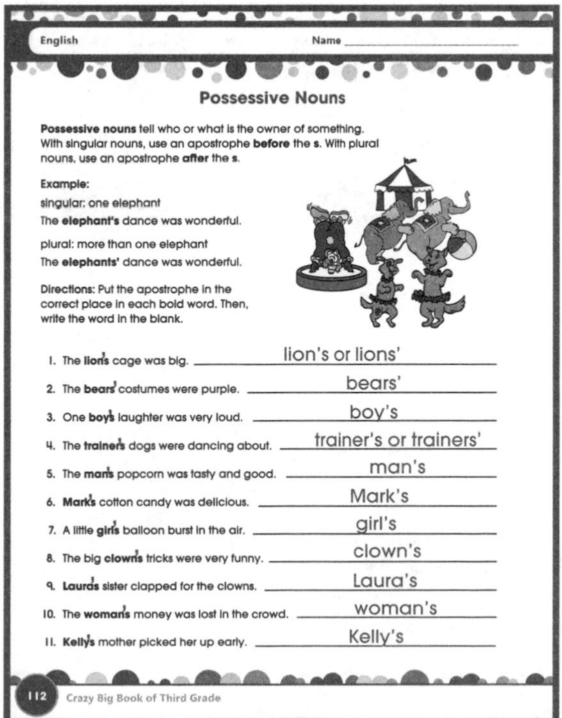

English Name ____________

Possessive Nouns

Possessive nouns tell who or what is the owner of something. With singular nouns, use an apostrophe **before** the **s**. With plural nouns, use an apostrophe **after** the **s**.

Example:

singular: one elephant

The **elephant's** dance was wonderful.

plural: more than one elephant

The **elephants'** dance was wonderful.

Directions: Put the apostrophe in the correct place in each bold word. Then, write the word in the blank.

1. The **lions** cage was big. lion's or lions'
2. The **bears** costumes were purple. bears'
3. One **boys** laughter was very loud. boy's
4. The **trainers** dogs were dancing about. trainer's or trainers'
5. The **mans** popcorn was tasty and good. man's
6. **Marks** cotton candy was delicious. Mark's
7. A little **girls** balloon burst in the air. girl's
8. The big **clowns** tricks were very funny. clown's
9. **Lauras** sister clapped for the clowns. Laura's
10. The **womans** money was lost in the crowd. woman's
11. **Kellys** mother picked her up early. Kelly's

112 Crazy Big Book of Third Grade

page 112

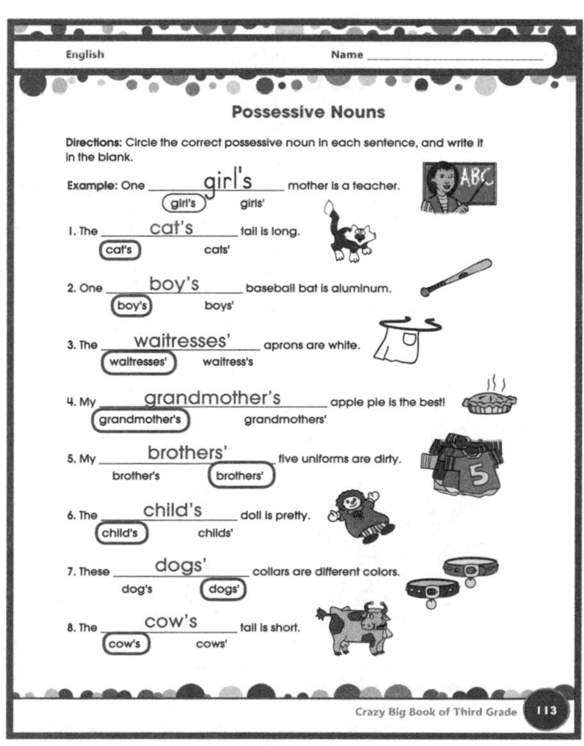

English Name ____________

Possessive Nouns

Directions: Circle the correct possessive noun in each sentence, and write it in the blank.

Example: One girl's mother is a teacher. (girl's) girls'

1. The cat's tail is long. (cat's) cats'
2. One boy's baseball bat is aluminum. (boy's) boys'
3. The waitresses' aprons are white. (waitresses') waitress's
4. My grandmother's apple pie is the best! (grandmother's) grandmothers'
5. My brothers' five uniforms are dirty. brother's (brothers')
6. The child's doll is pretty. (child's) childs'
7. These dogs' collars are different colors. dog's (dogs')
8. The cow's tail is short. (cow's) cows'

Crazy Big Book of Third Grade 113

page 113

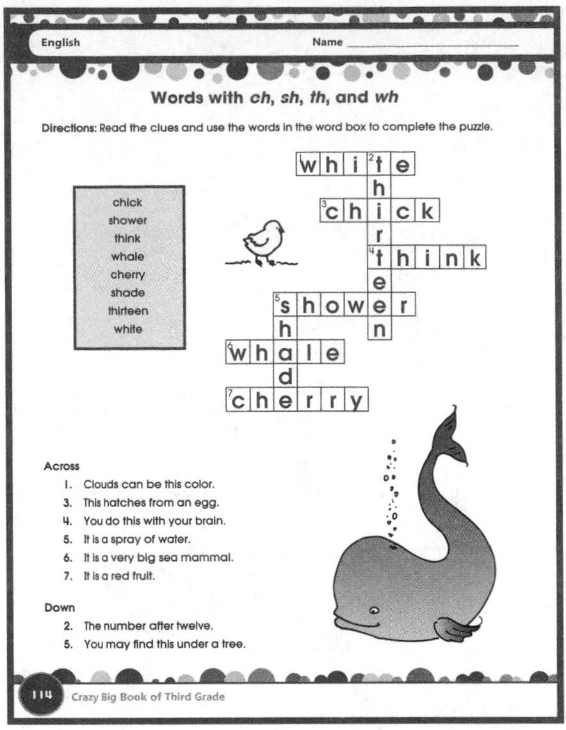

English Name ______

Words with *ch, sh, th,* and *wh*

Directions: Read the clues and use the words in the word box to complete the puzzle.

Word Box
chick
shower
think
whale
cherry
shade
thirteen
white

Across: 1. white 3. chick 4. think 5. shower 6. whale 7. cherry
Down: 2. thirteen 5. shade

Across
1. Clouds can be this color.
3. This hatches from an egg.
4. You do this with your brain.
5. It is a spray of water.
6. It is a very big sea mammal.
7. It is a red fruit.

Down
2. The number after twelve.
5. You may find this under a tree.

114 Crazy Big Book of Third Grade

page 114

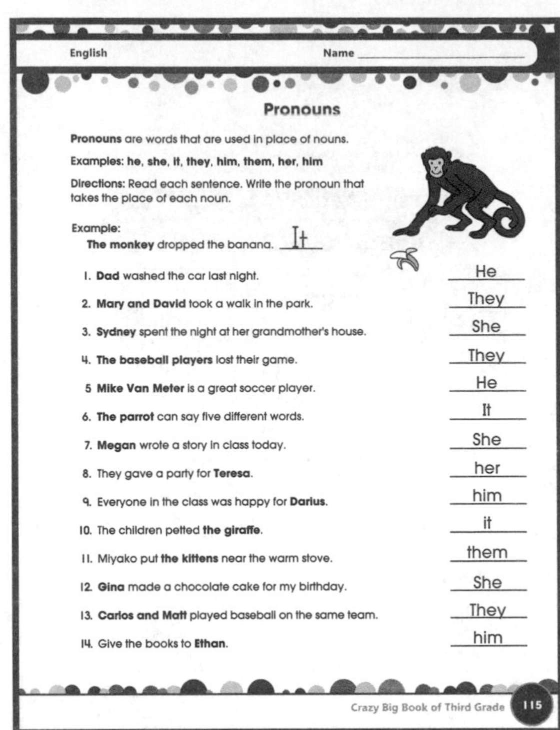

English Name ______

Pronouns

Pronouns are words that are used in place of nouns.

Examples: he, she, it, they, him, them, her, him

Directions: Read each sentence. Write the pronoun that takes the place of each noun.

Example:
The monkey dropped the banana. It

1. **Dad** washed the car last night. He
2. **Mary and David** took a walk in the park. They
3. **Sydney** spent the night at her grandmother's house. She
4. **The baseball players** lost their game. They
5. **Mike Van Meter** is a great soccer player. He
6. **The parrot** can say five different words. It
7. **Megan** wrote a story in class today. She
8. They gave a party for **Teresa**. her
9. Everyone in the class was happy for **Darius**. him
10. The children petted **the giraffe**. it
11. Miyako put **the kittens** near the warm stove. them
12. **Gina** made a chocolate cake for my birthday. She
13. **Carlos and Matt** played baseball on the same team. They
14. Give the books to **Ethan**. him

Crazy Big Book of Third Grade 115

page 115

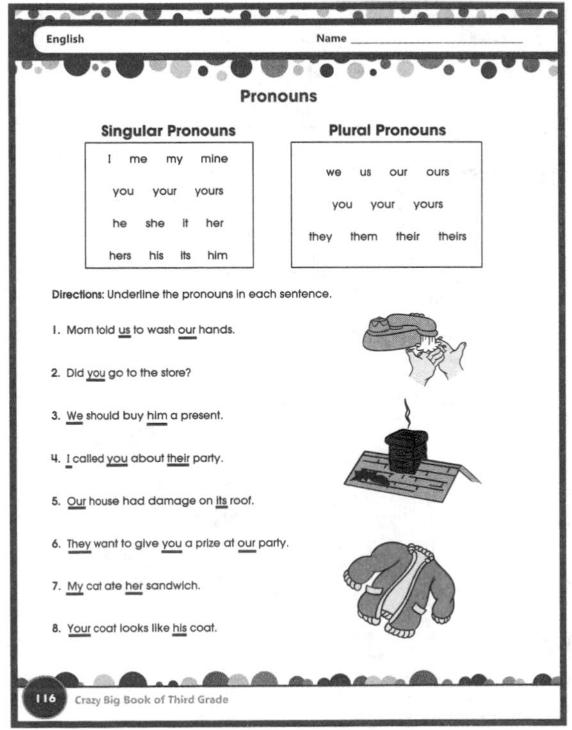

English Name ______

Pronouns

Singular Pronouns			
I	me	my	mine
you	your	yours	
he	she	it	her
hers	his	its	him

Plural Pronouns			
we	us	our	ours
you	your	yours	
they	them	their	theirs

Directions: Underline the pronouns in each sentence.

1. Mom told us to wash our hands.
2. Did you go to the store?
3. We should buy him a present.
4. I called you about their party.
5. Our house had damage on its roof.
6. They want to give you a prize at our party.
7. My cat ate her sandwich.
8. Your coat looks like his coat.

116 Crazy Big Book of Third Grade

page 116

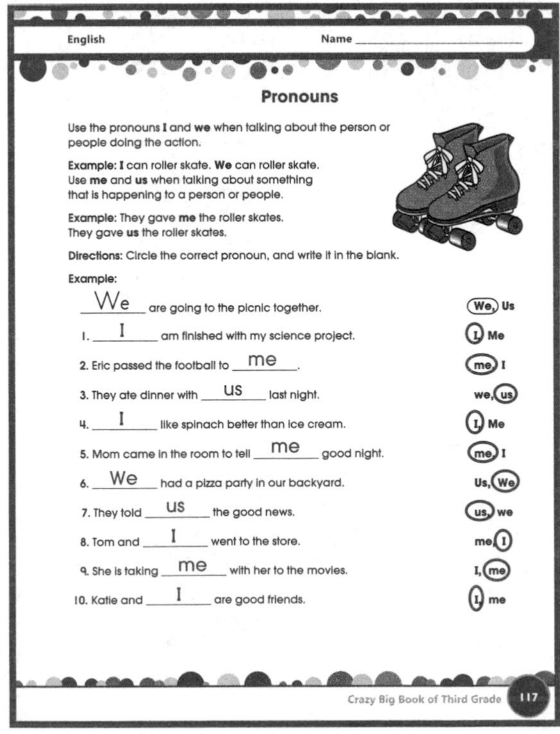

English Name ______

Pronouns

Use the pronouns **I** and **we** when talking about the person or people doing the action.

Example: I can roller skate. **We** can roller skate.
Use **me** and **us** when talking about something that is happening to a person or people.

Example: They gave **me** the roller skates.
They gave **us** the roller skates.

Directions: Circle the correct pronoun, and write it in the blank.

Example:
We are going to the picnic together. We, Us

1. I am finished with my science project. I, Me
2. Eric passed the football to me. me, I
3. They ate dinner with us last night. we, us
4. I like spinach better than ice cream. I, Me
5. Mom came in the room to tell me good night. me, I
6. We had a pizza party in our backyard. Us, We
7. They told us the good news. us, we
8. Tom and I went to the store. me, I
9. She is taking me with her to the movies. I, me
10. Katie and I are good friends. I, me

Crazy Big Book of Third Grade 117

page 117

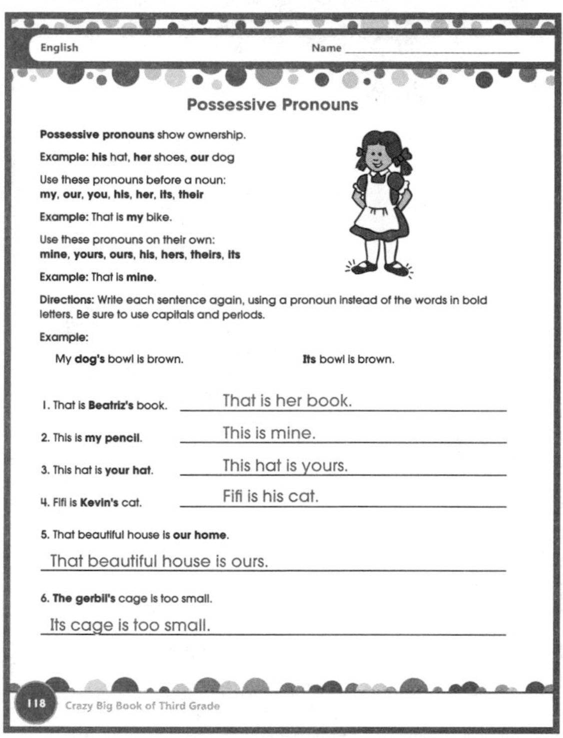
English Name ______________

Possessive Pronouns

Possessive pronouns show ownership.

Example: his hat, **her** shoes, **our** dog

Use these pronouns before a noun:
my, our, you, his, her, its, their

Example: That is **my** bike.

Use these pronouns on their own:
mine, yours, ours, his, hers, theirs, its

Example: That is **mine.**

Directions: Write each sentence again, using a pronoun instead of the words in bold letters. Be sure to use capitals and periods.

Example:

My **dog's** bowl is brown. **Its** bowl is brown.

1. That is **Beatriz's** book. That is her book.
2. This is **my pencil**. This is mine.
3. This hat is **your hat**. This hat is yours.
4. Fifi is **Kevin's** cat. Fifi is his cat.
5. That beautiful house is **our home**.
   That beautiful house is ours.
6. **The gerbil's** cage is too small.
   Its cage is too small.

118 Crazy Big Book of Third Grade

page 118

English Name ______________

Don't Just Sit There

Directions: Look at the picture clues. Then, complete the puzzle using the words from the word box.

Across: 3. dime 4. dress 6. dock 7. dent 8. donkey

Down: 1. drum 2. deer 3. dust 4. desk 5. down 7. dinner

Word box: dinner dime desk dock dust donkey deer dent down drum dress

Crazy Big Book of Third Grade 119

page 119

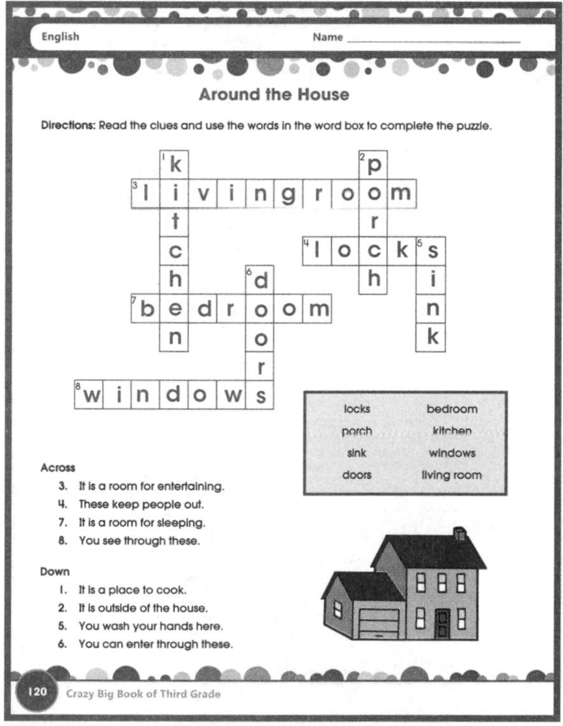
English Name ______________

Around the House

Directions: Read the clues and use the words in the word box to complete the puzzle.

Puzzle answers: 1 kitchen, 2 porch, 3 living room, 4 locks, 5 sink, 6 doors, 7 bedroom, 8 windows

locks	bedroom
porch	kitchen
sink	windows
doors	living room

Across
3. It is a room for entertaining.
4. These keep people out.
7. It is a room for sleeping.
8. You see through these.

Down
1. It is a place to cook.
2. It is outside of the house.
5. You wash your hands here.
6. You can enter through these.

120 Crazy Big Book of Third Grade

page 120

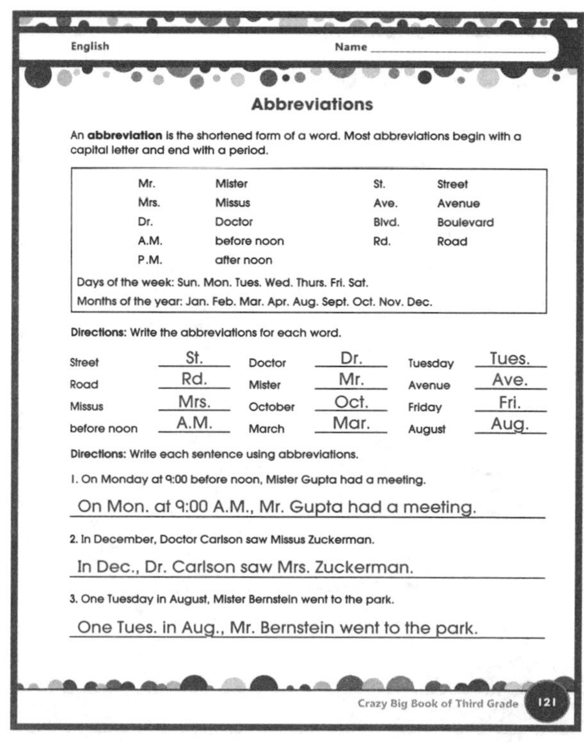
English Name ______________

Abbreviations

An **abbreviation** is the shortened form of a word. Most abbreviations begin with a capital letter and end with a period.

Mr.	Mister	St.	Street
Mrs.	Missus	Ave.	Avenue
Dr.	Doctor	Blvd.	Boulevard
A.M.	before noon	Rd.	Road
P.M.	after noon		

Days of the week: Sun. Mon. Tues. Wed. Thurs. Fri. Sat.
Months of the year: Jan. Feb. Mar. Apr. Aug. Sept. Oct. Nov. Dec.

Directions: Write the abbreviations for each word.

Street	St.	Doctor	Dr.	Tuesday	Tues.
Road	Rd.	Mister	Mr.	Avenue	Ave.
Missus	Mrs.	October	Oct.	Friday	Fri.
before noon	A.M.	March	Mar.	August	Aug.

Directions: Write each sentence using abbreviations.

1. On Monday at 9:00 before noon, Mister Gupta had a meeting.
   On Mon. at 9:00 A.M., Mr. Gupta had a meeting.
2. In December, Doctor Carlson saw Missus Zuckerman.
   In Dec., Dr. Carlson saw Mrs. Zuckerman.
3. One Tuesday in August, Mister Bernstein went to the park.
   One Tues. in Aug., Mr. Bernstein went to the park.

Crazy Big Book of Third Grade 121

page 121

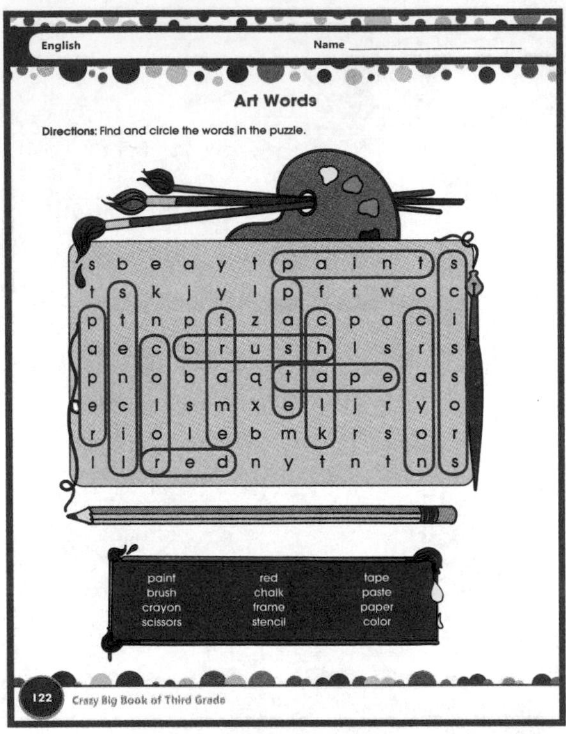

English Name ____________

Art Words

Directions: Find and circle the words in the puzzle.

s	b	e	a	y	t	p	a	i	n	t	s
t	s	k	j	y	l	p	f	t	w	o	c
p	t	n	p	f	z	a	c	p	a	c	i
a	e	c	b	r	u	s	h	l	s	r	s
p	n	o	b	a	q	t	a	p	e	a	s
e	c	l	s	m	x	e	l	j	r	y	o
r	i	o	l	e	b	m	k	r	s	o	r
l	l	r	e	d	n	y	t	n	t	n	s

paint	red	tape
brush	chalk	paste
crayon	frame	paper
scissors	stencil	color

122 Crazy Big Book of Third Grade

page 122

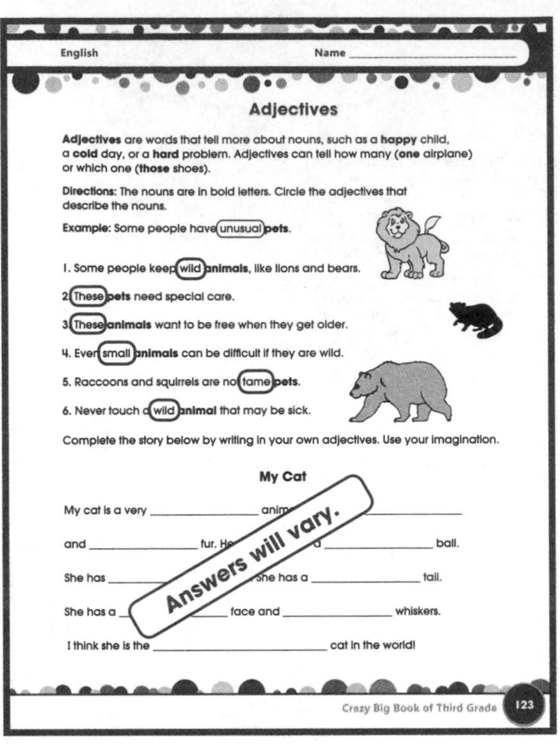

English Name ____________

Adjectives

Adjectives are words that tell more about nouns, such as a **happy** child, a **cold** day, or a **hard** problem. Adjectives can tell how many (**one** airplane) or which one (**those** shoes).

Directions: The nouns are in bold letters. Circle the adjectives that describe the nouns.

Example: Some people have (unusual) **pets**.

1. Some people keep (wild) **animals**, like lions and bears.
2. (These) **pets** need special care.
3. (These) **animals** want to be free when they get older.
4. Even (small) **animals** can be difficult if they are wild.
5. Raccoons and squirrels are not (tame) **pets**.
6. Never touch a (wild) **animal** that may be sick.

Complete the story below by writing in your own adjectives. Use your imagination.

My Cat

My cat is a very ________ anim... ________

and ________ fur. He... ...a ________ ball.

She has ________ ...she has a ________ tail.

She has a ________ face and ________ whiskers.

I think she is the ________ cat in the world!

Answers will vary.

Crazy Big Book of Third Grade 123

page 123

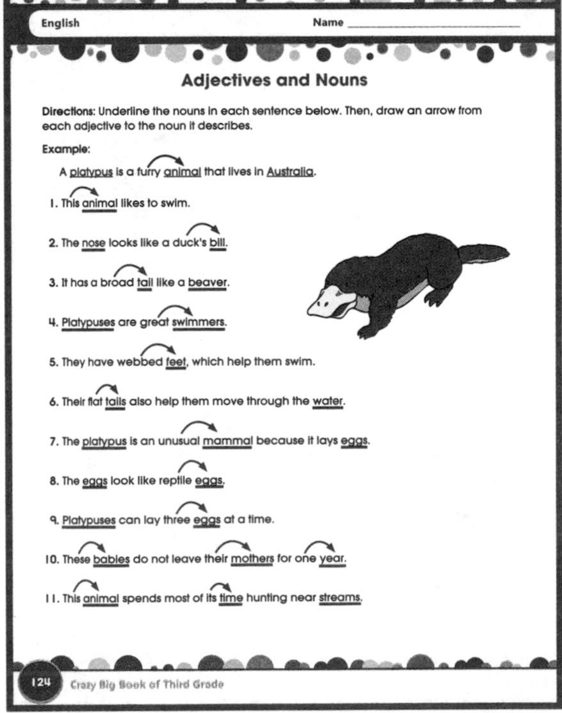

English Name ____________

Adjectives and Nouns

Directions: Underline the nouns in each sentence below. Then, draw an arrow from each adjective to the noun it describes.

Example:

A platypus is a furry animal that lives in Australia.

1. This animal likes to swim.
2. The nose looks like a duck's bill.
3. It has a broad tail like a beaver.
4. Platypuses are great swimmers.
5. They have webbed feet, which help them swim.
6. Their flat tails also help them move through the water.
7. The platypus is an unusual mammal because it lays eggs.
8. The eggs look like reptile eggs.
9. Platypuses can lay three eggs at a time.
10. These babies do not leave their mothers for one year.
11. This animal spends most of its time hunting near streams.

124 Crazy Big Book of Third Grade

page 124

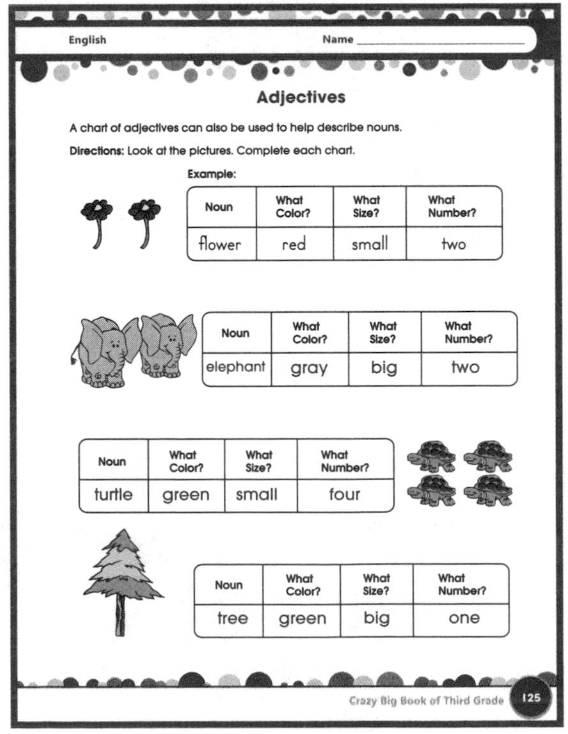

English Name ____________

Adjectives

A chart of adjectives can also be used to help describe nouns.

Directions: Look at the pictures. Complete each chart.

Example:

Noun	What Color?	What Size?	What Number?
flower	red	small	two

Noun	What Color?	What Size?	What Number?
elephant	gray	big	two

Noun	What Color?	What Size?	What Number?
turtle	green	small	four

Noun	What Color?	What Size?	What Number?
tree	green	big	one

Crazy Big Book of Third Grade 125

page 125

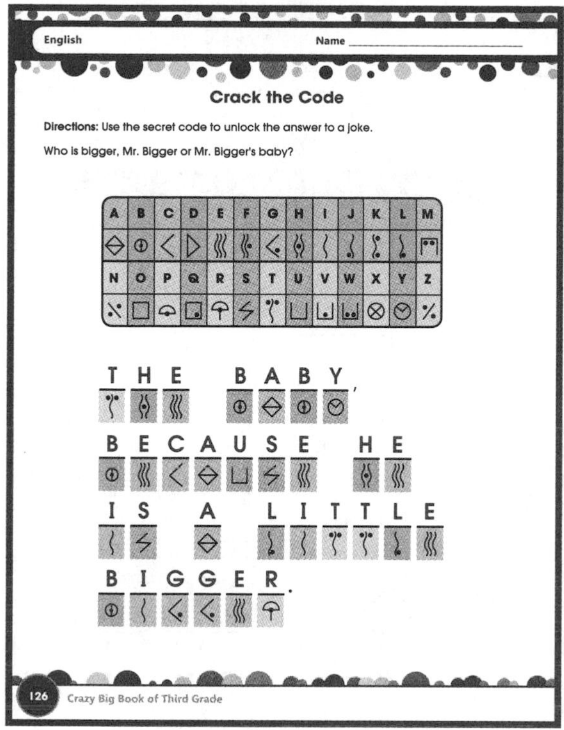

English Name ____________

Crack the Code

Directions: Use the secret code to unlock the answer to a joke.

Who is bigger, Mr. Bigger or Mr. Bigger's baby?

A	B	C	D	E	F	G	H	I	J	K	L	M
N	O	P	Q	R	S	T	U	V	W	X	Y	Z

THE BABY, BECAUSE HE IS A LITTLE BIGGER.

126 Crazy Big Book of Third Grade

page 126

English Name ____________

Animal Coverings

Directions: Find the type of covering for each animal to complete the puzzle.

shell
quills
fur
feathers
skin
scales

1 fur, 1 feathers, 2 quills, 3 skin, 3 shell, 4 scales

Across
1. snow hare
3. elephant
4. goldfish

Down
1. swan
2. porcupine
3. turtle

Crazy Big Book of Third Grade 127

page 127

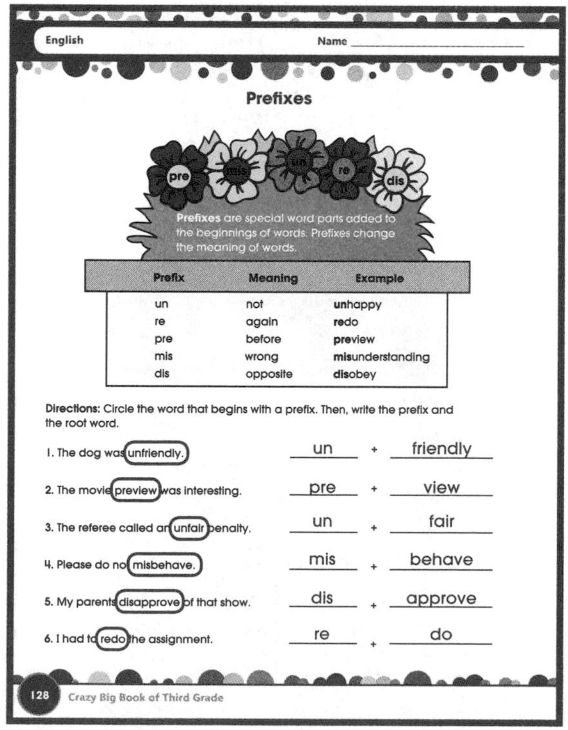

English Name ____________

Prefixes

pre mis un re dis

Prefixes are special word parts added to the beginnings of words. Prefixes change the meaning of words.

Prefix	Meaning	Example
un	not	**un**happy
re	again	**re**do
pre	before	**pre**view
mis	wrong	**mis**understanding
dis	opposite	**dis**obey

Directions: Circle the word that begins with a prefix. Then, write the prefix and the root word.

1. The dog was unfriendly. — un + friendly
2. The movie preview was interesting. — pre + view
3. The referee called an unfair penalty. — un + fair
4. Please do not misbehave. — mis + behave
5. My parents disapprove of that show. — dis + approve
6. I had to redo the assignment. — re + do

128 Crazy Big Book of Third Grade

page 128

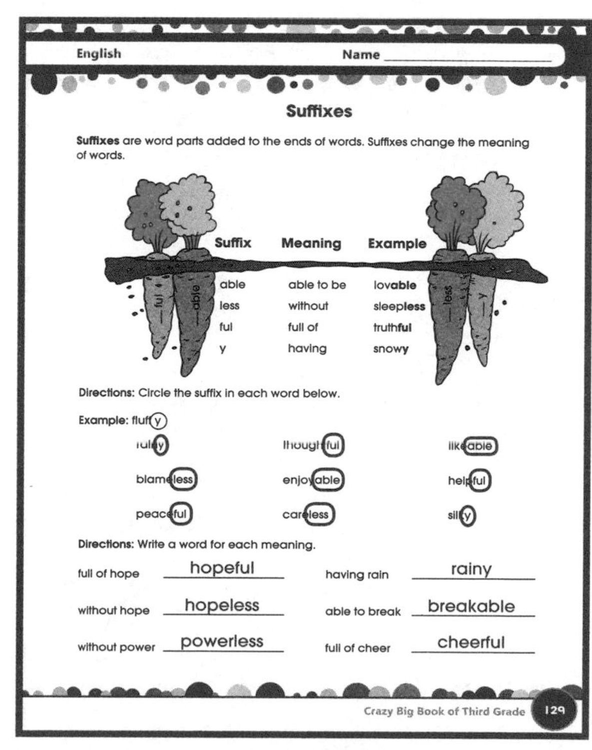

English Name ____________

Suffixes

Suffixes are word parts added to the ends of words. Suffixes change the meaning of words.

Suffix	Meaning	Example
able	able to be	lov**able**
less	without	sleep**less**
ful	full of	truth**ful**
y	having	snow**y**

Directions: Circle the suffix in each word below.

Example: fluff(y)

rul(y) thought(ful) like(able)
blame(less) enjoy(able) help(ful)
peace(ful) care(less) silk(y)

Directions: Write a word for each meaning.

full of hope hopeful — having rain rainy
without hope hopeless — able to break breakable
without power powerless — full of cheer cheerful

Crazy Big Book of Third Grade 129

page 129

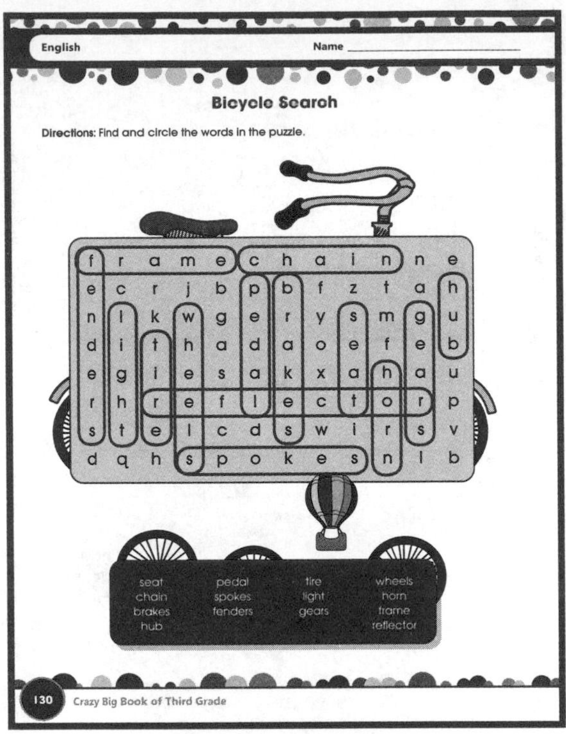

English Name ____________

Bicycle Search

Directions: Find and circle the words in the puzzle.

```
f r a m e c h a i n n e
e c r j b p b f z t a h
n l k w g e r y s m g u
d i t h a d a o e f e b
e g i e s a k x a h a u
r h r e f l e c t o r p
s t e l c d s w i r s v
d q h s p o k e s n l b
```

seat	pedal	tire	wheels
chain	spokes	light	horn
brakes	fenders	gears	frame
hub			reflector

130 Crazy Big Book of Third Grade

page 130

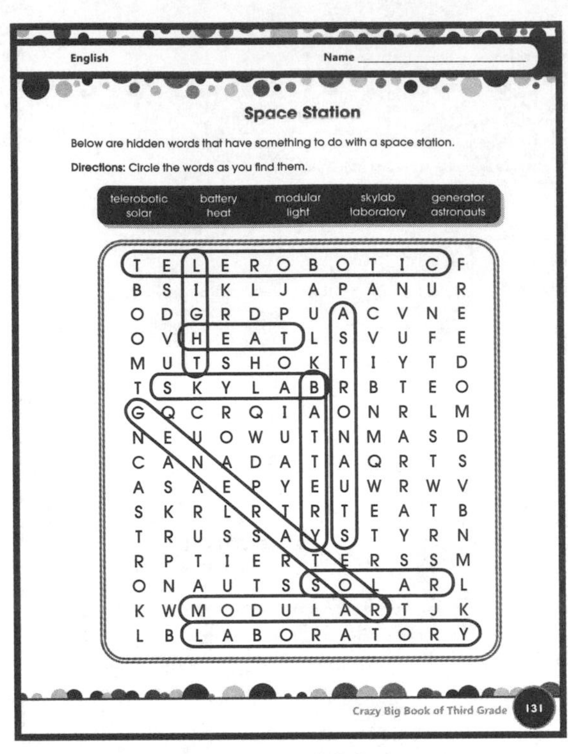

English Name ____________

Space Station

Below are hidden words that have something to do with a space station.

Directions: Circle the words as you find them.

telerobotic	battery	modular	skylab	generator
solar	heat	light	laboratory	astronauts

```
T E L E R O B O T I C F
B S I K L J A P A N U R
O D G R D P U A C V N E
O V H E A T L S V U F E
M U T S H O K T I Y T D
T S K Y L A B R B T E O
G Q C R Q I A O N R L M
N E U O W U T N M A S D
C A N A D A T A Q R T S
A S A E P Y E U W R W V
S K R L R T R T E A T B
T R U S S A Y S T Y R N
R P T I E R T E R S S M
O N A U T S S O L A R L
K W M O D U L A R T J K
L B L A B O R A T O R Y
```

Crazy Big Book of Third Grade 131

page 131

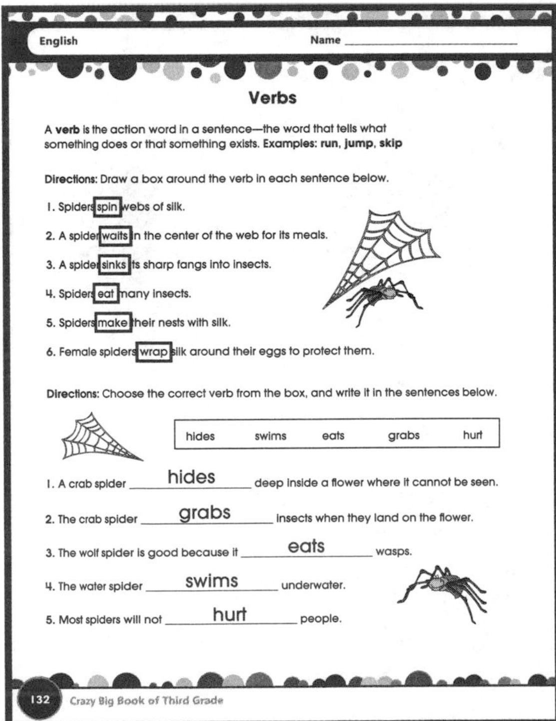

English Name ____________

Verbs

A **verb** is the action word in a sentence—the word that tells what something does or that something exists. **Examples: run, jump, skip**

Directions: Draw a box around the verb in each sentence below.

1. Spiders spin webs of silk.
2. A spider waits in the center of the web for its meals.
3. A spider sinks its sharp fangs into insects.
4. Spiders eat many insects.
5. Spiders make their nests with silk.
6. Female spiders wrap silk around their eggs to protect them.

Directions: Choose the correct verb from the box, and write it in the sentences below.

hides	swims	eats	grabs	hurt

1. A crab spider ___hides___ deep inside a flower where it cannot be seen.
2. The crab spider ___grabs___ insects when they land on the flower.
3. The wolf spider is good because it ___eats___ wasps.
4. The water spider ___swims___ underwater.
5. Most spiders will not ___hurt___ people.

132 Crazy Big Book of Third Grade

page 132

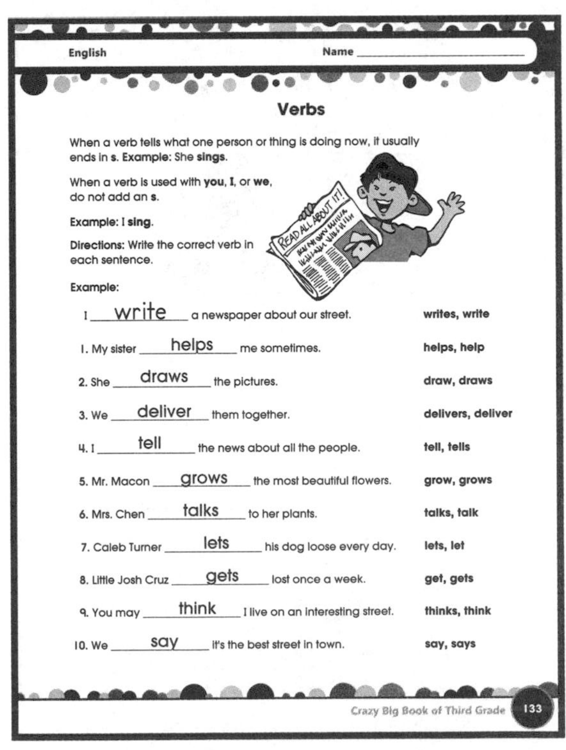

English Name ____________

Verbs

When a verb tells what one person or thing is doing now, it usually ends in **s**. **Example:** She **sings**.

When a verb is used with **you**, **I**, or **we**, do not add an **s**.

Example: I sing.

Directions: Write the correct verb in each sentence.

Example:

I ___write___ a newspaper about our street.	**writes, write**
1. My sister ___helps___ me sometimes.	**helps, help**
2. She ___draws___ the pictures.	**draw, draws**
3. We ___deliver___ them together.	**delivers, deliver**
4. I ___tell___ the news about all the people.	**tell, tells**
5. Mr. Macon ___grows___ the most beautiful flowers.	**grow, grows**
6. Mrs. Chen ___talks___ to her plants.	**talks, talk**
7. Caleb Turner ___lets___ his dog loose every day.	**lets, let**
8. Little Josh Cruz ___gets___ lost once a week.	**get, gets**
9. You may ___think___ I live on an interesting street.	**thinks, think**
10. We ___say___ it's the best street in town.	**say, says**

Crazy Big Book of Third Grade 133

page 133

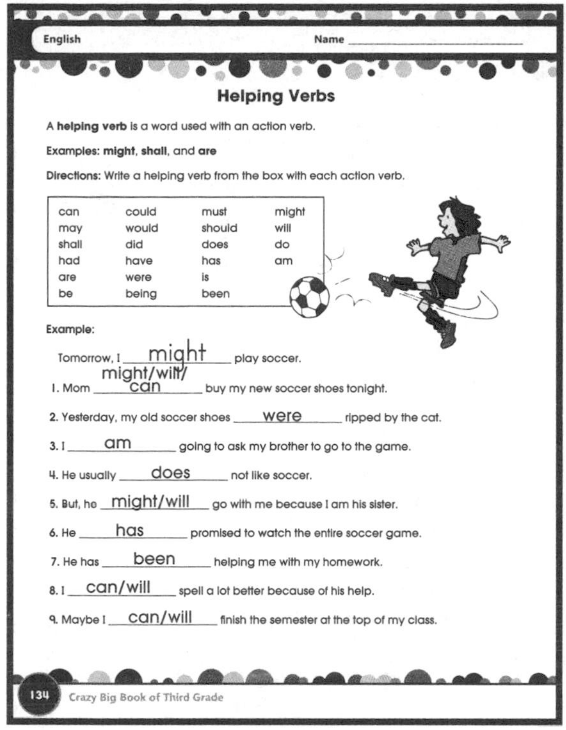

English Name ____________

Helping Verbs

A **helping verb** is a word used with an action verb.

Examples: might, shall, and **are**

Directions: Write a helping verb from the box with each action verb.

can	could	must	might
may	would	should	will
shall	did	does	do
had	have	has	am
are	were	is	
be	being	been	

Example:

Tomorrow, I __might__ play soccer.

1. Mom __might/will/can__ buy my new soccer shoes tonight.
2. Yesterday, my old soccer shoes __were__ ripped by the cat.
3. I __am__ going to ask my brother to go to the game.
4. He usually __does__ not like soccer.
5. But, he __might/will__ go with me because I am his sister.
6. He __has__ promised to watch the entire soccer game.
7. He has __been__ helping me with my homework.
8. I __can/will__ spell a lot better because of his help.
9. Maybe I __can/will__ finish the semester at the top of my class.

134 Crazy Big Book of Third Grade

page 134

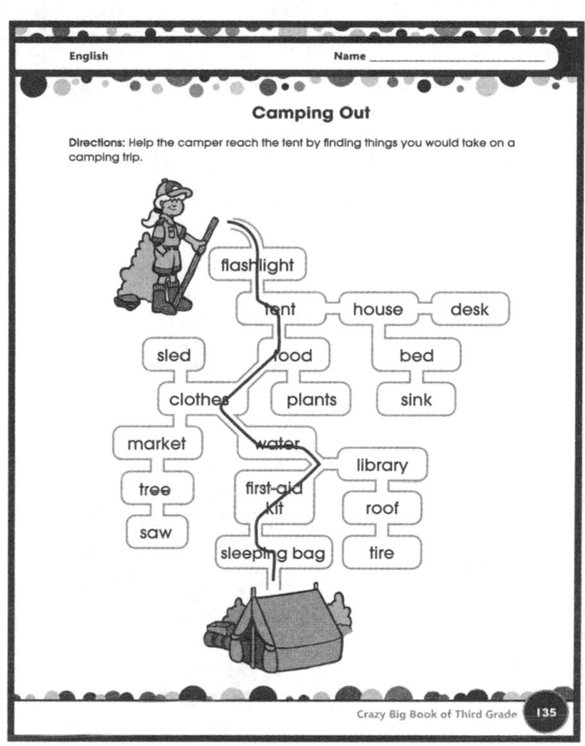

English Name ____________

Camping Out

Directions: Help the camper reach the tent by finding things you would take on a camping trip.

Crazy Big Book of Third Grade 135

page 135

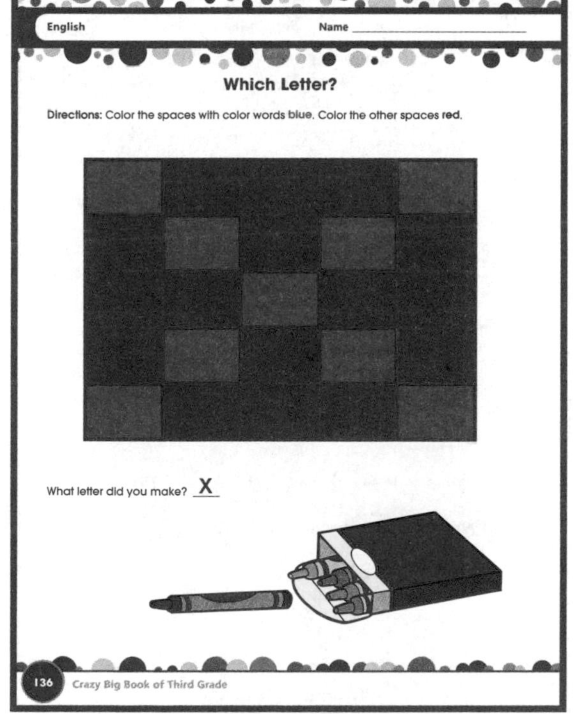

English Name ____________

Which Letter?

Directions: Color the spaces with color words blue. Color the other spaces **red.**

What letter did you make? __X__

136 Crazy Big Book of Third Grade

page 136

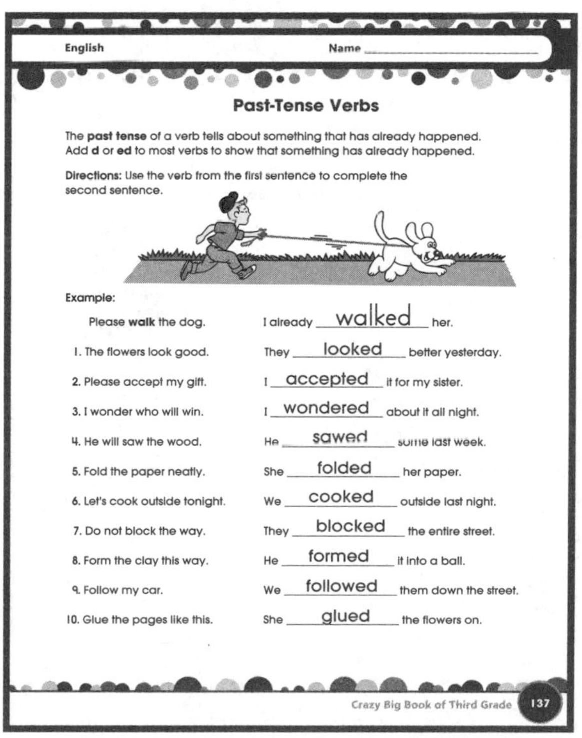

English Name ____________

Past-Tense Verbs

The **past tense** of a verb tells about something that has already happened. Add **d** or **ed** to most verbs to show that something has already happened.

Directions: Use the verb from the first sentence to complete the second sentence.

Example:

Please **walk** the dog. I already __walked__ her.

1. The flowers look good. They __looked__ better yesterday.
2. Please accept my gift. I __accepted__ it for my sister.
3. I wonder who will win. I __wondered__ about it all night.
4. He will saw the wood. He __sawed__ some last week.
5. Fold the paper neatly. She __folded__ her paper.
6. Let's cook outside tonight. We __cooked__ outside last night.
7. Do not block the way. They __blocked__ the entire street.
8. Form the clay this way. He __formed__ it into a ball.
9. Follow my car. We __followed__ them down the street.
10. Glue the pages like this. She __glued__ the flowers on.

Crazy Big Book of Third Grade 137

page 137

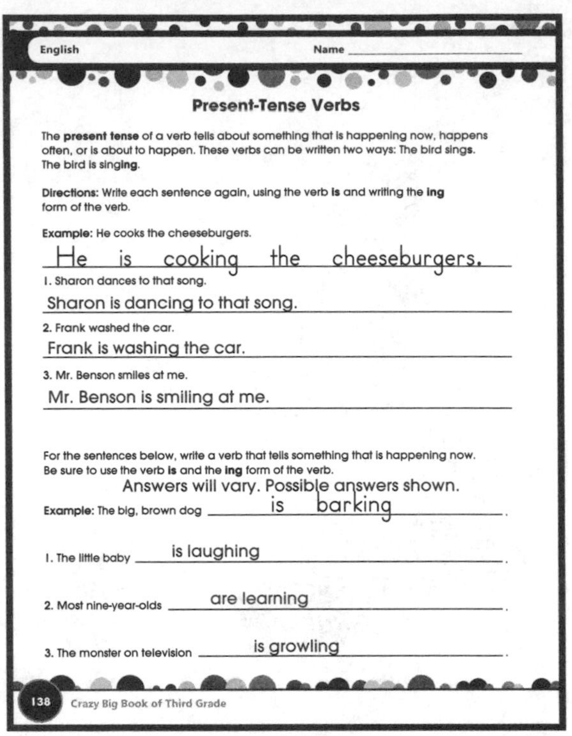

English Name ____________

Present-Tense Verbs

The **present tense** of a verb tells about something that is happening now, happens often, or is about to happen. These verbs can be written two ways: The bird sings. The bird is singing.

Directions: Write each sentence again, using the verb **is** and writing the **ing** form of the verb.

Example: He cooks the cheeseburgers.

He is cooking the cheeseburgers.

1. Sharon dances to that song.

Sharon is dancing to that song.

2. Frank washed the car.

Frank is washing the car.

3. Mr. Benson smiles at me.

Mr. Benson is smiling at me.

For the sentences below, write a verb that tells something that is happening now. Be sure to use the verb **is** and the **ing** form of the verb.

Answers will vary. Possible answers shown.

Example: The big, brown dog is barking.

1. The little baby is laughing.

2. Most nine-year-olds are learning.

3. The monster on television is growling.

138 Crazy Big Book of Third Grade

page 138

English Name ____________

Future-Tense Verbs

The **future tense** of a verb tells about something that has not happened yet but will happen in the future. **Will** or **shall** are usually used with future tense.

Directions: Change the verb tense in each sentence to future tense.

Example: She cooks dinner.

She will cook dinner.

1. He plays baseball.

He will play baseball.

2. She walks to school.

She will walk to school.

3. Hasaan talks to the teacher.

Hasaan will talk to the teacher.

4. I remember to vote.

I will remember to vote.

5. Jack mows the lawn every week.

Jack will mow the lawn every week.

6. We go on vacation soon.

We will go on vacation soon.

Crazy Big Book of Third Grade 139

page 139

English Name ____________

Irregular Verbs

Irregular verbs are verbs that do not change from the present tense to the past tense in the regular way, by adding **d** or **ed**.

Example: sing, **sang**

Directions: Read the sentence and underline the verbs. Choose the past-tense form from the box and write it next to the sentence.

blow — blew	fly — flew
come — came	give — gave
take — took	wear — wore
make — made	sing — sang
grow — grew	

Example:

Dad will make dinner tonight. made

1. I will probably grow another inch this year. grew

2. I will blow out the candles. blew

3. Everyone will give me presents. gave

4. I will wear my favorite red shirt. wore

5. My cousins will come from out of town. came

6. It will take them four hours. took

7. My Aunt Betty will fly in from Cleveland. flew

8. She will sing me a song when she gets here. sang

140 Crazy Big Book of Third Grade

page 140

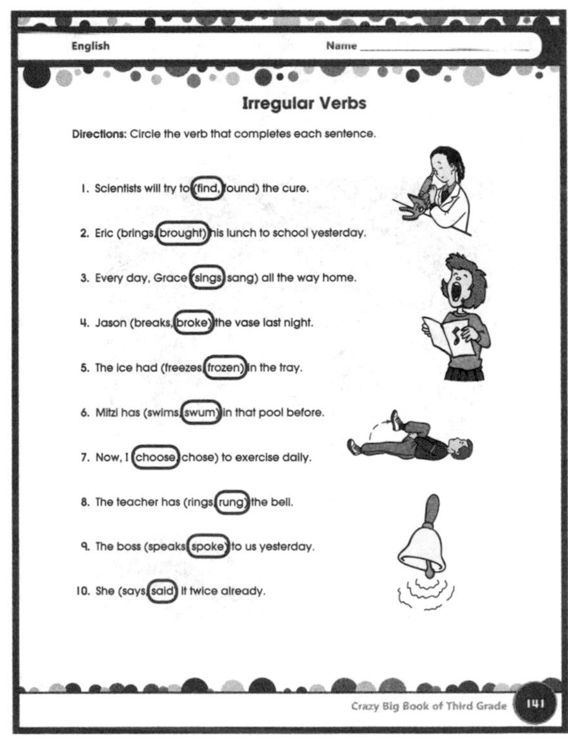

English Name ____________

Irregular Verbs

Directions: Circle the verb that completes each sentence.

1. Scientists will try to (find, found) the cure.
2. Eric (brings, brought) his lunch to school yesterday.
3. Every day, Grace (sings, sang) all the way home.
4. Jason (breaks, broke) the vase last night.
5. The ice had (freezes, frozen) in the tray.
6. Mitzi has (swims, swum) in that pool before.
7. Now, I (choose, chose) to exercise daily.
8. The teacher has (rings, rung) the bell.
9. The boss (speaks, spoke) to us yesterday.
10. She (says, said) it twice already.

Crazy Big Book of Third Grade 141

page 141

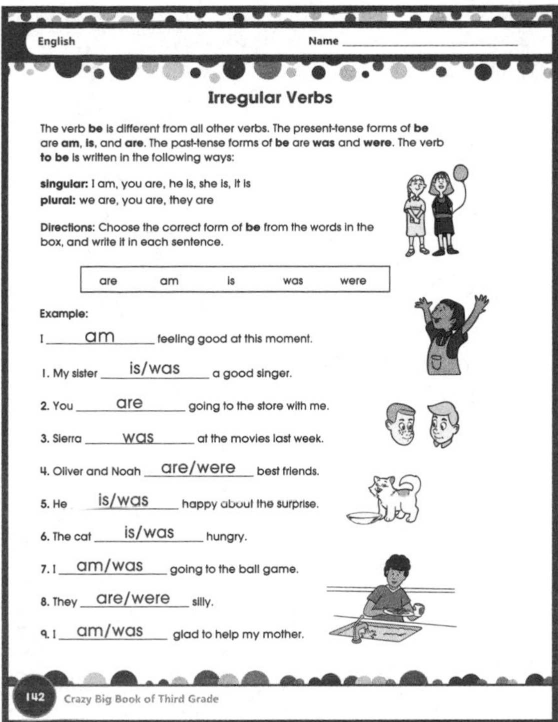

English Name ____________

Irregular Verbs

The verb **be** is different from all other verbs. The present-tense forms of **be** are **am**, **is**, and **are**. The past-tense forms of **be** are **was** and **were**. The verb **to be** is written in the following ways:

singular: I am, you are, he is, she is, it is
plural: we are, you are, they are

Directions: Choose the correct form of **be** from the words in the box, and write it in each sentence.

are am is was were

Example:

I ___am___ feeling good at this moment.

1. My sister ___is/was___ a good singer.
2. You ___are___ going to the store with me.
3. Sierra ___was___ at the movies last week.
4. Oliver and Noah ___are/were___ best friends.
5. He ___is/was___ happy about the surprise.
6. The cat ___is/was___ hungry.
7. I ___am/was___ going to the ball game.
8. They ___are/were___ silly.
9. I ___am/was___ glad to help my mother.

142 Crazy Big Book of Third Grade

page 142

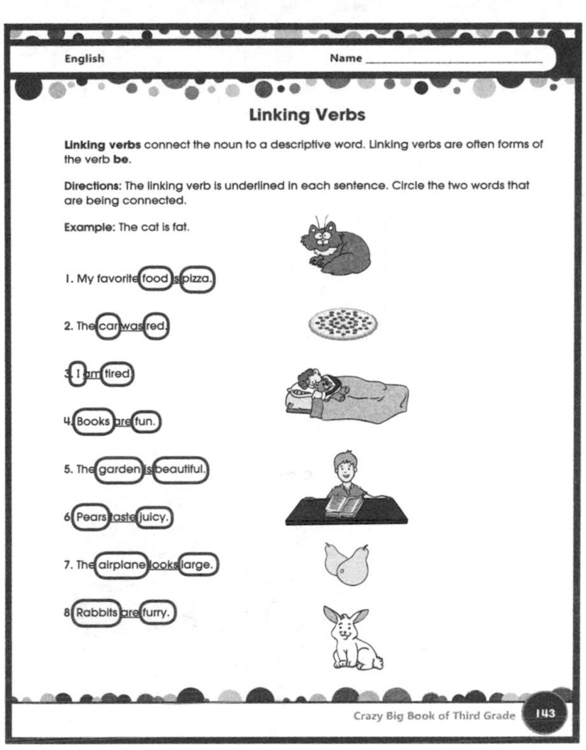

English Name ____________

Linking Verbs

Linking verbs connect the noun to a descriptive word. Linking verbs are often forms of the verb **be**.

Directions: The linking verb is underlined in each sentence. Circle the two words that are being connected.

Example: The cat is fat.

1. My favorite (food) is (pizza).
2. The (car) was (red).
3. (I) am (tired).
4. (Books) are (fun).
5. The (garden) is (beautiful).
6. (Pears) taste (juicy).
7. The (airplane) looks (large).
8. (Rabbits) are (furry).

Crazy Big Book of Third Grade 143

page 143

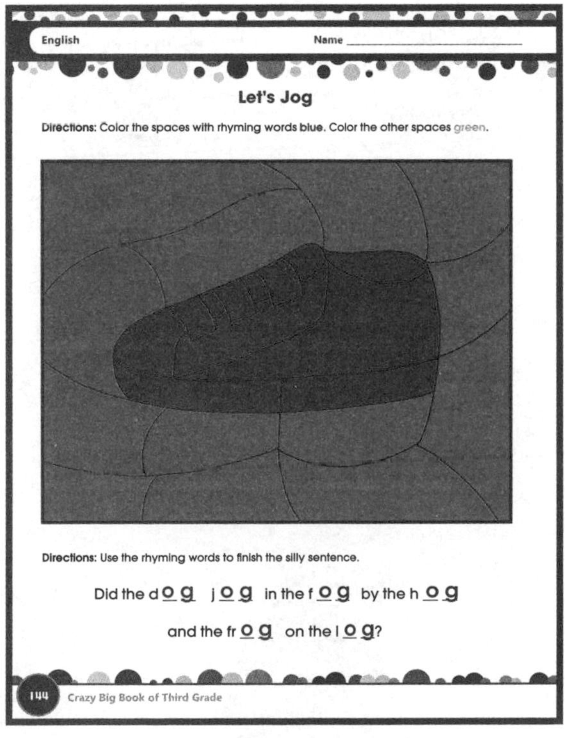

English Name ____________

Let's Jog

Directions: Color the spaces with rhyming words blue. Color the other spaces green.

Directions: Use the rhyming words to finish the silly sentence.

Did the d**og** j**og** in the f**og** by the h**og** and the fr**og** on the l**og**?

144 Crazy Big Book of Third Grade

page 144

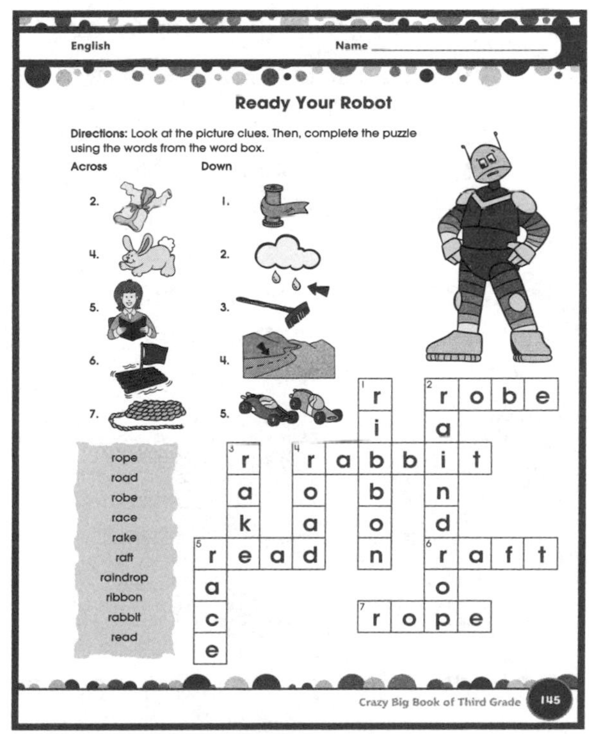

English Name ____________

Ready Your Robot

Directions: Look at the picture clues. Then, complete the puzzle using the words from the word box.

Across: 2. robe 4. rabbit 5. read 6. raft 7. rope

Down: 1. ribbon 2. raindrop 3. rake 4. road 5. race

rope
road
robe
race
rake
raft
raindrop
ribbon
rabbit
read

Crazy Big Book of Third Grade 145

page 145

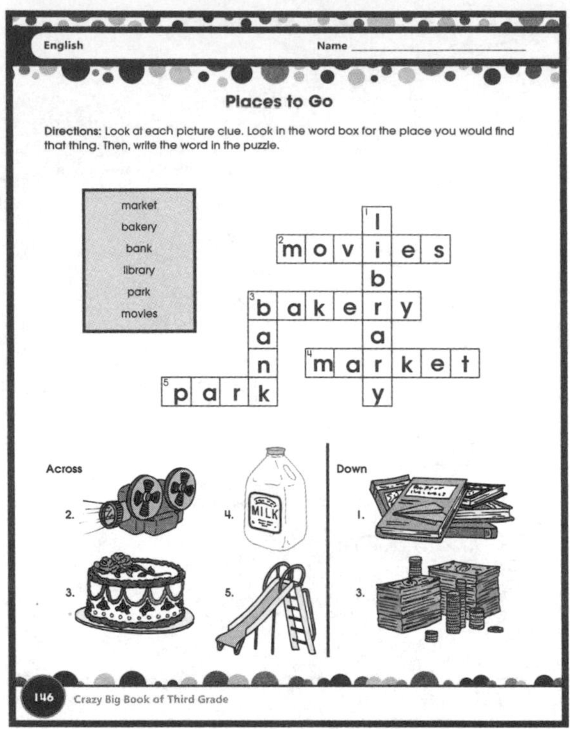

English Name ___

Places to Go

Directions: Look at each picture clue. Look in the word box for the place you would find that thing. Then, write the word in the puzzle.

market
bakery
bank
library
park
movies

Across: 2. movies 3. bakery 4. market 5. park

Down: 1. library 3. bank

Across 2. 3. 4. 5.

Down 1. 3.

146 Crazy Big Book of Third Grade

page 146

English Name ___

Adverbs

Adverbs are words that describe verbs. They tell where, how, or when.

Directions: Circle the adverb in each of the following sentences.

Example: The doctor worked (carefully.)

1. The skater moved (gracefully) across the ice.
2. Their call was returned (quickly.)
3. We (easily) learned the new words.
4. He did the work (perfectly.)
5. She lost her purse (somewhere.)

Directions: Complete the sentences below by writing your own adverbs in the blanks.

Example: The bees worked busily.

Answers will vary. Possible answers shown.

1. The dog barked loudly.
2. The baby smiled cheerfully.
3. She wrote her name quickly.
4. The horse ran steadily.

Crazy Big Book of Third Grade 147

page 147

English Name ___

Adverbs

Directions: Read each sentence. Then, answer the questions on the lines below.

Example: Charles ate hungrily. who? Charles what? ate how? hungrily

1. She dances slowly. who? She what? dances how? slowly
2. The girl spoke carefully. who? The girl what? spoke how? carefully
3. My brother ran quickly. who? My brother what? ran how? quickly
4. Jean walks home often. who? Jean what? walks when? often
5. The children played there. who? The children what? played where? there

148 Crazy Big Book of Third Grade

page 148

English Name ___

Pet Shop

Directions: Read the clues and use the words in the word box to complete the puzzle.

dog fish
cat rabbit
turtle gerbil bird

PETS

OPEN

Across
1. I have feathers. I can fly and sing. (bird)
4. I am small and furry with a long skinny tail. I like running around on a wheel. (gerbil)
7. I have a hard shell. I walk very slowly. (turtle)

Down
2. I have fur. I can bark and do tricks. (dog)
3. I am very quiet. I swim around in a bowl. (fish)
5. I have long floppy ears and a fluffy round tail. I like eating carrots. (rabbit)
6. I am fluffy and furry. When you pet me, I purr. (cat)

Crazy Big Book of Third Grade 149

page 149

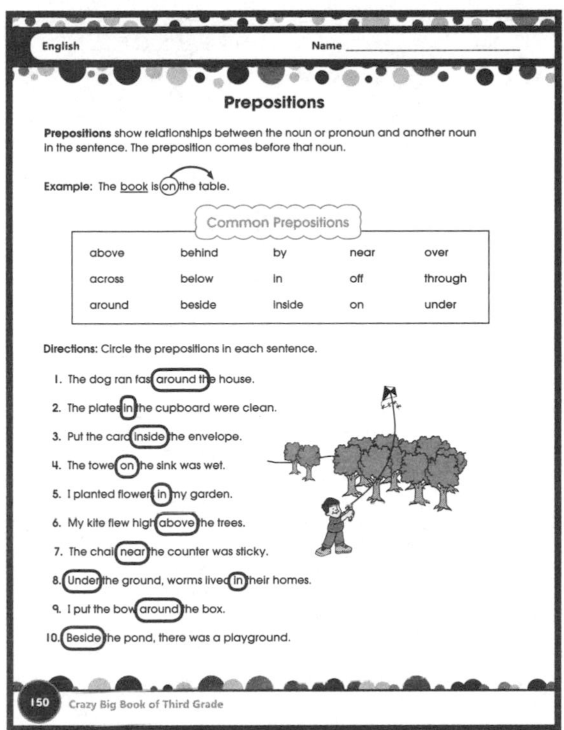

English Name ______________

Prepositions

Prepositions show relationships between the noun or pronoun and another noun in the sentence. The preposition comes before that noun.

Example: The book is (on) the table.

Common Prepositions

above	behind	by	near	over
across	below	in	off	through
around	beside	inside	on	under

Directions: Circle the prepositions in each sentence.

1. The dog ran fast (around) the house.
2. The plates (in) the cupboard were clean.
3. Put the card (inside) the envelope.
4. The towel (on) the sink was wet.
5. I planted flowers (in) my garden.
6. My kite flew high (above) the trees.
7. The chair (near) the counter was sticky.
8. (Under) the ground, worms lived (in) their homes.
9. I put the bow (around) the box.
10. (Beside) the pond, there was a playground.

150 Crazy Big Book of Third Grade

page 150

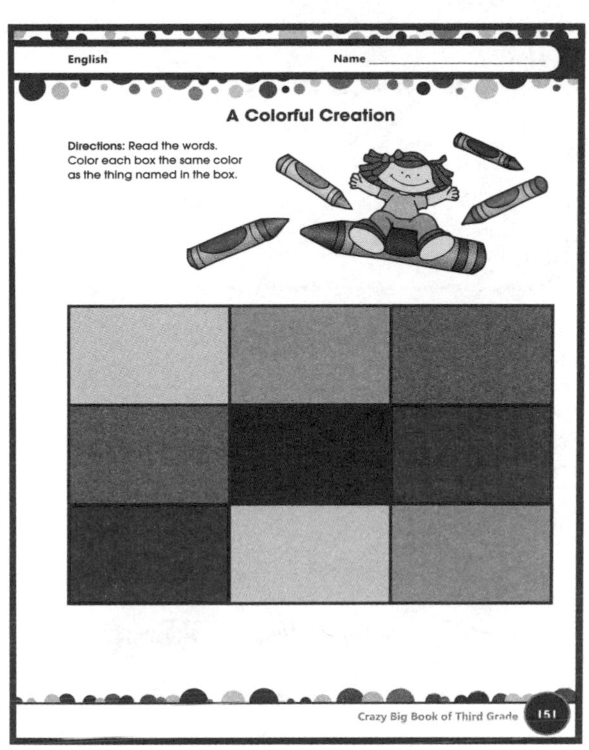

English Name ______________

A Colorful Creation

Directions: Read the words. Color each box the same color as the thing named in the box.

Crazy Big Book of Third Grade 151

page 151

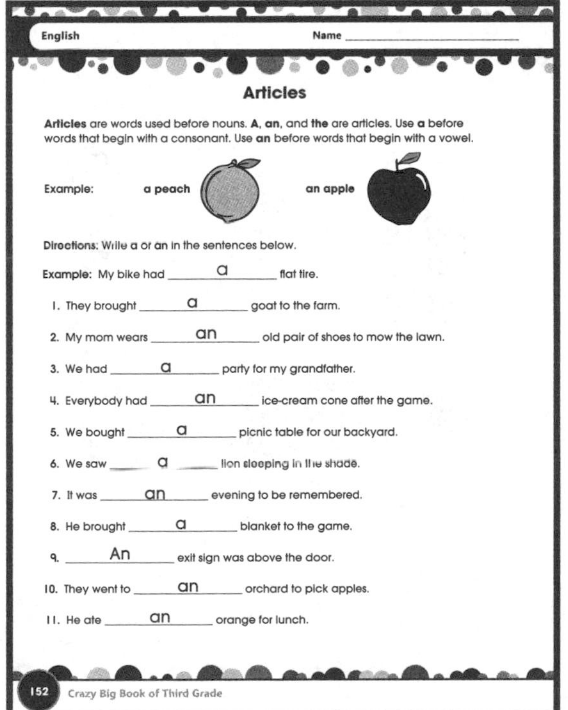

English Name ______________

Articles

Articles are words used before nouns. **A**, **an**, and **the** are articles. Use **a** before words that begin with a consonant. Use **an** before words that begin with a vowel.

Example: a peach an apple

Directions: Write a or an in the sentences below.

Example: My bike had ___a___ flat tire.

1. They brought ___a___ goat to the farm.
2. My mom wears ___an___ old pair of shoes to mow the lawn.
3. We had ___a___ party for my grandfather.
4. Everybody had ___an___ ice-cream cone after the game.
5. We bought ___a___ picnic table for our backyard.
6. We saw ___a___ lion sleeping in the shade.
7. It was ___an___ evening to be remembered.
8. He brought ___a___ blanket to the game.
9. ___An___ exit sign was above the door.
10. They went to ___an___ orchard to pick apples.
11. He ate ___an___ orange for lunch.

152 Crazy Big Book of Third Grade

page 152

English Name ______________

At the Beach

Directions: Read the sentences and use the words in the word box to complete the puzzle.

Across: 2. ships 4. hat 5. ball 6. large
Down: 1. dig 2. shell 3. shore

ships	shore	shell	dig	ball	large	hat

Across

2. I saw three ________ sail by.
4. I wore a ________ to protect myself from the sun.
5. I played catch with my beach ________.
6. I even saw a dolphin that was very ________.

Down

1. I used a shovel to ________ in the sand.
2. I found a ________ at the beach.
3. I saw a ship float up onto the ________.

Crazy Big Book of Third Grade 153

page 153

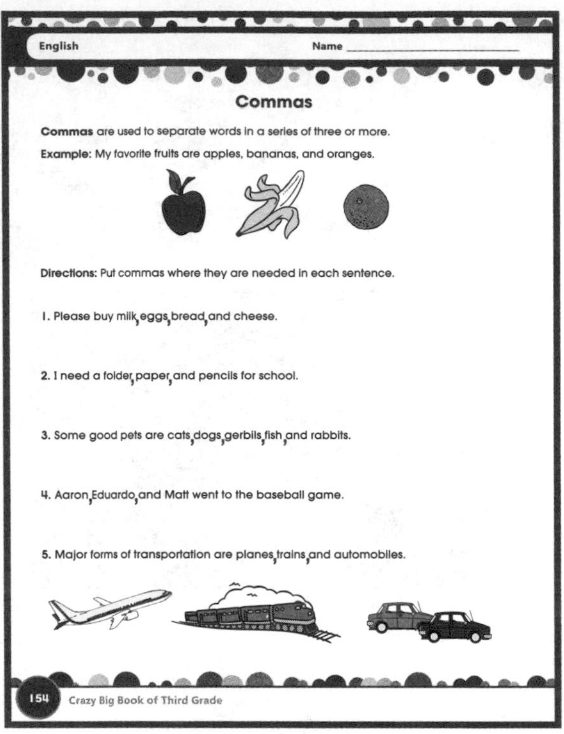

English Name ____________

Commas

Commas are used to separate words in a series of three or more.

Example: My favorite fruits are apples, bananas, and oranges.

Directions: Put commas where they are needed in each sentence.

1. Please buy milk, eggs, bread, and cheese.
2. I need a folder, paper, and pencils for school.
3. Some good pets are cats, dogs, gerbils, fish, and rabbits.
4. Aaron, Eduardo, and Matt went to the baseball game.
5. Major forms of transportation are planes, trains, and automobiles.

154 Crazy Big Book of Third Grade

page 154

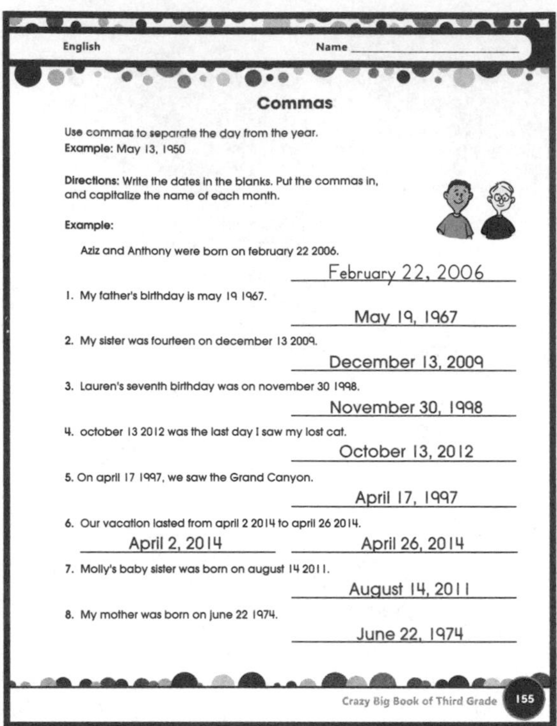

English Name ____________

Commas

Use commas to separate the day from the year.
Example: May 13, 1950

Directions: Write the dates in the blanks. Put the commas in, and capitalize the name of each month.

Example:

Aziz and Anthony were born on february 22 2006.
February 22, 2006

1. My father's birthday is may 19 1967.
May 19, 1967
2. My sister was fourteen on december 13 2009.
December 13, 2009
3. Lauren's seventh birthday was on november 30 1998.
November 30, 1998
4. october 13 2012 was the last day I saw my lost cat.
October 13, 2012
5. On april 17 1997, we saw the Grand Canyon.
April 17, 1997
6. Our vacation lasted from april 2 2014 to april 26 2014.
April 2, 2014 April 26, 2014
7. Molly's baby sister was born on august 14 2011.
August 14, 2011
8. My mother was born on june 22 1974.
June 22, 1974

Crazy Big Book of Third Grade 155

page 155

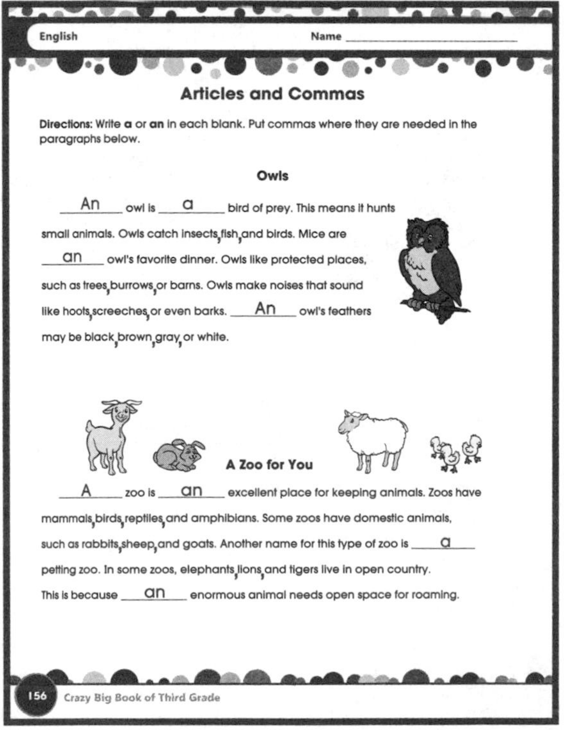

English Name ____________

Articles and Commas

Directions: Write **a** or **an** in each blank. Put commas where they are needed in the paragraphs below.

Owls

An owl is a bird of prey. This means it hunts small animals. Owls catch insects, fish, and birds. Mice are an owl's favorite dinner. Owls like protected places, such as trees, burrows, or barns. Owls make noises that sound like hoots, screeches, or even barks. An owl's feathers may be black, brown, gray, or white.

A Zoo for You

A zoo is an excellent place for keeping animals. Zoos have mammals, birds, reptiles, and amphibians. Some zoos have domestic animals, such as rabbits, sheep, and goats. Another name for this type of zoo is a petting zoo. In some zoos, elephants, lions, and tigers live in open country. This is because an enormous animal needs open space for roaming.

156 Crazy Big Book of Third Grade

page 156

English Name ____________

Fruity Fun

Directions: Look at the picture clues. Then, complete the puzzle using the words from the word box.

Across: 2. plum 3. apple 5. grapes

Down: 1. orange 2. pear 4. peach

Word box: apple, plum, orange, grapes, pear, peach

Crazy Big Book of Third Grade 157

page 157

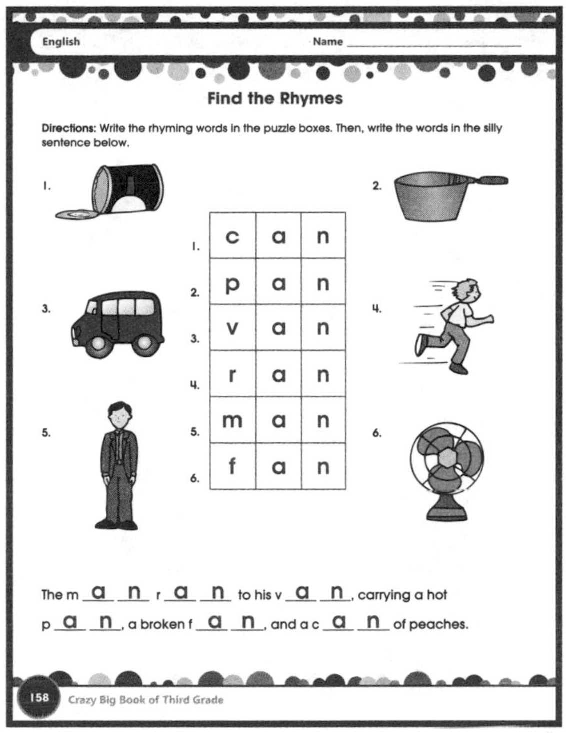
English Name

Find the Rhymes

Directions: Write the rhyming words in the puzzle boxes. Then, write the words in the silly sentence below.

1.	c	a	n
2.	p	a	n
3.	v	a	n
4.	r	a	n
5.	m	a	n
6.	f	a	n

The m a n r a n to his v a n, carrying a hot p a n, a broken f a n, and a c a n of peaches.

158 Crazy Big Book of Third Grade

page 158

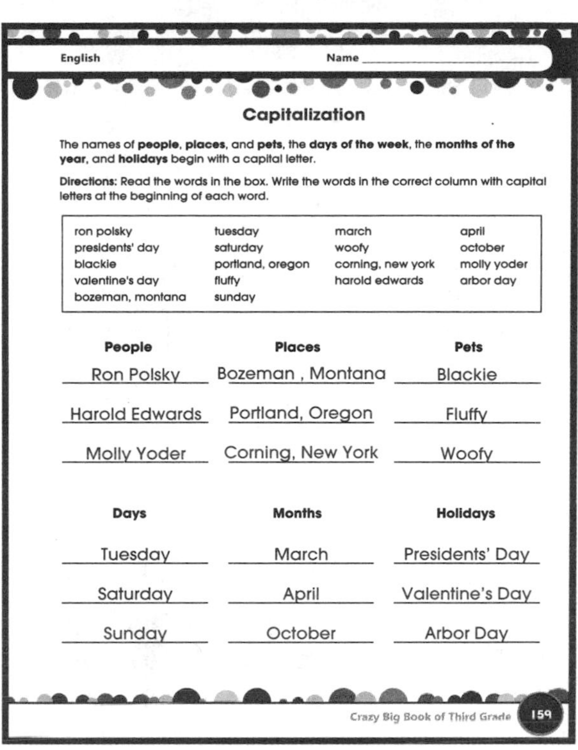
English Name

Capitalization

The names of **people**, **places**, and **pets**, the **days of the week**, the **months of the year**, and **holidays** begin with a capital letter.

Directions: Read the words in the box. Write the words in the correct column with capital letters at the beginning of each word.

ron polsky	tuesday	march	april
presidents' day	saturday	woofy	october
blackie	portland, oregon	corning, new york	molly yoder
valentine's day	fluffy	harold edwards	arbor day
bozeman, montana	sunday		

People	Places	Pets
Ron Polsky	Bozeman , Montana	Blackie
Harold Edwards	Portland, Oregon	Fluffy
Molly Yoder	Corning, New York	Woofy

Days	Months	Holidays
Tuesday	March	Presidents' Day
Saturday	April	Valentine's Day
Sunday	October	Arbor Day

Crazy Big Book of Third Grade 159

page 159

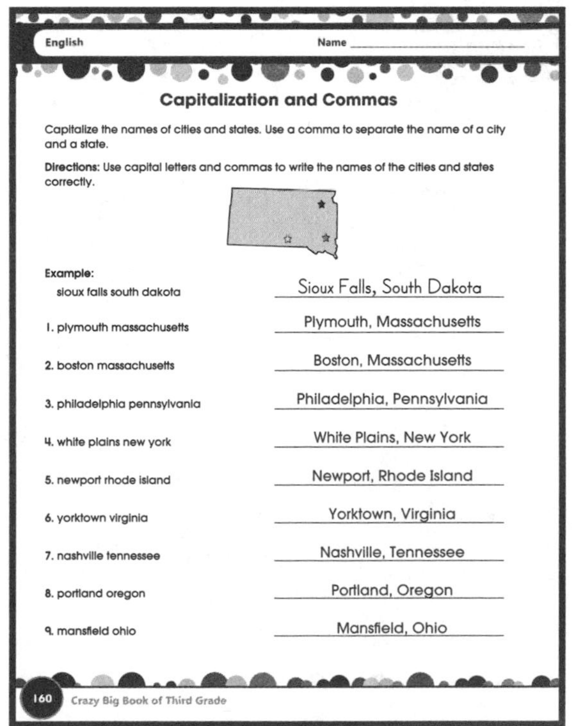
English Name

Capitalization and Commas

Capitalize the names of cities and states. Use a comma to separate the name of a city and a state.

Directions: Use capital letters and commas to write the names of the cities and states correctly.

Example:
sioux falls south dakota — Sioux Falls, South Dakota

1. plymouth massachusetts — Plymouth, Massachusetts
2. boston massachusetts — Boston, Massachusetts
3. philadelphia pennsylvania — Philadelphia, Pennsylvania
4. white plains new york — White Plains, New York
5. newport rhode island — Newport, Rhode Island
6. yorktown virginia — Yorktown, Virginia
7. nashville tennessee — Nashville, Tennessee
8. portland oregon — Portland, Oregon
9. mansfield ohio — Mansfield, Ohio

160 Crazy Big Book of Third Grade

page 160

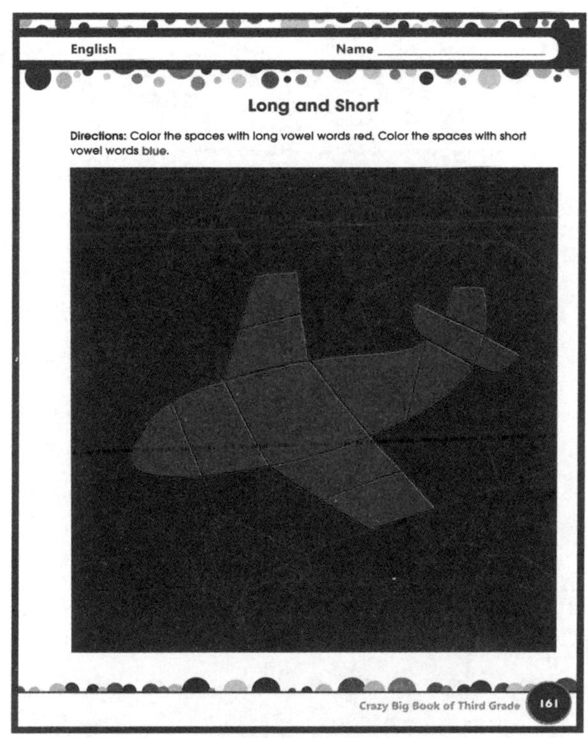
English Name

Long and Short

Directions: Color the spaces with long vowel words red. Color the spaces with short vowel words blue.

Crazy Big Book of Third Grade 161

page 161

Answer Key

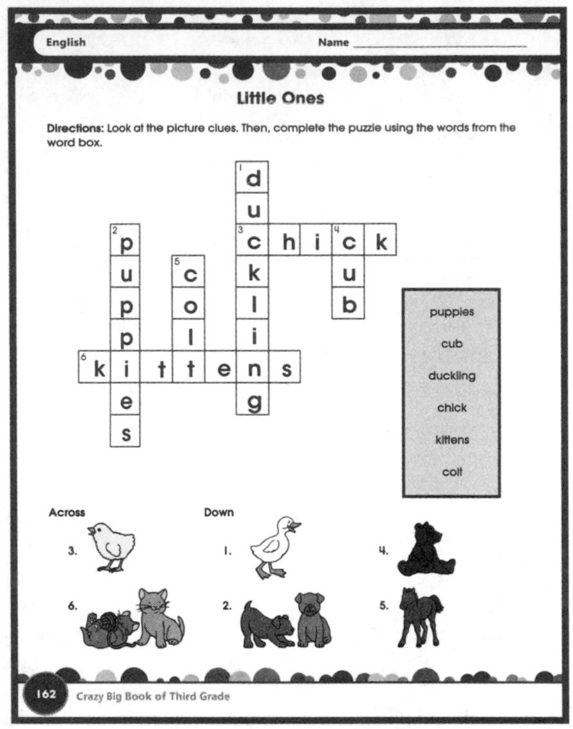
English Name ______________________

Little Ones

Directions: Look at the picture clues. Then, complete the puzzle using the words from the word box.

Word box
puppies
cub
duckling
chick
kittens
colt

Across: 3. 6.

Down: 1. 2. 4. 5.

162 Crazy Big Book of Third Grade

page 162

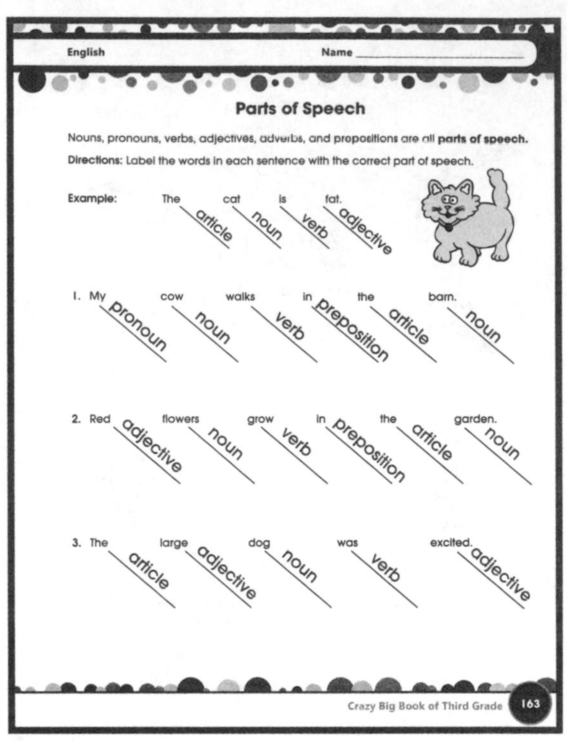
English Name ______________________

Parts of Speech

Nouns, pronouns, verbs, adjectives, adverbs, and prepositions are all **parts of speech.**

Directions: Label the words in each sentence with the correct part of speech.

Example: The (article) cat (noun) is (verb) fat. (adjective)

1. My (pronoun) cow (noun) walks (verb) in (preposition) the (article) barn. (noun)
2. Red (adjective) flowers (noun) grow (verb) in (preposition) the (article) garden. (noun)
3. The (article) large (adjective) dog (noun) was (verb) excited. (adjective)

Crazy Big Book of Third Grade 163

page 163

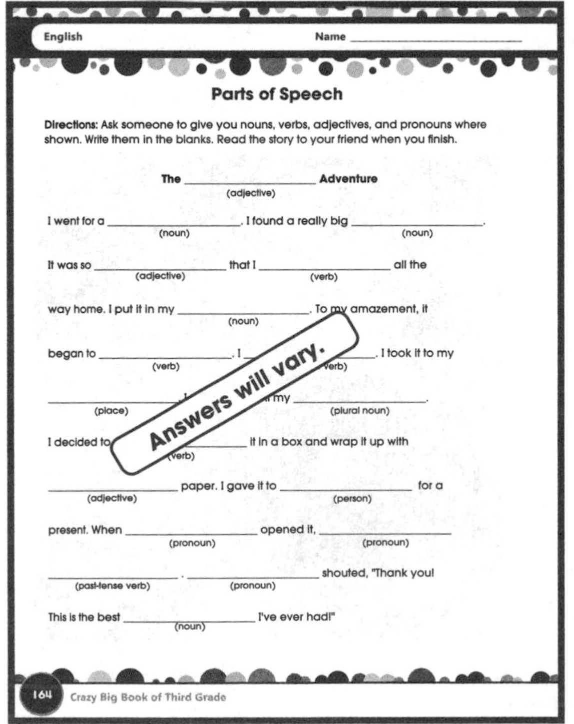
English Name ______________________

Parts of Speech

Directions: Ask someone to give you nouns, verbs, adjectives, and pronouns where shown. Write them in the blanks. Read the story to your friend when you finish.

The ____________ (adjective) Adventure

I went for a ____________ (noun). I found a really big ____________ (noun).

It was so ____________ (adjective) that I ____________ (verb) all the way home. I put it in my ____________ (noun). To my amazement, it began to ____________ (verb). I ____________ (verb). I took it to my ____________ (place) ... my ____________ (plural noun).

I decided to ____________ (verb) it in a box and wrap it up with ____________ (adjective) paper. I gave it to ____________ (person) for a present. When ____________ (pronoun) opened it, ____________ (pronoun) ____________ (past-tense verb). ____________ (pronoun) shouted, "Thank you! This is the best ____________ (noun) I've ever had!"

Answers will vary.

164 Crazy Big Book of Third Grade

page 164

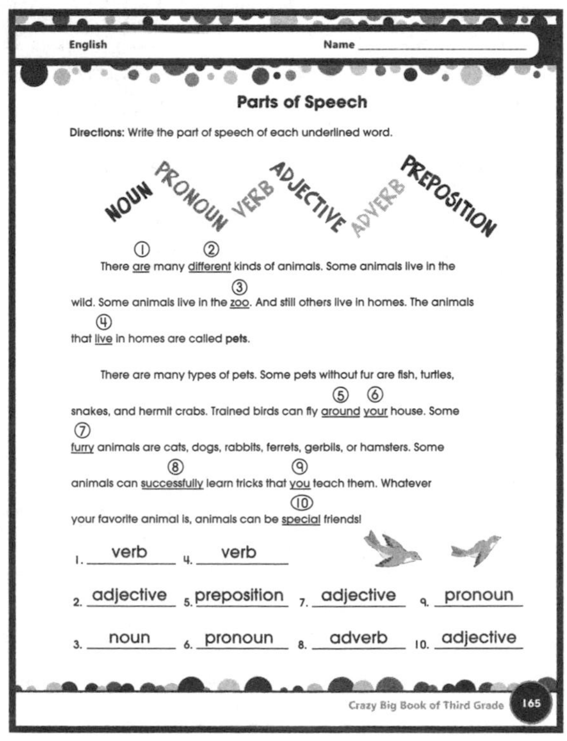
English Name ______________________

Parts of Speech

Directions: Write the part of speech of each underlined word.

There (1) are many (2) different kinds of animals. Some animals live in the wild. Some animals live in the (3) zoo. And still others live in homes. The animals that (4) live in homes are called **pets**.

There are many types of pets. Some pets without fur are fish, turtles, snakes, and hermit crabs. Trained birds can fly (5) around (6) your house. Some (7) furry animals are cats, dogs, rabbits, ferrets, gerbils, or hamsters. Some animals can (8) successfully learn tricks that (9) you teach them. Whatever your favorite animal is, animals can be (10) special friends!

1. verb
2. adjective
3. noun
4. verb
5. preposition
6. pronoun
7. adjective
8. adverb
9. pronoun
10. adjective

Crazy Big Book of Third Grade 165

page 165

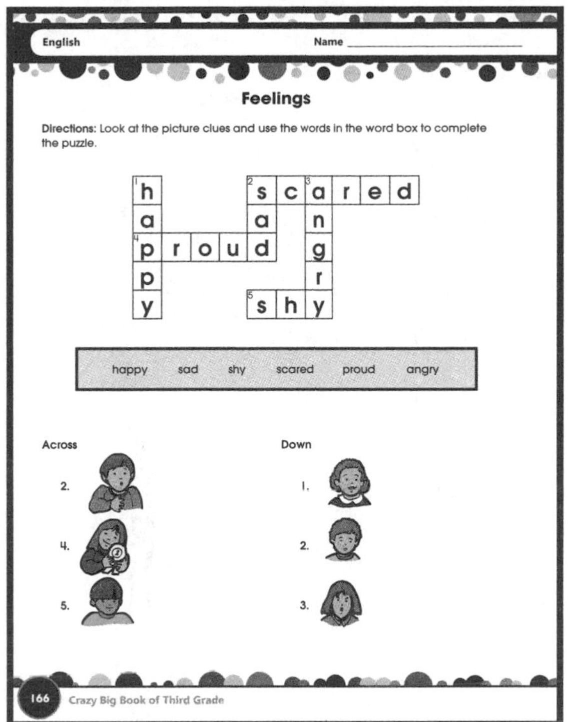

English Name ______________________

Feelings

Directions: Look at the picture clues and use the words in the word box to complete the puzzle.

[1]h [2]s c [3]a r e d
a a n
[4]p r o u d g
p r
y [5]s h y

happy	sad	shy	scared	proud	angry

Across: 2. 4. 5.

Down: 1. 2. 3.

166 Crazy Big Book of Third Grade

page 166

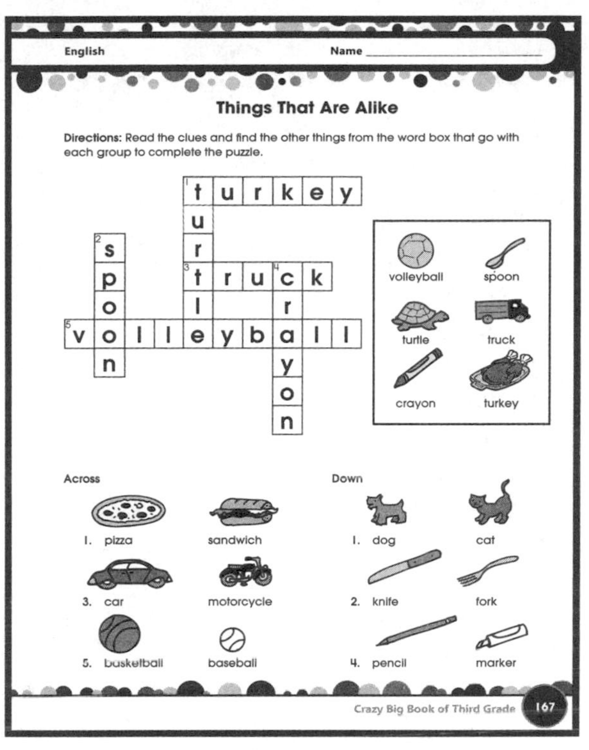

English Name ______________________

Things That Are Alike

Directions: Read the clues and find the other things from the word box that go with each group to complete the puzzle.

[1]t u r k e y
[2]s u
p r
o [3]t r u c [4]k
o l r
[5]v o l l e y b a l l
n y
o
n

volleyball	spoon
turtle	truck
crayon	turkey

Across
1. pizza sandwich
3. car motorcycle
5. basketball baseball

Down
1. dog cat
2. knife fork
4. pencil marker

Crazy Big Book of Third Grade 167

page 167

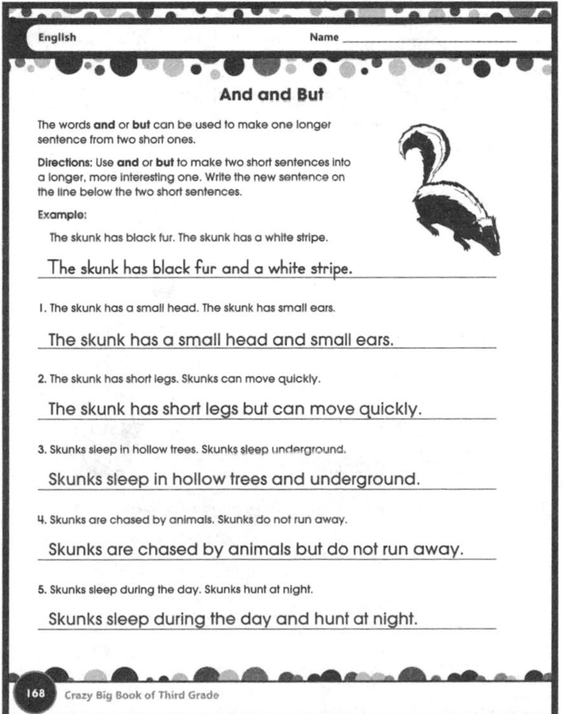

English Name ______________________

And and But

The words **and** or **but** can be used to make one longer sentence from two short ones.

Directions: Use **and** or **but** to make two short sentences into a longer, more interesting one. Write the new sentence on the line below the two short sentences.

Example:

The skunk has black fur. The skunk has a white stripe.

The skunk has black fur and a white stripe.

1. The skunk has a small head. The skunk has small ears.

   The skunk has a small head and small ears.

2. The skunk has short legs. Skunks can move quickly.

   The skunk has short legs but can move quickly.

3. Skunks sleep in hollow trees. Skunks sleep underground.

   Skunks sleep in hollow trees and underground.

4. Skunks are chased by animals. Skunks do not run away.

   Skunks are chased by animals but do not run away.

5. Skunks sleep during the day. Skunks hunt at night.

   Skunks sleep during the day and hunt at night.

168 Crazy Big Book of Third Grade

page 168

English Name ______________________

New Words

Directions: Starting with the top word in each square, change one letter at a time until the top word becomes the bottom word.

1.	C	A	P	E
2.	C	A	P	S
3.	C	A	N	S
4.	F	A	N	S
5.	F	I	N	S

6.	G	O	A	L
7.	G	O	A	T
8.	B	O	A	T
9.	B	E	A	T
10.	B	E	S	T

Crazy Big Book of Third Grade 169

page 169

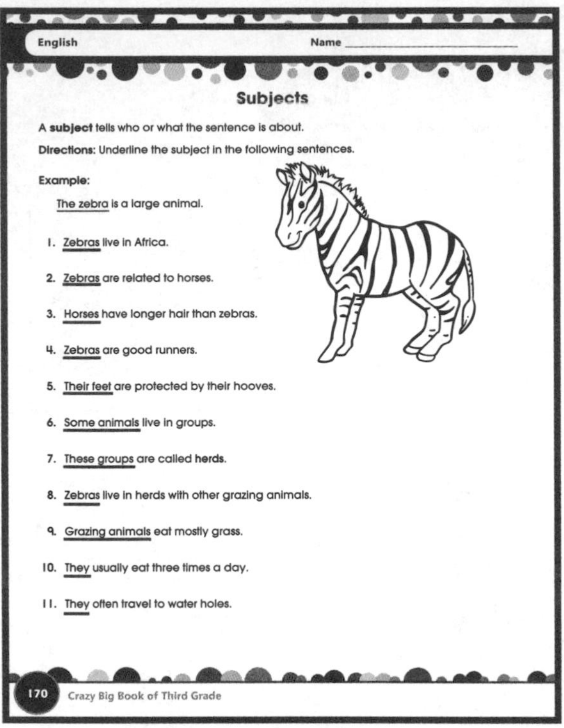

English Name ______

Subjects

A **subject** tells who or what the sentence is about.

Directions: Underline the subject in the following sentences.

Example:

The zebra is a large animal.

1. Zebras live in Africa.
2. Zebras are related to horses.
3. Horses have longer hair than zebras.
4. Zebras are good runners.
5. Their feet are protected by their hooves.
6. Some animals live in groups.
7. These groups are called **herds**.
8. Zebras live in herds with other grazing animals.
9. Grazing animals eat mostly grass.
10. They usually eat three times a day.
11. They often travel to water holes.

170 Crazy Big Book of Third Grade

page 170

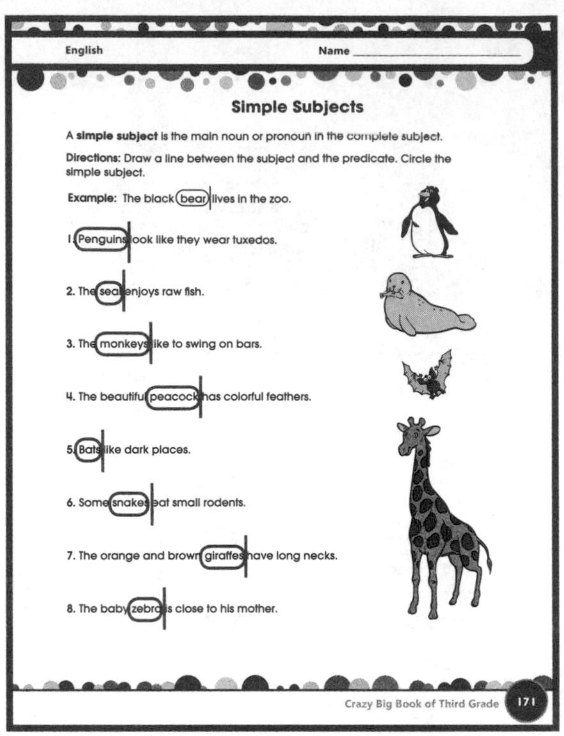

English Name ______

Simple Subjects

A **simple subject** is the main noun or pronoun in the complete subject.

Directions: Draw a line between the subject and the predicate. Circle the simple subject.

Example: The black bear lives in the zoo.

1. Penguins look like they wear tuxedos.
2. The seal enjoys raw fish.
3. The monkeys like to swing on bars.
4. The beautiful peacock has colorful feathers.
5. Bats like dark places.
6. Some snakes eat small rodents.
7. The orange and brown giraffes have long necks.
8. The baby zebra is close to his mother.

Crazy Big Book of Third Grade 171

page 171

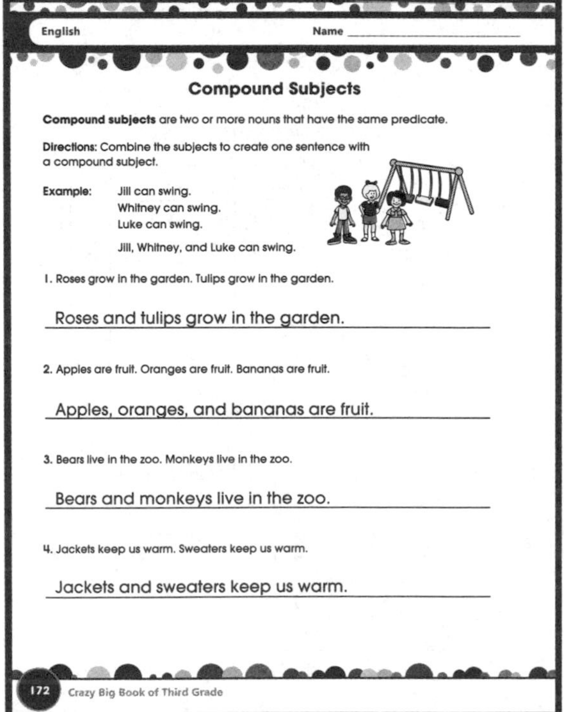

English Name ______

Compound Subjects

Compound subjects are two or more nouns that have the same predicate.

Directions: Combine the subjects to create one sentence with a compound subject.

Example: Jill can swing.
Whitney can swing.
Luke can swing.
Jill, Whitney, and Luke can swing.

1. Roses grow in the garden. Tulips grow in the garden.

Roses and tulips grow in the garden.

2. Apples are fruit. Oranges are fruit. Bananas are fruit.

Apples, oranges, and bananas are fruit.

3. Bears live in the zoo. Monkeys live in the zoo.

Bears and monkeys live in the zoo.

4. Jackets keep us warm. Sweaters keep us warm.

Jackets and sweaters keep us warm.

172 Crazy Big Book of Third Grade

page 172

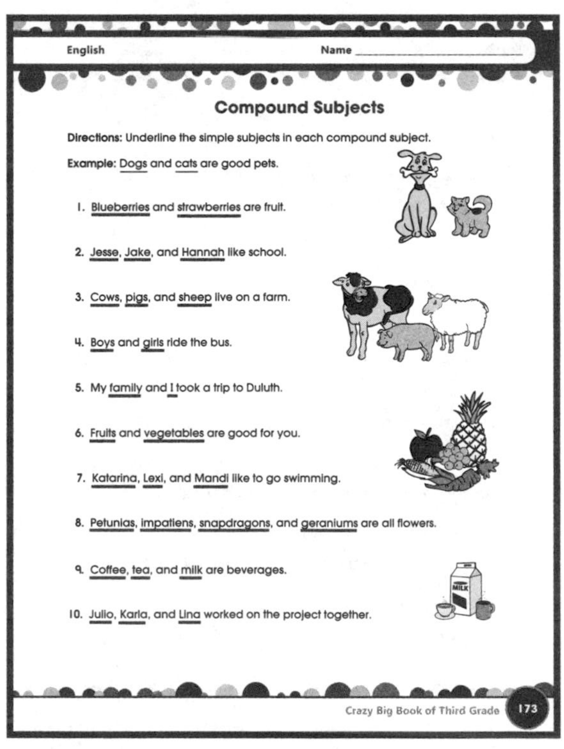

English Name ______

Compound Subjects

Directions: Underline the simple subjects in each compound subject.

Example: Dogs and cats are good pets.

1. Blueberries and strawberries are fruit.
2. Jesse, Jake, and Hannah like school.
3. Cows, pigs, and sheep live on a farm.
4. Boys and girls ride the bus.
5. My family and I took a trip to Duluth.
6. Fruits and vegetables are good for you.
7. Katarina, Lexi, and Mandi like to go swimming.
8. Petunias, impatiens, snapdragons, and geraniums are all flowers.
9. Coffee, tea, and milk are beverages.
10. Julio, Karla, and Lina worked on the project together.

Crazy Big Book of Third Grade 173

page 173

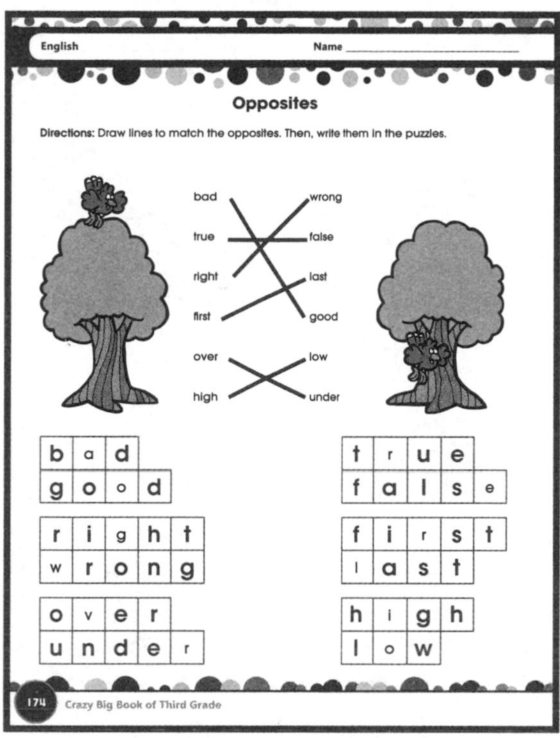
English Name ____________

Opposites

Directions: Draw lines to match the opposites. Then, write them in the puzzles.

bad	wrong
true	false
right	last
first	good
over	low
high	under

bad / good

true / false

right / wrong

first / last

over / under

high / low

174 Crazy Big Book of Third Grade

page 174

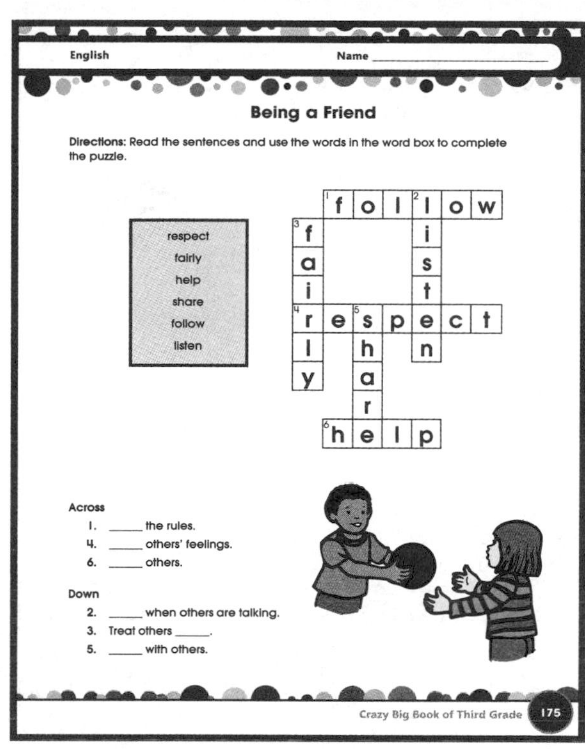
English Name ____________

Being a Friend

Directions: Read the sentences and use the words in the word box to complete the puzzle.

respect
fairly
help
share
follow
listen

Across

1. follow the rules.
4. respect others' feelings.
6. help others.

Down

2. listen when others are talking.
3. Treat others fairly.
5. share with others.

Crazy Big Book of Third Grade 175

page 175

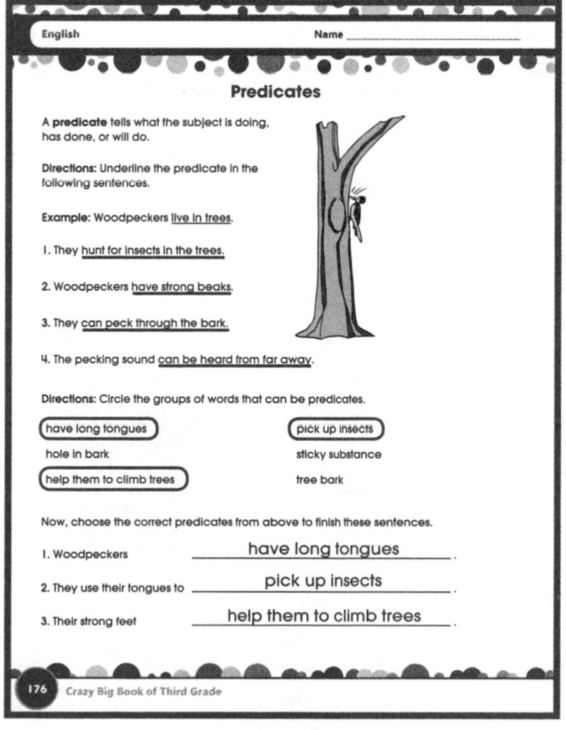
English Name ____________

Predicates

A **predicate** tells what the subject is doing, has done, or will do.

Directions: Underline the predicate in the following sentences.

Example: Woodpeckers live in trees.

1. They hunt for insects in the trees.
2. Woodpeckers have strong beaks.
3. They can peck through the bark.
4. The pecking sound can be heard from far away.

Directions: Circle the groups of words that can be predicates.

have long tongues (circled)
hole in bark
help them to climb trees (circled)
pick up insects (circled)
sticky substance
tree bark

Now, choose the correct predicates from above to finish these sentences.

1. Woodpeckers have long tongues.
2. They use their tongues to pick up insects.
3. Their strong feet help them to climb trees.

176 Crazy Big Book of Third Grade

page 176

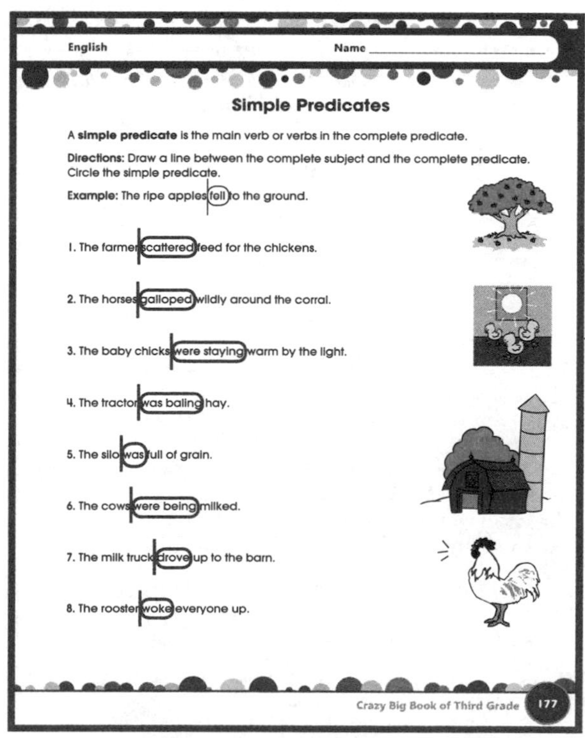
English Name ____________

Simple Predicates

A **simple predicate** is the main verb or verbs in the complete predicate.

Directions: Draw a line between the complete subject and the complete predicate. Circle the simple predicate.

Example: The ripe apples | fell to the ground.

1. The farmer | scattered feed for the chickens.
2. The horses | galloped wildly around the corral.
3. The baby chicks | were staying warm by the light.
4. The tractor | was baling hay.
5. The silo | was full of grain.
6. The cows | were being milked.
7. The milk truck | drove up to the barn.
8. The rooster | woke everyone up.

Crazy Big Book of Third Grade 177

page 177

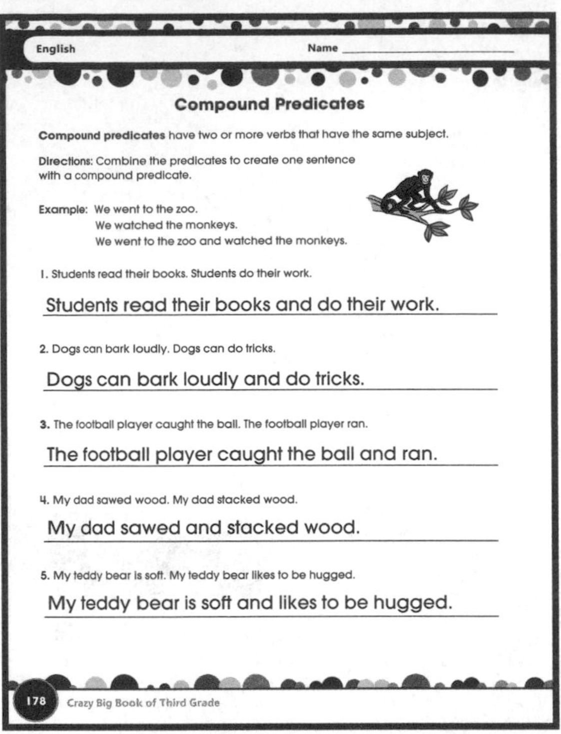

English Name ____________

Compound Predicates

Compound predicates have two or more verbs that have the same subject.

Directions: Combine the predicates to create one sentence with a compound predicate.

Example: We went to the zoo.
We watched the monkeys.
We went to the zoo and watched the monkeys.

1. Students read their books. Students do their work.
Students read their books and do their work.

2. Dogs can bark loudly. Dogs can do tricks.
Dogs can bark loudly and do tricks.

3. The football player caught the ball. The football player ran.
The football player caught the ball and ran.

4. My dad sawed wood. My dad stacked wood.
My dad sawed and stacked wood.

5. My teddy bear is soft. My teddy bear likes to be hugged.
My teddy bear is soft and likes to be hugged.

178 Crazy Big Book of Third Grade

page 178

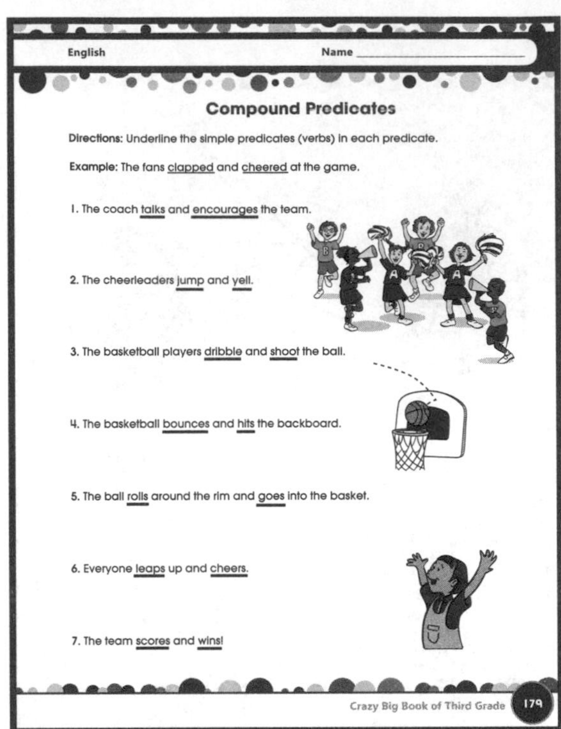

English Name ____________

Compound Predicates

Directions: Underline the simple predicates (verbs) in each predicate.

Example: The fans clapped and cheered at the game.

1. The coach talks and encourages the team.
2. The cheerleaders jump and yell.
3. The basketball players dribble and shoot the ball.
4. The basketball bounces and hits the backboard.
5. The ball rolls around the rim and goes into the basket.
6. Everyone leaps up and cheers.
7. The team scores and wins!

Crazy Big Book of Third Grade 179

page 179

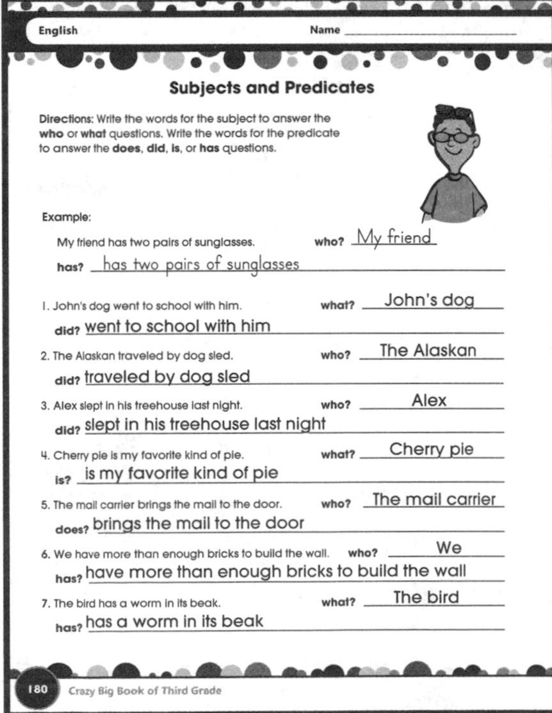

English Name ____________

Subjects and Predicates

Directions: Write the words for the subject to answer the **who** or **what** questions. Write the words for the predicate to answer the **does**, **did**, **is**, or **has** questions.

Example:

My friend has two pairs of sunglasses. **who?** My friend
has? has two pairs of sunglasses

1. John's dog went to school with him. **what?** John's dog
did? went to school with him

2. The Alaskan traveled by dog sled. **who?** The Alaskan
did? traveled by dog sled

3. Alex slept in his treehouse last night. **who?** Alex
did? slept in his treehouse last night

4. Cherry pie is my favorite kind of pie. **what?** Cherry pie
is? is my favorite kind of pie

5. The mail carrier brings the mail to the door. **who?** The mail carrier
does? brings the mail to the door

6. We have more than enough bricks to build the wall. **who?** We
has? have more than enough bricks to build the wall

7. The bird has a worm in its beak. **what?** The bird
has? has a worm in its beak

180 Crazy Big Book of Third Grade

page 180

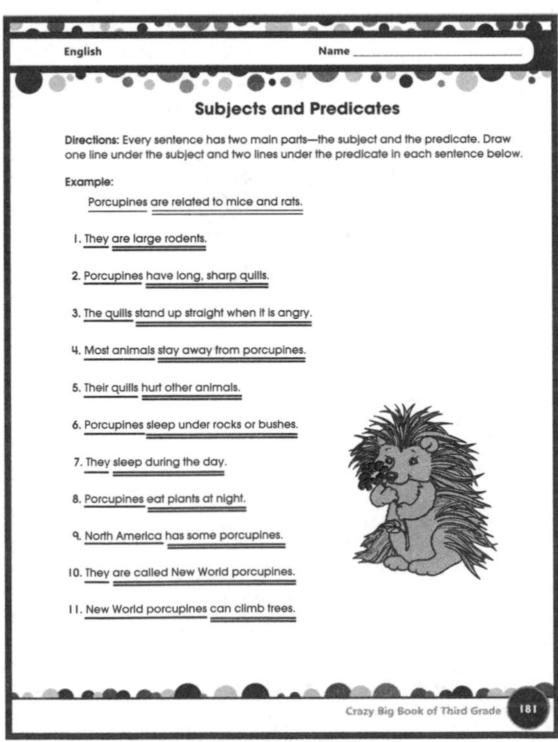

English Name ____________

Subjects and Predicates

Directions: Every sentence has two main parts—the subject and the predicate. Draw one line under the subject and two lines under the predicate in each sentence below.

Example:
Porcupines are related to mice and rats.

1. They are large rodents.
2. Porcupines have long, sharp quills.
3. The quills stand up straight when it is angry.
4. Most animals stay away from porcupines.
5. Their quills hurt other animals.
6. Porcupines sleep under rocks or bushes.
7. They sleep during the day.
8. Porcupines eat plants at night.
9. North America has some porcupines.
10. They are called New World porcupines.
11. New World porcupines can climb trees.

Crazy Big Book of Third Grade 181

page 181

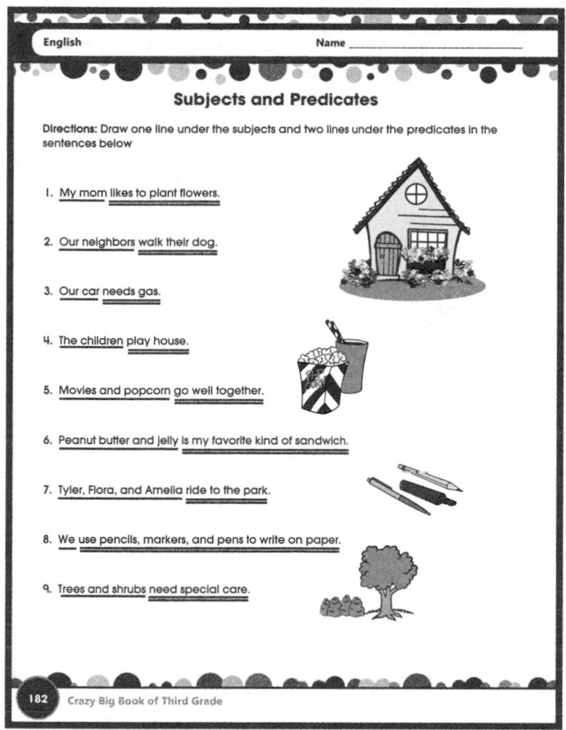

page 182

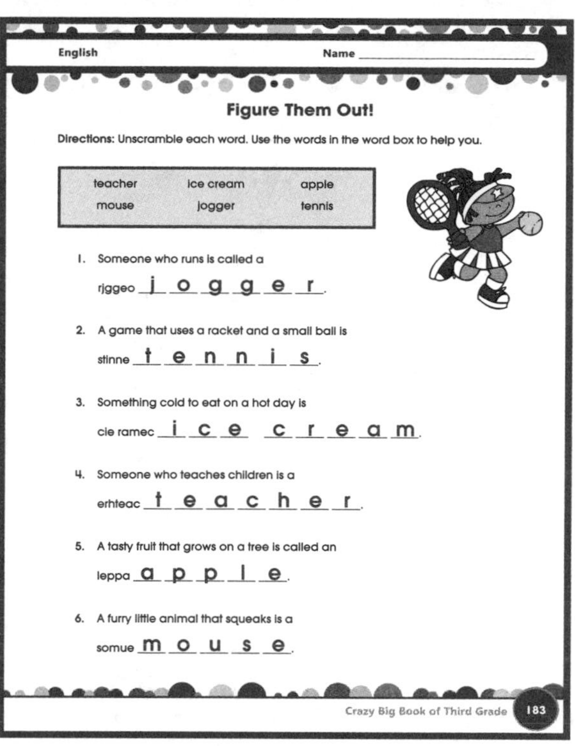

page 183

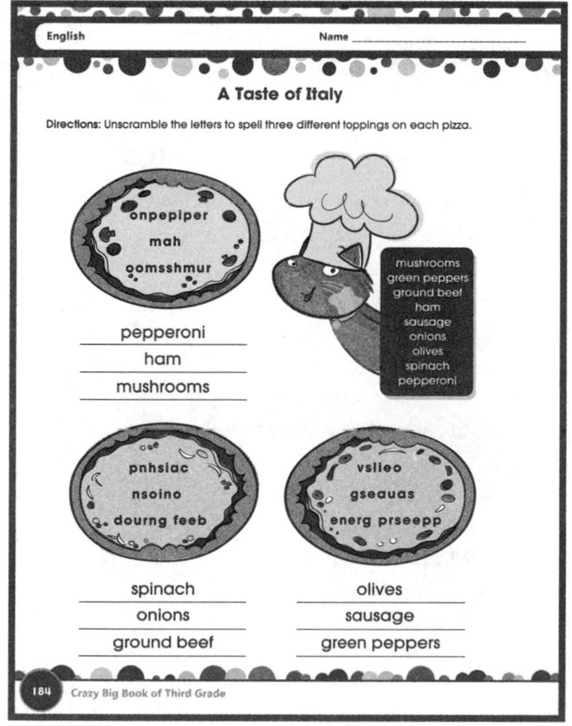

page 184

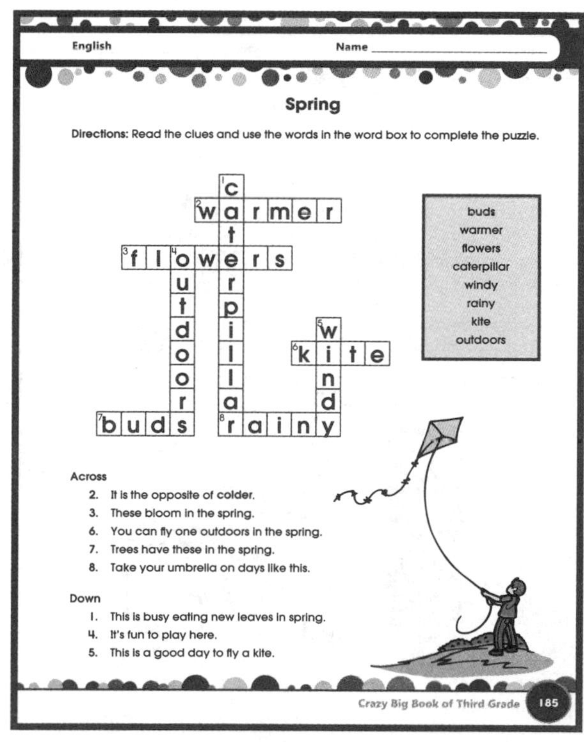

page 185

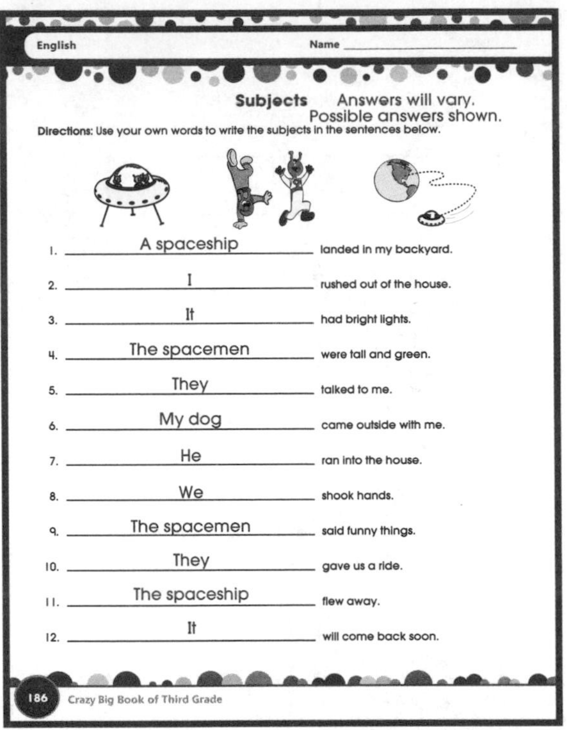

English Name ______

Subjects

Answers will vary. Possible answers shown.

Directions: Use your own words to write the subjects in the sentences below.

1. A spaceship landed in my backyard.
2. I rushed out of the house.
3. It had bright lights.
4. The spacemen were tall and green.
5. They talked to me.
6. My dog came outside with me.
7. He ran into the house.
8. We shook hands.
9. The spacemen said funny things.
10. They gave us a ride.
11. The spaceship flew away.
12. It will come back soon.

186 Crazy Big Book of Third Grade

page 186

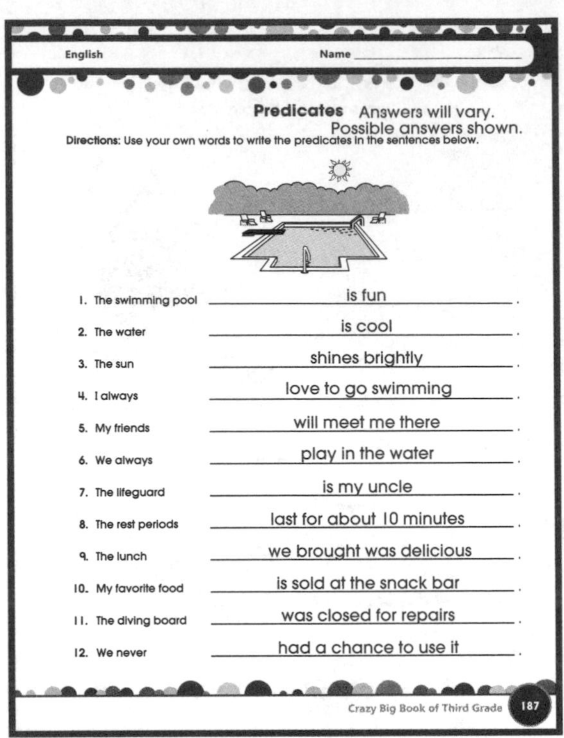

English Name ______

Predicates

Answers will vary. Possible answers shown.

Directions: Use your own words to write the predicates in the sentences below.

1. The swimming pool is fun.
2. The water is cool.
3. The sun shines brightly.
4. I always love to go swimming.
5. My friends will meet me there.
6. We always play in the water.
7. The lifeguard is my uncle.
8. The rest periods last for about 10 minutes.
9. The lunch we brought was delicious.
10. My favorite food is sold at the snack bar.
11. The diving board was closed for repairs.
12. We never had a chance to use it.

Crazy Big Book of Third Grade 187

page 187

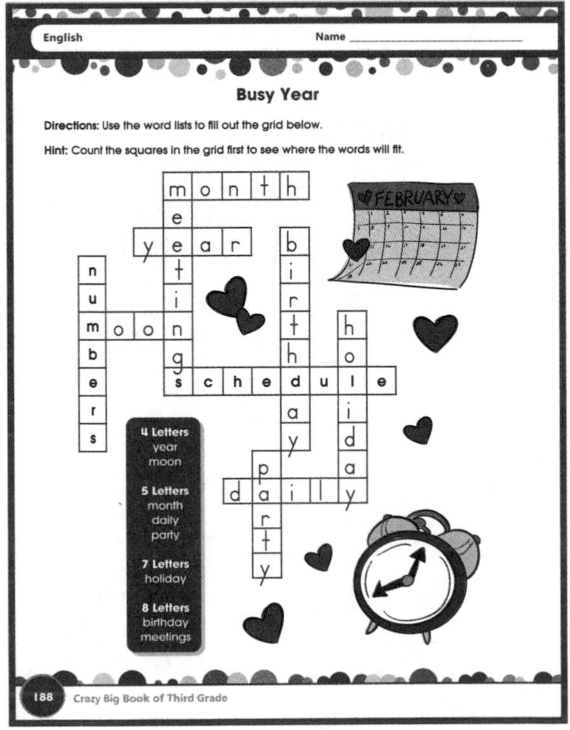

English Name ______

Busy Year

Directions: Use the word lists to fill out the grid below.

Hint: Count the squares in the grid first to see where the words will fit.

4 Letters
year
moon

5 Letters
month
daily
party

7 Letters
holiday

8 Letters
birthday
meetings

188 Crazy Big Book of Third Grade

page 188

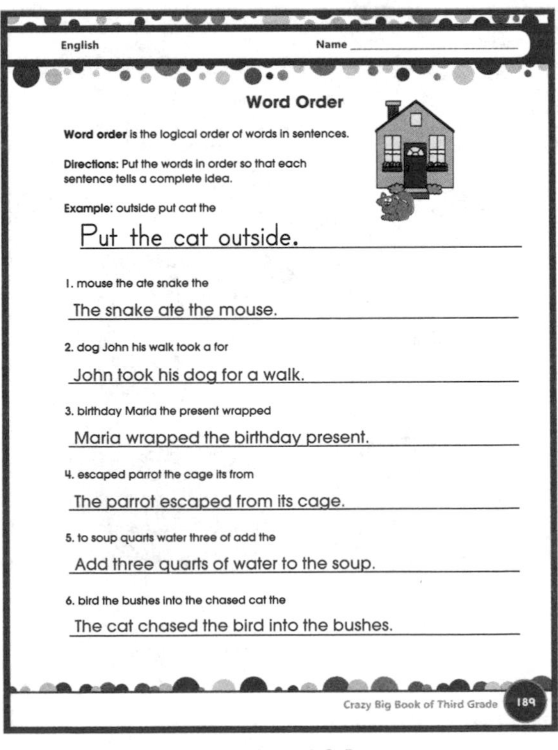

English Name ______

Word Order

Word order is the logical order of words in sentences.

Directions: Put the words in order so that each sentence tells a complete idea.

Example: outside put cat the

Put the cat outside.

1. mouse the ate snake the

The snake ate the mouse.

2. dog John his walk took a for

John took his dog for a walk.

3. birthday Maria the present wrapped

Maria wrapped the birthday present.

4. escaped parrot the cage its from

The parrot escaped from its cage.

5. to soup quarts water three of add the

Add three quarts of water to the soup.

6. bird the bushes into the chased cat the

The cat chased the bird into the bushes.

Crazy Big Book of Third Grade 189

page 189

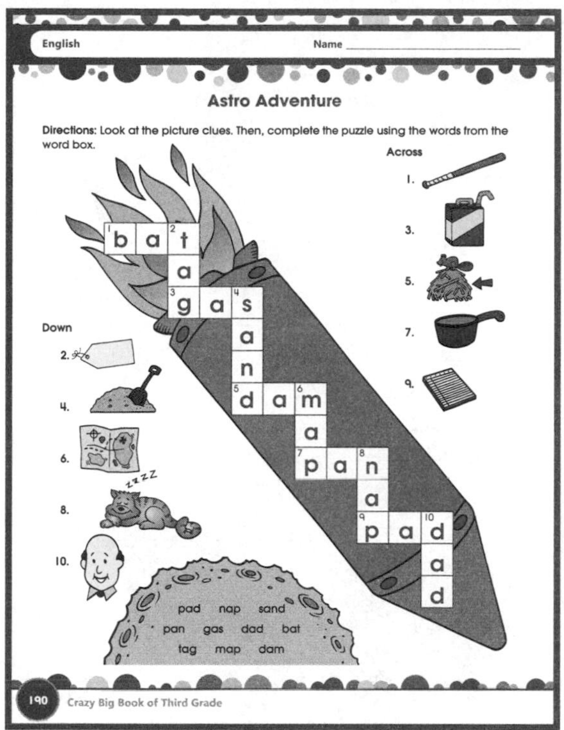
English Name ______

Astro Adventure

Directions: Look at the picture clues. Then, complete the puzzle using the words from the word box.

Across

1. 3. 5. 7. 9.

Down

2. 4. 6. 8. 10.

pad nap sand
pan gas dad bat
tag map dam

190 Crazy Big Book of Third Grade

page 190

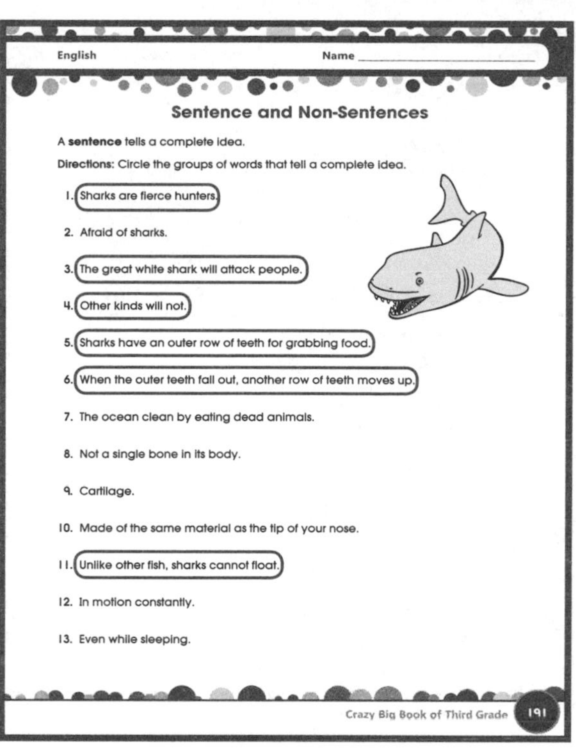
English Name ______

Sentence and Non-Sentences

A **sentence** tells a complete idea.

Directions: Circle the groups of words that tell a complete idea.

1. Sharks are fierce hunters.
2. Afraid of sharks.
3. The great white shark will attack people.
4. Other kinds will not.
5. Sharks have an outer row of teeth for grabbing food.
6. When the outer teeth fall out, another row of teeth moves up.
7. The ocean clean by eating dead animals.
8. Not a single bone in its body.
9. Cartilage.
10. Made of the same material as the tip of your nose.
11. Unlike other fish, sharks cannot float.
12. In motion constantly.
13. Even while sleeping.

Crazy Big Book of Third Grade 191

page 191

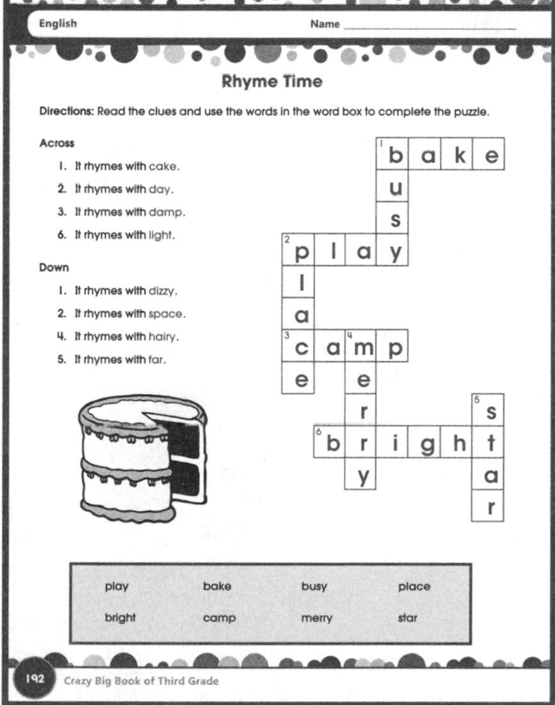
English Name ______

Rhyme Time

Directions: Read the clues and use the words in the word box to complete the puzzle.

Across

1. It rhymes with cake.
2. It rhymes with day.
3. It rhymes with damp.
6. It rhymes with light.

Down

1. It rhymes with dizzy.
2. It rhymes with space.
4. It rhymes with hairy.
5. It rhymes with far.

play	bake	busy	place
bright	camp	merry	star

192 Crazy Big Book of Third Grade

page 192

English Name ______

Nap Time in the Nest

Directions: Look at the picture clues. Then, complete the puzzle using the words from the word box.

Across

2. 4. 5. 6.

Down

1. 2. 1, 2, 3, 4, _, 6. 3. 5.

note nose numbers
needle net nail nine
nurse nest

Crazy Big Book of Third Grade 193

page 193

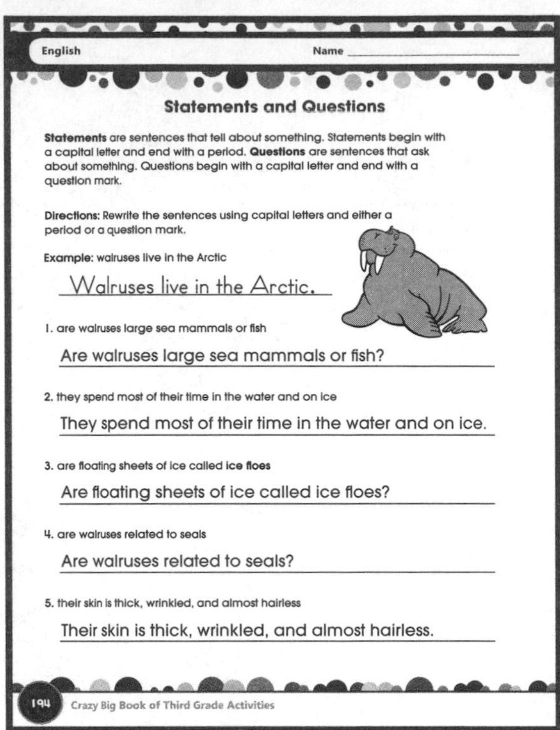
English Name ____________

Statements and Questions

Statements are sentences that tell about something. Statements begin with a capital letter and end with a period. **Questions** are sentences that ask about something. Questions begin with a capital letter and end with a question mark.

Directions: Rewrite the sentences using capital letters and either a period or a question mark.

Example: walruses live in the Arctic
Walruses live in the Arctic.

1. are walruses large sea mammals or fish
   Are walruses large sea mammals or fish?
2. they spend most of their time in the water and on ice
   They spend most of their time in the water and on ice.
3. are floating sheets of ice called **ice floes**
   Are floating sheets of ice called ice floes?
4. are walruses related to seals
   Are walruses related to seals?
5. their skin is thick, wrinkled, and almost hairless
   Their skin is thick, wrinkled, and almost hairless.

194 Crazy Big Book of Third Grade Activities

page 194

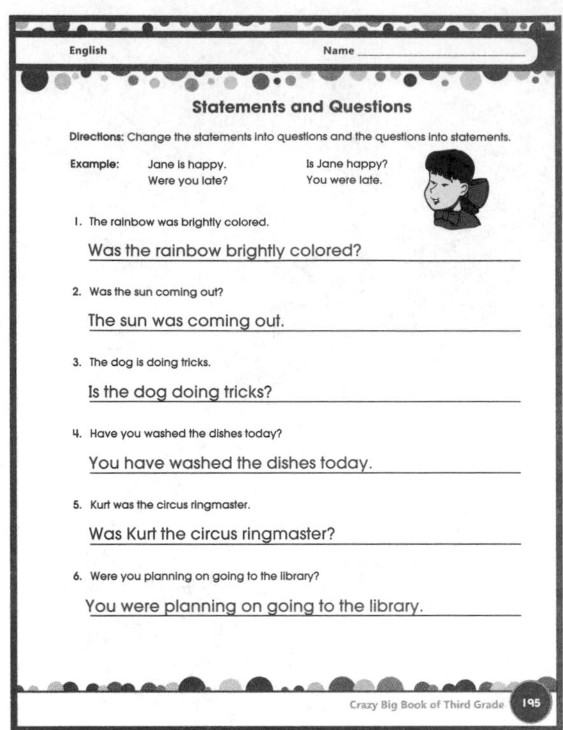
English Name ____________

Statements and Questions

Directions: Change the statements into questions and the questions into statements.

Example: Jane is happy. → Is Jane happy?
Were you late? → You were late.

1. The rainbow was brightly colored.
   Was the rainbow brightly colored?
2. Was the sun coming out?
   The sun was coming out.
3. The dog is doing tricks.
   Is the dog doing tricks?
4. Have you washed the dishes today?
   You have washed the dishes today.
5. Kurt was the circus ringmaster.
   Was Kurt the circus ringmaster?
6. Were you planning on going to the library?
   You were planning on going to the library.

Crazy Big Book of Third Grade 195

page 195

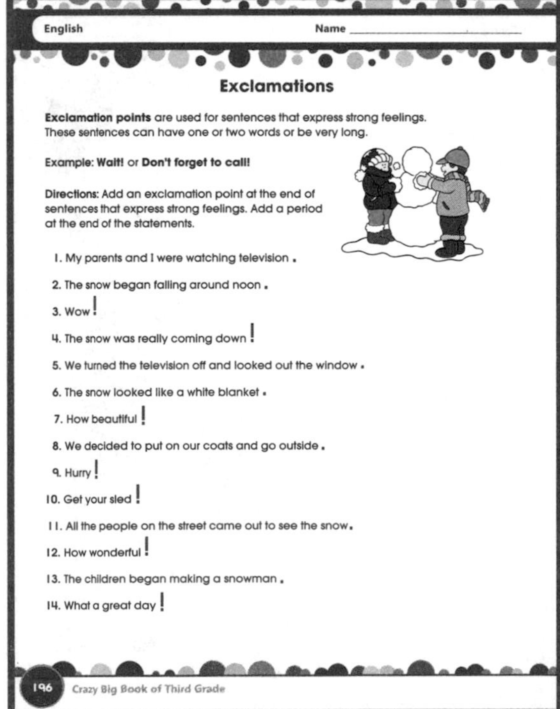
English Name ____________

Exclamations

Exclamation points are used for sentences that express strong feelings. These sentences can have one or two words or be very long.

Example: Wait! or **Don't forget to call!**

Directions: Add an exclamation point at the end of sentences that express strong feelings. Add a period at the end of the statements.

1. My parents and I were watching television .
2. The snow began falling around noon .
3. Wow !
4. The snow was really coming down !
5. We turned the television off and looked out the window .
6. The snow looked like a white blanket .
7. How beautiful !
8. We decided to put on our coats and go outside .
9. Hurry !
10. Get your sled !
11. All the people on the street came out to see the snow.
12. How wonderful !
13. The children began making a snowman .
14. What a great day !

196 Crazy Big Book of Third Grade

page 196

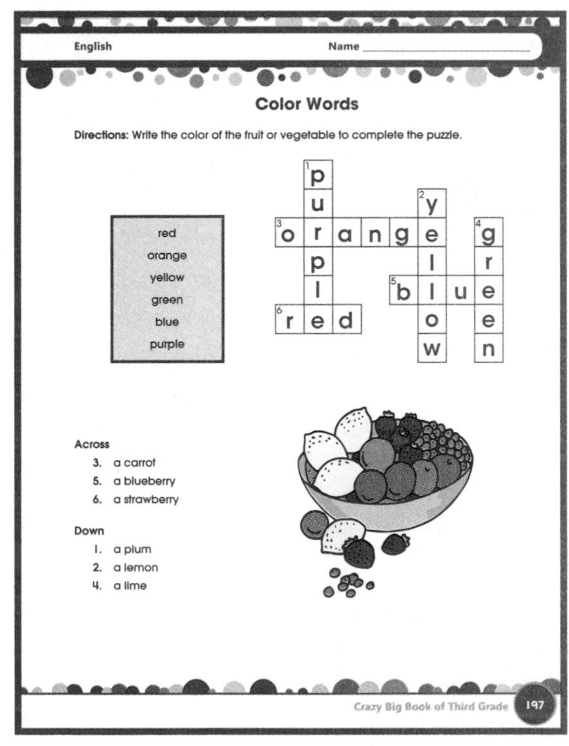
English Name ____________

Color Words

Directions: Write the color of the fruit or vegetable to complete the puzzle.

red
orange
yellow
green
blue
purple

	[1]p						
	u				[2]y		
[3]o	r	a	n	g	e		[4]g
	p				l		r
	l			[5]b	l	u	e
[6]r	e	d			o		e
					w		n

Across
3. a carrot
5. a blueberry
6. a strawberry

Down
1. a plum
2. a lemon
4. a lime

Crazy Big Book of Third Grade 197

page 197

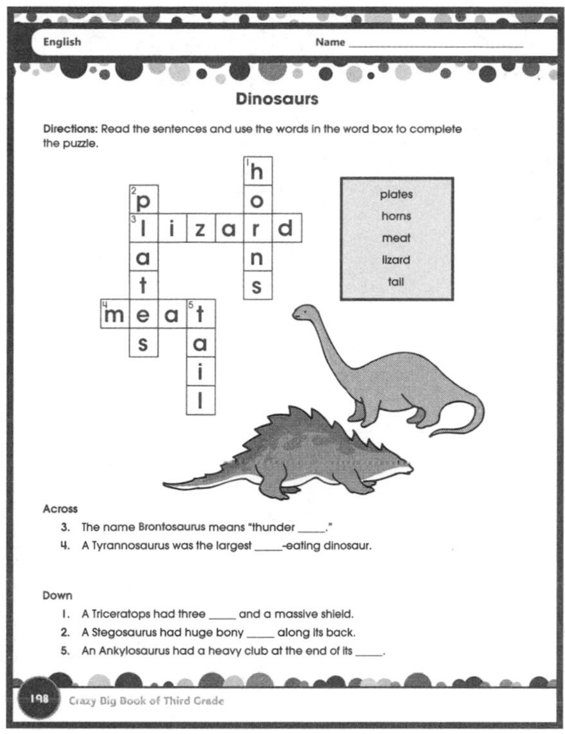

English Name ____________

Dinosaurs

Directions: Read the sentences and use the words in the word box to complete the puzzle.

Across

3. The name Brontosaurus means "thunder ____."
4. A Tyrannosaurus was the largest ____-eating dinosaur.

Down

1. A Triceratops had three ____ and a massive shield.
2. A Stegosaurus had huge bony ____ along its back.
5. An Ankylosaurus had a heavy club at the end of its ____.

198 Crazy Big Book of Third Grade

page 198

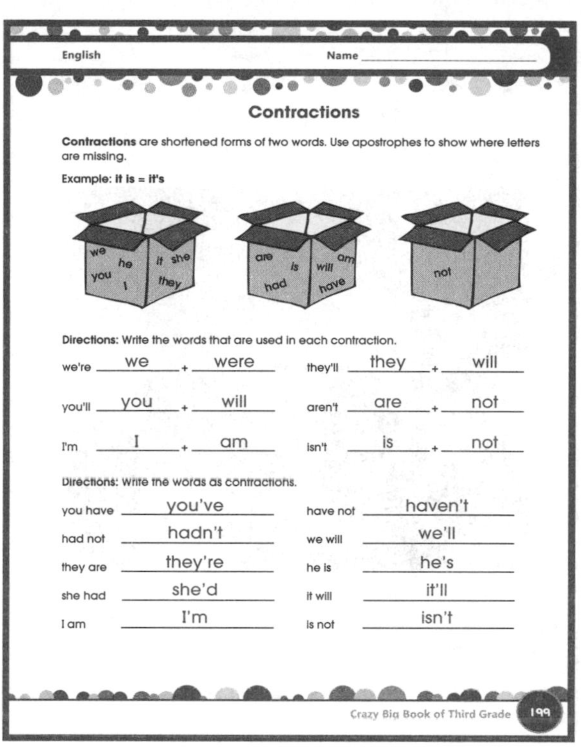

English Name ____________

Contractions

Contractions are shortened forms of two words. Use apostrophes to show where letters are missing.

Example: it is = it's

Directions: Write the words that are used in each contraction.

we're	we + were		they'll	they + will	
you'll	you + will		aren't	are + not	
I'm	I + am		isn't	is + not	

Directions: Write the words as contractions.

you have	you've	have not	haven't
had not	hadn't	we will	we'll
they are	they're	he is	he's
she had	she'd	it will	it'll
I am	I'm	is not	isn't

Crazy Big Book of Third Grade 199

page 199

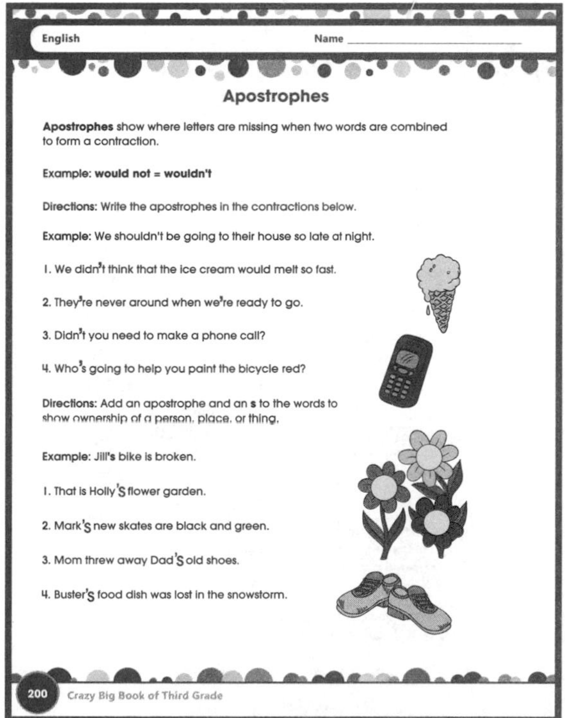

English Name ____________

Apostrophes

Apostrophes show where letters are missing when two words are combined to form a contraction.

Example: would not = wouldn't

Directions: Write the apostrophes in the contractions below.

Example: We shouldn't be going to their house so late at night.

1. We didn't think that the ice cream would melt so fast.
2. They're never around when we're ready to go.
3. Didn't you need to make a phone call?
4. Who's going to help you paint the bicycle red?

Directions: Add an apostrophe and an **s** to the words to show ownership of a person, place, or thing.

Example: Jill's bike is broken.

1. That is Holly's flower garden.
2. Mark's new skates are black and green.
3. Mom threw away Dad's old shoes.
4. Buster's food dish was lost in the snowstorm.

200 Crazy Big Book of Third Grade

page 200

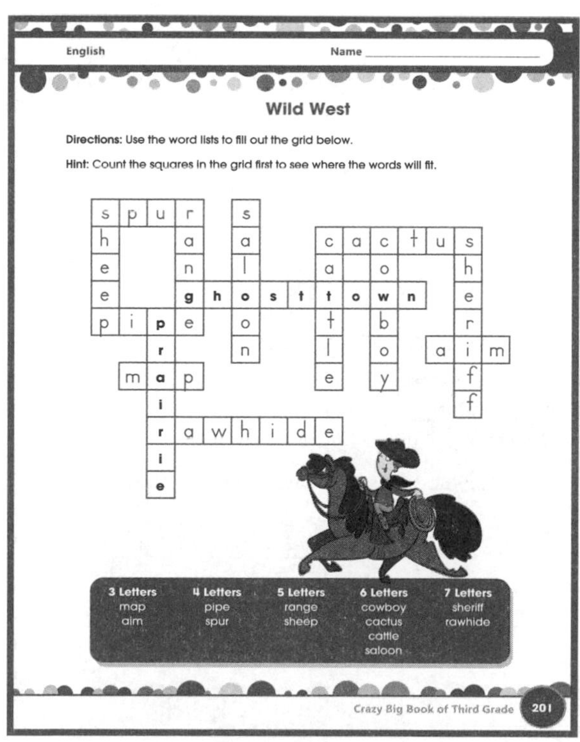

English Name ____________

Wild West

Directions: Use the word lists to fill out the grid below.

Hint: Count the squares in the grid first to see where the words will fit.

3 Letters	4 Letters	5 Letters	6 Letters	7 Letters
map	pipe	range	cowboy	sheriff
aim	spur	sheep	cactus	rawhide
			cattle	
			saloon	

Crazy Big Book of Third Grade 201

page 201

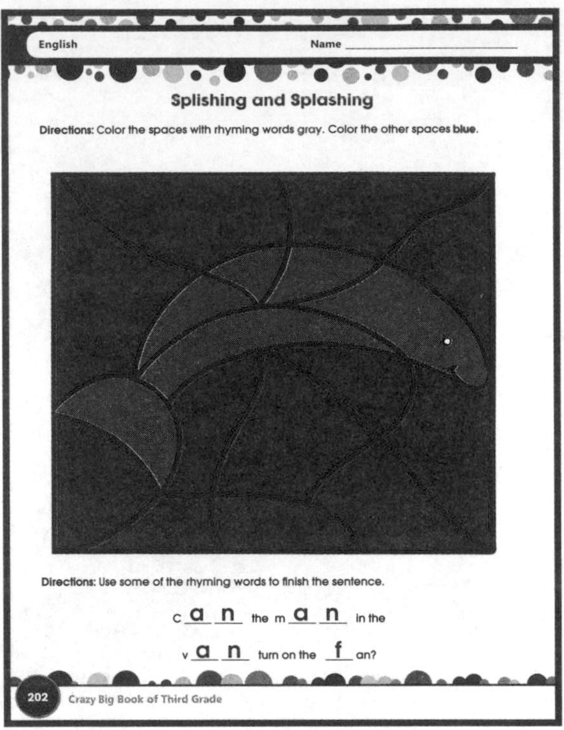

English Name ______

Splishing and Splashing

Directions: Color the spaces with rhyming words gray. Color the other spaces blue.

Directions: Use some of the rhyming words to finish the sentence.

c a n the m a n in the

v a n turn on the f an?

202 Crazy Big Book of Third Grade

page 202

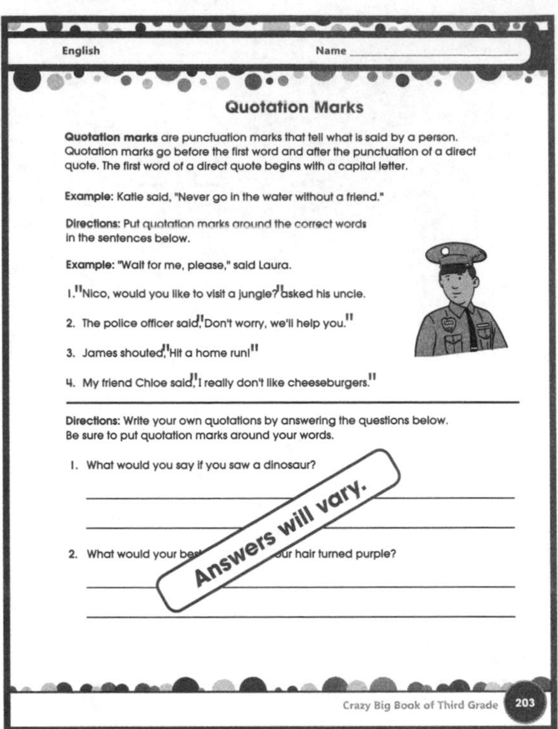

English Name ______

Quotation Marks

Quotation marks are punctuation marks that tell what is said by a person. Quotation marks go before the first word and after the punctuation of a direct quote. The first word of a direct quote begins with a capital letter.

Example: Katie said, "Never go in the water without a friend."

Directions: Put quotation marks around the correct words in the sentences below.

Example: "Wait for me, please," said Laura.

1. "Nico, would you like to visit a jungle?" asked his uncle.
2. The police officer said, "Don't worry, we'll help you."
3. James shouted, "Hit a home run!"
4. My friend Chloe said, "I really don't like cheeseburgers."

Directions: Write your own quotations by answering the questions below. Be sure to put quotation marks around your words.

1. What would you say if you saw a dinosaur?
2. What would your be[...]our hair turned purple?

Answers will vary.

Crazy Big Book of Third Grade 203

page 203

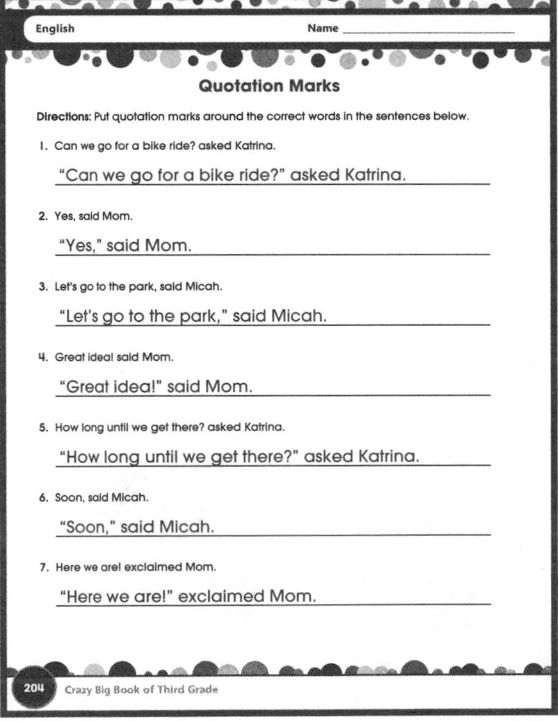

English Name ______

Quotation Marks

Directions: Put quotation marks around the correct words in the sentences below.

1. Can we go for a bike ride? asked Katrina.
   "Can we go for a bike ride?" asked Katrina.
2. Yes, said Mom.
   "Yes," said Mom.
3. Let's go to the park, said Micah.
   "Let's go to the park," said Micah.
4. Great idea! said Mom.
   "Great idea!" said Mom.
5. How long until we get there? asked Katrina.
   "How long until we get there?" asked Katrina.
6. Soon, said Micah.
   "Soon," said Micah.
7. Here we are! exclaimed Mom.
   "Here we are!" exclaimed Mom.

204 Crazy Big Book of Third Grade

page 204

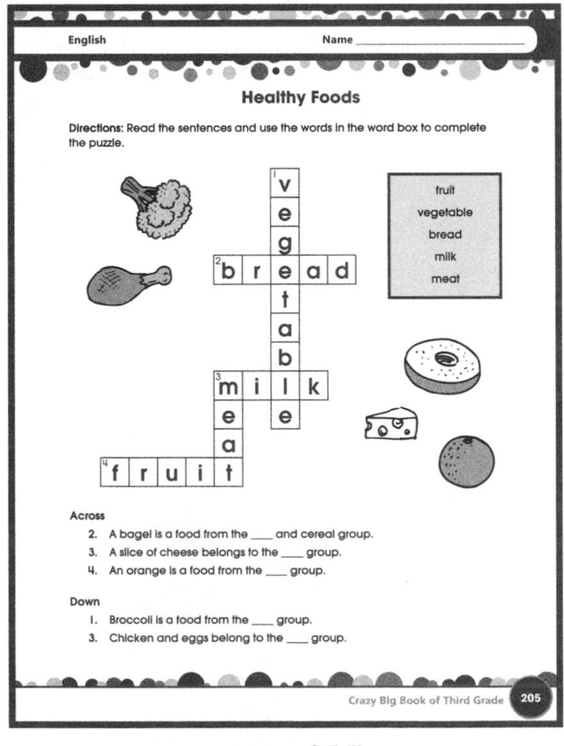

English Name ______

Healthy Foods

Directions: Read the sentences and use the words in the word box to complete the puzzle.

Word box: fruit, vegetable, bread, milk, meat

1 Down: vegetable
2 Across: bread
3 Across: milk
3 Down: meat
4 Across: fruit

Across
2. A bagel is a food from the ____ and cereal group.
3. A slice of cheese belongs to the ____ group.
4. An orange is a food from the ____ group.

Down
1. Broccoli is a food from the ____ group.
3. Chicken and eggs belong to the ____ group.

Crazy Big Book of Third Grade 205

page 205

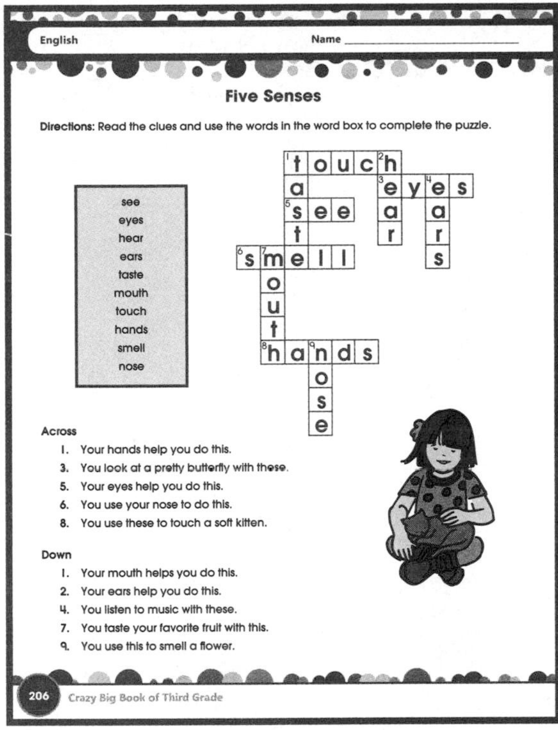

English Name ____________

Five Senses

Directions: Read the clues and use the words in the word box to complete the puzzle.

see
eyes
hear
ears
taste
mouth
touch
hands
smell
nose

Across
1. Your hands help you do this.
3. You look at a pretty butterfly with these.
5. Your eyes help you do this.
6. You use your nose to do this.
8. You use these to touch a soft kitten.

Down
1. Your mouth helps you do this.
2. Your ears help you do this.
4. You listen to music with these.
7. You taste your favorite fruit with this.
9. You use this to smell a flower.

206 Crazy Big Book of Third Grade

page 206

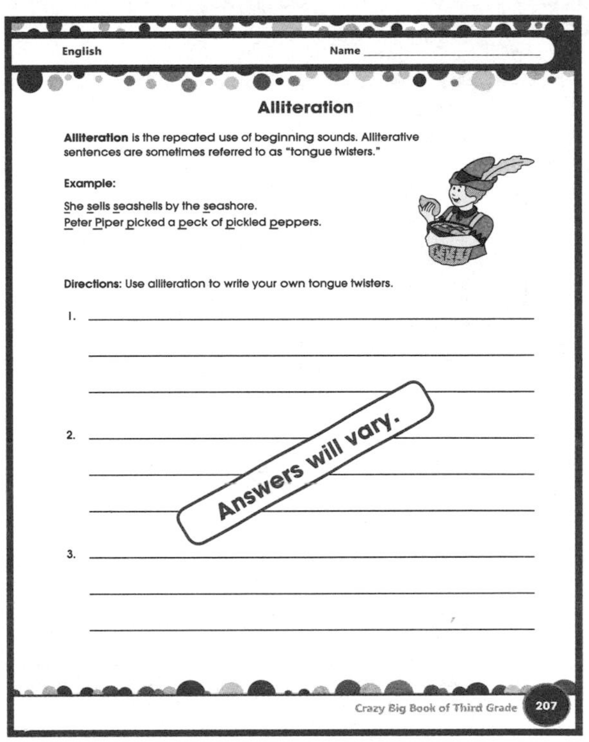

English Name ____________

Alliteration

Alliteration is the repeated use of beginning sounds. Alliterative sentences are sometimes referred to as "tongue twisters."

Example:

She sells seashells by the seashore.
Peter Piper picked a peck of pickled peppers.

Directions: Use alliteration to write your own tongue twisters.

1. ____________
2. ____________
3. ____________

Answers will vary.

Crazy Big Book of Third Grade 207

page 207

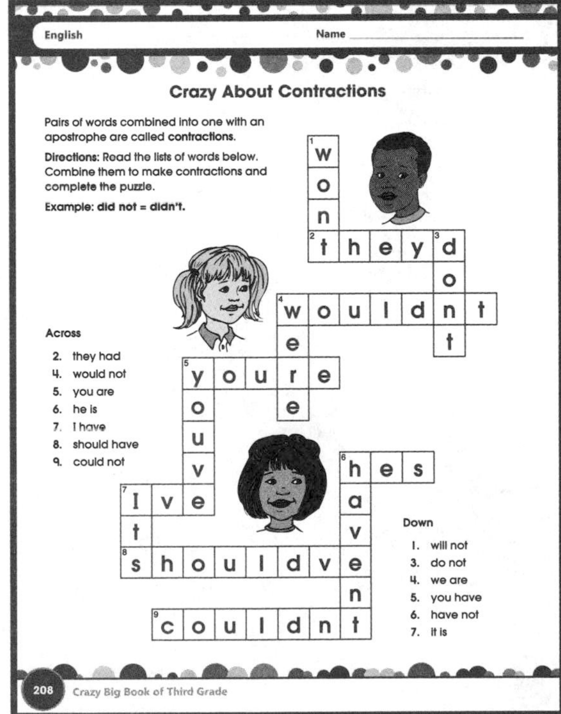

English Name ____________

Crazy About Contractions

Pairs of words combined into one with an apostrophe are called **contractions**.

Directions: Read the lists of words below. Combine them to make contractions and complete the puzzle.

Example: did not = didn't.

Across
2. they had
4. would not
5. you are
6. he is
7. I have
8. should have
9. could not

Down
1. will not
3. do not
4. we are
5. you have
6. have not
7. it is

208 Crazy Big Book of Third Grade

page 208

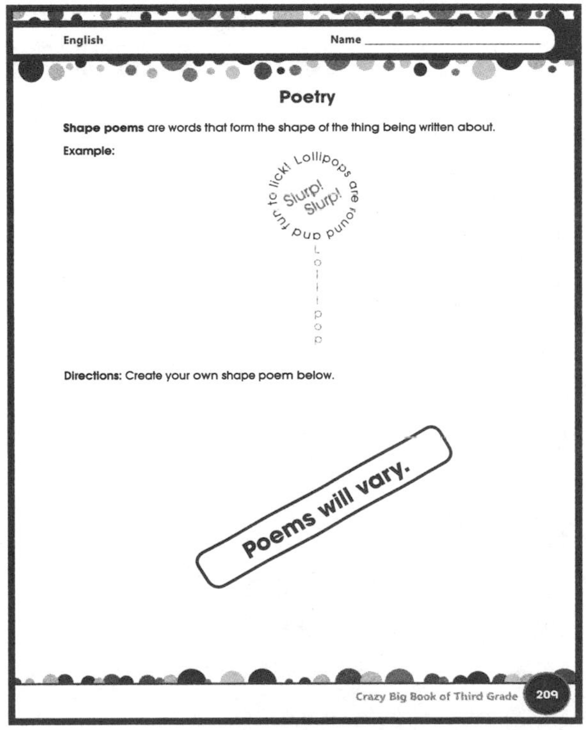

English Name ____________

Poetry

Shape poems are words that form the shape of the thing being written about.

Example:

Lollipops are round and fun to lick! Slurp! Slurp! Lollipop

Directions: Create your own shape poem below.

Poems will vary.

Crazy Big Book of Third Grade 209

page 209

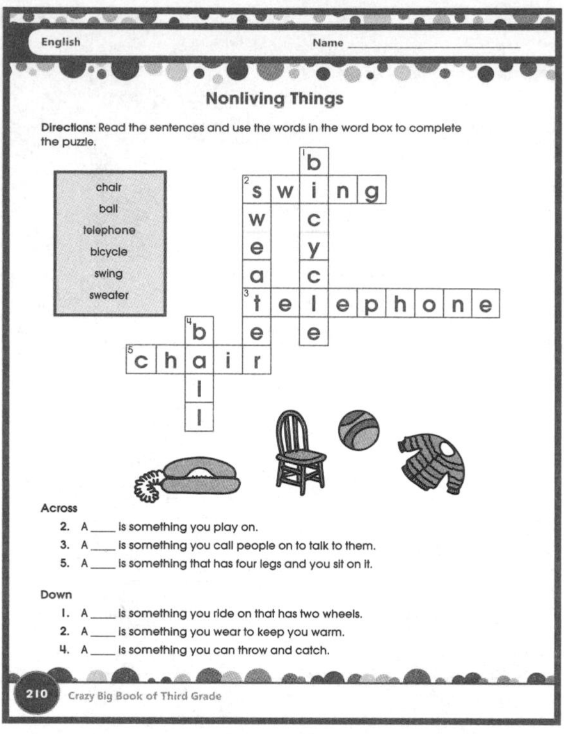
English Name ______________

Nonliving Things

Directions: Read the sentences and use the words in the word box to complete the puzzle.

chair
ball
telephone
bicycle
swing
sweater

Across

2. A ____ is something you play on.
3. A ____ is something you call people on to talk to them.
5. A ____ is something that has four legs and you sit on it.

Down

1. A ____ is something you ride on that has two wheels.
2. A ____ is something you wear to keep you warm.
4. A ____ is something you can throw and catch.

210 Crazy Big Book of Third Grade

page 210

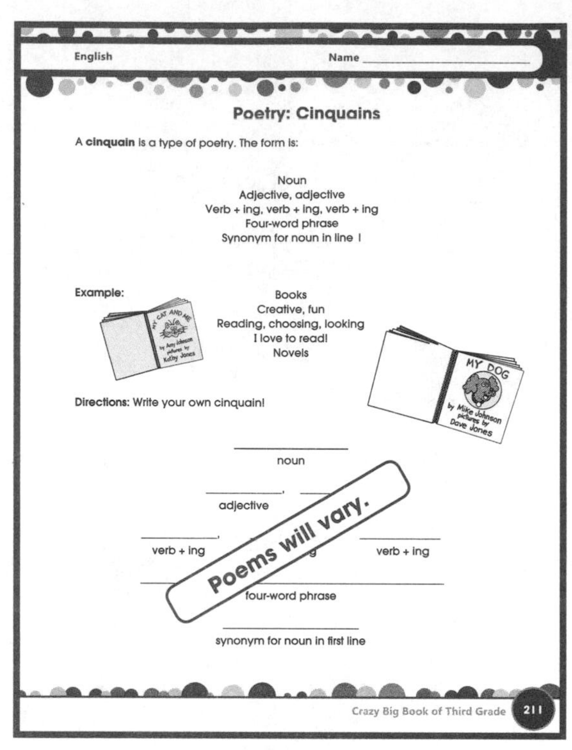
English Name ______________

Poetry: Cinquains

A **cinquain** is a type of poetry. The form is:

Noun
Adjective, adjective
Verb + ing, verb + ing, verb + ing
Four-word phrase
Synonym for noun in line 1

Example:

Books
Creative, fun
Reading, choosing, looking
I love to read!
Novels

Directions: Write your own cinquain!

______ noun

______, ______ adjective

______, ______, ______ verb + ing

______ four-word phrase

______ synonym for noun in first line

Crazy Big Book of Third Grade 211

page 211

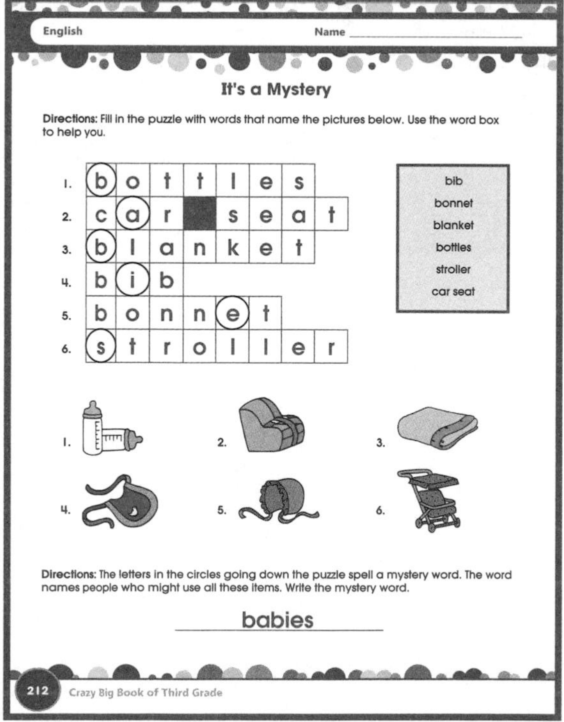
English Name ______________

It's a Mystery

Directions: Fill in the puzzle with words that name the pictures below. Use the word box to help you.

1. (b)ottles
2. c(a)r seat
3. (b)lanket
4. b(i)b
5. bonn(e)t
6. (s)troller

bib
bonnet
blanket
bottles
stroller
car seat

1. 2. 3. 4. 5. 6.

Directions: The letters in the circles going down the puzzle spell a mystery word. The word names people who might use all these items. Write the mystery word.

babies

212 Crazy Big Book of Third Grade

page 212

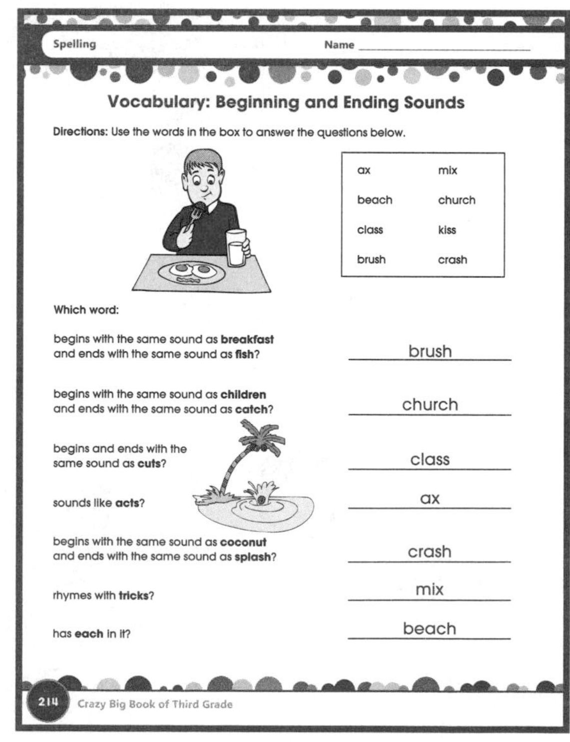
Spelling Name ______________

Vocabulary: Beginning and Ending Sounds

Directions: Use the words in the box to answer the questions below.

ax	mix
beach	church
class	kiss
brush	crash

Which word:

begins with the same sound as **breakfast** and ends with the same sound as **fish**? brush

begins with the same sound as **children** and ends with the same sound as **catch**? church

begins and ends with the same sound as **cuts**? class

sounds like **acts**? ax

begins with the same sound as **coconut** and ends with the same sound as **splash**? crash

rhymes with **tricks**? mix

has **each** in it? beach

214 Crazy Big Book of Third Grade

page 214

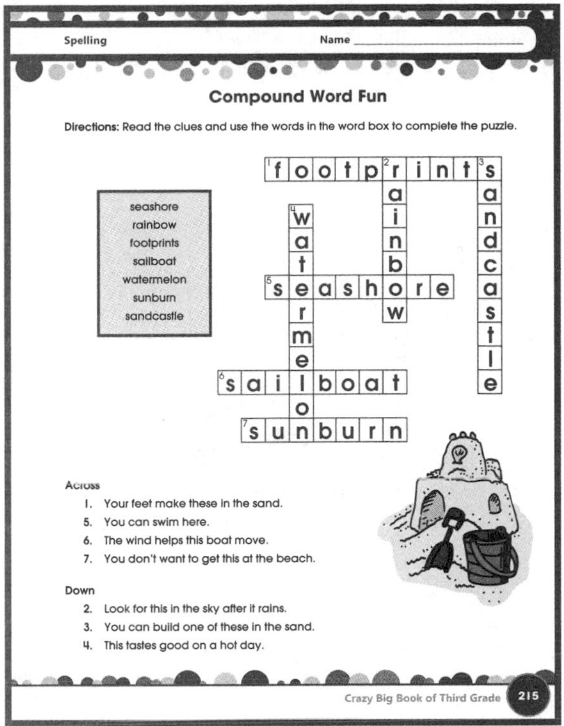

Spelling Name ____________

Compound Word Fun

Directions: Read the clues and use the words in the word box to complete the puzzle.

seashore
rainbow
footprints
sailboat
watermelon
sunburn
sandcastle

Puzzle answers: 1 Across: footprints; 2 Down: rainbow; 3 Down: sandcastle; 4 Down: watermelon; 5 Across: seashore; 6 Across: sailboat; 7 Across: sunburn

Across

1. Your feet make these in the sand.
5. You can swim here.
6. The wind helps this boat move.
7. You don't want to get this at the beach.

Down

2. Look for this in the sky after it rains.
3. You can build one of these in the sand.
4. This tastes good on a hot day.

Crazy Big Book of Third Grade 215

page 215

Spelling Name ____________

Vocabulary: Sentences

Directions: Use a word from the box to complete each sentence. Use each word only once.

ax	mix	beach	church	class	kiss	brush	crash

1. Those two cars are going to crash.
2. He chopped the wood with an ax.
3. Grandma gave me a kiss on my cheek.
4. Before you go, brush your hair.
5. How many students are in your class at school?
6. The waves bring sand to the beach.
7. To make orange, you mix yellow and red.
8. On Sunday, we always go to church.

216 Crazy Big Book of Third Grade

page 216

Spelling Name ____________

Vocabulary: Plurals

A word that names one thing is **singular**, like **house**. A word that names more than one thing is **plural**, like **houses**.

To make a word plural, add **s**.

Examples: one book — two books one tree — four trees

To make plural words that end in **s**, **ss**, **x**, **sh**, and **ch**, add **es**.

Examples: one fox — two foxes one bush — three bushes

Directions: Write the word that is missing from each pair below. Add **s** or **es** to make the plural words. The first one is done for you.

Singular	Plural
table	tables
beach	beaches
class	classes
ax	axes
brush	brushes
crash	crashes

Crazy Big Book of Third Grade 217

page 217

Spelling Name ____________

Vocabulary: Nouns and Verbs

A **noun** names a person, place, or thing. A **verb** tells what something does or what something is. Some words can be a noun one time and a verb another time.

Directions: Complete each pair of sentences with a word from the box. The word will be a noun in the first sentence and a verb in the second sentence.

mix	kiss	brush	crash

1. Did your dog ever give you a kiss (noun)?

   I have a cold, so I can't kiss (verb) you today.

2. I brought my comb and my brush (noun).

   I will brush (verb) the leaves off your coat.

3. Was anyone hurt in the crash (noun)?

   If you aren't careful, you will crash (verb) into me.

4. We bought trail mix (noun) at the store.

   I will mix (verb) the eggs together.

218 Crazy Big Book of Third Grade

page 218

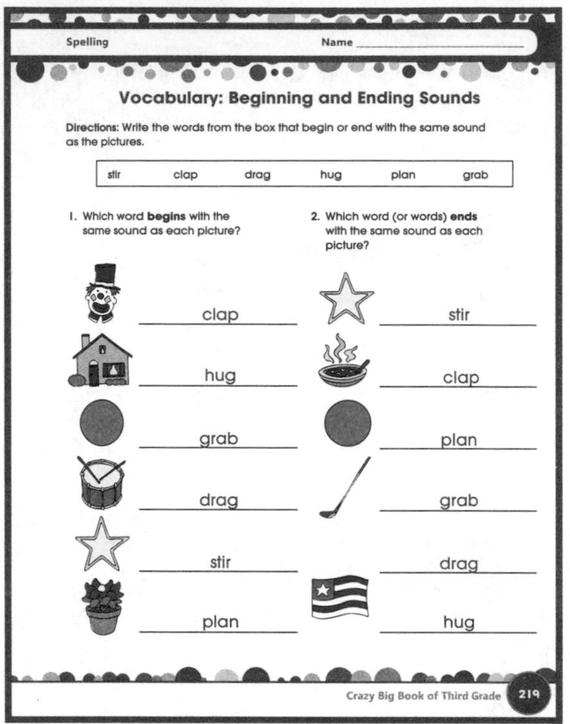

Spelling Name ____________

Vocabulary: Beginning and Ending Sounds

Directions: Write the words from the box that begin or end with the same sound as the pictures.

stir clap drag hug plan grab

1. Which word **begins** with the same sound as each picture?
2. Which word (or words) **ends** with the same sound as each picture?

1.	2.
clap	stir
hug	clap
grab	plan
drag	grab
stir	drag
plan	hug

Crazy Big Book of Third Grade 219

page 219

Spelling Name ____________

Firefighters

Directions: Read the sentences and use the words in the word box to complete the puzzle.

engine
slide
house
fight
clean
coats

1 clean 2 house 3 coats 4 fight 5 slide 6 engine

Across

3. They put on their ____, boots, and helmets.
5. As the fire alarm goes off, the firefighters ____ down the nearest fire pole.
6. They jump onto the fire ____.

Down

1. They check, ____, and put away all of their equipment.
2. After the fire is put out, the firefighters go back to the fire ____.
4. They turn on their siren and speed away to ____ the fire.

220 Crazy Big Book of Third Grade

page 220

Spelling Name ____________

Vocabulary: Verbs

Directions: Write the verb that answers each question. Write a sentence using that verb.

stir clap drag hug plan grab

Which verb means "to put your arms around someone"?

hug

Answers will vary.

Which verb means "to mix something with a spoon"?

stir

Answers will vary.

Which verb means "to pull something along the ground"?

drag

Answers will vary.

Which verb means "to take something suddenly"?

grab

Answers will vary.

Crazy Big Book of Third Grade 221

page 221

Spelling Name ____________

Vocabulary: Past-Tense Verbs

The past tense of a verb tells that something already happened. To tell about something that already happened, add **ed** to most verbs. If the verb already ends in **e**, just add **d**.

Examples:

We enter**ed** the contest last week.
I fold**ed** the paper wrong.
He add**ed** two boxes to the pile.
We taste**d** the fruit salad.
They decide**d** quickly.
She share**d** her sandwich.

Directions: Use the verb from the first sentence to complete the second sentence. Add **d** or **ed** to show that something already happened.

Example:

My mom looks fine today. Yesterday, she looked tired.

1. You enter through the middle door.
   We entered that way last week.
2. Please add this for me. I already added it twice.
3. Will you share your banana with me?
   I shared my apple with you yesterday.
4. It's your turn to fold the clothes. I folded them yesterday.
5. May I taste another one? I already tasted one.
6. You need to decide. We decided this morning.

222 Crazy Big Book of Third Grade

page 222

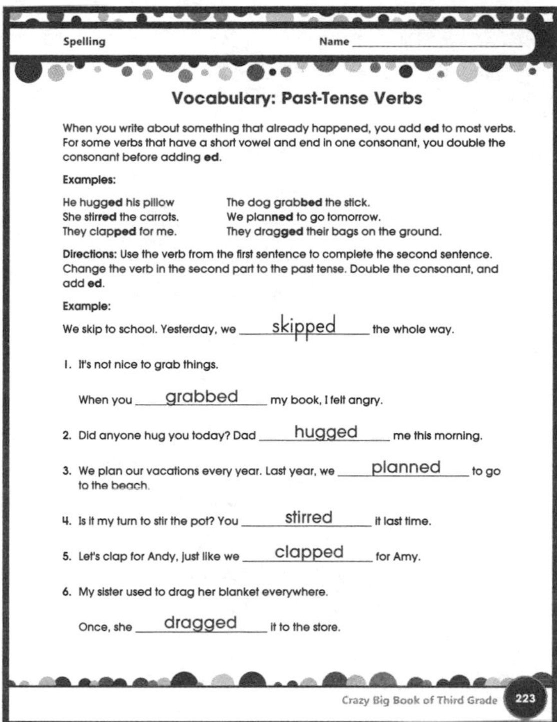
Spelling Name

Vocabulary: Past-Tense Verbs

When you write about something that already happened, you add **ed** to most verbs. For some verbs that have a short vowel and end in one consonant, you double the consonant before adding **ed**.

Examples:

He hug**ged** his pillow — The dog grab**bed** the stick.
She stir**red** the carrots. — We plan**ned** to go tomorrow.
They clap**ped** for me. — They drag**ged** their bags on the ground.

Directions: Use the verb from the first sentence to complete the second sentence. Change the verb in the second part to the past tense. Double the consonant, and add **ed**.

Example:

We skip to school. Yesterday, we skipped the whole way.

1. It's not nice to grab things. When you grabbed my book, I felt angry.
2. Did anyone hug you today? Dad hugged me this morning.
3. We plan our vacations every year. Last year, we planned to go to the beach.
4. Is it my turn to stir the pot? You stirred it last time.
5. Let's clap for Andy, just like we clapped for Amy.
6. My sister used to drag her blanket everywhere. Once, she dragged it to the store.

Crazy Big Book of Third Grade 223

page 223

Spelling Name

Vocabulary: Present-Tense Verbs

When something is happening right now, it is in the **present tense**. There are two ways to write verbs in the present tense.

Examples: The dog **walks**. The dog **is walking**. The cats **play**. The cats **are playing**.

Directions: Write each sentence again, writing the verb a different way.

Example:

He lists the numbers.

He is listing the numbers.

1. She is pounding the nail.
   She pounds the nail.
2. My brother toasts the bread.
   My brother is toasting the bread.
3. They search for the robber.
   They are searching for the robber.
4. The teacher lists the pages.
   The teacher is listing the pages.
5. They are spilling the water.
   They spill the water.
6. Nikhil and Amy load the packages.
   Nikhil and Amy are loading the packages.

224 Crazy Big Book of Third Grade

page 224

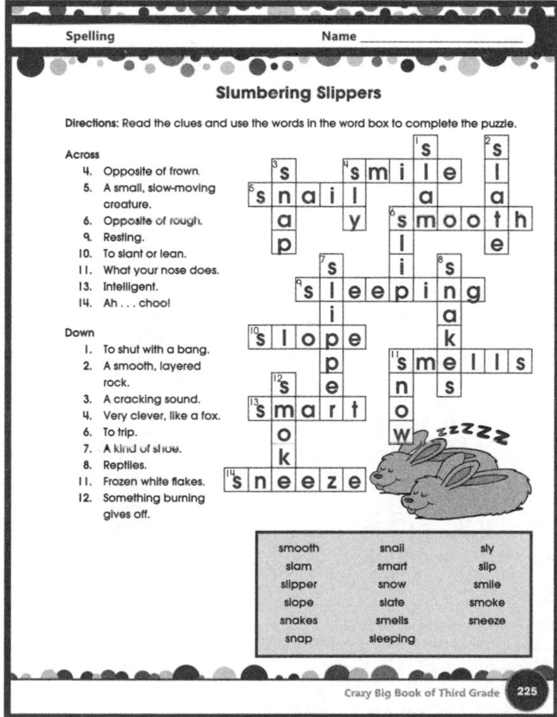
Spelling Name

Slumbering Slippers

Directions: Read the clues and use the words in the word box to complete the puzzle.

Across
4. Opposite of frown.
5. A small, slow-moving creature.
6. Opposite of rough.
9. Resting.
10. To slant or lean.
11. What your nose does.
13. Intelligent.
14. Ah . . . choo!

Down
1. To shut with a bang.
2. A smooth, layered rock.
3. A cracking sound.
4. Very clever, like a fox.
6. To trip.
7. A kind of shoe.
8. Reptiles.
11. Frozen white flakes.
12. Something burning gives off.

Across answers: 4. smile, 5. snail, 6. smooth, 9. sleeping, 10. slope, 11. smells, 13. smart, 14. sneeze

Down answers: 1. slam, 2. slate, 3. snap, 4. sly, 6. slip, 7. slipper, 8. snakes, 11. snow, 12. smoke

smooth	snail	sly
slam	smart	slip
slipper	snow	smile
slope	slate	smoke
snakes	smells	sneeze
snap	sleeping	

Crazy Big Book of Third Grade 225

page 225

Spelling Name

Vocabulary: Statements

A **statement** is a sentence that tells something.

Directions: Use the words in the box to complete the statements below. Write the words on the lines.

glue	decide	add
share	enter	fold

1. It took ten minutes for Kayla to add the numbers.
2. Ben wants to share his snack with me.
3. "I can't decide which color to choose," said DeShawn.
4. Glue can be used to make things stick together.
5. "This is how you fold your paper in half," said Mrs. Green.
6. The opposite of **leave** is enter.

Write your own statement on the line.

Answers will vary.

226 Crazy Big Book of Third Grade

page 226

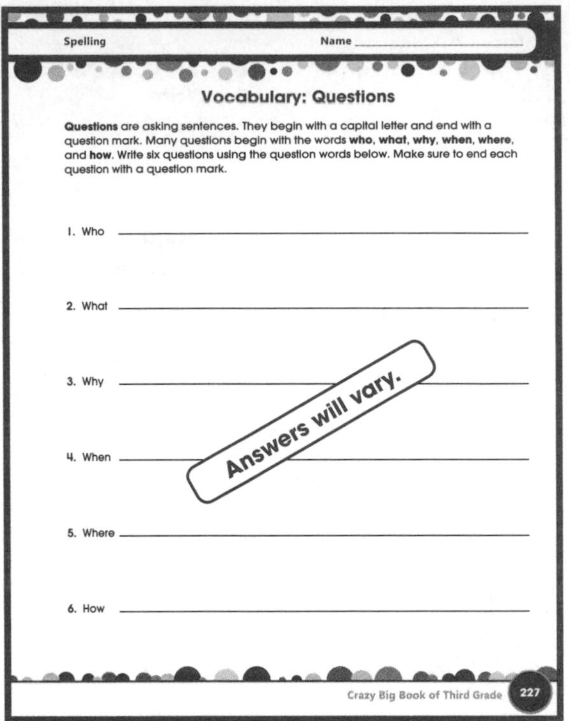
Spelling Name ____________

Vocabulary: Questions

Questions are asking sentences. They begin with a capital letter and end with a question mark. Many questions begin with the words **who**, **what**, **why**, **when**, **where**, and **how**. Write six questions using the question words below. Make sure to end each question with a question mark.

1. Who ____________
2. What ____________
3. Why ____________
4. When ____________
5. Where ____________
6. How ____________

Answers will vary.

Crazy Big Book of Third Grade 227

page 227

Spelling Name ____________

Vocabulary: Commands

A **command** is a sentence that tells someone to do something.

Directions: Use the words in the box to complete the commands below. Write the words on the lines.

glue	decide	add	share	enter	fold

1. Add a cup of flour to the batter.
2. Decide how much paper you will need to write your story.
3. Please glue the picture of the apple onto the paper.
4. Enter through this door and leave through the other door.
5. Please fold the letter and put it into an envelope.
6. Share your toys with your sister.

Write your own command on the lines.

Answers will vary.

228 Crazy Big Book of Third Grade

page 228

Spelling Name ____________

Vocabulary: Directions

A **direction** is a sentence written as a command.

Directions: Write the missing directions for these pictures. Begin each direction with one of the verbs below.

glue	enter	share	add	decide	fold

How To Make a Peanut Butter and Jelly Sandwich:

Answers may vary. Possible answers:

1. Spread peanut butter on bread.
2. Add some jam.
3. Cut the sandwich in half.
4. Share it with a friend.

How To Make a Valentine:

1. Fold a piece of red paper.
2. Draw half a heart.
3. Cut along the line you drew.
4. Glue it to the paper.

Crazy Big Book of Third Grade 229

page 229

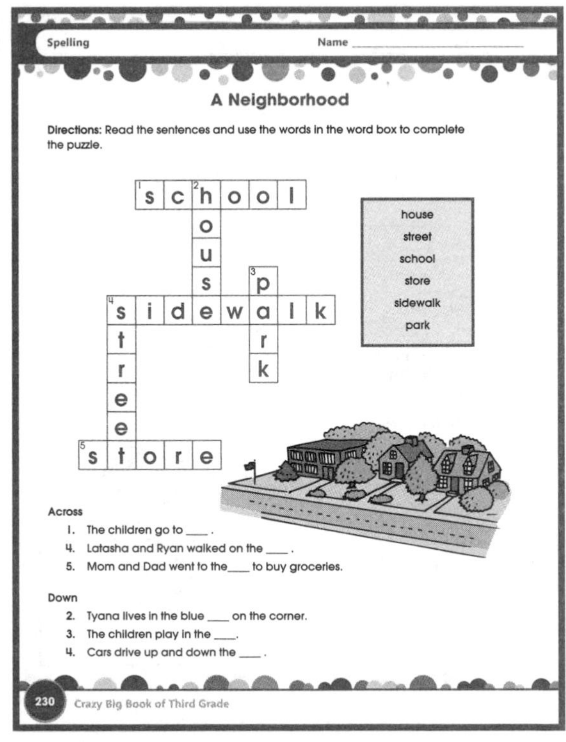
Spelling Name ____________

A Neighborhood

Directions: Read the sentences and use the words in the word box to complete the puzzle.

Crossword answers: 1 Across: school; 2 Down: house; 3 Down: park; 4 Across: sidewalk; 4 Down: street; 5 Across: store

house
street
school
store
sidewalk
park

Across

1. The children go to ____.
4. Latasha and Ryan walked on the ____.
5. Mom and Dad went to the ____ to buy groceries.

Down

2. Tyana lives in the blue ____ on the corner.
3. The children play in the ____.
4. Cars drive up and down the ____.

230 Crazy Big Book of Third Grade

page 230

Answer Key

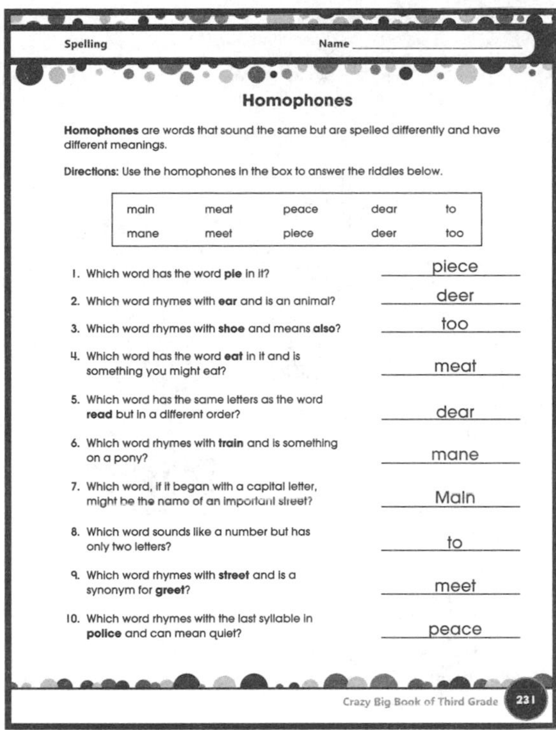
Spelling Name

Homophones

Homophones are words that sound the same but are spelled differently and have different meanings.

Directions: Use the homophones in the box to answer the riddles below.

main	meat	peace	dear	to
mane	meet	piece	deer	too

1. Which word has the word **pie** in it? piece
2. Which word rhymes with **ear** and is an animal? deer
3. Which word rhymes with **shoe** and means **also**? too
4. Which word has the word **eat** in it and is something you might eat? meat
5. Which word has the same letters as the word **read** but in a different order? dear
6. Which word rhymes with **train** and is something on a pony? mane
7. Which word, if it began with a capital letter, might be the name of an important street? Main
8. Which word sounds like a number but has only two letters? to
9. Which word rhymes with **street** and is a synonym for **greet**? meet
10. Which word rhymes with the last syllable in **police** and can mean quiet? peace

Crazy Big Book of Third Grade 231

page 231

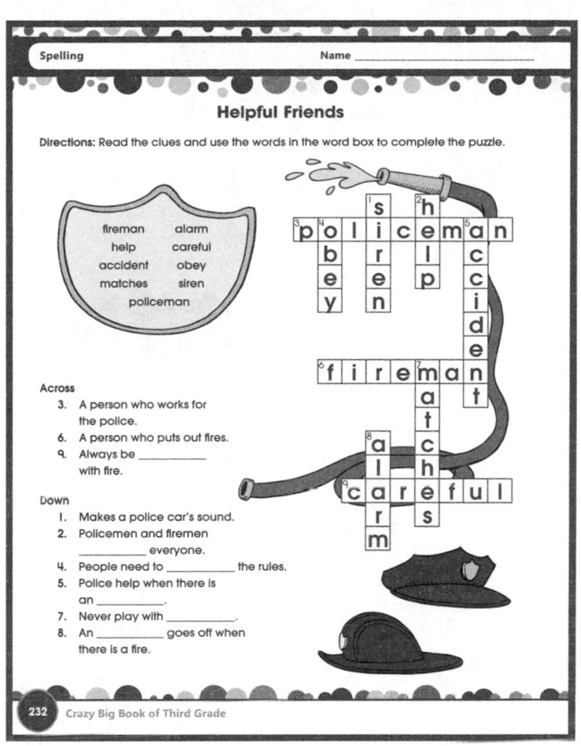
Spelling Name

Helpful Friends

Directions: Read the clues and use the words in the word box to complete the puzzle.

fireman, alarm, help, careful, accident, obey, matches, siren, policeman

Across
3. A person who works for the police.
6. A person who puts out fires.
9. Always be ________ with fire.

Down
1. Makes a police car's sound.
2. Policemen and firemen ________ everyone.
4. People need to ________ the rules.
5. Police help when there is an ________.
7. Never play with ________.
8. An ________ goes off when there is a fire.

232 Crazy Big Book of Third Grade

page 232

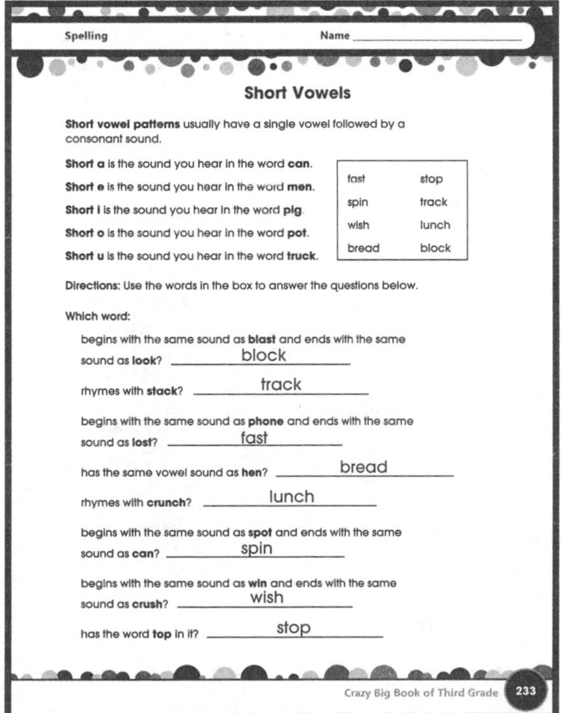
Spelling Name

Short Vowels

Short vowel patterns usually have a single vowel followed by a consonant sound.

Short a is the sound you hear in the word **can**.
Short e is the sound you hear in the word **men**.
Short i is the sound you hear in the word **pig**.
Short o is the sound you hear in the word **pot**.
Short u is the sound you hear in the word **truck**.

fast	stop
spin	track
wish	lunch
bread	block

Directions: Use the words in the box to answer the questions below.

Which word:

begins with the same sound as **blast** and ends with the same sound as **look**? block

rhymes with **stack**? track

begins with the same sound as **phone** and ends with the same sound as **lost**? fast

has the same vowel sound as **hen**? bread

rhymes with **crunch**? lunch

begins with the same sound as **spot** and ends with the same sound as **can**? spin

begins with the same sound as **win** and ends with the same sound as **crush**? wish

has the word **top** in it? stop

Crazy Big Book of Third Grade 233

page 233

Spelling Name

Long Vowels

Long vowels say the letter name sound.
Long a is the sound you hear in **cane**.
Long e is the sound you hear in **green**.
Long i is the sound you hear in **pie**.
Long o is the sound you hear in **bowl**.
Long u is the sound you hear in **cube**.

lame	goal
pain	few
street	fright
nose	gray
bike	fuse

Directions: Use the words in the box to answer the questions below.

1. Add one letter to each of these words to make words from the box.
   ray gray use fuse right fright
2. Change one letter from each word to make a word from the box.
   pail pain goat goal
   late lame bite bike
3. Write the word from the box that . . .
   has the long **e** sound. street
   rhymes with **you**. few
   is a homophone for **knows**. nose

234 Crazy Big Book of Third Grade

page 234

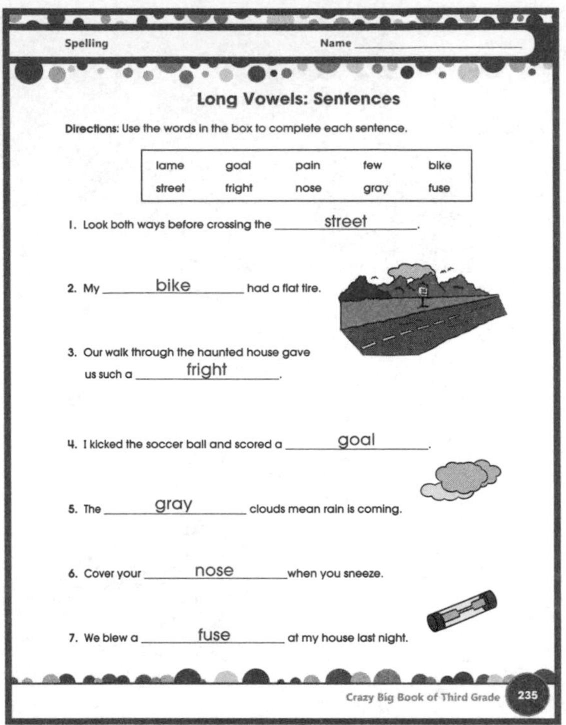

Spelling Name ____________

Long Vowels: Sentences

Directions: Use the words in the box to complete each sentence.

lame	goal	pain	few	bike
street	fright	nose	gray	fuse

1. Look both ways before crossing the street.
2. My bike had a flat tire.
3. Our walk through the haunted house gave us such a fright.
4. I kicked the soccer ball and scored a goal.
5. The gray clouds mean rain is coming.
6. Cover your nose when you sneeze.
7. We blew a fuse at my house last night.

Crazy Big Book of Third Grade 235

page 235

Spelling Name ____________

Around the City

Directions: Read the clues and use the words in the word box to complete the puzzle.

library
theater
park
museum
bank
drugstore
restaurant
school

1 drugstore
2 museum
3 library
4 school
5 theater
6 bank
7 restaurant
8 park

Across

3. You can borrow books here.
4. Teachers help children learn here.
7. You can get something to eat here.
8. This is where you can go to play or ride a bike.

Down

1. Your mother or father can get medicine here.
2. This building has things about science, antiques, or art.
5. This is where you can see a movie.
6. This is a place where people keep money.

LIBRARY

236 Crazy Big Book of Third Grade

page 236

Spelling Name ____________

Adjectives

Directions: Use the words in the box to answer the questions below. Use each word only once.

polite	careless	neat	shy	selfish	thoughtful

1. Someone who is quiet and needs some time to make new friends is shy.
2. A person who says "please" and "thank you" is polite.
3. Someone who always puts all the toys away is neat.
4. A person who won't share with others is being selfish.
5. A person who leaves a bike out all night is being careless.
6. Someone who thinks of others is thoughtful.

TOYS

Crazy Big Book of Third Grade 237

page 237

Spelling Name ____________

Spelling

Directions: Circle the word in each sentence that is not spelled correctly. Then, write the word correctly.

1. Zack isn't (shelfish) at all. — selfish
2. He (sharred) his lunch with me today. — shared
3. I was (careles) and forgot to bring mine. — careless
4. My father says if I (planed) better, that wouldn't happen all the time. — planned
5. Zack is kind of quiet, and I used to think he was (shie). — shy
6. Now, I know he is really (thotful). — thoughtful
7. He's also very (polyte) and always asks before he borrows anything. — polite
8. He would never just reach over and (grabb) something he wanted. — grab
9. I'm glad Zack (desided) to be my friend. — decided

238 Crazy Big Book of Third Grade

page 238

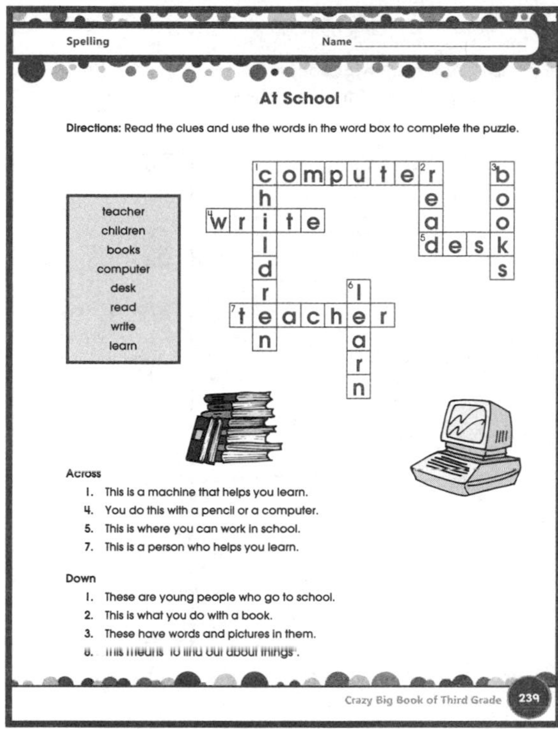

Spelling Name ____________

At School

Directions: Read the clues and use the words in the word box to complete the puzzle.

teacher
children
books
computer
desk
read
write
learn

Across
1. This is a machine that helps you learn.
4. You do this with a pencil or a computer.
5. This is where you can work in school.
7. This is a person who helps you learn.

Down
1. These are young people who go to school.
2. This is what you do with a book.
3. These have words and pictures in them.
6. This means to find out about things.

Crazy Big Book of Third Grade 239

page 239

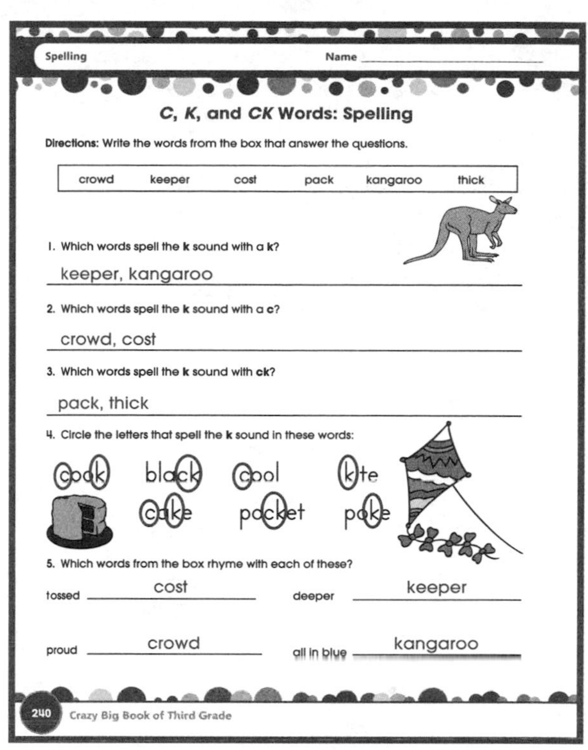

Spelling Name ____________

C, K, and CK Words: Spelling

Directions: Write the words from the box that answer the questions.

crowd keeper cost pack kangaroo thick

1. Which words spell the **k** sound with a **k**?
keeper, kangaroo
2. Which words spell the **k** sound with a **c**?
crowd, cost
3. Which words spell the **k** sound with **ck**?
pack, thick
4. Circle the letters that spell the **k** sound in these words:
cook black cool kite cake pocket poke
5. Which words from the box rhyme with each of these?
tossed cost deeper keeper
proud crowd all in blue kangaroo

240 Crazy Big Book of Third Grade

page 240

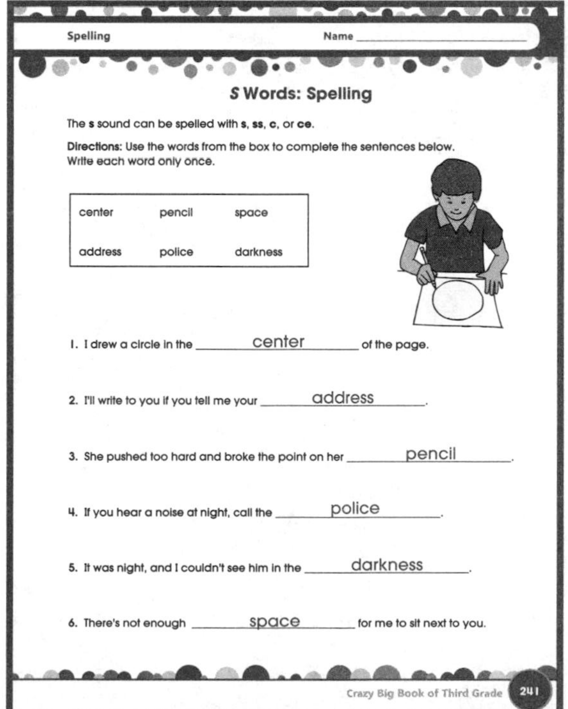

Spelling Name ____________

S Words: Spelling

The **s** sound can be spelled with **s**, **ss**, **c**, or **ce**.

Directions: Use the words from the box to complete the sentences below. Write each word only once.

center	pencil	space
address	police	darkness

1. I drew a circle in the center of the page.
2. I'll write to you if you tell me your address.
3. She pushed too hard and broke the point on her pencil.
4. If you hear a noise at night, call the police.
5. It was night, and I couldn't see him in the darkness.
6. There's not enough space for me to sit next to you.

Crazy Big Book of Third Grade 241

page 241

Spelling Name ____________

S Words: Spelling

Directions: Write the words from the box that answer the questions.

center pencil space address police darkness

1. Which words spell the **s** sound with **ss**?
address, darkness
2. Which words spell the **s** sound with a **c**?
center, pencil
3. Which words spell the **s** sound with **ce**?
space, police
4. Write two other words you know that spell the **s** sound with an **s**.
Answers will vary.
5. Circle the letters that spell the **s** sound in these words.
decide kiss careless ice cost fierce sentence
6. Put these letters in order to make words from the box.
sdsdera address sdserakn darkness
clipoe police clipne pencil
capse space retnce center

242 Crazy Big Book of Third Grade

page 242

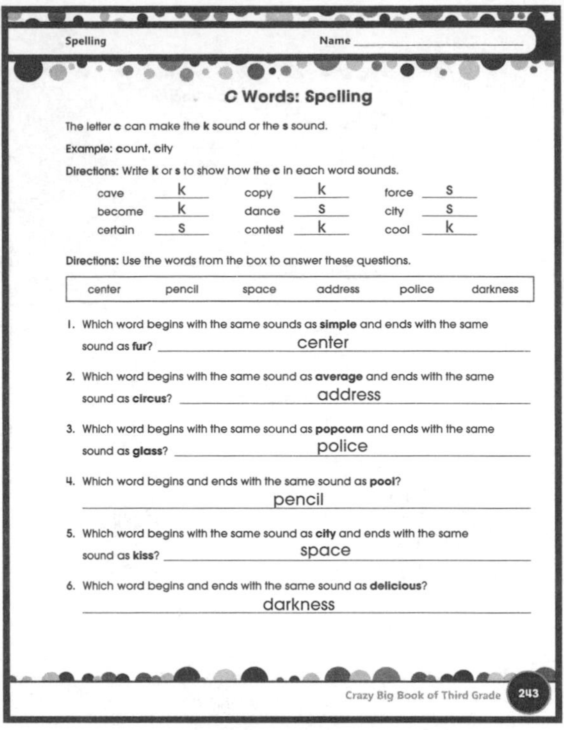

Spelling Name ______

C Words: Spelling

The letter **c** can make the **k** sound or the **s** sound.

Example: **c**ount, **c**ity

Directions: Write **k** or **s** to show how the **c** in each word sounds.

cave	k	copy	k	force	s
become	k	dance	s	city	s
certain	s	contest	k	cool	k

Directions: Use the words from the box to answer these questions.

center	pencil	space	address	police	darkness

1. Which word begins with the same sounds as **simple** and ends with the same sound as **fur**? center
2. Which word begins with the same sound as **average** and ends with the same sound as **circus**? address
3. Which word begins with the same sound as **popcorn** and ends with the same sound as **glass**? police
4. Which word begins and ends with the same sound as **pool**? pencil
5. Which word begins with the same sound as **city** and ends with the same sound as **kiss**? space
6. Which word begins and ends with the same sound as **delicious**? darkness

Crazy Big Book of Third Grade 243

page 243

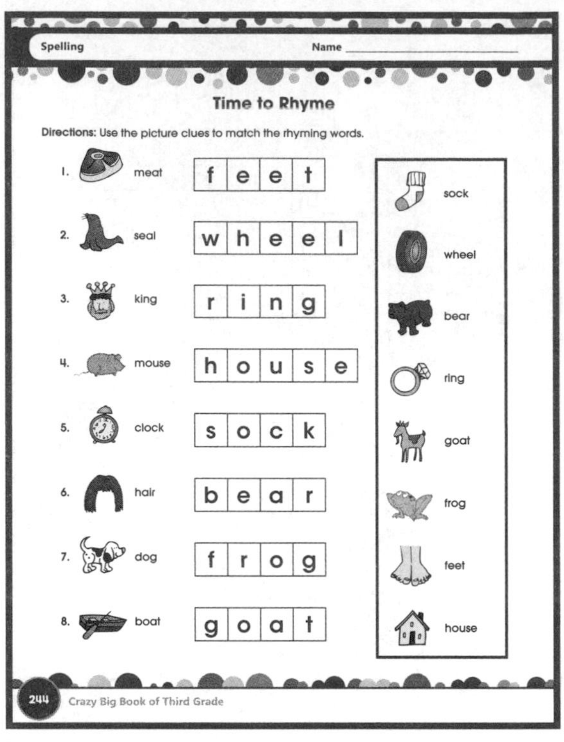

Spelling Name ______

Time to Rhyme

Directions: Use the picture clues to match the rhyming words.

1. meat — f e e t
2. seal — w h e e l
3. king — r i n g
4. mouse — h o u s e
5. clock — s o c k
6. hair — b e a r
7. dog — f r o g
8. boat — g o a t

244 Crazy Big Book of Third Grade

page 244

Spelling Name ______

Suffixes

A **suffix** is a word part added to the end of a word. Suffixes add to or change the meaning of the word.

Example: **sad** + **ly** = **sadly**

Below are some suffixes and their meanings.

ment	state of being, quality of, act of
ly	like or in a certain way
ness	state of being
ful	full of
less	without

Directions: The words in the box have suffixes. Use the suffix meanings above to match each word with its meaning below. Write the words on the lines.

friendly	cheerful	safely	sleeveless	speechless
kindness	amazement	sickness	peaceful	excitement

1. in a safe way — s a f e l y (6)
2. full of cheer — c h e e r f u l (2)
3. full of peace — p e a c e f u l (4)
4. state of being amazed — a m a z e m e n t (5)
5. state of being excited — e x c i t e m e n t (1)
6. without speech — s p e e c h l e s s (3)

Use the numbered letters to find the missing word below.

You are now on your way to becoming a m a s t e r (5 6 3 1 4 2) of suffixes!

Crazy Big Book of Third Grade 245

page 245

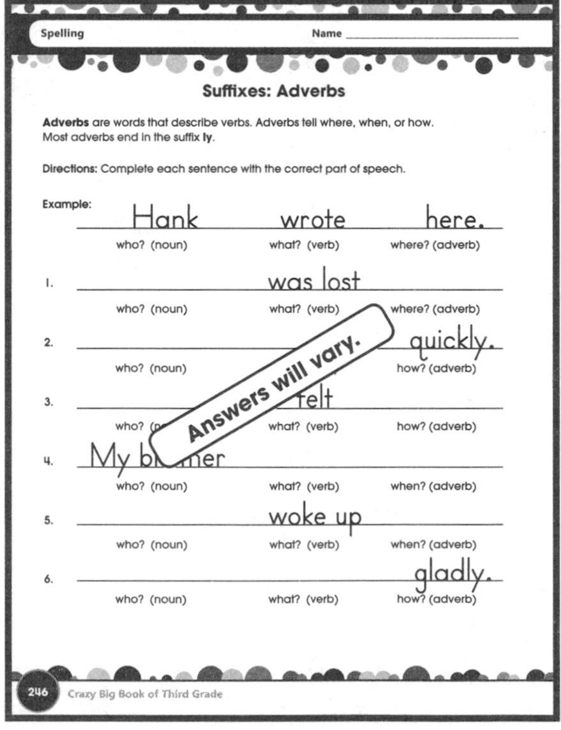

Spelling Name ______

Suffixes: Adverbs

Adverbs are words that describe verbs. Adverbs tell where, when, or how. Most adverbs end in the suffix **ly**.

Directions: Complete each sentence with the correct part of speech.

Example: Hank wrote here. (who? (noun) / what? (verb) / where? (adverb))

1. ______ was lost ______ (who? (noun) / what? (verb) / where? (adverb))
2. ______ ______ quickly. (who? (noun) / what? (verb) / how? (adverb))
3. ______ felt ______ (who? (noun) / what? (verb) / how? (adverb))
4. My brother ______ ______ (who? (noun) / what? (verb) / when? (adverb))
5. ______ woke up ______ (who? (noun) / what? (verb) / when? (adverb))
6. ______ ______ gladly. (who? (noun) / what? (verb) / how? (adverb))

Answers will vary.

246 Crazy Big Book of Third Grade

page 246

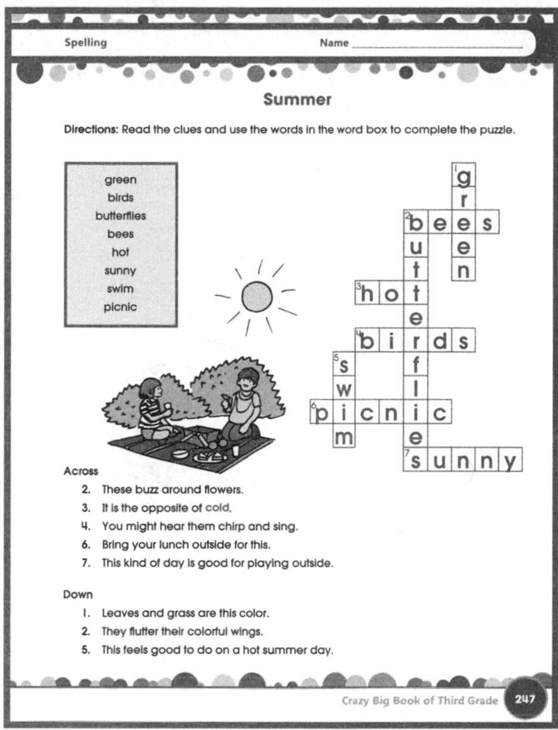

Spelling Name

Summer

Directions: Read the clues and use the words in the word box to complete the puzzle.

green
birds
butterflies
bees
hot
sunny
swim
picnic

Across
2. These buzz around flowers.
3. It is the opposite of cold.
4. You might hear them chirp and sing.
6. Bring your lunch outside for this.
7. This kind of day is good for playing outside.

Down
1. Leaves and grass are this color.
2. They flutter their colorful wings.
5. This feels good to do on a hot summer day.

Crazy Big Book of Third Grade 247

page 247

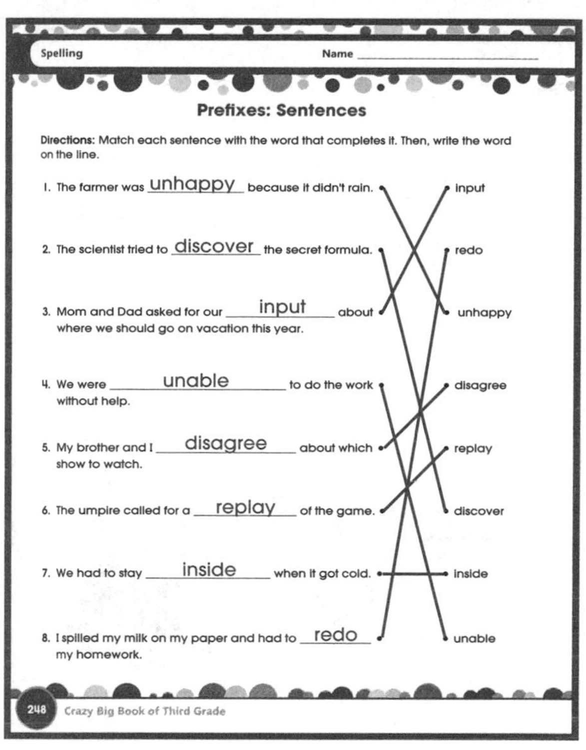

Spelling Name

Prefixes: Sentences

Directions: Match each sentence with the word that completes it. Then, write the word on the line.

1. The farmer was unhappy because it didn't rain.
2. The scientist tried to discover the secret formula.
3. Mom and Dad asked for our input about where we should go on vacation this year.
4. We were unable to do the work without help.
5. My brother and I disagree about which show to watch.
6. The umpire called for a replay of the game.
7. We had to stay inside when it got cold.
8. I spilled my milk on my paper and had to redo my homework.

input
redo
unhappy
disagree
replay
discover
inside
unable

248 Crazy Big Book of Third Grade

page 248

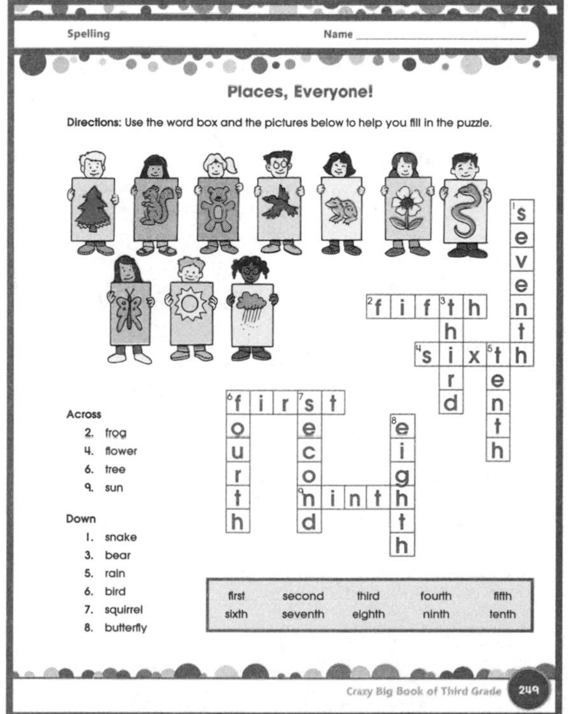

Spelling Name

Places, Everyone!

Directions: Use the word box and the pictures below to help you fill in the puzzle.

Across
2. frog
4. flower
6. tree
9. sun

Down
1. snake
3. bear
5. rain
6. bird
7. squirrel
8. butterfly

first second third fourth fifth
sixth seventh eighth ninth tenth

Crazy Big Book of Third Grade 249

page 249

Spelling Name

Synonyms

Synonyms are words that mean almost the same thing.

Example: sick — ill

Directions: Use words from the box to help you complete the sentences below.

glad fast noisy filthy angry

1. When I am mad, I could also say I am angry.
2. To be glad is the same as being happy.
3. After playing outside, I thought I was dirty, but Mom said I was filthy!
4. I tried not to be too loud, but I couldn't help being a little noisy.
5. If you're too fast, or speedy, you may not do a careful job.

Think of another pair of synonyms. Write them on the lines.
Answers will vary.

250 Crazy Big Book of Third Grade

page 250

Spelling Name ____________

Cool Cider

Directions: Read the clues and use the words in the word box to complete the puzzle.

Across
3. A baby's bed.
5. The cost of something.
6. A castle.
8. A yellow vegetable.
9. You can mold things with this.
10. A very small house.

Down
1. Something to drink.
2. Frozen water.
4. A cold dessert that comes in a cone.
7. A very large town.
8. A desert animal with a humped back.
9. A line that goes around.

city ice ice cream
corn circle palace
cabin clay camel
price crib juice

Crazy Big Book of Third Grade 251

page 251

Spelling Name ____________

Antonyms

Directions: Use antonyms from the box to complete the sentences below.

speedy	clean	quiet	thoughtful	happy

1. If we get too loud, the teacher will ask us to be quiet.
2. She was sad to lose her puppy, but she was happy to find it again.
3. Mark got dirty, so he had to scrub himself clean.
4. Janna was too speedy when she did her homework, so she worked slowly when she did it over.
5. Logan was too selfish to share his snack, but Kyra was thoughtful enough to share hers.

Think of another pair of antonyms. Write them on the lines.

Answers will vary.

252 Crazy Big Book of Third Grade

page 252

Spelling Name ____________

Stretch!

Directions: Read the clues and use the words in the word box to complete the puzzle.

Across
2. A shape that has equal sides.
4. A road.
5. To scatter little pieces.
7. Lightweight rope.
10. A bushy-tailed animal.
11. A stalk of grain.

Down
1. Opposite of weak.
2. The sound a mouse makes.
3. A small river.
4. Yell.
5. Opposite of crooked.
6. A season of the year.
7. To throw water.
8. Very odd.
9. To separate.
10. A homeless cat or dog.

splash	spring
squeak	square
strong	sprinkle
straight	straw
split	string
scream	squirrel
strange	stream
street	stray

Crazy Big Book of Third Grade 253

page 253

Spelling Name ____________

Contractions

A **contraction** is a short way to write two words together. Some letters are left out, but an apostrophe takes their place.

Directions: Write the words from the box that answer the questions.

hasn't	you've	aren't	we've	weren't

1. Write the correct contractions below.

Example:
I have I've was not wasn't
we have we've you have you've
are not aren't were not weren't
has not hasn't

2. Write two words from the box that are contractions using **have**.

we've you've

3. Write three words from the box that are contractions using **not**.

aren't hasn't weren't

254 Crazy Big Book of Third Grade

page 254

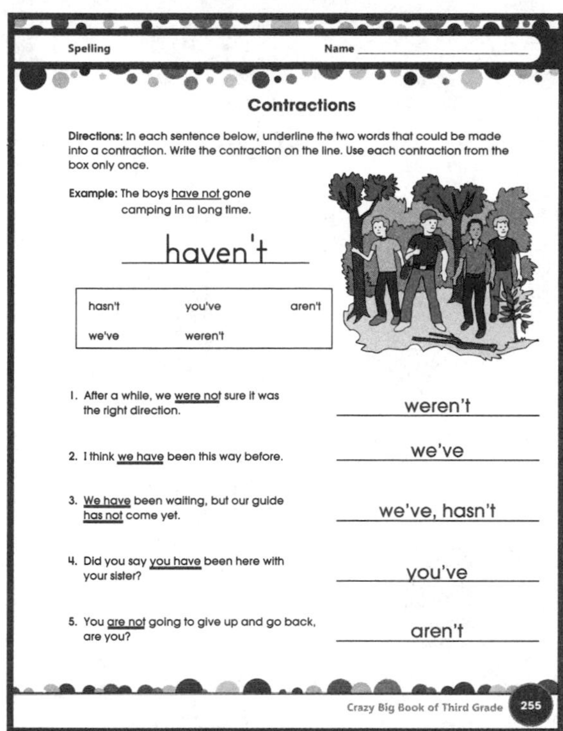

Spelling Name ____________

Contractions

Directions: In each sentence below, underline the two words that could be made into a contraction. Write the contraction on the line. Use each contraction from the box only once.

Example: The boys have not gone camping in a long time.

haven't

hasn't	you've	aren't
we've	weren't	

1. After a while, we were not sure it was the right direction. weren't
2. I think we have been this way before. we've
3. We have been waiting, but our guide has not come yet. we've, hasn't
4. Did you say you have been here with your sister? you've
5. You are not going to give up and go back, are you? aren't

Crazy Big Book of Third Grade 255

page 255

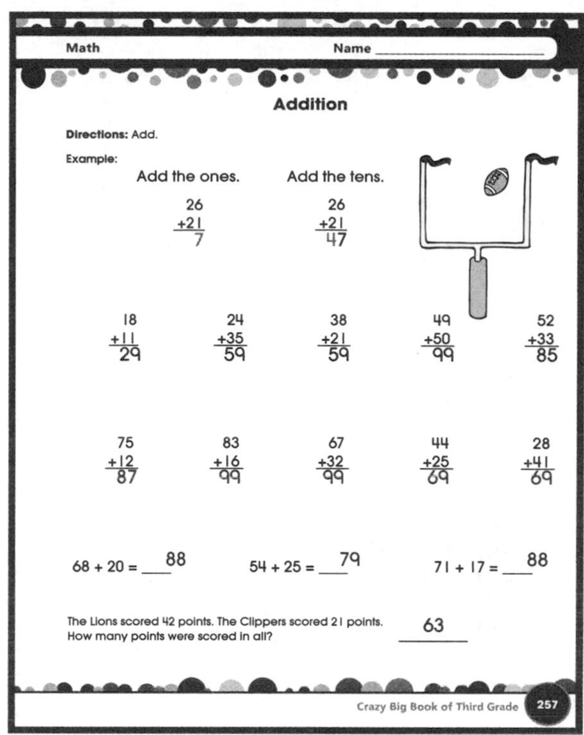

Math Name ____________

Addition

Directions: Add.

Example:

Add the ones. 26 + 21 = 7

Add the tens. 26 + 21 = 47

18 + 11 = 29   24 + 35 = 59   38 + 21 = 59   49 + 50 = 99   52 + 33 = 85

75 + 12 = 87   83 + 16 = 99   67 + 32 = 99   44 + 25 = 69   28 + 41 = 69

68 + 20 = 88   54 + 25 = 79   71 + 17 = 88

The Lions scored 42 points. The Clippers scored 21 points. How many points were scored in all? 63

Crazy Big Book of Third Grade 257

page 257

Math Name ____________

Crack the Code

Directions: Write each sum. Then, use the code to find the letter that goes with each sum. Write the letter in the circle.

+7		
3	10	f
4	11	i
6	13	s
7	14	h

+4		
4	8	c
3	7	r
8	12	o
4	8	c
8	12	o
1	5	d
7	11	i
0	4	l
2	6	e
9	13	s

+6		
4	10	f
1	7	r
6	12	o
3	9	g
7	13	s

7	13	9	4	10	5	8	14	12	6	11
r	s	g	l	f	d	c	h	o	e	i

258 Crazy Big Book of Third Grade

page 258

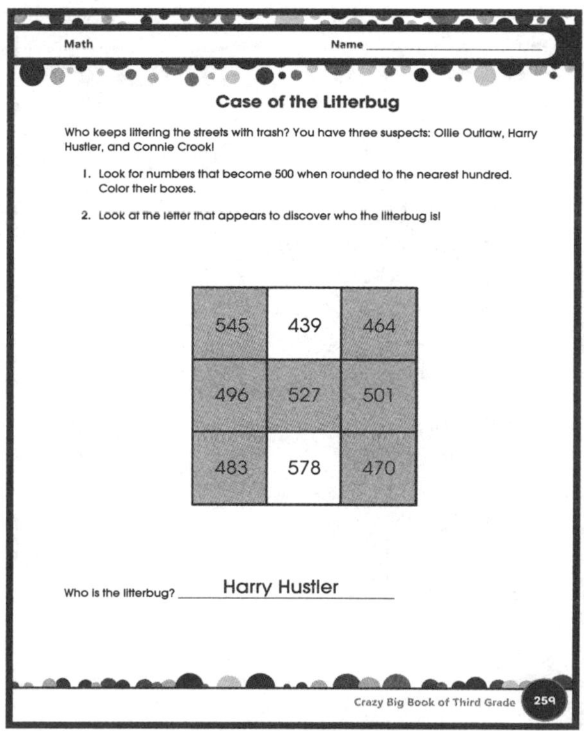

Math Name ____________

Case of the Litterbug

Who keeps littering the streets with trash? You have three suspects: Ollie Outlaw, Harry Hustler, and Connie Crook!

1. Look for numbers that become 500 when rounded to the nearest hundred. Color their boxes.
2. Look at the letter that appears to discover who the litterbug is!

545	439	464
496	527	501
483	578	470

Who is the litterbug? Harry Hustler

Crazy Big Book of Third Grade 259

page 259

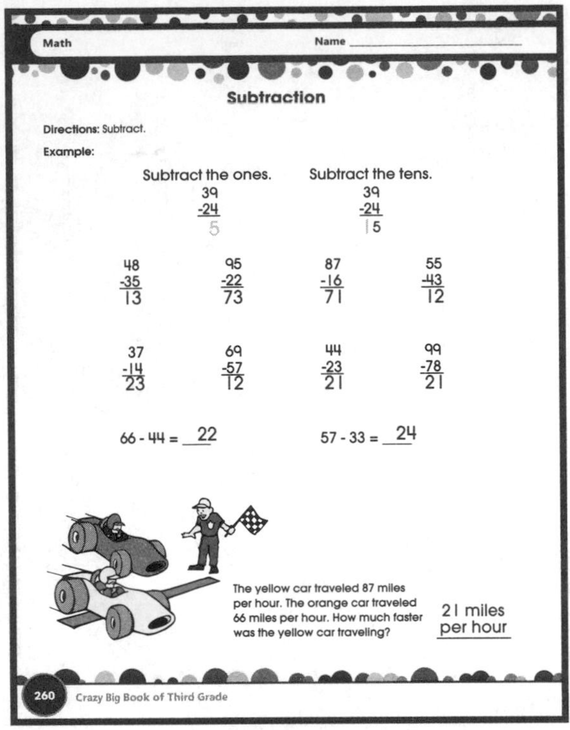

Math Name ______

Subtraction

Directions: Subtract.

Example:

Subtract the ones.	Subtract the tens.
39	39
-24	-24
5	15

48 − 35 = 13 95 − 22 = 73 87 − 16 = 71 55 − 43 = 12

37 − 14 = 23 69 − 57 = 12 44 − 23 = 21 99 − 78 = 21

66 - 44 = 22 57 - 33 = 24

The yellow car traveled 87 miles per hour. The orange car traveled 66 miles per hour. How much faster was the yellow car traveling? 21 miles per hour

260 Crazy Big Book of Third Grade

page 260

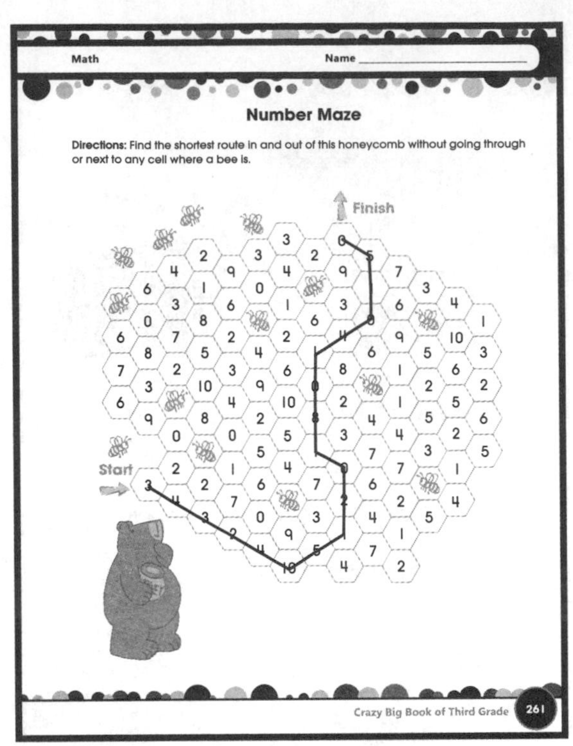

Math Name ______

Number Maze

Directions: Find the shortest route in and out of this honeycomb without going through or next to any cell where a bee is.

Crazy Big Book of Third Grade 261

page 261

Math Name ______

Double Scoop

Directions: What is your favorite flavor? Connect the dots from 5 to 100. Color.

262 Crazy Big Book of Third Grade

page 262

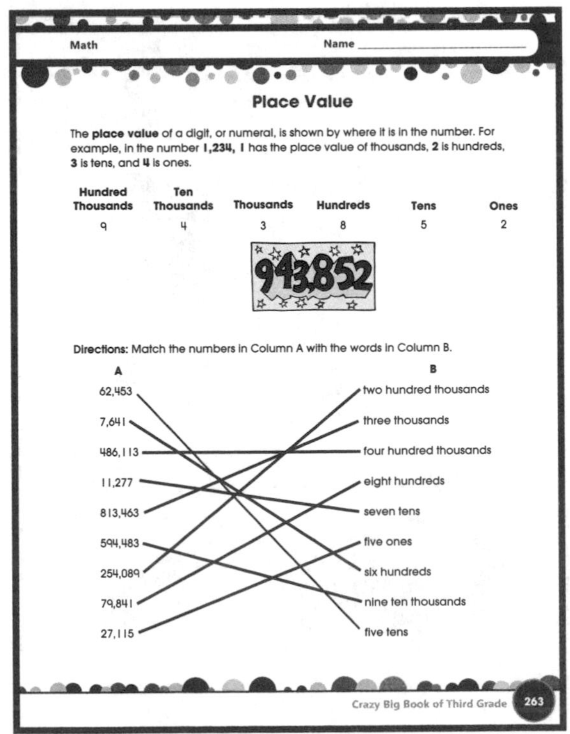

Math Name ______

Place Value

The **place value** of a digit, or numeral, is shown by where it is in the number. For example, in the number **1,234**, **1** has the place value of thousands, **2** is hundreds, **3** is tens, and **4** is ones.

Hundred Thousands	Ten Thousands	Thousands	Hundreds	Tens	Ones
9	4	3	8	5	2

943,852

Directions: Match the numbers in Column A with the words in Column B.

A	B
62,453	two hundred thousands
7,641	three thousands
486,113	four hundred thousands
11,277	eight hundreds
813,463	seven tens
594,483	five ones
254,089	six hundreds
79,841	nine ten thousands
27,115	five tens

Crazy Big Book of Third Grade 263

page 263

Math Name ______________________

Let's Ride

Directions: Monica loves to ride her horse, Spartan. Connect the dots from 100 to 2000. Color.

264 Crazy Big Book of Third Grade

page 264

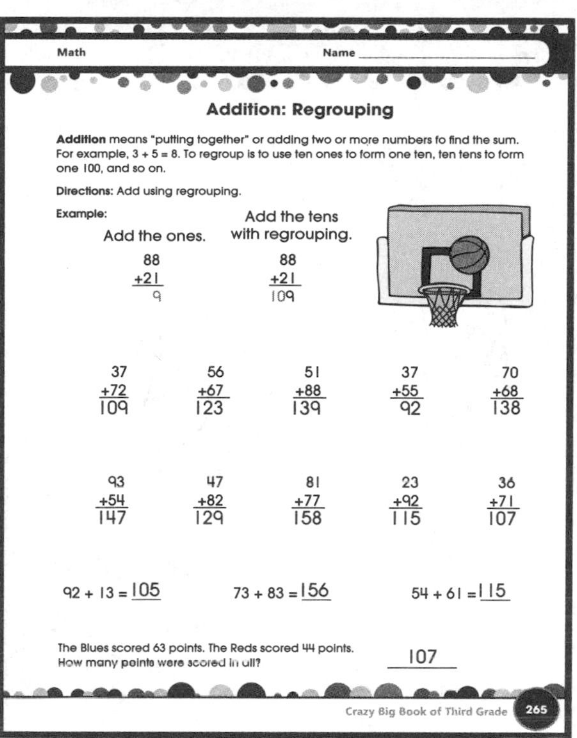

Math Name ______________________

Addition: Regrouping

Addition means "putting together" or adding two or more numbers to find the sum. For example, 3 + 5 = 8. To regroup is to use ten ones to form one ten, ten tens to form one 100, and so on.

Directions: Add using regrouping.

Example:

Add the ones: 88 + 21 = 9

Add the tens with regrouping: 88 + 21 = 109

37 + 72 = 109 | 56 + 67 = 123 | 51 + 88 = 139 | 37 + 55 = 92 | 70 + 68 = 138

93 + 54 = 147 | 47 + 82 = 129 | 81 + 77 = 158 | 23 + 92 = 115 | 36 + 71 = 107

92 + 13 = 105 | 73 + 83 = 156 | 54 + 61 = 115

The Blues scored 63 points. The Reds scored 44 points. How many points were scored in all? 107

Crazy Big Book of Third Grade 265

page 265

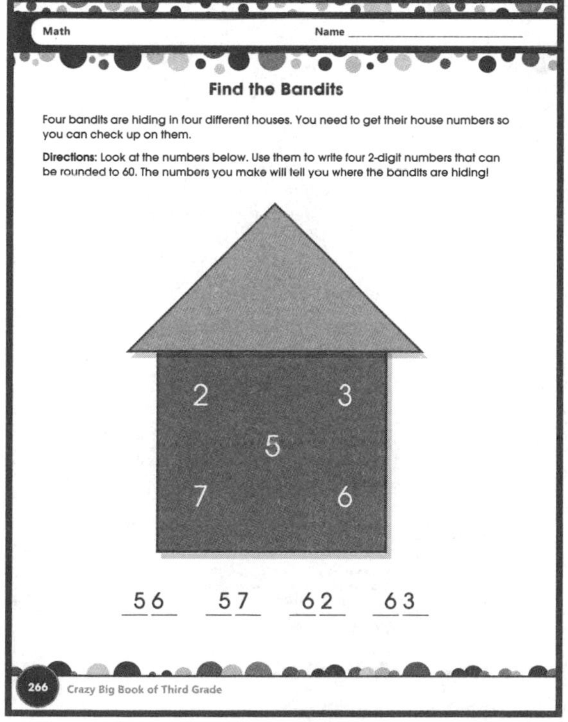

Math Name ______________________

Find the Bandits

Four bandits are hiding in four different houses. You need to get their house numbers so you can check up on them.

Directions: Look at the numbers below. Use them to write four 2-digit numbers that can be rounded to 60. The numbers you make will tell you where the bandits are hiding!

56 57 62 63

266 Crazy Big Book of Third Grade

page 266

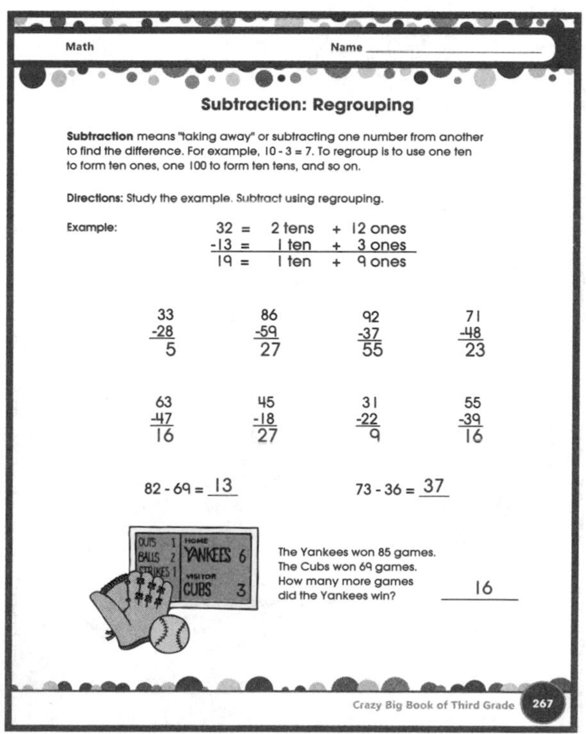

Math Name ______________________

Subtraction: Regrouping

Subtraction means "taking away" or subtracting one number from another to find the difference. For example, 10 - 3 = 7. To regroup is to use one ten to form ten ones, one 100 to form ten tens, and so on.

Directions: Study the example. Subtract using regrouping.

Example:

32 = 2 tens + 12 ones
-13 = 1 ten + 3 ones
19 = 1 ten + 9 ones

33 - 28 = 5 | 86 - 59 = 27 | 92 - 37 = 55 | 71 - 48 = 23

63 - 47 = 16 | 45 - 18 = 27 | 31 - 22 = 9 | 55 - 39 = 16

82 - 69 = 13 | 73 - 36 = 37

The Yankees won 85 games. The Cubs won 69 games. How many more games did the Yankees win? 16

Crazy Big Book of Third Grade 267

page 267

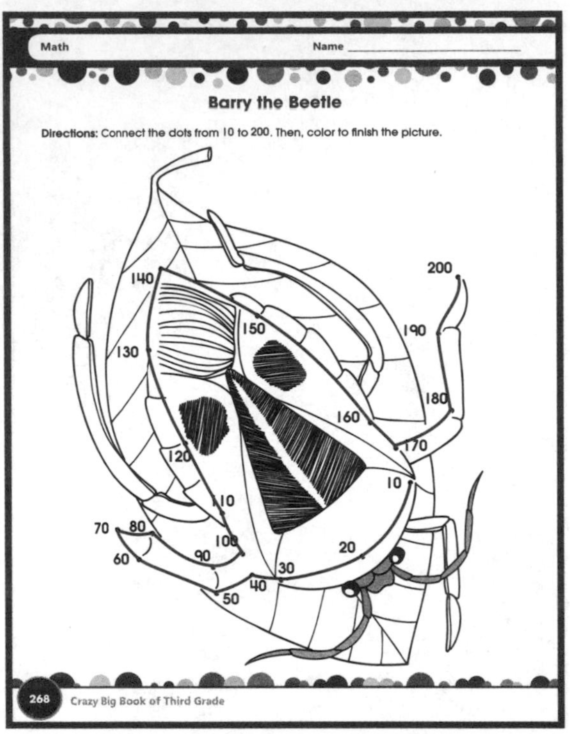

page 268

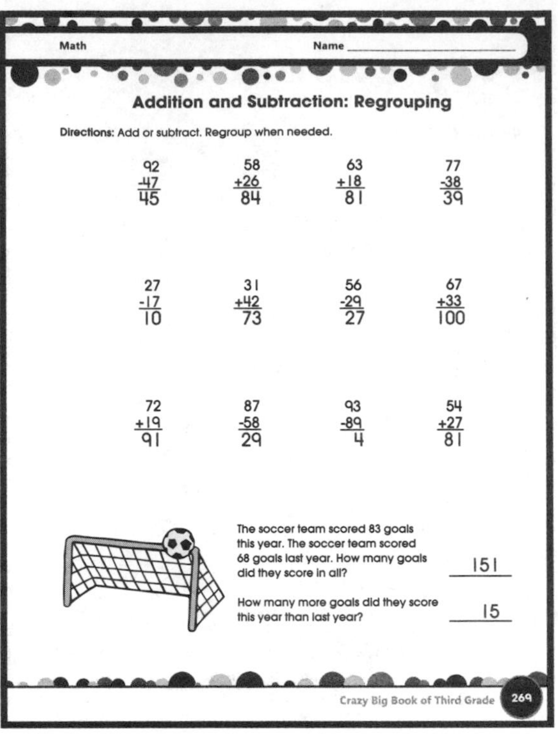

Math Name

Addition and Subtraction: Regrouping

Directions: Add or subtract. Regroup when needed.

92 − 47 = 45	58 + 26 = 84	63 + 18 = 81	77 − 38 = 39
27 − 17 = 10	31 + 42 = 73	56 − 29 = 27	67 + 33 = 100
72 + 19 = 91	87 − 58 = 29	93 − 89 = 4	54 + 27 = 81

The soccer team scored 83 goals this year. The soccer team scored 68 goals last year. How many goals did they score in all? 151

How many more goals did they score this year than last year? 15

Crazy Big Book of Third Grade 269

page 269

Math Name

Addition and Subtraction: Regrouping

Directions: Add or subtract using regrouping.

28 + 56 + 93 = 177	82 + 49 + 51 = 182	33 + 75 + 128 = 236	67 + 94 + 248 = 409
683 − 495 = 188	756 + 139 = 895	818 − 387 = 431	956 + 267 = 1,223
1,588 − 989 = 599	4,675 − 2,976 = 1,699	8,732 − 5,664 = 3,068	2,938 + 3,459 = 6,397

N.Y. TO MIAMI
N.Y. TO L.A.

To drive from New York City to Los Angeles is 2,832 miles. To drive from New York City to Miami is 1,327 miles. How much farther is it to drive from New York City to Los Angeles than from New York City to Miami? 1,505 miles

270 Crazy Big Book of Third Grade

page 270

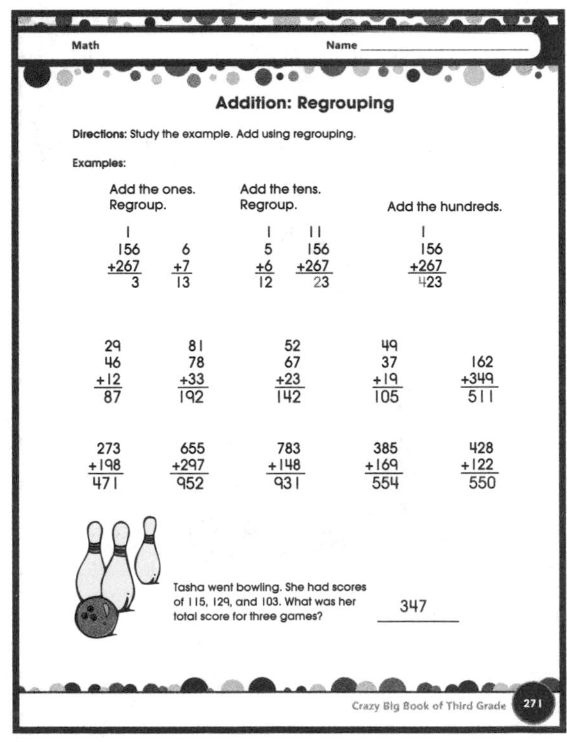

Math Name

Addition: Regrouping

Directions: Study the example. Add using regrouping.

Examples:

Add the ones. Regroup. 156 + 267 → 3; 6 + 7 = 13

Add the tens. Regroup. 5 + 6 = 12; 156 + 267 → 23

Add the hundreds. 156 + 267 = 423

29 + 46 + 12 = 87	81 + 78 + 33 = 192	52 + 67 + 23 = 142	49 + 37 + 19 = 105	162 + 349 = 511
273 + 198 = 471	655 + 297 = 952	783 + 148 = 931	385 + 169 = 554	428 + 122 = 550

Tasha went bowling. She had scores of 115, 129, and 103. What was her total score for three games? 347

Crazy Big Book of Third Grade 271

page 271

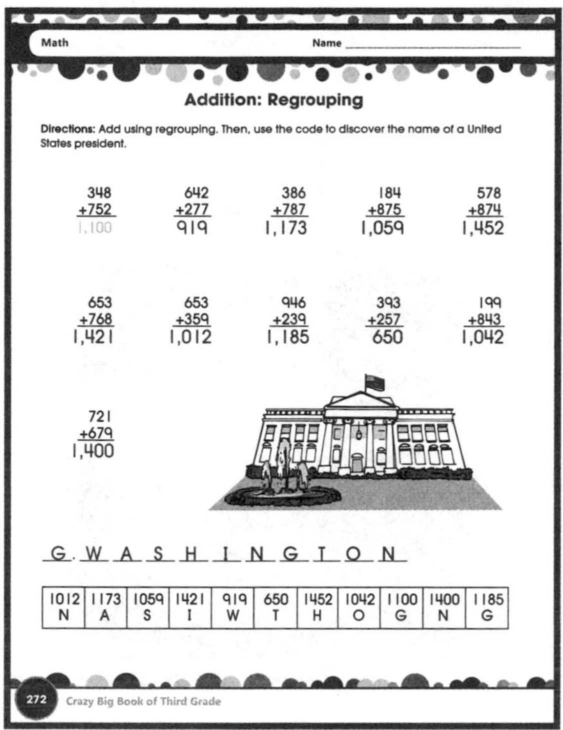
Math Name

Addition: Regrouping

Directions: Add using regrouping. Then, use the code to discover the name of a United States president.

348	642	386	184	578
+752	+277	+787	+875	+874
1,100	919	1,173	1,059	1,452

653	653	946	393	199
+768	+359	+239	+257	+843
1,421	1,012	1,185	650	1,042

721
+679
1,400

G. W A S H I N G T O N

1012	1173	1059	1421	919	650	1452	1042	1100	1400	1185
N	A	S	I	W	T	H	O	G	N	G

272 Crazy Big Book of Third Grade

page 272

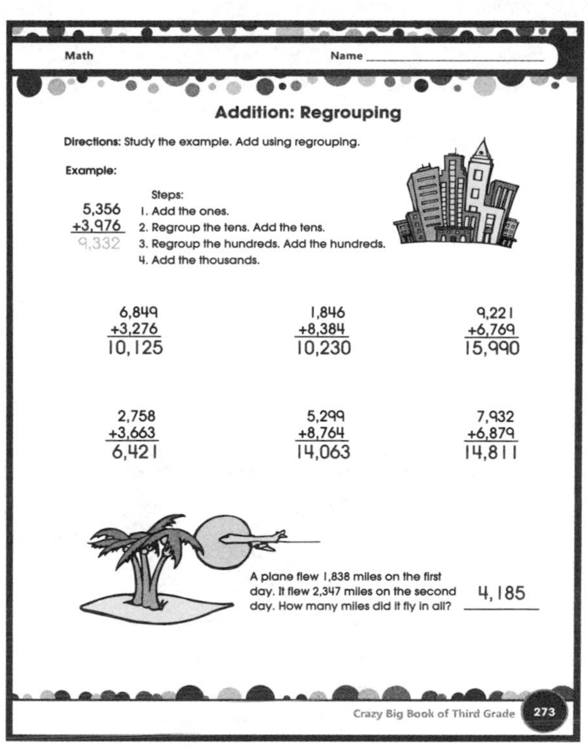
Math Name

Addition: Regrouping

Directions: Study the example. Add using regrouping.

Example:

5,356
+3,976
9,332

Steps:
1. Add the ones.
2. Regroup the tens. Add the tens.
3. Regroup the hundreds. Add the hundreds.
4. Add the thousands.

6,849	1,846	9,221
+3,276	+8,384	+6,769
10,125	10,230	15,990

2,758	5,299	7,932
+3,663	+8,764	+6,879
6,421	14,063	14,811

A plane flew 1,838 miles on the first day. It flew 2,347 miles on the second day. How many miles did it fly in all? 4,185

Crazy Big Book of Third Grade 273

page 273

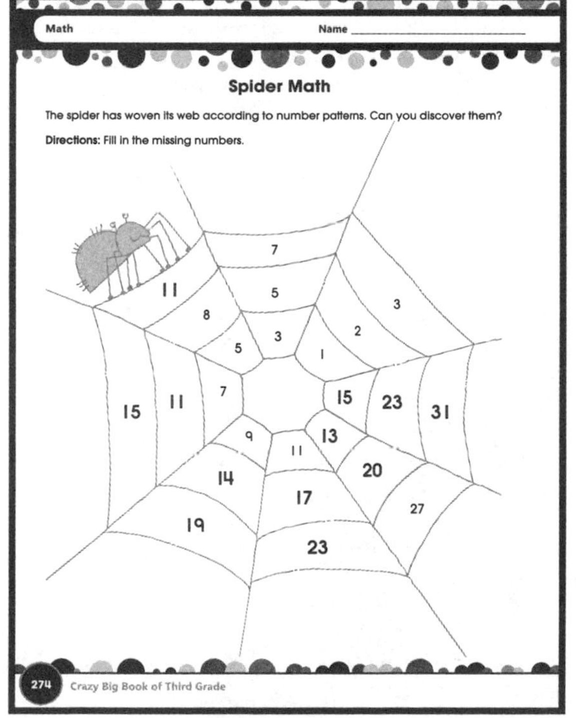
Math Name

Spider Math

The spider has woven its web according to number patterns. Can you discover them?

Directions: Fill in the missing numbers.

274 Crazy Big Book of Third Grade

page 274

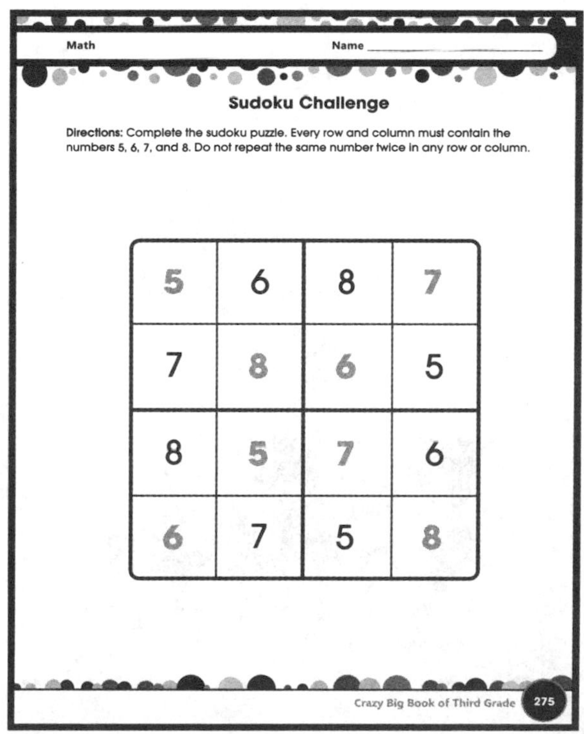
Math Name

Sudoku Challenge

Directions: Complete the sudoku puzzle. Every row and column must contain the numbers 5, 6, 7, and 8. Do not repeat the same number twice in any row or column.

5	6	8	7
7	8	6	5
8	5	7	6
6	7	5	8

Crazy Big Book of Third Grade 275

page 275

Answer Key

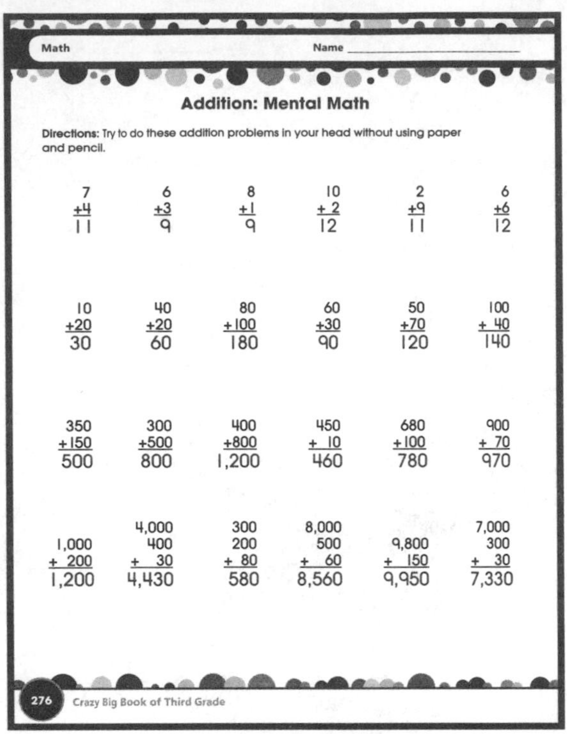

Math Name ____________

Addition: Mental Math

Directions: Try to do these addition problems in your head without using paper and pencil.

7 + 4 = 11	6 + 3 = 9	8 + 1 = 9	10 + 2 = 12	2 + 9 = 11	6 + 6 = 12
10 + 20 = 30	40 + 20 = 60	80 + 100 = 180	60 + 30 = 90	50 + 70 = 120	100 + 40 = 140
350 + 150 = 500	300 + 500 = 800	400 + 800 = 1,200	450 + 10 = 460	680 + 100 = 780	900 + 70 = 970
1,000 + 200 = 1,200	4,000 + 400 + 30 = 4,430	300 + 200 + 80 = 580	8,000 + 500 + 60 = 8,560	9,800 + 150 = 9,950	7,000 + 300 + 30 = 7,330

276 Crazy Big Book of Third Grade

page 276

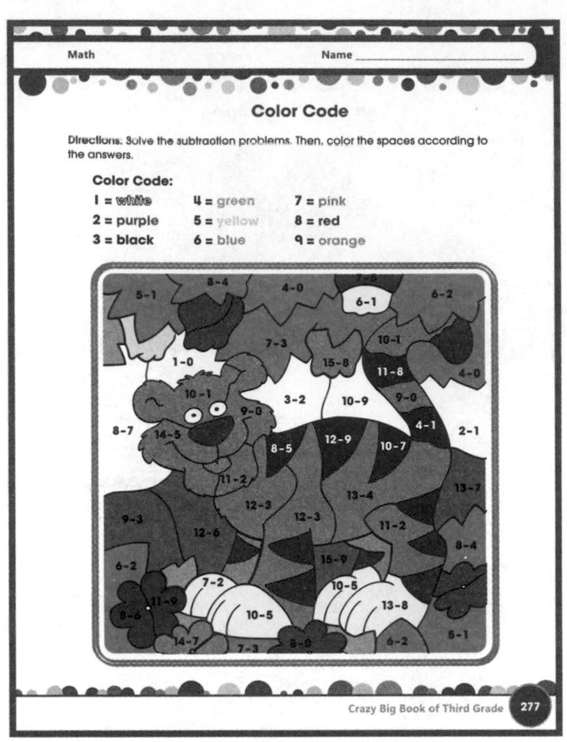

Math Name ____________

Color Code

Directions: Solve the subtraction problems. Then, color the spaces according to the answers.

Color Code:

1 = white
2 = purple
3 = black
4 = green
5 = yellow
6 = blue
7 = pink
8 = red
9 = orange

Crazy Big Book of Third Grade 277

page 277

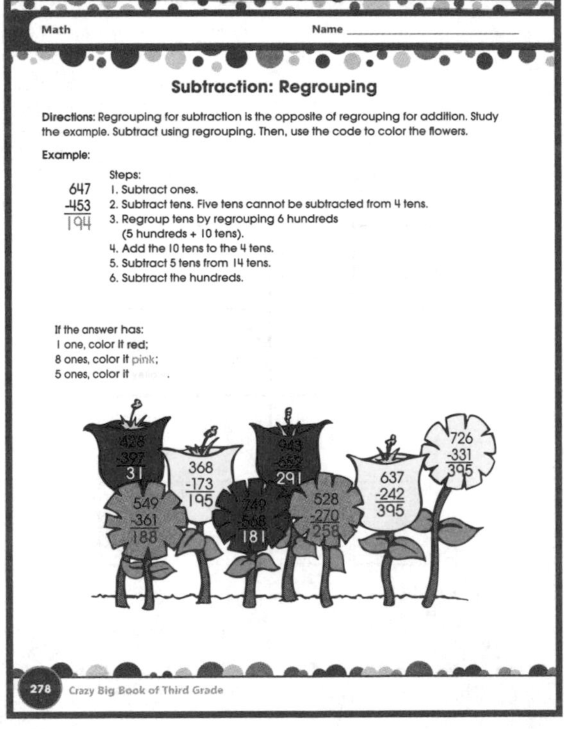

Math Name ____________

Subtraction: Regrouping

Directions: Regrouping for subtraction is the opposite of regrouping for addition. Study the example. Subtract using regrouping. Then, use the code to color the flowers.

Example:

647 − 453 = 194

Steps:
1. Subtract ones.
2. Subtract tens. Five tens cannot be subtracted from 4 tens.
3. Regroup tens by regrouping 6 hundreds (5 hundreds + 10 tens).
4. Add the 10 tens to the 4 tens.
5. Subtract 5 tens from 14 tens.
6. Subtract the hundreds.

If the answer has:
1 one, color it red;
8 ones, color it pink;
5 ones, color it yellow.

428 − 397 = 31
368 − 173 = 195
943 − 652 = 291
637 − 242 = 395
726 − 331 = 395
549 − 361 = 188
749 − 568 = 181
528 − 270 = 258

278 Crazy Big Book of Third Grade

page 278

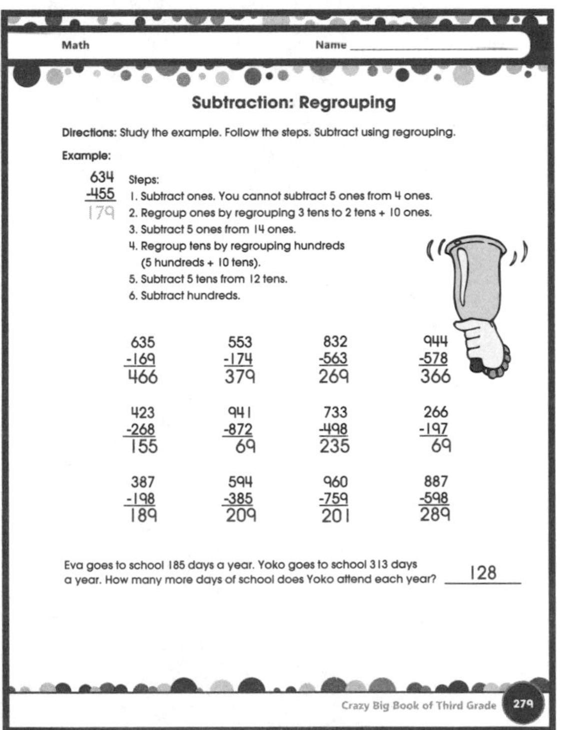

Math Name ____________

Subtraction: Regrouping

Directions: Study the example. Follow the steps. Subtract using regrouping.

Example:

634 − 455 = 179

Steps:
1. Subtract ones. You cannot subtract 5 ones from 4 ones.
2. Regroup ones by regrouping 3 tens to 2 tens + 10 ones.
3. Subtract 5 ones from 14 ones.
4. Regroup tens by regrouping hundreds (5 hundreds + 10 tens).
5. Subtract 5 tens from 12 tens.
6. Subtract hundreds.

635 − 169 = 466	553 − 174 = 379	832 − 563 = 269	944 − 578 = 366
423 − 268 = 155	941 − 872 = 69	733 − 498 = 235	266 − 197 = 69
387 − 198 = 189	594 − 385 = 209	960 − 759 = 201	887 − 598 = 289

Eva goes to school 185 days a year. Yoko goes to school 313 days a year. How many more days of school does Yoko attend each year? 128

Crazy Big Book of Third Grade 279

page 279

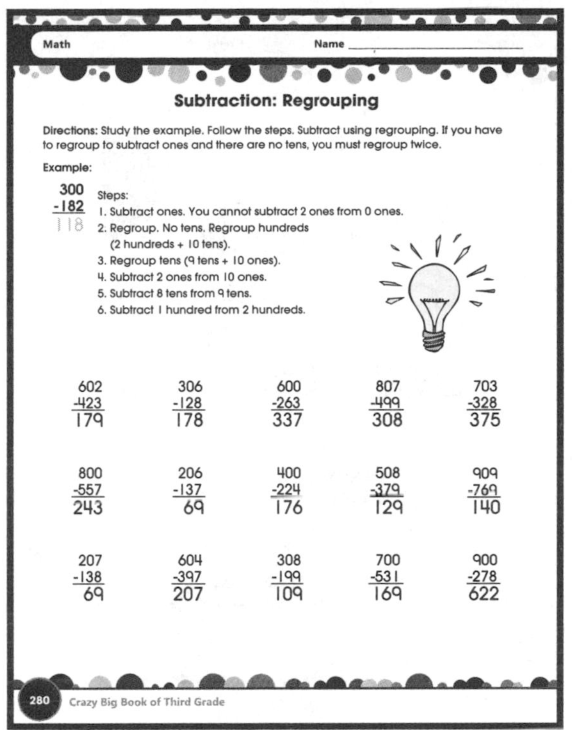
Math Name ______

Subtraction: Regrouping

Directions: Study the example. Follow the steps. Subtract using regrouping. If you have to regroup to subtract ones and there are no tens, you must regroup twice.

Example:

300
-182
118

Steps:
1. Subtract ones. You cannot subtract 2 ones from 0 ones.
2. Regroup. No tens. Regroup hundreds (2 hundreds + 10 tens).
3. Regroup tens (9 tens + 10 ones).
4. Subtract 2 ones from 10 ones.
5. Subtract 8 tens from 9 tens.
6. Subtract 1 hundred from 2 hundreds.

602 -423 = 179	306 -128 = 178	600 -263 = 337	807 -499 = 308	703 -328 = 375
800 -557 = 243	206 -137 = 69	400 -224 = 176	508 -379 = 129	909 -769 = 140
207 -138 = 69	604 -397 = 207	308 -199 = 109	700 -531 = 169	900 -278 = 622

280 Crazy Big Book of Third Grade

page 280

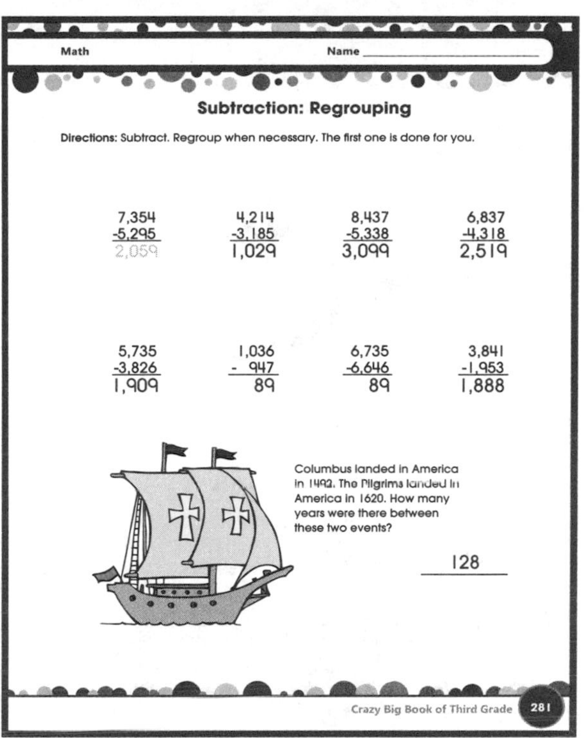
Math Name ______

Subtraction: Regrouping

Directions: Subtract. Regroup when necessary. The first one is done for you.

7,354 -5,295 = 2,059	4,214 -3,185 = 1,029	8,437 -5,338 = 3,099	6,837 -4,318 = 2,519
5,735 -3,826 = 1,909	1,036 - 947 = 89	6,735 -6,646 = 89	3,841 -1,953 = 1,888

Columbus landed in America in 1492. The Pilgrims landed in America in 1620. How many years were there between these two events?

128

Crazy Big Book of Third Grade 281

page 281

Math Name ______

Mary the Millipede

Directions: Connect the dots from 100 to 900. Then, color to finish the picture.

282 Crazy Big Book of Third Grade

page 282

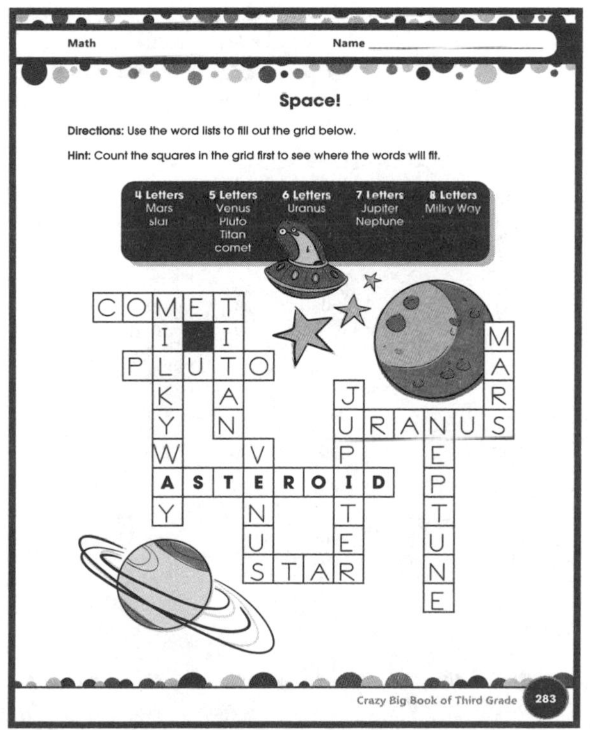
Math Name ______

Space!

Directions: Use the word lists to fill out the grid below.

Hint: Count the squares in the grid first to see where the words will fit.

4 Letters	5 Letters	6 Letters	7 Letters	8 Letters
Mars	Venus	Uranus	Jupiter	Milky Way
star	Pluto		Neptune	
	Titan			
	comet			

Crazy Big Book of Third Grade 283

page 283

Math Name

Down the Slope!

Directions: Find the differences. The number in the snowflakes will answer the question. Denali is the tallest mountain in North America. How high is it?

96 − 25 = 71; 71 − 18 = 53; 53 − 29 = 24; 24 − 18 = 6

82 − 16 = 66; 66 − 36 = 30; 30 − 29 = 1

76 − 38 = 38; 38 − 29 = 9

80 − 76 = 4

Denali is 6,194 meters high!

284 Crazy Big Book of Third Grade

page 284

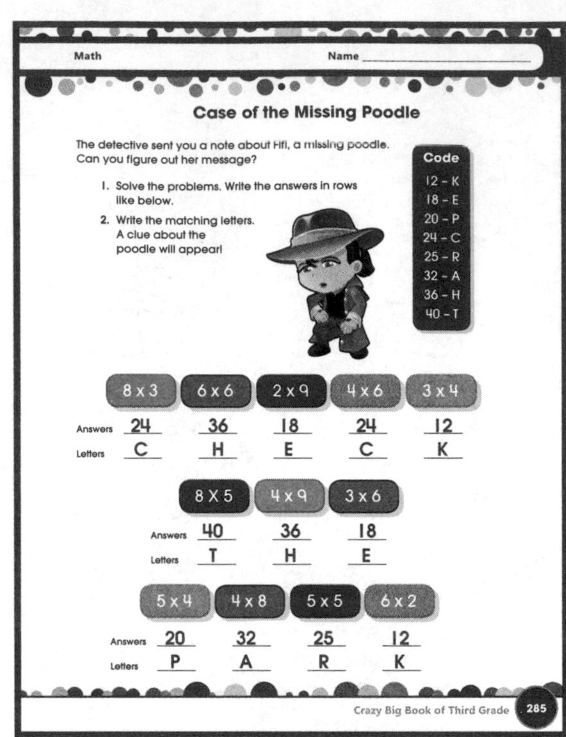
Math Name

Case of the Missing Poodle

The detective sent you a note about Fifi, a missing poodle. Can you figure out her message?

1. Solve the problems. Write the answers in rows like below.
2. Write the matching letters. A clue about the poodle will appear!

Code: 12 - K, 18 - E, 20 - P, 24 - C, 25 - R, 32 - A, 36 - H, 40 - T

	8 x 3	6 x 6	2 x 9	4 x 6	3 x 4
Answers	24	36	18	24	12
Letters	C	H	E	C	K

	8 X 5	4 x 9	3 x 6
Answers	40	36	18
Letters	T	H	E

	5 x 4	4 x 8	5 x 5	6 x 2
Answers	20	32	25	12
Letters	P	A	R	K

Crazy Big Book of Third Grade 285

page 285

Math Name

Subtraction: Mental Math

Directions: Try to do these subtraction problems in your head without using paper and pencil.

9 − 3 = 6	12 − 6 = 6	7 − 6 = 1	5 − 1 = 4	15 − 5 = 10	2 − 0 = 2
40 − 20 = 20	90 − 80 = 10	100 − 50 = 50	20 − 20 = 0	60 − 10 = 50	70 − 40 = 30
450 − 250 = 200	500 − 300 = 200	250 − 20 = 230	690 − 100 = 590	320 − 20 = 300	900 − 600 = 300
1,000 − 400 = 600	8,000 − 500 = 7,500	7,000 − 900 = 6,100	4,000 − 2,000 = 2,000	9,500 − 4,000 = 5,500	5,000 − 2,000 = 3,000

286 Crazy Big Book of Third Grade

page 286

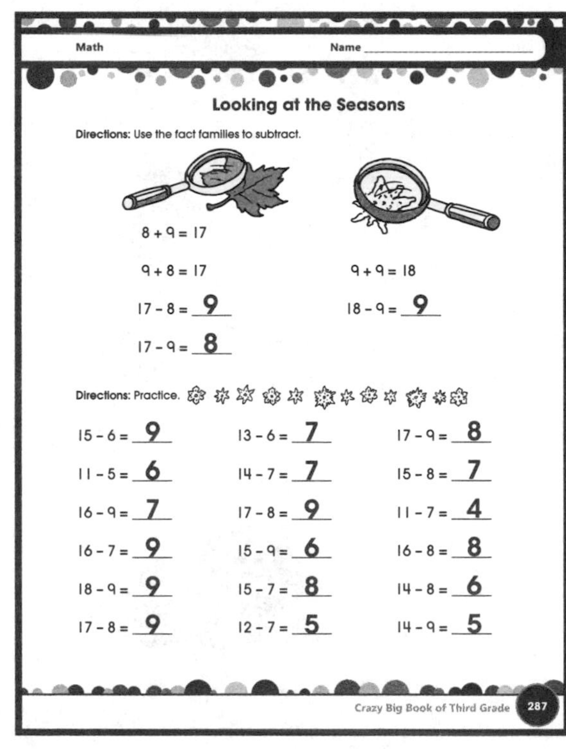
Math Name

Looking at the Seasons

Directions: Use the fact families to subtract.

8 + 9 = 17
9 + 8 = 17
17 − 8 = 9
17 − 9 = 8

9 + 9 = 18
18 − 9 = 9

Directions: Practice.

15 − 6 = 9	13 − 6 = 7	17 − 9 = 8
11 − 5 = 6	14 − 7 = 7	15 − 8 = 7
16 − 9 = 7	17 − 8 = 9	11 − 7 = 4
16 − 7 = 9	15 − 9 = 6	16 − 8 = 8
18 − 9 = 9	15 − 7 = 8	14 − 8 = 6
17 − 8 = 9	12 − 7 = 5	14 − 9 = 5

Crazy Big Book of Third Grade 287

page 287

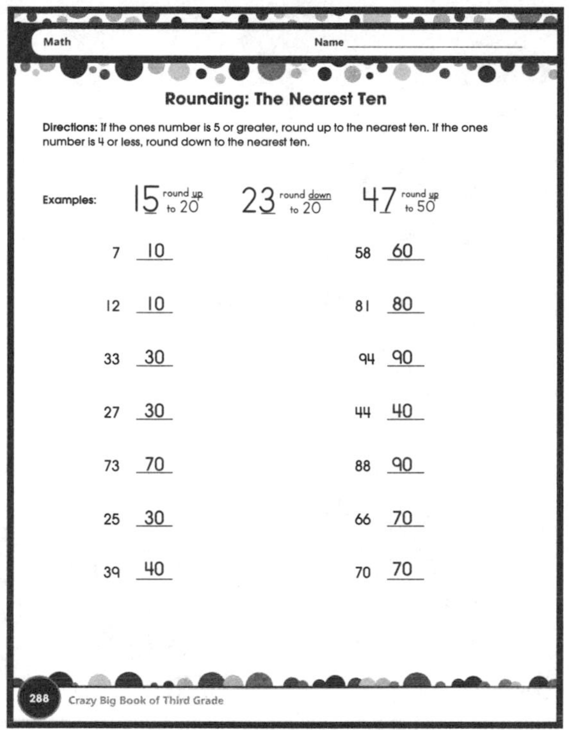

Math Name ____________

Rounding: The Nearest Ten

Directions: If the ones number is 5 or greater, round up to the nearest ten. If the ones number is 4 or less, round down to the nearest ten.

Examples: 15 round up to 20 | 23 round down to 20 | 47 round up to 50

7	10	58	60
12	10	81	80
33	30	94	90
27	30	44	40
73	70	88	90
25	30	66	70
39	40	70	70

288 Crazy Big Book of Third Grade

page 288

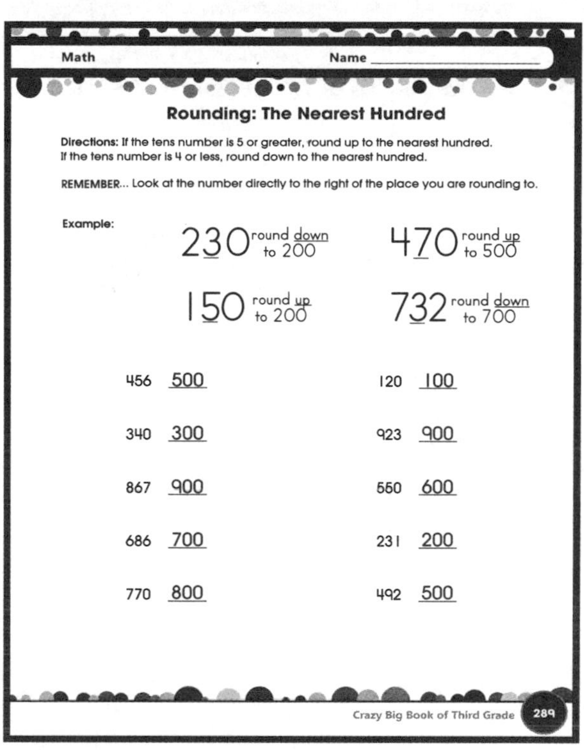

Math Name ____________

Rounding: The Nearest Hundred

Directions: If the tens number is 5 or greater, round up to the nearest hundred. If the tens number is 4 or less, round down to the nearest hundred.

REMEMBER... Look at the number directly to the right of the place you are rounding to.

Example: 230 round down to 200 | 470 round up to 500 | 150 round up to 200 | 732 round down to 700

456	500	120	100
340	300	923	900
867	900	550	600
686	700	231	200
770	800	492	500

Crazy Big Book of Third Grade 289

page 289

Math Name ____________

Grid Game

1. Draw a square around the greatest number.
2. Count by 2s to 40. Underline the numbers you use.
3. Draw a triangle around the number that is 4 less than 62.
4. Draw an X over each odd number.
5. Circle all of the uppercase letters. Write the letters you circled in order, starting with the top row and moving left to right.

SUMMER IS FUN

b	r	q	e	o	S	c	r	y	10	6	X
U	y	10	X	2	4	M	z	l	q	a	i
6	v	0	X	8	M	p	2	10	X	12	l
r	b	14	18	b	e	16	f	h	X	E	s
18	X	14	X	2	p	m	n	z	58	20	s
94	86	22	2	R	X	I	0	24	n	x	c
26	X	X	a	d	e	28	g	S	52	X	30
X	j	F	k	32	y	34	4	X	t	10	36
0	n	e	n	38	o	80	98	U	X	x	p
w	m	m	X	N	X	14	X	c	r	e	t
q	u	v	X	X	6	w	X	40	w	X	X

290 Crazy Big Book of Third Grade

page 290

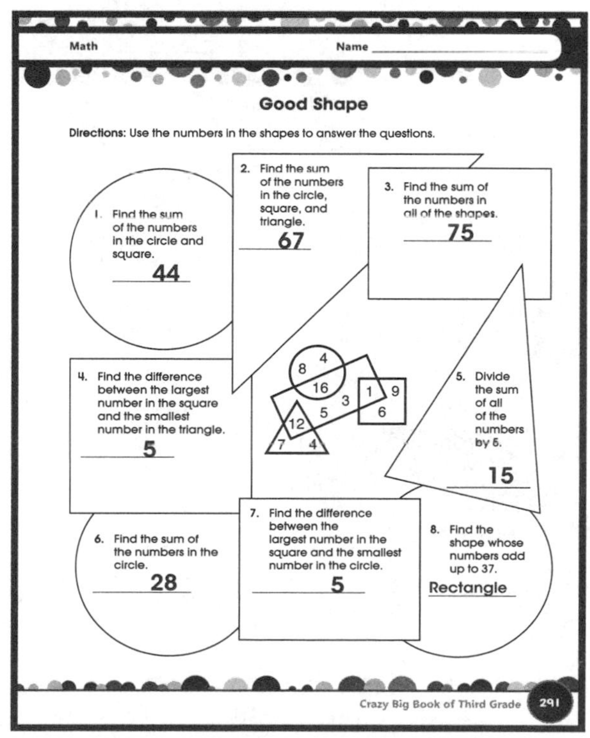

Math Name ____________

Good Shape

Directions: Use the numbers in the shapes to answer the questions.

1. Find the sum of the numbers in the circle and square. 44
2. Find the sum of the numbers in the circle, square, and triangle. 67
3. Find the sum of the numbers in all of the shapes. 75
4. Find the difference between the largest number in the square and the smallest number in the triangle. 5
5. Divide the sum of all of the numbers by 5. 15
6. Find the sum of the numbers in the circle. 28
7. Find the difference between the largest number in the square and the smallest number in the circle. 5
8. Find the shape whose numbers add up to 37. Rectangle

Crazy Big Book of Third Grade 291

page 291

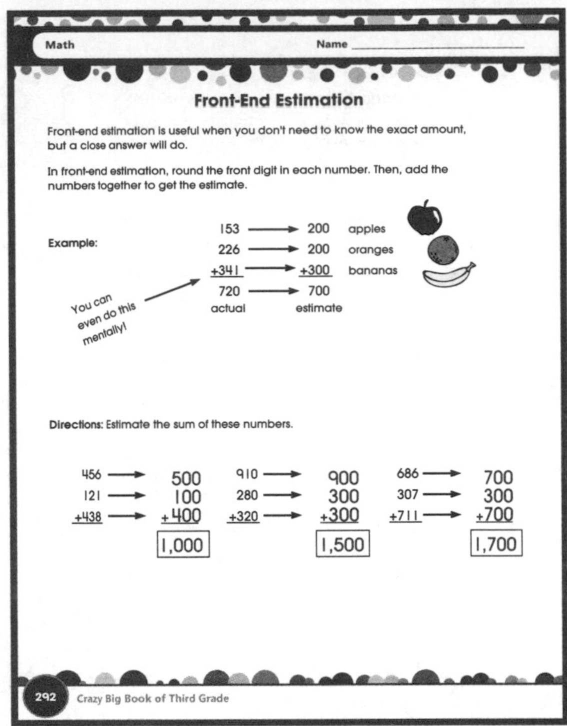

Math Name ______

Front-End Estimation

Front-end estimation is useful when you don't need to know the exact amount, but a close answer will do.

In front-end estimation, round the front digit in each number. Then, add the numbers together to get the estimate.

Example:

153 →	200	apples
226 →	200	oranges
+341 →	+300	bananas
720 →	700	
actual	estimate	

You can even do this mentally!

Directions: Estimate the sum of these numbers.

456 →	500	910 →	900	686 →	700
121 →	100	280 →	300	307 →	300
+438 →	+400	+320 →	+300	+711 →	+700
	1,000		1,500		1,700

292 Crazy Big Book of Third Grade

page 292

Math Name ______

Lily Pad

Directions: Help the frog hop to the lily pad.

Crazy Big Book of Third Grade 293

page 293

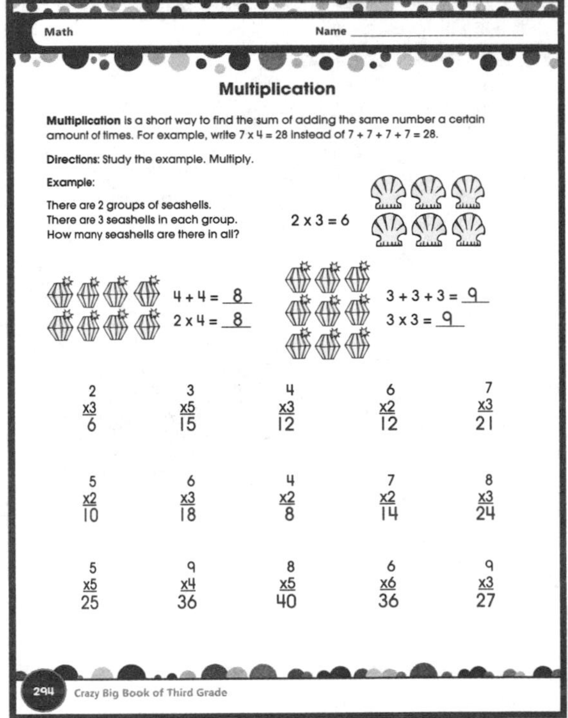

Math Name ______

Multiplication

Multiplication is a short way to find the sum of adding the same number a certain amount of times. For example, write 7 x 4 = 28 instead of 7 + 7 + 7 + 7 = 28.

Directions: Study the example. Multiply.

Example:

There are 2 groups of seashells.
There are 3 seashells in each group.
How many seashells are there in all?

2 x 3 = 6

4 + 4 = 8
2 x 4 = 8

3 + 3 + 3 = 9
3 x 3 = 9

2 x3 = 6	3 x5 = 15	4 x3 = 12	6 x2 = 12	7 x3 = 21
5 x2 = 10	6 x3 = 18	4 x2 = 8	7 x2 = 14	8 x3 = 24
5 x5 = 25	9 x4 = 36	8 x5 = 40	6 x6 = 36	9 x3 = 27

294 Crazy Big Book of Third Grade

page 294

Math Name ______

Multiplication

Directions: Multiply.

3 x5 = 15	4 x6 = 24	3 x8 = 24		
5 x5 = 25	4 x8 = 32	5 x4 = 20		
6 x7 = 42	3 x9 = 27	2 x8 = 16	7 x6 = 42	9 x4 = 36
6 x8 = 48	5 x6 = 30	7 x7 = 49	5 x3 = 15	8 x9 = 72

A riverboat makes 3 trips a day every day. How many trips does it make in a week? 21

Crazy Big Book of Third Grade 295

page 295

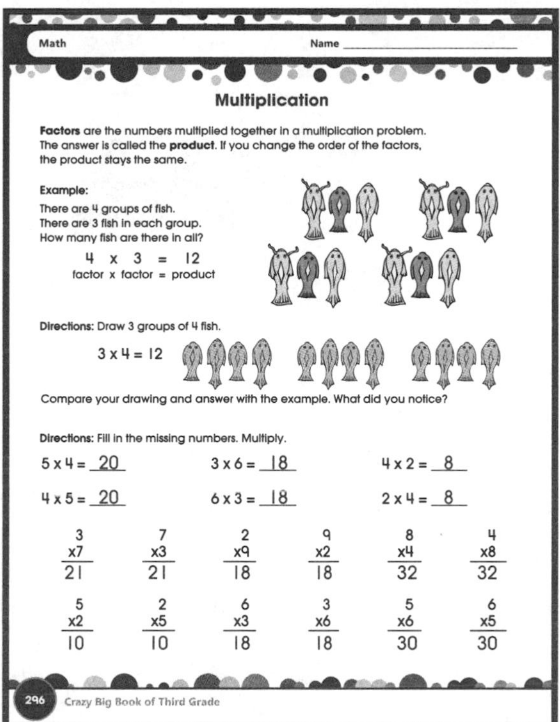

Math Name ____________

Multiplication

Factors are the numbers multiplied together in a multiplication problem. The answer is called the **product**. If you change the order of the factors, the product stays the same.

Example:
There are 4 groups of fish.
There are 3 fish in each group.
How many fish are there in all?

4 x 3 = 12
factor x factor = product

Directions: Draw 3 groups of 4 fish.

3 x 4 = 12

Compare your drawing and answer with the example. What did you notice?

Directions: Fill in the missing numbers. Multiply.

5 x 4 = 20 3 x 6 = 18 4 x 2 = 8

4 x 5 = 20 6 x 3 = 18 2 x 4 = 8

3 x7 = 21	7 x3 = 21	2 x9 = 18	9 x2 = 18	8 x4 = 32	4 x8 = 32
5 x2 = 10	2 x5 = 10	6 x3 = 18	3 x6 = 18	5 x6 = 30	6 x5 = 30

296 Crazy Big Book of Third Grade

page 296

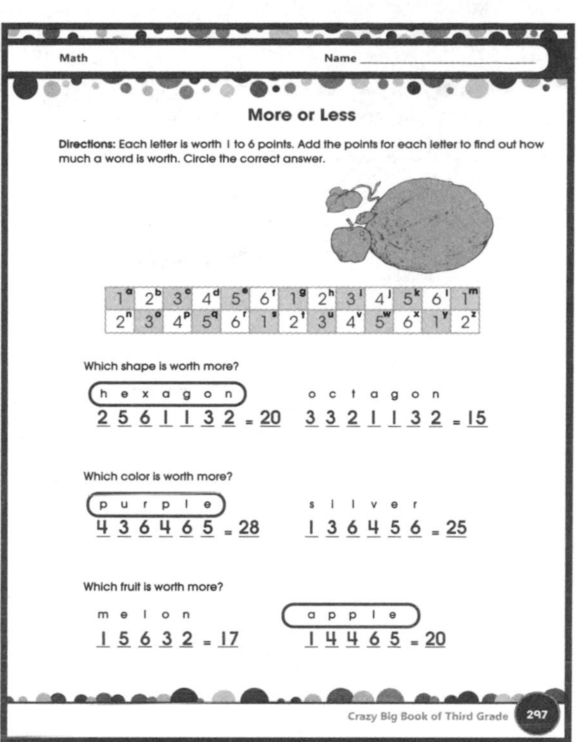

Math Name ____________

More or Less

Directions: Each letter is worth 1 to 6 points. Add the points for each letter to find out how much a word is worth. Circle the correct answer.

a	b	c	d	e	f	g	h	i	j	k	l	m
1	2	3	4	5	6	1	2	3	4	5	6	1
n	**o**	**p**	**q**	**r**	**s**	**t**	**u**	**v**	**w**	**x**	**y**	**z**
2	3	4	5	6	1	2	3	4	5	6	1	2

Which shape is worth more?

(h e x a g o n) 2 5 6 1 1 3 2 = 20 o c t a g o n 3 3 2 1 1 3 2 = 15

Which color is worth more?

(p u r p l e) 4 3 6 4 6 5 = 28 s i l v e r 1 3 6 4 5 6 = 25

Which fruit is worth more?

m e l o n 1 5 6 3 2 = 17 (a p p l e) 1 4 4 6 5 = 20

Crazy Big Book of Third Grade 297

page 297

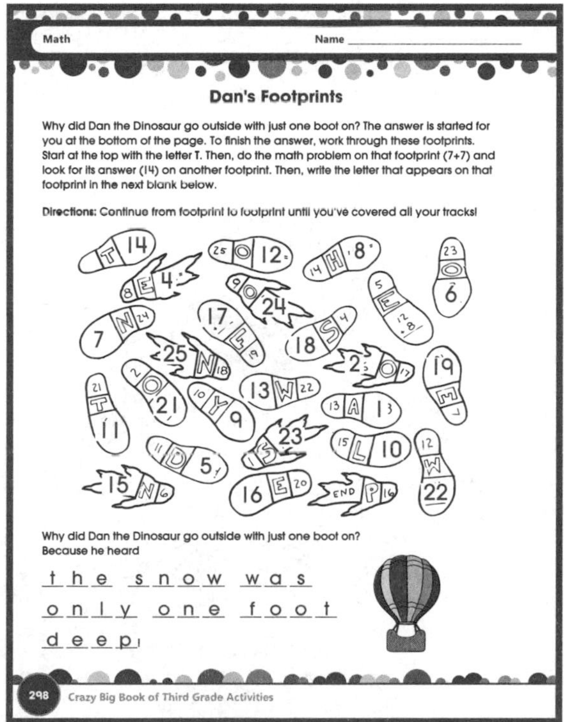

Math Name ____________

Dan's Footprints

Why did Dan the Dinosaur go outside with just one boot on? The answer is started for you at the bottom of the page. To finish the answer, work through these footprints. Start at the top with the letter T. Then, do the math problem on that footprint (7+7) and look for its answer (14) on another footprint. Then, write the letter that appears on that footprint in the next blank below.

Directions: Continue from footprint to footprint until you've covered all your tracks!

Why did Dan the Dinosaur go outside with just one boot on?
Because he heard

the snow was only one foot deep.

298 Crazy Big Book of Third Grade Activities

page 298

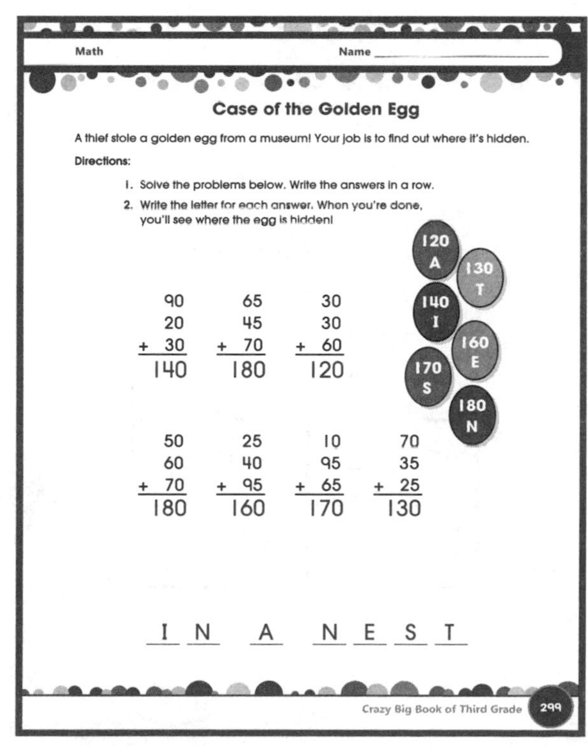

Math Name ____________

Case of the Golden Egg

A thief stole a golden egg from a museum! Your job is to find out where it's hidden.

Directions:

1. Solve the problems below. Write the answers in a row.
2. Write the letter for each answer. When you're done, you'll see where the egg is hidden!

120 A, 130 T, 140 I, 160 E, 170 S, 180 N

90 + 20 + 30 = 140	65 + 45 + 70 = 180	30 + 30 + 60 = 120	
50 + 60 + 70 = 180	25 + 40 + 95 = 160	10 + 95 + 65 = 170	70 + 35 + 25 = 130

I N A N E S T

Crazy Big Book of Third Grade 299

page 299

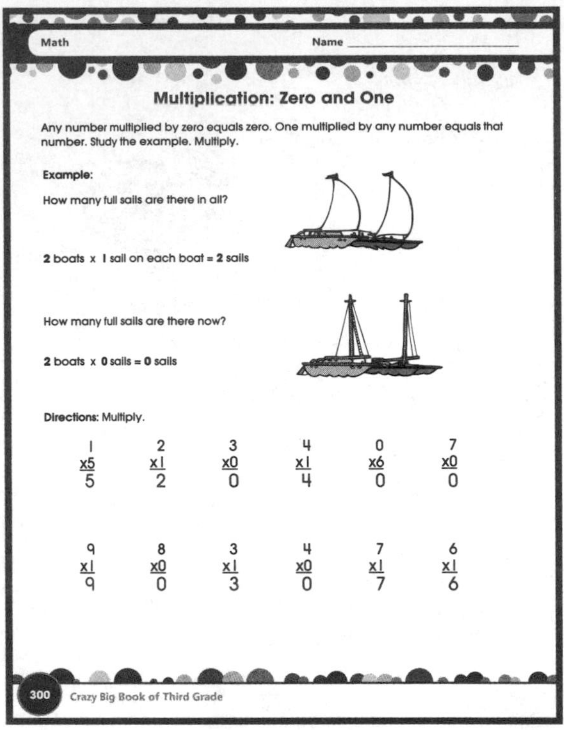
Math Name ____________

Multiplication: Zero and One

Any number multiplied by zero equals zero. One multiplied by any number equals that number. Study the example. Multiply.

Example:

How many full sails are there in all?

2 boats x **1** sail on each boat = **2** sails

How many full sails are there now?

2 boats x **0** sails = **0** sails

Directions: Multiply.

1	2	3	4	0	7
x5	x1	x0	x1	x6	x0
5	2	0	4	0	0

9	8	3	4	7	6
x1	x0	x1	x0	x1	x1
9	0	3	0	7	6

300 Crazy Big Book of Third Grade

page 300

Math Name ____________

Multiplication

Directions: Time yourself as you multiply. How quickly can you complete this page?

3	8	1	1	3	0
x2	x7	x0	x6	x4	x4
6	56	0	6	12	0

4	4	2	9	9	5
x1	x4	x5	x3	x9	x3
4	16	10	27	81	15

0	2	9	8	7	4
x8	x6	x6	x5	x3	x2
0	12	54	40	21	8

3	2	4	1	0	3
x5	x0	x6	x3	x0	x3
15	0	24	3	0	9

Crazy Big Book of Third Grade 301

page 301

Math Name ____________

Sudoku

Directions: Complete the sudoku puzzle. Every row and column must contain the numbers 1, 2, 3, and 4. Do not repeat the same number twice in any row or column.

2	1	4	3
4	3	1	2
1	2	3	4
3	4	2	1

302 Crazy Big Book of Third Grade

page 302

Math Name ____________

At the Seashore

Directions: Annie loves to build this at the beach. Connect the dots from 50 to 170. Color.

Crazy Big Book of Third Grade 303

page 303

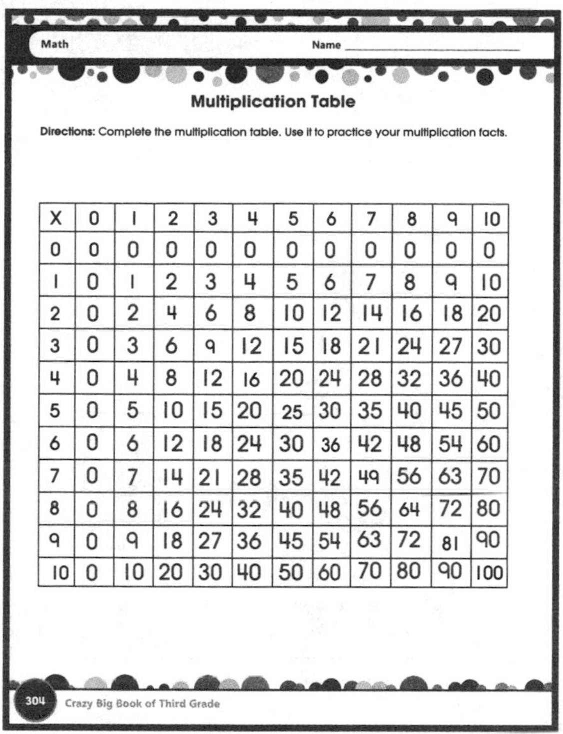

Math Name ____________

Multiplication Table

Directions: Complete the multiplication table. Use it to practice your multiplication facts.

X	0	1	2	3	4	5	6	7	8	9	10
0	0	0	0	0	0	0	0	0	0	0	0
1	0	1	2	3	4	5	6	7	8	9	10
2	0	2	4	6	8	10	12	14	16	18	20
3	0	3	6	9	12	15	18	21	24	27	30
4	0	4	8	12	16	20	24	28	32	36	40
5	0	5	10	15	20	25	30	35	40	45	50
6	0	6	12	18	24	30	36	42	48	54	60
7	0	7	14	21	28	35	42	49	56	63	70
8	0	8	16	24	32	40	48	56	64	72	80
9	0	9	18	27	36	45	54	63	72	81	90
10	0	10	20	30	40	50	60	70	80	90	100

304 Crazy Big Book of Third Grade

page 304

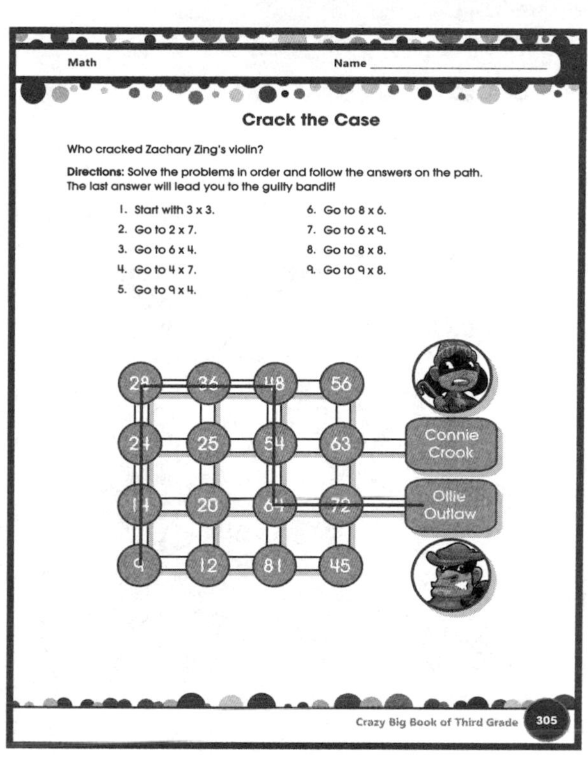

Math Name ____________

Crack the Case

Who cracked Zachary Zing's violin?

Directions: Solve the problems in order and follow the answers on the path. The last answer will lead you to the guilty bandit!

1. Start with 3 x 3.
2. Go to 2 x 7.
3. Go to 6 x 4.
4. Go to 4 x 7.
5. Go to 9 x 4.
6. Go to 8 x 6.
7. Go to 6 x 9.
8. Go to 8 x 8.
9. Go to 9 x 8.

Crazy Big Book of Third Grade 305

page 305

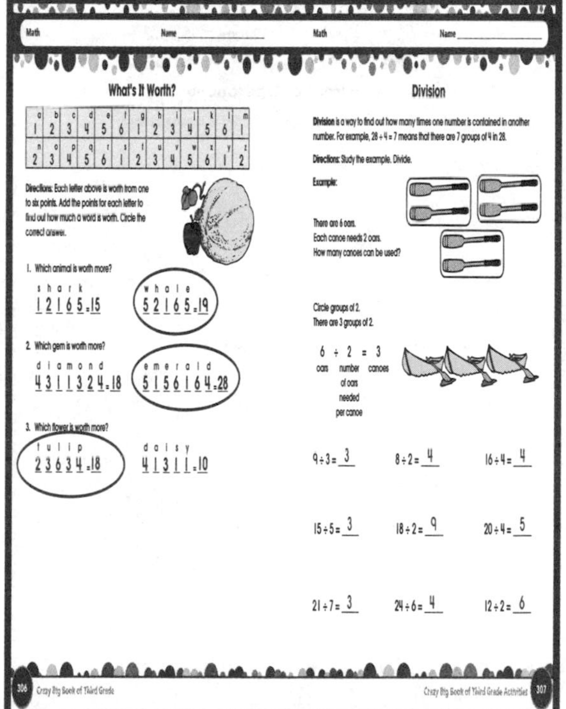

Math Name ____________

What's It Worth?

a	b	c	d	e	f	g	h	i	j	k	l	m
1	2	3	4	5	6	1	2	3	4	5	6	1
n	**o**	**p**	**q**	**r**	**s**	**t**	**u**	**v**	**w**	**x**	**y**	**z**
2	3	4	5	6	1	2	3	4	5	6	1	2

Directions: Each letter above is worth from one to six points. Add the points for each letter to find out how much a word is worth. Circle the correct answer.

1. Which animal is worth more?
   shark 1 2 1 6 5 = 15 — (whale 5 2 1 6 5 = 19)
2. Which gem is worth more?
   diamond 4 3 1 1 3 2 4 = 18 — (emerald 5 1 5 6 1 6 4 = 28)
3. Which flower is worth more?
   (tulip 2 3 6 3 4 = 18) — daisy 4 1 3 1 1 = 10

Math Name ____________

Division

Division is a way to find out how many times one number is contained in another number. For example, 28 ÷ 4 = 7 means that there are 7 groups of 4 in 28.

Directions: Study the example. Divide.

Example:

There are 6 oars.
Each canoe needs 2 oars.
How many canoes can be used?

Circle groups of 2.
There are 3 groups of 2.

6 (oars) ÷ 2 (number of oars needed per canoe) = 3 (canoes)

9 ÷ 3 = 3 8 ÷ 2 = 4 16 ÷ 4 = 4

15 ÷ 5 = 3 18 ÷ 2 = 9 20 ÷ 4 = 5

21 ÷ 7 = 3 24 ÷ 6 = 4 12 ÷ 2 = 6

306 Crazy Big Book of Third Grade   Crazy Big Book of Third Grade Activities 307

page 306

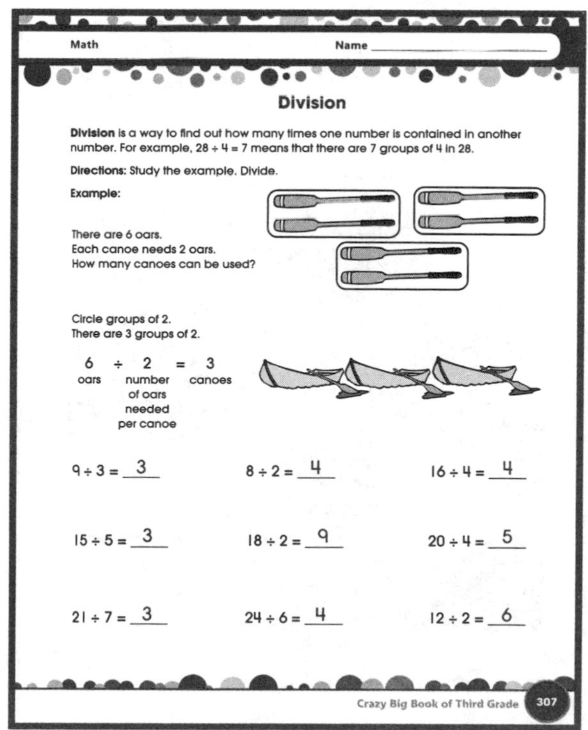

Math Name ____________

Division

Division is a way to find out how many times one number is contained in another number. For example, 28 ÷ 4 = 7 means that there are 7 groups of 4 in 28.

Directions: Study the example. Divide.

Example:

There are 6 oars.
Each canoe needs 2 oars.
How many canoes can be used?

Circle groups of 2.
There are 3 groups of 2.

6 (oars) ÷ 2 (number of oars needed per canoe) = 3 (canoes)

9 ÷ 3 = 3 8 ÷ 2 = 4 16 ÷ 4 = 4

15 ÷ 5 = 3 18 ÷ 2 = 9 20 ÷ 4 = 5

21 ÷ 7 = 3 24 ÷ 6 = 4 12 ÷ 2 = 6

Crazy Big Book of Third Grade 307

page 307

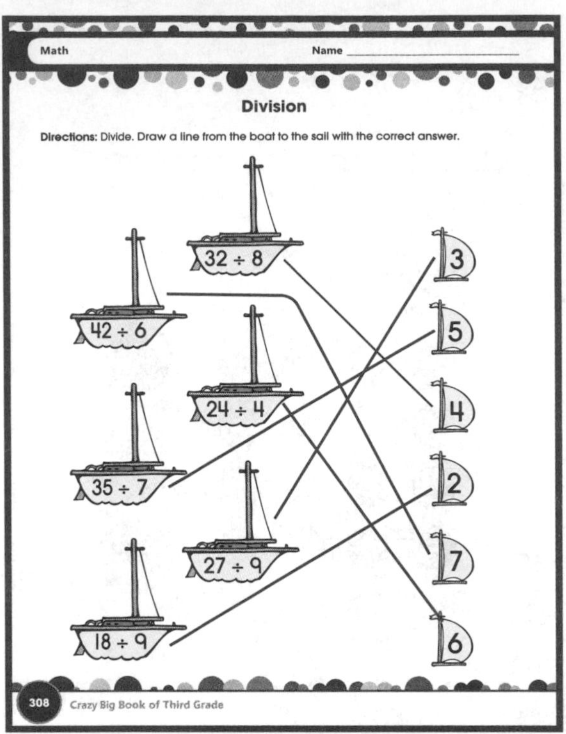
Math Name ______________

Division

Directions: Divide. Draw a line from the boat to the sail with the correct answer.

32 ÷ 8 — 4
42 ÷ 6 — 7
24 ÷ 4 — 6
35 ÷ 7 — 5
27 ÷ 9 — 3
18 ÷ 9 — 2

308 Crazy Big Book of Third Grade

page 308

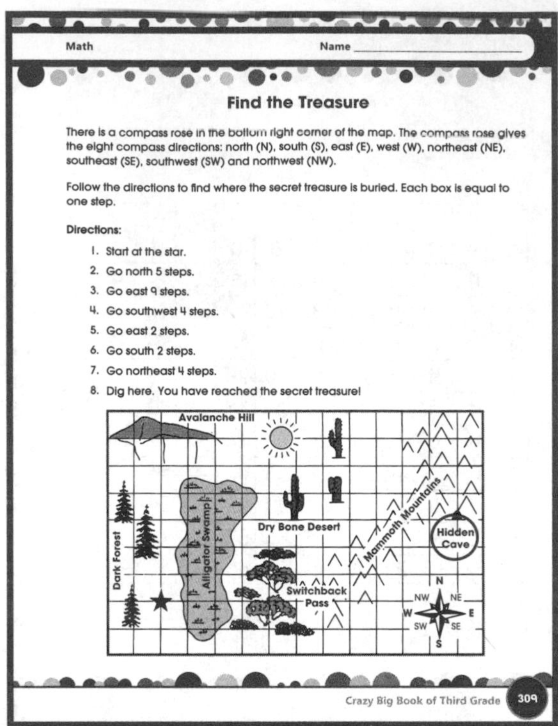
Math Name ______________

Find the Treasure

There is a compass rose in the bottom right corner of the map. The compass rose gives the eight compass directions: north (N), south (S), east (E), west (W), northeast (NE), southeast (SE), southwest (SW) and northwest (NW).

Follow the directions to find where the secret treasure is buried. Each box is equal to one step.

Directions:

1. Start at the star.
2. Go north 5 steps.
3. Go east 9 steps.
4. Go southwest 4 steps.
5. Go east 2 steps.
6. Go south 2 steps.
7. Go northeast 4 steps.
8. Dig here. You have reached the secret treasure!

Crazy Big Book of Third Grade 309

page 309

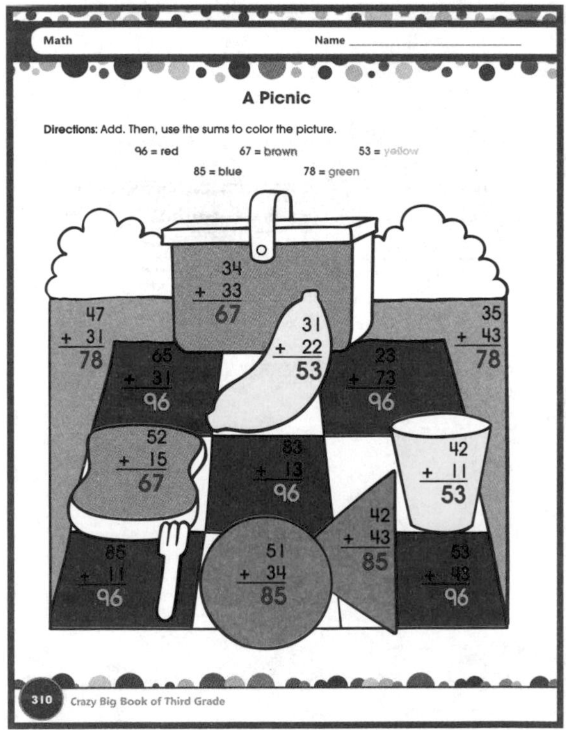
Math Name ______________

A Picnic

Directions: Add. Then, use the sums to color the picture.

96 = red 67 = brown 53 = yellow
85 = blue 78 = green

$34 + 33 = 67$
$47 + 31 = 78$
$31 + 22 = 53$
$35 + 43 = 78$
$65 + 31 = 96$
$23 + 73 = 96$
$52 + 15 = 67$
$83 + 13 = 96$
$42 + 11 = 53$
$42 + 43 = 85$
$85 + 11 = 96$
$51 + 34 = 85$
$53 + 43 = 96$

310 Crazy Big Book of Third Grade

page 310

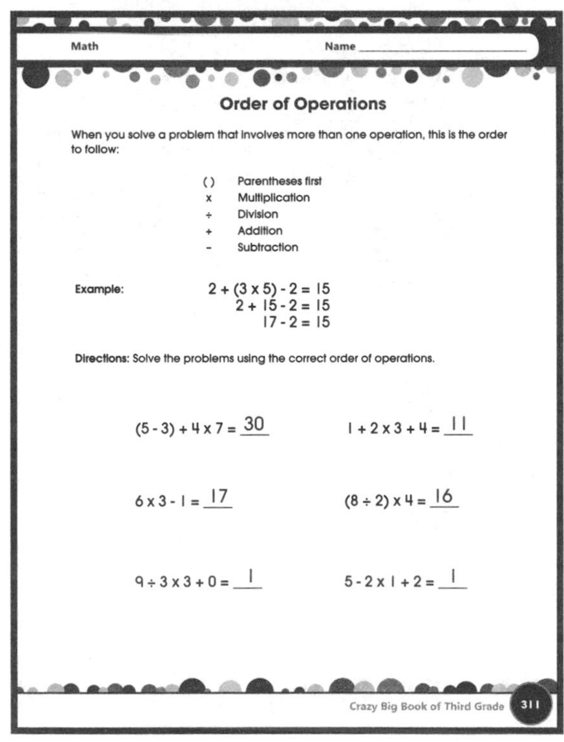
Math Name ______________

Order of Operations

When you solve a problem that involves more than one operation, this is the order to follow:

( ) Parentheses first
x Multiplication
÷ Division
+ Addition
- Subtraction

Example:

$2 + (3 \times 5) - 2 = 15$
$2 + 15 - 2 = 15$
$17 - 2 = 15$

Directions: Solve the problems using the correct order of operations.

$(5 - 3) + 4 \times 7 = $ 30
$1 + 2 \times 3 + 4 = $ 11
$6 \times 3 - 1 = $ 17
$(8 \div 2) \times 4 = $ 16
$9 \div 3 \times 3 + 0 = $ 1
$5 - 2 \times 1 + 2 = $ 1

Crazy Big Book of Third Grade 311

page 311

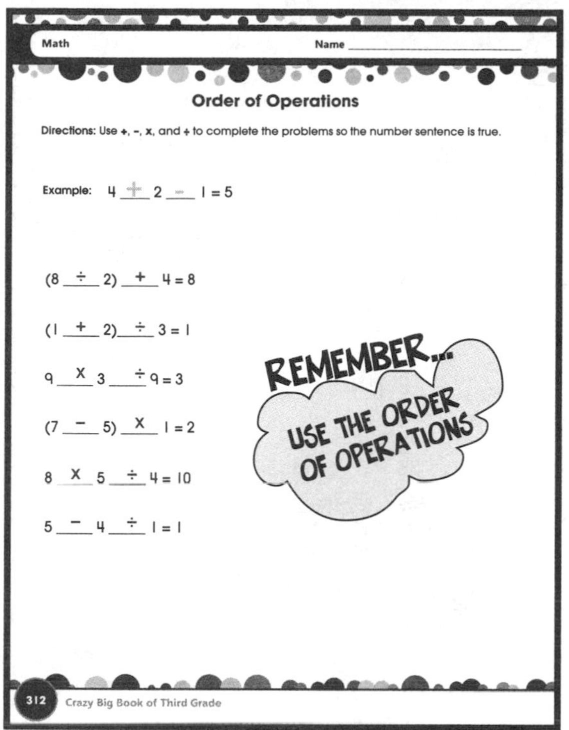

Math Name ____________

Order of Operations

Directions: Use +, −, x, and ÷ to complete the problems so the number sentence is true.

Example: 4 __+__ 2 __−__ 1 = 5

(8 __÷__ 2) __+__ 4 = 8

(1 __+__ 2) __÷__ 3 = 1

9 __x__ 3 __÷__ 9 = 3

(7 __−__ 5) __x__ 1 = 2

8 __x__ 5 __÷__ 4 = 10

5 __−__ 4 __÷__ 1 = 1

REMEMBER...
USE THE ORDER OF OPERATIONS

312 Crazy Big Book of Third Grade

page 312

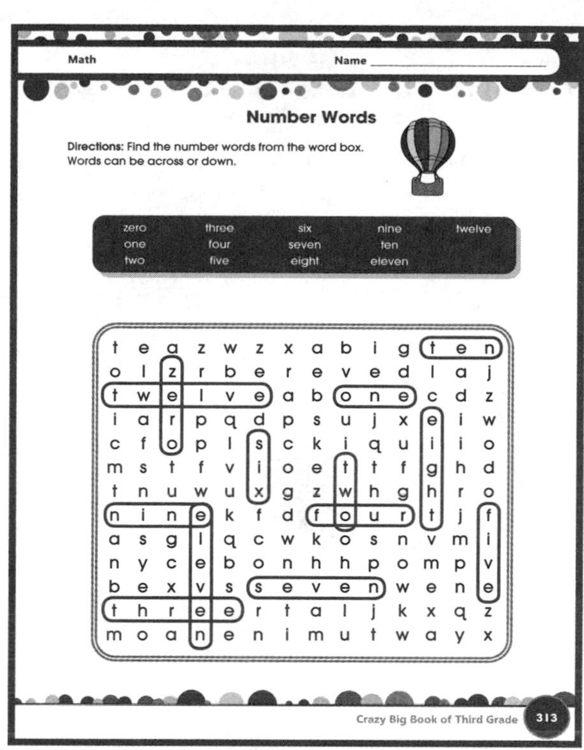

Math Name ____________

Number Words

Directions: Find the number words from the word box. Words can be across or down.

zero	three	six	nine	twelve
one	four	seven	ten	
two	five	eight	eleven	

t	e	a	z	w	z	x	a	b	i	g	t	e	n
o	l	z	r	b	e	r	e	v	e	d	l	a	j
t	w	e	l	v	e	a	b	o	n	e	c	d	z
i	a	r	p	q	d	p	s	u	j	x	e	i	w
c	f	o	p	l	s	c	k	i	q	u	i	i	o
m	s	t	f	v	i	o	e	t	t	f	g	h	d
t	n	u	w	u	x	g	z	w	h	g	h	r	o
n	i	n	e	k	f	d	f	o	u	r	t	j	f
a	s	g	l	q	c	w	k	o	s	n	v	m	i
n	y	c	e	b	o	n	h	h	p	o	m	p	v
b	e	x	v	s	s	e	v	e	n	w	e	n	e
t	h	r	e	e	r	t	a	l	j	k	x	q	z
m	o	a	n	e	n	i	m	u	t	w	a	y	x

Crazy Big Book of Third Grade 313

page 313

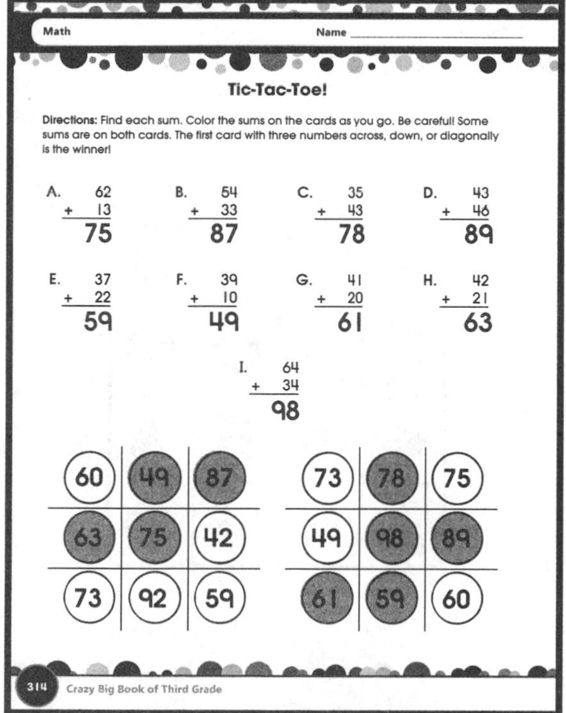

Math Name ____________

Tic-Tac-Toe!

Directions: Find each sum. Color the sums on the cards as you go. Be careful! Some sums are on both cards. The first card with three numbers across, down, or diagonally is the winner!

A. 62 + 13 = 75

B. 54 + 33 = 87

C. 35 + 43 = 78

D. 43 + 46 = 89

E. 37 + 22 = 59

F. 39 + 10 = 49

G. 41 + 20 = 61

H. 42 + 21 = 63

I. 64 + 34 = 98

60	49	87
63	75	42
73	92	59

73	78	75
49	98	89
61	59	60

314 Crazy Big Book of Third Grade

page 314

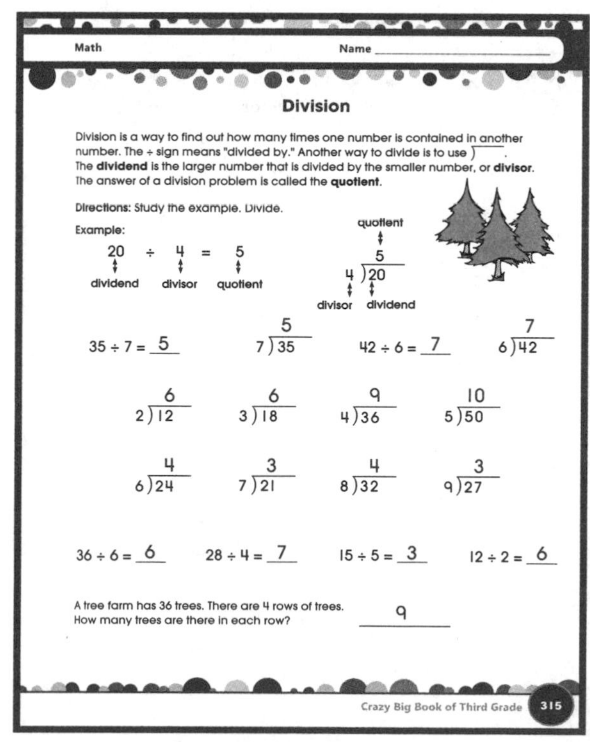

Math Name ____________

Division

Division is a way to find out how many times one number is contained in another number. The ÷ sign means "divided by." Another way to divide is to use $\overline{)\ \ }$. The **dividend** is the larger number that is divided by the smaller number, or **divisor**. The answer of a division problem is called the **quotient**.

Directions: Study the example. Divide.

Example:

20 ÷ 4 = 5 (dividend, divisor, quotient)

$4\overline{)20}$ = 5 (divisor, dividend, quotient)

35 ÷ 7 = __5__ $7\overline{)35}$ = 5 42 ÷ 6 = __7__ $6\overline{)42}$ = 7

$2\overline{)12}$ = 6 $3\overline{)18}$ = 6 $4\overline{)36}$ = 9 $5\overline{)50}$ = 10

$6\overline{)24}$ = 4 $7\overline{)21}$ = 3 $8\overline{)32}$ = 4 $9\overline{)27}$ = 3

36 ÷ 6 = __6__ 28 ÷ 4 = __7__ 15 ÷ 5 = __3__ 12 ÷ 2 = __6__

A tree farm has 36 trees. There are 4 rows of trees. How many trees are there in each row? __9__

Crazy Big Book of Third Grade 315

page 315

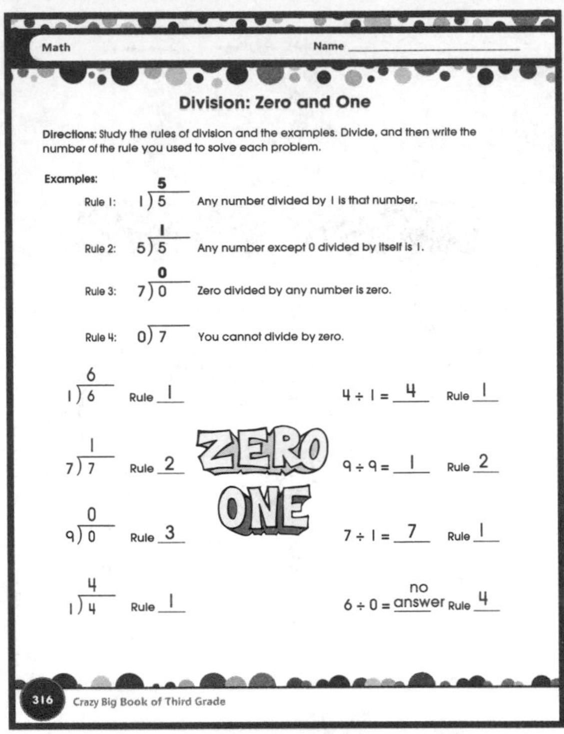

Math Name __________

Division: Zero and One

Directions: Study the rules of division and the examples. Divide, and then write the number of the rule you used to solve each problem.

Examples:

Rule 1: $1\overline{)5}$ = 5 Any number divided by 1 is that number.

Rule 2: $5\overline{)5}$ = 1 Any number except 0 divided by itself is 1.

Rule 3: $7\overline{)0}$ = 0 Zero divided by any number is zero.

Rule 4: $0\overline{)7}$ You cannot divide by zero.

$1\overline{)6}$ = 6 Rule 1

$4 \div 1 =$ 4 Rule 1

$7\overline{)7}$ = 1 Rule 2

$9 \div 9 =$ 1 Rule 2

$9\overline{)0}$ = 0 Rule 3

$7 \div 1 =$ 7 Rule 1

$1\overline{)4}$ = 4 Rule 1

$6 \div 0 =$ no answer Rule 4

316 Crazy Big Book of Third Grade

page 316

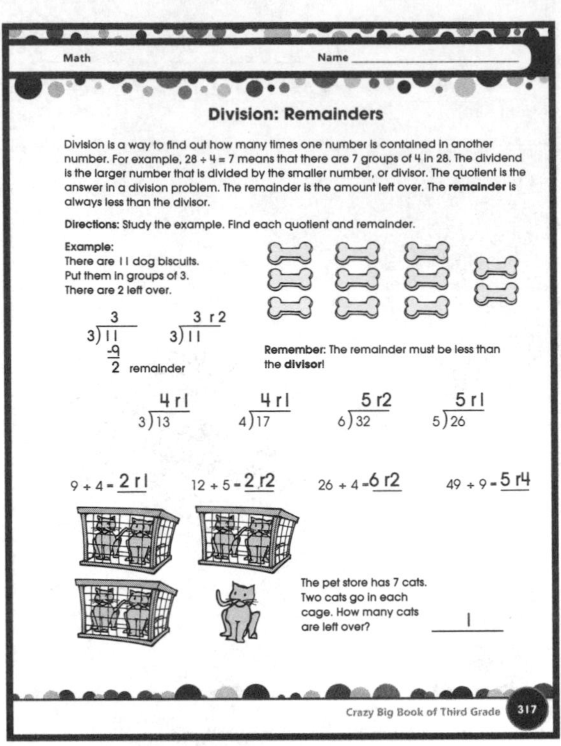

Math Name __________

Division: Remainders

Division is a way to find out how many times one number is contained in another number. For example, $28 \div 4 = 7$ means that there are 7 groups of 4 in 28. The dividend is the larger number that is divided by the smaller number, or divisor. The quotient is the answer in a division problem. The remainder is the amount left over. The **remainder** is always less than the divisor.

Directions: Study the example. Find each quotient and remainder.

Example:
There are 11 dog biscuits.
Put them in groups of 3.
There are 2 left over.

$3\overline{)11}$ = 3, -9, 2 remainder

$3\overline{)11}$ = 3 r2

Remember: The remainder must be less than the **divisor**!

$3\overline{)13}$ = 4 r1

$4\overline{)17}$ = 4 r1

$6\overline{)32}$ = 5 r2

$5\overline{)26}$ = 5 r1

$9 \div 4 =$ 2 r1

$12 \div 5 =$ 2 r2

$26 \div 4 =$ 6 r2

$49 \div 9 =$ 5 r4

The pet store has 7 cats. Two cats go in each cage. How many cats are left over? 1

Crazy Big Book of Third Grade 317

page 317

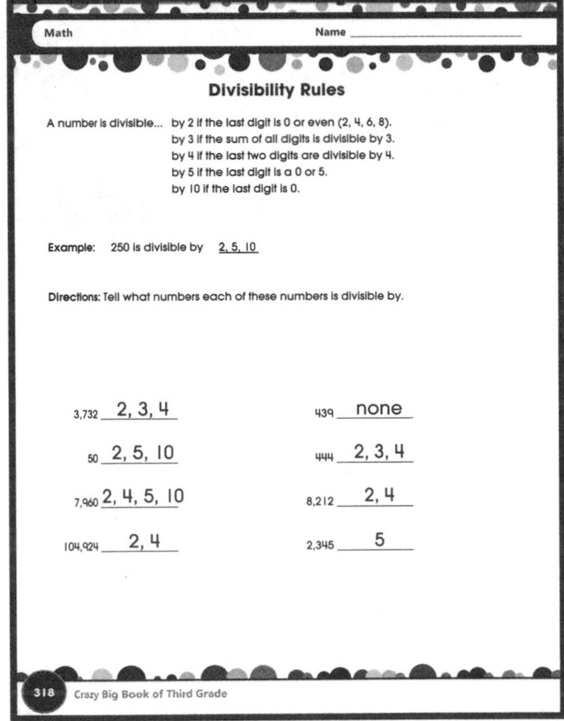

Math Name __________

Divisibility Rules

A number is divisible... by 2 if the last digit is 0 or even (2, 4, 6, 8).
by 3 if the sum of all digits is divisible by 3.
by 4 if the last two digits are divisible by 4.
by 5 if the last digit is a 0 or 5.
by 10 if the last digit is 0.

Example: 250 is divisible by 2, 5, 10

Directions: Tell what numbers each of these numbers is divisible by.

3,732 2, 3, 4

439 none

50 2, 5, 10

444 2, 3, 4

7,960 2, 4, 5, 10

8,212 2, 4

104,924 2, 4

2,345 5

318 Crazy Big Book of Third Grade

page 318

Math Name __________

Shape Sudoku

Directions: Complete the sudoku puzzle. Every row and column must contain a ▲, ▮, ♥, and ●. Do not repeat the same shape twice in any row or column.

●	♥	▲	▮
▮	▲	●	♥
♥	●	▮	▲
▲	▮	♥	●

Crazy Big Book of Third Grade 319

page 319

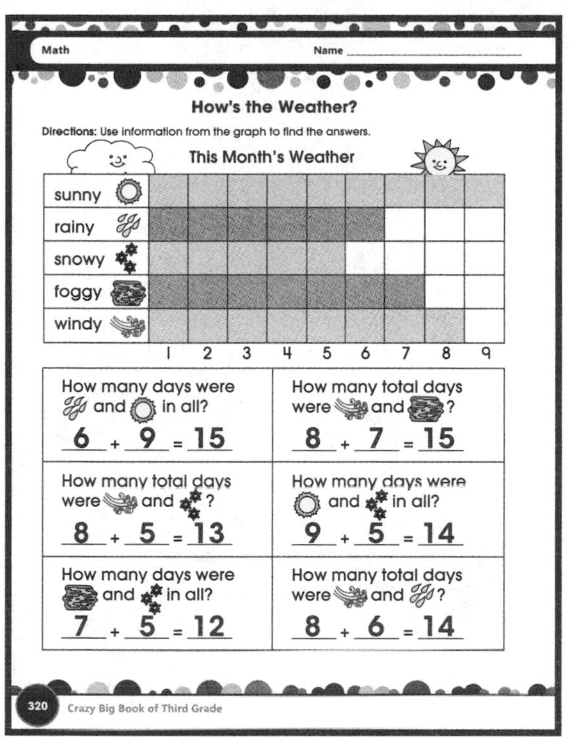
Math Name

How's the Weather?

Directions: Use information from the graph to find the answers.

This Month's Weather

	1	2	3	4	5	6	7	8	9
sunny	■	■	■	■	■	■	■	■	■
rainy	■	■	■	■	■	■			
snowy	■	■	■	■	■				
foggy	■	■	■	■	■	■	■		
windy	■	■	■	■	■	■	■	■	

How many days were rainy and sunny in all? 6 + 9 = 15	How many total days were windy and foggy? 8 + 7 = 15
How many total days were windy and snowy? 8 + 5 = 13	How many days were sunny and snowy in all? 9 + 5 = 14
How many days were foggy and snowy in all? 7 + 5 = 12	How many total days were windy and rainy? 8 + 6 = 14

320 Crazy Big Book of Third Grade

page 320

Math Name

Family Feud

Directions: Who will win? Find each sum working from left to right. Shade the answer on a bingo board. The first family to completely cover their card is the winner!

11 + 24 = 35 | 36 + 33 = 69 | 90 + 8 = 98

25 + 51 = 76 | 87 + 12 = 99 | 36 + 3 = 39

29 + 50 = 79 | 28 + 21 = 49 | 80 + 11 = 91

36 + 11 = 47 | 55 + 31 = 86 | 16 + 13 = 29

62 + 35 = 97 | 43 + 31 = 74 | 41 + 15 = 56

Crazy Big Book of Third Grade 321

page 321

Math Name

What's Missing?

Directions: Fill in the missing numbers to make the problems work.

33 + 62 = 95 | 24 + 42 = 66 | 52 + 24 = 76

31 + 52 = 83 | 63 + 14 = 77 | 53 + 46 = 99

23 + 73 = 96 | 53 + 25 = 78 | 85 + 12 = 97

10 + 48 = 58 | 13 + 62 = 75 | 54 + 35 = 89

322 Crazy Big Book of Third Grade

page 322

Math Name

Factor Trees

Factors are the smaller numbers multiplied together to make a larger number. Factor trees are one way to find all the factors of a number.

Directions: Fill in each blank to complete the factor trees below.

Example: 24 → 6 x 4 → 2 x 3 x 2 x 2

36 → 6 x 6 → 3 x 2 x 3 x 2

40 → 8 x 5 → 4 x 2 x 5 → 2 x 2 x 2 x 5

12 → 3 x 4 → 3 x 2 x 2

81 → 9 x 9 → 3 x 3 x 3 x 3

Crazy Big Book of Third Grade 323

page 323

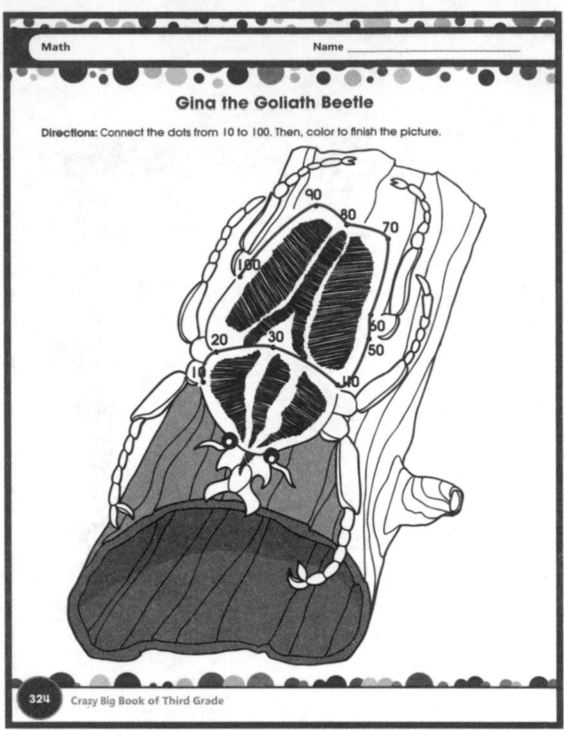
Math Name ____________

Gina the Goliath Beetle

Directions: Connect the dots from 10 to 100. Then, color to finish the picture.

324 Crazy Big Book of Third Grade

page 324

Math Name ____________

Go Bananas!

Directions: Write <, >, or = on each tree trunk. Color the banana with the greater number yellow. Color the banana with the lesser number green.

< less than > greater than = equal to

Crazy Big Book of Third Grade 325

page 325

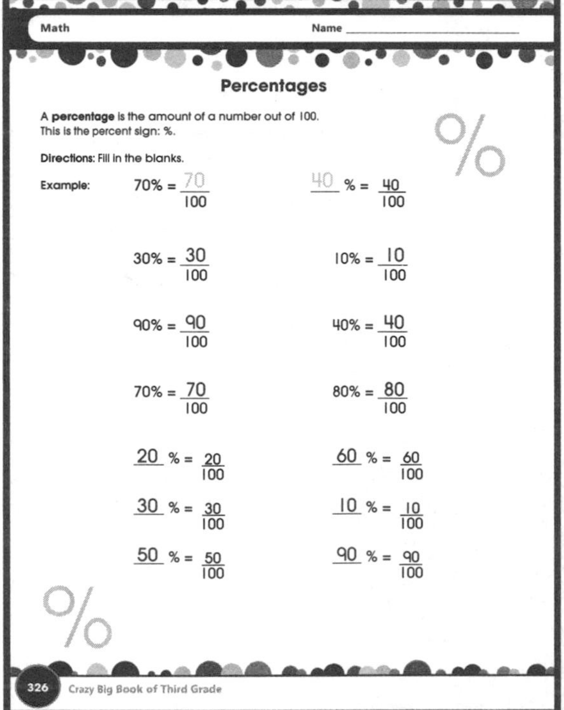
Math Name ____________

Percentages

A **percentage** is the amount of a number out of 100.
This is the percent sign: %.

Directions: Fill in the blanks.

Example: 70% = $\frac{70}{100}$

40 % = $\frac{40}{100}$

30% = $\frac{30}{100}$

10% = $\frac{10}{100}$

90% = $\frac{90}{100}$

40% = $\frac{40}{100}$

70% = $\frac{70}{100}$

80% = $\frac{80}{100}$

20 % = $\frac{20}{100}$

60 % = $\frac{60}{100}$

30 % = $\frac{30}{100}$

10 % = $\frac{10}{100}$

50 % = $\frac{50}{100}$

90 % = $\frac{90}{100}$

326 Crazy Big Book of Third Grade

page 326

Math Name ____________

Park Here, Please

Directions: In each parking lot, the sum of each row and column should be the same. Park the cars shown to match the sum on the flag.

Crazy Big Book of Third Grade 327

page 327

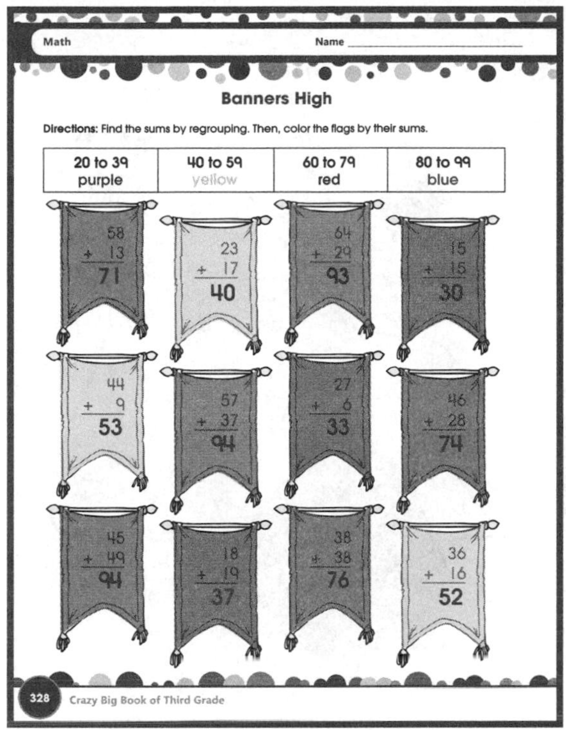
Math Name

Banners High

Directions: Find the sums by regrouping. Then, color the flags by their sums.

20 to 39 purple	40 to 59 yellow	60 to 79 red	80 to 99 blue

58 + 13 = 71; 23 + 17 = 40; 64 + 29 = 93; 15 + 15 = 30

44 + 9 = 53; 57 + 37 = 94; 27 + 6 = 33; 46 + 28 = 74

45 + 49 = 94; 18 + 19 = 37; 38 + 38 = 76; 36 + 16 = 52

328 Crazy Big Book of Third Grade

page 328

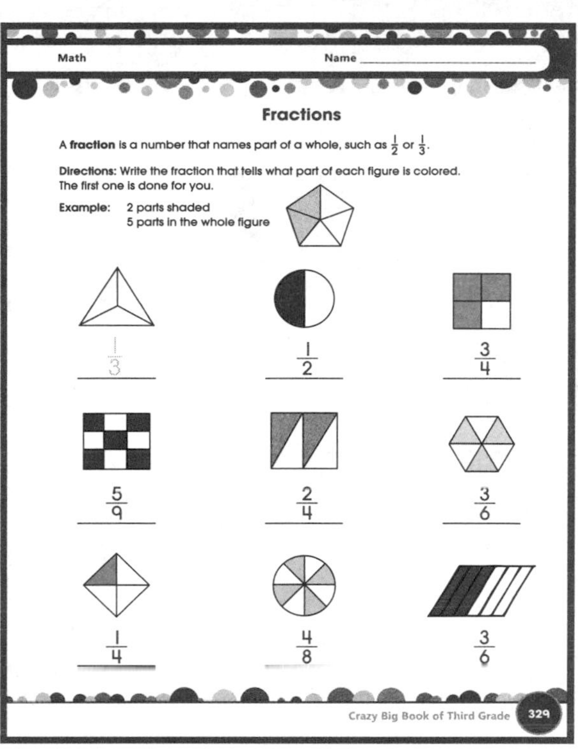
Math Name

Fractions

A **fraction** is a number that names part of a whole, such as $\frac{1}{2}$ or $\frac{1}{3}$.

Directions: Write the fraction that tells what part of each figure is colored. The first one is done for you.

Example: 2 parts shaded
5 parts in the whole figure

$\frac{1}{3}$ $\frac{1}{2}$ $\frac{3}{4}$

$\frac{5}{9}$ $\frac{2}{4}$ $\frac{3}{6}$

$\frac{1}{4}$ $\frac{4}{8}$ $\frac{3}{6}$

Crazy Big Book of Third Grade 329

page 329

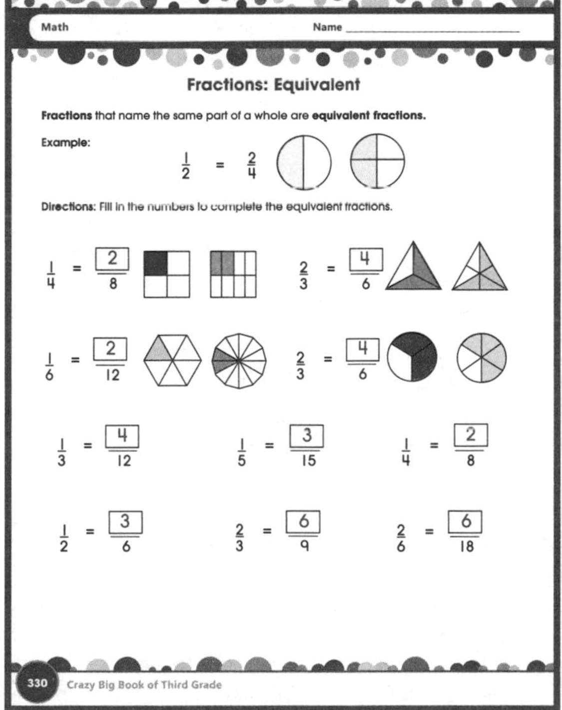
Math Name

Fractions: Equivalent

Fractions that name the same part of a whole are **equivalent fractions.**

Example: $\frac{1}{2} = \frac{2}{4}$

Directions: Fill in the numbers to complete the equivalent fractions.

$\frac{1}{4} = \frac{2}{8}$ $\frac{2}{3} = \frac{4}{6}$

$\frac{1}{6} = \frac{2}{12}$ $\frac{2}{3} = \frac{4}{6}$

$\frac{1}{3} = \frac{4}{12}$ $\frac{1}{5} = \frac{3}{15}$ $\frac{1}{4} = \frac{2}{8}$

$\frac{1}{2} = \frac{3}{6}$ $\frac{2}{3} = \frac{6}{9}$ $\frac{2}{6} = \frac{6}{18}$

330 Crazy Big Book of Third Grade

page 330

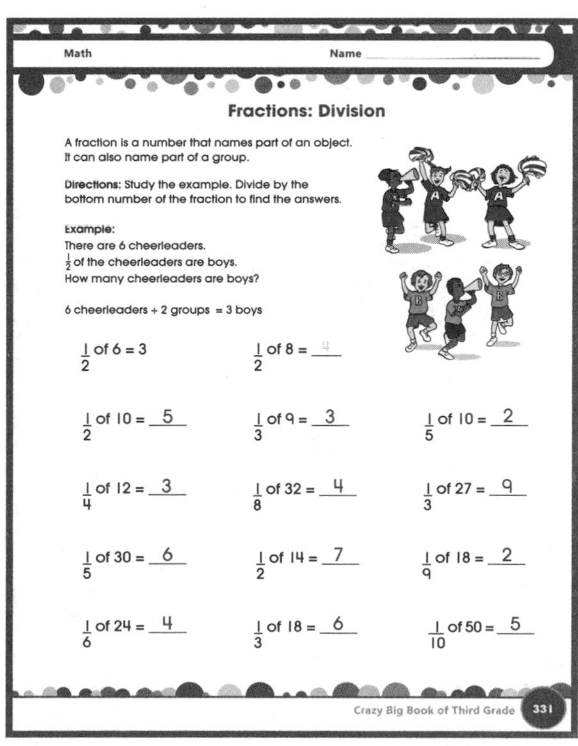
Math Name

Fractions: Division

A fraction is a number that names part of an object. It can also name part of a group.

Directions: Study the example. Divide by the bottom number of the fraction to find the answers.

Example:
There are 6 cheerleaders.
$\frac{1}{2}$ of the cheerleaders are boys.
How many cheerleaders are boys?

6 cheerleaders ÷ 2 groups = 3 boys

$\frac{1}{2}$ of 6 = 3 $\frac{1}{2}$ of 8 = 4

$\frac{1}{2}$ of 10 = 5 $\frac{1}{3}$ of 9 = 3 $\frac{1}{5}$ of 10 = 2

$\frac{1}{4}$ of 12 = 3 $\frac{1}{8}$ of 32 = 4 $\frac{1}{3}$ of 27 = 9

$\frac{1}{5}$ of 30 = 6 $\frac{1}{2}$ of 14 = 7 $\frac{1}{9}$ of 18 = 2

$\frac{1}{6}$ of 24 = 4 $\frac{1}{3}$ of 18 = 6 $\frac{1}{10}$ of 50 = 5

Crazy Big Book of Third Grade 331

page 331

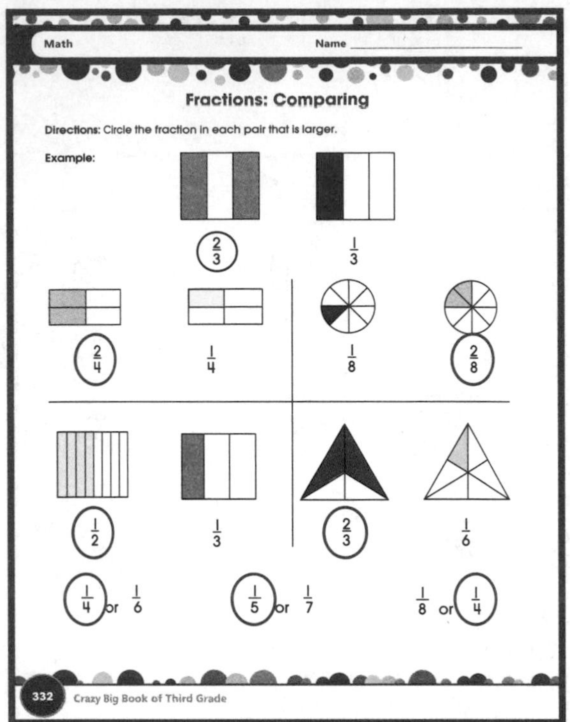
Math Name

Fractions: Comparing

Directions: Circle the fraction in each pair that is larger.

Example: (2/3) 1/3

(2/4) 1/4 | 1/8 (2/8)

(1/2) 1/3 | (2/3) 1/6

(1/4) or 1/6 | (1/5) or 1/7 | 1/8 or (1/4)

page 332

Math Name

Lift Off!

Directions: Subtract.

86 − 43 = 43
75 − 31 = 44
86 − 30 = 56
68 − 32 = 36
95 − 13 = 82
54 − 42 = 12
76 − 31 = 45
91 − 40 = 51
66 − 10 = 56
94 − 52 = 42
79 − 56 = 23
68 − 46 = 22
37 − 21 = 16

page 333

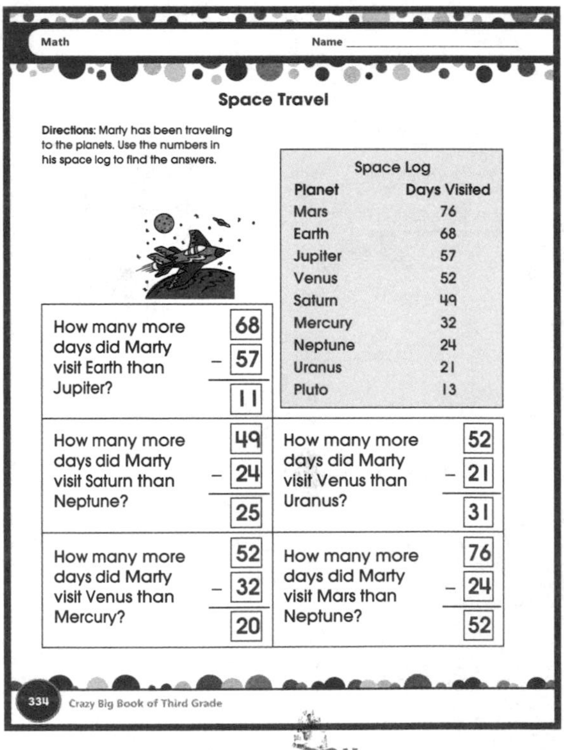
Math Name

Space Travel

Directions: Marty has been traveling to the planets. Use the numbers in his space log to find the answers.

Space Log

Planet	Days Visited
Mars	76
Earth	68
Jupiter	57
Venus	52
Saturn	49
Mercury	32
Neptune	24
Uranus	21
Pluto	13

How many more days did Marty visit Earth than Jupiter? 68 − 57 = 11

How many more days did Marty visit Saturn than Neptune? 49 − 24 = 25

How many more days did Marty visit Venus than Uranus? 52 − 21 = 31

How many more days did Marty visit Venus than Mercury? 52 − 32 = 20

How many more days did Marty visit Mars than Neptune? 76 − 24 = 52

page 334

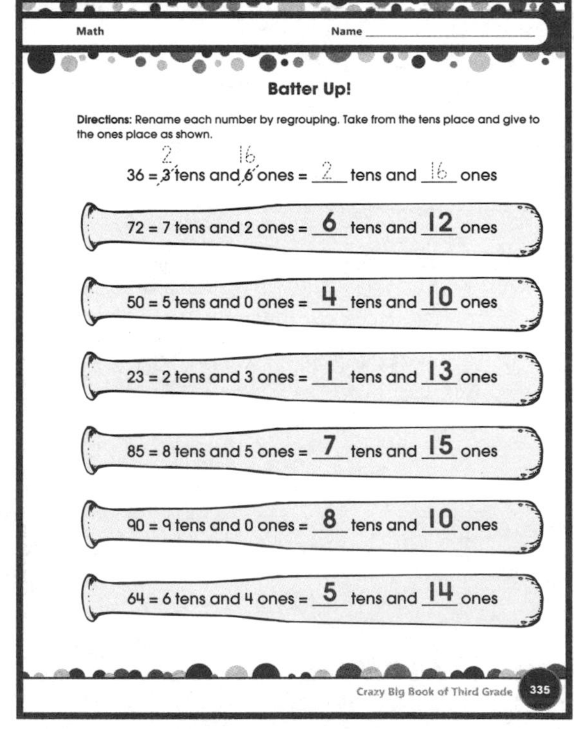
Math Name

Batter Up!

Directions: Rename each number by regrouping. Take from the tens place and give to the ones place as shown.

36 = 3 tens and 6 ones = 2 tens and 16 ones

72 = 7 tens and 2 ones = 6 tens and 12 ones

50 = 5 tens and 0 ones = 4 tens and 10 ones

23 = 2 tens and 3 ones = 1 tens and 13 ones

85 = 8 tens and 5 ones = 7 tens and 15 ones

90 = 9 tens and 0 ones = 8 tens and 10 ones

64 = 6 tens and 4 ones = 5 tens and 14 ones

page 335

Math Name ____________

Uh-Oh!

Directions: Answer each problem by regrouping. Use the differences to answer the riddle.

Why didn't the mountain climber yell for help?

HE WAS HANGING BY HIS TEETH!

H 35, E 28 W 9, A 67, S 63
H 35, A 67, N 25, G 46, I 52, N 25, G 46
B 17, Y 74 H 35, I 52, S 63
T 19, E 28, E 28, T 19, H 35!

G	T	R	W	E
62 − 16 = 46	48 − 29 = 19	83 − 34 = 49	91 − 82 = 9	56 − 28 = 28
A	**D**	**H**	**Y**	**I**
74 − 7 = 67	57 − 19 = 38	64 − 29 = 35	92 − 18 = 74	81 − 29 = 52
B	**S**	**F**	**N**	**C**
36 − 19 = 17	71 − 8 = 63	54 − 49 = 5	43 − 18 = 25	87 − 48 = 39

336 Crazy Big Book of Third Grade

page 336

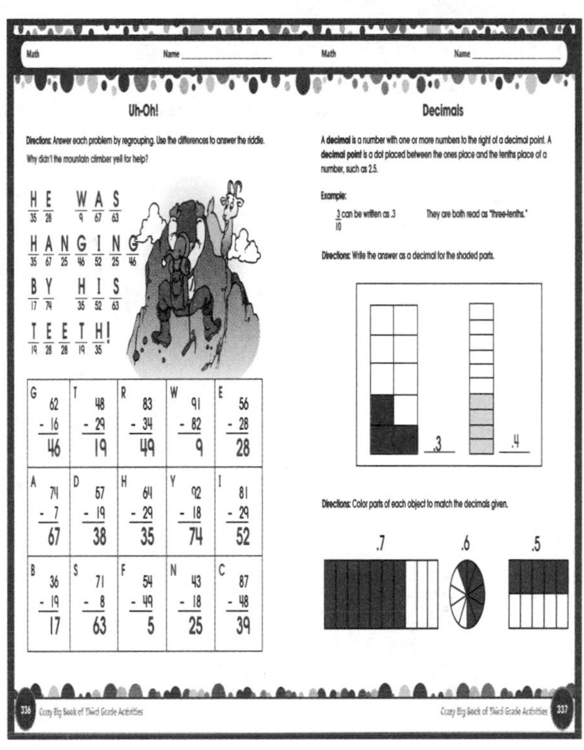
Math Name ____________ Math Name ____________

Uh-Oh!

Directions: Answer each problem by regrouping. Use the differences to answer the riddle.

Why didn't the mountain climber yell for help?

HE WAS HANGING BY HIS TEETH!

G	T	R	W	E
62 − 16 = 46	48 − 29 = 19	83 − 34 = 49	91 − 82 = 9	56 − 28 = 28
A	**D**	**H**	**Y**	**I**
74 − 7 = 67	57 − 19 = 38	64 − 29 = 35	92 − 18 = 74	81 − 29 = 52
B	**S**	**F**	**N**	**C**
36 − 19 = 17	71 − 8 = 63	54 − 49 = 5	43 − 18 = 25	87 − 48 = 39

Decimals

A **decimal** is a number with one or more numbers to the right of a decimal point. A **decimal point** is a dot placed between the ones place and the tenths place of a number, such as 2.5.

Example:

$\frac{3}{10}$ can be written as .3 They are both read as "three-tenths."

Directions: Write the answer as a decimal for the shaded parts.

.3 .4

Directions: Color parts of each object to match the decimals given.

.7 .6 .5

336 Crazy Big Book of Third Grade Activities Crazy Big Book of Third Grade Activities 337

page 337

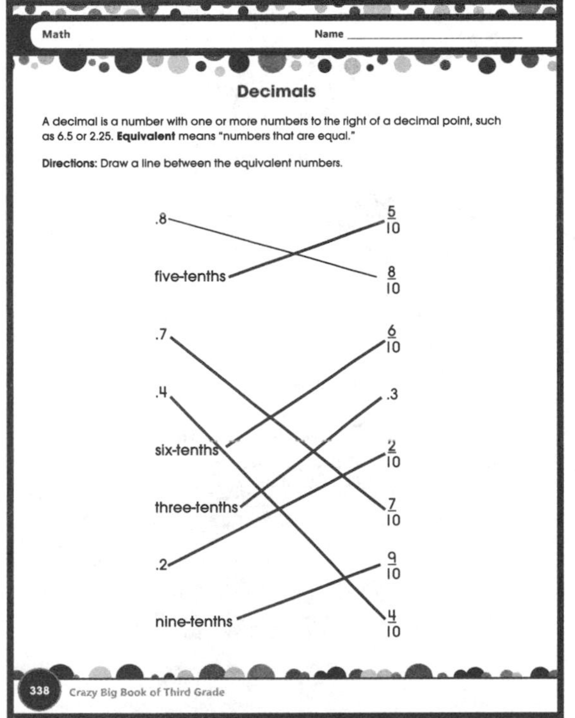
Math Name ____________

Decimals

A decimal is a number with one or more numbers to the right of a decimal point, such as 6.5 or 2.25. **Equivalent** means "numbers that are equal."

Directions: Draw a line between the equivalent numbers.

.8 — $\frac{8}{10}$
five-tenths — $\frac{5}{10}$
.7 — $\frac{7}{10}$
.4 — $\frac{4}{10}$
six-tenths — $\frac{6}{10}$
three-tenths — .3
.2 — $\frac{2}{10}$
nine-tenths — $\frac{9}{10}$

338 Crazy Big Book of Third Grade

page 338

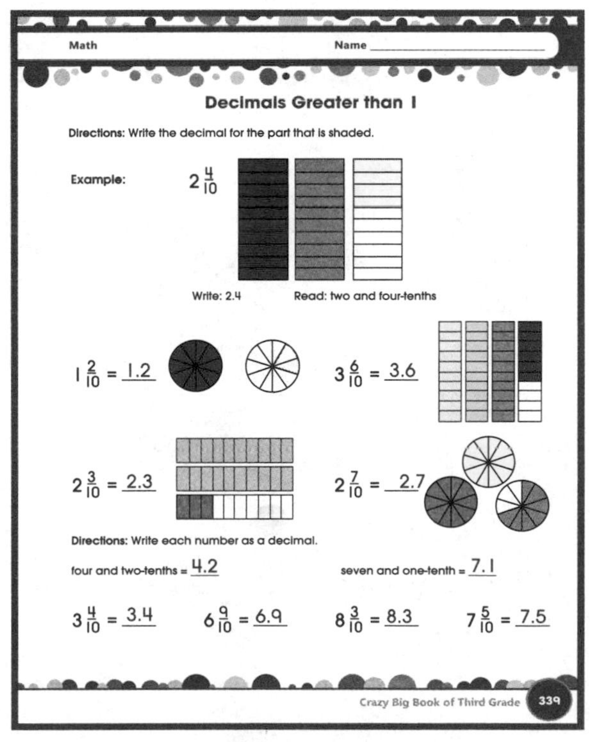
Math Name ____________

Decimals Greater than 1

Directions: Write the decimal for the part that is shaded.

Example: $2\frac{4}{10}$

Write: 2.4 Read: two and four-tenths

$1\frac{2}{10}$ = 1.2 $3\frac{6}{10}$ = 3.6

$2\frac{3}{10}$ = 2.3 $2\frac{7}{10}$ = 2.7

Directions: Write each number as a decimal.

four and two-tenths = 4.2 seven and one-tenth = 7.1

$3\frac{4}{10}$ = 3.4 $6\frac{9}{10}$ = 6.9 $8\frac{3}{10}$ = 8.3 $7\frac{5}{10}$ = 7.5

Crazy Big Book of Third Grade 339

page 339

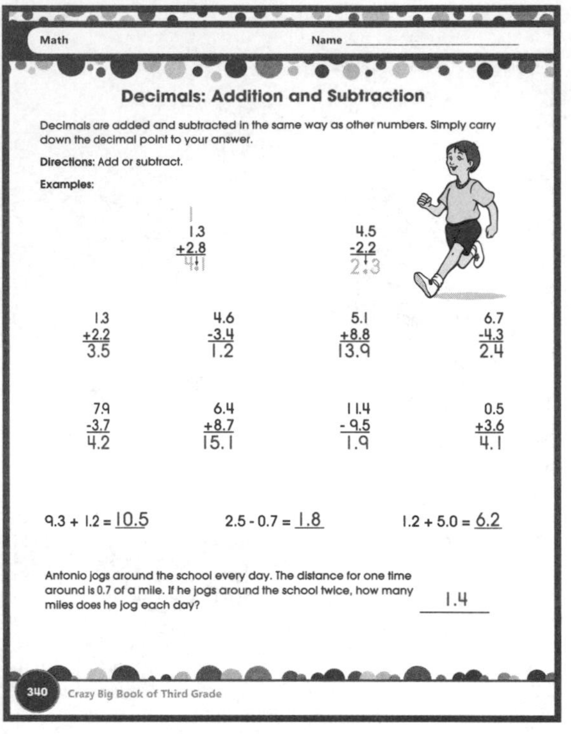

Math Name ______

Decimals: Addition and Subtraction

Decimals are added and subtracted in the same way as other numbers. Simply carry down the decimal point to your answer.

Directions: Add or subtract.

Examples:

1.3 + 2.8 = 4.1   4.5 − 2.2 = 2.3

1.3 + 2.2 = 3.5   4.6 − 3.4 = 1.2   5.1 + 8.8 = 13.9   6.7 − 4.3 = 2.4

7.9 − 3.7 = 4.2   6.4 + 8.7 = 15.1   11.4 − 9.5 = 1.9   0.5 + 3.6 = 4.1

9.3 + 1.2 = 10.5   2.5 - 0.7 = 1.8   1.2 + 5.0 = 6.2

Antonio jogs around the school every day. The distance for one time around is 0.7 of a mile. If he jogs around the school twice, how many miles does he jog each day? 1.4

340 Crazy Big Book of Third Grade

page 340

Math Name ______

Tic-Tac-Travel

Directions: Find each sum. Write X or O over the answers in the suitcase. The winner must get 3 spaces in a row or diagonally.

A. 7 + 8 = 15 = X   B. 6 + 4 = 10 = O   C. 3 + 3 = 6 = X   D. 5 + 4 = 9 = O

E. 3 + 2 = 5 = X   F. 6 + 7 = 13 = O   G. 8 + 6 = 14 = X   H. 6 + 6 = 12 = O

I. 7 + 4 = 11 = X

O 10	X 15	O 13	7
2	X 6	X 14	O 12
X 5	O 9	8	X 11

Crazy Big Book of Third Grade 341

page 341

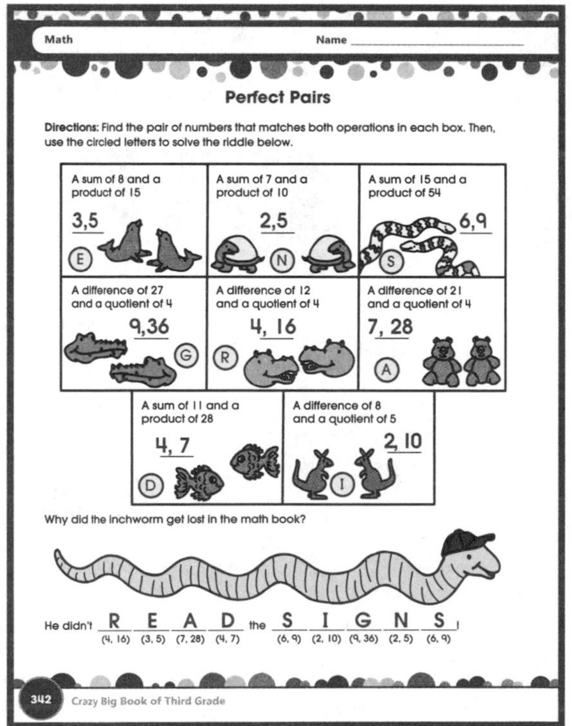

Math Name ______

Perfect Pairs

Directions: Find the pair of numbers that matches both operations in each box. Then, use the circled letters to solve the riddle below.

A sum of 8 and a product of 15	A sum of 7 and a product of 10	A sum of 15 and a product of 54
3,5 (E)	2,5 (N)	6,9 (S)
A difference of 27 and a quotient of 4	A difference of 12 and a quotient of 4	A difference of 21 and a quotient of 4
9,36 (G)	4, 16 (R)	7, 28 (A)
A sum of 11 and a product of 28	A difference of 8 and a quotient of 5	
4, 7 (D)	2, 10 (I)	

Why did the inchworm get lost in the math book?

He didn't R E A D the S I G N S.
(4, 16) (3, 5) (7, 28) (4, 7) (6, 9) (2, 10) (9, 36) (2, 5) (6, 9)

342 Crazy Big Book of Third Grade

page 342

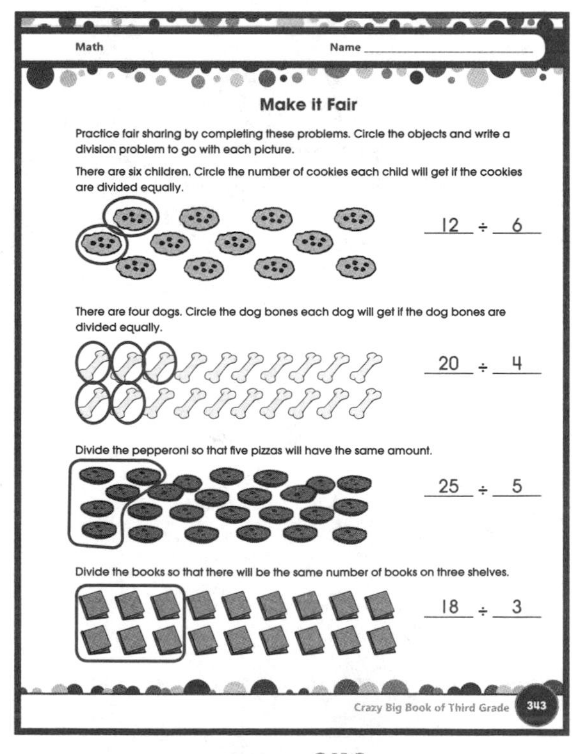

Math Name ______

Make it Fair

Practice fair sharing by completing these problems. Circle the objects and write a division problem to go with each picture.

There are six children. Circle the number of cookies each child will get if the cookies are divided equally. 12 ÷ 6

There are four dogs. Circle the dog bones each dog will get if the dog bones are divided equally. 20 ÷ 4

Divide the pepperoni so that five pizzas will have the same amount. 25 ÷ 5

Divide the books so that there will be the same number of books on three shelves. 18 ÷ 3

Crazy Big Book of Third Grade 343

page 343

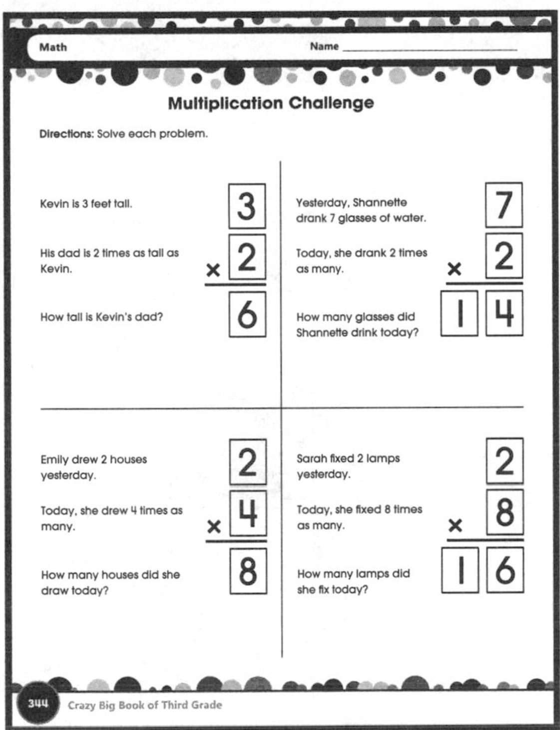
Math Name ____________

Multiplication Challenge

Directions: Solve each problem.

Kevin is 3 feet tall. His dad is 2 times as tall as Kevin. How tall is Kevin's dad? 3 × 2 = 6

Yesterday, Shannette drank 7 glasses of water. Today, she drank 2 times as many. How many glasses did Shannette drink today? 7 × 2 = 14

Emily drew 2 houses yesterday. Today, she drew 4 times as many. How many houses did she draw today? 2 × 4 = 8

Sarah fixed 2 lamps yesterday. Today, she fixed 8 times as many. How many lamps did she fix today? 2 × 8 = 16

344 Crazy Big Book of Third Grade

page 344

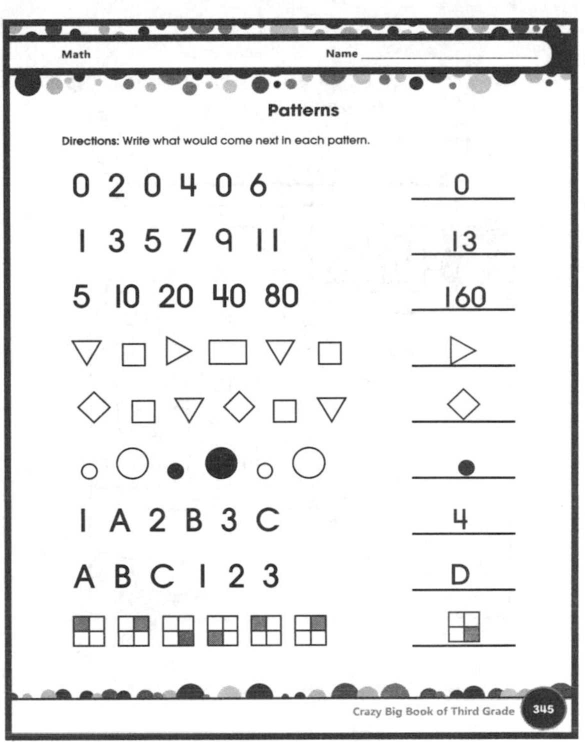
Math Name ____________

Patterns

Directions: Write what would come next in each pattern.

Pattern	Next
0 2 0 4 0 6	0
1 3 5 7 9 11	13
5 10 20 40 80	160
▽ □ ▷ ▭ ▽ □	▷
◇ □ ▽ ◇ □ ▽	◇
○ ◯ ● ⬤ ○ ◯	●
1 A 2 B 3 C	4
A B C 1 2 3	D

Crazy Big Book of Third Grade 345

page 345

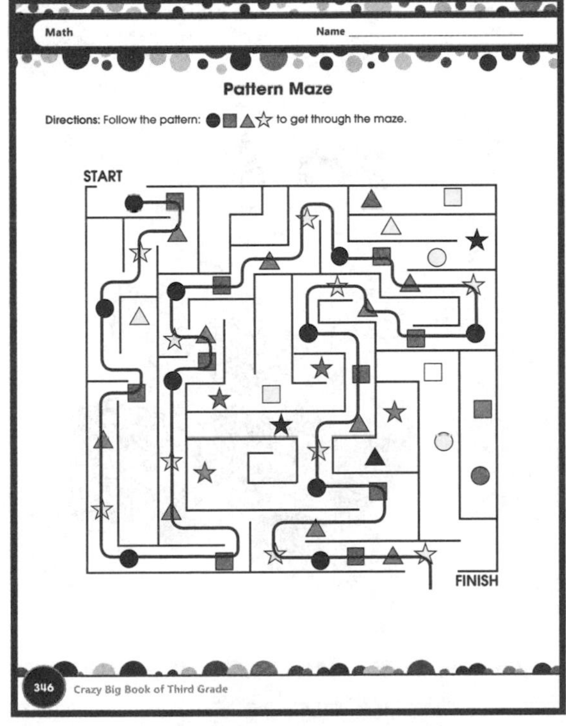
Math Name ____________

Pattern Maze

Directions: Follow the pattern: ●■▲☆ to get through the maze.

346 Crazy Big Book of Third Grade

page 346

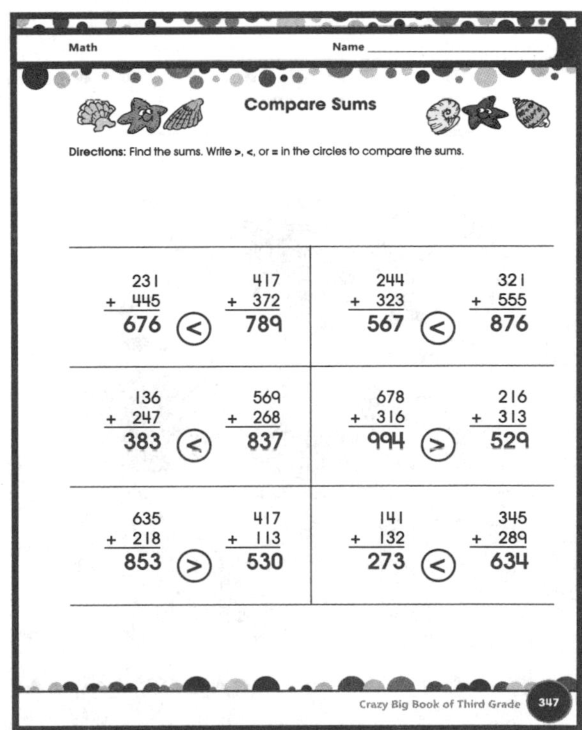
Math Name ____________

Compare Sums

Directions: Find the sums. Write >, <, or = in the circles to compare the sums.

231 + 445 = 676	<	417 + 372 = 789
244 + 323 = 567	<	321 + 555 = 876
136 + 247 = 383	<	569 + 268 = 837
678 + 316 = 994	>	216 + 313 = 529
635 + 218 = 853	>	417 + 113 = 530
141 + 132 = 273	<	345 + 289 = 634

Crazy Big Book of Third Grade 347

page 347

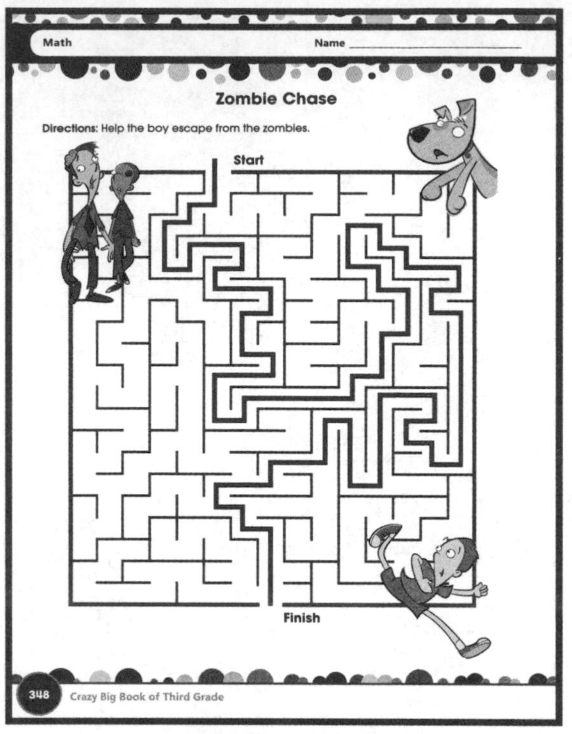
Math Name ____________

Zombie Chase

Directions: Help the boy escape from the zombies.

page 348

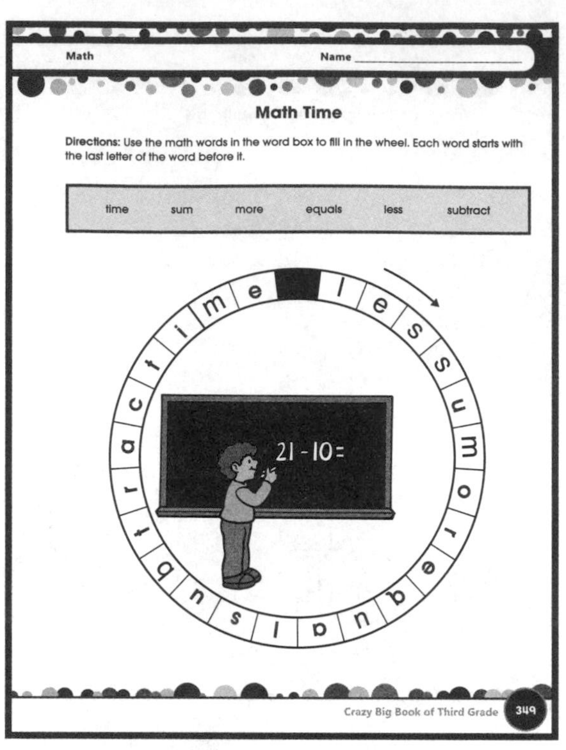
Math Name ____________

Math Time

Directions: Use the math words in the word box to fill in the wheel. Each word starts with the last letter of the word before it.

time	sum	more	equals	less	subtract

page 349

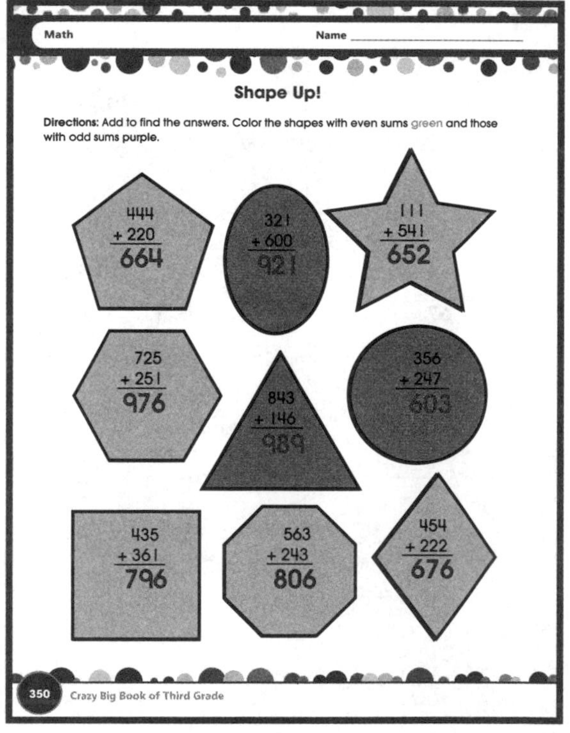
Math Name ____________

Shape Up!

Directions: Add to find the answers. Color the shapes with even sums green and those with odd sums purple.

page 350

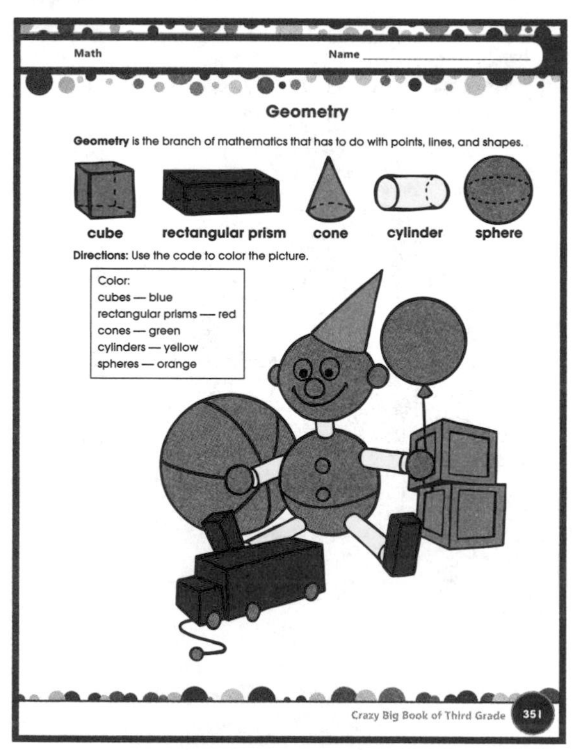
Math Name ____________

Geometry

Geometry is the branch of mathematics that has to do with points, lines, and shapes.

Directions: Use the code to color the picture.

Color:
cubes — blue
rectangular prisms — red
cones — green
cylinders — yellow
spheres — orange

page 351

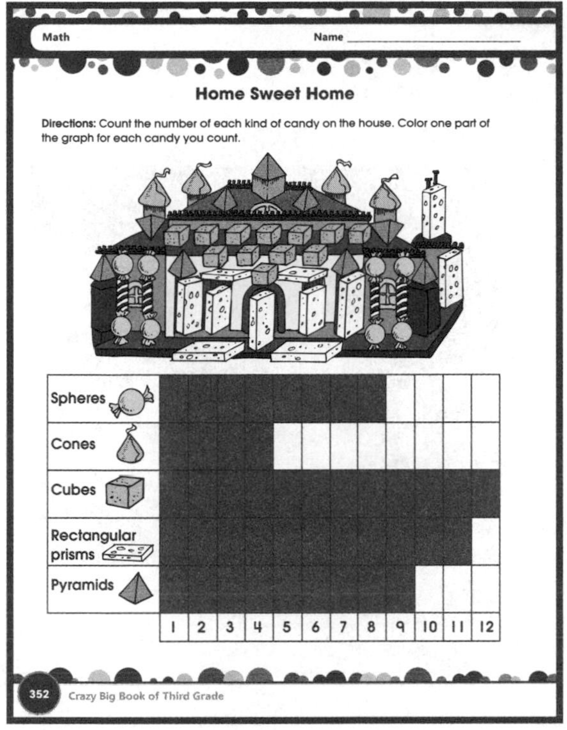
Math Name ____________

Home Sweet Home

Directions: Count the number of each kind of candy on the house. Color one part of the graph for each candy you count.

352 Crazy Big Book of Third Grade

page 352

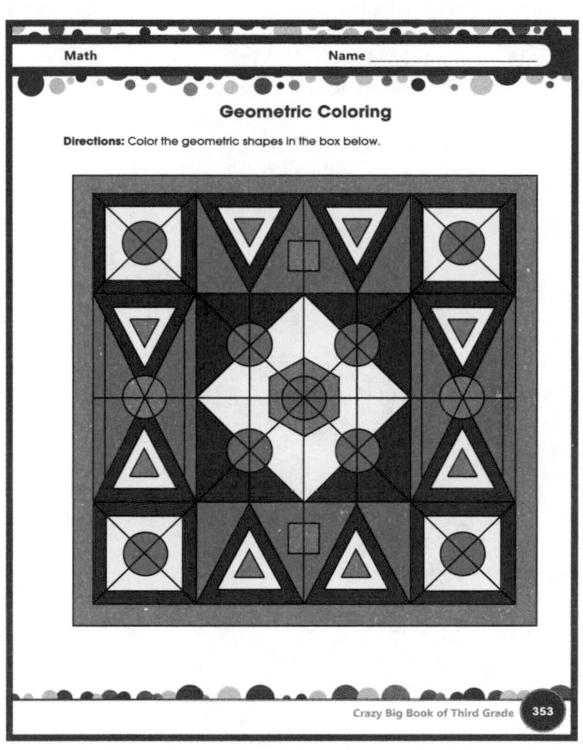
Math Name ____________

Geometric Coloring

Directions: Color the geometric shapes in the box below.

Crazy Big Book of Third Grade 353

page 353

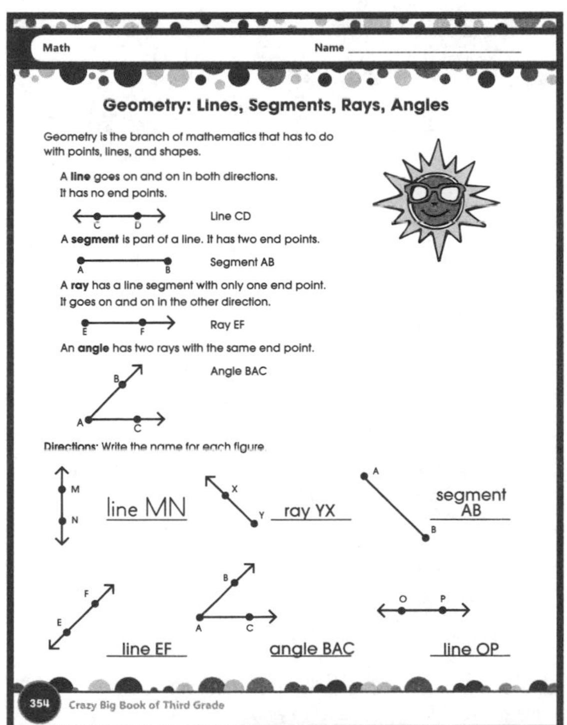
Math Name ____________

Geometry: Lines, Segments, Rays, Angles

Geometry is the branch of mathematics that has to do with points, lines, and shapes.

A **line** goes on and on in both directions. It has no end points.

Line CD

A **segment** is part of a line. It has two end points.

Segment AB

A **ray** has a line segment with only one end point. It goes on and on in the other direction.

Ray EF

An **angle** has two rays with the same end point.

Angle BAC

Directions: Write the name for each figure.

line MN — ray YX — segment AB

line EF — angle BAC — line OP

354 Crazy Big Book of Third Grade

page 354

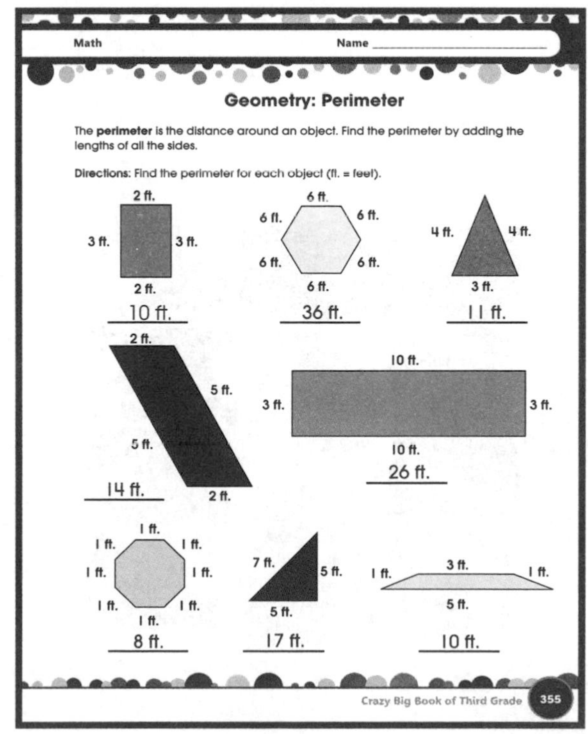
Math Name ____________

Geometry: Perimeter

The **perimeter** is the distance around an object. Find the perimeter by adding the lengths of all the sides.

Directions: Find the perimeter for each object (ft. = feet).

10 ft. — 36 ft. — 11 ft.

14 ft. — 26 ft.

8 ft. — 17 ft. — 10 ft.

Crazy Big Book of Third Grade 355

page 355

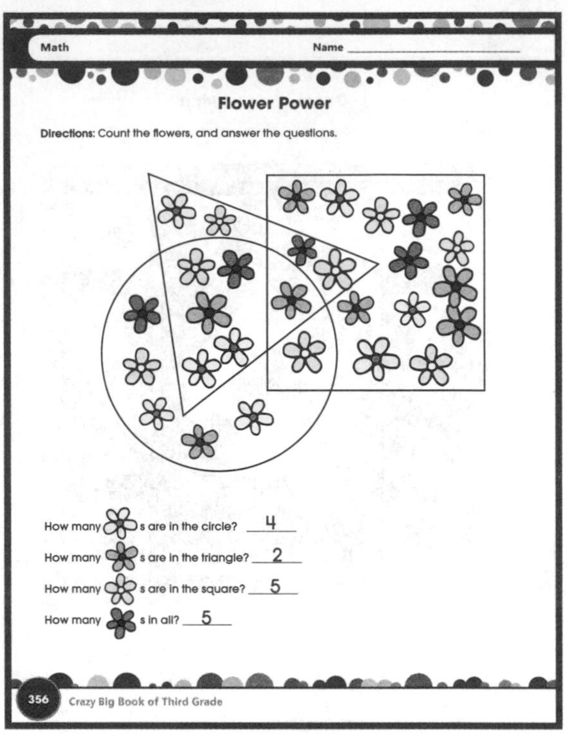
Math Name ______

Flower Power

Directions: Count the flowers, and answer the questions.

How many (flower)s are in the circle? 4

How many (flower)s are in the triangle? 2

How many (flower)s are in the square? 5

How many (flower)s in all? 5

356 Crazy Big Book of Third Grade

page 356

Math Name ______

Find the Mystery Number

Directions: Color the spaces with words that name shapes or colors **red**. Color the spaces with words that name numbers **purple**.

The mystery number is 4.

Crazy Big Book of Third Grade 357

page 357

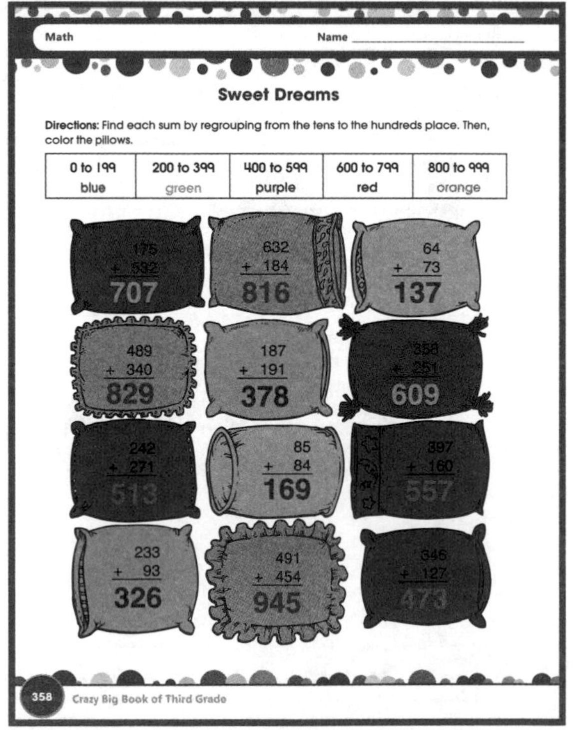
Math Name ______

Sweet Dreams

Directions: Find each sum by regrouping from the tens to the hundreds place. Then, color the pillows.

0 to 199	200 to 399	400 to 599	600 to 799	800 to 999
blue	green	purple	red	orange

175 + 532 = 707

632 + 184 = 816

64 + 73 = 137

489 + 340 = 829

187 + 191 = 378

358 + 251 = 609

242 + 271 = 513

85 + 84 = 169

397 + 160 = 557

233 + 93 = 326

491 + 454 = 945

346 + 127 = 473

358 Crazy Big Book of Third Grade

page 358

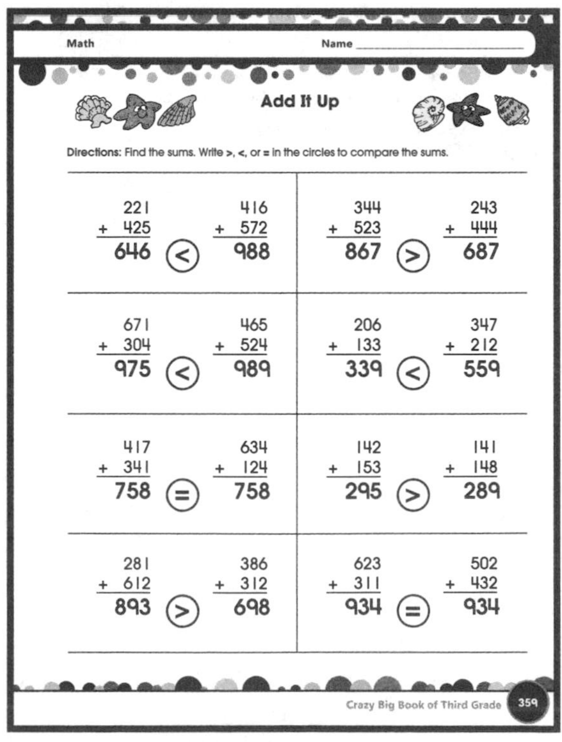
Math Name ______

Add It Up

Directions: Find the sums. Write >, <, or = in the circles to compare the sums.

221 + 425 = 646 < 416 + 572 = 988

344 + 523 = 867 > 243 + 444 = 687

671 + 304 = 975 < 465 + 524 = 989

206 + 133 = 339 < 347 + 212 = 559

417 + 341 = 758 = 634 + 124 = 758

142 + 153 = 295 > 141 + 148 = 289

281 + 612 = 893 > 386 + 312 = 698

623 + 311 = 934 = 502 + 432 = 934

Crazy Big Book of Third Grade 359

page 359

Math Name ____________

Let's Go!

Directions: Add to find each sum. Be sure to regroup from the ones to the tens place. Then, find and circle the sums hidden in the puzzle.

345 + 429	374 + 206	175 + 416	517 + 406	632 + 328
774	580	591	923	960

446 + 129	385 + 107	705 + 205	618 + 345	617 + 177
575	492	910	963	794

4	0	5	1	5	8	2	5	5
9	7	9	2	3	1	9	6	9
2	9	7	6	4	6	3	4	1
2	6	1	0	3	7	7	4	7
8	3	5	7	5	9	9	3	0
5	2	8	4	0	2	4	8	9
9	6	0	1	3	4	9	1	0

360 Crazy Big Book of Third Grade

page 360

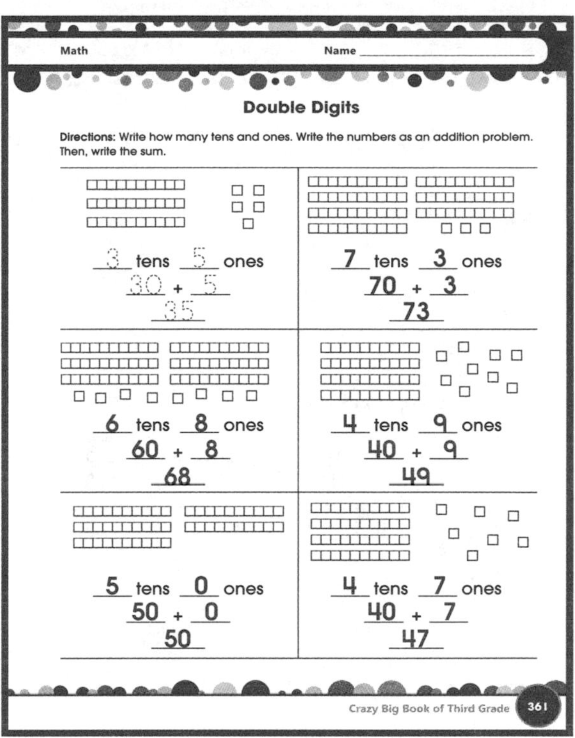

Math Name ____________

Double Digits

Directions: Write how many tens and ones. Write the numbers as an addition problem. Then, write the sum.

3 tens 5 ones
30 + 5
35

7 tens 3 ones
70 + 3
73

6 tens 8 ones
60 + 8
68

4 tens 9 ones
40 + 9
49

5 tens 0 ones
50 + 0
50

4 tens 7 ones
40 + 7
47

Crazy Big Book of Third Grade 361

page 361

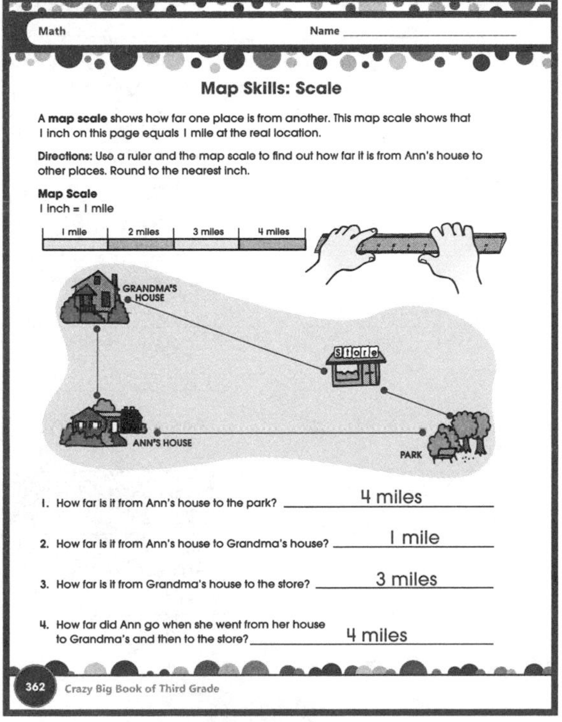

Math Name ____________

Map Skills: Scale

A **map scale** shows how far one place is from another. This map scale shows that 1 inch on this page equals 1 mile at the real location.

Directions: Use a ruler and the map scale to find out how far it is from Ann's house to other places. Round to the nearest inch.

Map Scale
1 inch = 1 mile

1. How far is it from Ann's house to the park? 4 miles
2. How far is it from Ann's house to Grandma's house? 1 mile
3. How far is it from Grandma's house to the store? 3 miles
4. How far did Ann go when she went from her house to Grandma's and then to the store? 4 miles

362 Crazy Big Book of Third Grade

page 362

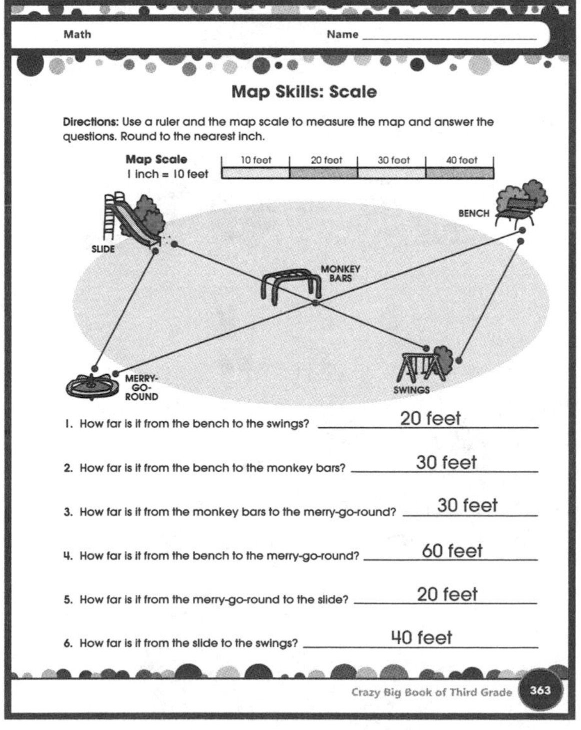

Math Name ____________

Map Skills: Scale

Directions: Use a ruler and the map scale to measure the map and answer the questions. Round to the nearest inch.

Map Scale
1 inch = 10 feet

1. How far is it from the bench to the swings? 20 feet
2. How far is it from the bench to the monkey bars? 30 feet
3. How far is it from the monkey bars to the merry-go-round? 30 feet
4. How far is it from the bench to the merry-go-round? 60 feet
5. How far is it from the merry-go-round to the slide? 20 feet
6. How far is it from the slide to the swings? 40 feet

Crazy Big Book of Third Grade 363

page 363

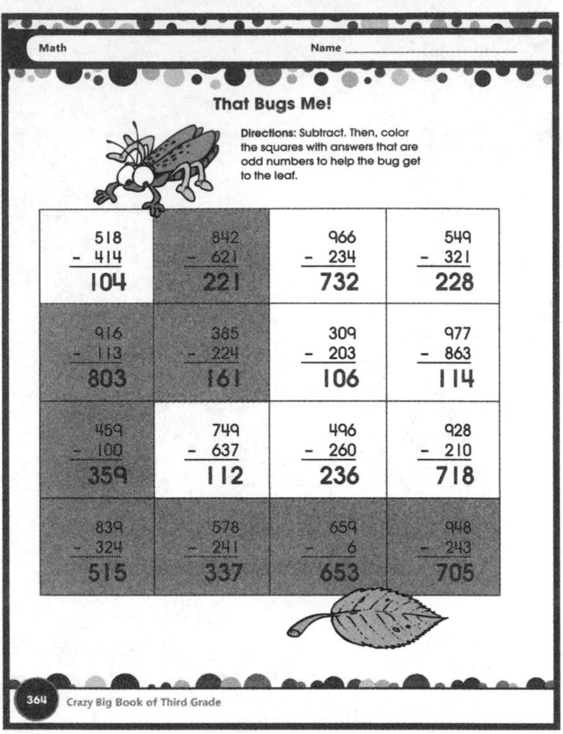

Math Name ____________

That Bugs Me!

Directions: Subtract. Then, color the squares with answers that are odd numbers to help the bug get to the leaf.

518 − 414 = 104	842 − 621 = 221	966 − 234 = 732	549 − 321 = 228
916 − 113 = 803	385 − 224 = 161	309 − 203 = 106	977 − 863 = 114
459 − 100 = 359	749 − 637 = 112	496 − 260 = 236	928 − 210 = 718
839 − 324 = 515	578 − 241 = 337	659 − 6 = 653	948 − 243 = 705

364 Crazy Big Book of Third Grade

page 364

Math Name ____________

That's Puzzling

Directions: Find each difference. Be sure to regroup from the hundreds place to the tens place. Use the answers to complete the puzzle.

Across

1. 328 − 184 = 144
3. 735 − 451 = 284
4. 945 − 193 = 752
6. 589 − 293 = 296
8. 483 − 382 = 101
9. 668 − 182 = 486
10. 903 − 81 = 822

Down

2. 612 − 190 = 422
5. 807 − 215 = 592
7. 959 − 269 = 690
8. 349 − 181 = 168

Crazy Big Book of Third Grade 365

page 365

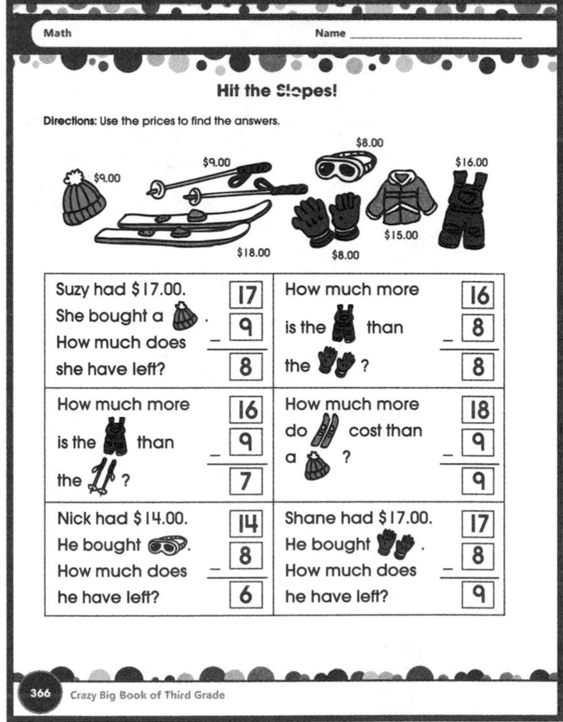

Math Name ____________

Hit the Slopes!

Directions: Use the prices to find the answers.

Suzy had $17.00. She bought a [hat]. How much does she have left? 17 − 9 = 8	How much more is the [snow pants] than the [gloves]? 16 − 8 = 8
How much more is the [snow pants] than the [poles]? 16 − 9 = 7	How much more do [skis] cost than a [hat]? 18 − 9 = 9
Nick had $14.00. He bought [goggles]. How much does he have left? 14 − 8 = 6	Shane had $17.00. He bought [gloves]. How much does he have left? 17 − 8 = 9

366 Crazy Big Book of Third Grade

page 366

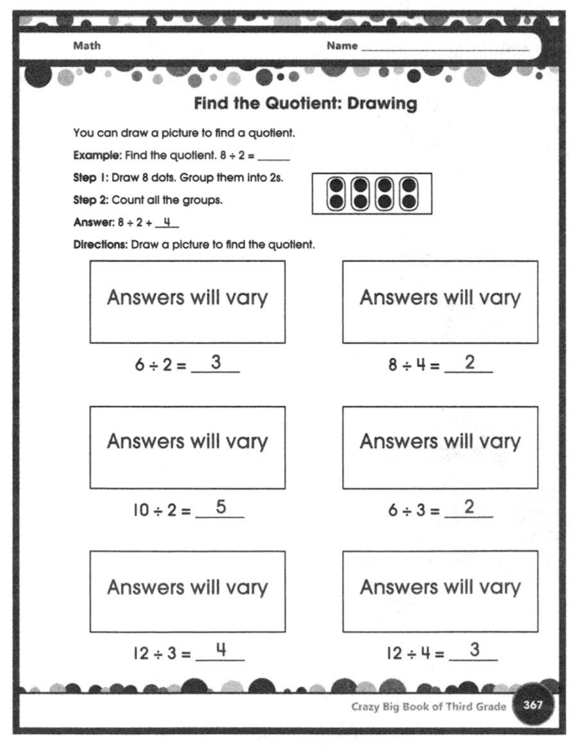

Math Name ____________

Find the Quotient: Drawing

You can draw a picture to find a quotient.

Example: Find the quotient. 8 ÷ 2 = ____

Step 1: Draw 8 dots. Group them into 2s.

Step 2: Count all the groups.

Answer: 8 ÷ 2 = 4

Directions: Draw a picture to find the quotient.

Answers will vary 6 ÷ 2 = 3	Answers will vary 8 ÷ 4 = 2
Answers will vary 10 ÷ 2 = 5	Answers will vary 6 ÷ 3 = 2
Answers will vary 12 ÷ 3 = 4	Answers will vary 12 ÷ 4 = 3

Crazy Big Book of Third Grade 367

page 367

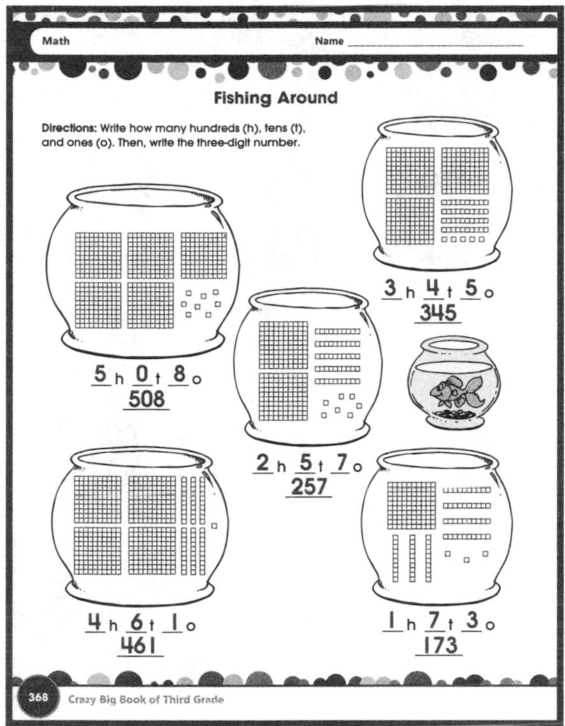

Math Name ____________

Fishing Around

Directions: Write how many hundreds (h), tens (t), and ones (o). Then, write the three-digit number.

5 h 0 t 8 o
508

3 h 4 t 5 o
345

2 h 5 t 7 o
257

4 h 6 t 1 o
461

1 h 7 t 3 o
173

368 Crazy Big Book of Third Grade

page 368

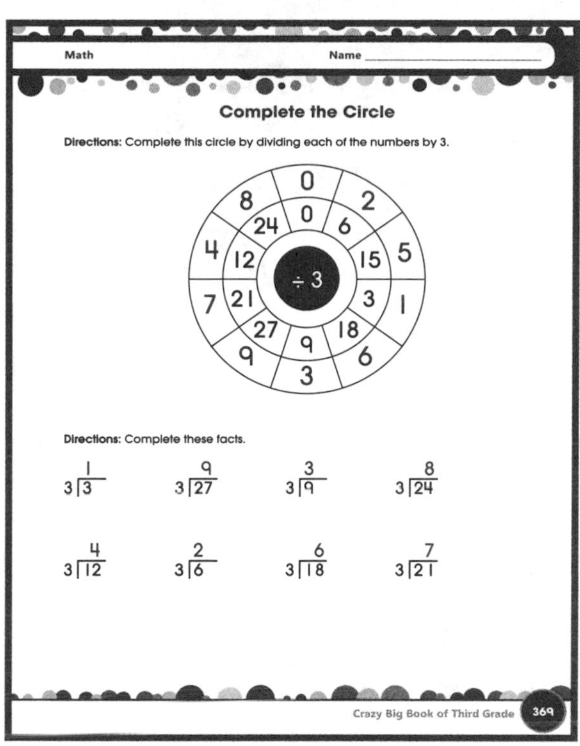

Math Name ____________

Complete the Circle

Directions: Complete this circle by dividing each of the numbers by 3.

Directions: Complete these facts.

$3\overline{)3}$ = 1 $3\overline{)27}$ = 9 $3\overline{)9}$ = 3 $3\overline{)24}$ = 8

$3\overline{)12}$ = 4 $3\overline{)6}$ = 2 $3\overline{)18}$ = 6 $3\overline{)21}$ = 7

Crazy Big Book of Third Grade 369

page 369

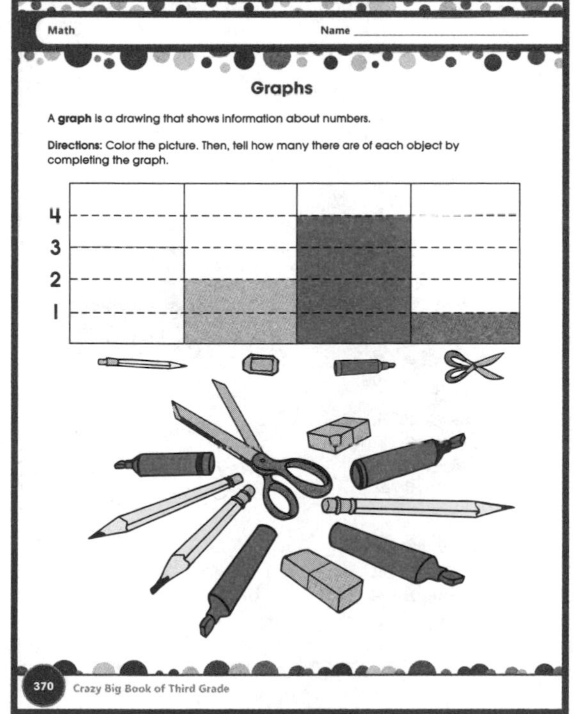

Math Name ____________

Graphs

A **graph** is a drawing that shows information about numbers.

Directions: Color the picture. Then, tell how many there are of each object by completing the graph.

370 Crazy Big Book of Third Grade

page 370

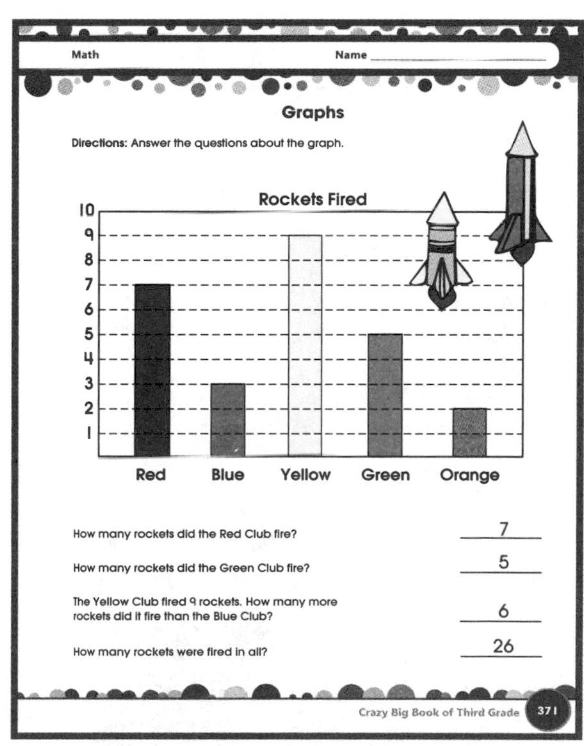

Math Name ____________

Graphs

Directions: Answer the questions about the graph.

How many rockets did the Red Club fire? 7

How many rockets did the Green Club fire? 5

The Yellow Club fired 9 rockets. How many more rockets did it fire than the Blue Club? 6

How many rockets were fired in all? 26

Crazy Big Book of Third Grade 371

page 371

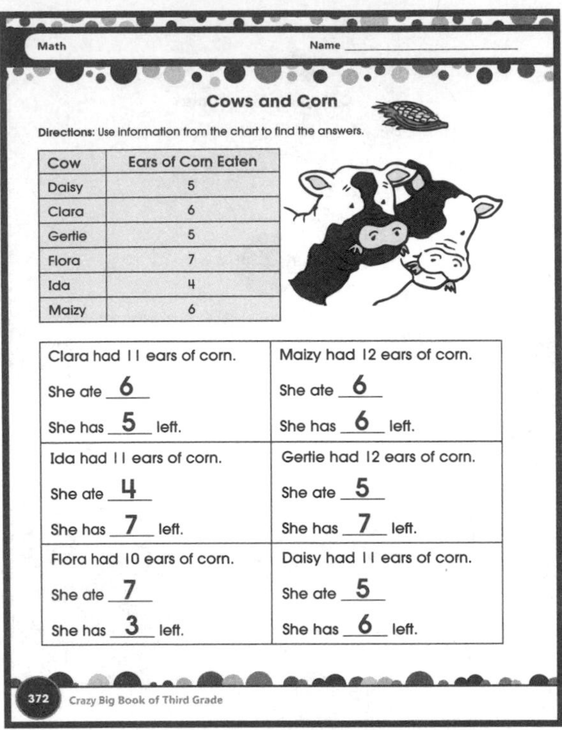

Math Name ________

Cows and Corn

Directions: Use information from the chart to find the answers.

Cow	Ears of Corn Eaten
Daisy	5
Clara	6
Gertie	5
Flora	7
Ida	4
Maizy	6

Clara had 11 ears of corn. She ate 6 She has 5 left.	Maizy had 12 ears of corn. She ate 6 She has 6 left.
Ida had 11 ears of corn. She ate 4 She has 7 left.	Gertie had 12 ears of corn. She ate 5 She has 7 left.
Flora had 10 ears of corn. She ate 7 She has 3 left.	Daisy had 11 ears of corn. She ate 5 She has 6 left.

372 Crazy Big Book of Third Grade

page 372

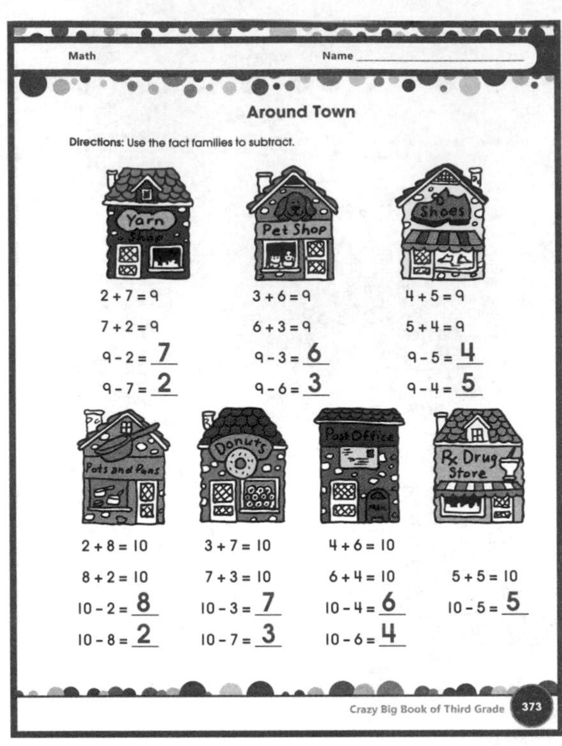

Math Name ________

Around Town

Directions: Use the fact families to subtract.

2 + 7 = 9	3 + 6 = 9	4 + 5 = 9
7 + 2 = 9	6 + 3 = 9	5 + 4 = 9
9 - 2 = 7	9 - 3 = 6	9 - 5 = 4
9 - 7 = 2	9 - 6 = 3	9 - 4 = 5

2 + 8 = 10	3 + 7 = 10	4 + 6 = 10	
8 + 2 = 10	7 + 3 = 10	6 + 4 = 10	5 + 5 = 10
10 - 2 = 8	10 - 3 = 7	10 - 4 = 6	10 - 5 = 5
10 - 8 = 2	10 - 7 = 3	10 - 6 = 4	

Crazy Big Book of Third Grade 373

page 373

Math Name ________

Skipping Through the 10s

Directions: Skip count by 10s. Begin with the number on the first line. Write each number that follows.

0, 10, 20, 30, 40, 50, 60, 70, 80, 90, 100
3, 13, 23, 33, 43, 53, 63, 73, 83, 93, 103
1, 11, 21, 31, 41, 51, 61, 71, 81, 91, 101
8, 18, 28, 38, 48, 58, 68, 78, 88, 98, 108
6, 16, 26, 36, 46, 56, 66, 76, 86, 96, 106
4, 14, 24, 34, 44, 54, 64, 74, 84, 94, 104
2, 12, 22, 32, 42, 52, 62, 72, 82, 92, 102
5, 15, 25, 35, 45, 55, 65, 75, 85, 95, 105
7, 17, 27, 37, 47, 57, 67, 77, 87, 97, 107
9, 19, 29, 39, 49, 59, 69, 79, 89, 99, 109

What is ten more than . . .?

26 36	29 39
44 54	77 87
53 63	91 101
24 34	49 59
66 76	35 45
54 64	82 92

374 Crazy Big Book of Third Grade

page 374

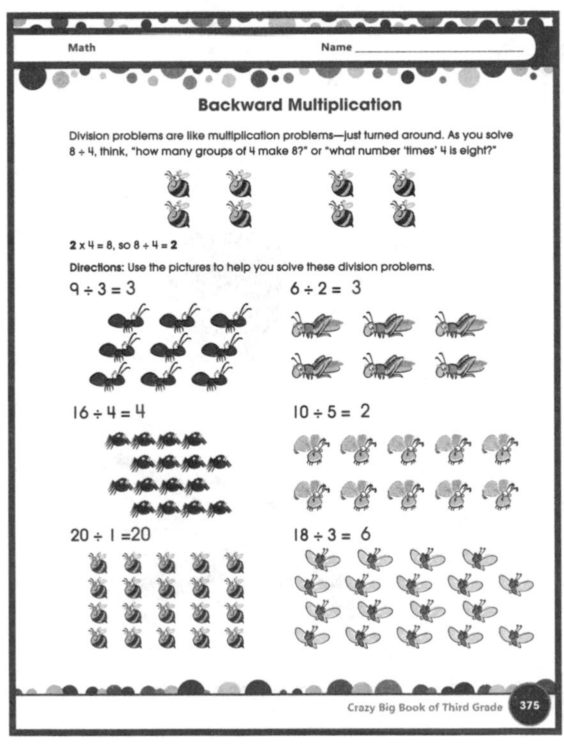

Math Name ________

Backward Multiplication

Division problems are like multiplication problems—just turned around. As you solve 8 ÷ 4, think, "how many groups of 4 make 8?" or "what number 'times' 4 is eight?"

2 x 4 = 8, so 8 ÷ 4 = 2

Directions: Use the pictures to help you solve these division problems.

9 ÷ 3 = 3

6 ÷ 2 = 3

16 ÷ 4 = 4

10 ÷ 5 = 2

20 ÷ 1 = 20

18 ÷ 3 = 6

Crazy Big Book of Third Grade 375

page 375

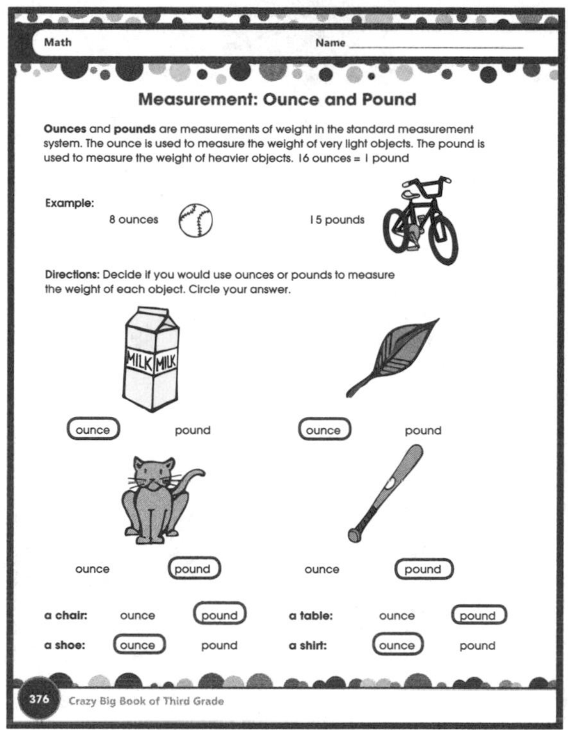
Math Name

Measurement: Ounce and Pound

Ounces and **pounds** are measurements of weight in the standard measurement system. The ounce is used to measure the weight of very light objects. The pound is used to measure the weight of heavier objects. 16 ounces = 1 pound

Example:
8 ounces
15 pounds

Directions: Decide if you would use ounces or pounds to measure the weight of each object. Circle your answer.

ounce (circled) pound
ounce (circled) pound
ounce pound (circled)
ounce pound (circled)

a chair: ounce pound (circled) **a table:** ounce pound (circled)
a shoe: ounce (circled) pound **a shirt:** ounce (circled) pound

376 Crazy Big Book of Third Grade

page 376

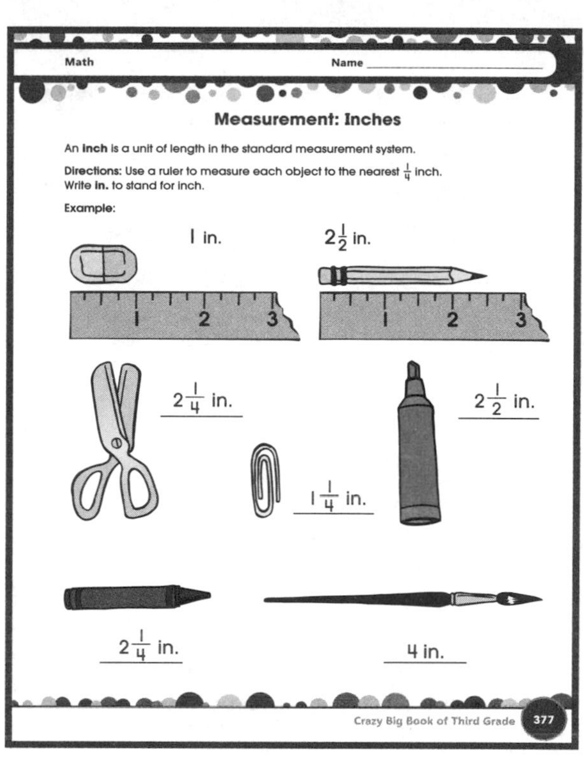
Math Name

Measurement: Inches

An **inch** is a unit of length in the standard measurement system.

Directions: Use a ruler to measure each object to the nearest $\frac{1}{4}$ inch. Write **in.** to stand for inch.

Example:
1 in.
$2\frac{1}{2}$ in.

$2\frac{1}{4}$ in.
$2\frac{1}{2}$ in.
$1\frac{1}{4}$ in.
$2\frac{1}{4}$ in.
4 in.

Crazy Big Book of Third Grade 377

page 377

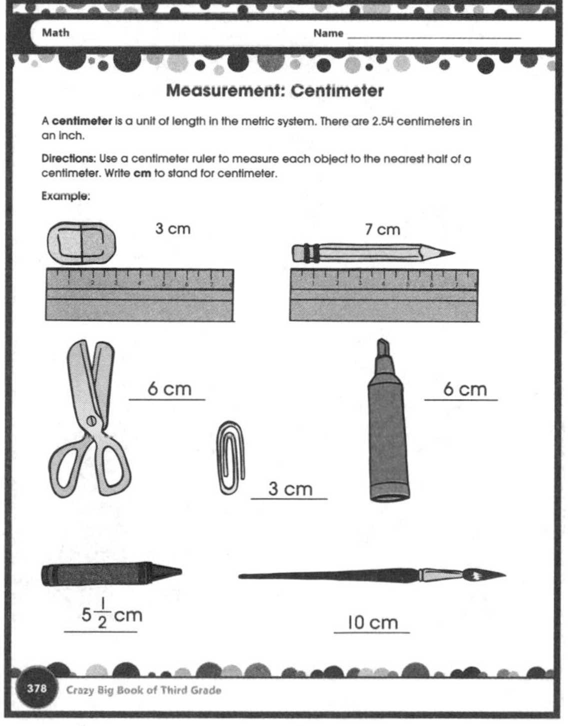
Math Name

Measurement: Centimeter

A **centimeter** is a unit of length in the metric system. There are 2.54 centimeters in an inch.

Directions: Use a centimeter ruler to measure each object to the nearest half of a centimeter. Write **cm** to stand for centimeter.

Example:
3 cm
7 cm

6 cm
6 cm
3 cm
$5\frac{1}{2}$ cm
10 cm

378 Crazy Big Book of Third Grade

page 378

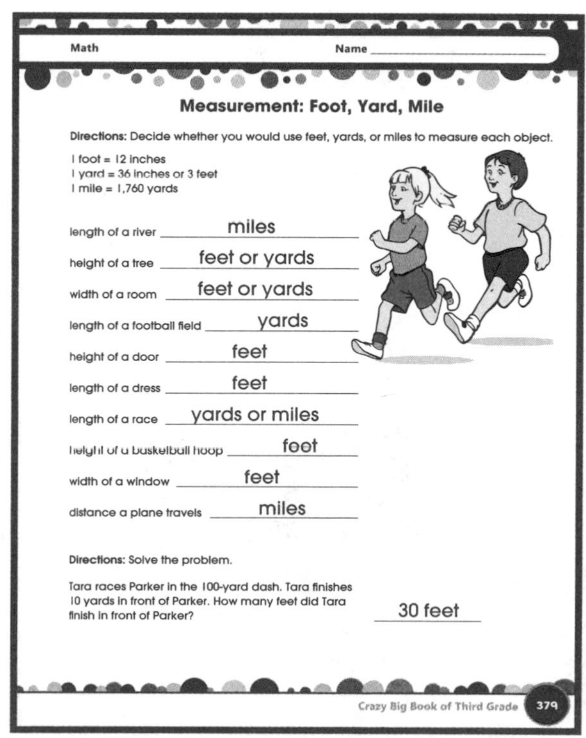
Math Name

Measurement: Foot, Yard, Mile

Directions: Decide whether you would use feet, yards, or miles to measure each object.

1 foot = 12 inches
1 yard = 36 inches or 3 feet
1 mile = 1,760 yards

length of a river: miles
height of a tree: feet or yards
width of a room: feet or yards
length of a football field: yards
height of a door: feet
length of a dress: feet
length of a race: yards or miles
height of a basketball hoop: feet
width of a window: feet
distance a plane travels: miles

Directions: Solve the problem.

Tara races Parker in the 100-yard dash. Tara finishes 10 yards in front of Parker. How many feet did Tara finish in front of Parker? 30 feet

Crazy Big Book of Third Grade 379

page 379

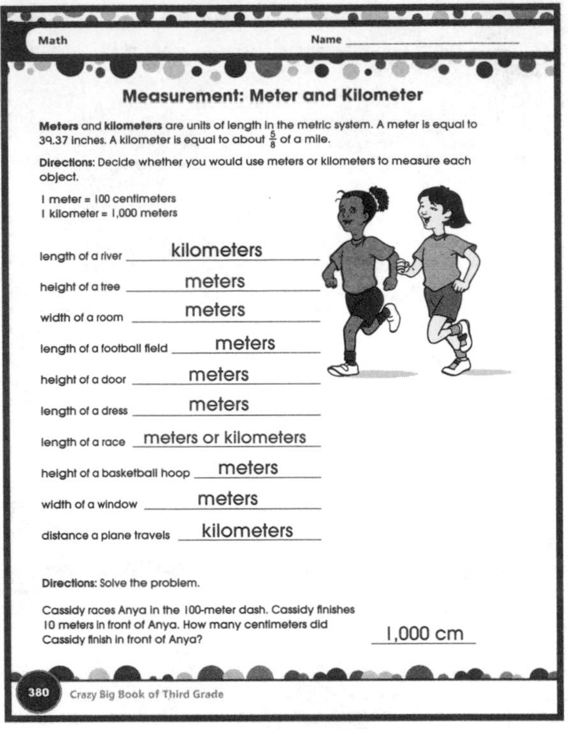

Math Name ______

Measurement: Meter and Kilometer

Meters and **kilometers** are units of length in the metric system. A meter is equal to 39.37 inches. A kilometer is equal to about $\frac{5}{8}$ of a mile.

Directions: Decide whether you would use meters or kilometers to measure each object.

I meter = 100 centimeters
I kilometer = 1,000 meters

length of a river kilometers
height of a tree meters
width of a room meters
length of a football field meters
height of a door meters
length of a dress meters
length of a race meters or kilometers
height of a basketball hoop meters
width of a window meters
distance a plane travels kilometers

Directions: Solve the problem.

Cassidy races Anya in the 100-meter dash. Cassidy finishes 10 meters in front of Anya. How many centimeters did Cassidy finish in front of Anya? 1,000 cm

380 Crazy Big Book of Third Grade

page 380

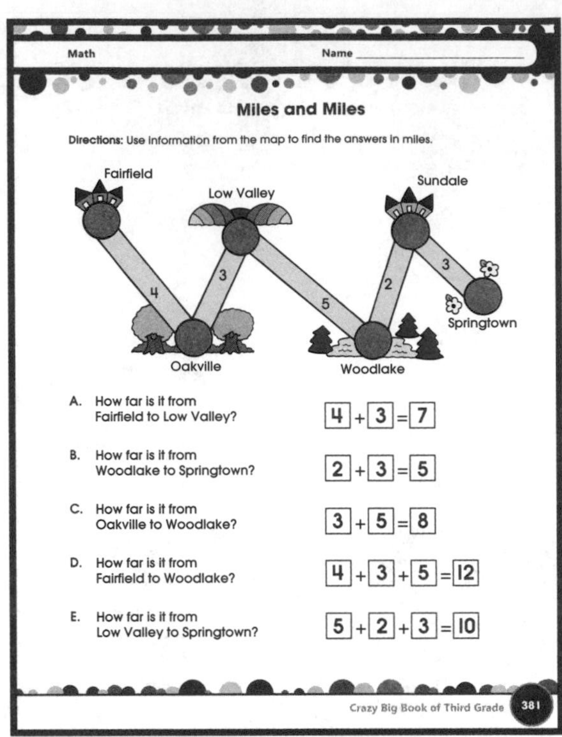

Math Name ______

Miles and Miles

Directions: Use information from the map to find the answers in miles.

A. How far is it from Fairfield to Low Valley? 4 + 3 = 7

B. How far is it from Woodlake to Springtown? 2 + 3 = 5

C. How far is it from Oakville to Woodlake? 3 + 5 = 8

D. How far is it from Fairfield to Woodlake? 4 + 3 + 5 = 12

E. How far is it from Low Valley to Springtown? 5 + 2 + 3 = 10

Crazy Big Book of Third Grade 381

page 381

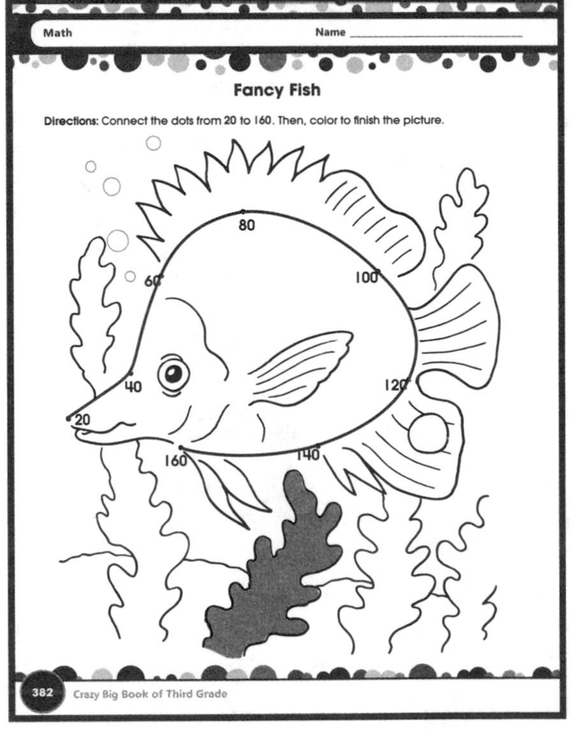

Math Name ______

Fancy Fish

Directions: Connect the dots from 20 to 160. Then, color to finish the picture.

382 Crazy Big Book of Third Grade

page 382

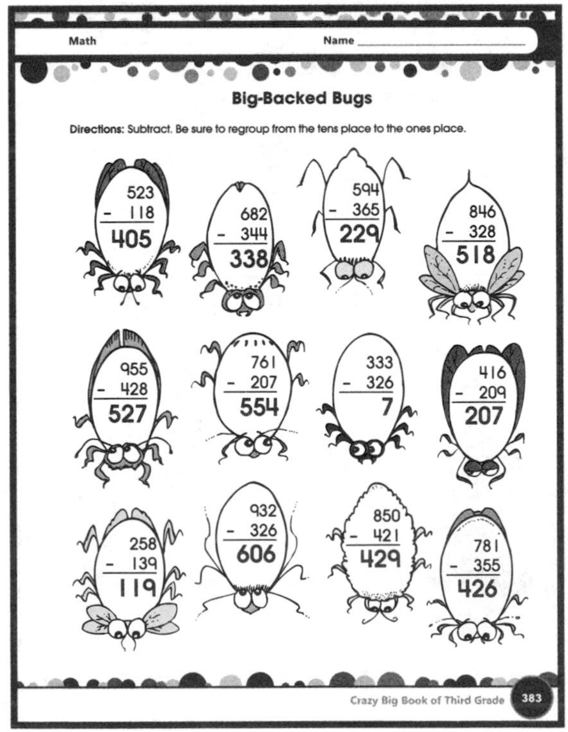

Math Name ______

Big-Backed Bugs

Directions: Subtract. Be sure to regroup from the tens place to the ones place.

Crazy Big Book of Third Grade 383

page 383

Math Name ____________

Barry's and Gary's

Directions: Read each story. Use the pictures and price tags below to find the prices. Write and solve an addition or subtraction problem.

Darcy shopped at Gary's. She bought a [glasses] and a [glue]. How much did she spend in all?	$5.29 + $1.14 $6.43	Devin had $4.33. He bought a [book] at Barry's. How much did he have left?	$4.33 − $2.83 $1.50
How much more is a [book] at Barry's than at Gary's?	$2.83 − $2.67 $.16	Brandon bought two [markers] at Gary's. How much did he spend altogether?	$3.08 + $3.08 $6.16
How much more is a [backpack] at Gary's than at Barry's?	$4.37 − $3.36 $1.01	Hannah had $7.81. She bought a [backpack] at Barry's. How much does she have left?	$7.81 − $3.36 $4.45

384 Crazy Big Book of Third Grade

page 384

Math Name ____________

What a Ball Game!

Directions: Use information from the scoreboard to find the answers.

Runs scored

Inning	1	2	3	4	5	6	7	8	9
Cubs	8	14	14	5	12	6	5	13	11
Reds	13	7	8	13	6	14	12	7	5

Who scored more runs in the 4th inning? Reds How many more? 13 − 5 = 8	Who scored more runs in the 8th inning? Cubs How many more? 13 − 7 = 6
Who scored more runs in the 3rd inning? Cubs How many more? 14 − 8 = 6	Who scored more runs in the 6th inning? Reds How many more? 14 − 6 = 8
Who scored more runs in the 1st inning? Reds How many more? 13 − 8 = 5	Who scored more runs in the 7th inning? Reds How many more? 12 − 5 = 7

Crazy Big Book of Third Grade 385

page 385

Math Name ____________

I Spy Something Green

Directions: To find out what I spy, color the boxes with differences of 5, 6, or 7. Then, write the letters from the colored boxes in the blanks, working from left to right.

I spy a T R A C T O R!

S: 12 − 9 = 3	T: 11 − 4 = 7	L: 12 − 8 = 4	E: 9 − 5 = 4
R: 12 − 7 = 5	F: 10 − 7 = 3	A: 10 − 3 = 7	Q: 11 − 8 = 3
G: 9 − 6 = 3	C: 10 − 4 = 6	T: 11 − 5 = 6	O: 10 − 6 = 4
H: 11 − 7 = 4	M: 8 − 4 = 4	O: 11 − 6 = 5	R: 12 − 5 = 7

386 Crazy Big Book of Third Grade

page 386

Math Name ____________

Weather Chart

Directions: Use information from the graph to find the answers.

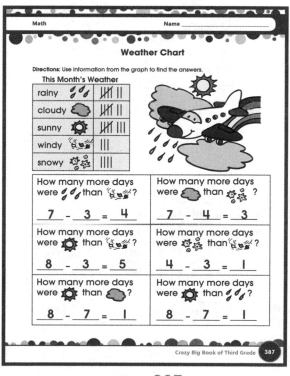

This Month's Weather

rainy	𝍸 II
cloudy	𝍸 II
sunny	𝍸 III
windy	III
snowy	IIII

How many more days were [rainy] than [windy]? 7 − 3 = 4	How many more days were [cloudy] than [snowy]? 7 − 4 = 3
How many more days were [sunny] than [windy]? 8 − 3 = 5	How many more days were [snowy] than [windy]? 4 − 3 = 1
How many more days were [sunny] than [cloudy]? 8 − 7 = 1	How many more days were [sunny] than [rainy]? 8 − 7 = 1

Crazy Big Book of Third Grade 387

page 387

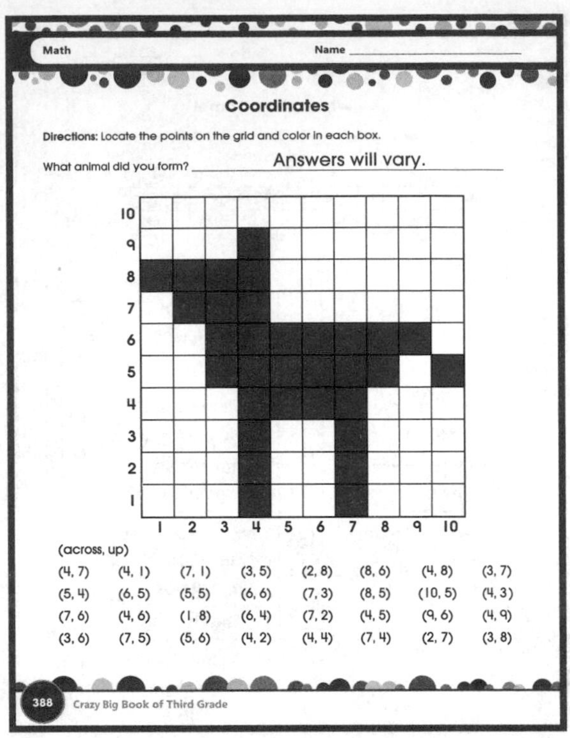

Math Name ____________

Coordinates

Directions: Locate the points on the grid and color in each box.

What animal did you form? Answers will vary.

(across, up)

(4, 7)	(4, 1)	(7, 1)	(3, 5)	(2, 8)	(8, 6)	(4, 8)	(3, 7)
(5, 4)	(6, 5)	(5, 5)	(6, 6)	(7, 3)	(8, 5)	(10, 5)	(4, 3)
(7, 6)	(4, 6)	(1, 8)	(6, 4)	(7, 2)	(4, 5)	(9, 6)	(4, 9)
(3, 6)	(7, 5)	(5, 6)	(4, 2)	(4, 4)	(7, 4)	(2, 7)	(3, 8)

388 Crazy Big Book of Third Grade

page 388

Math Name ____________

Time to Add

Directions: Add. Then, to answer the question, write the circled numbers in order.

How many minutes are in a day? 1, 4 4 0

21 + 70 = (91)

36 + 21 = 57

59 + 20 = 79

28 + 31 = 59

14 + 60 = (74)

34 + 43 = 77

33 + 11 = (44)

23 + 72 = 95

45 + 41 = 86

63 + 26 = 89

50 + 40 = (90)

Crazy Big Book of Third Grade 389

page 389

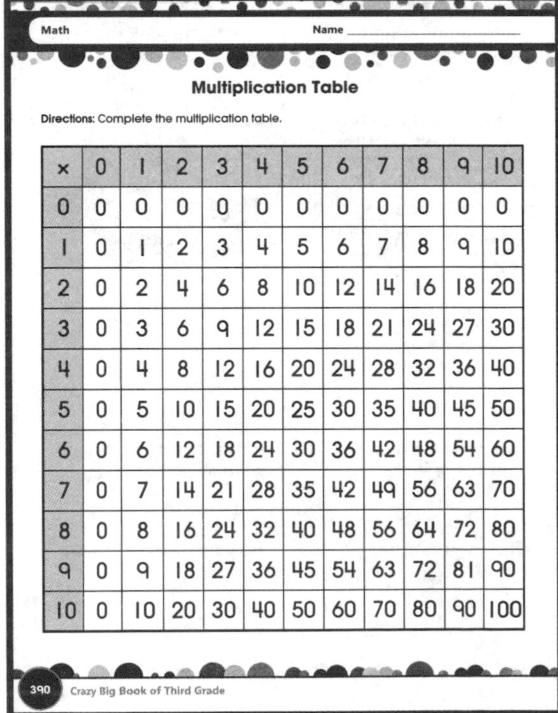

Math Name ____________

Multiplication Table

Directions: Complete the multiplication table.

×	0	1	2	3	4	5	6	7	8	9	10
0	0	0	0	0	0	0	0	0	0	0	0
1	0	1	2	3	4	5	6	7	8	9	10
2	0	2	4	6	8	10	12	14	16	18	20
3	0	3	6	9	12	15	18	21	24	27	30
4	0	4	8	12	16	20	24	28	32	36	40
5	0	5	10	15	20	25	30	35	40	45	50
6	0	6	12	18	24	30	36	42	48	54	60
7	0	7	14	21	28	35	42	49	56	63	70
8	0	8	16	24	32	40	48	56	64	72	80
9	0	9	18	27	36	45	54	63	72	81	90
10	0	10	20	30	40	50	60	70	80	90	100

390 Crazy Big Book of Third Grade

page 390

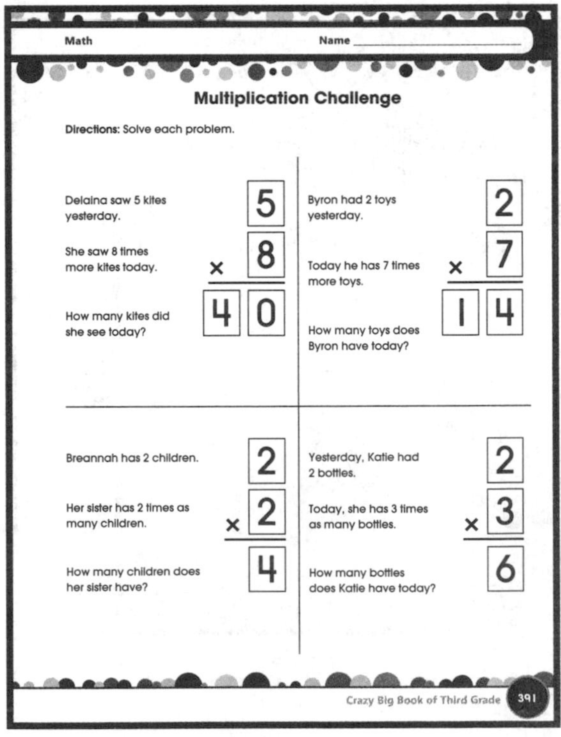

Math Name ____________

Multiplication Challenge

Directions: Solve each problem.

Delaina saw 5 kites yesterday. She saw 8 times more kites today. How many kites did she see today?

5 × 8 = 40

Byron had 2 toys yesterday. Today he has 7 times more toys. How many toys does Byron have today?

2 × 7 = 14

Breannah has 2 children. Her sister has 2 times as many children. How many children does her sister have?

2 × 2 = 4

Yesterday, Katie had 2 bottles. Today, she has 3 times as many bottles. How many bottles does Katie have today?

2 × 3 = 6

Crazy Big Book of Third Grade 391

page 391

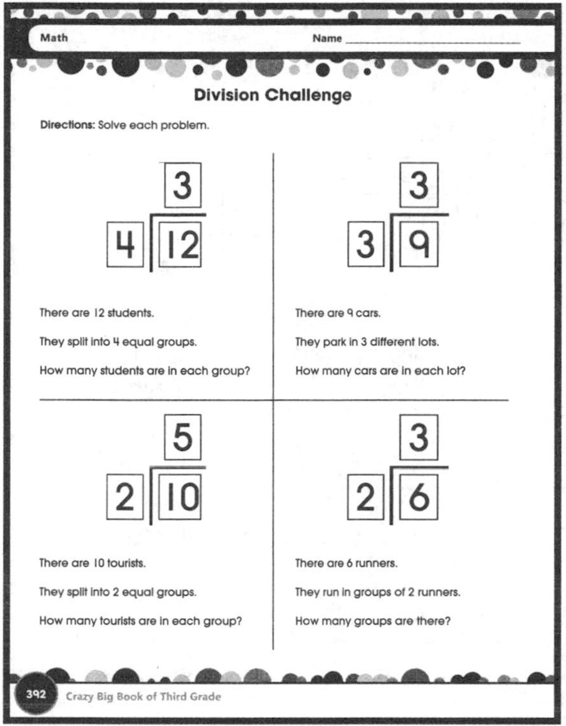

Math Name ____________

Division Challenge

Directions: Solve each problem.

4 ⟌ 12 = 3

There are 12 students.

They split into 4 equal groups.

How many students are in each group?

3 ⟌ 9 = 3

There are 9 cars.

They park in 3 different lots.

How many cars are in each lot?

2 ⟌ 10 = 5

There are 10 tourists.

They split into 2 equal groups.

How many tourists are in each group?

2 ⟌ 6 = 3

There are 6 runners.

They run in groups of 2 runners.

How many groups are there?

392 Crazy Big Book of Third Grade

page 392

Math Name ____________

Roman Numerals

Another way to write numbers is to use Roman numerals.

I	1	VII	7
II	2	VIII	8
III	3	IX	9
IV	4	X	10
V	5	XI	11
VI	6	XII	12

Directions: Fill in the Roman numerals on the watch.

What time is it on the watch?

3 o'clock

Crazy Big Book of Third Grade 393

page 393

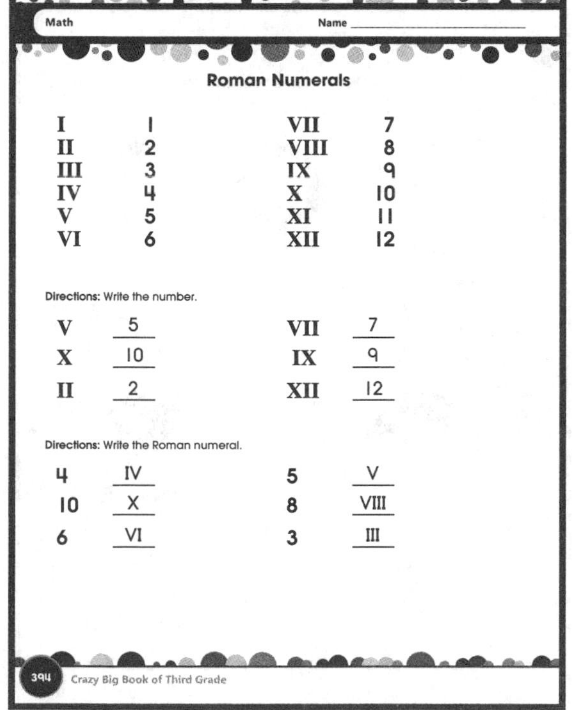

Math Name ____________

Roman Numerals

I	1	VII	7
II	2	VIII	8
III	3	IX	9
IV	4	X	10
V	5	XI	11
VI	6	XII	12

Directions: Write the number.

V	5	VII	7
X	10	IX	9
II	2	XII	12

Directions: Write the Roman numeral.

4	IV	5	V
10	X	8	VIII
6	VI	3	III

394 Crazy Big Book of Third Grade

page 394

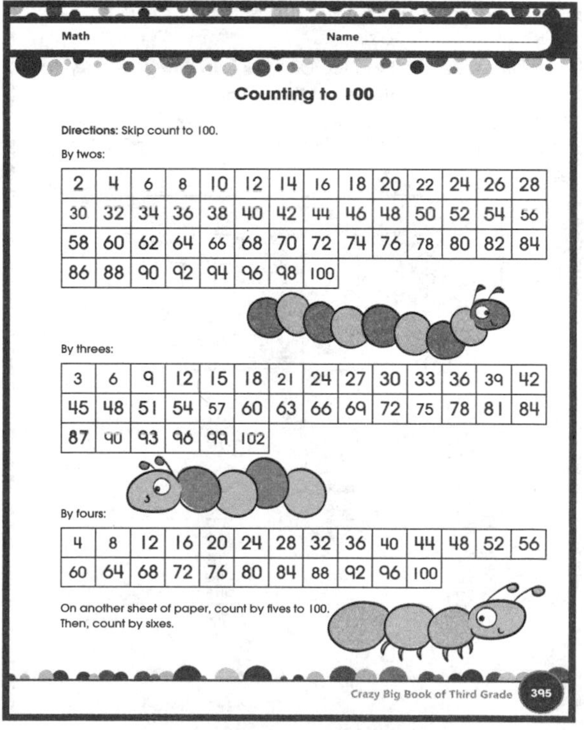

Math Name ____________

Counting to 100

Directions: Skip count to 100.

By twos:

2	4	6	8	10	12	14	16	18	20	22	24	26	28
30	32	34	36	38	40	42	44	46	48	50	52	54	56
58	60	62	64	66	68	70	72	74	76	78	80	82	84
86	88	90	92	94	96	98	100						

By threes:

3	6	9	12	15	18	21	24	27	30	33	36	39	42
45	48	51	54	57	60	63	66	69	72	75	78	81	84
87	90	93	96	99	102								

By fours:

4	8	12	16	20	24	28	32	36	40	44	48	52	56
60	64	68	72	76	80	84	88	92	96	100			

On another sheet of paper, count by fives to 100. Then, count by sixes.

Crazy Big Book of Third Grade 395

page 395

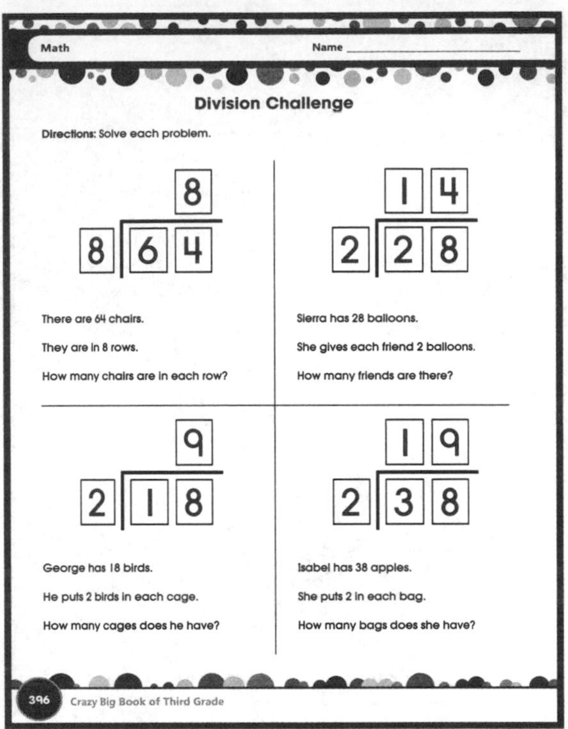

page 396

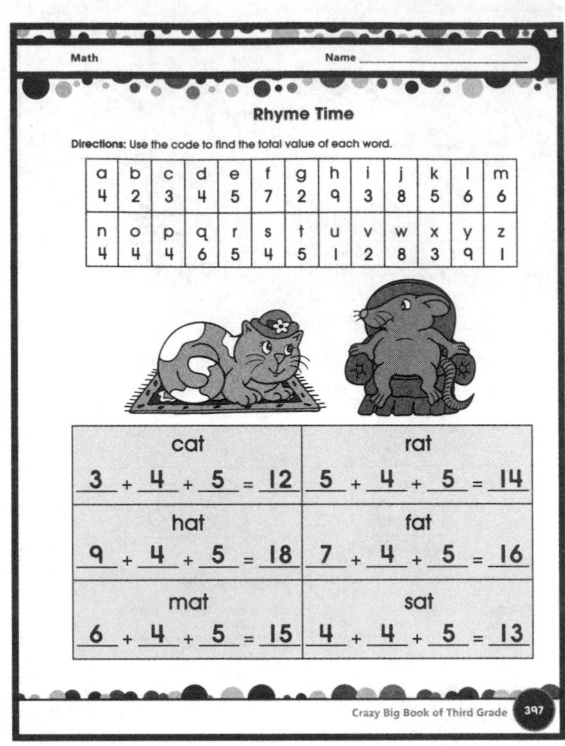

page 397

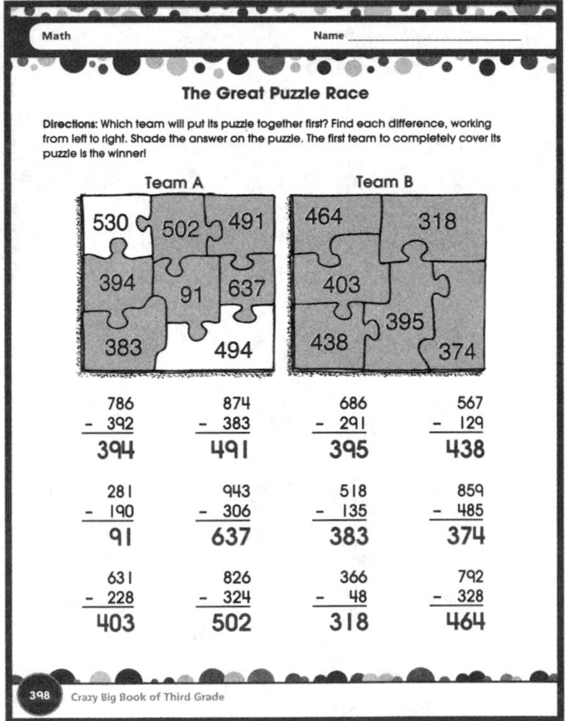

page 398

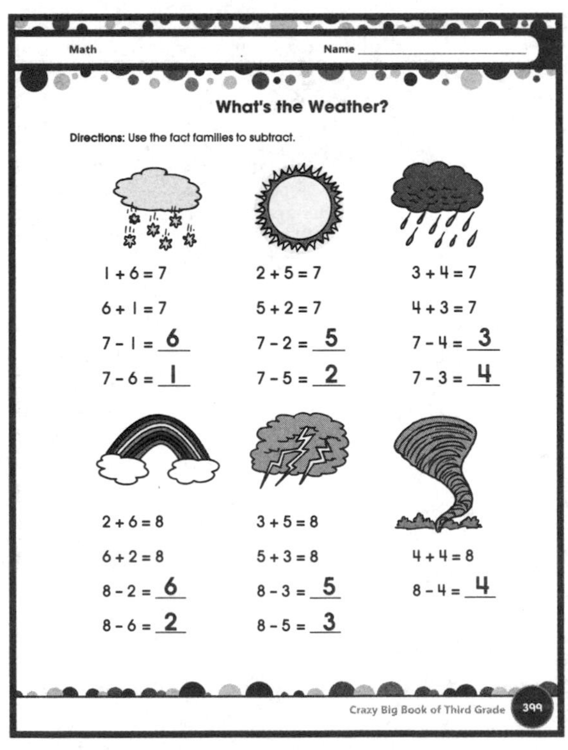

page 399

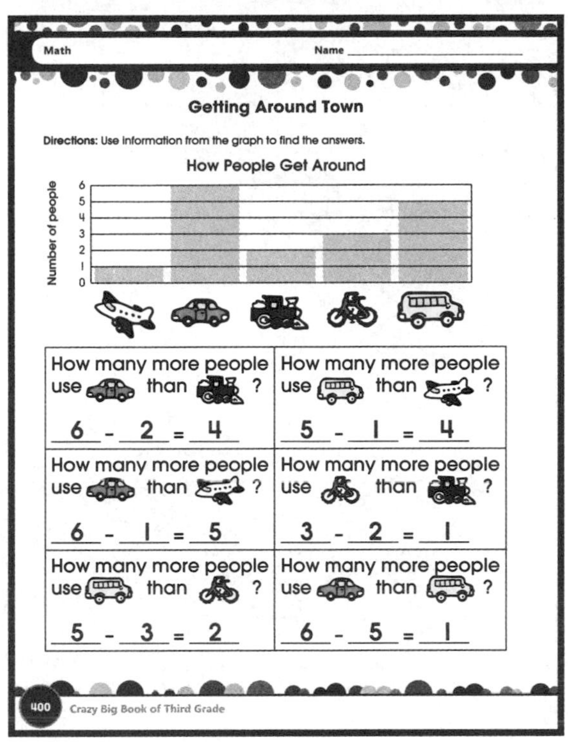
Math Name

Getting Around Town

Directions: Use information from the graph to find the answers.

How People Get Around

How many more people use [car] than [train]?	How many more people use [bus] than [airplane]?
6 - 2 = 4	5 - 1 = 4
How many more people use [car] than [airplane]?	How many more people use [bicycle] than [train]?
6 - 1 = 5	3 - 2 = 1
How many more people use [bus] than [bicycle]?	How many more people use [car] than [bus]?
5 - 3 = 2	6 - 5 = 1

400 Crazy Big Book of Third Grade

page 400

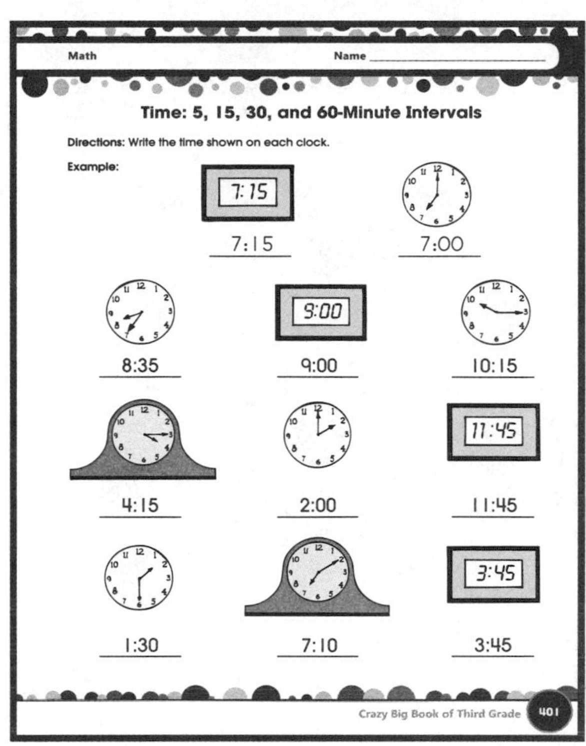
Math Name

Time: 5, 15, 30, and 60-Minute Intervals

Directions: Write the time shown on each clock.

Example:

7:15 7:00

8:35 9:00 10:15

4:15 2:00 11:45

1:30 7:10 3:45

Crazy Big Book of Third Grade 401

page 401

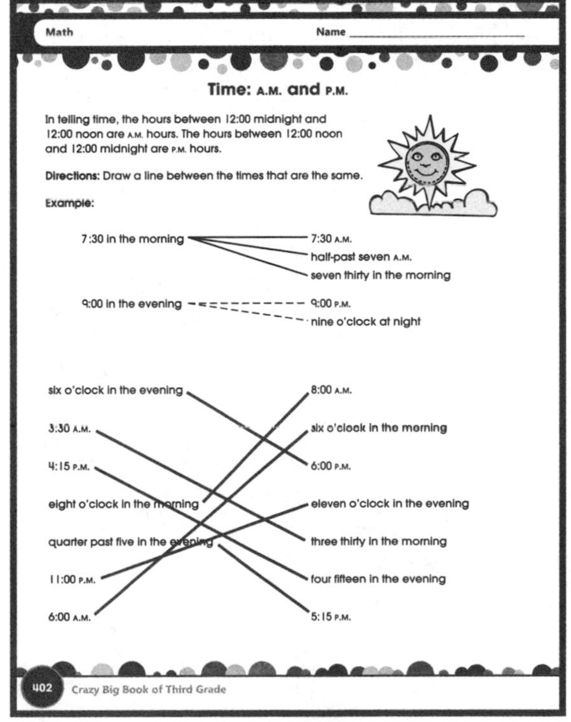
Math Name

Time: A.M. and P.M.

In telling time, the hours between 12:00 midnight and 12:00 noon are A.M. hours. The hours between 12:00 noon and 12:00 midnight are P.M. hours.

Directions: Draw a line between the times that are the same.

Example:

7:30 in the morning — 7:30 A.M. — half-past seven A.M. — seven thirty in the morning

9:00 in the evening — 9:00 P.M. — nine o'clock at night

six o'clock in the evening — 6:00 P.M.
3:30 A.M. — three thirty in the morning
4:15 P.M. — four fifteen in the evening
eight o'clock in the morning — 8:00 A.M.
quarter past five in the evening — 5:15 P.M.
11:00 P.M. — eleven o'clock in the evening
6:00 A.M. — six o'clock in the morning

402 Crazy Big Book of Third Grade

page 402

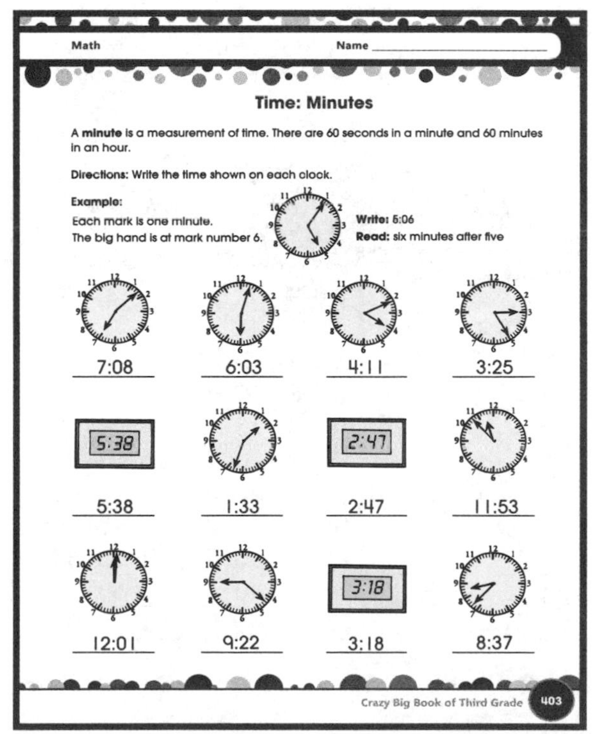
Math Name

Time: Minutes

A **minute** is a measurement of time. There are 60 seconds in a minute and 60 minutes in an hour.

Directions: Write the time shown on each clock.

Example:
Each mark is one minute.
The big hand is at mark number 6.
Write: 5:06
Read: six minutes after five

7:08 6:03 4:11 3:25

5:38 1:33 2:47 11:53

12:01 9:22 3:18 8:37

Crazy Big Book of Third Grade 403

page 403

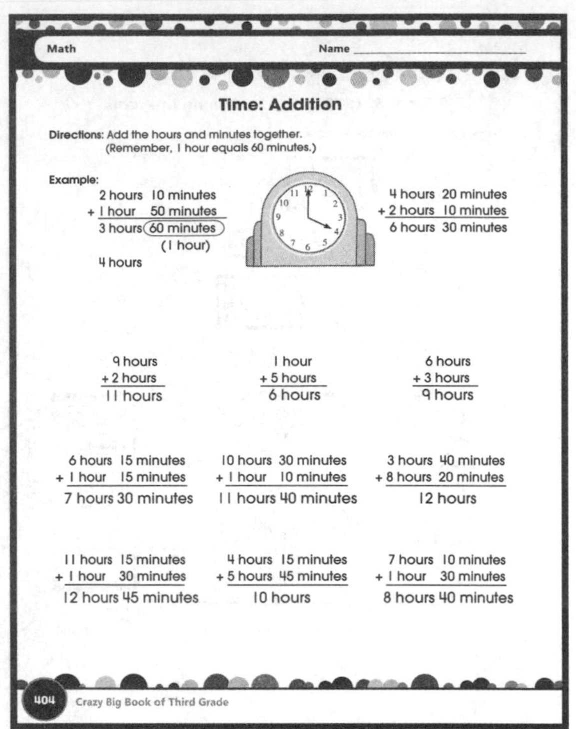

Math Name ______________

Time: Addition

Directions: Add the hours and minutes together.
(Remember, 1 hour equals 60 minutes.)

Example:

2 hours 10 minutes
+ 1 hour 50 minutes
3 hours (60 minutes)
(1 hour)
4 hours

4 hours 20 minutes
+ 2 hours 10 minutes
6 hours 30 minutes

9 hours + 2 hours = 11 hours
1 hour + 5 hours = 6 hours
6 hours + 3 hours = 9 hours

6 hours 15 minutes + 1 hour 15 minutes = 7 hours 30 minutes
10 hours 30 minutes + 1 hour 10 minutes = 11 hours 40 minutes
3 hours 40 minutes + 8 hours 20 minutes = 12 hours

11 hours 15 minutes + 1 hour 30 minutes = 12 hours 45 minutes
4 hours 15 minutes + 5 hours 45 minutes = 10 hours
7 hours 10 minutes + 1 hour 30 minutes = 8 hours 40 minutes

404 Crazy Big Book of Third Grade

page 404

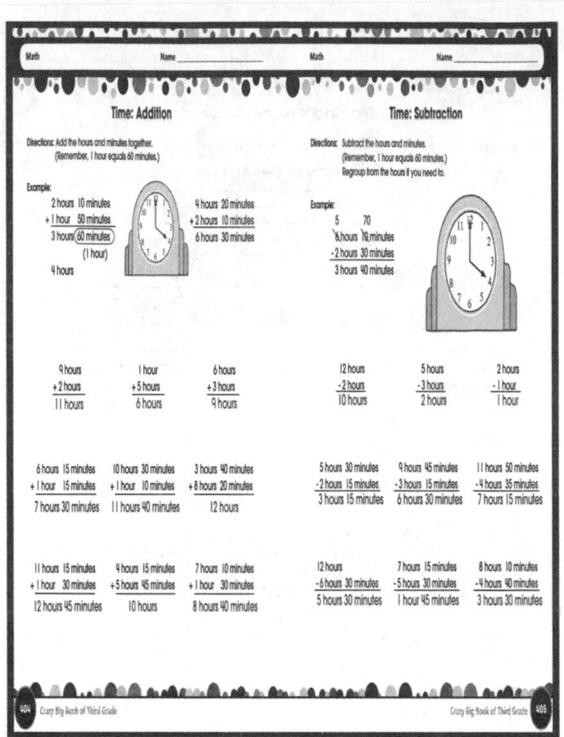

Math Name ______________

Time: Addition

Directions: Add the hours and minutes together.
(Remember, 1 hour equals 60 minutes.)

Example:

2 hours 10 minutes
+ 1 hour 50 minutes
3 hours (60 minutes)
(1 hour)
4 hours

4 hours 20 minutes
+ 2 hours 10 minutes
6 hours 30 minutes

9 hours + 2 hours = 11 hours
1 hour + 5 hours = 6 hours
6 hours + 3 hours = 9 hours

6 hours 15 minutes + 1 hour 15 minutes = 7 hours 30 minutes
10 hours 30 minutes + 1 hour 10 minutes = 11 hours 40 minutes
3 hours 40 minutes + 8 hours 20 minutes = 12 hours

11 hours 15 minutes + 1 hour 30 minutes = 12 hours 45 minutes
4 hours 15 minutes + 5 hours 45 minutes = 10 hours
7 hours 10 minutes + 1 hour 30 minutes = 8 hours 40 minutes

Math Name ______________

Time: Subtraction

Directions: Subtract the hours and minutes.
(Remember, 1 hour equals 60 minutes.)
Regroup from the hours if you need to.

Example:

5 70
~~6~~ hours ~~10~~ minutes
- 2 hours 30 minutes
3 hours 40 minutes

12 hours - 2 hours = 10 hours
5 hours - 3 hours = 2 hours
2 hours - 1 hour = 1 hour

5 hours 30 minutes - 2 hours 15 minutes = 3 hours 15 minutes
9 hours 45 minutes - 3 hours 15 minutes = 6 hours 30 minutes
11 hours 50 minutes - 4 hours 35 minutes = 7 hours 15 minutes

12 hours - 6 hours 30 minutes = 5 hours 30 minutes
7 hours 15 minutes - 5 hours 30 minutes = 1 hour 45 minutes
8 hours 10 minutes - 4 hours 40 minutes = 3 hours 30 minutes

404 Crazy Big Book of Third Grade
Crazy Big Book of Third Grade 405

page 405

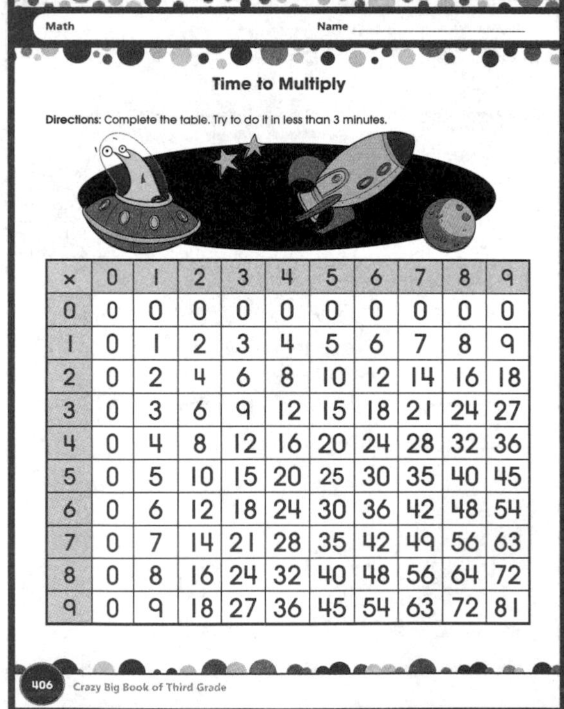

Math Name ______________

Time to Multiply

Directions: Complete the table. Try to do it in less than 3 minutes.

×	0	1	2	3	4	5	6	7	8	9
0	0	0	0	0	0	0	0	0	0	0
1	0	1	2	3	4	5	6	7	8	9
2	0	2	4	6	8	10	12	14	16	18
3	0	3	6	9	12	15	18	21	24	27
4	0	4	8	12	16	20	24	28	32	36
5	0	5	10	15	20	25	30	35	40	45
6	0	6	12	18	24	30	36	42	48	54
7	0	7	14	21	28	35	42	49	56	63
8	0	8	16	24	32	40	48	56	64	72
9	0	9	18	27	36	45	54	63	72	81

406 Crazy Big Book of Third Grade

page 406

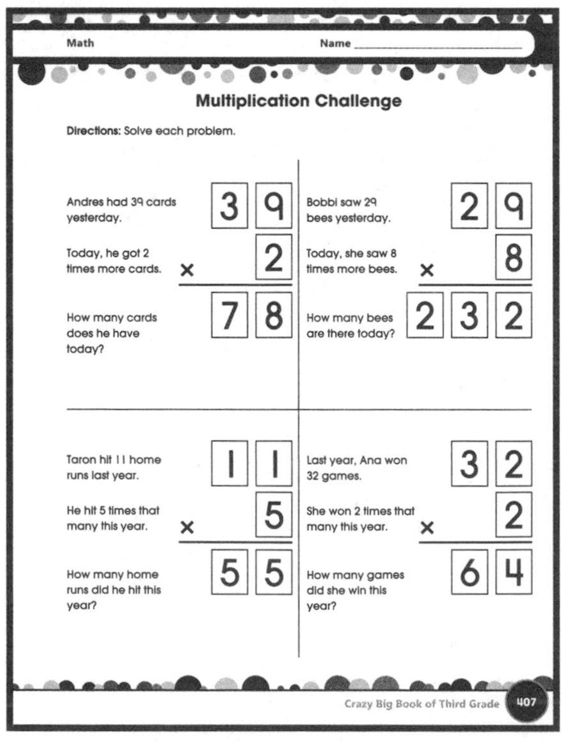

Math Name ______________

Multiplication Challenge

Directions: Solve each problem.

Andres had 39 cards yesterday. — 39
Today, he got 2 times more cards. — × 2
How many cards does he have today? — 78

Bobbi saw 29 bees yesterday. — 29
Today, she saw 8 times more bees. — × 8
How many bees are there today? — 232

Taron hit 11 home runs last year. — 11
He hit 5 times that many this year. — × 5
How many home runs did he hit this year? — 55

Last year, Ana won 32 games. — 32
She won 2 times that many this year. — × 2
How many games did she win this year? — 64

Crazy Big Book of Third Grade 407

page 407

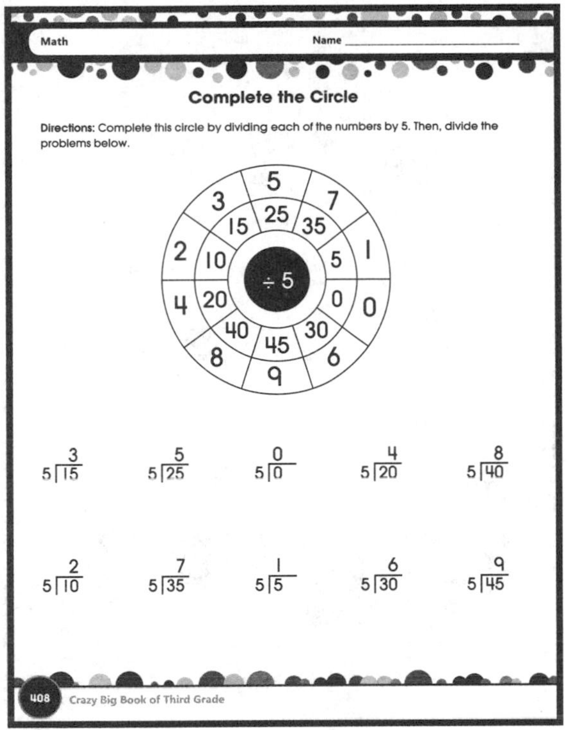
Math Name ____________

Complete the Circle

Directions: Complete this circle by dividing each of the numbers by 5. Then, divide the problems below.

5)15 = 3	5)25 = 5	5)0 = 0	5)20 = 4	5)40 = 8
5)10 = 2	5)35 = 7	5)5 = 1	5)30 = 6	5)45 = 9

408 Crazy Big Book of Third Grade

page 408

Math Name ____________

Division Challenge

Directions: Solve each problem.

7)35 = 5

Vince read 35 pages in his book.

It took him 7 days.

How many pages did he read each day?

2)18 = 9

Tasha worked 18 hours.

She worked for 2 days.

How many hours did she work each day?

6)54 = 9

Emory bought 54 cards.

They came in 6 boxes.

How many cards are in each box?

4)32 = 8

A basketball game is 32 minutes long.

The game is split in 4 parts.

How many minutes long is each part?

Crazy Big Book of Third Grade 409

page 409

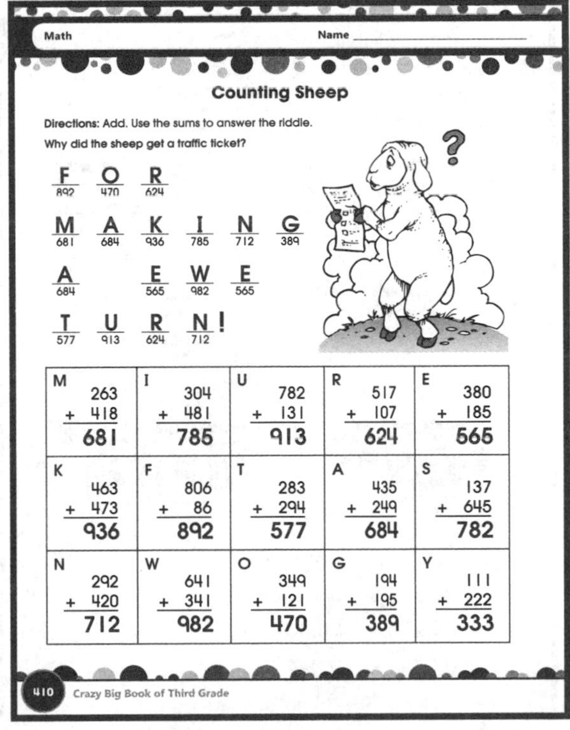
Math Name ____________

Counting Sheep

Directions: Add. Use the sums to answer the riddle.

Why did the sheep get a traffic ticket?

F (892) O (470) R (624)

M (681) A (684) K (936) I (785) N (712) G (389)

A (684) E (565) W (982) E (565)

T (577) U (913) R (624) N (712)!

M 263 + 418 = 681	I 304 + 481 = 785	U 782 + 131 = 913	R 517 + 107 = 624	E 380 + 185 = 565
K 463 + 473 = 936	F 806 + 86 = 892	T 283 + 294 = 577	A 435 + 249 = 684	S 137 + 645 = 782
N 292 + 420 = 712	W 641 + 341 = 982	O 349 + 121 = 470	G 194 + 195 = 389	Y 111 + 222 = 333

410 Crazy Big Book of Third Grade

page 410

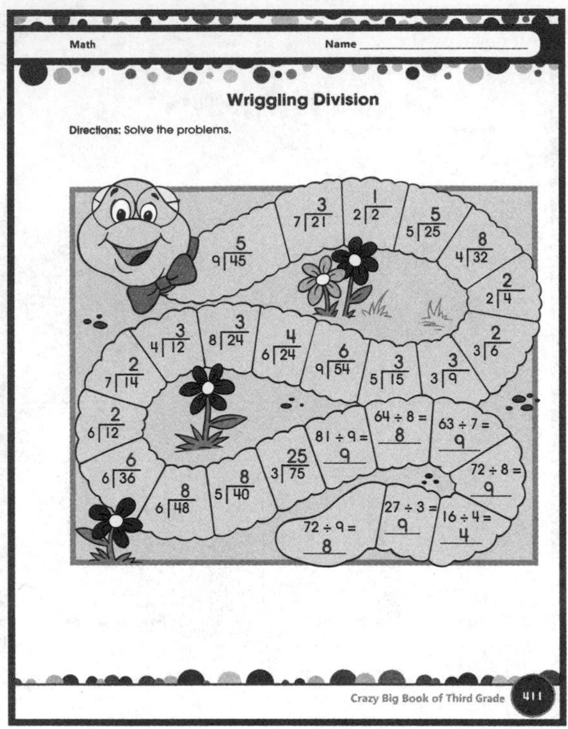
Math Name

Wriggling Division

Directions: Solve the problems.

9⟌45 = 5, 7⟌21 = 3, 2⟌2 = 1, 5⟌25 = 5, 4⟌32 = 8, 2⟌4 = 2, 3⟌6 = 2, 3⟌9 = 3, 5⟌15 = 3, 9⟌54 = 6, 6⟌24 = 4, 8⟌24 = 3, 4⟌12 = 3, 7⟌14 = 2, 6⟌12 = 2, 6⟌36 = 6, 6⟌48 = 8, 5⟌40 = 8, 3⟌75 = 25, 81 ÷ 9 = 9, 64 ÷ 8 = 8, 63 ÷ 7 = 9, 72 ÷ 8 = 9, 16 ÷ 4 = 4, 27 ÷ 3 = 9, 72 ÷ 9 = 8

Crazy Big Book of Third Grade 411

page 411

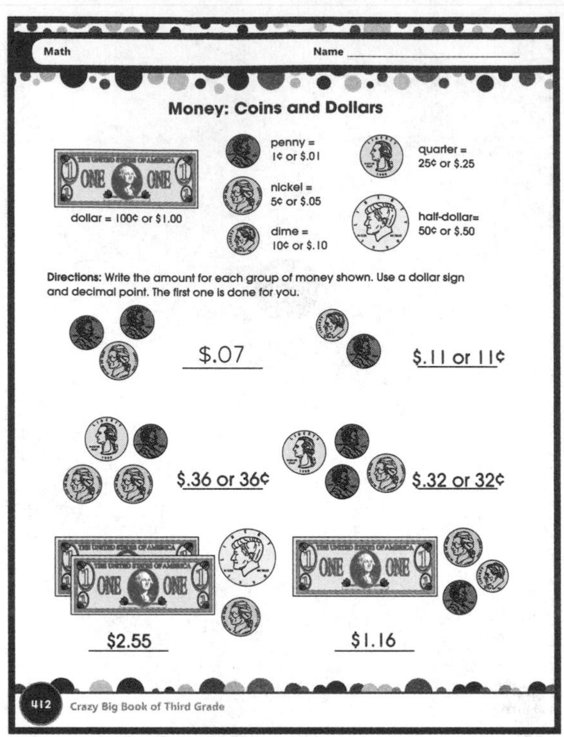
Math Name

Money: Coins and Dollars

dollar = 100¢ or $1.00

penny = 1¢ or $.01

nickel = 5¢ or $.05

dime = 10¢ or $.10

quarter = 25¢ or $.25

half-dollar= 50¢ or $.50

Directions: Write the amount for each group of money shown. Use a dollar sign and decimal point. The first one is done for you.

$.07

$.11 or 11¢

$.36 or 36¢

$.32 or 32¢

$2.55

$1.16

412 Crazy Big Book of Third Grade

page 412

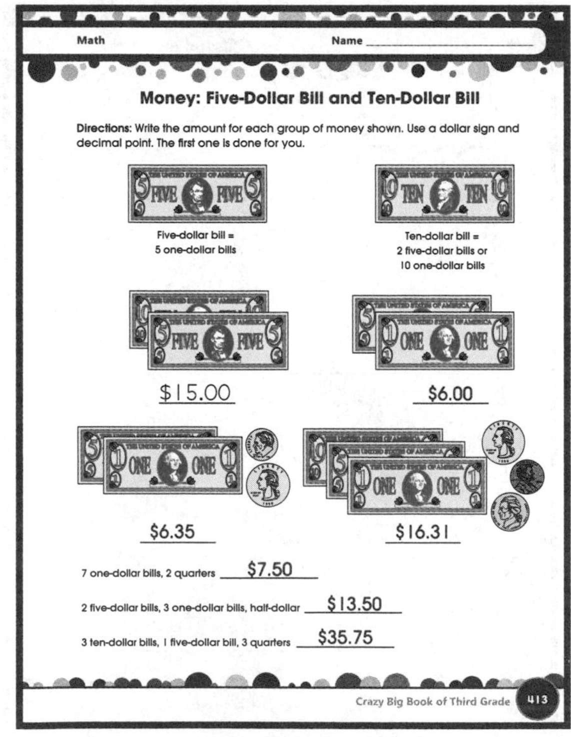
Math Name

Money: Five-Dollar Bill and Ten-Dollar Bill

Directions: Write the amount for each group of money shown. Use a dollar sign and decimal point. The first one is done for you.

Five-dollar bill = 5 one-dollar bills

Ten-dollar bill = 2 five-dollar bills or 10 one-dollar bills

$15.00

$6.00

$6.35

$16.31

7 one-dollar bills, 2 quarters $7.50

2 five-dollar bills, 3 one-dollar bills, half-dollar $13.50

3 ten-dollar bills, 1 five-dollar bill, 3 quarters $35.75

Crazy Big Book of Third Grade 413

page 413

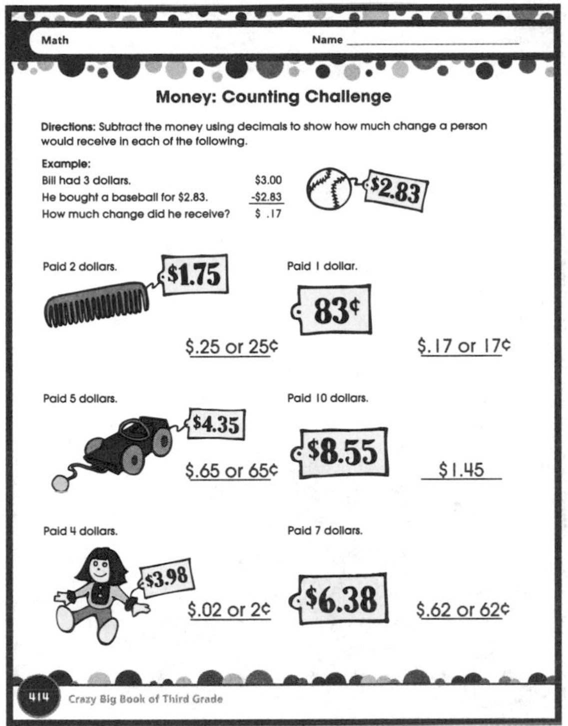

Math Name ______________

Money: Counting Challenge

Directions: Subtract the money using decimals to show how much change a person would receive in each of the following.

Example:

Bill had 3 dollars. $3.00
He bought a baseball for $2.83. -$2.83
How much change did he receive? $ .17

Paid 2 dollars. $1.75 — $.25 or 25¢

Paid 1 dollar. 83¢ — $.17 or 17¢

Paid 5 dollars. $4.35 — $.65 or 65¢

Paid 10 dollars. $8.55 — $1.45

Paid 4 dollars. $3.98 — $.02 or 2¢

Paid 7 dollars. $6.38 — $.62 or 62¢

414 Crazy Big Book of Third Grade

page 414

Math Name ______________

Money: Comparing

Directions: Compare the amount of money in the left column with the price of the object in the right column. Is the amount of money in the left column enough to purchase the object in the right column? Circle **yes** or **no**.

Example: $1.75

Alice has 2 dollars. She wants to buy a jump rope for $1.75. Does she have enough money? (Yes) No

$6.95 Yes (No)

$.55 (Yes) No

$12.85 (Yes) No

Crazy Big Book of Third Grade 415

page 415

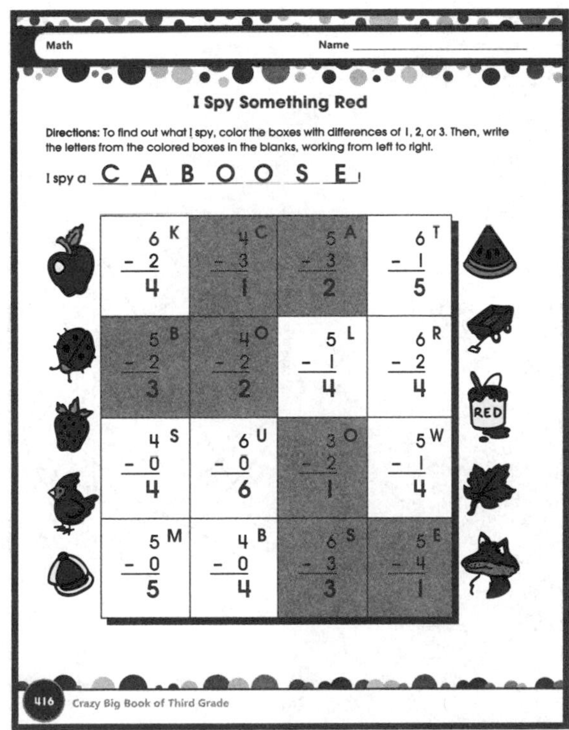

Math Name ______________

I Spy Something Red

Directions: To find out what I spy, color the boxes with differences of 1, 2, or 3. Then, write the letters from the colored boxes in the blanks, working from left to right.

I spy a C A B O O S E!

K: 6 − 2 = 4	C: 4 − 3 = 1	A: 5 − 3 = 2	T: 6 − 1 = 5
B: 5 − 2 = 3	O: 4 − 2 = 2	L: 5 − 1 = 4	R: 6 − 2 = 4
S: 4 − 0 = 4	U: 6 − 0 = 6	O: 3 − 2 = 1	W: 5 − 1 = 4
M: 5 − 0 = 5	B: 4 − 0 = 4	S: 6 − 3 = 3	E: 5 − 4 = 1

416 Crazy Big Book of Third Grade

page 416

Math Name

The Shoe Store

Directions: Use the prices to find the answers.

$9 $5 $6 $8 $7

Dan buys and. How much does he spend in all? $9 + $6 = $15	Anna buys and. How much does she spend in all? $8 + $7 = $15
David buys and. How much does he spend in all? $9 + $8 = $17	Rachel buys and. How much does she spend in all? $7 + $6 = $13
Lee buys and. How much does she spend in all? $7 + $9 = $16	Josie buys and. How much does she spend in all? $5 + $8 = $13

Crazy Big Book of Third Grade 417

page 417

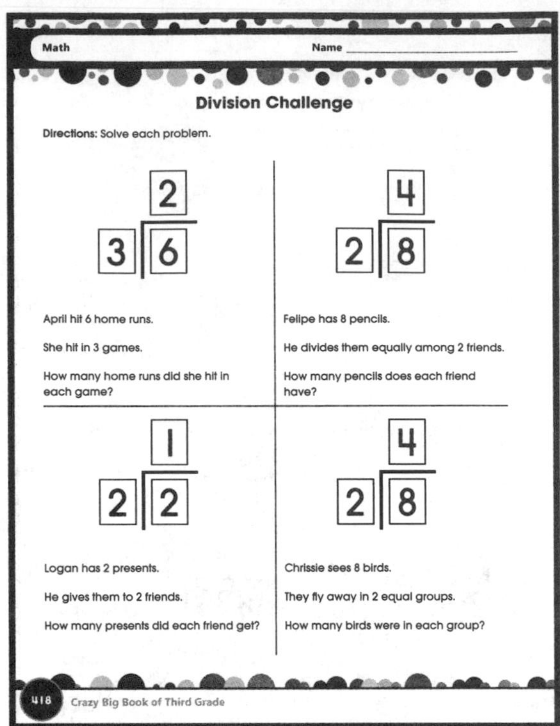

Math Name

Division Challenge

Directions: Solve each problem.

3)6 = 2

April hit 6 home runs.

She hit in 3 games.

How many home runs did she hit in each game?

2)8 = 4

Felipe has 8 pencils.

He divides them equally among 2 friends.

How many pencils does each friend have?

2)2 = 1

Logan has 2 presents.

He gives them to 2 friends.

How many presents did each friend get?

2)8 = 4

Chrissie sees 8 birds.

They fly away in 2 equal groups.

How many birds were in each group?

418 Crazy Big Book of Third Grade

page 418

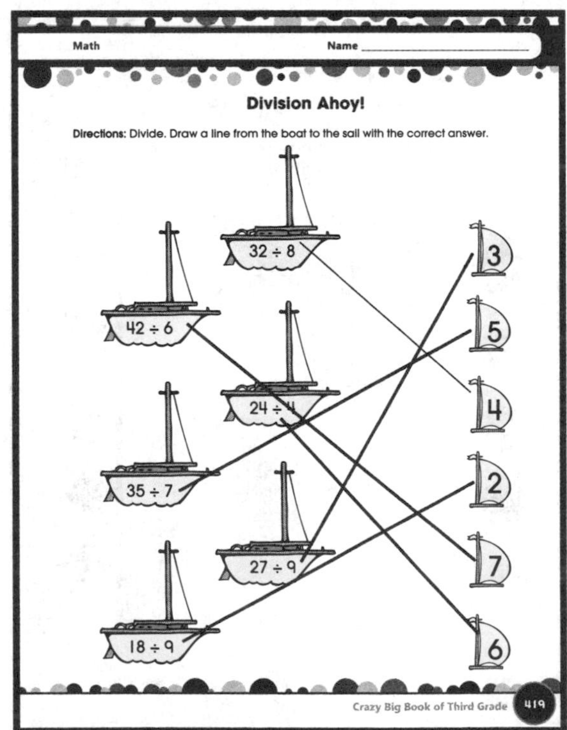

Math Name

Division Ahoy!

Directions: Divide. Draw a line from the boat to the sail with the correct answer.

32 ÷ 8

42 ÷ 6

24 ÷ 4

35 ÷ 7

27 ÷ 9

18 ÷ 9

3

5

4

2

7

6

Crazy Big Book of Third Grade 419

page 419

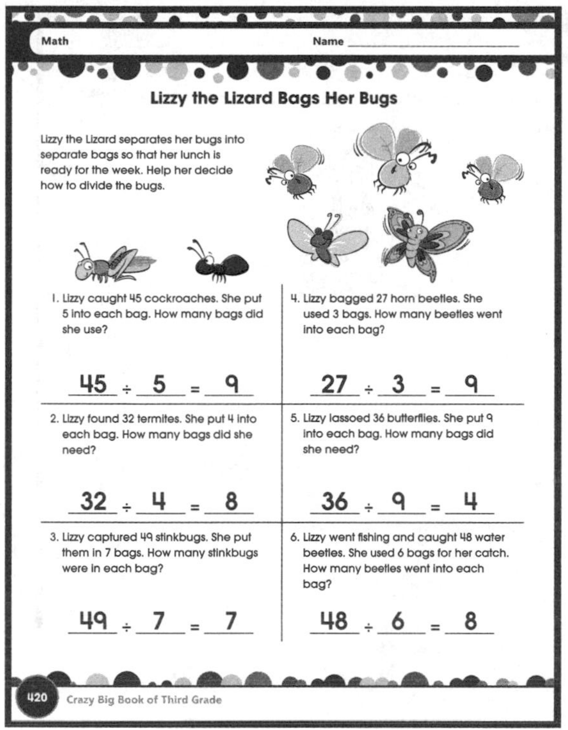

Math Name ______________

Lizzy the Lizard Bags Her Bugs

Lizzy the Lizard separates her bugs into separate bags so that her lunch is ready for the week. Help her decide how to divide the bugs.

1. Lizzy caught 45 cockroaches. She put 5 into each bag. How many bags did she use?

   45 ÷ 5 = 9

2. Lizzy found 32 termites. She put 4 into each bag. How many bags did she need?

   32 ÷ 4 = 8

3. Lizzy captured 49 stinkbugs. She put them in 7 bags. How many stinkbugs were in each bag?

   49 ÷ 7 = 7

4. Lizzy bagged 27 horn beetles. She used 3 bags. How many beetles went into each bag?

   27 ÷ 3 = 9

5. Lizzy lassoed 36 butterflies. She put 9 into each bag. How many bags did she need?

   36 ÷ 9 = 4

6. Lizzy went fishing and caught 48 water beetles. She used 6 bags for her catch. How many beetles went into each bag?

   48 ÷ 6 = 8

420 Crazy Big Book of Third Grade

page 420

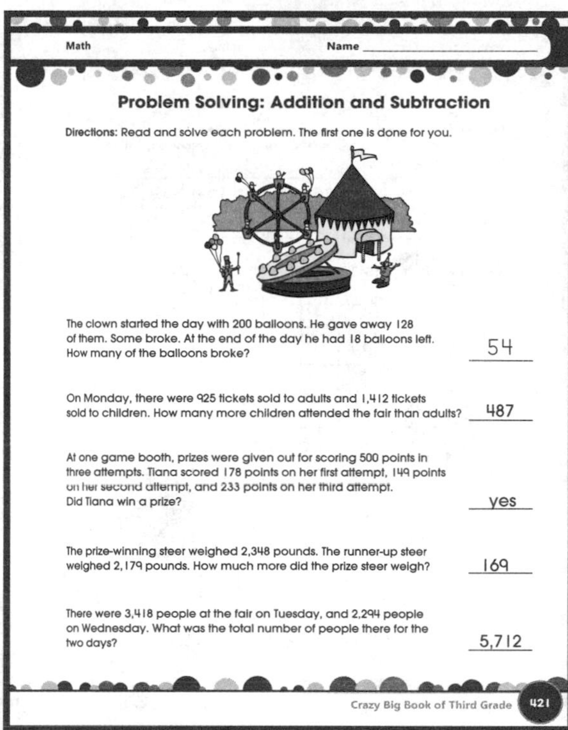

Math Name ______________

Problem Solving: Addition and Subtraction

Directions: Read and solve each problem. The first one is done for you.

The clown started the day with 200 balloons. He gave away 128 of them. Some broke. At the end of the day he had 18 balloons left. How many of the balloons broke? 54

On Monday, there were 925 tickets sold to adults and 1,412 tickets sold to children. How many more children attended the fair than adults? 487

At one game booth, prizes were given out for scoring 500 points in three attempts. Tiana scored 178 points on her first attempt, 149 points on her second attempt, and 233 points on her third attempt. Did Tiana win a prize? yes

The prize-winning steer weighed 2,348 pounds. The runner-up steer weighed 2,179 pounds. How much more did the prize steer weigh? 169

There were 3,418 people at the fair on Tuesday, and 2,294 people on Wednesday. What was the total number of people there for the two days? 5,712

Crazy Big Book of Third Grade 421

page 421

Math Name ______________

Complete the Circle

Directions: Complete the circle by multiplying each of the numbers by 3.

Now, complete these facts.

$5 \times 3 = 15$ $9 \times 3 = 27$ $3 \times 1 = 3$ $3 \times 8 = 24$ $6 \times 3 = 18$ $3 \times 2 = 6$

$0 \times 3 = 0$ $3 \times 5 = 15$ $2 \times 3 = 6$ $3 \times 4 = 12$ $8 \times 3 = 24$ $3 \times 9 = 27$

422 Crazy Big Book of Third Grade

page 422

Math Name ______

Double Trouble

Directions: Solve each multiplication problem. Below each answer, write the letter from the code that matches the answer. Read the coded question and write the answer in the space provided.

1	4	9	16	25	36	49	64	81	100	121	144
E	G	H	I	N	O	S	T	U	W	X	Y

10 × 10	3 × 3	6 × 6
100	9	36
W	H	O

4 × 4	7 × 7
16	49
I	S

7 × 7	4 × 4	8 × 8	8 × 8	4 × 4	5 × 5	2 × 2
49	16	64	64	16	25	4
S	I	T	T	I	N	G

5 × 5	1 × 1	11 × 11	8 × 8
25	1	121	64
N	E	X	T

8 × 8	6 × 6
64	36
T	O

12 × 12	6 × 6	9 × 9
144	36	81
Y	O	U

?

Answer: Who is sitting next to you?

Crazy Big Book of Third Grade Activities 423

page 423

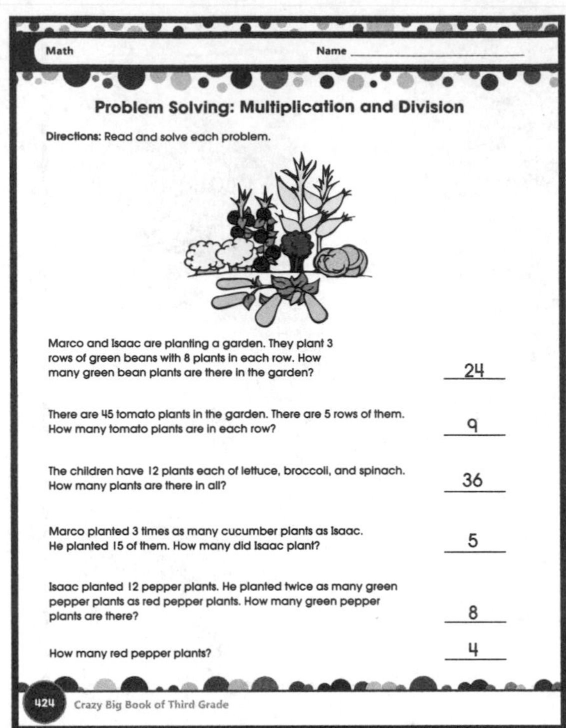

Math Name ______

Problem Solving: Multiplication and Division

Directions: Read and solve each problem.

Marco and Isaac are planting a garden. They plant 3 rows of green beans with 8 plants in each row. How many green bean plants are there in the garden? 24

There are 45 tomato plants in the garden. There are 5 rows of them. How many tomato plants are in each row? 9

The children have 12 plants each of lettuce, broccoli, and spinach. How many plants are there in all? 36

Marco planted 3 times as many cucumber plants as Isaac. He planted 15 of them. How many did Isaac plant? 5

Isaac planted 12 pepper plants. He planted twice as many green pepper plants as red pepper plants. How many green pepper plants are there? 8

How many red pepper plants? 4

424 Crazy Big Book of Third Grade

page 424

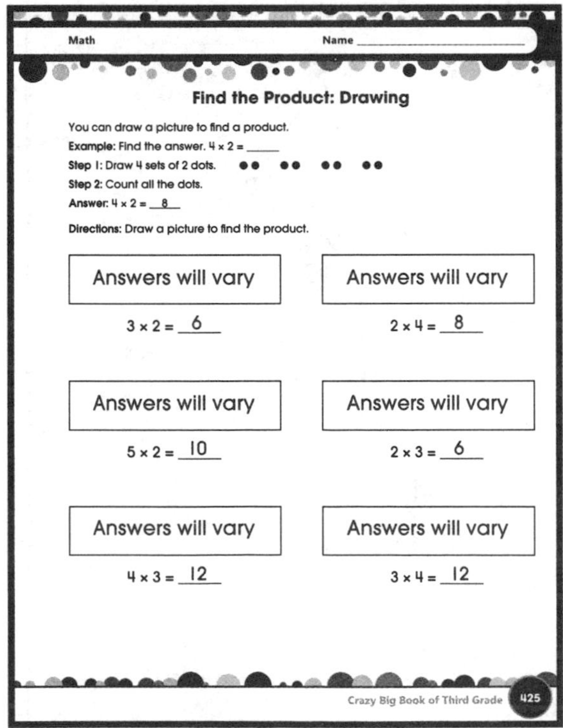

Math Name ______

Find the Product: Drawing

You can draw a picture to find a product.

Example: Find the answer. 4 × 2 = ______

Step 1: Draw 4 sets of 2 dots. ●● ●● ●● ●●

Step 2: Count all the dots.

Answer: 4 × 2 = 8

Directions: Draw a picture to find the product.

Answers will vary

3 × 2 = 6

Answers will vary

2 × 4 = 8

Answers will vary

5 × 2 = 10

Answers will vary

2 × 3 = 6

Answers will vary

4 × 3 = 12

Answers will vary

3 × 4 = 12

Crazy Big Book of Third Grade 425

page 425

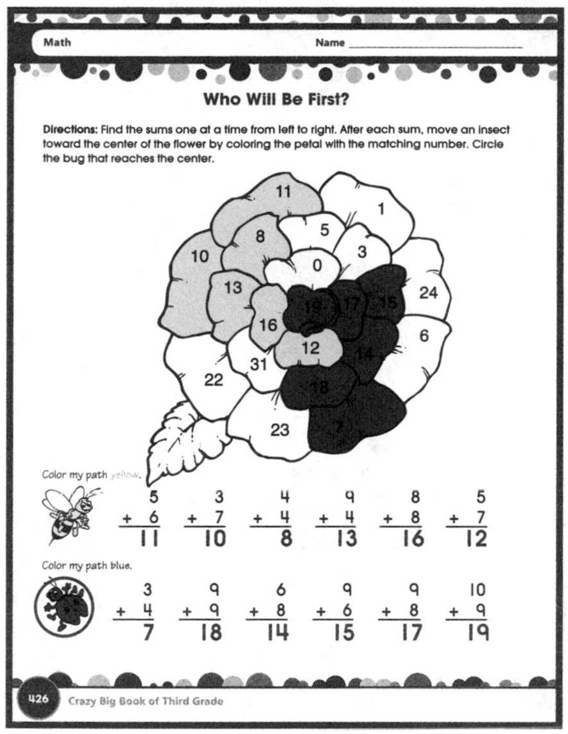
Math Name

Who Will Be First?

Directions: Find the sums one at a time from left to right. After each sum, move an insect toward the center of the flower by coloring the petal with the matching number. Circle the bug that reaches the center.

Color my path yellow.

5 + 6 = 11	3 + 7 = 10	4 + 4 = 8	9 + 4 = 13	8 + 8 = 16	5 + 7 = 12

Color my path blue.

3 + 4 = 7	9 + 9 = 18	6 + 8 = 14	9 + 6 = 15	9 + 8 = 17	10 + 9 = 19

426 Crazy Big Book of Third Grade

page 426

Math Name

Problem Solving: Fractions and Decimals

A **fraction** is a number that names part of a whole, such as $\frac{1}{2}$ or $\frac{1}{3}$.

Directions: Read and solve each problem.

There are 20 large animals on the Mendozas' farm. Two-fifths are horses, two-fifths are cows, and the rest are pigs. Are there more pigs or cows on the farm? more cows

Farmer Mendoza had 40 eggs to sell. He sold half of them in the morning. In the afternoon, he sold half of what was left. How many eggs did Farmer Mendoza have at the end of the day? 10

There is a fence running around seven-tenths of the farm. How much of the farm does not have a fence around it? Write the amount as a decimal. 0.3

The Mendozas have 10 chickens. Two are roosters, and the rest are hens. Write a decimal for the number that are roosters and for the number that are hens. 0.2 roosters 0.8 hens

Mrs. Mendoza spends three-fourths of her day working outside and the rest working inside. Does she spend more time inside or outside? outside

Crazy Big Book of Third Grade 427

page 427

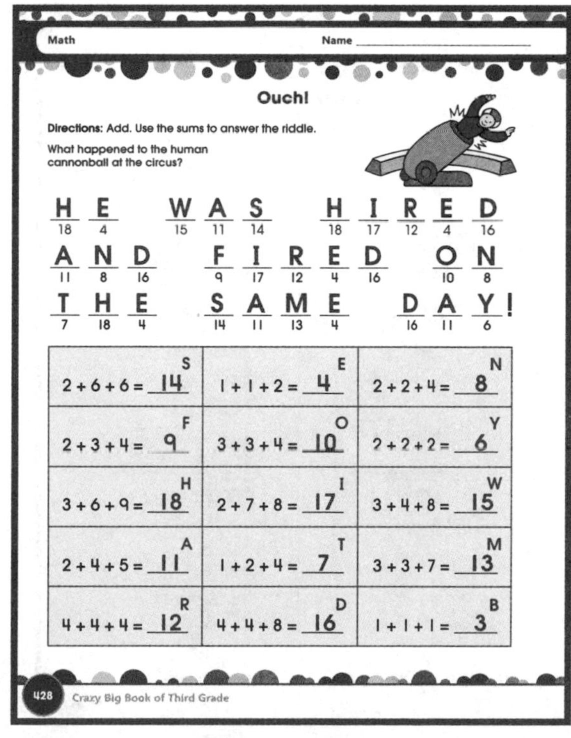
Math Name

Ouch!

Directions: Add. Use the sums to answer the riddle.

What happened to the human cannonball at the circus?

HE WAS HIRED AND FIRED ON THE SAME DAY!

H	E		W	A	S		H	I	R	E	D
18	4		15	11	14		18	17	12	4	16

A	N	D		F	I	R	E	D		O	N
11	8	16		9	17	12	4	16		10	8

T	H	E		S	A	M	E		D	A	Y	!
7	18	4		14	11	13	4		16	11	6	

S 2 + 6 + 6 = 14	E 1 + 1 + 2 = 4	N 2 + 2 + 4 = 8
F 2 + 3 + 4 = 9	O 3 + 3 + 4 = 10	Y 2 + 2 + 2 = 6
H 3 + 6 + 9 = 18	I 2 + 7 + 8 = 17	W 3 + 4 + 8 = 15
A 2 + 4 + 5 = 11	T 1 + 2 + 4 = 7	M 3 + 3 + 7 = 13
R 4 + 4 + 4 = 12	D 4 + 4 + 8 = 16	B 1 + 1 + 1 = 3

428 Crazy Big Book of Third Grade

page 428

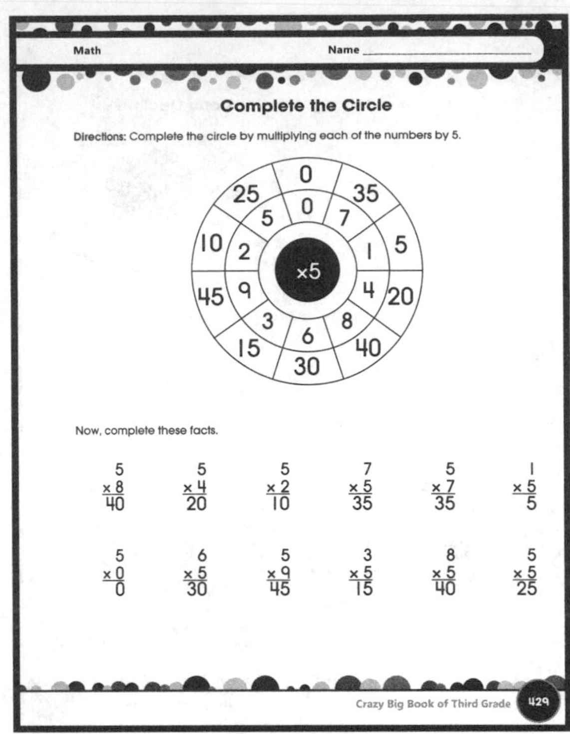

Math Name ______

Complete the Circle

Directions: Complete the circle by multiplying each of the numbers by 5.

Now, complete these facts.

$5 \times 8 = 40$ $5 \times 4 = 20$ $5 \times 2 = 10$ $7 \times 5 = 35$ $5 \times 7 = 35$ $1 \times 5 = 5$

$5 \times 0 = 0$ $6 \times 5 = 30$ $5 \times 9 = 45$ $3 \times 5 = 15$ $8 \times 5 = 40$ $5 \times 5 = 25$

Crazy Big Book of Third Grade 429

page 429

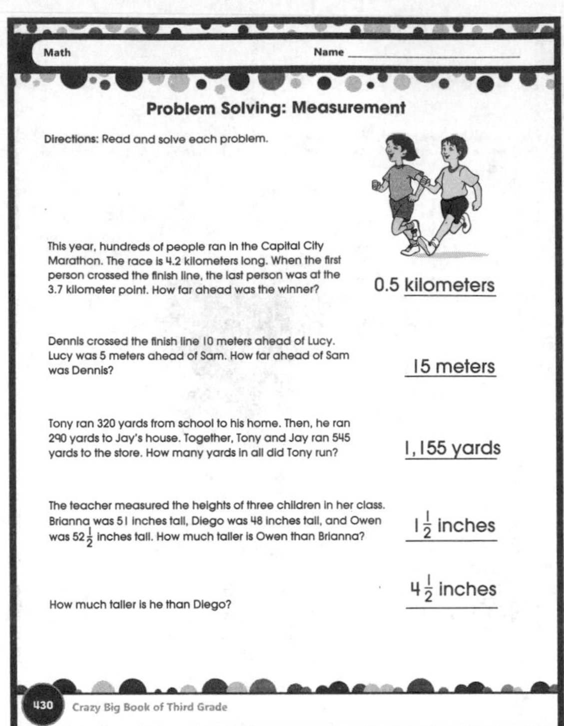

Math Name ______

Problem Solving: Measurement

Directions: Read and solve each problem.

This year, hundreds of people ran in the Capital City Marathon. The race is 4.2 kilometers long. When the first person crossed the finish line, the last person was at the 3.7 kilometer point. How far ahead was the winner? 0.5 kilometers

Dennis crossed the finish line 10 meters ahead of Lucy. Lucy was 5 meters ahead of Sam. How far ahead of Sam was Dennis? 15 meters

Tony ran 320 yards from school to his home. Then, he ran 290 yards to Jay's house. Together, Tony and Jay ran 545 yards to the store. How many yards in all did Tony run? 1,155 yards

The teacher measured the heights of three children in her class. Brianna was 51 inches tall, Diego was 48 inches tall, and Owen was $52\frac{1}{2}$ inches tall. How much taller is Owen than Brianna? $1\frac{1}{2}$ inches

How much taller is he than Diego? $4\frac{1}{2}$ inches

430 Crazy Big Book of Third Grade

page 430

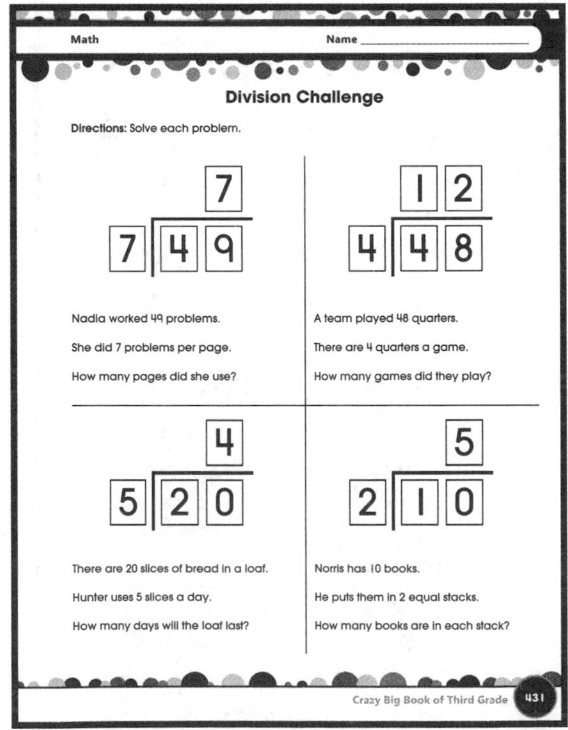

Math Name ______

Division Challenge

Directions: Solve each problem.

$49 \div 7 = 7$

Nadia worked 49 problems.

She did 7 problems per page.

How many pages did she use?

$48 \div 4 = 12$

A team played 48 quarters.

There are 4 quarters a game.

How many games did they play?

$20 \div 5 = 4$

There are 20 slices of bread in a loaf.

Hunter uses 5 slices a day.

How many days will the loaf last?

$10 \div 2 = 5$

Norris has 10 books.

He puts them in 2 equal stacks.

How many books are in each stack?

Crazy Big Book of Third Grade 431

page 431

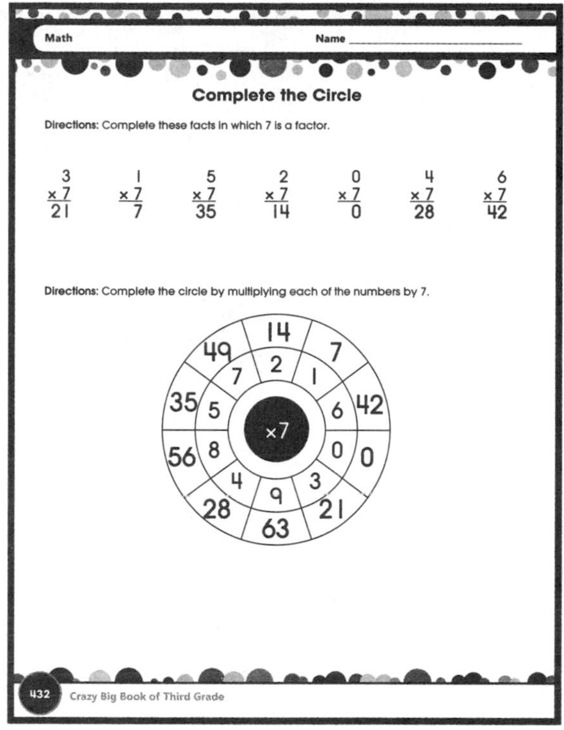

Math Name ____________

Complete the Circle

Directions: Complete these facts in which 7 is a factor.

$3 \times 7 = 21$ $\quad 1 \times 7 = 7$ $\quad 5 \times 7 = 35$ $\quad 2 \times 7 = 14$ $\quad 0 \times 7 = 0$ $\quad 4 \times 7 = 28$ $\quad 6 \times 7 = 42$

Directions: Complete the circle by multiplying each of the numbers by 7.

432 Crazy Big Book of Third Grade

page 432

Math Name ____________

Problem Solving

Directions: Read and solve each problem.

$2.45 $1.59 $4.99

Ralph has $8.75. He buys a teddy bear and a puzzle. How much money does he have left? $2.17

Kelly wants to buy a teddy bear and a ball. She has $7.25. How much more money does she need? $.19 or 19¢

Lydia paid 1 five-dollar bill, 2 one-dollar bills, 2 quarters, 1 dime, and 8 pennies for a book. How much did it cost? $7.68

Mei-Lin leaves for school at 7:45 A.M. It takes her 20 minutes to get there. On the clock, draw the time that she arrives at school.

Frank takes piano lessons every Saturday morning at 11:30. The lesson lasts for an hour and 15 minutes. On the clock, draw the time his piano lesson ends. Is it A.M. or P.M.? Circle the correct answer.

Crazy Big Book of Third Grade 433

page 433

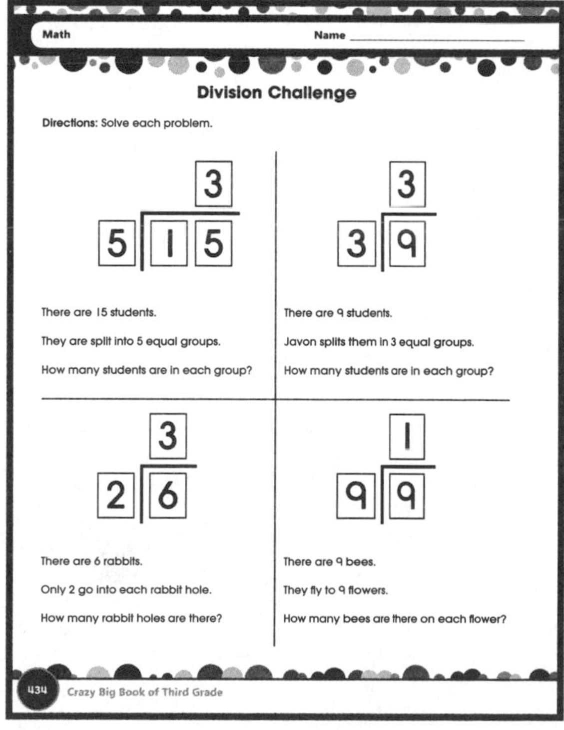

Math Name ____________

Division Challenge

Directions: Solve each problem.

$15 \div 5 = 3$

There are 15 students.
They are split into 5 equal groups.
How many students are in each group?

$9 \div 3 = 3$

There are 9 students.
Javon splits them in 3 equal groups.
How many students are in each group?

$6 \div 2 = 3$

There are 6 rabbits.
Only 2 go into each rabbit hole.
How many rabbit holes are there?

$9 \div 9 = 1$

There are 9 bees.
They fly to 9 flowers.
How many bees are there on each flower?

434 Crazy Big Book of Third Grade

page 434